AN INTRODUCTION TO
STOCK EXCHANGE INVESTMENT

An Introduction to Stock Exchange Investment

Third edition

Janette Rutterford

with Marcus Davison

© Janette Rutterford 1983, 1993, 2007

First edition 1983
Second edition 1993
Reprinted 7 times
Third edition 2007
Published by PALGRAVE MACMILLAN
Houndmills, Basingstoke, Hampshire RG21 6XS and
175 Fifth Avenue, New York, N.Y. 10010
Companies and representatives throughout the world

PALGRAVE MACMILLAN is the global academic imprint of the Palgrave Macmillan division of St. Martin's Press, LLC and of Palgrave Macmillan Ltd.
Macmillan® is a registered trademark in the United States, United Kingdom and other countries. Palgrave is a registered trademark in the European Union and other countries.

ISBN-13: 978–0–333–77802–9
ISBN-10: 0–333–77802–2

This book is printed on paper suitable for recycling and made from fully managed and sustained forest sources. Logging, pulping and manufacturing processes are expected to conform to the environmental regulations of the country of origin.

A catalogue record for this book is available from the British Library.

Library of Congress Cataloging-in-Publication Data

A catalog record for this book is available from the Library of Congress.

10   9   8   7   6   5   4   3   2   1
16   15   14   13   12   11   10   09   08   07

Printed and bound in China

Learning Resources
Centre

12930598

To my father and mother, without whom
I would never have finished this book.

Contents

Figures

Tables

Boxes

Examples

Preface to the third edition

The desire to write this book first arose from the lack of a good text book suitable for my undergraduate investment course. The books then available fell into two main categories. The first consisted of large US texts which described the US stock markets and were somewhat parochial in nature. The second category was aimed at the UK market, but these books were usually of the 'how to buy and sell shares' and 'get rich quick' variety. They are strong on recommendations and weak on theory.

More than 20 years on, as I am preparing the third edition with Marcus Davison, not that much has changed. This book aims to take the best of both worlds, describing markets, mostly UK but also some international, and also explaining the theoretical framework that underpins all stock market investment strategies. This book not only provides an introduction to the world of investment, describing how markets work, the types of financial securities, and the main types of investor, but also explains the principles underlying stock exchange investment. We concentrate on the two main characteristics of any security – risk and return – and using these, show how financial investments such as shares, bonds, options and futures can be compared and valued. We also explain how to approach the design of an investment portfolio, and discuss alternative investment strategies, both those advocated in theory and those used in practice in the stock market.

STRUCTURE OF THE BOOK

The book is divided into six main parts. Part 1 includes an introductory chapter which explains the role of the stock exchange and how it works, as well as providing an introduction to the concept of market efficiency. The second chapter in Part I introduces the concept of a security's risk and return, and shows how these can be quantified.

Part II covers fixed income securities, or bonds, with Chapter 3 looking in depth at how the UK government bond, or 'gilts' market works, and Chapter 4 on how the bonds can be compared and traded using yield as a measure of return, and duration and convexity as measures of risk.

Part III covers equities or shares. Chapter 5 describes shares and how they are issued and valued. Chapters 6 and 7 concentrate not on how to value individual types of security but how to combine securities such as shares into portfolios. Portfolio theory and the capital asset pricing model, described in these chapters, show how diversification can lead to portfolios with better risk and return characteristics than individual securities.

Part IV looks at risk management products, in particular financial futures and options. Chapter 8 describes the main types of financial futures contract related to stock markets – short term interest rate, bond, equity index futures and swaps – and discusses why they are of interest to stock market investors. Chapter 9 covers options, showing how they are valued and also how they can be used to improve investment performance, again in the risk–return sense.

Part V is devoted to institutional and international investment, two quite specific facets of the stock market. Institutional investors now dominate stock exchange investment, and we need to understand the characteristics of pension funds, insurance companies, investment and unit trusts, in particular, to measure their impact on the securities in which they invest. We cover investing institutions in Chapter 10. Similarly, we need to understand the different perspective of the international investor, for whom currency risk is an additional risk, when compared with that of investors investing in securities on their domestic stock exchange. We cover international investment in Chapter 11.

The final part of this book, Part VI, takes a more strategic look at stock exchange investment. Chapter 12 looks at investment objectives, strategies and how investment performance is measured, key elements in investment management. Chapter 13 addresses current issues in investment theory and practice, concentrating in particular on how investors are dealing with implementing investment theories such as portfolio theory and the capital asset pricing model in practice, and whether or not markets and investors are as rational as investment theories would suggest.

Terms marked in **bold italics** on their first occurrence in the body of the book are covered in the Glossary at the back of the book.

READERSHIP

Given that we put a theoretical risk and return framework on the subject of stock exchange investment, we hope to interest both students at university and students of fund management, as well as practitioners and individuals coming into contact with investment, such as bankers, accountants, lawyers, analysts, actuaries, and of course investors. The aim has been to keep the maths clear and easy to understand, concentrating on explaining concepts through the use of examples rather than equations. Most of the examples shown in this book can be worked out using a simple calculator, although options are more easily valued using simple computer software.

Janette Rutterford
February 2007

Acknowledgements

I would first of all like to thank my co-author, Marcus Davison, for taking on what has turned out to be a major rewrite of this book for its third edition. It is all the better for a fresh look and a critical eye. I must also thank the providers of the information for permission to reproduce extracts from their publications. These extracts are crucial to the book since one of its aims is to show how published financial data, in particular data in financial publications such as the *Financial Times* and real time data analysis provided by services such as Bloomberg, look in practice.

Finally, I would like to thank all those who helped us to produce this third edition, in particular Martin Drewe of Palgrave Macmillan who has encouraged us to meet deadlines. But I would also like to thank the many people who complimented me on the first and second editions and encouraged me to believe that a third edition, more than 20 years after the first, would be welcome.

Janette Rutterford

My first acknowledgement is of course to Janette, for the leap of faith that induced her to commission me to work with her on this new edition. I have been sustained along the way by too many people to mention here, but I would single out the successive cohorts of students who have unwittingly acted as 'beta testers' of much of the material presented here. I owe a very special debt of gratitude to my sons: to Paul for doing a lot more than merely keeping his legal-eagle's eye on the brief foray into the world of corporate taxation; and to Nicholas for subjecting the entire text to the uniquely jaundiced critical scrutiny of a maths undergraduate. But my biggest debt is to my partner Alison, without whom I might still have been sufficiently rash to accept Janette's commission, but without whose unstinting encouragement and support I would never have had the self-discipline or the patience to fulfil it.

Marcus Davison

The authors and publishers are grateful to the following for permission to reproduce copyright material:

Office for National Statistics for Table 1.2, Table 3.4, Table 3.5, Table 10.1, Table 10.3, Table 10.4, Table 10.5, Table 10.6, Table 10.7, Figure 13.4 and Figure 13.5.

London stock exchange for Table 1.3 and Table 1.4.

London Business School for Table 7.1, Table 7.2, Table 7.3 and Appendix 7.1.

Debt Management Office for Figure 3.1, Table 3.2, Table 3.3, Table 3.8, Table 3.9, Figure 4.1, Figure 4.2, Table 4.2, Table 4.3, Table 4.6 and Example 3.1. Reproduced by permission.

CFA Institute for Figures 6.9 and 11.2, originally published in B. Solnik (1974), 'Why not diversify internationally, rather than domestically?' *Financial Analysts Journal*, **30** (4), pp. 48–54. Reproduced by permission of the publisher. All rights reserved.

Euronext.LIFFE for Table 8.1, Table 8.2, Table 8.3, Table 8.5, Table 8.6, Table 8.7, Table 8.9, Table 8.11, Table 8.12, Table 9.1, Table 9.2, Table 9.5 and Table 9.6.

British Bankers Association for Table 8.4. Reproduced by permission.

Financial Times for Table 8.13, Example 11.1 and Example 11.2, all copyright © 28 October 2004, *Financial Times*; Example 2.3, copyright © 30 November 2006, *Financial Times*; Table 3.6, copyright © 18 November 2005, *Financial Times*; Table 3.7, copyright © 1 July 2006, *Financial Times*; Table 4.10, copyright © 4 December 2006, *Financial Times*; Example 5.1, copyright © 7 January 2006 and 9 January 2006, *Financial Times*; Box 5.6, copyright © 1 November 2002, *Financial Times*; and Appendix 5.3, copyright © 30 November 2006, *Financial Times*. Reproduced by permission. All rights reserved.

Investment Management Association for Figure 10.1.

FTSE All-World Review for Table 11.1.

Blackwell for Figure 12.6 from 'Components of Investment Performance' by E. F. Fama (1972) in *Journal of Finance*, **27** (3), p. 551. Reproduced by permission of the publisher.

Bank for International Settlements for Table 8.14. Copyright © Bank for International Settlements 2004. All rights reserved.

Elek Books for Table 1.2, originally published in *The Stock Exchange: Its History and Functions* by E. V. Morgan and W. A. Thomas (1962).

Addison-Wesley Publishing Company, Inc. for Appendix 9.1, from Thomas E. Copeland, J. Fred Weston, and Kuldeep Shastri, *Financial Theory and Corporate Policy* (2004). By permission of the publishers.

McKinsey for Figure 13.4.

ABN-AMRO for Table 7.5 and Figure 11.3, from E. Dimson, P. Marsh and M. Staunton, *Global Investment Returns Yearbook 2004*; Figure 3.2, from E. Dimson, P. Marsh and M. Staunton, *Global Investment Returns Yearbook 2005*; and Figure 13.1, from E. Dimson, P. Marsh and M. Staunton, *Global Investment Returns Yearbook 2006*.

Every effort has been made to trace all the copyright-holders, but if any have been inadvertently overlooked the publishers will be pleased to make the necessary arrangements at the earliest opportunity.

Part I
Investment Basics

1 Products, markets and players

CHAPTER CONTENTS

Learning objectives for this chapter

After studying this chapter you should be able to

○ describe how the financial markets mediate between savers and borrowers
○ describe the role played by securities within the financial markets
○ classify the activities of financial markets according to a range of useful criteria
○ classify different types of securities according to their key characteristics of risk and return
○ apply the theory of efficient markets to real-life situations
○ appreciate the main historical influences on the structure and configuration of modern securities markets.

INTRODUCTION

This book is an introduction to the theory and practice of investment in securities, the collective term for *shares* (also referred to as *equities*) issued by companies and *bonds* issued by companies, governments and other organisations.

Investment is the opposite of consumption. Consumption is the outlay of money to acquire goods or services to be consumed either immediately or at some time in the not-too-distant future. Investment is the outlay of money with the sole objective and expectation of receiving a money return at some future date or dates. An essential feature of any investment transaction is therefore 'present cash outflow, future cash inflow'. In an important extension to this principle, the sacrifice of an expected present cash inflow has in principle the same effect as a present cash outflow, and a reduction in future cash outflow has the same effect as a future cash inflow.

Investment may be in *real assets* or in *financial assets*. A company seeking to increase its profits by cutting its future costs might replace an old machine by investing in a more efficient replacement which is expected to produce the same output at lower cost, or more output but at the same cost, as the existing machine. This is an investment in a real asset, and the future cash inflow in this case takes the form of the consequent reduction in the expected stream of future costs. An investor buying shares in the same company is acquiring a financial asset, that is, a *direct* claim to an expected future stream of cash in the form of dividends and the eventual proceeds of sale of the shares. But in both cases – the company buying a new machine and the investor buying shares – each is forgoing the use of cash today in expectation of receiving cash, or of having to spend less cash, in the future.

This book is about investment in financial assets, and its particular focus is on those financial assets known as **marketable securities**. These are shares and bonds issued in a form that enables them to be readily bought and sold among investors through an organised market or **stock exchange**. But in order to understand fully how shares and bonds behave, we also need to look at some associated products and markets beyond the strict confines of the stock exchange itself. In response to the ever-increasing volatility and complexity of the markets since the 1970s, a wide and ever-growing range of new financial products has been developed to enable market participants both to manage the risks arising from securities activity and to speculate on future movements in securities prices, without directly buying or selling the securities themselves. These products are called **derivative products** (or **derivatives** for short) because their essential properties are derived from those of the underlying securities or other financial products on which they are based. Derivatives can be **exchange-traded** (either on the stock exchange itself or on a separately organised specialist exchange) or bought and sold on a private bilateral basis, as for example between an investor and her bank (**over-the-counter** or **OTC**). Because of the very close relationship between derivatives and their underlying securities, a whole section of this book is devoted to a detailed analysis of these risk management products.

The book naturally features three recurring themes – products, markets and players. Here are some of the more important questions that we will consider about each of them.

Products

How and why are marketable securities and the related derivative products created?
What are their inherent characteristics, and how do they differ from each other?
How are they related to each other?
How does their behaviour – and in particular their value and the returns they earn – respond to changes in external market conditions?

Markets

What is the purpose of having organised exchanges for transactions in securities and in derivative products?
How do the markets operate?
How do we know whether the markets are doing their job efficiently?
How do the markets benefit those who issue and invest in securities – and the economy in general?

Players

Who issues and invests in securities?

Who uses derivative products?

What are the typical objectives of different market participants, and what strategies do they adopt in order to achieve their objectives?

We round off the introduction to this chapter with a brief look at how this chapter and the rest of the book as a whole are organised.

The question of what makes the investor 'tick' is central to any study of securities investment. For this reason we devote the whole of the next chapter, Chapter 2, to the standard model of the investor as a rational self-interested wealth-maximiser who evaluates potential investment opportunities purely in terms of just two criteria – **risk** and **total return**. The mathematical expression of this proposition underpins the whole of finance theory and is developed in detail in that chapter. Possible shortcomings to this approach are explored in Chapter 13 where we examine some open issues in finance.

The next two parts of the book explore in detail the two principal types of marketable securities. Part II, comprising Chapters 3 and 4, looks at the world of bonds or – to give them their more generic title – **fixed income securities**. Part III, comprising Chapters 5, 6 and 7, analyses equities. Part IV, comprising Chapters 8 and 9, covers the main derivatives products, **financial futures, options** and **swaps**. Part V, comprising Chapters 10 and 11, provides an introduction to the institutional and international dimension of securities investment. Part VI, comprising Chapters 12 and 13, takes a more detailed look at different types of investors and the types of investment strategy they adopt, and ends with a review of open issues in investment theory and practice.

We now turn to securities market products, to explore the different types of securities on offer to investors in securities markets, including shares, bonds and derivative products. We then explore the risks of these products before describing the basics of stock markets, in particular the benefits of such markets and their classifications. The chapter then looks at the concept of market efficiency and the efficient market hypothesis before ending with a historical profile of the London stock market.

SECURITIES MARKET PRODUCTS

The main investment products traded in the stock market – shares and bonds – are financial claims on the companies, governments and other organisations that issue them in order to raise funds for their medium and long-term financing needs. These claims become the assets of investors who buy them, and liabilities of, or claims on, the entities that issue them. They form just a part (though a very important part) of the broader universe of products used by the financial markets to channel funds from economic sectors in financial surplus (*surplus sectors*) to economic sectors in financial deficit (*deficit sectors*). It is important to appreciate where marketable securities fit into the wider financial markets, and how the financial markets as a whole fit into the **real economy**, where non-financial or real assets (goods and services) are produced and distributed. By contrast, a financial asset is one that consists solely of a claim on a future stream of cash.

When governments, companies and other organisations raise money from investors to finance their activities, they create many different forms of financial claims for investors to purchase. Claims created in a form that can continue to be readily bought and sold after their original issues are known as securities. If these securities have been accepted for trading on a recognised market such as a stock exchange, they are called marketable securities.

Securitised financial claims form an important part of the wider universe of financial assets, which also includes non-securitised claims such as bank deposits, loans and mortgages. We call all of these assets *financial assets* because they simply represent claims on future cash flows. Those cash flows may or may not be fixed in their amount or timing, but what distinguishes them from other assets – real assets – is that ownership of them does not automatically confer any rights over, or entitlement to, non-financial assets such as the factories owned by a company or the facilities owned by a government.

This distinction between financial and real assets follows the distinction drawn in classical economics between **product markets** and **factor markets.** In product markets goods and services are distributed to their end-users. In factor markets the two inputs into the production process – labour and capital – are bought and sold. Financial assets are traded in, and created by, the market for capital. So producers and distributors of real goods and services raise funds from investors in the **primary capital market**. The investors then buy and sell among themselves, in the **secondary market** and in the associated derivatives markets, the risks and the associated returns that they have acquired through these indirect stakes in the real economy.

Box 1.1 Confusing terminology 1: When are securities not securities?

The terminology of finance can be very confusing. This is the first of a series of boxes in the text which will highlight these confusions as they arise.

There is no real risk of confusion when the language of finance uses specially coined words (such as **annuity** – see Chapter 10) or when it uses common words in senses quite different from their everyday meanings (such as **straddle** – see Chapter 9). But a problem may arise when we use common words in senses that are only subtly, but significantly, different from their everyday usage. Possibly the best example of this is **risk**, which we analyse in detail in Chapter 2.

A further problem arises when we use the same word to mean different things in different contexts. *Security* is one such term. In the context of this book, we are normally using it to mean a readily transferable financial claim such as a share or a bond. But the word is also used in a quite different sense, to denote an asset or assets that a borrower or debtor has pledged as collateral security for a debt or other obligation, on terms giving the lender or creditor direct recourse to those assets if the debtor defaults on the payment obligation. The commonest example from the world of personal finance is the **mortgage** that secures a loan on the borrower's house. Companies regularly pledge their assets as security for their borrowings, so securities can be secured or unsecured. And there is nothing to stop securities being used as (collateral) security, for example, for a bank loan.

Basic products: shares and bonds

Companies, governments and other organisations raise funds to finance their activities by issuing a wide range of securities which differ from each other

    ○ in the timing and variability of the future returns they offer to investors

○ in the nature and scale of the risks the investors accept
○ in the rights of monitoring and control enjoyed by the investors – and in their rights of recourse if things go wrong or if their expectations are not fulfilled.

When investors buy different types of securities issued by a company, they are sharing out among themselves the rights to the cash flows arising from the company's future operations, as well as the risks associated with those cash flows. In the simplest case, a company issues a single type of security, known in the United Kingdom as ***ordinary shares*** and in the United States as ***common stock***. Such shares give each investor a proportionate right to the residual value of the company, that is to any distributions of cash from net earnings (after all expenses, taxes and claims of other providers of finance have been satisfied) and to the eventual proceeds of liquidation of the firm (after all outstanding liabilities have been met).

The upside potential of shares is entirely unlimited, because however large the residual income and net assets might be, all of it belongs to the shareholders. But the downside risk of shares is *not* unlimited. The principle of **limited liability** limits the amount of shareholders' funds at risk to the value of the **share capital** each of them has agreed to subscribe. If a businessman (or woman) trades in his own name as a principal on his own account, and fails to pay his business liabilities, his trade creditors can normally have recourse through the courts to all his personal assets as well as to his business assets. But a limited liability company is an entirely separate legal entity from its shareholders; its assets are not their assets and its liabilities are not their liabilities. So shareholders in a limited liability company do not risk anything above and beyond the money they have promised to subscribe for their own shares. If they have already subscribed all the funds originally promised, they have no further liability at all (unless, of course, it can be proved that the company was established or operated with the deliberate intention of defrauding creditors, in which case further legal sanctions may apply to the shareholders and to the directors they appoint to manage the company on their behalf). Shareholders cannot lose more than 100 per cent of their initial stake in the business. This may sound like cold comfort, but later in this book, in Part V on derivative products, we shall come across highly leveraged instruments where buyers can actually lose far more than 100 per cent of their initial investment and – even more alarmingly – sellers too expose themselves to a potentially unlimited liability.

In contrast to ordinary shares, all other types of security issued by a company have one feature in common: both the upside profit potential and the downside risk are to a greater or lesser degree limited or mitigated by a binding contract (hence the use of the word 'bond' to denote the most important class of such securities). The investors forgo the upside potential enjoyed by the shareholders in favour of a fixed return in the form of periodic interest, and they receive additional compensatory benefits in two forms.

○ Their claims on the company are legally enforceable; they have contractual rights to certain payments by the company, typically for periodic interest on the funds provided plus repayment of those funds on a fixed or determinable date in the future.
○ Their claims rank ahead of those of the ordinary shareholders, who (as in the case where there are no other financial claims on the company) are entitled to what is left after all other claims have been satisfied.

Box 1.2 Confusing terminology 2: Treasury stock and treasury stock

Although the stock exchange is the market where securities of all types are traded, the words 'stock' and 'stocks' as applied to individual securities have different meanings in the United Kingdom and in the United States. The US usage of 'stocks' corresponds to 'shares' in the United Kingdom, though both countries use the generic term 'equities' in the same way. More confusingly still, in the United Kingdom some types of debt security (notably government bonds) are commonly referred to as 'stock', so a government bond issue might be called '8% Treasury Stock due 2013', but in the United States, 'treasury stock' refers not to debt securities issued by the Treasury Department of the US government but to a company's holding of its own shares that it has repurchased on the market, and instead of cancelling, holds in its own 'treasury' for possible future reissue.

Because the claims of debt providers enjoy greater priority and protection than those of equity holders, this class of investors has a much smaller say in the running of the firm and much less control over the actions of its managers. Company legislation provides general protection against fraudulent misuse of investors' money and also requires the regular publication of accounts which, though nominally forming part of a report from the directors to the shareholders, are in practice provided for the protection of all stakeholders in the company. Debt providers may also be able to impose specific covenants restricting the company from taking certain actions that might jeopardise the recovery of their claims, but unlike shareholders, they have no automatic or statutory right to be informed or consulted about the ongoing management of the firm. When the providers of debt are considering what return they should receive for lending money to a company, and what additional safeguards they should seek, a major factor for them is the protection already afforded by the fact that the shareholders' financial claims are subordinated to their own; so the size of this 'equity cushion' behind them in the queue for funds plays a key role in their calculations.

Not all organisations that issue securities issue shares. By far the most important exception is the government itself, which does not have limited-liability shareholders in the conventional sense but (as we shall see in Chapter 4) does issue debt on a much bigger scale than any other organisation in the entire market. One unusual but helpful way to think of the government is not as a limited liability company but as an unlimited liability partnership, with all the taxpayers as the partners. In practical terms, the ability of a government to service debt denominated in its own currency is unlimited, because it can always call on the partners to pay sufficient taxes to meet its debt obligations. It is for this reason that government debt is generally regarded as the nearest thing to a risk-free security; the *equity cushion* is effectively unlimited. This risk-free aspect of government debt is also reflected in the fact that investors accept a lower return for investing in it than in any other comparable security.

Derivative products and other exotic animals

Investing in securities exposes investors to many risks, of which the most obvious is the risk of an unexpected fall in the value of an investment. Similarly, *not* investing also exposes them to risks, such as the risk that the price of a security they intend to purchase in the future will increase unexpectedly so that it will be more expensive to acquire. The secondary market offers investors an efficient way of managing some of the risks they have incurred by purchasing securities, but conventional secondary market transactions do not provide certainty of future outcomes (in terms of the prices at which securities can be bought and sold for settlement at some more or less remote future date), or true insurance in the sense of protection against negative outcomes without the loss of positive opportunities.

To meet these and other investor needs, since the 1970s the markets have evolved a large and still growing family of derivatives products, of which the most important are futures and options. *Financial futures* enable investors and others to fix now the prices at which individual securities (or whole market indices of securities) can be bought or sold for settlement at a future date. *Options* give buyers the right to buy or to sell securities (or indices) at a fixed price at a future date but only if it is to their advantage to do so. While futures and options therefore differ crucially from each other in respect of the relative fixity of their outcomes, they are similar to each other (and different from cash market transactions) in that they enable market participants to trade indirectly in large amounts of securities by making just a very small down payment, by way of *premium* (in the case of options) or *initial margin* (in the case of futures). These are highly geared instruments, because the profit or loss on the investor's down-payment will reflect the change in value of the full amount of the position in the underlying securities.

Cash products and derivative products can be combined into hybrid instruments incorporating features from both. A bond that is convertible into ordinary shares is a combination of a conventional bond and an option to purchase the shares, and the returns and risks of such instruments are a complex amalgam of the individual building blocks.

RISKS OF SECURITIES MARKETS

We have already identified a key characteristic that marketable securities share with all other financial assets. This is the sacrifice of a known amount of cash today (the purchase price) in return for the right to receive a more or less uncertain stream of cash in the future. Common sense suggests that the price an investor will be prepared to pay in order to acquire such a right to future cash flows will depend on three things: their amount, their timing, and the degree of uncertainty in each. In Chapter 2 we shall give formal mathematical expression to these factors, but for the purpose of this introductory analysis we need to consider them only in qualitative terms.

The variability and uncertainty of future cash flows from an investment can be caused by many factors. One way to classify them is as either internal or external. Internal factors are those that are expressed or implied in the terms of the investment itself. External factors result from the interaction of external events with the internal provisions of the investment contract. The two types of factor are not mutually exclusive: an investment can be subject to uncertainty as a result of both types of factor at the same time.

Internal risk factors

At one extreme, the contractual terms of an investment may dictate the exact amounts and due dates of all future cash flows to which the investor is entitled. For example, a bond issued by a company will typically provide for the investor to receive annual interest at a

---

Box 1.3 Confusing terminology 3: Risk and uncertainty

In everyday conversation, 'risk' is nearly always bad: I risk losing my job, you risk having a traffic accident. But in the specialised language of finance, risk is usually synonymous with uncertainty, and uncertainty cuts both ways, as it refers to the possibility that an outcome can be better, and not just worse, than what we expect or hope for.

A key problem besetting most investment calculations is how to model future uncertainty. Is the spread of possible outcomes distributed symmetrically around the expected outcome, or is it skewed in one direction? Does the probability of possible outcomes diminish in a predictable way with increasing divergence from the expected outcome? To what extent is the distribution of past outcomes a reliable guide to the future?

While uncertainty embraces pleasant as well as unpleasant surprises, the very fact that an investment may give surprises at all is generally regarded by investors as a bad thing.

---

specified percentage rate for a fixed number of years, with repayment of the principal on the final interest payment date. Here the basic contract allows for no intrinsic uncertainty as to timing or amount, though the small print of the contract may provide for early termination if, for instance, the company is acquired by another company, or gets into financial difficulties, or materially changes the type of business in which it is engaged. In any event, if the company fails to meet its contractual commitments, investors can sue it in the court, just as they would sue any other defaulting debtor.

At the other extreme, the stream of future cash flows to which an ordinary shareholder is entitled is defined (partly by company law and partly by the terms of the company's own articles of association), but only in purely qualitative terms as a pro rata share of the periodic dividend and of the proceeds of an eventual liquidation. The amount and timing of the dividends actually paid will depend both on the company's future profits and on the directors' policy for distributing those profits to shareholders rather than retaining them for further investment in the company's business. The shareholders are partially compensated for this high degree of uncertainty by legal provisions which give them a much greater control over the running of the company than that enjoyed by the providers of debt finance. But this control is exercised by the shareholders as a body and rather infrequently (for instance, at annual general meetings), and the degree of control exercised by an individual shareholder with a small fractional holding is negligible.

External risk factors

When we consider the external factors affecting the variability and uncertainty of future cash flows, the situation becomes very much more complicated.

In the case of the bond with ostensibly fixed cash flows, two quite separate problems emerge. The first is that the issuer might be unable to pay the contracted amounts of interest and principal in full and on time. This could be for any of a number of reasons, the most common being an unexpected deterioration in its profitability or in its cash position.

Another possibility is that the company is theoretically able to discharge its debt but is prevented by some external agency from doing so. For instance, its profits might have been accumulated in a foreign country which imposes restrictions on the repatriation of earnings and thus prevents the company from meeting its obligations.

The second potential source of uncertainty stems from the secondary market mechanism that enables investors to realise the value of their securities by selling them on to other investors. Whereas the future cash flows from an investment might be relatively certain in amount and timing (as, for instance, in the case of bonds issued by the government), the value attached by the market to those cash flows, and hence the value that can be realised by a seller on the secondary market, fluctuates in response to external factors, the most important of which is the prevailing *level of interest rates*. If interest rates generally have risen since the investor originally purchased a government bond in the primary market, then – all other things being equal – the value of the investment on the secondary market will have fallen. This is examined in greater depth in Chapter 3.

Under external factors we should also consider some of the main factors affecting company earnings and hence the dividends paid on shares. Apart from the general commercial success of the company, a variety of technical factors in the financial markets can have a significant impact. A principal such factor is the impact of *fluctuating foreign exchange rates*. A company that incurs most of its expenses in its home country but sells its output mainly abroad will experience a drop in its net earnings if the currencies of the countries where it sells suffer a loss in value without a corresponding rise in its selling prices. We shall see just how important this and similar factors are when we consider in detail the strong international dimension of the London stock exchange and of the largest companies whose shares are traded there.

Possibly the most pervasive external factor affecting the value of returns on securities is inflation, or the fluctuation in the *purchasing power of money*. This factor is unique in that it affects all securities in a particular country over a specified time period. Investors in a conventional UK government bond enjoy near-certainty in terms of the amount and timing of their future cash flows, but have no guarantee of what those cash flows will buy in comparison with the purchasing power they sacrificed when they made the original investment; by contrast, investors in a UK government **index-linked bond** do enjoy protection against inflation, but the protection is only watertight if they buy the bond at original issue and hold it for its entire life (see Chapter 3). Conventional wisdom has it that investment in equities provides a long-term protection against inflation, but economists are divided on this issue. The return on equities is a residual, representing whatever is left over after all other claims on a firm have been satisfied, and the way in which inflation affects the value of that residual is very complex.

THE MARKET: BASIC FEATURES

Market players

The markets in securities and derivatives are similar in many ways to other organised markets. They bring together as much as possible of the aggregate potential supply and demand in order to reduce transaction and search costs, improve liquidity and build confidence. Most importantly, they aim to promote the discovery of fair and uniform prices. But each of these functions takes on a special importance in the case of investment products because their dependence on unknown and unknowable future events makes their value both uncertain and opaque.

A closer study of the roles taken by the players in the securities markets further reinforces the view that these markets differ quite significantly from conventional markets in goods and services. In most conventional markets, each participant usually takes on the role of either a producer/seller or consumer/buyer. The goods or services flow in one direction through the market, from the producers at one end to the consumers at the other, while the money flows in the opposite direction. The securities markets conform to this pattern only to a very limited extent. It is true that a key function of the financial markets is to channel surplus funds from households and other economic agents who have more than enough for their current consumption requirements (surplus sectors), to others who can put to productive use funds in excess of what they have currently available (deficit sectors). So companies and governments issuing new securities in the *primary market* are indeed supplying assets for the market to distribute to purchasers. But once a new marketable security has been sold to an initial investor, this is not the end but only the beginning of the story. A key feature of the stock market is that a security can continue to be bought and sold among market participants in a *secondary market* for as long as it has value, that is, for as long as it is expected to produce some future cash flows for the holder. So financial assets do not just pass through the market as if along a one-way street; they also circulate within it. In this respect the market for securities may appear to be similar to markets for second-hand or previously-owned goods such as cars, houses or antique furniture. But the big difference is that the value of a security, unlike that of a house or a car, is not affected by the fact that it has been previously owned *per se*, still less by how well it has been looked after, or even by how old it is. The value of a security depends exclusively on its expected future cash flows, so it is not a backward-looking but a forward-looking concept.

The structure of the securities markets is further complicated by the fact that the companies and governments that supply new securities to the market are also active as buyers of other issuers' new securities and as buyers and sellers of previously issued securities. And as if all this were not enough, in many securities markets, and especially in those of the most advanced economies, it is possible for investors to sell securities they do not already own. All of this makes the job of organising, regulating and understanding the market rather more complex than in the case of a conventional market for goods or services.

The range of firms providing services within the financial markets includes not only pure intermediaries between buyers and sellers (like property agents – or marriage brokers!), but also various types of institution that transform the essential characteristics of savings as they flow from investors to borrowers. The relationship between investors and borrowers is largely determined by a permanent and unavoidable conflict of interest. The most obvious conflict (but it is only one of many) is that investors want to be able to cash in their investments at any time and at short notice, whereas borrowers like to have the use of investors' money for as long as possible. Ideally borrowers would like to have indefinite use of investors' funds, with no legally enforceable contractual requirement to repay them. Different types of *financial intermediaries* have developed different types of financial product to reconcile this conflict, enabling both investors and borrowers to come closer to their objectives.

In the introduction we have already identified some of the general benefits of an organised market in securities. We now discuss these in a little more detail.

Benefits of organised markets

Reduction in search costs

In the absence of an organised market, investors would be confronted with an almost impossible task in their search for suitable outlets for their surplus funds, and borrowers would face a comparable challenge in their quest for finance on exactly the terms they require. The stock exchange and other financial marketplaces substantially eliminate search costs for both groups.

Reduction in transaction costs and uncertainty

If investors and borrowers were left to strike deals with each other individually and in isolation, the costs of executing each transaction could be very high, as it would involve lengthy negotiation and the expense of engaging lawyers and other professional experts to draft documentation acceptable to both sides. And in such a do-it-yourself, hit-and-miss world, there would be no guarantee that investors would get what they had bargained for. The stock exchange reduces transaction costs and uncertainties in several ways. It effectively vouches for the terms of the investment (without of course guaranteeing actual payment) by imposing **listing requirements** on issuers and on the securities they issue. The exchange also reduces the actual costs of transactions by means of economies of scale. The financial markets provide standard settlement mechanisms which not only reduce transaction costs but also ensure that investors get exactly what they order, and that they pay only against delivery.

Price discovery and market efficiency

An important test of the efficiency of a market is the fairness of its prices. The market absorbs information and responds by producing a price, called **price discovery**. A highly developed stock exchange like the London market has complex rules to ensure as far as possible that all information relevant to the determination of a fair price for a security is made available to all potential investors through the market, quickly, simultaneously and at minimum cost. It also has rules to prevent price-rigging, insider dealing and market manipulation by one or more parties acting in concert to establish an artificial price level. These rules encourage the belief that the market price is a fair price, and this belief attracts both issuers and investors. The higher the proportion of aggregate supply of, and demand for, a security that is channelled into the market, the fairer the price will actually be, thus generating a virtuous circle. But if issuers or investors suspect that a significant volume of business is being transacted off-market by parties who have access to better prices or information, they will want to do the same. This takes supply and demand away from the market, and makes it less likely that the market price will be a fair one, so that the investors' and issuers' suspicions become self-fulfilling, generating a vicious circle. This issue of market efficiency is so central to the theory and practice of the securities markets that further sections are devoted to it later in this chapter and in Chapters 12 and 13.

Protection and monitoring – 'after-sales service'

The stock exchange offers a measure of investor protection by requiring issuers to provide a regular and continuing flow of information about their business and about any factors that might affect the prices of their securities. Companies whose securities are listed on the London stock exchange are required not only to provide more financial and other information than is required under the basic company law and accounting disclosure rules, but also to adhere to additional codes of *corporate governance* which further safeguard the rights of public shareholders by regulating the relationship between them and the directors they appoint to manage companies on their behalf.

Liquidity

The term *liquidity*, as applied to a financial market, is frequently misunderstood, perhaps because it has a familiar but quite different meaning, similar to solvency, when applied to a company or an individual. In the context of a financial market, liquidity refers to the ease with which a participant can buy or sell in the required quantity without affecting the market price. Shares in the largest, most actively traded, companies are generally more liquid than those in very small companies. There are a number of reasons for this, and we explore these in more detail later in this book. A stock exchange can employ a variety of measures to ensure that there is some liquidity in the shares of even the most obscure small company.

For liquidity purposes, what matters is not the total size of the share issue but the amount of the *free float*: that is, the proportion of the issue that the market considers to be not in the hands of long-term investors but potentially available for trading at any time. Examples of large companies whose free float is significantly restricted by such long-term holdings are Sainsbury and Associated British Foods, where the interests of the founding families (in ABF's case, the Weston family) currently control respectively about 20 per cent and 54 per cent of the total equity.

Box 1.4 Liquidity and lobster pots

The late Julian Baring, for many years a stockbroker in the City of London, is reputed to have kept a lobster pot hanging from the ceiling above the desk where he used to meet his clients. It was intended as a reminder to them that it was much easier to get into the shares of a small company than to get out of them again. Liquidity is a measure of the relative ease of buying *and selling* a security.

Transformation ...

So far we have considered only the basic types of marketable investment products which are issued directly by end-users of funds (companies, governments and other organisations) to end-investors (individuals and others who are looking for profitable homes for their surplus financial resources). But in the introduction to this chapter we noted that the financial markets perform an additional function of transforming investors' surplus resources into financial instruments that achieve a better compromise between the investors' and the borrowers' objectives. This transformation takes three principal forms.

... of maturity

The provision of an active secondary market in shares and bonds already goes a long way towards meeting the conflicting needs of investors (who want ready access to their money) and borrowers (who want to be able to use it for as long as possible and to maintain control over the timing and amount of repayments), but this is only one of several ways in which the financial markets achieve maturity transformation.

For example, a key function of the banking system is to take short-term deposits from savers and to invest them either in longer-term loans or in marketable and other securities. In this case the transformation is accomplished by means of an intermediary (the bank) accepting as a principal the full liability to repay deposits on demand. The risk of a temporary mismatch between the depositors' demands for funds and the corresponding inflow of interest and principal repayments from the bank's longer-term borrowers falls fairly and squarely on the bank's own shoulders and is borne directly by its shareholders.

... of risk

The financial markets offer a variety of ways in which investors can reduce the risks arising from their investments, or (more strictly) can reduce their risks without suffering a commensurate reduction in the returns they earn. The most obvious example is the way in which the banking sector offers this facility, by pooling the deposits of many savers and investing them in a very wide range of loans and other assets. This reduces individual savers' risk to a fraction of what it would be if, instead of entrusting their comparatively small wealth to the bank, they lent it all to a small number of individuals. The bank further reduces the risk incurred by the saver by means of its superior ability to monitor its borrowers and because any losses are borne first by its own shareholders.

Transformation of risk is also achieved by a range of **collective investment** vehicles such as pension funds, insurance companies, **unit trusts** (called **mutual funds** in the United States), **open-end investment companies** (abbreviated to **OEICs**) and **investment trusts** (called **closed-end investment companies** in the United States). This confusing plethora of names will be discussed at greater length in Chapter 10 when we analyse the business of different types of investing institution. For the moment it is sufficient to note that all of these are investment vehicles that pool investors' comparatively small sums and invest them in much larger and professionally managed portfolios of securities in order to reduce risks by means of diversification. As a form of intermediation they differ from the banking model in that the full amount of all profits and losses arising from the asset portfolio flows through to the savers, with no equity cushion to protect them from unforeseen losses – but with no upper limit on their profits either.

... of size

Whatever form the intermediation takes, one benefit is that small investors are freed from many of the practical constraints and diseconomies of scale which would otherwise reduce the efficiency of their savings. A small investor who attempted to achieve the same degree of diversification as a bank or a collective investment vehicle would very quickly find that transaction costs (commission, stamp duty and so on) consumed a disproportionately large amount of his or her funds, and the time required to monitor all the investments would leave very little time for anything else.

Classifications of organised markets

Financial markets are sometimes classified either as pairs of mutually exclusive opposites or according to some other more or less formal criterion. We have met a few of these already, such as primary and secondary, underlying and derivative, exchange-traded and over-the-counter (or OTC). It is useful to expand a little on some of these and to add some more to the list.

Primary and secondary

A **primary market** is a market in which new securities are issued and sold to investors for the first time, while an active **secondary market**:

○ provides a means for investors continuously to adjust the risk and return characteristics of the securities in their portfolios in the light of changing circumstances and
   market conditions
○ plays a key role in reconciling the conflicting time horizons of investors and
   borrowers
○ provides a reference point for the fair pricing of new issues of securities.

Most importantly, by providing investors with the possibility of an early exit from their investments, a secondary market reduces the returns they are prepared to accept. This ulti-mately has the effect of reducing the cost of capital to the economy at large, so that more investments in real projects are made and the productive capacity of the economy expands more quickly than would otherwise be the case.

Exchange-traded and over-the-counter (OTC)

The primary focus of this book is investment in exchange-traded securities, but in view of the close relationship between different financial markets it is important also to have an understanding of some of the OTC markets. Although a universal feature of OTC markets is that deals are struck bilaterally between two parties without any intervention or supervision by an exchange, they differ radically among themselves in terms of how public or private they are. The biggest and best known OTC financial markets are the interbank markets in deposits and in foreign exchange.

We might note in passing that the foreign exchange market is another case of confusing terminology: although the buying and selling of different currencies against each other is universally described as foreign exchange, it does not take place on a formally organised exchange like the stock exchange. But despite the absence of a formal exchange, the market is in fact very public, in that the participants in it have full and immediate access to all the other participants' prices and to the flow of information affecting those prices. The foreign exchange market is also quite heavily regulated, in that its members adhere to common codes of conduct which are enforced by their trade associations, by central banks and by financial services industry regulators. Similarly, the market in **interest rate** and **currency swaps** (which are described in greater detail in Chapters 8 and 11 respectively) is entirely an OTC market, but there is a high level of price transparency and the product is largely standardised through the use of commonly agreed documentation. Nevertheless, the main advantage of an OTC market is preserved, which is that each transaction can be tailored to the exact needs of the participants.

Capital and money markets

The markets in which securities are traded are described collectively as the capital markets, because they provide the means for companies, governments and other organisations to procure their medium and long-term capital needs, and for investors to find suitable homes for their surplus capital. The money markets (which, incidentally, are almost without exception OTC markets) are where substantially the same players, but primarily the banks, adjust their short-term liquidity surpluses and deficits. The distinction between capital and money markets is by no means clear-cut. Some products trade in only one of these markets. For example, both **interbank deposits** and **certificates of deposit** (the latter sharing with securities the characteristic of transferability) are traded exclusively in the money markets, whereas shares are traded only in the capital markets. But high-quality debt securities with a remaining maturity of under one year are clearly suitable instruments for the management of short-term liquidity, so the distinction becomes blurred. The informal distinction is that the money markets are concerned with transactions with a maturity of less than one year, whereas the capital markets deal in longer maturities, but the connection between the two remains very close. For instance, one of the principal ways in which the banks adjust their temporary liquidity mismatches is by entering into **repurchase** or **repo** agreements, whereby one bank raises short-term funds from another (or from the central bank) by selling and simultaneously buying back for a later date its holdings of government bonds. The headline interest rate published by the Bank of England, which is universally regarded as the benchmark for the entire structure of sterling interest rates, is in fact the rate at which the Bank lends money to the banking sector through repo transactions.

Quote-driven and order-driven

Within the subset of markets organised as formal exchanges, an important distinction is the way in which prices are formed and transactions actually come about. In the traditional, quote-driven stock market, a specific type of member firm known as a **market-maker** (or a **jobber** in the pre-1986 London stock exchange) has an obligation to quote continuous two-way prices at which it is prepared to buy and sell a security from or to other market participants. Usually this commitment is to deal in a predetermined and advertised quantity known (on the London exchange) as *normal market size*. The market-maker trades as a principal for its own account and entirely at its own risk, and the normal commercial imperative of securing business without actually going bankrupt in the process is a powerful force in ensuring that the market remains transparent and competitive. For smaller companies in particular, the existence of committed market-makers is widely considered to be an essential condition for the maintenance of liquidity in their shares.

The development of electronic trading technology in recent years has led to a rapid spread of an alternative process known as *order-driven trading*. In an order-driven market, members input into a central computer system their buy and sell orders for a security; these may be their own orders as principals or they may be orders they have been asked to execute for customers. The computer system has two functions; it broadcasts the details of all the current orders to the market at large, and it automatically executes buy and sell orders whenever they can be matched in terms of price and amount. Both the London stock exchange and the exchange for associated derivatives products are now predominantly order-driven, and more will be said about each of them later in this chapter and in Chapter 8.

Market sectors and indices

Market sectors and market indices are an important means employed by the market for classifying securities, and especially shares. The well-established practice of informally classifying the stock market into industry sectors is largely a matter of convenience. Individual researchers and analysts (and even whole teams of them) cannot claim to cover the entire market in any depth, so they specialise instead in industries or sectors, to make it easier to compare one company with its peers – and easier also for investors to compare one analyst with another! It is important to remember that the classification into sectors is both informal (it has no basis in the way the exchange itself is actually organised) and to an extent subjective.

Some sectors are more homogenous than others in terms of the businesses carried on by the companies in them, but even the most apparently homogenous sector (like food retailing, for example) still embraces a range of companies that would not regard themselves as being exclusively in direct competition with each other; Tesco competes with Sainsbury as a food retailer, but also with many other non-food retailers in the sale of electrical and household goods; Marks & Spencer is classified as a general retailer, despite having a significant food-retailing operation which brings it into competition with Tesco. A diversified company might therefore potentially qualify for inclusion in more than one sector. A key objective of such a company's investor relations activities is to 'persuade' the financial community to allocate the company to the sector where it will enjoy the highest rating.

The structure and composition of stock market indices is an altogether more formal matter. We shall see later (Chapter 5) how the main UK stock market indices, of which the most important is the FTSE 100 index of the 100 largest share issues by total value, are compiled, and what their significance is for investors and analysts. The important thing to note, in connection with sectors and indices, is that these are not merely passive ways of conveniently classifying securities; how investors regard a share, and therefore what they are prepared to pay for it, is in part determined by the sector and index to which it belongs.

MARKET EFFICIENCY: AN INTRODUCTION

Significance of market efficiency

We have already mentioned the importance of the *price discovery* function in financial markets. The key input into a market is information, and the key output from a market is the price. The effectiveness of a market depends on many things, including the quality of its settlement mechanisms, the level of transaction costs and the reputation of its members for integrity and financial soundness, but above all it requires all participants to be confident that the prices quoted are fair. Note that we say 'fair' and not 'correct'. In the absence of perfect foresight about the future, nobody can actually know the correct price for a security. But if the market price reflects all available past and present information that might be relevant to the future, then the price can be said to be fair in the sense that it offers a fair return for the risks perceived to be incurred, and the market is said to be efficient. Another way of expressing this is to say that a price that reflects all available relevant information, although it will almost certainly turn out to have been 'wrong' with the benefit of hindsight, is not likely to be *systematically* either too high or too low.

The idea of markets as being efficient or inefficient causes much emotion and argument in investment circles. This is no doubt partly because, in practice, the great majority of investment advisers act as if markets are inefficient, and therefore they are justified in their attempts to make *excess profits*: that is, profits that more than compensate for the risks actually incurred. But if markets are in fact fully efficient in the above sense, the rationale on which most investment advice and policy is based can be shown to be invalid, because the widespread practice of trying to *pick winners* by studying past prices or other available information cannot lead to *systematically* higher returns.

This debate has become more heated as the proportion of indirect investment (that is, investments held indirectly through pension funds and insurance companies) has increased. Individual investors have only themselves to blame if they try to pick winners and are unsuccessful at it. But if pension fund managers adopt a picking-winners strategy when securities markets are in fact efficient, beneficiaries of the fund will suffer. Firstly, the turnover of the fund (and hence transaction costs) will be unnecessarily high, as the pension fund managers think they see opportunities to invest in winners. Second, the portfolio may well be badly diversified if the managers have concentrated on holding a few potential winners. Chapter 6 will show that diversification is the key to optimising the relationship between portfolio return and risk. Failure to diversify not only increases risk unnecessarily but also – according to the standard market model (the Capital Asset Pricing Model or CAPM) to be studied in Chapter 7 – gratuitously exposes the investor to additional risks for which the market pays no return at all.

The rapid growth in the amount of indirect investment has increased the need to monitor the investment strategy and performance of financial intermediaries such as pension funds. Given that these institutions could adopt the *fair return for risk* strategy prescribed by the CAPM, this model offers a suitable benchmark against which to assess their actual investment strategies. In fact, the CAPM has been used to develop a series of performance measures, adjusted for risk, which can be used to assess any portfolio's performance and hence investment managers' ability, if any, to *beat the market.* Prior to the development of the CAPM, performance was often judged solely on return with little direct account being taken of risk. Even today, tables showing investment trust and unit trust performance, while giving exhaustive details about the returns achieved, show only rudimentary information about the relative riskiness of each trust's investment strategies. Without such information it is not possible to make meaningful comparisons of performance.

Chapter 2 is concerned with the problem of capturing the concepts of risk and fair returns mathematically. The whole of Chapter 10 is devoted to a description of the major institutions involved in the securities markets and how they affect the investment scene.

Chapter 12 considers how performance can be measured using the CAPM. The remainder of this section explores in primarily qualitative terms the question of how efficiently the stock market in fact incorporates available information into securities prices, and introduces the main implications of the different levels of efficiency (known as weak, semi-strong and strong) for investment strategy.

Test of market efficiency – the 'random walk'

It is not possible to observe directly what information is and is not reflected in the price of a particular security at a particular time, so the question of how efficiently markets absorb information has to be approached indirectly. This can be done in three ways:

○ by examining short-term price movements
○ by searching for long-term trends in prices and returns
○ by means of event studies, which examine the behaviour of market prices around the time of identifiable external shocks such as the announcement of a takeover or of a major new contract.

The first way to test the efficiency of markets is to examine successive very short-term price movements for autocorrelation, that is, for signs of a significant correlation between successive price changes. Although the market does have a very long-term tendency to go up, this tendency is negligible in the context of short-term price fluctuations, so that in an efficient market the current price also reflects the market's expectation of what will be a fair price in a few minutes' time. 'If one could be sure that a price would rise, it would have already risen' (Samuelson 1965). We can infer from this that in an efficient market the price will move only in response to genuinely new information, and as information is genuinely new only if it bears no relation to what came immediately before, we would expect in an efficient market that successive price movements are as likely to be in opposite directions as in the same direction: that is, that autocorrelation between price movements would be very low.

Such a situation – where the correlation between successive price movements is close to zero – is popularly referred to as the 'random walk of a drunken man', or more formally as the *random walk theory*, but an important implication of this choice of terminology is often overlooked. It is of course true that a drunken man walks at random, in the sense that it is impossible to predict from his last step the direction in which his next step will take him. But an important extension of this observation is that the most likely place to find a drunken man is very close to the spot where he was last seen, as his random steps will have a tendency over time to cancel each other out and to lead him back to his starting point. In formal statistical terms, the best available unbiased estimate of his current position is the position at which he was last seen. Transferring this analogy to the price of a security in an efficient market, we can say that if the market is reacting only to genuinely new information, then the best unbiased estimate of a fair price is the current price, which is as likely to be too high as it is to be too low.

The idea that security prices in an organised market might follow a random walk was first implied by Bachelier (1900) in a study of commodities traded on the French commodities markets. From the 1930s to the 1960s, the random walk theory was also tested successfully on company share prices. Cowles (1933 and 1944) pointed towards what has become the most controversial consequence of random share-price movement – that even professional investors cannot consistently outguess the market.

Proofs of the random walk theory can take several forms. As with all tests of theories involving future expected prices or returns, past actual prices or returns are used for the tests (since these are easier to measure). So, for the random walk theory, sets of past share prices are tested for dependence. One such test involves calculating the correlation coefficients of consecutive (or lagged) share price changes over daily and longer intervals. Tests have been carried out on both UK and US share databases, and the serial correlations, as correlation coefficients for time series data are called, have been found to be around zero. For example, Moore (1962) looked at weekly share price changes from 1951 to 1958 on 29 US shares selected at random and found an average serial correlation coefficient of -0.06.

More recent tests of the random walk theory have benefited from more accurate price series data. Price changes over varying periods of time from intra-day to several years, and for individual shares and portfolios of shares, have been tested for serial correlation, giving rise to a range of results. Although there is now some evidence that the autocorrelations, particularly for longer time horizon price changes, are significantly different from zero, they are still close enough to zero to prevent forecastable trends from appearing in time series of prices, and for share price series to look remarkably like random walks.

The second way of approaching the problem is to look at the big picture to see if there are in fact patterns in share prices over time. Clearly if we take a very long view, say over the last 100 years or so, there is one obvious pattern: shares are more likely to go up than down, though even this pattern is prone to reversals which are neither minor nor short-lived – nor widely predicted. In an early study of supposed trends in share prices, Roberts (1959) demonstrated that a fictitious time series generated from random numbers could produce a pattern that was very similar to a chart tracking actual share prices.

What perhaps matters more than just the direction of raw share prices is the question whether there are patterns to be found in the *returns* on shares, and in particular whether such patterns can be systematically exploited to earn more than a fair return for the risks incurred. The central problem in any such study is that in order to determine whether a given return is fair or not, it requires assumptions to be made about what constitutes a fair return for risk; in short, it needs a model of the risk–return relationship. Consequently, a study that appears to show that (contrary to the random walk theory) it is possible to earn excess returns by studying past price movements, is also open to the interpretation that it is the underlying risk/return model that is flawed, and systematic excess returns are in fact not possible. Fama (1998) examined a wide rage of studies from the 1980s and 1990s which seemed to cast doubt on the randomness of share price movements, and concluded that quite small changes in the underlying assumptions about risk and return were sufficient to make the supposed anomalies disappear.

The third type of test, the *event study*, was first undertaken by Ball and Brown (1968) and by Fama et al. (1969) and has subsequently been repeated many times. The purpose of these studies is to establish how quickly and accurately share prices find a new equilibrium level after publication of major events, such as unexpected earnings or dividend

---

Box 1.5 How wrong can you be?

On the last trading day of 1999, the FTSE 100 index of leading UK shares reached an all-time closing high of 6930. Market commentators, in their routine year-end reviews and forecasts, almost unanimously predicted a further year of positive returns in 2000. In the event, the market registered a negative return of almost 5 per cent. Undeterred, at the end of 2000, they predicted a recovery in 2001. The actual return on the market for 2001 was negative 12.9 per cent. And the whole process was repeated at the end of 2001: a predicted recovery was followed by an even greater negative return of 22.3 per cent. At the end of 2002, sentiment finally turned negative and many now predicted a fourth straight year of losses for 2003. The market did indeed begin the year by sinking a further 15 per cent, but from March onwards it staged a strong if sporadic recovery, and not only made up for the first quarter's losses but actually finished the year with an overall positive return of 21.2 per cent.

What lesson is to be learned from this? Study of the UK stock market from 1900 to 2004 shows that the correlation between successive years' returns is very low. The probability of a negative return in any particular year is about 38 per cent, regardless whether the markets went up or down the previous year – or went down for each of the previous three years.

---

announcements, or mergers and acquisitions. Generally, such studies have found that share prices are quick to adjust not only to the more obvious implications of such shocks but also to their less direct consequences. Again, however, all such studies must adopt a particular risk/return model as a benchmark.

The efficient markets hypothesis

That share prices appear to follow a random walk is an interesting result, and proving it or attempting to disprove it occupied many researchers throughout the 1960s and 1970s. But what remained to be shown was *why* share prices followed a random walk. There was plenty of evidence, but a formal theory was missing. What was needed was a model of share price behaviour to explain the random walk. This gap was filled by a more general model based on the concept of efficiency of the markets in which shares are traded – the efficient markets hypothesis (EMH).

In a perfect market, information would be freely and instantaneously available to all, there would be a homogenous product, no taxes, perfect competition amongst investors and no transaction costs associated with trading. Under these conditions, each share will be fairly valued, in the sense that all information will be fully absorbed into the share price and investors will be in agreement that the current share price is as likely to go up as go down. Thus, the share price can, until new information is released, be considered to be at an equilibrium value. As new items of information about the company's prospects come in, the company's share price will absorb this information and move to a new equilibrium value. It can be shown that, in such a *perfect market*, successive price changes will be independent and prices will follow a random walk. This follows, first because the news inherent in the new piece of information concerning the company might be either good or bad, but it will certainly be independent of the last piece of information (otherwise it would not be new), and so the price change towards the new equilibrium value will be independent of the last price change. Second, because of the number of traders in the market and the lack of barriers to trading, the information (known to everyone) will be absorbed so quickly that the new equilibrium value will be achieved straightaway.

However, in a market where transaction costs are high enough to deter trading or where information is slow to reach the majority of investors, and speculative dealing by those who have the new information is in some way prevented, it might take several days or weeks for new information to be impounded in the share price. There would then be a trend in the share price as it moved towards its new equilibrium value. In such an imperfect and inefficient market, share price changes would be serially dependent rather than random, and excess returns could be made either by spotting the trends from charts or by trading on new information before it was fully impounded into the share price.

So a random walk theory for share prices reflects a securities market where new information is rapidly incorporated into prices and where abnormal or excess returns cannot be made from spotting trends or from trading on new information. In practice we know such securities markets are not perfect in the sense of having no transaction costs, no taxes and so on. We also know that it is an impossible task to make all information immediately available to everyone and to give everyone the ability to interpret instantaneously the information correctly. Nevertheless, judging from the evidence on random walks, securities markets do appear to be relatively efficient at reflecting new information in prices. The question then becomes one of how efficient the markets are.

Fama (1970) decided to define different markets in terms of their level of efficiency, where the level reflected the type or scope of information that was quickly and fully reflected in price. He defined three levels of efficiency, each level designed to correspond with the different types of *picking winners* investment strategies which were used in practice to try to achieve excess returns.

Example 1.1 shows the three different 'strengths' of the EMH corresponding to different levels of efficiency.

○ In the *weak form* of efficiency, each share price is assumed to reflect fully the information content of all past share prices.
○ In the *semi-strong form*, the information impounded is assumed to include not only that given by all past share prices, which are of course public knowledge, but all publicly available information relevant to the share value. This includes, for example, company announcements, brokers' reports, industry forecasts and company accounts.
○ The *strong form* of the EMH requires all known information to be impounded in the current share price, whether publicly and generally available or not. The strong form will thus include what is known as *insider information*, for

---

Example 1.1 Efficient markets hypothesis

Prices fully reflect all available information

Weak form	**Semi-strong form**	**Strong form**
Prices fully reflect past prices	Prices fully reflect all publicly available information	Prices fully reflect all information

example details of an impending takeover bid known only to senior management of both parties to the bid.

As we saw earlier, markets that are efficient in quickly reflecting new information prevent investors from making excess profits using that information. Thus, in a weak-form efficient market, investors would be unable to pick winners by looking at charts of past share prices or by devising trading rules based on share price movements. In a semi-strong form efficient market, investors with access only to publicly available information would not be able consistently to make excess profits by buying shares, say on announcement of favourable new information. For example, if an investor decided to buy shares on each announcement of unexpectedly high earnings, this information would be available to all and the share prices concerned would quickly reflect that information and increase. Even if the shares did not reach their new equilibrium values immediately (because it can take time for new information to be fully analysed), the prices at which the investor could buy the shares would be unbiased estimates of these new equilibrium values, as likely to be above as below them. Finally, if the strong form of the EMH held, no investors could generate excess returns whatever information they used, whether a 'new' analysis of the company accounts or a hot tip from the managing director, since in a market with this level of efficiency, share prices would already reflect all information relevant to the shares, whether publicly available or not.

It can be seen from the above that the ability of investors to pick winners and make excess returns using new information is directly related to the speed and efficiency of a market at absorbing that information.

The EMH does not say that investors will never beat the market and will never make large profits. What it does say is that, on average, over a period of time, investing is a *fair game*. 'You win some, you lose some.' This fair game concept is useful in that it allows the different levels of the EMH to be tested. Instead of trying to measure the amount of information impounded in share prices, we can look to see if, by using different pieces of information, excess returns can be made. If they can, the market is not efficient with respect to that information. If they cannot, it is one piece of evidence supporting efficiency, but not a conclusive proof. However much evidence is piled up in its favour, the EMH can never be formally proved, leaving open the possibility that some investor might have an as yet untested way of picking winners consistently over time.

The EMH, as described above, is a more comprehensive model of share price behaviour than the random walk theory, referring not just to past share price movements but to all information pertaining to the share. It is a model that helps us to understand how markets operate in practice and how closely they approximate to theoretically perfect markets. Figure 1.1 places the EMH in perspective relative to the other models of share price behaviour.

In Figure 1.1, the perfect market has the most stringent requirements concerning market behaviour. The attraction of the perfect market is that it is an assumption underlying the major security pricing models, such as the CAPM. In the real world, we know that the conditions assumed in perfect markets do not prevail. There are transaction costs associated with trading in securities, and information concerning securities is not freely and instantaneously available to all. However, if transaction costs are not excessive, if information is fairly readily available and if there is sufficient competition among investors, markets will be reasonably efficient in the sense that the securities' prices will

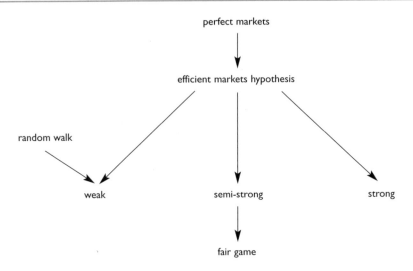

Figure 1.1 Models of share price behaviour

reflect the information available, and reflect it quickly enough to prevent excess returns being consistently made through trading on that information.

The EMH remains exactly what it says it is – a hypothesis – and this means that it cannot be proved but only disproved. During the 1980s and 1990s, many studies appeared that challenged it, mostly by claiming to detect anomalous trends or patterns which created opportunities for genuinely systematic excess returns. We shall examine more recent research we discuss the wider implications of EMH for investment strategy in Chapter 12.

LONDON: PROFILE OF AN INTERNATIONAL FINANCIAL MARKET

We shall base our analysis primarily on the London stock exchange and the corresponding exchange in derivative products, the London International Financial Futures Exchange (LIFFE), which is now known as 'Euronext.liffe' following its 2001 merger with the Euronext group of continental European exchanges. Many of the standard texts on the securities markets concentrate on the US markets, which are the largest in the world. London and Tokyo occupy second and third place (their order depending on the measure used), so the choice of London may appear somewhat limiting. But as we shall see from the more detailed description of the London market later in this chapter, this is not the case. The London stock exchange, like the UK financial markets of which it is a central element, has retained a uniquely international focus throughout its long history. The primary function of the US and Tokyo markets has always been to meet the enormous capital requirements of their respective domestic economies, but the London market has long enjoyed a primacy in the business of cross-border investment. For much of its history it actually played only a subsidiary role in the raising of capital for the UK domestic economy. Despite the troubled history of its domestic economy for much of the latter part of the twentieth century, the United Kingdom has the world's largest surplus in external trade in financial services and is unique in the relative size and significance of its financial sector. The London markets offer possibly the widest range of financial products of any of the world's major financial centres, and thus provide the opportunity for comprehensive illustration of the theoretical principles and practical techniques explained in this book.

Early development: to the beginning of the Industrial Revolution

The London stock exchange likes to trace its own history to an incident in 1760 when a group of some 150 brokers who had been thrown out of the Royal Exchange in the City of London because of their rowdy behaviour decided to form a club of their own. The Royal Exchange itself had been established in 1571 as a place where merchants, bankers, brokers and financiers of all sorts would eventually come together to conduct the burgeoning business associated with the rapid expansion of England's overseas trade, not only with Europe but also with the Americas and with Asia. London's main competition as a trading and financial centre came from the Netherlands, initially from Antwerp (until that city was occupied by the Spanish in 1585) and then from Amsterdam, which arguably developed the world's first stock exchange in the early seventeenth century. The protracted wars between England and Holland from 1654 to 1672 eventually tipped the balance of commercial power in favour of London, which by 1700 was the world's largest city and port.

The early 1720s brought a major setback in the further development of London as a financial centre. The rampant speculation and the associated fraudulent dealings that came to be known as the South Sea Bubble ruined many fortunes and reputations. One of the longer-term adverse consequences was a ban on the formation of joint-stock (limited liability) companies, other than by the cumbersome and expensive means of a specific Act of Parliament. This hindered the emergence of an effective capital market for more than a century. The ban began to be relaxed from the 1820s onwards, partly in response to the failure of nearly a hundred banks in England and Wales in 1826, but it was not fully lifted until the mid-1850s, by which time the Industrial Revolution was well under way.

In the intervening years the stock exchange had found more than enough to do elsewhere. Between 1739 and 1815 the British government had been at war more often than at peace, and this had produced an ever-increasing deficit which had to be financed through bond issuance. And the stock exchange had also been very busy channelling capital to overseas ventures which were perceived to be more profitable than any opportunities available domestically. The 1820s, for instance, had seen the first in what was to become a regular cycle of boom-and-bust forays into South American investments. This fascination with foreign investment may seem strange in an era when communications were so tenuous, but it is worth remembering that before the railways were built, the long-established network of maritime communications meant that London merchants 'felt' closer to Amsterdam and to Hamburg than they did to any city in the north of England.

This openness to continental influence also showed itself in the steady stream of merchants and bankers who migrated to London from Europe, including several who became so acclimatised that they eventually came to typify the very essence of London merchant banking: the Barings from Bremen in 1762, the Rothschilds from Frankfurt in 1798, and the Schroders from Hamburg in 1804.

The Industrial Revolution and after: 1840–1914

The expansion of the railway and mining industries from the 1830s onwards dramatically increased the requirement for fixed capital investment, but the evidence is that this was initially met on a local and regional level. Between 1830 and 1847 the number of provincial stock broking firms increased from just seven to more than 500, and many provincial stock exchanges opened for the first time. From the middle of the nineteenth century it is possible to talk about the emergence of a genuinely national market in securities, but its importance should not be exaggerated. First, apart from banking, mining and railways, most industries were less capital-intensive than is often supposed, and certainly much less capital-intensive than their modern counterparts. When businesses got into financial trouble, it was less often for lack of long-term fixed capital than because of insufficient liquidity or working capital: that is, short-term revolving bank facilities to finance the production and distribution cycle. Second, many entrepreneurs and family-owned businesses were reluctant to expose themselves to the scrutiny and control of outside shareholders who were complete strangers, so they preferred to finance themselves internally (by retaining profits for reinvestment in the business), by forming partnerships or by raising money through the agency of trusted contacts such as local lawyers. This reluctance to issue new equity but rather to fund expansion internally or by means of debt or *preference shares* (all of which involved less loss of control than the issuance of new equity) in fact characterised the financing of British industry right up until the period after the Second World War.

As far as the London stock exchange was concerned, the century after 1815 was a period of almost continuous peace. The growth in government debt slowed down considerably, and was compensated for by a rapid expansion in overseas investment opportunities. Overall, the history of the exchange in the nineteenth century was dominated by a series of bubbles, scams, and failures and near-failures of broking and banking firms. The last and in some ways most significant of these was the Barings crisis of 1890, when that bank found itself unable to meet its liabilities because it had over-invested in Argentinian bonds which proved to be illiquid. The Bank of England averted a broader crisis of confidence by organising the other major London banks into a guarantee fund to keep Barings afloat.

Table 1.1 summarises the growth and the changing composition of the stock exchange in the 60 years leading up to the First World War. It should be explained that most of these securities were *debentures* (secured bonds) and other types of non-ordinary-share securities such as preference shares.

Towards the end of the nineteenth century, differences in the pattern of corporate organisation and structure began to emerge between the United Kingdom and the United States, which would have important repercussions for the later development of the stock markets in those countries. At first sight, both countries were characterised by an outbreak of merger mania in the 25 to 30 years before the First World War, but closer inspection reveals key differences, which are partly attributable to the fact that successive UK governments stuck to a policy of free trade while those of its main emerging competitors – the United States, newly unified Germany and Japan – sought to foster the growth of domestic companies behind a wall of protectionism. As a result, whereas US mergers tended to have an expansionist and aggressive flavour, many of those in the United Kingdom were essentially defensive. US mergers tended to be *vertical* – that is, to seek

Table 1.1 Nominal value of securities on London stock exchange, 1853 and 1913

| | 1853 | | 1913 | |
	£ million	%	£ million	%
Domestic:				
Gilts and municipals	854	70	1,290	11
Railways	194	16	1,217	11
Other companies	66	6	2,079	19
Total domestic	1,114	92	4,586	41
Foreign:				
Governments	70	6	3,746	33
Railways	31	3	2,931	26
Total foreign	101	9	6,677	59
Grand total	1,215	100	11,262	100

Source: Morgan and Thomas (1962).

savings, efficiencies and growth opportunities through the integration of several connecting links in the supply, production and distribution chain – whereas UK mergers tended rather to take the form of *horizontal* alliances between direct competitors in an industry. To this extent, many UK mergers performed some of the essentially defensive functions of trade associations and cartels. One result of this trend was that big business, in the now familiar form of an enterprise organised into formal divisions under the ultimate control of a strong unifying centralised management, emerged rather later in the United Kingdom than in the other three major industrial countries.

The wars and their aftermath: 1914–79

The First World War radically refocused the attention of the London financial markets, and the stock exchange in particular, on the domestic scene. From the 1920s onwards the financing needs of domestic industry increased sharply just at a time when the strains of waging the first 'total war' had seriously weakened the country's external finances and reduced the volume of surplus capital available for overseas investment. Fundraising by companies on the stock exchange continued to be dominated by offerings of non-equity securities. In addition to the reasons noted above, a deliberate government policy of keeping interest rates low from 1931 onwards, to deter the potential influx of foreign capital and its destabilising effect on the currency, made debt the most attractive source of new capital. There was also a huge increase in the amount of the National Debt, and the first signs emerged of *crowding out* of the private sector by the ever-expanding public sector.

The Second World War reinforced most of these trends but there were new factors too. At the outbreak of war exchange controls were imposed, radically restricting the ability of UK residents (individuals as well as companies) to purchase foreign currencies to finance investment or spending abroad. The United Kingdom emerged from the war with crippling external debts which led to further loss of overseas assets; the external value of sterling became a chronic problem and as a result exchange controls remained in place for a total of 40 years. Although industry was generally very liquid at the end of the war, from 1950 onwards its appetite for new outside capital increased sharply as the economy finally began to emerge from wartime controls and resume a growth path.

For the first time, companies began to look to the equity market to fill a large part of this financing gap. Many factors were at work here. On the positive side, the increasing popularity of fully funded pension schemes meant that pension funds had a need for a long-term asset whose value would grow in line with the growth of the economy, and bonds – with their fixed maturities and repayment amounts – did not meet this requirement. On the negative side, although the returns on bonds were relatively certain in monetary terms, high and unstable inflation and interest rates, which dogged the UK economy for most of the period from the late 1950s until the 1980s, undermined the value of these returns in real terms, belying the ostensibly low-risk nature of bond investment.

The rapid growth in equity financing also meant that the divorce between ownership and control, which UK industrialists had tended to resist, now gathered pace. It is no coincidence that the same period saw an equally rapid growth in the popularity of the hostile takeover bid. Shareholders with no history of long-term loyalty to a company proved to be susceptible to persuasion by predators who saw opportunities to extract more value out of their companies by replacing incumbent management and merging the business into larger units.

Despite the presence of exchange controls and the economic problems that beset the UK for much of the second half of the twentieth century, the City responded with typical flexibility and opportunism to develop new lines of business to replace those that were in decline. Foremost among these was the development of the ***euromarkets***.

In the 1950s and 1960s a number of factors had come together to cause a substantial build-up in the holdings of US dollar balances by governments, companies and other organisations that were not resident in the United States. These factors included (for governments) the importance of keeping a large part of their external reserves of gold and foreign currency in the form of US dollars (which until August 1970 were backed by the US government's promise to convert them into gold at the fixed price of US$40 for one ounce). The chronic external trade deficit of the United States also led to an accumulation of dollar balances overseas. For various reasons it became either unattractive or inadvisable for these balances to be held directly in accounts at the US offices of banks. One reason (particularly among governments that were not wholly sympathetic to the United States) was the fear of possible expropriation. A more technical reason was the imposition by the US authorities of maximum interest rates on deposits held in US domestic banking offices, and of a withholding tax on interest paid on such deposits. As a result, from the 1950s onwards it became increasingly popular to redeposit these dollars in banking offices in London. As time passed, the practice spread to other financial centres and to other currencies, so that a general definition of a ***eurocurrency*** is any currency held in a bank outside the country of the currency itself. So sterling balances held in Paris banks were eurosterling balances, deutschmark balances held in Luxemburg banks were euromarks, and so on. A key benefit of holding balances in this way was that it not only escaped the possibly unwelcome attentions of the US authorities but also was subject to a lighter regulatory regime in its adoptive country than was applied to banking and other transactions in the local currency.

Dollar balances held outside the United States did not lie idle in their offshore bank accounts, but were actively lent out to governments, companies and other borrowers in the eurodollar loan market, and before long an active market in eurocurrency bonds

---

Box 1.6 Confusing terminology 4: Euromarkets and euromarkets

For the first 30 years or so of their existence, the euromarkets – complete with their eurocurrencies, eurobonds and eurodeposits – were relatively easy to understand and caused little confusion. It was only necessary to remember only one central principle – that a euro-instrument was one issued outside the country of the currency in which it was denominated – and almost everything else was plain sailing. Then in the late 1990s 12 of the 15 countries in the European Union joined together in a single currency called the euro, which was introduced on 1 January 1999 and finally replaced their national currencies on 1 January 2002. Together these countries are known as the eurozone and their governments now issue bonds not in their former national currencies but in the euro. The euro is therefore their domestic currency for all purposes, including capital markets transactions.

It is usually apparent from the context whether a writer or speaker using the word 'euro' either on its own or in a compound (like 'eurobond') is referring to the European single currency or is using the term in its older and still current sense of an instrument or market outside the country of its currency. The usual (but by no means universal) convention in writing about the single currency is to spell it with a lower case 'e' ('euro' not 'Euro'), and in compound expressions to keep it separate from other words; so, for example, a euro bond is a bond denominated in euros, whereas a eurobond is a bond issued outside the country of the currency in which it is denominated.

---

sprang up. London continues to dominate the global eurobond business, with an estimated 75 per cent share in total *origination* (new issues) of this product.

Changes since 1979

Exchange controls were completely abolished, without prior warning, by the incoming Conservative government in 1979. This simultaneously increased the attractiveness of the United Kingdom as a destination for inward investment, and opened up the more or less unlimited possibilities of overseas investment for UK individuals and institutions. As Table 1.2 shows, the proportion of UK equities held by foreign investors had sharply declined by some 50 per cent during the 1960s and 1970s to a level of just 3.6 per cent in 1981, but in the following decade it more than tripled and continued to rise steadily to its present level of almost one third of the entire market.

This radical change in the external environment for investment was soon matched by far-reaching changes in the way the securities markets themselves were organised.

When the first edition of this book appeared in the early 1980s, a UK graduate embarking on a career in the City of London could still say that he (or – less probably – she, for it was only ten years since membership of the exchange had been opened to women) was going to work 'on the stock exchange'. That venerable phrase denoted a specific geographical location: 'on' had its origin in 'on the floor of', and the stock exchange tower itself – all 26 floors of it – had physically dominated the central City skyline when it was opened by the Queen just ten years earlier. But the phrase also described equally precisely and exclusively a discrete set of activities – the trade in UK government securities and in shares issued almost exclusively by UK companies. To be absolutely precise, the phrase described two closely interlinked but strictly distinct activities: the trading in

Table 1.2 Beneficial ownership of UK shares 1963–2004, by percentage of equity owned

	1963	1969	1975	1981	1989	1990	1991	1992	1993	1994	1997	1998	1999	2000	2001	2002	2003	2004
Rest of the world	7.0	6.6	5.6	3.6	12.8	11.8	12.8	13.1	16.3	16.3	24.0	27.6	29.3	32.4	31.9	32.1	32.3	32.6
Insurance companies	10.0	12.2	15.9	20.5	18.6	20.4	20.8	19.5	20.0	21.9	23.5	21.6	21.6	21.0	20.0	19.9	17.3	17.2
Pension funds	6.4	9.0	16.8	26.7	30.6	31.7	31.3	32.4	31.7	27.8	22.1	21.7	19.6	17.7	16.1	15.6	16.1	13.7
Individuals	54.0	47.4	37.5	28.2	20.6	20.3	19.9	20.4	17.7	20.3	16.5	16.7	15.3	16.0	14.8	14.3	14.9	14.1
Unit trusts	1.3	2.9	4.1	3.6	5.9	6.1	5.7	6.2	6.6	6.8	6.7	3.0	2.7	1.7	1.8	1.6	2.0	1.9
Investment trusts					1.6	1.6	1.5	2.1	2.5	2.0	1.9	1.9	1.9	2.1	2.2	1.8	2.3	3.3
Other financial institutions	11.3[1]	10.1[1]	10.5[1]	6.8[1]	1.1	0.7	0.8	0.4	0.6	1.3	2.0	4.1	5.1	4.6	9.9	10.5	11.1	10.7
Charities	2.1	2.1	2.3	2.2	2.3	1.9	2.4	1.8	1.6	1.3	1.9	1.4	1.3	1.4	1.0	1.1	1.2	1.1
Private non-financial companies	5.1	5.4	3.0	5.1	3.8	2.8	3.3	1.8	1.5	1.1	1.2	1.4	2.2	1.5	1.0	0.8	0.7	0.6
Public sector	1.5	2.6	3.6	3.0	2.0	2.0	1.3	1.8	1.3	0.8	0.1	.01	0.1	–	–	–	–	0.1
Banks	1.3	1.7	0.7	0.3	0.7	0.7	0.2	0.5	0.6	0.4	0.1	0.6	1.0	1.4	1.3	2.1	2.2	2.7
Total²	100.0	100.0	100.0	100.0	100.0	100.0	100.0	100.0	100.0	100.0	100.0	100.0	100.0	100.0	100.0	100.0	100.0	100.0

1 Includes investment trusts
2 Components may not sum to the total because of rounding

Source: Office for National Statistics.

securities as principal or market-maker by *stockjobbers*, and the purchase and sale of such securities on behalf of clients by *stockbrokers* acting as their agents, in a *single-capacity* system in which firms could engage in one but not both of these activities. The external demarcation line between the stock exchange and the rest of the financial services industry, and in particular the banking sector, was drawn almost as clearly as this internal division between jobbing and broking. The corporate finance departments of the larger UK merchant banks worked closely with stockbrokers in connection with new issues and takeovers, but otherwise the direct links between the banking industry and the stock market were relatively tenuous.

This was all changed by the wave of deregulation which swept through the UK economy in general, and the financial sector in particular, in the course of the 1980s. The initial thrust of government attention on the City had been concentrated quite narrowly on the restrictive stock exchange practice of charging agreed minimum commission rates for securities transactions. But as the implications of dismantling this monopolistic practice gradually sank in, it became clear that exposing the stock exchange to the free flow of competitive market forces would create risks and opportunities which made it both necessary and desirable to attract into the exchange significant new resources in the form of external capital. The abolition of minimum commission rates in 1986 thus ultimately became the trigger for a whole series of changes which collectively came to be known as Big Bang:

○ Ownership of member firms, which had previously been unlimited partnerships of either brokers or jobbers, was opened up to outside limited companies.
○ All firms became broker/dealers and were able, if they wished, to operate in a dual capacity as agents and as principals.
○ Minimum scales of commission were abolished.
○ Individual members ceased to have voting rights.

Trading moved from being conducted face-to-face on a market floor to being performed via computer and telephone from separate dealing rooms located either 'upstairs' (that is, in the member firms' suites of offices on the upper floors of the Stock Exchange tower) or, increasingly, from within member firms' own premises located elsewhere in the City.

The effect of these changes was as rapid as it was dramatic. Within a couple of years and with very few exceptions, the existing firms of brokers and jobbers alike were bought up by other financial institutions (primarily, but by no means exclusively, by the UK commercial and merchant banks) and thus contributed to the formation of what became the 'one-stop shops' that characterise the City landscape today. That was but the first wave of ownership changes; a second, more protracted wave in the 1990s led to the current situation where the UK capital markets are dominated by the presence of a handful of foreign-owned, mostly US-based, investment banks.

Concurrently with the liberalising measures of Big Bang came equally radical moves to improve and systematise the chaotic and inadequate arrangements for investor protection in the United Kingdom. These moves imposed new layers of regulation on the investment industry at the same time as Big Bang was deregulating it. The new regime came into force with the passing of the Financial Services Act 1986, which among many other changes subsumed the previously virtually independent and self-governing stock exchange for the first time into a broader statutory framework. This framework is loosely described as *self-regulation* but is more accurately defined as *practitioner-based regulation*. The basic regulations were imposed from above by legislation but the detailed procedural rule books, and their enforcement, were delegated to a number of approved practitioner-led associations, each of which specialised in a segment of the investment industry, with separate bodies looking after (for example) the investment management and securities trading sectors.

Just as Big Bang was followed by two distinct waves of ownership changes among the major players in the industry, the regulatory regime created by the 1986 Financial Services Act proved only to be a first attempt at a truly comprehensive and watertight system of investor protection. The experience gained under the 1986 Act, as well as the changing patterns of activity in the markets themselves, led eventually to a second piece of primary legislation, the Financial Services and Markets Act of 2001. Under the new regime created by the 2001 Act, the former multiplicity of self-regulatory bodies was replaced by a single statutory body, the *Financial Services Authority*. (Confusingly, this is now universally referred to as the *FSA*, which had also been the accepted abbreviation for the 1986 Act which was now consigned to the history books.) This reflected the fact that most larger financial institutions were active in several different sectors and so – under the 1986 regime – were subject to multiple and overlapping supervision. Most of these institutions were also banks, and the licensing and supervision of banks as banks had been left completely outside the 1986 investor-protection framework in the hands of the UK central bank, the Bank of England. The 2001 Act therefore not only subsumed under the FSA the functions of all the former investor-protection organisations, but also transferred to the FSA the prudential supervision of the banks. A further spur for this change was the government decision taken in 1997 to transfer from the Treasury to the Bank of England the responsibility for monetary policy in general and for the setting of interest rates in particular. It was felt that this responsibility did not sit well with the role of banking supervisor in view of the possible conflicts of interest it could produce, especially in times of crisis.

As far as the stock exchange was concerned, the changes that culminated in the 2001 Act completed a process whereby more and more of its traditional functions have in effect been delegated or outsourced. The FSA now has responsibility not only for licensing and supervision of firms and individuals engaged in securities trading, but also – as the UK listing authority – for the vetting and approval of share and other securities issues for listing on the exchange, for the ongoing compliance of listed companies with the listing rules (with regard, for example, to the timely and orderly publication of information to investors), and for the integrity, efficiency and transparency of the securities markets generally.

In 1997, the stock exchange began the transition to an order-driven market with the introduction of the **Stock Exchange Trading System** (**SETS** for short), initially for trading in the most liquid stocks (the top 100 shares) but subsequently extended to most of the top 250 shares. Smaller issues, in which the natural level of market supply and demand may be insufficient to guarantee the maintenance of a liquid two-way market at all times, continue to be traded either on a hybrid system (**SETSmm**, which is a version of SETS supported by dedicated market-makers) or as before on a purely quote-driven system. Examples 1.2 and 1.3 show sample screen displays for stocks traded on SETS and on SETSmm respectively.

Example 1.2 Sample SETS screen

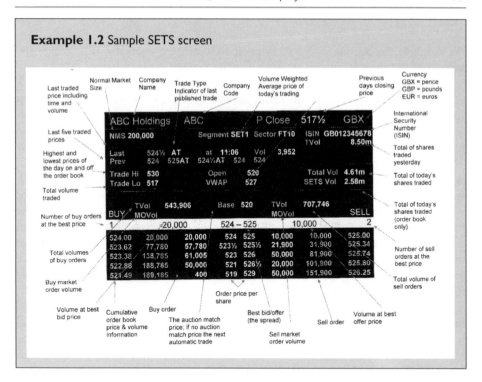

Example 1.3 Sample SETSmm screen, highlighting differences from standard SETS screen

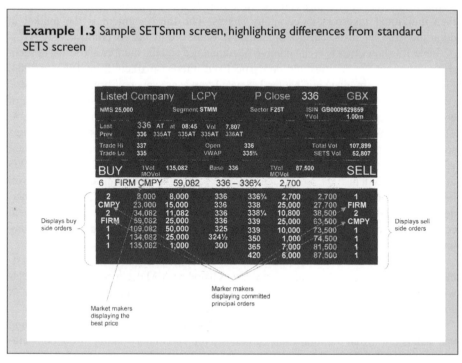

The present

We conclude this section with a description and statistical overview of the range and volume of securities now listed and traded on the London stock exchange.

As we have already seen, the principal types of securities traded on the London stock exchange are shares and bonds. Shares are divided into three categories. The Official List (or Main Market) comprises shares issued by UK companies that have their primary listing on the London exchange. Many of these companies (and most of the largest ones) also maintain a secondary listing on one or more foreign exchanges – in most cases the New York market. The Main Market is the most tightly regulated of the three share markets. A separate, more lightly regulated market, the Alternative Investment Market (or AIM), was established in 1995 for shares in smaller UK and foreign companies, particularly for young rapidly growing companies that could not meet the stringent requirements of the main market in terms of their track record. The third market is the market in foreign companies (mostly, but by no means exclusively, large international companies) that maintain their primary listings in their home countries but find it advantageous to have a secondary listing in London because of the increased visibility it gives to their shares and to their business in general.

The bond market also divides naturally into three segments. The most important is the market in UK government bonds or **gilts**, which is described in detail in Chapter 3, and is subject to a unique regulatory regime of its own. The second segment, the eurobond market, is more lightly regulated than the Main Market, because of the generally high credit standing of issuers in that market, and also because it is dominated by banks and institutional investors that are considered to require a less rigorously protective regime than individual investors in company shares. The third segment is the market in domestic fixed interest securities other than those issued by the government.

Table 1.3 shows trends in the number of companies and the number and value of securities issued on the equities and domestic fixed interest markets from 1963 to 2004. Figures for gilts are given in Chapter 3. Several trends are apparent from these numbers. As far as the Main Market is concerned, there has been a steady decrease in the number of companies listed, and in the average number of types of security issued by each company. The latter development is the result of the near-disappearance of domestic fixed interest securities; not only has the number of such issues shrunk by over 80 per cent, but their value in comparison with the market value of equities has fallen from 12 per cent in 1963 to barely 1 per cent in 2004. Note that the relative value of fixed income securities was still rising in the 1960s to a peak of almost 20 per cent of equity value in 1973. It is no coincidence that 1975 saw the highest rate of inflation recorded in the UK in the twentieth century (25 per cent); inflation and the associated high and volatile interest rates swung investor sentiment decisively against domestic fixed income securities.

A second clear trend is the popularity of the more lightly regulated Alternative Investment Market. Although the total value of issues listed on AIM declined along with worldwide stock market prices in the first three years of the new century, the number of companies seeking a listing continued to increase steadily.

The trends in the figures for foreign companies are perhaps less clear. The first thing that stands out is that the total value of issues with a secondary listing in London actually exceeded the value of domestic issues throughout the 40-year period under review, although the last five years has seen a decline not only in the number of companies listed

Table 1.3 Companies and securities listed on the London stock exchange, 1963–2004 (figures up to 1994 include Irish companies)

		Equities			Fixed interest	
		No. of companies	No. of secs.	Market value (£m)	No. of secs.	Nominal value (£m)
Main Market	1963	4,409	4,064	32,204	4,173	3,780
	1968	3,673	3,470	35,643	4,252	5,290
	1973	3,585	3,301	40,841	4,243	8,113
	1978	2,930	2,486	64,203	3,474	7,337
	1983	2,295	1,995	156,800	2,787	7,806
	1988	2,054	2,041	398,488	2,253	17,805
	1993	1,927	2,050	810,103	1,605	22,550
	1998	2,087	2,591	1,422,480	951	27,742
	1999	1,945	2,393	1,820,077	858	21,671
	2000	1,904	2,272	1,796,811	819	19,952
	2001	1,809	2,117	1,523,524	758	18,975
	2002	1,701	1,962	1,147,827	704	16,507
	2003	1,557	1,751	1,355,833	634	15,845
	2004	1,465	1,575	1,460,705	567	15,082
AIM	1995	121	129	2,382	14	66
	1996	252	253	5,299	24	82
	1997	308	309	5,655	25	93
	1998	312	311	4,438	20	94
	1999	347	364	13,468	22	102
	2000	524	535	14,935	15	69
	2001	629	631	11,607	15	36
	2002	704	711	10,252	23	39
	2003	754	736	18,358	26	44
	2004	1,021	953	31,753	27	23
Foreign	1966	417		29,124		
	1968	420		42,490		
	1973	397		115,771		
	1978	374		192,950		
	1983	437		486,796		
	1988	526		926,069		
	1993	485		1,918,431		
	1998	522		2,804,584		
	1999	499		3,577,484		
	2000	501		3,525,701		
	2001	453		2,580,359		
	2002	419		1,901,689		
	2003	381		1,974,811		
	2004	351		1,971,636		

Source: London stock exchange.

but also in their relative market value (even after allowing for the general decline in stock market values since the peak of late 1999).

Table 1.4 shows turnover statistics for equities since 1965 (UK Main Market), 1988 (foreign) and 1995 (AIM). The underlying trends in these figures are rather less easy to discern than in Table 1.3, because of changes in the pattern of share ownership between institutions and individuals, and in the trading and investing habits of these groups. We shall return to the theme of share ownership in Chapters 5, 10 and 12. Turnover during 2004 in domestic fixed interest securities amounted to just £30 billion. Some 35 per cent of this total was in *convertible bonds*, and a further 35 per cent in preference shares.

Finally, it is worth noting that even the apparently 'domestic' section of the equities market in fact has a very international flavour. A popular misconception is that the shares quoted on the Main Market of the stock exchange somehow represent a notional economic entity called 'UK plc' (similar to 'US Inc'). This could hardly be further from the truth, for three main reasons.

First, very large sections of the UK economy are either privately owned or under the control of foreign companies which may have secondary listings in London but invariably have their primary listings elsewhere. A prominent but by no means atypical example is the volume manufacture of cars in the United Kingdom. This is now in the hands of foreign companies. But the shares of four of the largest car manufacturers in the United Kingdom – Ford, General Motors, Honda and Toyota – do have secondary listings on the London market. Similarly, the second-largest UK supermarket chain, Asda, is a subsidiary of the world's largest retailer, Wal-Mart of the United States, but this company does not have a secondary listing in London. In the second rank of UK supermarket chains, one of the biggest operators (Waitrose) is a division of the retailing group John Lewis, which is not a listed company at all but is organised instead as a unique kind of partnership; and the nationwide chain of co-operative foodstores are just that – co-operatives.

Second, many companies that have a primary listing on the Main Market of the London stock exchange conduct a large part of their operations, and earn a substantial proportion of their revenue, outside the United Kingdom. Listed UK companies are required to include in their published accounts a segmental analysis of their sales, profits and net assets by type of business and by geographic region, and a glance at these shows just how misguided the 'UK plc' notion is. According to figures published by the five largest companies quoted on the Main Market (Shell, BP, HSBC, Vodafone and GlaxoSmithKline, which together account for nearly one-third of the total value of all listed shares), none of them earns anything like 50 per cent of its profits in the United Kingdom: all of them are global companies which happen to be headquartered in the United Kingdom. Shell, BP and HSBC publish their accounts in US dollars as the natural currency of their respective businesses; Vodafone publishes its accounts in US dollars and in sterling. Some quoted companies conduct substantially all of their operations outside the United Kingdom and have an insignificant business presence in this country. This is especially true of mining companies, which have been a speciality of the London market since the earliest days of the Industrial Revolution and which continue to seek a London listing because of the depth of experience and understanding that this market brings to bear on a highly specialised sector.

Third, the extent to which companies are financed by equity varies widely between sectors, between companies within a sector, and with the rise and fall of the economic

Table 1.4 Turnover in equities on the London stock exchange, 1965–2004

		Value (£m)	No. of bargains	Average value per bargain (£)
Main Market	1965	3,479	3,417,395	1,018
	1968	9,118	5,313,166	1,716
	1973	17,079	4,954,799	3,447
	1978	19,215	4,129,963	4,652
	1983	52,340	4,277,402	12,236
	1988	325,589	7,099,717	45,859
	1993	563,967	10,343,533	54,524
	1998	1,037,137	16,277,103	63,718
	1999	1,410,590	21,076,558	66,927
	2000	1,895,534	29,427,308	64,414
	2001	1,904,845	32,130,988	59,284
	2002	1,815,034	37,508,832	48,390
	2003	1,876,922	46,160,508	40,661
	2004	2,316,194	53,907,459	42,966
AIM	1995	270	29,009	544
	1996	1,944	187,975	5,529
	1997	2,415	217,426	6,443
	1998	1,948	225,494	6,921
	1999	5,398	845,556	21,258
	2000	13,606	2,013,584	39,510
	2001	4,855	706,582	28,167
	2002	3,518	449,876	24,792
	2003	6,616	823,948	57,662
	2004	18,126	1,675,955	97,326
Foreign	1988	79,649	727,037	109,553
	1993	579,570	2,791,157	207,645
	1998	2,183,248	7,118,502	306,701
	1999	2,420,134	7,563,399	319,980
	2000	3,519,722	11,300,814	311,457
	2001	3,676,342	17,454,095	210,629
	2002	2,780,317	15,159,382	183,406
	2003	1,759,120	9,949,410	176,806

Source: London stock exchange.

cycle. The more mature, stable and cash-generative an industry is, the less it needs to finance itself with risk capital (that is, with equity) and the more it can afford to finance itself with debt: we shall see later that *leveraging* in this way has the effect of enhancing the return to the shareholders, although it also increases the risks they bear. Conversely, companies and sectors that are at a very early stage in their development do not have the track record or cash flow to support a high level of debt, and have to rely to a greater extent on risk capital.

Finally, the market value of foreign listings exceeded the market value of domestic listings in 2004. In addition, the London stock exchange has some foreign companies listed on both the Main Market and AIM.

The combined impact of all these factors is that the shares listed on the London stock exchange do not directly reflect the structure or the performance of the UK domestic economy. This can be seen from the fact that just four industry sectors – banks, pharmaceuticals, telecommunications and oils – account for 50 per cent by value of all UK company ordinary shares listed on the Main Market. Particularly significant is that fact that whereas a single telecommunications company (Vodafone) accounts for nearly 5 per cent of the market, all the other non-telecommunications utilities together – water, electricity and gas – make up less than 4 per cent. This is because the other utilities are generally more mature, more stable and more cash generative than mobile telephony, so that they have less need to finance themselves with public risk capital; also, many of them are now owned by subsidiaries of foreign companies or indeed companies that are 100 per cent international.

SUMMARY

This chapter has provided an initial introduction to the products, the markets and the players in the world of stock exchange securities investment.

We identified securities as an important subset of the financial products and instruments that a developed economy uses to channel more efficiently its capital resources from surplus sectors (primarily households), which have a temporary excess, to deficit sectors (primarily governments and commercial firms). What makes securities special is that they can readily be bought and sold. Securities come in many shapes and forms, but perhaps the most important distinction is between bonds, which constitute fixed, contractual and legally enforceable claims against the borrowers or issuers, and equities, which constitute a right only to a share in the residual income and assets of issuers after all contractual claims have been discharged.

We then saw how an organised market in such securities can bring benefits to both sectors and to the economy as a whole, primarily by reducing transaction costs and by transforming savings in such a way that both savers and borrowers can get closer to the rather different products that each would ideally like to have.

A key characteristic of a securities market is its informational efficiency, that is, the extent to which its prices fully reflect all relevant information, and we made a preliminary study of the efficient markets hypothesis – a theme to which we return in Chapters 12 and 13.

Finally we sketched the unique evolution of the London financial and securities markets. We saw how the London market first established, and then, by a process of endless adaptation, maintained its position as the world's pre-eminent market for international financial transactions.

REVIEW EXERCISES

1. What are the main functions of an organised market in securities? Outline the main benefits of such markets for:
   a. issuers of securities

b. investors

c. the economy in general.

2. Describe how and why London maintained its pre-eminence as an international financial marketplace despite the relative decline of the UK economy in the first 80 years of the twentieth century.

3. Describe the main changes which have taken place in the UK stock exchange since the early 1980s. Why do you think these changes have occurred?

4. Compare and contrast shares and bonds, from the points of view of:

a. the issuer

b. the investor.

5. Describe the main stages in the evolution of the efficient markets hypothesis. Do you agree that, in a strong-form efficient market, the market price for a security is invariably a fair price? Give your reasons.

6. Visit the website of the London stock exchange (www.londonstockexchange.com) and look for the latest versions of the statistics reproduced in Tables 1.3 and 1.4. How have they evolved in the intervening period? What do you think are the main factors that have influenced that evolution?

7. What are the principal factors influencing the relative certainty or uncertainty of future cash flows from a security? Explain how each of them might impact the expected return from:

a. shares

b. bonds.

Sample answers to these exercises can be found on the companion website.

2 Investment return and risk

CHAPTER CONTENTS

Learning objectives for this chapter

After studying this chapter you should be able to

○ calculate the holding period return on an investment
○ apply the basic principle connecting the price and return of an investment
○ be aware of the different types of risk affecting securities
○ calculate the expected return of a security and its risk as measured by the standard deviation of its returns
○ calculate the expected utility of an investment.

INTRODUCTION

This chapter discusses the two most important attributes of every investment: return and risk. When considering any security, the investor is always concerned with the return expected on the investment and the **risk** of the investment, that is, how likely it is that the return expected will be achieved. In a certain world, the return would always be exactly as expected and there would be no risk. The investor would merely have to compare the returns available on different investments and choose those that offered the highest returns.

Unfortunately, the existence of uncertainty means that returns on investments are not always as expected. The hoped-for dividends on the shares in the speculative Australian mining company might never materialise, or the company whose bond you hold may go into liquidation. All securities are subject to risk. Different types of securities will have different kinds of risk attached to them (for example, UK government securities do not suffer the risk of default but are vulnerable to changes in interest rates). However the effect of all these different kinds of risk is the same: the *actual* returns achieved will be different from those *expected* by the investor. The riskier the security is, the more likely it is that the hoped-for return will not be achieved, or the greater the likely shortfall from the expected return.

So investors need to be able to quantify both the uncertain return and the level of that uncertainty for each security before they can make investment decisions. Depending on their attitude towards risk and return, they will then be able to choose the securities that offer them the combination of risk and return that best suits them.

The chapter starts by introducing the standard measure of return, known as the *holding period return*, which is all investors would need to be able to make investment decisions under certainty. We then go on to consider investment decisions made under uncertainty and different types of risk to which securities are subject, namely uncertainty of income, default risk, interest rate risk and inflation risk.

Given uncertainty, it is not possible to determine in advance the future holding period return on any security, since a range of returns is possible. The concept of a probability distribution of returns is then introduced. This enables investors to quantify both the return they *expect* to get and the probability of not achieving that return. Investors can then decide, according to the level of return they wish to achieve and the amount of risk they are willing to bear, which securities they prefer. If they are averse to taking on risk, they will prefer the securities that offer the least risk for any given return or the most return for any given level of risk. We shall assume that the average investor on the stock exchange is what is known as *risk averse*.

The concept of *utility*, which combines the attitudes of each investor to both risk and return into one measure, is then discussed. Utility also takes into account the wealth of the investor, so each security must be analysed to see how its returns will affect the investor's wealth. Utility enables investors, if they know their *utility function* (which they can estimate by evaluating their attitude to certain risk–return alternatives), to calculate the expected utility of each investment opportunity. All they then have to do is to choose the one that offers them the highest expected utility.

The chapter concludes with a section on two ways of reducing risk without reducing expected return. These are *pooling* and *hedging*, and investors can apply these methods of reducing risk by diversifying their securities portfolio (as discussed in detail in Chapter 6) and by making use of the various futures markets referred to in the text.

HOLDING PERIOD RETURN

Investors, when deciding on which securities they wish to hold in their portfolios, have to be able to compare them directly. Each security is characterised by a market price, the cost of the security, and a pattern of cash flows. Suppose share A cost 486p and, at the end of six months, paid a dividend of 20p just before it was sold for 500p. How can it be compared with share B, bought at 30p, held for one year and then sold for 35p with no dividend payment? Obviously the different costs of the shares must be taken into account, as well as the different time periods involved.

Calculating the percentage holding period return for each security avoids the problem of comparing different-sized investments. This return is simply the gain during the period held (money received less cost) divided by the cost. So:

$$R = \frac{D_1 + P_1 - P_0}{P_0} \tag{2.1}$$

where P_0 is the cost, P_1 the value of the investment at the end of the holding period and D_1 any interest or dividend payments made during the period. Using equation 2.1, the holding period returns of shares A and B can be calculated and compared as in Example 2.1.

The holding period returns of A and B are still not yet directly comparable since B was

Example 2.1 Holding period returns of shares A and B

Share	Holding period return	Holding period (months)
A	$R_A = \dfrac{(20 + 500) - 486}{486}$	
	$= 0.070$	
	$R_A = 7.0\%$	6
B	$R_B = \dfrac{(0 + 35) - 30}{30}$	
	$= 0.167$	
	$R_B = 16.7\%$	12

invested for twice as long as A. When A was sold, the proceeds could have been reinvested for another six months but we do not know what return would have been available to the investor at that time. An alternative solution would be to calculate the equivalent six-monthly return on B. This is done in Example 2.2 by equating the return on money invested for two six-month periods, at a return r_B per period, to money invested for an equivalent one-year period at return R_B, the one-year holding period return.

We can now compare A, which offered a return of 7% over six months, with B which offered a higher equivalent return over the same period of 8%.

Most investors would no doubt choose the investment that offered the highest return over any particular period. If we look at Table 2.1 to see which investments have typically yielded the highest returns in the past, we note that ordinary shares have, on average, out-performed long-term gilts on annual return over the past 100 years.

With this evidence before them, investors would surely always buy shares. And yet many investors choose gilts or hold at least some gilts in their investment portfolio. The reason that people invest in gilts can be seen from the third column in Table 2.1, which shows the *variation* in annual return achieved on shares and gilts. Although gilts have offered a lower return on average, they have also offered less chance of a large negative return or loss. This means that investors cannot just look at return alone when making investment decisions, they must also consider *risk*.

Table 2.1 Returns and risk of different types of security

1900–2000	Annual average return (%)	Range of annual returns (%)
Long-term gilts	6.1	+0.5 to +17.2
Ordinary shares	12.1	-48.8 to 145.6

Source: Dimson, Marsh and Staunton (2001).

Example 2.2 Six-month holding period return

Suppose that £100 is invested for six months at 5%. At the end of six months, it will be worth

$$£100 (1 + 0.05) = £105$$

If reinvested for another six months at 5% it will be worth

$$£105 (1 + 0.05) = £110.25$$

or

$$£100 (1 + 0.05)^2$$

If we define r_B to be the six-monthly return equivalent to an annual holding period return on B of R_B, we can write

$$(1 + r_B)^2 = 1 + R_B$$

We know $R_B = 16.7\%$ or 0.167, giving

$$(1 + r_B)^2 = 1.167$$

Solving,

$$r_B = 0.080$$
$$r_B = 8.0\%$$

TYPES OF RISK

There are several different types of risk that can lead to variability in return on a security. Some securities, such as gilts, will have few risks attached to them, whereas company shares will be subject to many possible reasons for fluctuations in return. One of the risks to which ordinary shares are subject is *uncertainty of income*.

Uncertainty of income

The risk of uncertainty of income is a risk to which all ordinary shareholders are subject. This can be seen by looking at the holding period return on an ordinary share, which can be written as

$$R = \frac{D_1 + P_1 - P_0}{P_0} \tag{2.1}$$

where D_1 is the dividend expected to be paid during the holding period, P_0 the share purchase price and P_1 the price at the end of the period. When we considered shares A and B, we knew the values of D_1, P_0 and P_1 because in that case we were looking at *past* returns achieved on the investments. Unfortunately, investors are always making investment decisions concerning the future. All they know is P_0, the current market price of the share. They have no idea what the share price will be when they sell it, or what dividend payments they will receive. In contrast with its fixed interest securities, such as debentures, a company does *not* contract to pay its ordinary shareholders any fixed or even any minimum level of dividend.

Ordinary shareholders own the assets of the company after all other claims on it have been satisfied, but the company is under no obligation to pay out these shareholders' funds as dividends. Probably only part of the total profit attributable to ordinary shareholders in any one year will be paid out as dividends, the remainder being retained within the company. If a company is doing well, the ordinary shareholders will expect both to receive a dividend D_1 and for the share price P_1 to exceed P_0, reflecting the retention of earnings by the company. Some fast-growing companies have a policy of paying no dividends at all over a period of years. In these cases the holding period return is purely the capital gain or loss, $P_1 - P_0$.

However, if the company does badly, it does not have to make any payments to ordinary shareholders as it does to its debt-holders. The profitability of any company is subject to certain risks. For example, an economic recession could lead to a reduction in sales, or a political decision could mean higher tax payments. Technical change could render the company's products obsolescent or, on a simpler level, an event such as a fire could wipe out the assets of the company. These factors render the profits of the company uncertain, and since ordinary shareholders are entitled only to the balance of income and capital after all other security-holders have been paid, ordinary shares are the most risky of all securities. On the other hand, ordinary shareholders stand to gain more than fixed interest security-holders, whose return is more limited.

Corporate fixed interest debt-holders suffer, as we have mentioned above, less uncertainty of income since they are promised specific interest payments by the company. However, they are subject to another type of risk, the risk of *default*.

Default risk

If a company does badly, it may be unable to pay the interest on a fixed interest security or to repay the interest on maturity. Only government bonds, fixed interest securities issued or guaranteed by a government, such as UK gilts, are not subject to default risk; governments are the only borrowers that can always avoid default in the last resort by printing more money – provided the debt is in their own currency.

All types of fixed interest corporate debt are subject to default risk, from debenture stocks secured on the assets of the company to unsecured *loan stocks* and *high-yield bonds*, but each will be subject to a different level of risk of losing on the investment. On default, debenture holders can appoint a receiver whose job it is to realise the security they hold and, if it is worth at least the sum they are owed, will suffer no risk. Unsecured loan holders have no security, and rank behind the secured creditors of the company.

Corporate fixed interest securities do not represent a major part of the stock exchange in the United Kingdom, but globally they are an important form of investment, via the eurobond market described in Chapter 4 or the US corporate bond market. Each major company will have several corporate bonds, each with carefully defined rights to the assets of the company in the event of default. For example, a *subordinated* debenture means that it comes lower down in the queue than an *unsubordinated* debenture, and will only be entitled to payment, in the event of default, after the unsubordinated debenture holders have been fully repaid. Example 2.3 shows an extract from the *Financial Times* giving market information on just a few corporate bonds with an investment *credit rating*. Opinions on the creditworthiness and hence the default risk of these bonds range from awarding a rating of AAA for, say, a highly rated bond to C or D for bonds that are already on default, and these ratings are provided by Moody's, Standard & Poor's and Fitch. *Junk bonds* are simply non-***investment grade bonds***, in other words poorly rated by the credit-rating agencies and hence more subject to default risk. More on this in Chapter 4.

Ordinary shareholders do not suffer default risk since they are not entitled to any particular level of income or to any prespecified repayment which might run the risk of not being paid. Preference shareholders, also described in Chapter 4, lie somewhere between fixed interest debt-holders and ordinary shareholders; although they are entitled to fixed interest payments, if these are not made the company is not legally in default, since preference shareholders are part-owners and not creditors of the company.

Other risks

It is easy to see why securities issued by companies, even if they promise a fixed income, have an element of risk. In an uncertain and competitive world some companies may well fail, and given that companies have limited liability, investors in these companies will in the last resort only have recourse to the assets remaining within the company, which may not be sufficient to repay their investments in full. It is less easy, though, to understand why fixed interest securities issued by the British government offer uncertain returns.

The British government first borrowed from the City of London in the sixteenth century, although the secondary market in government securities only became fully developed in the nineteenth century when London was the financial centre of the world. These securities came to be known as gilts because there was absolutely no risk of default. There was never any doubt that the government would pay the interest or repay on maturity, since the government could create the money when needed. In fact, in the nineteenth century a group of people called the 'three percenters' lived on unearned income from investment in gilt-edged stocks which provided an annual return of capital of around 3 per cent. With a £5000 investment in gilts, the annual income of £150 was sufficient to maintain a family in middle-class ease.

How securities' returns and prices are related

Before we can fully analyse the risks inherent in investing in gilts, or any other securities, we must understand how the return (or yield) of any security is related to its price.

Let us consider 2½% Consols, one of the undated gilts (refer to Chapter 3 for a more detailed description of gilts). The term *undated* means that the government promises to pay £2.50 per annum (for every £100 held) indefinitely. The quoted price of 2½% Consols always refers to £100 **nominal** of the stock. However, each year the £2.50 received by investors will appear less valuable to them. £2.50 received now is worth more than £2.50 received next year because it can be invested to yield more than £2.50 in one year's time. Suppose the current one-year interest rate is 10%. £2.50 could be invested to become £2.50 × (1.10) or £2.75 in 12 months' time, and so £2.50 received in one year's time is only worth £2.50/(1.1) or £2.27 today. This £2.27 is known as the ***present value*** of £2.50. The present value of receiving £x in the future is always less than £x because

Example 2.3 Market information on some investment-grade corporate bonds

Nov 29	Red date	Coupon	Ratings S*	M*	F*	Bid price	Bid yield	Day's chge yield	Mth's chge yield	Spread vs Govts
■ US $										
KFW Int Fin	01/07	4.75	AAA	Aaa	AAA	99.90	5.35	+0.02	+0.04	+0.11
CIT Group	04/07	7.38	A	A2	A	100.19	6.72	–	+0.52	+1.71
GE Capital	06/07	5.00	AAA	Aaa	n/a	99.83	5.33	+0.02	+0.12	+0.22
Depfa Pfandrbnk	10/07	3.38	AAA	n/a	AAA	98.50	5.23	–	-0.35	+0.11
Goldman Sachs	01/08	4.13	AA-	Aa3	AA-	98.89	5.15	-0.06	-0.09	+0.02
Citigroup	02/08	3.50	n/a	Aa1	AA+	98.17	5.14	+0.01	–	+0.02
Canada	11/08	5.25	AAA	Aaa	AAA	100.92	4.75	+0.01	–	+0.05
DaimlerChrysler	09/09	7.20	BBB	Baa1	BBB+	103.99	5.62	–	-0.09	+0.97
Wal Mart	08/09	6.88	AA	Aa2	AA	104.43	5.09	-0.04	-0.09	+0.53
Du Pont	10/09	6.88	A	A2	A	104.78	5.06	-0.07	-0.13	+0.50
Philipps Petr	05/10	8.75	A-	A1	A-	111.43	5.13	-0.01	-0.09	+0.56
Unilever	11/10	7.13	A+	A1	A+	106.99	5.13	+0.02	-0.06	+0.54
Bank America	01/11	7.40	A+	Aa3	A+	109.91	4.72	-0.17	-0.12	+0.22
JP Morgan	02/11	6.75	A	A1	A	105.96	5.14	-0.06	-0.16	+0.63
France Telecom	03/11	7.75	A-	A3	A-	109.90	5.13	-0.03	-0.13	+0.62
Petronas	05/12	7.00	A-	A1	A-	108.28	5.24	-0.06	-0.15	+0.74
Goldman Sachs	11/14	5.50	AA-	Aa3	AA-	100.86	5.37	-0.03	-0.15	+0.86
Italy	09/23	6.88	A+	Aa2	AA-	117.83	5.26	-0.01	-0.07	+0.75
Pacific Bell	03/26	7.13	A	A2	A	110.89	6.15	+0.01	-0.17	+1.54
Deutsche Tel	07/13	5.25	A-	A3	A-	97.91	5.63	–		+1.12
DaimlerChrysler	01/31	8.50	BBB	Baa1	BBB+	121.41	6.70	-0.04	-0.16	+2.11
FHLMC	03/31	6.75	AAA	Aaa	AAA	124.72	4.98	-0.02	-0.14	+0.37
GE Capital	03/32	6.75	AAA	Aaa	AAA	117.41	5.47	-0.05	-0.23	+0.88
Gen Motors	11/31	8.00	BB+	Ba1	BB	109.28	7.19	+0.01	-0.26	+2.60
■ Euro										
Dresdner Fin	01/07	4.00	A+	A1	A	100.00	3.88	+0.16	+0.16	+0.51
Eurohypo	02/07	4.00	AAA	Aaa	AAA	100.04	3.63	-0.01	+0.06	+0.16
BNG	05/07	2.88	AAA	Aaa	AAA	99.61	3.72	–	+0.05	+0.14
ING Bank	07/07	5.63	AA	Aa2	AA	101.02	3.76	+0.01	–	+0.26
TPSA Eurofin	12/08	7.75	BBB+	Baa1	BBB+	104.53	5.36	-0.06	-0.06	+0.67
BAT Int Fin	02/09	4.88	BBB+	Baa1	A-	101.73	4.04	+0.04	+0.02	+0.38
VW Int Fin	05/09	4.13	A-	A3	A-	100.53	3.89	+0.04	+0.05	+0.23
SMBC Int Fin	06/09	8.50	A-	A2	BBB+	107.93	5.13	-0.07	-0.12	+0.56
Depfa Pfandrbnk	01/09	3.75	AAA	Aaa	AAA	100.08	3.71	+0.06	+0.01	+0.02
Mannesman Fin	05/09	4.75	A-	A3	A-	101.79	3.97	+0.02	+0.01	+0.31
Deutsche Fin	07/09	4.25	AA-	Aa3	AA-	101.06	3.82	+0.09	+0.04	+0.16
Repsol Int Fin	05/10	6.00	BBB	Baa1	BBB+	105.75	4.15	+0.01	-0.03	+0.49
Elec de France	10/10	5.75	AA-	Aa1	AA	106.79	3.84	+0.12	+0.07	+0.17
HVB	09/11	5.00	AAA	Aa1	AAA	104.87	3.86	+0.02	+0.05	+0.20
■ YEN										
Tokyo Elec	11/06	2.80	MATD	MATD	MATD	100.00	2.80	–	+2.12	–
Nippon Teleg	07/07	2.50	AA-	Aa1	AA-	101.34	0.43	-0.04	+0.06	-0.04
Toyota Motor	06/08	0.75	AAA	Aaa	n/a	100.11	0.68	-0.03	+0.03	+0.07
KFW Int Fin	03/10	1.75	AAA	Aaa	AAA	102.60	0.95	-0.02	+0.05	-0.01
Chubu Elec	07/15	3.40	NR	Aa3	AA-	113.10	1.67	+0.04	-0.02	–
■ £										
DaimlerChrysler	12/06	7.50	BBB	Baa1	BBB+	100.01	5.86	-0.57	+0.37	+0.97
HBOS	04/08	6.38	AA	Aa2	AA+	101.18	5.33	+0.02	+0.03	+0.25
Network Rail	03/09	4.88	AAA	Aaa	AAA	99.23	5.17	+0.02	+0.06	+0.17
Boots	05/09	5.50	BBB	Baa2	BBB	99.61	5.58	+0.01	+0.07	+0.60
France Telecom	03/11	7.50	A-	Baa1	A-	107.60	5.48	+0.01	-0.01	+0.63

US $ denominated bonds NY close; all other London close. *S - Standard & Poor's, M - Moody's, F - Fitch.
Source: Reuters

Source: *Financial Times*, 30 November 2006.

of the *opportunity cost* of not being able to invest the money in the interim. In other words, the investor has forgone the opportunity of investing £x for one year.

Investors can now calculate the present value of receiving a string of future £2.50s if they know the prevailing interest rate, R, on equivalent investments. The present value of £100 nominal of 2½% Consols is P_0, and P_0 can be written as

$$P_0 = \frac{D}{(1+R)} + \frac{D}{(1+R)^2} + \cdots \frac{D}{(1+R)^n} + \cdots \tag{2.2}$$

where D represents the yearly interest payment of £2.50. Of course, the present value, P_0, of the gilt must be its market price if the market is efficient. So, knowing P_0, investors can determine R, called the **discount rate** because it is used to discount future cash flows, and which represents the actual rate of return they will get on their gilt-edged investments, assuming the gilt is held indefinitely.

Equation 2.2 is exactly equivalent to equation 2.1 for the holding period return:

$$R = \frac{D_1 + P_1 - P_0}{P_0} \tag{2.1}$$

This can be seen in Example 2.4, where equation 2.1 is first rearranged to be an expression for the initial price P_0, and then the holding period is extended by one year at a time until the investment is assumed to be held indefinitely.

Equation 2.5 states that the price of an undated fixed interest stock is equal to its *coupon* (the **nominal interest rate**) divided by the required yield. The lower the coupon, relative to the required yield, the lower the price. If we substitute, say, a current market price of £60 for 2½% Consols we can find its required yield.

$$£60 = \frac{£2.50}{R}$$

$R = 4.17\%$

Investors require an annual return of 4.17% on this undated gilt-edged stock. Because the coupon is below this, the price of £100 nominal is low at £60. When Consols were issued, the required yield would have been around 2½–3% and the market price approximately equal to the nominal price of £100. Interest rates are now higher and so the present value, or market price, of a stream of £2.50 interest payments is worth less than its value 100 years or more ago.

This introduction to the yield on gilts now allows us to analyse the two main types of risk affecting all fixed interest securities including gilts, interest rate risk and inflation risk.

Interest rate risk

Let us consider the case of an investor who purchases £100 nominal of 2½% Consols when the prevailing yield on the gilt is 10%. His purchase price, P_0, will be

$$P_0 = \frac{£2.50}{0.10} = £25$$

Example 2.4 Value and return of a security

The holding period return is

$$R = \frac{D_1 + P_1 - P_0}{P_0} \tag{2.1}$$

Multiplying by P_0,

$$RP_0 = D_1 + P_1 - P_0$$

$$P_0 (1 + R) = D_1 + P_1$$

$$P_0 = \frac{D_1}{(1 + R)} + \frac{P_1}{(1 + R)}$$

where P_1 is the price of the security at the end of the holding period, say one year. Now suppose the security is held for two years. We can write

$$P_0 = \frac{D_1}{(1 + R)} + \frac{D_2}{(1 + R)^2} + \frac{P_2}{(1 + R)^2}$$

where D_2 is the income received in year 2 and P_2 the price of the security at the end of the two years. If the security is held for n years we can write

$$P_0 = \frac{D_1}{(1 + R)} + \frac{D_2}{(1 + R)^2} + \cdots \frac{D_n}{(1 + R)^n} + \frac{P_n}{(1 + R)^n}$$

In the special case of an undated gilt, such as 2½% Consols, this becomes

$$P_0 = \frac{D_1}{(1 + R)} + \frac{D_2}{(1 + R)^2} + \cdots \frac{D_n}{(1 + R)^n} + \cdots \tag{2.2}$$

where D is the fixed annual interest payment received indefinitely.

Equation 2.2, for an undated gilt which will pay interest D in perpetuity, can be simplified.

$$P = \frac{D}{(1 + R)} + \frac{D}{(1 + R)^2} + \cdots \frac{D}{(1 + R)^n} + \cdots \tag{2.3}$$

If we multiply throughout by $(1 + R)$

$$(1 + R)P = D + \frac{D}{(1 + R)} + \cdots + \frac{D}{(1 + R)^{n-1}} + \frac{D}{(1 + R)^n} + \cdots \tag{2.4}$$

and subtract (2.3) from (2.4), most of the terms on the right-hand side cancel out because we have the same infinite series. We are left with

$$(1 + R)P - P = D$$

$$P = \frac{D}{R} \tag{2.5}$$

Suppose that after one year, interest rates and hence required yields on gilts increase. The required yield on 2½% Consols rises to 15%. The market price of this gilt will be

$$P_1 = \frac{£2.50}{0.15} = £16.70 \tag{A}$$

Alternatively, suppose in that time the required yield on 2½% Consols falls to 5%. The market price in this case will be

$$P_1 = \frac{£2.50}{0.05} = £50 \tag{B}$$

If the investor then sells the gilt, his return, if scenario (A) takes place, will be

$$\text{Return } R_A = \frac{D_1 + P_1 - P_0}{P_0} = \frac{2.50 + 16.70 - 25}{25}$$

$$R_A = -23\%$$

If scenario (B) takes place, his return will be

$$\text{Return } R_B = \frac{D_1 + P_1 - P_0}{P_0} = \frac{2.50 + 50 - 25}{25}$$

$$R_B = 110\%$$

A change in interest rates has had a dramatic impact on the investor's return on his supposedly risk-free gilt. Only when interest rates, and hence prices of gilts, are stable can a gilt truly be considered risk-free.

So investors in an undated stock run the risk that, when they wish to dispose of the stock, interest rates will have risen and the value of their gilt fallen. How does interest rate risk operate on gilts that are not undated and have a finite life with explicit redemption dates?

Suppose an investor knows that he has a need for funds at a specified date in the future. For example, he has to repay a £10,000 loan in exactly five years' time. If he puts his money into gilts with longer than five years to run, or indeed undated stocks, he runs the risk that interest rates will rise during the five years he will hold the stock and that, when he comes to sell the gilts to pay off his loan, their value will be less than the £10,000 he needs. On the other hand, if he invests in short-term gilts, with less than five years to run, he runs the opposite risk of a possible fall in interest rates. If the gilts mature before he needs the £10,000, he will have to reinvest them. This leaves the investor open to the risk that interest rates will fall before the gilts are repaid, so that he will only be able to reinvest the proceeds at a lower yield than if he had chosen gilts with the full five-year life. This example illustrates the fact that, unless investors *match* the maturity of their gilt-edged investments exactly with the maturity of their liabilities – in this case, the investor chooses gilts with a five-year life – they will expose themselves to risks due to changes in interest rates. In fact, even if the investor matches maturities, the gilt will pay interest before maturity which he may not wish to spend. The interest may therefore have to be reinvested, perhaps at a lower rate than that yielded by the gilt.

Pension funds and insurance companies have commitments at specified dates in the future which they can quantify more or less exactly, for example maturing insurance policies and pension payments. These institutions can thus choose gilts that match their commitments and to a great extent avoid interest rate risk. Other investors are unlikely to be able to specify exactly *when* they will need money in the future and are probably unable to state the future value of these commitments. Life assurance payments or pensions may be expressed in nominal terms which can be matched by the maturity of nominal amounts of gilts. In contrast, an investor wishing to buy a house in five years' time which costs £140,000 today does not know how much money she will then need to be able to afford an equivalent house. House price inflation will increase the nominal cost of the house. For example, £250,000 may be needed in five years to be able to buy what £140,000 would buy today.

Inflation risk

This brings us to the second type of risk attached to gilts, and in fact all other fixed interest securities. Suppose Mr Stone, wishing to buy a house that currently costs £140,000, invests a sufficient amount in gilts maturing in five years' time to repay him £140,000. He will probably find that this will not be enough to buy the house of his dreams. Even if he expects inflation to be such that he will need £200,000 in five years' time and he invests in gilts that will repay £200,000, Mr Stone still runs the risk that inflation will not be as he had anticipated and he will need more (or less) than £200,000 to buy that house.

Let us look at a simple numerical example which brings out the impact of inflation. Suppose Mrs Silver buys a gilt for £95 which has only one year to maturity, at which time she will received the principal of £100 plus an interest payment of £5. Mrs Silver's return on that gilt held for one year will be

$$R = \frac{D_1 + P_1 - P_0}{P_0}$$

$$= \frac{(5 + 100) - 95}{95}$$

$$R = 10.5\%$$

Now suppose she expects inflation to be 5% during the next year, so that £105 in one year's time will have the same purchasing power as £100 now. Mrs Silver can calculate her expected real return by expressing all cash flows in *current purchasing power* terms.

$$\text{Expected real return } R_{real} = \frac{100 - 95}{95} \times 100$$

$$R_{real} = 5.3\%$$

There is no risk as yet in this investment decision. If the market as a whole requires a real rate of return of 5.3% on a one-year gilt, **Fisher** (1930) has postulated that nominal interest rates (actual market interest rates) will fully reflect expected inflation. Thus, if inflation is expected to be 5%, the nominal interest rate can be calculated as follows:

$$(1 + \text{nominal rate of return}) = (1 + \text{real rate of return })(1 + \text{expected inflation rate}) \quad (2.6)$$

$$= (1.053)\,(1.05)$$
$$= 1.106$$

Nominal interest rate = **10.6%**

The market prices the gilt at £95 to take into account the expected 5% inflation. If no inflation were expected, the market price would be higher at £99.72.

$$P_0 = \frac{D_1 + P_1}{1 + R}$$

$$= \frac{105}{1.053}$$

$$= \textbf{£99.72}$$

According to Fisher's theory, nominal interest rates rise to take account fully of expected inflation and this pushes down the prices of gilts.

So far, inflation risk is not a problem to Mrs Silver, provided she is aware of expected inflation and provided expected inflation is included in nominal interest rates, as Fisher suggests. She will be able to compare investments and make investment decisions with equanimity. However, there are two factors that can make inflation risk a risk in practice.

First, interest rates may not exactly adjust to expected inflation as Fisher predicts. However, it is difficult to test Fisher's theory since, although tests can be carried out to see whether interest rates have taken account of *actual* inflation, it is more diffi-cult to determine whether interest rates have taken account of *expected* inflation, because of the difficulty of measuring expected inflation. (If interest rates do adjust in this way, one might expect investors to require the same real rate of interest on, say, gilts, over time, with the nominal, required return actually varying from this constant because of expected inflation.)

Second, even if expected inflation is fully catered for in market prices, unexpected inflation can affect the real returns of investors and prevent Mr Stone from realising enough in real terms to buy his house.

Suppose Mrs Silver buys the gilt described above for £95 and that inflation during that year turns out to be 10%. The purchasing power of £105 received at the end of that year will only be £105/(1.1) or £95.45. So Mrs Silver's *actual* real return will be

$$R_{actual} = \frac{95.45 - 95}{95}$$

$$R_{actual} = \textbf{0.5\%}$$

Inflation risk, in the sense that the actual real returns achieved on investments could be less than the expected real returns, is a risk for all types of fixed interest securities. So Mrs Silver cannot avoid inflation risk by investing in particular fixed interest securities. However, if next year's inflation can be estimated more accurately than inflation in several years' time (and if nominal interest rates do fully take account of expected infla-tion), then Mrs Silver will suffer less inflation risk if she invests in short-term rather than long-term or undated securities, simply because current estimates of inflation are less likely to be wrong in the short rather than the long term. In that sense, Mrs Silver will suffer less inflation risk, the shorter-term the gilt she buys.

However, although inflation risk is present to a greater or lesser extent when investing in any fixed interest security, it need not be attached to ordinary share investment. The dividends paid on shares are not fixed. If inflation is high, the company should be able to achieve high nominal profits and to pay out high nominal dividends. In fact, if the company has issued a substantial number of fixed interest securities, the value of the ordinary shares may increase by more than inflation to balance the loss incurred by the fixed interest security-holders whose investments are worth less because of unexpected inflation.

MEASUREMENT OF RISK AND RETURN

The previous section discussed the different types of risk attached to investment in securities: uncertainty of income, default risk, interest rate risk and inflation risk. As well as being subject to various types of risk, different securities suffer these risks to greater or lesser extents. However, whatever the risk, it is always reflected in the variability of returns achieved on any security, and derives from the fact that we live in an uncertain world.

When looking into the future, we can predict different possible states of the world, for example the company whose loan stock we are considering buying may or may not default; the actual inflation rate, which we expected to be 5%, may turn out to be 10% or 8% or 3%. If only one possible state could occur, we would live in a certain world with certain returns on investment and zero risk.

Now we have identified the different types of risk that exist and realised that they are the result of the possibility of different states of the world occurring in the future, how can we quantify the risk and likely return of any investment?

We use probabilities to attach numbers to the likelihood of each state of the world occurring. For example, suppose we look at what happened to £100 invested in company X shares at the beginning of each year for the past 50 years. What were the end-of-year values of the investment in each of those 50 years? Suppose we find that the end-of-year value was £104 in ten of those years, £106 in 15 of those years and so on, as in Example 2.5 (ignoring dividends).

What can we say about the likely end-of-year value of £100 invested now in company X? If the factors underlying company X's share performance are fundamentally unchanged, we can convert these long-run frequencies of past returns into probabilities concerning the future. We can say that there is a probability of 10 in 50, or a 0.2 chance, that the value will be £104, giving 4% return and so on, as in Example 2.6.

These probabilities (p_i) add up to 1 because we have taken into account all eventualities and no more than one of these eventualities could occur. (The states of the world considered are, in other words, *exhaustive* and *mutually exclusive*.) All we have done here is apply the way we think about, say, cards to investments in shares. Since there are four aces in a pack we deduce that there is a probability of 4 in 52 or 1 in 13 that an ace will be picked at random from the full pack. What we mean by this is that if we pick cards at random often enough from the full pack we will expect 1 out of every 13 picked to be an ace. We are using *long-run average frequencies* to estimate the likelihood of future events.

Probabilities derived from inspecting past frequencies are known as *objective probabilities*. They have been calculated by looking at actual past events. With

Example 2.5 Frequency distribution of the value of one-year investments of £100 in company X in each of the last 50 years

End-of-year value £	Frequency with which value occurred
104	10
106	15
108	15
110	10
	50

investments in securities, objective probabilities can be calculated by looking at the frequency distribution of returns the security has achieved in the past. If a particular share has provided variable returns in the past and if it has not fundamentally changed its business, it is likely to be equally volatile in the future. Frequency distributions will therefore provide a good picture of what may happen in the future. Alternatively, data on past performance may not be available or factors affecting the security's return may have altered. In this case, *subjective probabilities* based on the best estimates of investors or their advisers will have to be used to provide the probability distribution of future returns.

Expected return

Armed with our probability distribution, we still need to measure risk and return to be able to compare investments. We have an idea of the different returns that are likely, but is there one figure which will give us the best estimate of the return we shall actually achieve? The most likely outcome, known as the *mode* (the one with the highest probability), is either 6% or 8% in this example – both have a probability of 0.3. This measure of return is inconvenient if there is, as in this case, more than one mode in the probability distribution. The *median*, defined to be that return where there is a 50% chance that the actual return will be less than or more than this figure must, in our example, lie somewhere between 6 and 8%.

Example 2.6 Probability distribution of end-of-year values of £100 invested now in company X

End-of-year value £	Holding period return on investment (%)	Probability p_i
104	4	0.2
106	6	0.3
108	8	0.3
110	10	0.2
		1.0

The median, as with the mode, does not take into account all the possible returns in the distribution.

The third possible estimate of the future return is the *mean* or *expected return*. This is the average of all the possible returns weighted by probabilities. It is equivalent to the *average* return one would expect to get if one kept on investing each year in company X. The expected return gives a single figure which takes into account all possible returns, and which is useful statistically, as we shall see later. For these reasons, and because it is intuitively easy to understand, the expected return is the measure normally used for estimating future, uncertain returns.

$$\text{Expected return} = p_1R_1 + p_2R_2 + P_3R_3 + \ldots + p_nR_n$$

where each $R_i(i = 1, \ldots, n)$ is a possible return and p_1 the probability that this return will occur. In this case, the expected return $E(R)$ is

$$
\begin{aligned}
E(R) &= p_1R_1 + p_2R_2 + P_3R_3 + P_4R_4 \\
&= (0.2 \times 4) + (0.3 \times 6) + (0.3 \times 8) + (0.2 \times 10) \\
&= 7\%
\end{aligned}
$$

More generally we can write $E(R)$ as

$$E(R) = \sum_{i=1}^{i=n} p_iR_i \tag{2.7}$$

where $\sum$ is a summation sign indicating that we should add together as many p_iR_i terms as there are.

At the beginning of the chapter, we compared securities by looking at their actual returns. Because we were looking at historic returns, we knew the P_0, P_1 and D_1 for each security and hence its return, R. When comparing future investments to be made in an uncertain world, the values of P_1 and even D_1 may not be known in advance. Estimates of the possible returns that could be achieved and the probabilities of these returns must be made and, from these estimates, the *expected* return can be calculated. Securities can therefore be compared by looking not at their actual but at their expected returns.

Definition of risk

However, we know that in a risky world, we would not necessarily always buy the security that offered the highest expected return because each security will have a different level of risk attached to it. For example, suppose an investor is comparing the two investment opportunities, each costing £100, described in Example 2.7.

In this example, both A and B offer the same expected return. The investor cannot choose between them on the basis of expected return alone. He needs to consider the risks of A and B, first to see whether they are worth purchasing at all and second to see which of A and B he prefers.

Intuitively we can see that security B is riskier than A but how do we measure that risk? Is it the risk relative to the initial investment of £100 or relative to the expected value of

Example 2.7 Comparison of risk and return of securities A and B

	End-of-year value £	Return (%)	Probability
Security A	110	+10	0.3
	120	+20	0.4
	130	+30	0.3
			1.0

Expected return of A: $0.3 \times 10 + 0.4 \times 20 + 0.3 \times 30$ **= 20%**

Security B	60	-40	0.3
	120	20	0.4
	180	+80	0.3
			1.0

Expected return of B: $0.3 \times -40 + 0.4 \times 20 + 0.3 \times 80$ **= 20%**

£120? If security *B* becomes worth £60, the investor will actually lose £40 in cash but he will lose £60 relative to the expected value of *B*. The £60 will be the more relevant figure, since not only will the investor have lost £40, if *B* turns out to be worth £60, but he will also have lost the opportunity of investing his £100 in something else of equivalent risk which could have yielded him £20. His concern will therefore be with how different the return could be from £120.

Another problem in deciding on how to measure risk is whether the investor is concerned only with downside risk (risk that the return will be less than he expects) or the risk that the return will be more *or* less than he expects. Consider the probability distributions in Figure 2.1. They all have the same expected return of 10%.

Figure 2.1(i) shows a normal distribution. This is the well-known probability distribution that occurs when a number of random and separate possibilities are envisaged. It is symmetric, which means that the distribution below the expected value is the mirror image of the distribution above the expected value. Thus, in this case of a normal probability distribution, any measure of downside risk (the risk that the return will be less than expected) will give the same result as a measure of total dispersion about the expected value (the risk that the return will be less *or* more than expected).

On the other hand, if the distributions are skewed (not symmetrical), as in Figures 2.1(ii) and 2.1(iii), measures of downside risk and total dispersion do not give the same result. In Figure 2.1(ii), the downside risk is greater than the risk of doing better than expected, whereas in Figure 2.1(iii) the opposite is the case. A measure of total dispersion would not be able to distinguish between Figures 2.1(ii) and 2.1(iii).

However, a measure of total dispersion, the standard deviation, is the most common measure of risk used in the theory of investment. There are three major reasons for this. First, if security return distributions are normal, as in Figure 2.1(i), the expected return and standard deviation are the only two measures needed to describe fully the probability distribution of any security. It is also true, in this case, that the standard deviation is equivalent to a measure of downside risk. Second, most frequency distributions of past security returns do appear to conform more to

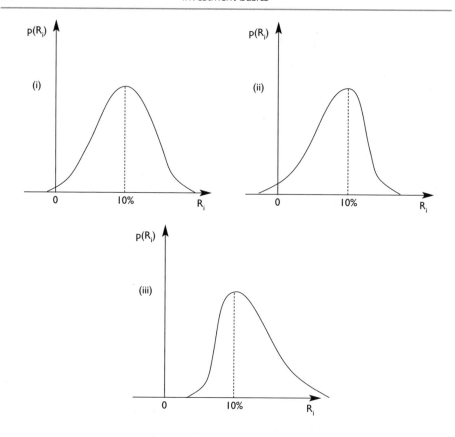

Figure 2.1 Normal and skewed probability distributions

normal than to skewed distributions. Even if they are not exactly normal, it is a statistical fact that the returns of a portfolio made up of a collection of such securities will be normal, and most people do hold portfolios of securities. Third, the standard deviation is a particularly easy measure to handle, as we shall see below.

The remainder of this book will assume that the standard deviation adequately quantifies the total risk of investing in a security – the uncertainty surrounding the actual returns which will be achieved. The greater the uncertainty, the greater the standard deviation and vice versa. If there is no uncertainty – that is, the return is known for certain – the dispersion, and hence the standard deviation, will be zero. However, we cannot be sure that investors do regard the standard deviation as an adequate measure. They may prefer another measure of risk altogether (such as the maximum possible cash loss from an investment, which does not require knowledge of the full probability distribution of returns) or they may require more than one measure of risk, perhaps needing a measure for skewness as well as dispersion. Nevertheless, the above-mentioned attractions of the standard deviation have led to its supremacy as a measure of risk, and until more is known about how investors do quantify risk, the standard deviation is an adequate and simple measure.

Measurement of risk

The formula for the standard deviation of a probability distribution is rather complicated to look at but simple to understand. The square of the standard deviation, known as the *variance*, is usually calculated first. The variance is the sum of the *squares* of the dispersions around the expected return, $E(R)$, weighted by their probabilities (as for the expected return). Squares are used because if actual dispersions were added they would cancel each other out and sum to zero. So we can calculate the variance, V, as

$$V = \sum_{i=1}^{i=n}\left((E(R) - R_i)^2 p_i(R_i)\right) \tag{2.8}$$

The standard deviation S is then the square root of V. In Example 2.8 we use the investment in shares of company X, described in Example 2.6, as an example.

As an exercise, check that the standard deviations of securities A and B, described in Example 2.7, are 8% and 46% respectively. The standard deviation is always expressed in the same units as the expected return and is intuitively easier to use than the variance, especially with a normal distribution. With a normal distribution, we can say that there is approximately a 2 in 3 (more accurately, 68.3%) chance that the return will actually be within + or − 1 standard deviation of the expected value. For example, if the expected return on a security is 10% and its standard deviation (on a normal distribution) is 2%, there is a 2 in 3 chance that the return will actually be between 8 and 12%. Similarly, there is only 1 chance in 100 that the return will lie outside the range 5–15%. These generalisations cannot be applied to securities A and B of Example 2.7 since their probability distributions are only very simple approximations to a normal distribution.

Knowing only the expected returns of A and B did not allow the investor to make any investment decisions under uncertainty. Knowing both their expected returns and their risks now enables the investor to do two things:

○ decide whether A and B offer sufficient reward in the form of expected return for their risks

Example 2.8 Calculation of variance and standard deviation

End-of-year return R_i	Dispersion $E(R) - R_i$	Square of dispersion $(E(R) - R_i)^2$	Probability p_i	$(E(R) - R_i)^2 p_i$
4	3	9	0.2	1.8
6	1	1	0.3	0.3
8	-1	1	0.3	0.3
10	-3	9	0.2	1.8
$E(R)$ = 7%	0	20	1.0	V = 4.2

V = 4.2
S = $\sqrt{V}$
S = $\sqrt{4.2}$ = 2.1%

The standard deviation, S, is 2.1%.

○ assuming both *A* and *B* are attractive investments, decide which of *A* and *B* to choose.

The theories discussed in this book assume investors are averse to taking on risk. In other words, they require more expected return before they will take on more risk. Since *A* has a lower standard deviation, for the same expected return, the investor will prefer *A*.

EXPECTED UTILITY

Although all investors are presumed risk averse, each investor will make different *trade-off decisions* between risk and expected return. This trade-off will be affected by such factors as unwillingness to bear risk, which will be reflected in how much additional expected return investors require for taking on an additional unit of risk. Similarly, another factor will be how much the investment could affect the investor's total wealth. A potential loss of £1000 would probably worry a millionaire less than someone with earnings of £100 per week.

The concept of utility allows investors to combine their attitudes to risk and return at different levels of wealth into one measure: *utility of wealth*. Utility in this case can be thought of as the satisfaction the individual gets from different amounts of wealth. The different probable outcomes of any investment will lead to different probable levels of wealth. If investors know how much utility they will get from each level of wealth, they can calculate their expected utility from each investment, just as they can determine the expected return of any investment. They will then choose any investment that increases their expected utility, and will prefer those that increase it most. Each investor will have a different utility function which will lead to his or her preferring different investments.

As an example, let us consider Mr Black who is evaluating the investments described in Example 2.9. Unlike the case in Example 2.7, the investments do not offer the same expected return nor do they have the same standard deviation. The choice is no longer as simple: it depends on whether Mr Black requires more or less than the additional 2% expected return offered by *J* in exchange for an additional 5% standard deviation. With a simple expected return/standard deviation analysis, Mr Black can choose only if he lays down rules such as 'no more than 7% standard deviation' (in which case he prefers *I*) or

---

Example 2.9 Comparison of securities *I* and *J* with different expected returns and different risks

Security	Cost of investment £	End-of-year value £	Return R_i (%)	Probability P_i	Expected return $E(R)$	Standard deviation S (%)
I	100	105	5	0.5	10	5
		115	15	0.5		
J	100	102	2	0.5	12	10
		122	22	0.5		

'at least 12% return' (in which case he prefers *J*). However, knowledge of the utility function allows him to choose the one which maximises his expected utility. Suppose Mr Black has the following utility of wealth function where *W* is his wealth:

$$U(W) = 0.1\ W - 0.000025W \tag{2.9}$$

Equation 2.9 is a quadratic equation in *W*. This means that, when plotted on a graph (as in Figure 2.2), Mr Black's utility function is a curve with a decreasing slope, the larger *W*. We shall see later that this type of curve implies that Mr Black is risk averse. In other words, he requires a higher expected return, the higher the risk of the investment.

In this example, we are concerned with whether Mr Black, given his particular utility function, prefers *I* or *J*. To ascertain this, we must know his current actual wealth – suppose it is £500. We now calculate the expected utility he would derive from each investment. We do this in the same way as we calculated expected return in equation 2.7. Thus, expected utility is simply the sum of the utilities attached to the possible wealth after investment, weighted by their probabilities. Expected utility of wealth, written *EU(W)*, is:

$$EU(W) = \sum_{i=1}^{i=n} p_i U(W_1) \tag{2.10}$$

The expected utilities of wealth after investing in *I* or *J* are shown in Example 2.10. Mr Black's current utility of wealth is *U(W)* where *W* = £500:

$$
\begin{aligned}
U(W) &= 0.1(500) - 0.000025(500)^2 \\
&= 50 - 6.25 \\
&= \mathbf{43.75\ U}
\end{aligned}
$$

The actual values we calculate for utility do not matter. What counts is the relative ranking of utilities. Units of utility are usually termed 'utiles' (U). They can be of any size,

---

Example 2.10 Mr Black's expected utility of wealth from investments *I* and *J*

(1) End-of-year value of security £	(2) Probability of outcome, P_i	(3) End-of-year wealth, W_i (net of cost of investment) £	(4) Utility of wealth $U(W_i) =$ $0.1W_i - 0.000025W_i^2$ (U)	(5) = (2) x (4) $p_i U(W_i)$
Initial wealth £500, cost of investment £100				
I 105	0.5	505	44.12	22.06
115	0.5	515	44.87	22.44
				$EU(W_i)$ = 44.50 U
J 102	0.5	502	43.90	21.95
122	0.5	522	45.39	22.69
				$EU(W_i)$ = 44.64 U

like temperature. What counts is whether *A* is hotter than *B*, not the absolute heat values of *A* or *B*.

In both cases, expected utilities are greater than Mr Black's existing utility and both investments are worthwhile. However, investment *J* offers the highest expected utility to Mr Black and would be preferred by him.

So expected utility enables Mr Black to make investment decisions under uncertainty using one simple measure rather than separately evaluating the expected return of each investment, its risk and its effect on his wealth.

If we plot Mr Black's utility function on a graph, we get a curve as in Figure 2.2. This is the curve of a risk-averse investor. Mr Black is averse to risk in the sense that he requires additional expected return for taking on additional risk. We saw that this was true when we looked at the expected utilities he derived for securities *I* and *J*. He preferred *J* because, in his view, the additional 2% it offered in expected return more than compensated for the additional 5% in standard deviation.

Another way of showing that this is the graph of a risk-averse investor is to consider Mr Black's attitude to a 'fair gamble', that is, a gamble with an expected value of zero. For example, suppose Mr Black were offered a 50% chance of winning £50 and a 50% chance of losing £50. If his current wealth is £500, we can see from the graph that he loses more utility (-3.8*U*) if his wealth is reduced to £450 than if he gains from increasing his wealth to £550 (+3.7*U*). A risk-averse investor, like Mr Black, will always refuse a fair gamble.

Most gambles in real life, such as on horse races or the football pools, have a negative expected value because of the government tax on gambling and the profits of the companies organising the betting. The question arises of how we can assume investors have risk-averse utility functions when the incidence of gambling is so high. Various solutions to this paradox have been proposed, for example that the shape of the utility function changes according to the level of wealth and incorporates both a risk-averse and risk-preferring section, as in Figure 2.3.

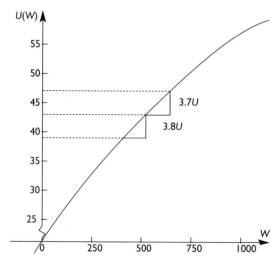

Figure 2.2 Mr Black's utility function

Alternatively, gamblers might ascribe better odds (probabilities) to the possible outcomes of the gamble than actually hold because they believe they are 'lucky'.

The underlying topic of this chapter has been: how do investors compare different securities? We have suggested that they should determine the probability distribution of returns for each security, although only the expected return and standard deviation need in practice be calculated.

All individuals then have to decide whether the expected return offered on each security is sufficient to reward them for its risk, assuming they are risk-averse, and then have to compare the risk–return trade-offs offered by those securities. Knowledge of their utility of wealth function enables investors to choose between securities, taking into account in a single measure their attitudes to risk and return at each level of wealth. In this way, they can easily choose between securities, such as between I and J in Example 2.9. In practice, however, investors do not know what their utility function is, and certainly not its mathematical expression. What risk-averse investors can do is to choose the security or portfolio which offers the highest expected return for a given risk, or the lowest risk for a particular desired return. We shall return, in Chapter 6, to the topic of investors' choice between portfolios of varying returns and risks to achieve this *optimal* portfolio.

REDUCTION OF RISK

Since we assume throughout this book that investors are risk averse, it would be interesting to finish this chapter by investigating whether there are any simple mechanisms whereby risk can be reduced, without sacrificing return. If there are, any sensible investor will follow them.

There are, in fact, two principal ways in which risk can be reduced. The first, *pooling*, is the reason for the existence of such bodies as insurance companies and investment trusts, and the second, *hedging*, requires the participation of speculators in the market.

In Chapter 1 we considered the role of a stock market as a means of transferring risk from entrepreneurs to investors and between investors. Pooling and hedging offer means whereby the overall level of risk can be not only transferred but actually *reduced*.

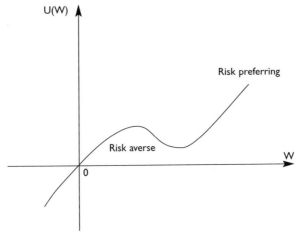

Figure 2.3 Graph of cubic utility function

Pooling

Consider the risk of your house being totally destroyed. Each house owner bears this risk, which can be well quantified by probabilities using past frequencies of houses being destroyed. Although this risk is small, the house may well represent the most valuable asset in the investor's portfolio and he or she may therefore wish to insure against an occurrence which has a high expected cost. In other words the house owner will pay a fixed premium to an insurance company in return for the insurance company guaranteeing to pay should his house be damaged or destroyed. If many house owners pool their risks in this way, the insurance company will actually bear less risk than if each house owner had separately borne the risk. This is because the risk of each house being destroyed is *independent* of the risk of another house being destroyed (events that might affect all houses such as nuclear war are specifically excluded in insurance policies), and when these independent risks are considered, the standard deviation of the pooled risk is less than the sum of the individual risks.

Why this is so will be shown when we discuss portfolio theory in Chapter 6. We shall merely state the result here. If each house is insured for the same amount and the risk of each house being destroyed is equal and has standard deviation S_H, then the risk borne by the company insuring n such houses is S where

$$S = \frac{S_H}{\sqrt{n}}$$

For example, if the company insures 10,000 houses, its standard deviation or risk will be 1/100th of the risk of the individual house owner. The overall risk of these n houses being destroyed has been reduced by pooling. An important proviso must be attached to this statement. The overall risk will be reduced by the presence of the insurance company only if the probability of the event occurring is not increased as a result of the insurance being taken out. If people, knowing that they are insured, are more careless, the overall risk borne by the insurance company may not be less than the sum of the individual risks. This is called the 'moral hazard' problem.

Of course, insurance has nothing to do with the stock market. Insurance policies are arranged via Lloyd's, a completely separate market, or with insurance companies (who may then use Lloyd's). Also, the returns on securities are not independent; they are affected by common economic factors. Nevertheless, it will be seen again in Chapter 6 that the combination by investors of securities into a portfolio will always be worthwhile in the sense that their overall risk will be reduced to less than the weighted average of the risks of the component securities. This method of reducing the risk of investing in securities is called diversification, and forms the basis of portfolio theory.

Hedging

As with pooling, the possibility of reducing risk by hedging applies only to a specific kind of risk. This is one where two parties are subject to exactly opposite risks, say one person bears the risk of event A happening and the other of event A not happening. If these two people can get together and agree on a transaction before the outcome of A is known, they will both have hedged their risk.

For example, a producer of cocoa wishes to know how much cocoa to grow next year. He will be influenced by the price of cocoa prevailing next year, which he would like to know now. Similarly, a manufacturer of chocolates wishes to plan his production of sweets and would like to be assured of future supplies at fixed prices. If the producer and manufacturer get together to agree today on a price for cocoa to be delivered next year, they will both have hedged their risks. The producer's uncertainty of the future price he can get for his cocoa and hence how much he should grow has been resolved. The manufacturer's uncertainty concerning future prices and supplies of raw materials is removed. Both parties have hedged the risk of a change in the price of cocoa – on the manufacturer's side the risk of cocoa prices going *up* and on the producer's side the risk of cocoa prices going *down*. They have used what is known as the *forward market* for their transaction. Forward markets exist in major commodities such as sugar, cocoa, metals and in foreign exchange. They are markets in which future transactions are agreed now but not paid for or delivered until a specified date in the future. These markets provide hedges in exactly the same way as we described in the cocoa market. For example, in the *foreign exchange forward market*, UK buyers of US goods bear the risk of the cost of the dollars they need for their purchase going up in sterling terms, whereas British sellers of goods priced in dollars bear the risk of the value of dollars falling in sterling terms. Forward transactions in dollars will enable them both to hedge their risks.

These forward markets (or *futures markets*, as the more regulated ones are known) have evolved in response to the need for certain risks, such as fluctuations in commodity prices or exchange rates, to be hedged. Such markets require the existence of speculators since there may not be an even balance of opposite risks to be hedged. More traders may wish to hedge against the price of cocoa rising in value than against its falling, and so speculators will have to step in to take the risk of the cocoa price falling. In fact, if speculators accurately forecast which way prices are going to move, they will improve the market in cocoa, for they will buy when prices are low, hold stocks and sell when prices are high. In this way, they will remove excess quantities of cocoa from a depressed market and provide needed cocoa in a buoyant market. However, inexpert speculators will have the opposite and damaging effect. The existence of speculators willing to take on risk means that risk can be not only reduced by hedging but also transferred to investors willing to accept risk, as on the stock exchange.

We may ask ourselves: of what use is hedging to the stock market investor? Commodities and foreign exchange markets operate separately from stock markets and do not involve transactions in quoted securities. There are two main reasons that stock market investors should be interested in hedging.

First, investors now have the opportunity to undertake hedging transactions in quoted securities. As far as shares are concerned, they can use futures contracts on stock market indices and options on both stock market indices and individual shares. Futures and options are described in Chapters 8 and 9. In addition, the interest rate risk inherent in bond investment can be hedged through the use of bond futures and options in all the major markets. Even inflation risk can to some extent be hedged, in the UK at least, through the use of index-linked gilts described in more detail in Chapters 3 and 4.

The second reason that stock market investors should be interested in hedging is because the foreign exchange markets, both spot and forward, must be understood before international investment can be undertaken. Most overseas investments require the purchase of foreign currency and so involve two considerations, that of the risk and return of the investment itself *and* that of the risk of holding the foreign currency in which it is denominated. The subject of international investment and the hedging of currency risk is discussed in Chapter 11.

SUMMARY

This chapter has described the two major characteristics of any investment, its expected return and risk. The different types of risk underlying various types of investment were discussed, from supposedly risk-free bonds to company shares. The major types of risk described were uncertainty of income, default risk, interest rate risk and inflation risk.

The chapter then considered how uncertain return and risk could be measured so that different investments could be compared. Probability distributions, derived either objectively from observation of past returns or subjectively by estimating future possible returns, were used to quantify expected return. The standard deviation of the probability distribution of returns is a suitable measure of risk provided the distribution is normal or investors ignore skewness.

Investors' attitude to the risk and expected return of investment can be neatly described in their utility function. Each investor may have a different attitude to risk and return and hence a different utility function. Such a utility function is expressed in terms of the investor's wealth and not the rates of return of the investment. Obviously different returns will imply different changes in the investor's wealth. In the special case where the investor only compares the expected returns and standard deviations of investments, his or her utility function can be shown to be quadratic, and such an investor will be risk averse.

This book assumes that, when considering investments, investors can be viewed as risk averse. If this is the case they will be interested in any means whereby risk can be reduced, and the last section of the chapter considered two possible methods of reducing risk, pooling and hedging.

REVIEW EXERCISES

1. Mr Woolly is choosing between two possible investment opportunities:
   a. A government bond which will mature in exactly one year. On that date the nominal amount (£100) and a 3% interest payment will be made. The price of £100 nominal of this stock is £98 today.
   b. 100 shares costing 98p each in a company specialising in software for personal computers. The return on the shares is uncertain but the investor has read a report on the company which estimates the one-year return to be as follows, subject to how the economy behaves and how the company's products are received by the market:

Reception of new products	Economic situation	
	Growth	Recession
Good	$r = 30\%$	$r = 15\%$
	$p = 0.2$	$p = 0.3$
Bad	$r = 10\%$	$r = -10\%$
	$p = 0.3$	$p = 0.2$

where r = total rate of return and p = probability.

    i.   Using expected values and standard deviations, calculate the expected return and risk of the two investments.

    ii.   Bearing in mind that inflation is expected to be 5% in the next 12 months, which investment would you advise Mr Woolly to make?

    iii. What other factors would you take into consideration?

2. Bond A pays annual interest of 5% and has exactly five years to maturity.
   a. Calculate the present value of the bond at annual rates of return of 4%, 5% and 6%.
   b. Calculate the present value of the same bond in exactly one year's time at each of the three annual rates of return 4%, 5% and 6%.
   c. When you compare the present value of the bond and of the individual cash flows at the three different rates of return (4%, 5% and 6%) what do you notice about:
       i. the relationship between return and present value?
       ii. the relative impact of a given change in return on the nearer and the more distant cash flows?
       iii. the relative impact of successive equal changes in return on the overall present value of the bond?
       iv. the effect of the passage of time on the present value of a bond, if there is no change in underlying change in rates of return?

3. The table reproduced at the end of this exercise sets out the probabilities of different possible levels of total annual return on two shares M and N.
   a. Calculate the expected return on each share.
   b. Calculate the variance and standard deviation of returns on each share.
   c. Which of the two shares seems to offer the better combination of return and risk?
   d. Is there any reason that a simple comparison of expected return and standard deviation of returns might not offer a comprehensive guide to the relative attractiveness of these two shares?

Expected return p.a.	Probability share M	Probability share N
5.0%	0.02	0.04
6.0%	0.04	0.05
7.0%	0.08	0.06
8.0%	0.13	0.09
9.0%	0.15	0.13
10.0%	0.16	0.12
11.0%	0.15	0.10
12.0%	0.13	0.09
13.0%	0.08	0.08
14.0%	0.04	0.07
15.0%	0.02	0.06
16.0%		0.04
17.0%		0.03
18.0%		0.02
19.0%		0.01
20.0%		0.01

4. An investor requires a real rate of return of 4% p.a. and expects inflation over the next
   year to be 6% p.a.
   a. What nominal rate of return does he require from the investment?
   b. Assuming that he achieved the required nominal rate of return, what real rate of
       return will he actually achieve if inflation during the year turned out to be not the
       expected 6% p.a., but:
       i.   2% p.a.?
       ii. 10% p.a.?

5. In 1921, an investor in short-term (i.e. risk-free) UK government debt would have
   earned a nominal annual return of 5.34%. In the course of the year, the general
   price level fell by 26%. What real rate of return would the investor have earned in
   the year?

6. Go to the website of the UK government's Office for National Statistics (ONS)
   (www.statistics.gov.uk), and find the section on inflation rates. Study how the
   different measures of inflation are constructed, and how they have varied over the
   years. How relevant do you consider these measures to be for a long-term investor
   in shares or bonds?

Sample answers to the review exercises can be found on the companion website.

Part II
Bonds and Fixed Income

3 Bonds and government securities

CHAPTER CONTENTS

Learning objectives for this chapter

After studying this chapter you should be able to

○ classify debt securities according to their basic characteristics including coupon and maturity
○ calculate prices and returns on different types of UK government bonds
○ describe the principal mechanisms of the UK government bond market
○ use your understanding of the UK government bond market to analyse another country's bond market.

INTRODUCTION TO BONDS

Chapters 3 and 4 are devoted to a detailed description and analysis of debt securities: that is, securities that give the holders a contractual and legally enforceable right to certain future payments by the issuer. The generic term for these securities – bonds – emphasises the legal commitment of the issuer to make those payments, regardless of its ability or willingness to pay or of external market conditions.

Bonds come in many different forms. Here are brief descriptions of the types you will most frequently encounter in practice.

In the simplest and also the commonest case, the exact amounts and timings of all the bond payments are fixed at the time of original issue. A company issuing a £100 million 10% bond for five years is taking on an obligation to pay £10 million in interest on each of the first four anniversaries of the issue (or perhaps £5 million every half-year), plus a final interest payment and repayment of the original £100 million principal on the fifth anniversary. Such issues are referred to as ***straight bonds*** or just ***straights***, or – even more colloquially – ***plain vanilla bonds***. To distinguish them from the variant described in the next paragraph, they are also sometimes called ***single-dated bonds***.

A variant on the plain vanilla bond gives the issuer the right to choose the repayment date, often within certain predetermined limits. Such an issue is sometimes referred to as

---

Box 3.1 Bond market terminology

Bond market terminology can be confusing at first, especially in its use of fully interchange-able synonyms. For example, the periodic interest payments on bonds are commonly referred to as coupons. This is because bonds that are evidenced by paper certificates (and not, as is increasingly the case, by a centrally maintained electronic register of bondholders) have an attached page or pages of coupons, one for each interest payment. The investors claim their interest payments every six or 12 months by detaching the appropriate coupon and sending it to the issuing company's designated paying agent.

Another important synonym is 'redeem', which is used interchangeably with 'repay'. To redeem is to buy back, and it refers to the fact that on the final repayment date (or maturity) of the bond the issuer buys back the original certificate from the investor, just as individuals buy back a simple IOU when they repay the underlying debt.

---

a *double-dated* or *callable* issue, as the issuer has the right to call in the bonds for repayment before the final maturity date.

In a refinement of the double-dated bond, the issuer has the right to repay the bond at any time on or after a specified future date, but is under no obligation to repay the principal amount and may simply continue paying the interest in perpetuity. This is called an *undated* or *perpetual* issue.

Bonds may also be issued on a floating-rate basis, whereby the interest rate is not fixed in absolute terms at the time of issue, but is reset periodically according to a predetermined formula: for example, every six months at 0.25% p.a. above the current rate for six-month wholesale money market deposits. Such issues are known as *floating rate notes* or *floaters* for short.

A more complex type of bond incorporates a feature designed to protect investors against the fall in the purchasing power of money during the term of their investment. In this case, the monetary amounts of the interest payments or of the final repayment, or both, may be linked by a predetermined formula to changes in an official measure of inflation, so that an indexation uplift compensates the investors for the erosion of the currency's purchasing power. These are called *index-linked bonds*.

Other variations on the basic bond structure may give the bondholders the *option* (that is, the right but not the obligation) to convert some or all of their bonds into other securities on predetermined terms in the future, either into ordinary shares of the issuing company (or, more rarely, of another company) or into a new bond issue with different conditions from the original one. Such an issue is called a *convertible*.

In one special case which (as we will find in Chapter 4) has a unique significance in the analysis of bond markets and investment strategies, a bond may be issued on terms whereby no interest payments are made at all while the bond is outstanding or on maturity, but the investors achieve the whole of their return by receiving a larger amount on final repayment than they invested at the outset. These are known as *zero-coupon bonds*, or *zeros* for short.

Finally, it is possible for an investor to create synthetic zeros by separating the rights to each of the cash flows represented by a conventional coupon-bearing bond. Each of the coupons, as well as the final repayment, becomes in effect a separate zero-coupon bond. This technique is called *stripping*, from the fact that in the case of a bond evidenced by a paper certificate it is achieved by the simple expedient of stripping all the coupons from the main bond and from each other. Stripped bonds in the UK government securities market are officially referred to as *strips*, which stands for separately registered and traded interest and principal securities.

In this and the following chapter we shall concentrate primarily on bonds issued by the UK government in its own domestic currency and market. The sheer size of this market and the unique characteristics of government securities give them a theoretical and practical significance extending far beyond the realms of the bond markets into other financial markets including equities.

Before beginning our analysis of the UK government bond market, we look at how important it is in a global context. Table 3.1 shows the relative importance of the top six government bond markets, by market value in billions of dollars, at the end of 2006, as represented in the MSCI Sovereign Debt Issues Index. From this you can see that the largest bond market is in Japanese government bonds, followed by the US Treasury bond market. The UK government bond market ranks only sixth, behind the more indebted Germany, Italy and France, but still represents just under 6 per cent of the developed market index for sovereign or government issues.

Table 3.1 Major government bonds in a global bond index

Country	Number of issues included*	Market value $billion	Nominal outstanding billion local currency	% of total
Japan	196	2,926.35	¥332,954.34	27.24
USA	132	2,354.36	$2,217.49	21.92
Germany	43	1,061.86	€740.00	9.89
Italy	36	947.61	€654.61	8.82
France	39	893.22	€619.79	8.32
UK	34	637.50	£295.33	5.94
Developed world	668	$10,739.85	$10,139.85	100.00

* includes all sovereign issues of more than $2 billion and excludes index-linked bonds
Note: the amounts are not the total size of each market, but a representative amount.
Source: MSCI Sovereign Debt Issues Index (from Bloomberg, 4 December 2006).

HISTORY OF UK GOVERNMENT BONDS

History of the National Debt

Government bonds can be defined as the marketable portion of the UK National Debt – that is, the portion issued in a securitised form which can be readily bought and sold by investors in a liquid secondary market.

Debt itself seems to be an unavoidable fact of life for central government. Long before the United Kingdom became a full parliamentary democracy and assumed all the responsibilities of a modern welfare state in the twentieth century, long even before it became a constitutional monarchy in 1689, the financial embarrassments of kings and queens (who were then synonymous with the state) are a recurring theme in the history books. Richard the Lionheart, who ruled England from 1189 until 1199, was so desperate for funds to finance his military campaigns in the Middle East that he is reputed to have said he would 'even sell the City of London if he could find somebody rich enough to buy it'. Similarly, it is estimated that by 1433 the prolonged war with France left the Crown in debt to the tune of £100 billion in today's money, equivalent to almost a quarter of the entire present-day National Debt. Sustained efforts to put the national finances on a sound footing remained the exception rather than the rule: under the prudent management of her adviser Lord Burghley, Elizabeth I had amassed a rare surplus equivalent to a full year's revenue by the time she had been on the throne for 25 years in 1584.

Just over a hundred years later, the granting of a Royal Charter to the Bank of England in 1695 marked the first beginnings of a market for government debt in its present form, when a group of entrepreneurs headed by William Paterson won the right to issue transferable debt instruments on the government's behalf, and thus in effect became managers of the National Debt and bankers to the government. The immediate impulse for the founding of the Bank of England was the government's pressing need for a loan of £1.2 million to finance its war against France. War continued to be a principal driving force of state finances right through to the twentieth century. A hundred years after the Bank of England was established, another war against France prompted the introduction of another permanent feature of the public finances – income tax.

Figure 3.1 shows, first, how in the half century before the First World War, peace and growing industrial prosperity led to a steady decline in national debt as a proportion of gross domestic product (GDP).

Two major and interlinked developments then transformed the entire meaning and context of the National Debt in the twentieth century. The direct demands of two world wars put an almost intolerable strain on public finances, so that by the late 1940s the United Kingdom was in commercial terms on the verge of bankruptcy. At the same time, government activity had steadily extended into almost every corner of national life, not only indirectly as a consequence of waging a hitherto unknown kind of 'total war', but also more

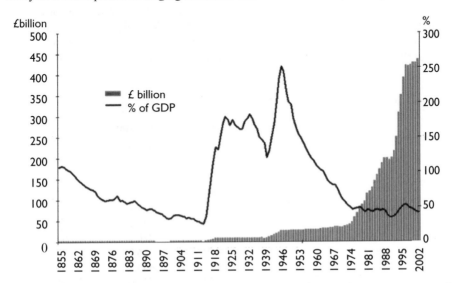

Figure 3.1 Gross National Debt since 1855: nominal £ billion and as a percentage of GDP

Source: Debt Management Office.

consciously with the growing aspirations of a now fully enfranchised population, in the fields of employment, education, welfare and general economic growth and stability.

For much of the post-war period, structural economic problems contributed to the chronic instability of the public finances. The strict financial disciplines adopted by successive governments since the late 1970s, aided by a policy of returning nationalised enterprises to private ownership and of harnessing private capital to finance major long-term public sector infrastructure projects, ushered in a new period of relative stability. Nevertheless, as the more detailed Table 3.2 shows, the strains of the early 1990s recession and the ill-fated experiment with membership of the Exchange Rate Mechanism of the European Community (as the European Union was then known) took their toll on the public finances in the middle of that decade. Table 3.2 picks up the figures from 1975 onwards, the first year since 1916 when the National Debt was less than 50 per cent of GDP.

Responsibility for the issuance of gilts and for management of government debt was transferred in 1998 from the Bank of England to the Debt Management Office (DMO), a newly established special-purpose executive agency of the Treasury.

Current trends

Marketable sterling government bonds currently account for about 70 per cent of the National Debt. A relatively small volume of UK government bonds has been issued in foreign currencies on the international (eurobond) market, where the UK enjoys no special legal status but is in theory at least just one issuer among all the many other commercial and governmental borrowers. However, its financial standing puts it in the very top rank of such borrowers in terms of creditworthiness. In the domestic sterling debt markets, by contrast, the government is the pre-eminent issuer. Not only is its credit standing undoubted (since the foundation of the Bank of England in the 1690s, no British government has ever defaulted on, or had to reschedule, payment of its sterling debts), it is also by far the largest borrower and is in a unique position to influence the structure and mechanics of the market. The perceived risk-free nature of government debt gives it a special place both as an investment vehicle for market participants seeking to eliminate or to mitigate portfolio risk, and as a benchmark for the appropriate pricing of less creditworthy issuers. For all these

Table 3.2 The UK National Debt, 1975–2004

Year	£ billion	% of GDP	Year	£ billion	% of GDP
1975	45.3	46	1994	306.9	46
1980	95.3	43	1995	349.2	50
1985	158.0	46	1996	390.7	52
1986	171.4	44	1997	419.5	52
1987	185.8	46	1998	418.4	49
1988	197.4	44	1999	421.6	47
1989	197.3	39	2000	426.2	45
1990	193.0	35	2001	426.0	43
1991	198.7	35	2002	434.5	42
1992	214.5	36	2003	448.0	41
1993	248.8	40	2004	497.1	43

Source: Debt Management Office, HM Treasury.

Table 3.3 Maturity of gilts in issue, end 2005

Type of gilt	Nuimber of gilts	Maturity in years	Nominal amount in issue (£ bn nominal)	% of total
Long	11	Over 15	130.5	32.7
Medium	10	5–15	106.5	26.7
Short	12	1–5	91.1	22.9
Ultra-short	10	Under 1	67.4	16.9
Undated	8	No fixed maturity	3.0	0.7
Total in issue	**51**		**398.5**	**100.0**

Source: Debt Management Office.

reasons, sterling-denominated UK government bonds became known in the days of the Gold Standard as *gilt-edged* (or *gilts* for short), meaning that they were, if not absolutely as good as gold, then at least edged with gold. The term has proved considerably more durable than the Gold Standard and is still in universal use today.

Table 3.3 shows the number and type of gilts in issue at the end of 2005. Gilts are typically divided by maturity to redemption into five categories: long, medium, short, ultra-short and undated. Ultra-short are considered along with money market instruments, that is, fixed interest securities that have a maturity of less than 12 months. Undated bonds are bonds issued with no fixed maturity date but which can be redeemed at the government's option, although they form only a small percentage of the total gilts in issue.

Apart from gilts, the government has two other sources of sterling financing. It issues Treasury bills (tradable IOUs with maturities of one, three and six months) in the context of its short-term cash management, and also offers a range of non-marketable savings products to private investors under the heading of National Savings and Investments.

As mentioned earlier, the government also has foreign currency liabilities, which it uses primarily to manage its external reserve position.

An insight into the significance of gilts for investors can be gained from Table 3.4 showing the distribution of gilt holdings at 31 December 2004.

It can be seen that the major financial institutions hold substantial portfolios of gilts. The attractions of holding gilts to these investors are various. For example, insurance companies have long-term commitments. If they buy gilts with the same maturities as

Table 3.4 Distribution of principal gilt holdings by market value, 31 December 2004

	£million	%
Insurance companies and pension funds	219,688	60.0
Overseas	78,373	21.4
Households	35,201	9.6
Local authorities and public corporations	2,983	0.8
Building societies	1,034	0.3
Banks and other financial institutions	29,140	8.0
Total	**366,419**	**100.0**

Source: Office for National Statistics.

these commitments they can be certain of being able to meet their liabilities in nominal terms. Also, banks and building societies keep a certain proportion of their investments in what are known as liquid assets (easily realisable short-term investments of minimal risk) in order to be able to pay depositors wishing to withdraw funds from their accounts. Short-term gilts are considered to be suitable liquid assets.

Another reason that both institutions and individual investors include gilt-edged securities in their portfolios will become clear on reading Chapters 6 and 7. Since gilts are less risky than company shares, both portfolio theory and the capital asset pricing model (discussed in those chapters) show that any portfolio that is intended to be less risky than one consisting entirely of company shares should include some risk-free assets such as gilts.

However, these reasons that investors hold gilts do not explain the higher turnover of gilts in the London market. The extract from the DMO Quarterly Report for the fourth quarter (Q4) of 2005 reproduced as Table 3.5 gives total turnover for the quarter of £871.5 billion, or more than 200 per cent of all gilts in issue. This already impressive figure is increased by half as much again when we take into account the turnover recorded in the same period in long gilt futures contracts, which are discussed in Chapter 8. Note that the majority of turnover in Table 3.5 is in the 7–10 year and over 15 year categories, and that turnover by customers exceeds turnover by professional *gilt-edged market makers (GEMMs)*.

The prices, and hence the returns, of gilts are affected above all by present and future interest rates, although different gilts are affected to different extents by changes in these rates. Interest rates and expectations concerning future interest rates change frequently. This provides scope to investors who feel they can accurately predict interest rate changes to make profits either by switching between gilts or by switching between gilts and other securities such as shares. The high turnover in gilts is partly caused by the transactions of such investors. Even the financial institutions that have long-term commitments actively deal in part of their gilt portfolios.

Unless gilts are held to match a specific nominal liability, they can no longer be considered investments that can be bought and then ignored. The volatility of interest rates, and hence the prices of gilts, imply that investors must carefully choose when to buy and when to sell gilts if they wish to maximise their returns.

Most investment advice to the small investor concentrates on share investment, for two

Table 3.5 Gilts turnover, Q4 2005

Band	Customer £bn	Customer % aggregate	Professional £bn	Professional % aggregate	Combined £bn	Combined % aggregate
0–12mths	18.6	3.1	4.6	1.7	23.3	2.7
1–3 years	70.6	11.9	23.5	8.5	94.1	10.8
3–5 years	97.6	16.4	38.3	13.8	135.9	15.6
5–7 years	36.4	6.1	14.2	5.1	50.5	5.8
7–10 years	167.8	28.2	109.0	39.4	276.8	31.8
10–15 years	23.3	3.9	8.5	3.1	31.8	3.6
15+ years	142.5	24.0	60.1	21.7	202.6	23.3
Index-linked	37.5	6.3	18.6	6.7	56.1	6.4
Strips	0.5	0.1	0.0	0.0	0.5	0.1
Total	**594.6**	**100.0**	**276.92**	**100.0**	**871.5**	**100.0**

Source: Debt Management Office.

reasons. First, share investment has been the traditional first love of the small investor, and second, the gilt-edged market is dominated to an even greater extent than the share market by large institutions dealing in large amounts. The average size of a gilt-edged bargain in the actively traded issues is several million pounds. Also, the type of analysis needed to understand gilt price movements is different from that required for shares, and the small investor unversed in these techniques is at a considerable disadvantage. However, the principles underlying these techniques are relatively straightforward, and as we shall see, the traditional valuation methods, such as redemption yields, used by investors in the market, are now being superseded by more sophisticated and accurate analyses of interest rates. Any investor who understands both techniques need have no fears of investing in fixed interest securities.

The remaining sections of this chapter will first describe the different types of gilts currently available on the market and how they can be distinguished from one another, following the basic classification of bonds with which we opened this chapter. The chapter continues with a section on how to calculate returns on investments in fixed interest securities such as gilts, describing the two most common measures, the interest yield and the redemption yield. We then look at the main market participants and how they fit into the overall structure of the market itself. The method of issue of gilts is then outlined for conventional as well as index-linked gilts. Chapter 4 continues the discussion on bonds with a more sophisticated approach to determining returns and to measuring the impact of interest rate changes on gilt prices.

DESCRIPTION OF UK GOVERNMENT BONDS

General characteristics

Table 3.6 (overleaf) reproduces the table published in the *Financial Times (FT)* on Saturday 19 November 2005 showing a summary of gilts market data as at the close of business on the previous day. In November 2005 there were a total of 52 different gilts in issue. These comprised 34 conventional fixed rate dated issues, 8 conventional fixed rate undated issues, and 10 index-linked issues. The amounts of bonds outstanding in each issue varied enormously, from just £0.7 million nominal of the undated 2¾% Annuities issue, to almost £17 billion each of the 8% Treasury 2021 and the 4¼% Treasury 2032. The 2¾% Annuities issue and another almost equally small undated issue are omitted from the *FT* table. The *FT* lists all issues in chronological order of final maturity date, subdividing the dated issues further into four maturity bands: up to 5 years; 5 to 10 years; 10 to 15 years, over 15 years and undated, a slightly different classification from the DMO one used in Tables 3.3 and 3.5.

In former times, for ease of identification individual dated gilts issues were given a variety of names, including 'Treasury Stock', 'Exchequer Stock', 'Funding Stock' and 'Conversion Stock'. The generally much older undated issues were also given names like 'Annuities', 'Consolidated' (or 'Consols' for short) or 'War Loan'. Some of these names contained an allusion to the original purpose of the issue, but for trading and analysis purposes the different names are irrelevant. The word 'stock' is especially confusing as in other contexts it is usually taken to denote equities rather than debt securities. More recent conventional issues have almost invariably been called 'x% Treasury Stock YYYY', where x is the nominal coupon rate and YYYY is the year of final maturity

Table 3.6 Gilts in issue at 18 November 2005

UK GILTS - cash market

Nov 18	Notes	Price £	W'k % Chng	Amnt £m	Interest due	Last xd	Red Yield
Shorts'' (Lives up to Five Years)							
Tr 8½pc '05		100.17	–.1	9,821	Je7 De7	27.5	4.48
Tr 7¾pc '06		102.68	....	3,955	Mr8 Se8	30.8	4.28
Cn 9¾pc '06	✠	105.16	....	6	My15 Nv15	4.11	4.33
Tr 7½pc '06		103.23	....	11,807	Je7 De7	27.5	4.30
Tr 4½pc '07		100.33	0.1	11,500	Se7 Mr7	28.4	4.23
Tr 8½pc '07		106.65	0.1	4,638	Ja16 Jy16	7.7	4.28
Tr 7¼pc '07		105.73	0.2	11,103	Je7 De7	5'4	4.29
Tr 5pc '08		101.54	0.3	14,221	Mr7 Se7	27.5	4.29
Tr 5½pc '08–12		102.84	0.4	1,026	Mr10 Se10	9'4	4.41
Tr 9pc '08	✠	112.46	0.3	687	Ap13 Oc13	4.10	4.37
Tr 4pc '09		99.10	0.5	16,616	Mr7 Se7	3'4	4.29
Tr 8pc '09	✠	112.92	0.5	393	Mr25 Se25	16.3	4.31
Tr 5¾pc '09		105.35	0.5	11,437	Je7 De7	27.5	4.29
Tr 4¾pc '10		101.90	0.7	9,250	Jy7 De7	27.5	4.29
Five to Ten Years							
Tr 6¼pc '10		108.80xd	0.7	4,958	My25 Nv25	16.11	4.28
Tr 4¼pc '11		99.81	0.8	3,250	Mr7 Se7	–	4.29
Cn 9pc Ln '11		123.36	0.7	5,396	Jy12 Ja12	1.7	4.29
Tr 7¾pc '12–15		117.59	0.8	805	Jy26 Ja26	15.7	4.46
Tr 5pc '12		103.93	0.9	13,346	Mr7 Se7	3'4	4.28
Tr 9pc '12	✠	126.95xd	0.8	403	Fe6 Au6	28.7	4.33
Tr 8pc '13		124.59	1.0	6,181	Mr27 Se27	16.9	4.28
Tr 5pc '14		105.25	1.2	13,050	Se7 Mr7	3'4	4.28
Tr 4¾pc '15		103.87	1.4	13,000	Mr7 Se7	16.9	4.26

	Notes	Price £	W'k % Chng	Amnt £m	Interest due	Last xd	Red Yield
Ten to Fifteen Years							
Tr 8pc '15		130.63	1.2	7,377	Je7 De7	27.5	4.23
Tr 8¾pc '17		141.15	1.3	7,751	Fe25 Au25	16.8	4.26
Ex 12pc '13–17	✠	151.99	0.9	58	Je12 De12	2.6	4.30
Tr 4¾pc '20		105.30	1.7	8,069	Mr7 Se7	–	4.25
Over Fifteen Years							
Tr 8pc '21		142.18	1.6	16,741	Je7 De7	27.5	4.26
Tr 5pc '25		110.26	1.9	15,422	Mr7 Se7	3'4	4.22
Tr 6pc '28		126.68	1.9	11,756	De7 Je7	26.11	4.18
Tr 4¼pc '32		101.51	2.2	16,961	De7 Je7	27.5	4.16
Tr 4¼pc '36		101.86	2.3	15,338	Mr7 Se7	27.5	4.14
Tr 4¾pc '38		111.25	2.3	14,250	Je7 De7	5'4	4.12
Tr 4¼pc '55		104.77	2.7	4,750	Je7 De7	–	4.03
Undated							
Cons 4pc	✠	88.11xd	2.9	358	Au1 Fe1	21.7	–
War Ln 3½pc		83.54	3.1	1,939	Je1 De1	23.5	–
Cn 3½pc '61 Aft.	✠	85.15	3.2	87	Ap1 Oc1	21.3	–
Tr 3pc '66 Aft.	✠	68.39	3.0	53	Ap5 Oc5	26.9	–
Cons 2½pc	✠	58.75	3.1	272	5JaApJyOc	26.9	–
Tr 2½pc	✠	58.34	3.1	493	Ap1 Oc1	17.3	–

	Notes	Price £	W'k % Chng	Amnt £m	Interest due	Last xd	Yield (2)
Index–Linked	(b)						
2pc '06	(69.5)	274.86	....	2,037	Ja19 Jy19	8.7	1.26
2½pc '09	(78.8)	248.42	0.2	3,098	My20 Nv20	11'4	1.63
2½pc '11	(74.6)	266.94	0.4	4,342	Fe23 Au23	12.8	1.63
2½pc '13	(89.2)	226.89	0.4	6,397	Fe16 Au16	8'4	1.60
2½pc '16	(81.6)	255.50	0.7	7,471	Ja26 Jy26	15.7	1.50
2½pc '20	(83.0)	260.34	0.6	6,165	Ap16 Oc16	6.10	1.44
2½pc '24	(97.7)	231.43	0.7	5,751	Ja17 Jy17	7.7	1.35
4⅛pc '30	(135.1)	225.70	0.6	3,921	Ja16 Jy22	1'4	1.26
2pc '35	(173.6)	130.81	0.5	6,975	–	1'4	1.20
1¼pc'55†	(192.20000)	111.00	0.9	1,963	–	–	–

(b) Figures in parentheses show RPI base for indexing, (ie 8 months prior to issue) and have been adjusted to reflect rebasing of RPI to 100 in January 1987. Conversion factor 3.945. Yield (2) 3%. RPI for Feb 2005: 188.6 for Oct 2005: 193.3

† I.L. 1 1/4pc 2055 has a base RPI of 192.20000 with a 3 month lag. The 'clean' price shown has no inflation adjustment. The yield is calculated using no inflation assumption.

Closing mid-prices are shown in pounds per £100 nominal of stock. All UK Gilts are tax-free to non-residents on application. Gilts benchmarks and most liquid stocks, are shown in bold type. Weekly percentage changes are calculated on a Friday to Friday basis. ✠ Indicative price. xd Ex dividend. Red yield: Gross redemption yield.

Source: Debt Management Office (DMO).

Source: *Financial Times*.

('YYYY/YYYY' in the case of a double-dated issue). Index-linked gilt issues were uniformly called 'x% Index-Linked Treasury Stock YYYY', where x is the real coupon rate. (Index-linked gilts and the significance of the real, as opposed to the nominal, coupon are described in more detail later in this chapter.)

With effect from 31 March 2005, all new issues of gilts bear the uniform name 'X% Treasury Gilt 20XX' (for conventional stocks) and 'X% Index-linked Treasury Gilt 20XX' (for index-linked stocks). In announcing this change, the DMO explicitly acknowledged that the term 'stock' tended to cause confusion with equity products, especially in the minds of non-UK investors.

The prices of gilts are quoted in terms of the price to be paid for £100 nominal of the issue, so that (for instance) £100.00 nominal of the 8% Treasury 2021 would have cost £142.18 at the close of business on 18 November 2005. 'Nominal' simply denotes the actual amount of the payments to which the holder is entitled. Although prices are quoted in terms of £100 nominal, it is in fact possible to buy any nominal amount of a gilt issue, down to the last penny. The officially quoted prices of gilts (rounded to two decimal places in the FT table) are expressed to six decimal places, thus enabling us to determine down to the last penny the actual consideration to be paid for a £1 million nominal amount of stock. We shall see the significance of this when we calculate the actual consideration paid on gilts transactions later in this section.

With certain very minor exceptions, gilts pay interest semi-annually, and the coupon dates for each issue are shown. This means, for example, that holders of £100.00 nominal of the 6% Treasury 2028 will receive coupon payments of £3.00 every 7 June and 7 December until the final maturity on 7 December 2028, when they will receive the final coupon payment of £3.00 and the capital repayment of £100.00. Gilt coupons are paid to the investors who are registered as the holders of the bonds on the sixth working day before the coupon date; the time lag is to allow for administrative arrangements to make the payments. As a result, sellers of gilts in transactions up to and including the seventh business day before the next coupon lose all rights to the coupon, and buyers compensate them by paying, in addition to the agreed purchase price, an amount equal to the accrued interest since the last coupon date. The seller is said to have sold, and the buyer to have bought, *cum dividend* (or *cum div* for short), meaning 'with the dividend'. If investors sell gilts between one and six business days before the coupon date, they will still receive the whole dividend; sellers must therefore compensate buyers, who will not begin to earn coupon income until the next coupon period begins. In this case the buyer is said to buy *ex dividend* or *ex div* (without the dividend), and the seller gives the buyer a discount from the agreed price equivalent to the interest accruing in the few days between transaction date and coupon date.

The convention employed for calculating interest on gilts transactions is the same as is used for US Treasury bonds, and is called *actual/actual*. The amount of *accrued interest* added to a cum dividend transaction is:

the full amount of the next coupon
multiplied by
the number of days elapsed between the last coupon date and the transaction settlement date (normally the next business day following the transaction date)
divided by
the total number of days in the coupon period.

So, for example, the total consideration for a transaction in £1 million nominal of the 8% Treasury 2021 concluded at the price shown in Table 3.6 on Friday 18 November 2005 for settlement on Monday 21 November 2005 would be calculated as follows:

Principal: £1 million @ 142.18	£1,421,800.00
Accrued interest:	
Next coupon amount (£1 million x 8% / 2): £40,000.00	
Days elapsed (7 June–21 November): 167	
Total days in coupon period (7 June–7 December): 183	
Accrued interest: £40,000.00 x 167 / 183	£36,502.73
Total consideration	**£1,458,302.73**

Conversely, the amount of negative accrued interest deducted from an ex dividend transaction is:

the full amount of the next coupon
multiplied by
the number of days from the transaction settlement date to the next coupon
divided by
the total number of days in the coupon period.

The procedure for calculating the consideration on a gilts transaction that settles within the ex dividend period is illustrated by reference to the 6¼% Treasury 2010. This was due to pay its next dividend on 25 November 2005, just four days after the normal settlement date of a transaction concluded on 18 November. As in the previous example, purely for illustration purposes we assume the deal was for a nominal amount of £1 million and was struck at the price shown in the table.

Principal: £1 million @ 108.80	£1,088,000.00
Accrued interest:	
Next coupon amount (£1 million x 6.25%/ 2): £31,250.00	
Days to next coupon (21–25 November): 4	
Total days in coupon period (25 May–25 November): 184	
Negative accrued interest: £31,250.00 x 4 / 184	–£679.35
Total consideration	**£1,087,320.65**

The price before the adjustment for accrued interest (whether positive or negative) is referred to as the ***clean price***. The price after adjustment is called the ***dirty price***. By market convention, the published prices for gilts are always clean prices.

Conventional issues

In terms of the classification set out at the beginning of this chapter, conventional gilts comprise all single-dated, double-dated and undated sterling UK government securities, but exclude index-linked gilts. This category includes both fixed and floating-rate bonds, but the latter are rare and the last such issue was in fact redeemed in 2001.

Single-dated

A single-dated conventional gilt issue is uniquely and comprehensively described by the coupon rate and the date on which it is repayable. These are the two basic pieces of information we need in order to analyse it as an investment. The coupon rate generally reflects the level of market interest rates at the time of original issue. This accounts for the wide variety of coupons on currently outstanding gilt issues. It has to be stressed that for valuation and other purposes, the 'history' of a bond is of no interest to the analyst or investor. For instance, to take as an example the single-dated issue with the shortest remaining time to final maturity in Table 3.6, it is of no consequence to today's investor when or in what market conditions the 8½% Treasury 2005 was first issued. For valuation and analysis purposes, all that mattered on 18 November 2005 was that the purchase of £100 nominal of this issue gave the purchaser the right to receive on 7 December 2005 the final half-year's interest of £4.25 and the final repayment of principal of £100.00. The only other piece of information that might interest the investor is the amount of the issue that is still outstanding. If it is very small (a so-called *rump stock*, identified in Table 3.6 with the symbol ⌖), the issue might not be very liquid so it might not be possible always to deal at the most competitive prices in large amounts.

Double-dated

Double-dated issues differ from single-dated issues in just one respect. Instead of having a single maturity date, a double-dated issue has a range of dates within which the government may choose to redeem it at its nominal value, usually on the giving of three months' notice. The government's choice of repayment date will depend on the cost of refinancing the issue with new gilts. If the maturing double-dated issue can be refinanced at a lower coupon rate, then the government will redeem as soon as possible. But if current interest rates are higher than the coupon on the existing issue, it will be more economical to keep the existing issue outstanding for as long as possible.

At the time of writing, the general level of market interest rates is lower than at almost any other time during the life of any outstanding double-dated issue, so all of them could theoretically be refinanced at a lower cost. That is why in the *FT* table all the double-dated issues were listed chronologically as if they would be repaid on the earliest permitted date. Of course this treatment does rely on a big assumption: that an interest rate scenario similar to the current one will also prevail at the various dates in the future when each of these double-dated bonds first becomes eligible for possible redemption.

Undated

The eight remaining undated issues are also the oldest issues still outstanding, some dating right back to the nineteenth century. Some of these were originally issued with maturities expressed in the form 'YYYY or after', indicating that there was an earliest redemption date but no fixed final date. For instance, 3½% War Loan was originally issued in 1932 (by consolidating various earlier issues dating from the First World War) as '3½% War Loan 1952 or after'. As with double-dated issues, an eventual decision to redeem these issues will depend on the economics of refinancing. All of the undated issues date back to times when rates were even lower than they are at present, so there is no imminent prospect of redemption. But it is worth noting that in 1948 (when rates were even lower than at the time of original issue) 3½% War Loan 1952 or after was listed as a 'short', as it seemed possible that it would be redeemed on or very soon after the first available date. Three of the undated issues differ from all other gilt issues in that they pay interest quarterly instead of semi-annually.

Box 3.2 Nominal and real rates of return on gilts

The lowest real rate of return recorded in the twentieth century on short-term UK government debt was in 1915, when a rapid pick-up in inflation early in the First World War drove the real rate down to minus 15.4% p.a. The highest real rate recorded was 42.4% p.a. in 1921 (as we learned in the review exercises at the end of Chapter 2), when the nominal rate was just 5.34% p.a. but it was accompanied by deflation of 26%. The link between nominal interest rates and inflation became closer towards the end of the twentieth century, so real rates too ceased to fluctuate so widely.

Index-linked issues

We saw in Chapter 2 that even if the return on an investment is both fixed in money (or nominal) terms and free of all risk of default or delayed receipt, its value in real terms may still be reduced by inflation. Theoretically, the value of returns in real terms can also be increased by deflation – that is, by a rise in the purchasing power of money – but in practice this has occurred very infrequently in the past hundred years.

The impact of inflation on the value of returns from government securities is especially problematic because it seriously compromises the otherwise risk-free quality which is so important for many types of investors. As we shall see in Chapter 7, any investors seeking to balance the overall risk of an investment portfolio need to have access to a risk-free asset in order to achieve their target levels of risk and return. Moreover, certain types of investor, and especially pension funds, have future liabilities that are indexed to inflation, and therefore they need to be able to invest in corresponding assets that protect them against inflation while simultaneously offering a high degree of security and stability. Equities have shown the necessary growth in capital value and dividend income over long periods of time, and have been traditionally regarded as the best investment for keeping pace with inflation in the long run, but in the short to medium term they can be very volatile, as the protracted *bear market* from 2000 onwards clearly demonstrated.

Inflation had been a periodic and growing problem throughout the post-war period, but the experience of the 1970s represented a step change upwards in both the general level of inflation and its unpredictability. Retail price inflation hit a peak of 25 per cent p.a. in 1975. A committee (the Wilson Committee) was appointed by the government to look into the resulting problems for the investing community. In its report published in 1980 it recommended that the government should issue inflation-indexed gilts specifically to resolve the problem faced by pension funds. As the following brief chronology shows, this new product developed very rapidly.

March 1981   £1 billion nominal of the first index-linked gilt (2% Index-linked Treasury 1996) was issued by single price auction. Indexation was to the General Index of Retail Prices (RPI) and ownership was initially restricted to pension funds or similar institutions writing pension business.

March 1982   The fourth index-linked gilt (2% Index-linked Treasury 1988) was issued.

March 1982   The restrictions on the ownership of index-linked gilts were removed.

May 1983   A convertible index-linked gilt was issued, giving investors the option to convert their holdings into a conventional gilt on any one of three dates.

In November 2005 there were ten index-linked gilts outstanding and they accounted for about 25 per cent by nominal value of all gilts in issue. The popularity of the product is hardly surprising, when it is considered that UK retail prices rose by 125 per cent in the 20 years following the first index-linked issue in March 1982.

Which index?

While the principle of linking the coupon and repayment value of a bond to the change in a price index is as simple as it is appealing, practical application of the principle is problematic in several respects.

First, it is not at all obvious which index of inflation is appropriate. The monthly indices of consumer prices are the best known measure of inflation in the United Kingdom, but – as their name shows – they does not pretend to measure inflation in the economy as a whole, but only the impact of inflation on a basket of consumer goods and services. Pension funds (a main source of demand for inflation-proof bonds) might be more interested in linking the value of their investments to an earnings index, as their liabilities under so-called *defined benefits* or *final salary* pension schemes are linked to earnings, which usually rise faster than consumer prices

An arguably more rigorous measure than a consumer prices index is the *GDP deflator*, which tracks changes in all prices (producer as well as consumer prices) and weights them according to their contribution to overall economic activity. But the GDP deflator has two disadvantages: it is not well known outside the relatively small circle of professional economists and statisticians, and – as with many other economic statistics – preliminary announcements of its value are subject to subsequent correction. As a result, the monthly Retail Price Index has been adopted as the inflation measure for index-linked gilts.

How to calculate accrued interest, coupons and principal repayments?

The second, and purely practical, problem arises from the fact that, from the beginning of each six-month coupon period, it has to be possible to calculate the amount of accrued interest to be settled with secondary market transactions on any date during the period, as well as the amount of the coupon to be paid at the end of the period and the principal to be paid on final maturity. In theory, the index-linking of a bond should compensate the holder for inflation actually experienced during the holding period, but this is clearly not possible in practice, as the most recent RPI figure available at the beginning of a coupon period might have been published as much as a month earlier, and it records the actual level of prices in the month previous to that.

When index-linked gilts were first introduced, it seemed logical to devise a system that would fix the amount of each coupon at the beginning of the coupon period, so that accrued interest could be calculated on the basis of the full amount of the coupon multiplied by the number of days since last coupon, divided by the total number of days in the coupon period. As the most recent available value for the index could be as much as two months earlier than the start of the coupon period, for all index-linked stocks issued before mid-2005, all payments of coupons, as well as the final repayment amount, were indexed with an eight-month time-lag. Each coupon is calculated by indexing the nominal coupon by the change in the index between the eighth month prior to the original issue date and the eighth month prior to the coupon payment date. The final repayment amount is similarly calculated by indexing the nominal amount of the bond by the change in the index over the same lagged period.

Subject to the possible distorting effect of the eight-month time-lag, the process of indexation has the effect that an investor purchasing an index-linked gilt on first issue and holding it to maturity will achieve a real return equivalent to the rate published in the title of the issue. We shall consider as an example the 4 ⅛% Index-Linked Treasury Stock 2030 issued in June 1992. The base value RPI is given in Table 3.6 as 135.1 – the RPI figure for October 1991 (published in November 1991). This gilt pays interest in January and July, for which the relevant RPI figures are those relating to the previous May and November respectively. So the semi-annual coupon payment in January 2004, for example, was calculated as:

$$\frac{4.125}{2} \times \frac{181.5 \text{ (i.e. RPI for May 2003)}}{135.1 \text{ (i.e. RPI for October 1991)}}$$

= 2.7708 (rounded down to four decimal places).

Similarly, the redemption proceeds on maturity in July 2030 of a £100 nominal holding of this bond will be:

$$£100.00 \times \frac{\text{RPI for November 2029}}{135.1 \text{ (i.e. RPI for October 1991)}}$$

In each case, the indexation uplift compensates the investor for the decline in the purchasing power of money between a date eight months before the original issue date and a date eight months before the coupon date or (as the case may be) the final repayment date.

Index-linked gilts from mid-2005

For index-linked gilts issued from mid-2005 onwards (starting with the 1¼% Index-linked Treasury Gilt due 2055 and issued in September 2005), the eight-month time-lag has been replaced with a system of three-month time-lags, which follows international practice more closely and is specifically modelled on a system used by the Canadian government for its index-linked issues since 1991.

Under the new system, all payments – whether of accrued interest (between secondary market sellers and purchasers) or of coupon or final repayment (by the Treasury) – are calculated by multiplying the original nominal amount by an *Index Ratio* which is unique to each issue for each payment date. It is calculated by dividing the Reference RPI for that date by the Reference RPI for the original issue date. The Reference RPI for the first day of any month is the RPI for the third month prior to that date: and the Reference RPI for any date after the first day of a month is obtained by linear interpolation between the RPIs for the third and second months prior to that date. All Reference RPI calculations are performed to five decimal places.

Let us take as an example the calculation of accrued interest on a transaction, for settlement on 21 November 2005, in the only index-linked issue to have been made so far at that date under the new system, the 1¼% issue made on 23 September 2005 and due in 2055.

The first step is to calculate the Reference RPI for the issue date. The RPIs for the third and second months before the issue date, i.e. June and July 2005, were in fact identical, so this part of the calculation is unusually easy! The Reference RPI for 23 September 2005 is the June 2005 RPI (which is the Reference RPI for 1 September) plus 22/30 of the difference between the June and July RPIs.

$$192.2 + \left[(192.2 - 192.2) \times \frac{22}{30} \right] = 192.2$$

The second step is to calculate the Reference RPI for the settlement date, 21 November 2005. Here we have to interpolate between the RPI figures for August and September 2005, which were 192.6 and 193.1 respectively.

$$192.6 + \left[(193.1 - 192.6) \times \frac{20}{30} \right] = 193.33333$$

The Index Ratio for this issue for 21 November 2005 is therefore

$$\frac{193.33333}{192.2} = 1.00382$$

The accrued interest per £100 nominal is then calculated on the basis of:

Semi-annual coupon × Index Ratio × (actual number of days since last coupon / actual number of days in coupon period)

which in this case is

$$\frac{£1.25}{2} \times 1.00382 \times \frac{59}{184} = £0.201173$$

All of the above examples relate to index-linked gilts issued after the RPI was rebased in January 1987. Rebasing is simply the process of re-starting the index at 100, in order to prevent it from becoming too high and arithmetically unwieldy, and has no other significance. Prior to 1987 the index had last been rebased to 100 in January 1974, and by January 1987 it had reached 394.5. Apart from the consideration of arithmetical neatness, such a high index figure was a constant and unwelcome reminder of the UK's very poor inflation record in the years after 1974, so it made political as well as practical sense to rebase it at 100. When calculating the indexation uplift on an index-linked gilt issued before January 1987 for a period ending after that date, it is therefore necessary to multiply the base month index by 100/394.5 in order to achieve comparability with the rebased index figure for the current (i.e. post-1987) date. This is the meaning of the footnote ('Conversion factor 3.945') in Table 3.6. Note that the rebased RPI figures shown in the table have been rounded to one decimal place for the sake of clarity; the actual conversion factor, for instance, for the 2½% Index-Linked Treasury 2011 is 74.550063371356. This is the original RPI figure of 294.1 (the index for May 1981, eight months before the stock was issued in January 1982) divided by 3.945.

Global index-linked issues

More than 20 countries around the world have issued index-linked bonds in one form or another. The key global index-linked bond prices are shown in Table 3.7, with break-even inflation rates (see page 93). The most popular index is a local retail price index, but some governments have used wholesale prices. Italy has used the deflator of GDP at factor cost, and Australia has used both the consumer price index and the index of average weekly earnings. But perhaps the most spectacular example of an index-linked bond was the 7% 15-year bond issued by the French government in 1973. This was indexed to the price of gold, as the French have traditionally viewed gold as the most secure investment. The disadvantage of this is that a government has even less control over the price of gold than it does over the RPI. Between 1976 and 1988 the price of gold fluctuated between US$104 and US$667 an ounce. The 1981 interest payment alone was worth over 60 per cent of the original amount issued and the final redemption value was 831 per cent of the face value. However, the minister responsible for this bond, Giscard d'Estaing, subsequently went on to become President of France!

Table 3.7 Major inflation-linked bond markets as at 30 June 2006

	Price Nov 30	Yield Nov 30	Nov 29	Month return	Break-even inflation[2]	Value bn[1]	Stock Market[3]	No of stocks
Can 4.25% '21	134.61	1.64	1.69	0.86	2.38	5.2	36.5	4
Fr 35% '09	102.95	1.85	1.92	0.24	1.78	13.8	120.1	10
Swe 4% '08	122.66	1.39	1.39	0.32	2.08	28.1	277.6	6
UK 2.5% '09	253.59	1.95	1.98	0.05	2.97	3.3	131.5	11
UK 2.5% '16	263.26	1.49	1.53	0.27	3.00	7.7	131.5	11
UK 2% '24	245.71	1.14	1.18	0.15	3.16	6.6	131.5	11
UK2% '35	144.51	0.90	0.94	-0.28	3.14	8.7	131.5	11
US 3.625% '08	100.77	2.92	2.98	0.44	1.77	16.8	400.9	20
US3.625% '28	126.21	2.10	2.15	1.96	2.56	16.8	400.9	20

Representative stocks from each major market.
1 Local currencies.
2. Diff. between conventional and IL bond.
3 Total market value. In line with market convention, for UK gilts inflation factor is applied to price; for other markets it is applied to par amount.
Original source: Merrill Lynch Global Bond Indices.

Source: *Financial Times*, 1 July 2006.

Indexation makes the analysis and valuation process for index-linked gilts rather more complex than for conventional bonds. In particular, the uncertainty about future indexation makes comparison with conventional bonds quite problematic, as index-linked gilts offer a fixed real rate of return but uncertain nominal return, whereas conventional gilts offer the reverse – an uncertain real return but a fixed nominal one. At the end of the next section, in which we consider the question of returns on gilt-edged securities in more detail, we shall explain the conventions used by the market to make this difficult comparison.

Strips

In the introduction to this chapter we referred to the practice of 'stripping' conventional bonds into their constituent parts, so that the rights to each coupon payment and to the final principal repayment could all be traded independently of each other. Official strip facilities have been available in the US government securities market since 1985, and France since 1991. Official strip markets also now exist in Germany, Italy, Spain, the Netherlands, Belgium and Canada. The strip market began in the United Kingdom on 8 December 1997. Not all gilts issues can be stripped. In November 2005, 19 of the 35 conventional gilts issues, totalling about £250 billion nominal value, were eligible for stripping. Strictly speaking, strips are not a separate category of bonds, because they are made up of the constituent parts of the conventional issues described earlier in this section. They have exactly the same characteristics as regards security of payment as the conventional bonds from which they have been created.

CALCULATION OF BOND RETURNS

We now examine the various methods used to calculate the return on gilt-edged securities: these are, in fact, applicable to all fixed interest securities. We consider first of all the case of conventional gilts that are not index-linked.

We have defined the holding period return of a security as

$$R = \frac{D_1 + P_1 - P_0}{P_0} \qquad (2.1)$$

where

D_1 = any dividend or interest payments made during the period
P_0 = the cost price of the security
P_1 = the selling price of the security.

Holding period return is useful for comparative purposes since it can be applied to all securities. It can also be used to calculate the deviation of the actual return from the expected return. Unfortunately, in order to calculate R, P_1 must be known. This is a simple matter if we are calculating the *historic* return achieved on disposal of a security. It is not so easy when we are trying to calculate the return we *expect* to get from a security. P_1 must be estimated and, to obtain a reasonable estimate, we need an understanding of how prices are affected by interest rate changes, as well as a forecast of how and when rates themselves will change. We leave a discussion of these topics until Chapter 4. For the moment, we concentrate on two measures of return commonly used for gilts and fixed interest securities, both of which get around the problem of having to estimate P_1.

Conventional issues

Interest yield

Interest yield, the simpler measure of the two, avoids the problem of having to estimate P_1 to calculate the capital gain or loss on the gilt by simply ignoring it. It concentrates only on the first part of the holding period return, the return from income.

The **interest yield** (also known as the *running yield, flat yield, income yield* or *coupon yield*) is simply the coupon divided by the clean price.

For example, the 8% Treasury 2021 was priced at £142.18 in Table 3.6. The annual coupon is 8% and so the interest yield, *IR*, is:

$$IR = 8/142.18$$
$$= 0.0563$$
$$\mathbf{IR = 5.63\%}$$

Of what use is the interest yield? It does not reflect the total return from holding a gilt since it ignores any capital gain or loss. It also ignores the acccrued interest, which would give an indication of the income as a percentage of money invested. But it does give a simple indication to investors of their return in terms of income by comparing the interest they receive with the actual price they paid for the gilt rather than its nominal value. For example, with 8% Treasury 2021, the coupon suggests a return of 8% on the nominal value of £100, but interest rates are now much lower than when this gilt was issued. As a result, the price of the gilt has risen by over 40 per cent to £142.18 per £100 nominal, to give a running yield of just 5.63% p.a. on an investment made at the current price.

As well as being relevant for determining income from gilts, the other major use of the interest yield is to determine the **cost of carry**. This is particularly useful for traders and shorter-term investors. For example, suppose a trader wants to buy a gilt in the expectation that the price will rise over the next few days. She will have to fund this purchase with short-term borrowing. However, she will receive accrued interest (in the form of an interest yield) from the gilt. Therefore her cost of carry will be:

Cost of carry = borrowing cost – interest yield

suppose her borrowing cost is 5% and she wishes to buy 8% Treasury 2021. will be:

% – 5.63%

lculated in this case is negative, indicating that the investor
ng yield of 0.63% on her investment.
ner the interest yield, the lower the cost of carry. The lower the

cost of carry, the less the trader has to worry about achieving a price rise just in order to break even.

As we have already seen, the interest yield ignores the possible impact of capital gain or loss on the overall return of a gilt. Most investors will experience a gain or a loss on disposal. Interest yield also ignores the time value of money, since it assumes that the interest paid in any year up to 2021 is as valuable to the investor as this year's interest payment. The **redemption yield** or **yield to maturity** is the second measure of return used in relation to gilts, and overcomes the disadvantages of the interest yield as a measure of return.

Redemption yield

Using the mathematical principles of Example 2.4 on page 48, and adopting the notation C_n for a cash flow occurring n periods from today, and r for the periodic rate of return, we can generalise the value of a security with the equation:

$$P_0 = \frac{C_1}{(1+r)^1} + \frac{C_2}{(1+r)^2} + \frac{C_3}{(1+r)^3} + \frac{C_n}{(1+r)^n} + \frac{P_n}{(1+r)^n} \tag{3.1}$$

In the case of a bond which will pay £100 on redemption, and with a coupon, we can write equation 3.1 as:

$$P_0 = \frac{C}{(1+r)^1} + \frac{C}{(1+r)^2} + \frac{C}{(1+r)^3} + \cdots + \frac{C_n + 100}{(1+r)^n} \tag{3.1a}$$

The price P_0 is simply the present value of a future income stream made up of regular interest payments C, and a redemption payment of 100 on maturity.

In other contexts, you may already have encountered r by another name – the **internal rate of return** or **IRR**. It is the discount rate at which the present value of the future cash flows exactly equates to the current price. As it is the rate of return or yield that investors achieve if they buy the security at the current price and hold it to redemption, it is called the redemption yield of the security. As a measure of overall return it is an improvement on the interest yield because it takes into account the time value of money. The shorter the remaining life of the gilt, the more valuable is the final redemption payment in present value terms. The redemption yield also avoids the problem of having to estimate an unknown future selling price P_1 by assuming that the gilt is not sold but is held to maturity. In other words, P_1 always equals £100 (except in the case of index-linked gilts, which we discuss below).

In real life the calculation of the redemption yield is actually somewhat more complex than appears from equation 3.1 for two reasons:

○ Gilt coupons are paid semi-annually, not annually as ~ examples quoted above.
○ Most purchases and sales of gilts take place on days coincide with coupon dates.

This has two consequences:

○ As we saw earlier in this chapter, the total purchase price is a dirty price which includes the interest accrued since the last coupon date.
○ The future cash flows do not occur at exact multiples of six months from the purchase date.

The first problem is solved quite simply by calculating the price on the basis that the discounting period is six months, not one year. Mathematically this is quite straightforward, but we need to exercise care in interpreting the results. We shall return to this after investigating the second problem.

The second and superficially more awkward problem is solved by initially discounting all the future cash flows (other than the immediate next coupon) not back to the present day but only as far as the next coupon date. This part of the calculation is easy because we are still discounting in whole periods. If we add to this discounted sum the nominal value of the next coupon itself, we will have not the present value of all future cash flows but their *future* value as *at the date of the next coupon*. We then convert this amount to a true present value by discounting it back to the present in one fractional discounting period corresponding to the period from purchase to next coupon. Fractional discounting is the process of discounting at the rate of $1/(1 + r)^n$ where n is not a whole number.

The full equation for calculating the price of a conventional single-dated gilt is as follows.

$$P = v^{\frac{s-t}{s}}\left\{ d_1 + d_2 v + \frac{cv^2}{f(1-v)}\,(1 - v^{n-1}) + 100v^n \right\}$$

(3.2)

where

P	=	dirty price per £100 nominal
d_1	=	next coupon payment
d_2	=	next but one coupon payment
c	=	annual coupon per £100 nominal
r	=	redemption yield (see explanation of v below)
f	=	number of coupons payable per year (normally $= 2$)

$$v = \frac{1}{1 + \dfrac{r}{f}}\,.$$

s	=	number of calendar days in the full coupon period in which the transaction occurs
t	=	number of calendar days from the last coupon date until the transaction date
n	=	number of coupon periods to redemption from the next coupon payment.

It is unlikely that you will ever have to reproduce this equation from memory, but it is a good idea to know what the different components are doing.

The symbol v is used as a shorthand for the redemption yield expressed as a annual discounting factor, simply in order to make the equation a little less 'y.

The expression $\dfrac{cv^2}{f(1-v)}(1-v^{n-1})$ represents the sum of the future value (as at the next coupon date) of all the future coupons except for the next two. This expression makes use of the fact that the discounted amounts of the future coupons are a geometric series, as each is equivalent to the previous one multiplied by a constant factor $1/(1+r)$.

The expression $v^{\frac{s-t}{s}}$ has the effect of discounting the future value of all payments (as at the next coupon date) back to the transaction date.

We need to return now to the earlier question of annual versus semi-annual discounting periods. In order to be able to compare fixed interest securities with different frequencies of interest payment, it is usual to quote the annual redemption yield, r. We saw how the equation used a single symbol v as shorthand for the semi-annual discount factor $\dfrac{1}{1+\frac{r}{f}}$, but we need to take a closer look at the denominator of that expression. In the commonest case, where payments are semi-annual, $f = 2$, so $\dfrac{r}{f}$ is exactly half of the annual redemption yield. But is it strictly correct to assume, as the equation apparently does, that if (for example) the annual redemption yield is 10%, then the semi-annual redemption yield is 5%? That this is not strictly correct can easily be demonstrated by calculating the present value of a payment of £110 due on one year's time on each of two bases, namely (i) by discounting for one period at 10% per period and (ii) by discounting it for two periods at 5% per period. In the former case

$$\frac{£110.00}{(1+0.1)} = £100.00$$

whereas in the latter case, with semi-annual discounting,

$$\frac{£110.00}{(1+0.05)^2} = £99.78$$

As the present value of one and the same nominal future payment is less when discounted twice at 5% than once at 10%, it follows that a discount rate of 5% per half-year is a higher effective rate than 10% per year. In fact the annual equivalent rate of 5% per half-year is given by the formula

$$(1+0.05)^2 - 1 = 0.1025$$
$$= 10.25\%.$$

The market convention for quoting annual redemption yields on gilts and many other securities that pay interest half-yearly ignores this fact, and simply quotes the annual redemption yield as two times the *true* semi-annual yield and not the compounded figure, which gives a more accurate return estimate. This can cause complications when semi-annual bonds such as gilts are compared with annual-pay bonds such as eurobonds.

You may have noticed that the equations we have used have been arranged in a suitable way for calculating the price when all the other variables (the cash flows and the redemption yield) are provided. In practice, we might be confronted with a situation where the cash flows and the price are provided, and we are required to calculate the redemption yield implied by the price, that is, to solve equation 3.1 or 3.2 for the unknown r. This is the same operation as to find the internal rate of return in a discounted cash flow calculation, and there is no easy way to do this other than by a process of iteration (in other words, by trial and error). Fortunately, any computer or pocket calculator with specialised finance functions can do this very quickly.

Index-linked issues

We have seen how to calculate the interest and redemption yields for gilts whose payments are fixed in nominal terms. The problem we now consider is how to calculate returns for index-linked gilts, whose payments are fixed in real terms but not in nominal terms. It would seem logical to try to calculate a real interest yield and a real redemption yield. On closer examination we shall see that the real interest yield has very little theoretical significance or practical usefulness. The redemption yield on an index-linked gilt can be calculated on either of two bases – nominal or real – and is much more useful. Comparisons can be drawn between the two measures of redemption yield on an index-linked bond, or between the nominal redemption yields on an index-linked bond and a conventional issue, and these do produce some useful analytical insights which repay the difficulties posed by the calculation process itself.

Real interest yield

We cannot calculate a nominal interest yield on index-linked gilts for the simple reason that the future nominal interest payments are unknown and will vary. A nominal interest yield makes sense only if the periodic cash income is constant.

For example, if we were to calculate the real price of the 4⅛% Index-Linked Treasury 2030 as at 18 November 2005, we would use the RPI figures for October 1991 (eight months before the bonds were issued in June 1992) and for March 2005 (eight months before the current date) as follows:

$$\text{Real price} \quad = \quad \text{Current cash price} \times \quad \frac{\text{RPI}_{\text{October 1991}}}{\text{RPI}_{\text{March 2005}}}$$

$$= \quad £225.70 \quad \times \quad \frac{135.1}{190.5}$$

$$\textbf{Real price} \quad = \quad \textbf{£160.06}$$

We could then calculate the real interest yield as

$$\frac{\text{Real coupon}}{\text{Real price}} = \quad \frac{4.125}{160.06}$$

$$= \quad 2.58\%$$

But how much use is this figure? As with nominal interest yields, it ignores both the time value of money and any capital loss or gain on sale or redemption. In addition, it lacks the main attraction of the nominal interest yield, namely the speed and ease with which it can be calculated, and the eight-month time-lag means it is not a true real yield. Finally, it does not give the investor an accurate idea of the level of running income to be received from the investment. For all these reasons, the real interest yield is rarely used, and it has been explained here for the sake of completeness only.

Redemption yields

We said earlier that it is possible to calculate the redemption yield of an index-linked bond either on a nominal basis or on a real basis.

In order to be able to calculate the redemption yield of an index-linked bond in nominal (or money terms), we first need to forecast the future nominal cash flows. There are two ways of doing this. One is to take the most recent rate of inflation and extrapolate into the future as far as the redemption date of the bond issue. The other method, which is in fact the one almost universally used by analysts and investors, is to make a 'realistic' but subjective estimate of future inflation and apply that to the entire remaining life of the bond issue. This is of course extremely difficult, especially when looking at a time horizon of up to 30 years. However, it must be remembered that one of the assumptions behind all redemption yield calculations is that the required rate of return is constant over the life of the bond, whatever its maturity. It is no more unrealistic to assume a constant inflation rate for the same period.

We shall keep the mathematics in this section relatively easy by taking as an example from Table 3.6 the 2½% Index-Linked Treasury 2009. As this issue pays coupons on 20 May and 20 November, we can use the figures in Table 3.6 (closing market prices quoted on 18 November 2005 for settlement on 21 November) without having to worry about the additional complexities of fractional discounting periods and dirty prices. Footnote 2 to Table 3.6 tells us that future inflation has been forecast at a constant rate of 3% per annum (p.a.), and we shall use this rate here.

The amount of the next coupon, due on 20 May 2006, has already been set on the basis of the RPI for September 2005 ('RPI_1'). The issue was originally made in October 1982, so the base month RPI is February 1982 ('RPI_0'). The next semi-annual coupon is therefore calculated from the expression

$$\frac{£2.50}{2} \times \frac{RPI_1}{RPI_0} = £1.25 \times \frac{193.1}{78.76} = £3.0647 \text{ rounded down to four decimal places.}$$

Note that the actual RPI for February 1982 was 294.1, and this was converted to 78.7579 when the index was rebased in January 1987.

We can now use a slightly modified version of the basic equation 3.1 to calculate the nominal redemption yield on this bond as follows:

Clean price (18 November 2005)	£248.42 per £100 nominal
Next coupon payment	£3.0647 on 20 May 2006
Subsequent coupon payments	The issue matures on 20 May 2009, so there will be six further coupon payments after 20 May 2006. The forecast nominal amounts will be based on the known 20 May 2006 coupon and inflated by the factor $(1 + i)^n$ where i is the forecast semi-annual inflation rate. (Note that if we assume an annual

inflation rate of I, the equivalent semi-annual rate i is not $^i/_2$ but $\sqrt{(1 + I)} - 1$; the same consideration about the compounding frequency applies here as on page 89.)

Expected principal repayment $£100 \times \dfrac{193.1}{78.76}(1 + i)^6 = £245.18(1 + i)^6$

(where $\dfrac{193.1}{78.76}$ is the indexation up to May 2006 and $(1 + i)^6$ is the linking thereafter)

Let

$P_0 =$ today's price
$R =$ the semi-annual nominal redemption yield
$r =$ the semi-annual real redemption yield and
$D_i =$ the periodic nominal coupon payment
$V =$ the nominal redemption amount.

Then we can write

$$P_0 = \sum_{i=1}^{i=n} \frac{D_i}{(1 + R)^i} + \frac{V}{(1 + R)^n}$$

Substituting in known values, we get

$$248.42 = \frac{3.0647}{(1 + R)} + \frac{3.0647(1 + i)}{(1 + R)^2} + \dots \frac{3.0647(1 + i)^8}{(1 + R)^9} + \frac{245.18(1 + i)^8}{(1 + R)^9}$$

If we now adopt the *FT*'s forecast that $i = 3\%$ p.a. (which, again observing the compounding rules, equates to 1.0489% per half-year) we can use a calculator or PC with an iteration function to solve this equation for R and thus calculate the implied semi-annual nominal redemption yield. This is 2.3261% per half-year, or about 4.65% expressed according to the convention for annual-equivalent rates.

We shall consider the significance of this figure further when we have completed the task of calculating a real redemption yield in the next subsection.

As we saw in Chapter 2, the relationship between a real and a nominal rate of return was postulated by Fisher as follows:

$$(1 + R) = (1 + r)(1 + i)$$

As we now have values for R and i, we can solve this equation for r as follows:

$$(1 = 0.023261) = (1 + r)(1 + 0.01489)$$

$$(1 + r) = \frac{1.023261}{1.01489}$$

$$r = \frac{1.023261}{1.01489} - 1 = 0.008248$$

The real yield is therefore estimated at 0.8248% per half-year or 1.65% per year, which is very close to the figure of 1.63% given in Table 3.5. The small remaining discrepancy is because we have assumed inflation at 3 per cent from Sept 2005 (i.e. from 8 months before next coupon) whereas the strict formula uses the actual historical inflation rate for the period from September 2005 to the present.

So far we have worked out that if inflation stays at a constant level of 3% p.a. for the next three or four years, this index-linked gilt will produce an annual redemption yield of about 4.65% in nominal terms or about 1.65% in real terms. What can we do with this information?

Perhaps the most obvious thing is to compare the nominal redemption yield with that of a conventional bond with about the same maturity, to see if we can work out which of them is better value, and under what conditions. The closest match among the conventional issues is the 4% Treasury 2009, which matures on 7 March 2009, just over two months before the index-linked issue we are studying. The redemption yield on the 4% Treasury was quoted as 4.29% p.a. This is of course a nominal yield, and is fixed in nominal terms for any investors who bought it on 18 November 2005 at the price shown in the *FT* and held it to final maturity. Would such investors have fared better if they had instead bought the 2½% Index-Linked Treasury 2009 on the same day? The answer is, 'It depends.' If inflation were to average 3% for the whole time from 2005 until 2009, investors in the index-linked issue would do better, with a nominal redemption yield of 4.65% p.a., or 0.36% p.a. better than investors in the conventional issue. But if inflation is lower than the forecast of 3% p.a., then the index-linked investors will enjoy lower nominal income and have less of an advantage, and eventually a point will come where they will be worse off than conventional investors. When is that point reached, in terms of the forecast future inflation level? To work this out, we need to find the inflation level at which the nominal cash flows from the conventional issue will represent the same real rate of return as the 1.65% achieved by the index-linked issue. The quickest way to calculate this is once again to use Fisher's equivalence:

$$(1 + R) = (1 + r)(1 + i)$$

In this case, we have values for R (4.29% p.a., the nominal return on the conventional gilt) and for r (1.65% p.a., the real rate of return on the index-linked gilt) and need to solve the equation for i, the inflation rate at which R and r are equivalent to each other. Again, we have to take care with the annual versus semi-annual convention, calculating a semi-annual inflation rate from the semi-annual yield values.

$$(1 + R) = (1 + r)(1 + i)$$

$$\frac{(1 + R)}{(1 + r)} = (1 + i)$$

$$i = \frac{(1 + R)}{(1 + r)} - 1$$

$$= \frac{1.02195}{1.008248} - 1$$

$$i = 0.01359092$$

This gives us a semi-annual rate inflation of 1.359%, but note that it would be incorrect simply to follow the bond market convention and double it to arrive at an annual inflation rate. The annual inflation rate corresponding to a semi-annual rate of 1.359% is $1.01359^2 - 1$, which is 2.74%.

We call this figure the *breakeven inflation rate* for the two issues we have compared, because this is the inflation rate at which neither is better than the other. If inflation is higher than this, index-linked investors will do better, whereas if inflation does not reach this level, conventional investors will suffer less erosion of the value of their fixed nominal returns and will do better than their index-linked counterparts.

Strips

As synthetic zero-coupon bonds, strips are mathematically the easiest type of gilt-edged investment to evaluate. Each strip consists of a right to receive either a single coupon payment or the final principal repayment of a specific gilt issue at a fixed future date. (For obvious practical reasons, double-dated gilts cannot be stripped.) Its price is therefore the present value of that future cash flow, discounted at the market rate of return for loans to the government for the corresponding period. Strips have a redemption yield but no interest yield. The relationship between price and yield is expressed by the following equation:

$$P = \frac{100}{\left(1 + \frac{r}{2}\right)^{\frac{d}{s}+n}}$$

where

P = price per £100 nominal of the strip
r = redemption yield
d = number of days from the transaction date to the next coupon date of the underlying gilt issue
s = number of days in the current coupon period of the underlying gilt
n = number of coupon periods remaining after the current period of the underlying gilt.

Because the prices of strips are driven exclusively by a discount factor applied to a single future cash flow, the market convention is actually to express the price in terms of the redemption yield. Table 3.8 shows three extracts from the DMO's list of strips prices for 18 November 2005, consisting of (i) the stripped principal repayments of all 19 then strippable issues, (ii) the eight shortest-dated stripped coupons (covering dates in 2006–08) and (iii) the six longest-dated stripped coupons (covering dates in 2036–38).

Strips with the stock name suffix 'P' represent the final repayments of stripped gilts issues. The stock name suffix 'C' refers to coupon strips, but coupon strips differ from principal strips in that they refer to coupons on any strippable issue falling due for payment on the date indicated. For example, the strip named 'UK Treasury Strip 07DEC2007C' refers to a stripped coupon falling due on 7 December 2007 on any strippable issue. The purpose of making coupons interchangeable in this way (the technical term for this is *fungible*) is to increase the depth and liquidity of the market. The policy of standardising coupon and repayment dates on one of just two semi-annual cycles (either 7 June/December or 7 March/September) further facilitates this.

Table 3.8 Prices of gilts strips, 18 November 2005 (extracts)

Stock name	Price	Yield
UK 8½ Treasury Strip 07DEC2005P	99.817744	4.216747
UK 7½ Treasury Strip 07DEC2006P	95.637632	4.319543
UK 4½ Treasury Strip 07MAR2007P	94.681466	4.272342
UK 7¼ Treasury Strip 07DEC2007P	91.638646	4.318430
UK 5 Treasury Strip 07MAR2008P	90.692987	4.306411
UK 4 Treasury Strip 07MAR2009P	86.900463	4.309812
UK 5¾ Treasury Strip 07DEC2009P	84.180431	4.304314
UK 4¾ Treasury Strip 07JUN2010P	82.466440	4.288078
UK 5 Treasury Strip 07MAR2012P	76.629384	4.275104
UK 5 Treasury Strip 07SEP2014P	68.922584	4.277954
UK 4¾ Treasury Strip 07SEP2015P	66.221403	4.253464
UK 8 Treasury Strip 07DEC2015P	65.883772	4.198070
UK 4¾ Treasury Strip 07MAR2020P	54.803856	4.252351
UK 8 Treasury Strip 07JUN2021P	51.999097	4.251688
UK 5 Treasury Strip 07MAR2025P	44.917558	4.191712
UK 6 Treasury Strip 07DEC2028P	38.857116	4.144469
UK 4¼ Treasury Strip 07JUN2032P	34.123947	4.091862
UK 4¼ Treasury Strip 07MAR2036P	29.362654	4.086526
UK 4¼ Treasury Strip 07DEC2038P	26.295254	4.083599
UK Treasury Strip 07MAR2006C	98.742778	4.367760
UK Treasury Strip 07JUN2006C	97.690107	4.344700
UK Treasury Strip 07SEP2006C	96.686630	4.295517
UK Treasury Strip 07DEC2006C	95.675042	4.281267
UK Treasury Strip 07MAR2007C	94.677341	4.275784
UK Treasury Strip 07JUN2007C	93.662872	4.286240
UK Treasury Strip 07SEP2007C	92.644974	4.306915
UK Treasury Strip 07DEC2007C	91.639985	4.317699
UK Treasury Strip 07JUN2036C	29.088652	4.083940
UK Treasury Strip 07DEC2036C	28.481361	4.086846
UK Treasury Strip 07JUN2037C	27.952629	4.082027
UK Treasury Strip 07DEC2037C	27.428761	4.077934
UK Treasury Strip 07JUN2038C	26.940020	4.071019
UK Treasury Strip 07DEC2038C	26.542440	4.054707

Source: Debt Management Office.

As a separately traded instrument in their own right, strips are a relatively recent innovation. But the principle underlying their pricing is in fact an even more fundamental building block than the more familiar redemption yield in establishing the structure of market interest rates. For this reason we shall defer detailed analysis of strips yields until Chapter 4, where we analyse the term structure of interest rates in greater depth.

THE GILT MARKET AND PLAYERS

In this final section on UK government securities, we describe

○ the functions of the main participants in the gilts market

○ the primary issuance mechanism for new gilts
○ the scale and pattern of secondary market trading.

Market participants

Before the Big Bang reforms of 1986 the gilt-edged market, just like the London equities market, was organised on single-capacity lines whereby member firms of the stock exchange functioned either as principals (jobbers) or as agents (brokers). Following the Big Bang the gilt-edged market has been organised around a group of specialist dealing firms called gilt-edged market-makers or GEMMs. GEMMs enjoy certain special rights but also accept certain obligations in the interests of maintaining an orderly and efficient market, which balances the requirements of the government (as the sole issuer) with those of the institutions and others who invest in government securities. In order to keep their own dealings and positions confidential, the GEMMs deal with each other through the medium of a small group of *inter-dealer brokers* (or IDBs) specially approved by the authorities and exclusively dedicated to this function of preserving anonymity among the GEMMs.

Until 1997, the Bank of England continued to exercise its traditional role of manager of the government's debt and was thus a principal trading counterparty for the GEMMs. In 1997, the government transferred from the Treasury to the Bank of England the overall responsibility for setting monetary policy and interest rates. It was felt that the combination under one roof of this new responsibility with the Bank's established function as the manager of the government's debt programme could lead to a conflict of interest. The government resolved this by transferring the debt management responsibilities to a newly established executive agency of the Treasury, the Debt Management Office (or DMO).

The following five years saw a series of further changes in the market. Some of these were technical in nature: for instance, the basis on which accrued interest is calculated was amended so that it was brought more into line with international practice. Other changes were more far-reaching, like the active promotion of a market in gilt *repurchase agreements* (or *repos*) which link the gilt-edged market closely to the mainstream sterling money market.

The DMO was established on 1 April 1998 as an executive agency of the Treasury, operating at arm's length from ministers. The DMO's brief is 'to carry out the Government's debt management policy of minimising financing costs over the long term, taking account of risk, and to manage the aggregate cash needs of the Exchequer in the most cost-effective way, in both cases consistently with the objectives of monetary and any wider policy considerations'. In practical terms, this entails:

○ adjusting the maturity and nature of the government's debt portfolio
○ maintaining an issuance programme which is open, predictable and transparent
○ promoting the development of a liquid and efficient gilts market.

The activities of the principal investors in the gilts market are described in greater detail in Chapter 10.

Primary issuance: the auction process

In former times, the relationship between the government's debt managers and the institutions that account for the lion's share of investment in government securities was often an uneasy one. It was probably not helped by the fact that regardless of the difficulty it periodically caused to both sides, neither could do without the other. The story of how Nathan Rothschild of the Frankfurt banking family made a fortune out of dealing in British government securities immediately after the victory over Napoleon at the Battle of Waterloo in 1815 may be apocryphal. But it has enjoyed wide credence simply because it so vividly conjures up the cloak-and-dagger aura which characterised the gilts market even into modern times. It was said that Rothschild went to great lengths to get news of the outcome of the battle before the general public, and when he heard of the British victory he appeared on the stock exchange with an ostentatiously sombre expression and sold large volumes of gilts. The market took this as evidence that the battle had been lost, and in the ensuing panic the price of gilts plummeted. Meanwhile Rothschild had his agents quietly buy up the stock at the lower prices, and made a killing when news of the victory at Waterloo became known.

More recently, the combination of chronic economic problems and volatile interest rates which characterised the market from the 1960s to the 1980s led to pronounced fluctuations in both the issuance and the market value of gilts. Interest rates were more prone to sharp and unexpected rises (for instance, to protect the value of sterling in a crisis of international confidence in the currency) than to equally sharp and unexpected falls. Investors were therefore more likely to sustain exceptional losses than to enjoy windfall profits. This rather tarnished the image of gilt-edged securities as a theoretically low-risk investment. Although government securities are risk-free in terms of the certainty of payment, fluctuations in interest rates play havoc with the secondary market value of all bonds including those issued by governments, so that the returns for investors who do not

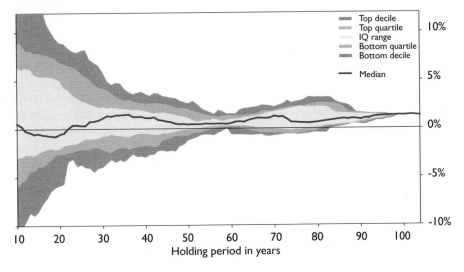

Figure 3.2 Dispersion of real returns on UK government bonds over periods of 10–105 years, 1900–2004
Source: Dimson and Marsh (2005).

hold such securities from original issuance to final maturity is very uncertain. In addition, high and volatile inflation rates have a further negative impact on the real value and the security of returns, even to those investors who hold to maturity. Figure 3.2 graphically illustrates the effect of these factors over the 105 years from 1900 to 2004.

This shows the distribution of real (i.e. inflation-adjusted) returns on investing in UK government bonds for holding periods of varying length. At the extreme left-hand side, we see the distribution of returns on the 96 separate holding periods consisting of ten successive calendar years between 1900 and 2004, i.e. the periods 1 January 1900 to 31 December 1909, 1 January 1901 to 31 December 1910, and so on, ending with the 96th such period, from 1 January 1995 to 31 December 2004. The darker shaded area at the bottom of the distribution represent the lowest decile, that is, the worst 10% of results for holding periods of that length, and from this we can see that there were more than ten holding periods of ten years in which the real return from holding gilts was worse than minus 5%. Surprising as this might be, if we look a little further to the right we find an even more startling result. The thick line in the middle of the distribution shows the average return for holding periods of each length, and this shows quite clearly that for holding periods of between 12 and 20 years the average real return was actually negative over the entire 105-year period of the study. So much for government bonds being a risk-free investment!

If we return to the issue of the government's relationship with the market, a major question was whether the government's financing objectives, and the general health of the market, would be helped or hindered by a more open and cooperative regime based on recognition of the two sides' unavoidable dependence on each other. General dissatisfaction with the way relevant news reached the market occasionally spilled over into allegations that some brokers and investors had privileged access to early warning of the government's intentions.

In the course of the 1990s the debate was settled – at least for the moment – in favour of openness. Nearly all gilts are now issued by means of a competitive public auction process which is specifically designed to protect the government from possible collusion by market makers, and individual market makers from the risks of the *winner's curse* (the tendency for the winning bid in an auction to exceed the true value of the item). At the beginning of each financial year the DMO publishes an outline of its gilts issuance plans for the coming year, including an assessment of the underlying assumptions on which the plans are based. A further more detailed programme is published at the beginning of each quarter, so that market makers and investors have a clear idea of exactly when the DMO plans to issue how much of what type of issue. The resulting transparency and predictability is believed to reduce the amount the Treasury is charged for market uncertainty (known as the **supply uncertainty premium**). There is also a system of formal consultation, in which the DMO and the market makers meet to discuss issues ranging from questions of broad strategy to more narrowly technical problems and proposals, and the outcome of these meetings is normally made public.

Table 3.9 shows the auction timetable for the financial year 2005–06 which was published by the DMO in April 2005.

Example 3.1 shows the press notice issued by the DMO after the auction of £2.25 billion of a further tranche of the then longest-dated gilt, the 4¼% Treasury Stock 2036. As the government's objective is to maximise the amount of cash it raises in relation to its future payment obligations, it allots bonds to the bidders in descending order of their bid prices (which is the same as ascending order of their bid yields). In this example the

Table 3.9 Gilt auction timetable for the financial year 2005–06

Date	Gilt/type	Date	Gilt/type
2005		Tuesday 25 October	Index-linked
Tuesday 12 April	2% IL 2035	Tuesday 8 November[2]	Conventional
Thursday 14 April	5% 2025	Thursday 24 November[2]	Index-linked
Thursday 28 April	4¾% 2010	Tuesday 6 December[2]	Conventional
Tuesday 24 May	2½% IL 2016	**2006**	
Thursday 26 May	4¼% 2055	Tuesday 10 January	Conventional
Tuesday 7 June	4¾% 2020	Tuesday 24 January	index-linked
Thursday 23 June	4¼% IL 2030	Thursday 26 January	Conventional
Thursday 14 July	4¼% 2055	Thursday 7 February	Index-linked
Tuesday 26 July	2½% IL 2020	Thursday 16 February[2]	Conventional
Tuesday 2 August	4% 2009	Wednesday 1 March[2]	Conventional
Tuesday 6 September	4¼% 2036	Tuesday 7 March[2]	Index-linked
Thursday 22 September	X% IL 2055		
Tuesday 27 September	4¾% 2020	1 This auction was cancelled on 20 April 2005	
Tuesday 11 October[1]	Index-linked	2 Subject to confirmation following the	
Thursday 13 October	Conventional	Chancellor's decisions on the Budgetary	
		timetable.	

Source: Debt Management Office.

Example 3.1 Announcement by DMO of result of gilt auction, 2 July 2003

<u>PRESS NOTICE</u>

RESULT OF THE SALE BY AUCTION OF £2,250 MILLION OF 4 1/4% TREASURY STOCK 2036

The United Kingdom Debt Management Office ('DMO') announces that the auction of £2,250 million of 4¼% Treasury Stock 2036 has been allotted in full.

1. All bids which have been accepted at the lowest accepted price have been allotted approximately 6.0% of the amount bid for. Competitive bids made at prices above the lowest accepted price have been allotted in full. Competitive bids made at prices below the lowest accepted price have been rejected.

2. The range of bids accepted was as follows:

	Price	Yield
Highest Accepted	£94.05	4.60%
Non-competitive allotment price (i.e. the rounded average acceptance price)	£93.86	4.62%
Lowest Accepted	£93.55	4.63%

3. The total amounts allotted and bids received were as follows:

Amount allotted to competitive bids	£2,079.0 million
Amount allotted to non-competitive bids	
Gilt-edged market makers	£168.75 million
Others	£2.25 million
Total	£2,250.0 million
Total bids received	£3,388.41 million
Times covered	1.51 times

highest bid price of £94.05 corresponded to the lowest yield of 4.60% p.a., and all bids at this level were allotted in full. The lowest accepted bid of £93.55 corresponded to a yield of 4.63%. Would-be purchasers who bid below this level (that is, demanded a return of over 4.63% p.a.) went away empty-handed from the auction.

SUMMARY

In this chapter we have used the domestic market in sterling-denominated UK government debt to make a comprehensive analysis of the main characteristics of marketable fixed-rate debt securities. After setting the market in its historical context, we explored in detail the differing ways in which price and return are related to each other for different types of security, ranging from conventional single-dated bonds to perpetuals and index-linked bonds. We also looked at the mechanics of trading such securities, including the problems associated with accrued interest and cum and ex dividend transactions. We also sketched the structure of the present-day market in gilts and took an historical perspective on trends.

REVIEW EXERCISES

For these exercises you will find it useful to visit the following websites in order to obtain updated information relating to the various tables in Chapter 3:

www.dmo.gov.uk: the Debt Management Office of the UK government, for updated information relating to Tables 3.3 and 3.5 (look for the section containing the DMO's quarterly and annual reports)
www.londonstockexchange.com: the London stock exchange, for information relating to gilt turnover.
www.ft.com: the Financial Times, for updated information relating to gilt prices.

1. What trend can you detect in the total amount of UK bonds in issue since the dates shown in the text? Can you relate the changes to developments either in the condition of the UK's public finances or in the general economic situation of the UK?
2. How has the overall composition of gilts in issue changed in terms of (a) the split between different maturities of conventional bonds and (b) the split between conventional and index-linked bonds? (Tip: an extensive commentary on this can be found on the DMO website.)
3. Do you detect any trends in the composition of the investor base for gilts? Make a note of your findings for future reference, when you read Chapter 10 on investment institutions.
4. Compare carefully the coupons of the conventional bonds now in issue with the coupons of the gilts in issue as at 18 November 2005 (Table 3.6). How might you explain any changes?
5. With reference to the data presented in Table 3.5, how has the pattern of turnover in gilts changed since 2004/05? Has the total volume changed significantly? How has the average bargain size evolved? Has the relative level of activity in different types or maturities of gilts changed at all? Make a note (from the DMO quarterly report) of the most actively traded gilt in the most recent quarter: you will need this information again when you do the review exercises at the end of Chapter 8.
6. Calculate the total consideration for a transaction of exactly £1 million nominal in each of the following gilts, dealt on Monday 4 September 2006 for settlement on Tuesday 5 September.

Issue	Clean price	Next coupon date
4% Treasury 2009	98.17	7 September 2006
4¾% Treasury 2010	100.04	7 December 2006
5% Treasury 2025	108.11	7 September 2006
6% Treasury 2028	124.48	7 December 2006
4⅛% Index-Linked 2030	235.44	22 January 2007

Note for the purposes of the index-linked issue that the RPI for May 2006 was 197.7.

7. Calculate the interest yield for each of the conventional gilts listed in Exercise 6 above.

8. Calculate the consideration for a transaction of exactly £1 million nominal in each of the following gilt strips, dealt on Monday 4 September 2006 for settlement on Tuesday 5 September.

Strip	Yield (%)	Redemption date
4¼% Principal Strip	3.981349	7 March 2036
4¼% Principal Strip	3.663010	7 December 2055

9. From the data presented in Table 3.6 for the 8% Treasury maturing on 27 September 2013 and for the 2½% Index-Linked Treasury maturing 16 August 2013, calculate an approximate breakeven inflation rate for the period November 2005–August 2013.

Sample answers to the review exercises can be found on the companion website.

4 Bond strategies

CHAPTER CONTENTS

Learning objectives for this chapter

After studying this chapter you should be able to

○ describe in detail the relationship between the price, yield and maturity of a bond
○ derive the implied current and future spot interest rates from an observed set of yields
○ use the concepts of duration, modified duration and convexity to model the reaction of bond prices to interest rate changes
○ describe how duration and convexity can be used in practice as an aid to bond investment strategy.

INTRODUCTION

In Chapter 3, we saw how bonds (or *fixed income securities*) differ from one another, through their coupons and maturities. We also learned how to calculate common measures of return on bonds, including the interest yield and the redemption yield, also known as the yield to maturity. And we explored the mathematics of the relationship between redemption yield and present value or price. In this chapter, we look more closely at ways of making investment choices between different fixed interest securities.

We saw in earlier chapters that the value of all fixed interest securities is subject to interest rate risk and inflation risk (as well as default risk for non-government securities). But what is the precise impact of a change in interest rates or of unexpected inflation on a particular fixed interest security? In this chapter we shall see how this depends on the specific pattern of its cash flows: that is, on its particular coupon and maturity. Before we can make informed investment choices between fixed interest securities, we need to understand how each security will be affected by such changes.

We also need to understand whether there is a relationship between the current prices of bonds and current expectations of future market conditions which will determine future prices. We shall find that fixed interest security prices do largely reflect market expectations of interest and inflation rates. However, these expectations are not immediately obvious from redemption yields, but have to be inferred indirectly from the future interest rates which are implied by bond prices and their associated yields.

Investors can then use this information about market expectations of future interest rates to follow one of two broad types of investment strategy. In order to understand these strategies more easily, we normally assume that investors' overall objective in investing in fixed income securities is to achieve a target level of return over a pre-determined period. This might be because they want to be sure of having money available to meet definite or probable liabilities at a fixed future date or dates. For the professional investor, this could be the need for a company or its pension fund to have the necessary resources to pay out pensions to its past, present and future employees. An analogous situation for the private investor is when parents wish to put funds aside to provide for the future education of an infant child (or for the wedding of a grown-up child). But equally, investors trading in the bond market for pure gain and without the need to cover some externally determined liability are likely to set themselves a target level of return within a predetermined time horizon. This is particularly important in the bond market, because we shall see that especially in markets where prices accurately reflect expectations, apparent gains in one period can often be realised only at the expense of directly compensating losses in following periods. In short, in the world of fixed income securities, we always have to watch out for the apparently profitable strategy which on closer inspection turns out disappointingly to be little more than a *zero-sum game*.

The two broad types of fixed income investment strategy are:

○ **Passive strategy ('follow the market').** Investors accept the market's expectations of future interest rates embodied in the *yield curve* of current bond prices. As we shall see in the course of this chapter, these are reflected in the differing redemption yields underpinning current prices for bonds of differing maturities. Investors then attempt either to minimise interest rate risk by matching the maturities of the bonds with the maturities of their liabilities, or to minimise inflation risk by investing short term or buying index-linked bonds.

○ **Active strategy ('beat the market').** Investors compare their own expectations of future interest and inflation rates with the expectations of the market, and choose those bonds that will perform best if their forecast proves to be more accurate than that of the market. If, for example, they believe that interest rates will decline over the next year by more than is predicted by the market and is currently reflected in bond prices, they will invest in those bonds that are the most sensitive to changes in interest rates, which will therefore experience the biggest price rises if the forecast is correct. They will invest in securities that are more sensitive than the present value of their liabilities, and will therefore appreciate more than their liabilities if the forecast turns out to have been accurate. We shall see that this sensitivity can be assessed by a simple and reliable measure called *duration*.

The structure of Chapter 4 is as follows. We first examine the measures used to describe bonds in Chapter 3 to see how they can help in investment decision making. We shall find that the only measure of any potential use is the redemption yield. However, the redemption yield does not directly help us to obtain market forecasts of future interest rates, so we turn to **spot interest rates** and *forward interest rates* for this information. We can then determine the **term structure of interest rates**, both now and in the future, which allows us to estimate the sensitivity of different bonds to expected changes in interest rates and thus to choose in which bonds to invest. We find that this sensitivity can be captured in the **duration** and **convexity** of a security. Finally, we see how these findings can be harnessed into the service of our chosen investment strategy for the fixed income markets.

PRICE, YIELD AND MATURITY: BASIC PRINCIPLES OF THE RELATIONSHIP

In Review Exercise 2 at the end of Chapter 2 we looked at four basic principles about the relationship between the present value (or market price), the rate of return (or redemption yield), and the maturity of a bond or of any other future cash flow. We found that:

Principle 1: As return increases, present value decreases, and vice versa.
Principle 2: A given change in the rate of return has a smaller impact on nearer than on more remote cash flows.
Principle 3: As return increases, the present value falls at a reducing rate.
Principle 4: As a bond approaches its final maturity, if the applicable rate of return remains static, the clean price of the bond approaches 100.

Table 4.1 illustrates these principles with an expanded table of results from the data used in Chapter 2, showing the price behaviour of a 5% coupon bond at redemption yields ranging from 3% p.a. to 7% p.a. at two different points in its overall life – five years from maturity and four years from maturity. For each date, part A of the table calculates the present values of the bond's individual cash flows at each yield, and part B calculates the change in present value for each cash flow for each 1% increase in yield. For example, when the yield increases from 4% to 5%, the present value of the two-year cash flow falls from 4.62 to 4.54, or by 1.90%. Both the present values and the percentage changes have been calculated with full accuracy, and rounded to two decimal places for display purposes only. We shall come back to the numbers in Table 4.1 later in the chapter.

It is relatively easy to plot the price behaviour of a specific bond at different dates or under different market interest rates, but how can we compare different bonds with each other for investment purposes? The next section considers, and dismisses, all but one of the various possible measures of comparison. The remaining measure – redemption yield – will point us in the direction of the measure which will – finally – meet our requirement.

COMPARING BONDS …

In this section we look at the measures discussed in Chapter 3 to see whether they can help us to compare bonds. Table 4.2 shows relevant information for the largest and most actively traded conventional single-dated gilts (**benchmark issues**) as at Friday 5 December 2003. We have chosen this date in order to avoid unnecessary

Table 4.1 Present value, and percentage change in present value, of a 5% coupon bond with nominal value 100.00, at redemption yields from 3% p.a. to 7% p.a., with a remaining life of (1) five years and (2) four years

(1) Five years to maturity

Year	Cash flow	Annual redemption yield				
		3.00%	4.00%	5.00%	6.00%	7.00%
A. Present values of cash flows						
1	5.00	4.85	4.81	4.76	4.72	4.67
2	5.00	4.71	4.62	4.54	4.45	4.37
3	5.00	4.58	4.44	4.32	4.20	4.08
4	5.00	4.44	4.27	4.11	3.96	3.81
5	105.00	90.57	86.30	82.27	78.46	74.86
Total		109.16	104.45	100.00	95.79	91.80
B. Percentage change in present value of cash flows						
1			-0.96%	-0.95%	-0.94%	-0.93%
2			-1.91%	-1.90%	-1.88%	-1.86%
3			-2.86%	-2.83%	-2.80%	-2.78%
4			-3.79%	-3.76%	-3.72%	-3.69%
5			-4.72%	-4.67%	-4.63%	-4.59%
Total			-4.31%	-4.26%	-4.21%	-4.16%

(2) Four years to maturity

Year	Cash flow	Annual redemption yield				
		3.00%	4.00%	5.00%	6.00%	7.00%
A. Present values of cash flows						
1	5.00	4.85	4.81	4.76	4.72	4.67
2	5.00	4.71	4.62	4.54	4.45	4.37
3	5.00	4.58	4.44	4.32	4.20	4.08
4	105.00	93.29	89.75	86.38	83.17	80.10
Total		107.43	103.63	100.00	96.53	93.23
B. Percentage change in present value of cash flows						
1			-0.96%	-0.95%	-0.94%	-0.93%
2			-1.91%	-1.90%	-1.88%	-1.86%
3			-2.86%	-2.83%	-2.80%	-2.78%
4			-3.79%	-3.76%	-3.72%	-3.69%
Total			-3.54%	-3.50%	-3.47%	-3.43%

computational complexities in the subsequent detailed analysis. Friday 5 December 2003 was the dealing date for settlement on Monday 8 December 2003, the business day closest to 7 December which is a coupon date for a large number of gilt-edged issues. By using this date we almost eliminate the difference between clean and dirty prices and we substantially simplify the discounting process because we will be dealing in whole coupon periods. We quote the yields to three places of decimals for greater clarity in our analysis.

... by price?

Superficially the most striking difference between the bond issues is in their prices, which are shown in terms of £ per £100 nominal, and their coupons. Just by

Table 4.2 Benchmark conventional single-dated gilt issues; prices and yields quoted on Friday 5 December 2003, for settlement Monday 8 December 2003

Maturity	Coupon	Clean price	Interest yield	Redemption yield	Difference
07 Jun 04	5.00%	100.54	4.973	3.893	-1.080
07 Dec 05	8.50%	107.72	7.891	4.419	-3.472
07 Dec 06	7.50%	108.05	6.941	4.594	-2.347
07 Dec 07	7.25%	109.17	6.641	4.707	-1.935
07 Mar 08	5.00%	101.05	4.948	4.722	-0.226
07 Mar 09	4.00%	96.36	4.151	4.791	0.640
07 Dec 09	5.75%	104.86	5.484	4.808	-0.676
25 Nov 10	6.25%	108.19	5.777	4.850	-0.927
12 Jul 11	9.00%	125.92	7.147	4.874	-2.273
07 Mar 12	5.00%	100.74	4.963	4.889	-0.074
27 Sep 13	8.00%	123.97	6.453	4.891	-1.562
07 Sep 14	5.00%	100.64	4.968	4.922	-0.047
07 Dec 15	8.00%	127.62	6.269	4.924	-1.345
25 Aug 17	8.75%	137.65	6.357	4.937	-1.419
07 Jun 21	8.00%	136.15	5.876	4.900	-0.976
07 Mar 25	5.00%	101.98	4.903	4.849	-0.054
07 Dec 28	6.00%	117.13	5.123	4.814	-0.308
07 Jun 32	4.25%	91.81	4.629	4.779	0.150
07 Mar 36	4.25%	91.82	4.629	4.748	0.119

Source: Debt Management Office.

comparing their prices, can the investor determine which bond gives the best value or pays the highest return in relation to the risk incurred? The issue with the highest price, at £137.65 per £100 nominal, is the 8¾% issue maturing in 2017, and the lowest priced issue is the 4¼% of 2032 with a price of just £91.81. Is it in any sense useful or meaningful to say that these are respectively the most and least expensive gilts on offer? Clearly not, as the two prices represent the purchase costs of two quite different future streams of cash. For an outlay of £137.65, the purchaser of the 8¾% of 2017 is entitled to receive £4.375 (one-half of £8.75) every six months for 13 years and a final payment of £104.375 in about 13½ years, whereas the investor in the 4¼% issue of 2032 will pay £91.81 now for the right to receive a semi-annual income of just £2.125 (one-half of £4.25) for 28 years and a final payment of 102.125. In very rough terms, the investor in the longer-dated gilt receives about half the annual income of the shorter-dated investor, but for more than twice as long, and each of them also receives a £100 capital repayment at the end. These streams of income are so completely different from each other that to compare their respective initial outlays is to compare apples with oranges. And a simple comparison does not even begin to help us answer more searching questions. Which bond is a safer bet if interest rates go up unexpectedly in the near future? Should an investor who has a liability maturing in 2032 buy the issue maturing in that year or would he or she be better off if he or she were to buy the shorter-dated bond with a view to reinvesting the proceeds on maturity in 2017 for a further 15 years?

... by coupon?

If the prices do not enable us to differentiate usefully between bonds, can the coupons help us instead? The coupons range from 4–4¼% for the shortest and the longest of the issues shown, to 8–9% for five of the medium-dated issues. Do the latter issues necessarily offer better value than the former? Again, we are not comparing like with like, because we have to invest substantially different amounts for the right to receive the coupons. Whereas we have to invest only £92–96 per £100 nominal to acquire the right to receive the lower coupon issues, we have to invest anything from £124 to over £136 to secure the higher coupon streams.

... by maturity?

Maturity can be a useful comparative measure for bonds since investors can choose bonds according to their pattern of consumption preferences or their future liabilities. One way of avoiding interest rate risk is to match exactly the maturities of assets and liabilities. But in practice interest rate risk cannot be completely avoided in this way since interest payments during the life of the bond might not exactly match consumption needs, and so they might have to be reinvested, perhaps at less advantageous rates. For example, if a bond with a longer maturity than the liability is chosen, investors run the risk that interest rates will have risen and the price fallen when the bond has to be sold to meet the liability. If a bond with too short a maturity is chosen, investors run the risk that interest rates will have fallen and the money received on redemption will have to be reinvested for the remaining term at a lower interest rate than they could have obtained on a bond with the same maturity as the liability. Only if investors were to purchase a zero-coupon fixed interest security (one that pays no interest during its life) could they avoid interest rate risk altogether.

However, investors might be unable or unwilling to match the maturity of their investments to that of their liabilities, or they might wish to compare two bonds with the same maturity. In order to choose between bonds in these circumstances, they must be able to compare the interest rate risk and the return on each of the bonds they are considering, and to do this, they must turn to the only remaining measure, the redemption yield.

... by redemption yield?

At first sight it might appear paradoxical that in our search for suitable criteria to distinguish between bond issues we have eliminated several measures that exhibited significantly different values (such as price and coupon) and have narrowed the field down to the measure that (at least on our chosen date) seems to vary least between different issues, namely their redemption yields. These rise gently from 4.791% for the shortest, five-year issue in Table 4.2 to a peak of about 4.937% at the 14-year horizon before declining back to 4.748% again at the very long end – hardly a dramatic progression.

We can plot these redemption yields on a graph to form a *yield curve* showing the broad shape of returns on similar securities with different maturities at a particular point in time, and we can study how this curve changes over time and in response to market conditions. Figure 4.1 shows just such a *par yield curve* for gilts for 31 March 2003 and 31 March 2004. From the par yield curve (plotting notional bonds with coupons equal

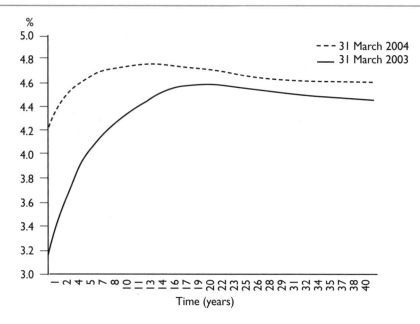

Figure 4.1 Par gilt yield curves as at 31 March 2003 and 2004
Source: Debt Management Office.

to their yields and hence priced at par), we can see that gilt yields had risen during the year, and by more in the shorter maturities. But before we can interpret the yield curve in any finer detail we need to understand more precisely what is really at work behind the redemption yields.

We learned in Chapter 3 that the redemption yield of a bond is the unique periodic discount rate which, when applied uniformly to all the future cash flows of that bond, exactly equates the sum of their present values to the current market price. Table 4.4 shows this calculation in detail for each of the four short-dated issues featured in Table 4.3, as all of these conveniently have identical coupon payment dates on 7 June and 7 December annually. Note that in accordance with the usual convention for discounting gilt-edged bond cash flows and for expressing their redemption yields, a discounting period of six months is used and the resulting discount rate is simply doubled (and not compounded) to give the annual equivalent rate. Note also that the present values or market prices calculated here are the dirty prices: that is, they include just one day's

Table 4.3 Selected short-dated benchmark conventional gilt issues, under five years remaining life as at 5 December 2003

Maturity	Coupon	Clean price	Interest yield	Redemption yield	Difference
07 June 04	5.00%	100.54	4.973	3.893	-1.080
07 Dec 05	8.50%	107.72	7.891	4.419	-3.472
07 Dec 06	7.50%	108.05	6.941	4.594	-2.347
07 Dec 07	7.25%	109.17	6.641	4.707	-1.935

Source: Debt Management Office.

Table 4.4 Benchmark conventional single-dated gilt issues, under five years remaining life as at 5 December 2003: calculation of dirty prices from redemption yields

Maturity	07 June 04		07 Dec 05		07 Dec 06		07 Dec 07	
Coupon	5.00%		8.50%		7.50%		7.25%	
Annual equivalent yield	3.893%		4.419%		4.594%		4.707%	
Date	Cash flow	PV	Cash flow	PV	Cash flow	PV	Cash flow	PV
07 June 04	102.50	100.55	4.25	4.16	3.75	3.67	3.63	3.54
07 Dec 04			4.25	4.07	3.75	3.58	3.63	3.46
07 June 05			4.25	3.98	3.75	3.50	3.63	3.38
07 Dec 05			104.25	95.54	3.75	3.42	3.63	3.30
07 Jun 06					3.75	3.35	3.63	3.23
07 Dec 06					103.75	90.55	3.63	3.15
07 June 07							3.63	3.08
07 Dec 07							103.63	86.04
Market value (dirty price)		100.55		107.74		108.08		109.19

accrued coupon interest which would have had to be paid on a purchase for settlement on 8 December 2003.

In fact this seemingly innocuous discount table conceals a potentially serious problem which we can see more clearly if we rewrite the calculation for the two shortest bonds in the mathematical notation familiar from earlier chapters.

The present value of a bond is calculated by applying equation 3.1:

$$P_0 = \frac{C_1}{(1+r)} + \frac{C_2}{(1+r)^2} + \frac{C_3}{(1+r)^3} + \ldots \frac{C_n}{(1+r)^n} + \frac{100}{(1+r)^n} \qquad (3.1)$$

We can combine the last two terms of this equation as they have the same denominator, so that for the 5% issue maturing on 7 June 2004 this gives:

$$P_0 = \frac{102.50}{\left(1 + \dfrac{0.03893}{2}\right)} = 100.55$$

Similarly, for the 8½% issue maturing on 7 December 2005:

$$P_0 = \frac{4.25}{\left(1 + \dfrac{0.04419}{2}\right)} + \frac{4.25}{\left(1 + \dfrac{0.04419}{2}\right)^2} + \frac{4.25}{\left(1 + \dfrac{0.04419}{2}\right)^3} + \frac{104.25}{\left(1 + \dfrac{0.04419}{2}\right)^4}$$

$$P_0 = 4.16 + 4.07 + 3.98 + 95.53 = 107.74$$

We know that the discount rate that should be used for calculating the present value of any future cash flow from an investment is the rate of interest we could get by investing in another investment of equivalent risk – in other words, the *opportunity cost* of the

investment. Viewed from our chosen perspective of 8 December 2003, there is no difference in risk between amounts due to be paid on 7 June 2004 under each of our four
chosen short-dated gilts or under any of the many other longer-dated gilts that pay
coupons semi-annually on 7 June and 7 December: each represents a claim on the UK
government, and the legal terms of those claims are identical with each other. So if we
are to be consistent, we should discount all such cash flows at the same rate as each other
– a uniform rate for lending money to the UK government from 8 December 2003 to
7 June 2004 (with no intervening cash flows – in other words, a zero-coupon bond). Similarly, as there is no difference in risk between amounts due to be paid on 7 December
2004 under each of our chosen benchmark issues, these too should be discounted at the
appropriate rate for purchasing a zero-coupon bond issued by the UK government on
8 December 2003 for redemption on 7 December 2004.

But the redemption yield calculation does not work like that. It is simply the *uniform*
discount rate that, given the price, coupon and maturity of a bond, discounts all of the
future cash flows of that particular bond back to the price, without regard to the actual
underlying uniform rates for loans of each maturity to the UK government. The redemption yield can be understood as a blended rate derived from these underlying rates; it is
the purely mathematical solution for the variable r in any equation like equation 3.1 if P_0
is already known. But clearly it will vary according to the pattern of cash flows of each
bond: two bonds with the same maturity but different coupons will exhibit different
redemption yields, because the differing patterns of their underlying cash flows will
result in a different blend of underlying rates.

SPOT RATES AND THE TERM STRUCTURE OF INTEREST RATES

Since redemption yields do not represent a reliable picture of prevailing interest rates for
different maturities of bond, we must go back to the basic discounted cash flow valuation model for bonds and examine the underlying interest rates that determine their prices.
Adapting equation 3.1, we can write:

$$P_0 = \frac{C_1}{(1+r_1)} + \frac{C_2}{(1+r_2)^2} + \frac{C_3}{(1+r_3)^3} + \ldots \frac{C_n}{(1+r_n)^n} + \frac{100}{(1+r_n)^n} \qquad (4.1)$$

where r_1 is the periodic rate of interest required on one-period investments, r_2 is the periodic rate of interest required for money invested now for two periods, and so on; r_1 will not
necessarily be equal to r_2 or to r_3 (as is assumed in the calculation of the redemption yield)
since interest rates will be expected to change over time. These interest rates, the r_i, are
called **spot interest rates** because they are rates for investments made now or 'on the spot'.
In other words, investors contract to lend money now for n periods in return for which
they receive a single payment after n periods representing repayment of principal plus
periodically compounded interest at r_n per period throughout the n periods of the loan.

As we have already seen, the purchase of a gilt-edged bond always involves a loan to
the UK government, and investors will be guaranteed the interest and principal payments,
whichever bond they invest in. So they will require the same interest rate for lending for n
years to the UK government for any bond. This means that, at any point in time, a uniform
set of spot rates can be used to value any bond. All cash flows paid on the same future date
but under different bonds will be discounted at the same rate.

It might be instructive to be able to plot on a graph a *spot rate curve* and an expected spot rate (or forward rate) curve in 12 months' time (or for whichever holding period is preferred) in order to be able to study changes in bond prices and calculate expected holding period returns and investment strategies. But before we draw such a curve, the spot rates r_i have to be determined.

There are essentially three ways of determining spot rates: substitution, regression, and from zero-coupon bonds. Although all three methods are different, the principle is the same in that the spot rates are determined from actual market prices for bonds. The spot rates are the market consensus rates for lending to the UK government, in the case of bonds, for one year, two years, and so on.

We shall use the fictitious data in Example 4.1 to show how the substitution method can be used to calculate spot rates out to two years. We start with a one-year annual coupon bond. For this bond, the one-year spot rate is simply the same as the redemption yield and so the one-year spot rate can readily be calculated.

Example 4.1 Data for estimation of existing spot rates

Bond	Coupon (%)	Maturity (years)	Price £
A	8.5	1	98.625
B	10.0	2	98.375

$$P_0 = \frac{C + 100}{(1 + r_1)}$$

$$98.625 = \frac{108.50}{(1 + r_1)}$$

$$1 + r_1 = \frac{108.50}{98.625}$$

$$r_1 = \frac{108.50}{98.625} - 1 = 0.1001 = \mathbf{10.01\%}$$

For the two-year bond, we write down the price in terms of the one-year cash flow discounted by the one-year spot rate (which we now know) and the two-year cash flow discounted by the two-year spot rate (which we do not yet know). Since we know the price of the bond and the one-year spot rate, we can solve the equation for the two-year spot rate.

$$P_0 = \frac{C_1}{(1 + r_1)} + \frac{C_2 + 100}{(1 + r_2)^2}$$

$$98.375 = \frac{10}{(1.1001)} + \frac{110}{(1 + r_2)^2}$$

$$98.375 = 9.09 + \frac{110}{(1 + r_2)^2}$$

$$89.285 = \frac{110}{(1 + r_2)^2}$$

$$(1 + r_2)^2 = \frac{110}{89.285}$$

$$r_2 = \sqrt{\frac{110}{89.285}} - 1 = 0.1100 = \mathbf{11.00\%}$$

Now let us compare this result with a redemption yield calculation for Bond *B*: that is, a calculation that reconciles the present value with the future cash flows by means of a single uniform discount rate, which in this case is found (either by trial and error or by using a computer) to be 10.948%.

Example 4.2 Calculation of Bond *B* present value using redemption yield

Year	Cash flow	Discount factor at 10.948%	PV
1	10	0.901	9.013
2	110	0.812	89.362
Present value			98.375

The redemption yield model says that out of our total investment of £98.375 we invest £9.013 for one year at an annual rate of 10.948%, and £89.362 for two years at the same annual rate of 10.948%. But we now know that while this can be a mathematically valid way of arriving at the current price, it does not correspond to the economic reality (as revealed by the spot rates), which is that we have invested £9.09 for one year at the one-year spot rate of 10.01%, and the remaining £89.285 at the two-year spot rate of 11.00%.

As we observed earlier in this section, the redemption yield is nothing more than a weighted blend of the two spot rates. In the case of a two-year bond, it is relatively easy to guess roughly where that blended rate will lie: as we have invested about one-tenth of our money at 10% for one year and the remaining nine-tenths at 11% for two years, the blended rate will reflect roughly a 20:1 weighting in favour of the two-year rate. But such rough-and-ready analysis becomes quite impractical if we try to apply it to a bond which pays semi-annual coupons for the next 28 years, and whose redemption yield is a blend of 56 different spot rates.

In practice, the substitution process would have to be carried out right through the maturity spectrum and it would be difficult to find bonds with exactly the right maturities. For this reason, spot rates are normally determined by regression. The population of bond prices, coupons and maturities is put into the computer, and the set of spot rates that best fits the data is estimated by regression analysis. In practice, as we can see from Table 3.6, the policy of concentrating gilts issue on a relatively small number of large but liquid issues results in a situation where some parts of the maturity spectrum have only a few bonds, so the estimates will not be perfect. However, the method is good enough to derive for most bond markets a sensible set of spot rates.

One immediate use for such a regression model is to reprice all the bonds in the model with the spot rates estimated from the model. Since the spot rates are the best estimates, repricing the bonds will make some bonds look **expensive** relative to their market price while others will look **cheap** (a bond is expensive if its redemption yield is lower than a theoretically calculated fair return for the risk incurred, and cheap if its redemption yield is higher). This could simply be a problem with the accuracy of the regression technique, but if the cheapness or dearness varies over time, this technique could throw up genuine opportunities for enhancement of returns.

The third method of establishing the spot rates is possible only if there is a set of *zero-coupon bonds*, one for every maturity in the yield curve. If there is, the redemption yields on the zero-coupon bonds are theoretically the same as the spot rates that we are attempting to reconstruct. The facility for stripping gilt-edged bonds (see Chapter 3) in effect creates just the series of zero-coupon bonds we need for this exercise. This third method is clearly the simplest and most attractive, but there is a major drawback in practice. The spot rates derived from stripped gilts might be different from those derived from coupon bonds using regression techniques because different supply and demand factors influence the two types of bond, affecting their relative prices and hence the spot rates derived from these two sets of prices. For example, insurance companies might particularly value 20-year zero-coupon bonds, since they have a higher average life than is available with coupon bonds. We should also bear in mind that the market for strips is still quite small, so it might not fulfil the price-discovery function as efficiently as the market for the underlying bonds themselves.

Figure 4.2 shows the zero-coupon, or spot, yield curves, determined by regression analysis, for UK gilts for 31 December 2004 and 31 March 2005.

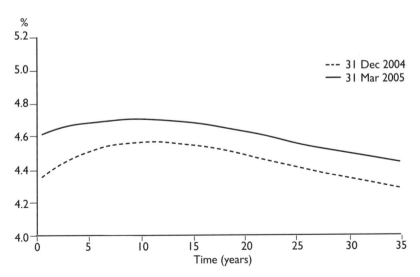

Figure 4.2 UK zero-coupon (spot) yield curves as at 31 December 2004 and 31 March 2005
Source: Debt Management Office.

FORWARD INTEREST RATES

Even when we have calculated or estimated the spot rates lurking behind the prices and redemption yields of coupon bonds, we have not yet quite got right to the bottom of the interest rate structure, because we do not know yet why (for example) the two-year spot rate differs from the one-year spot rate. Later in this chapter we shall see that there is a variety of possible explanations, but the one most commonly advanced, and most intuitively appealing, is that the two-year spot rate represents a combination of the current actual one-year spot rate with an expectation of what the one-year spot rate will be in exactly one year's time. If we can somehow determine these implied future spot rates (sometimes referred to as the *future term structure of interest rates*), we shall be able to see how interest rates are expected to change in the future. This will bring us one step closer to determining our overall bond investment strategy, as outlined in the introduction to this chapter.

The concept of an implied future interest rate can be understood and illustrated most easily by observing very short-term money-market interest rates, as the following analysis will show.

Box 4.1 Instantaneous interest rates

What is so special about the period of one year that we should choose it as our unit for dividing up the future? After all, time is an infinitely divisible continuum. Such a question would be justified, because the choice is in fact arbitrary. The two-year rate might consist of the current one-year rate plus the expectation of the one-year rate in one year's time, but what is the current one-year rate, if it is not the current six-month rate plus the expectation of the six-month rate in six months' time? And so we could continue, until we were asking: what is the rate for two instants, if it is not the current rate for one instant plus the expectation of the rate for one instant in one instant's time? This line of reasoning leads to the idea of an instantaneous interest rate, and this is in fact the form in which the Bank of England currently calculates by means of regression analysis the market's expectation of what instantaneous interest rates will be at six-monthly intervals in the future.

Interest calculations, unlike time itself, do in practice have a minimum unit of calculation, and that is a period of one day. Managers of very short-term liquidity (for instance, in banks) do in fact decide to lend out their surplus funds in the money market for one day or for two, depending on whether they agree with the market's expectation, as embodied in the two-day rate, of what tomorrow's one-day rate will be.

If we were to be really strict, we would say that the minimum unit of calculation for interest is not the day but the night, as interest is charged overnight on balances outstanding at the close of business each day. *Overnight* is in fact the name popularly given to the one-day interest rate in the money market.

Money market rates

We start by introducing a refinement to our established notation for denoting interest rates or yields so that we can indicate not only the length of the holding period but also the starting point of that holding period in relation to the present time. We shall denote such a rate with $r_{x,y}$ where x is the time in years from today until the start of the holding period, and y is the time in years from today until the end of the holding period. For example, the interest rate on an investment starting today and running for six months will be denoted by $r_{0,0.5}$, and the interest rate on an investment starting in three months' time and maturing in one year's time will be denoted by $r_{0.25,1.0}$.

In the interbank deposit market, the major banks borrow and lend among themselves large amounts of sterling and other currencies at fixed rates for varying maturities, ranging from overnight to a year or, less frequently, even longer periods. Among the most frequently traded maturities are one, three and six months. So, for example, on 16 January 2004 typical interbank rates for three-month and six-month sterling deposits were 4.00% and 4.25% p.a. respectively. What, if anything, might a comparison of these rates tell us about market expectations of interest rates for the future period bridging the gap between these two maturities: i.e. the period running from 16 April to 16 July 2004? The same question could be posed in a slightly different form: how could a borrower use these rates on 16 January 2004 to fix the rate at which he will be able to borrow, say, £1 million from 16 April to 16 July? One way would be to borrow immediately, for a period of six months, at the prevailing rate of 4.25% per annum (p.a.) the amount that, when invested for three months at the current three-month deposit rate, would yield a total return of exactly £1 million on 16 April. Note that the sterling interbank deposit market uses the same basic convention as the gilt-edged market for calculating interest amounts: actual number of days divided by 365, but uses simple interest rather than compound interest, as for all money-market instruments. As the three-month interest rate is 4.00% p.a., we can calculate the amount to be borrowed P from the equation

$$P = \frac{£1,000,000}{\left(1 + \frac{r_{0,0.25} \times 90}{365}\right)}$$

by substituting 0.04 for $r_{0,0.25}$:

$$P = \frac{£1,000,000}{\left(1 + \frac{0.04 \times 90}{365}\right)} = \frac{£1,000,000}{1.009863} = £990,233.33$$

In this way the borrower will have the use of £1 million from 16 April until 16 July, when he will have to repay the original six-month loan with interest. We calculate the amount he will have to repay F from the equation

$$F = P\left(1 + \frac{r_{0,0.5} \times 182}{365}\right)$$

So

$$F = £990,233.33 \times \left(1 + \frac{0.0425 \times 182}{365}\right) = £1,011,218.14$$

The end result is that the borrower will have had the use of £1 million for three months from mid-April to mid-July, and will have known from the outset that he would have to pay a total of £1,011,218.14 at the end. His actual interest cost is £11,218.14 for three months, and the effective annual interest rate is calculated from the equation:

$$\frac{£11,218.14}{£1,000,000} \times \frac{365}{92} \times 100 = 4.4507\%$$

What this has shown is that the combination of a three-month spot rate of 4.00% p.a. and a six-month spot rate of 4.25% p.a. implies an expected three-month spot rate of 4.4507% p.a. for the period starting three months from today. If the market's expectation of the future spot rate were higher than this, participants would be motivated to borrow large amounts of six-month money at 4.25% p.a. and lend three-month money at 4.00% p.a., in the expectation of being able to invest the proceeds of the three-month deposit at a rate higher than the breakeven rate of 4.4507% p.a. This would simultaneously increase demand for six-month money (forcing the rate up) and increase the supply of three-month money (forcing the rate down) until the two rates came back into equilibrium.

The general formula for calculating a short-term forward interest rate $r_{i,j}$ is given by the following equation:

$$r_{i,j} = \left\langle \frac{\left[1 + \left(\dfrac{r_{0,j} \times d_{0,j}}{100 \times y}\right)\right]}{\left[1 + \left(\dfrac{r_{0,i} \times d_{0,i}}{100 \times y}\right)\right]} - 1 \right\rangle \times \left[\frac{y \times 100}{d_{i,j}}\right] \tag{4.2}$$

where $d_{i,j}$ represents the number of days between two future dates which are respectively i and j days from the present day, and y represents the number of days in a year according to the daycount convention employed by the particular market (365 in the case of the sterling money market).

Bond market rates

The next step is to extend the basic concept of future spot rates for short-term money-market transactions to the more complex world of longer-term bonds. How can we use the technique introduced in the last section to establish market expectations of interest rates at more remote future dates? The answer is that we can apply exactly the same mathematical method to our current spot rate curve to calculate the theoretical value of the implied future spot rate or forward rate not only for a specific one-year period in the future but for any future period, starting and finishing on any dates as long as they lie within the period covered by our spot rate curve.

Table 4.5 shows the spot and forward rates derived by regression analysis from the closing prices for conventional gilt-edged issues on Friday 5 December 2003, for settlement on Monday 8 December. The start dates, expressed in terms of years from the present day, are shown in the column headers and the end dates are shown at the beginning of each line. The first column of figures, starting in year 0, therefore represents the zero-coupon or spot rate curve. The second column shows the forward rates for periods starting in one year's time, that is, on 8 December 2004, and running to the end of the year shown at the beginning of each line. The last in each line of figures is the forward one-year rate for each year from 2004 until 2028.

The following illustration shows how the table is constructed. (Note that the spot rates

Table 4.5 Spot and implied forward interest rates derived from gilt-edged market prices as at 5 December 2003

Year	0	1	2	3	4	5	6	7	8	9	10	11	12	13	14	15	16	17	18	19	20	21	22	23	24
1	4.15																								
2	4.40	4.65																							
3	4.56	4.76	4.87																						
4	4.67	4.84	4.93	5.00																					
5	4.75	4.90	4.98	5.03	5.06																				
6	4.80	4.93	5.00	5.05	5.07	5.08																			
7	4.84	4.96	5.02	5.06	5.08	5.08	5.07																		
8	4.87	4.97	5.03	5.06	5.07	5.08	5.08	5.07																	
9	4.89	4.98	5.03	5.05	5.07	5.06	5.05	5.05	5.03																
10	4.90	4.98	5.02	5.05	5.05	5.05	5.04	5.03	5.01	4.99															
11	4.90	4.98	5.01	5.03	5.04	5.03	5.02	5.01	4.99	4.97	4.94														
12	4.90	4.97	5.00	5.02	5.02	5.01	5.00	4.99	4.97	4.94	4.92	4.89													
13	4.90	4.96	4.99	5.00	5.00	4.99	4.98	4.96	4.94	4.92	4.89	4.86	4.83												
14	4.89	4.95	4.97	4.98	4.98	4.97	4.95	4.93	4.91	4.89	4.86	4.83	4.80	4.78											
15	4.88	4.93	4.95	4.96	4.95	4.94	4.93	4.91	4.88	4.86	4.83	4.80	4.77	4.75	4.72										
16	4.86	4.91	4.93	4.93	4.93	4.92	4.90	4.88	4.86	4.83	4.80	4.77	4.75	4.72	4.69	4.66									
17	4.85	4.89	4.91	4.91	4.90	4.89	4.87	4.85	4.83	4.80	4.77	4.74	4.72	4.69	4.66	4.63	4.60								
18	4.83	4.87	4.88	4.88	4.88	4.86	4.84	4.82	4.80	4.77	4.74	4.72	4.69	4.66	4.63	4.60	4.57	4.54							
19	4.81	4.85	4.86	4.86	4.85	4.84	4.82	4.80	4.77	4.74	4.72	4.69	4.66	4.63	4.60	4.57	4.55	4.52	4.49						
20	4.79	4.83	4.84	4.84	4.83	4.81	4.79	4.77	4.74	4.72	4.69	4.66	4.63	4.60	4.58	4.55	4.52	4.50	4.47	4.45					
21	4.78	4.81	4.82	4.81	4.80	4.79	4.77	4.74	4.72	4.69	4.66	4.64	4.61	4.58	4.55	4.53	4.50	4.47	4.45	4.43	4.41				
22	4.76	4.79	4.79	4.79	4.78	4.76	4.74	4.72	4.69	4.67	4.64	4.61	4.58	4.56	4.53	4.50	4.48	4.46	4.43	4.41	4.39	4.37			
23	4.74	4.77	4.77	4.77	4.75	4.74	4.72	4.69	4.67	4.64	4.62	4.59	4.56	4.54	4.51	4.48	4.46	4.43	4.41	4.39	4.37	4.36	4.34		
24	4.72	4.75	4.75	4.74	4.73	4.71	4.69	4.67	4.65	4.62	4.59	4.57	4.54	4.51	4.49	4.46	4.44	4.42	4.40	4.38	4.36	4.34	4.32	4.31	
25	4.70	4.73	4.73	4.72	4.71	4.69	4.67	4.65	4.63	4.60	4.57	4.55	4.52	4.50	4.47	4.45	4.42	4.40	4.38	4.36	4.34	4.33	4.31	4.30	4.28

used here were calculated to 14 decimal places by the Bank of England by means of regression analysis: for the purpose of illustrations here and elsewhere in this chapter we have worked to six decimal places, but have sometimes rounded the numbers displayed for the sake of overall presentation.) The current spot rates for six and seven years were 4.802591% and 4.842769% respectively. The forward one-year rate starting in six years' time is the rate that establishes an equilibrium between those two spot rates: in other words, it is the rate at which an investor in a six-year zero bond will be able to invest the proceeds of her maturing investment for one further year, and still be neither better nor worse off than if she had bought a seven-year zero bond at the outset. Using our modified notation $r_{x,y}$ for rates of return, we can express this equilibrium relationship as follows:

$$1 + r_{6,7} = \frac{\left(1 + r_{0,7}\right)^7}{\left(1 + r_{0,6}\right)^6}$$

Substituting actual values for $r_{0,6}$ and for $r_{0,7}$:

$$1 + r_{6,7} = \frac{\left(1 + 0.04842769\right)^7}{\left(1 + 0.04802591\right)^6}$$

$$r_{6,7} = \frac{1.392417}{1.325050} - 1$$

$$r_{6,7} = 1.050842 - 1 = 0.0508042 = \mathbf{5.08\%}$$

We can now plot together the spot (zero-coupon) curve and the curve of forward one-year rates, and we do this in Figure 4.3.

Now at last we are able to make sense of the overall shape of the yield curve. We can divide the series into three phases:

1. We can see quite clearly that short-term (one-year) rates are expected to rise quite sharply over the next six years. This has the effect of pulling upwards the spot rates for those periods, each of which is 'blended' from the underlying series of forward one-year rates. But as long as the forward rate is rising, the current spot rate will still lag behind it.

2. In the second period, from year 7 to year 12, the forward rates decline, but as these rates are still higher than the 'blended' spot rate they continue to have a *positive* marginal impact on the spot rate, which continues to rise, albeit increasingly gently.

3. The beginning of the third period is clearly marked by the crossover point around year 12. At this point, future expected rates are now below the blended spot rates, so they begin to have a *negative* impact on those rates, which accordingly begin to decline. But as all the current spot rates for periods longer than 13 years incorporate the (higher) forward rates for all earlier years, the 'blend' is now *higher* than the forward rate for each successive year.

Using forward rates to predict future spot rates

So much for the theory, but how useful in practice are these forward rates in estimating the rates that will actually prevail in one, six or 26 years' time? This depends on two

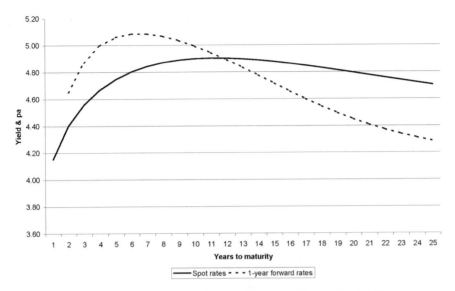

Figure 4.3 Spot and one-year forward gilt yields as at 5 December 2003

factors: the efficiency of the market for bonds and the element of bias that might be included in implied forward rates as estimators of future spot rates.

If the market is active, with many investors and low transaction costs, and if expectations about future interest rates are widely disseminated, these expectations will be incorporated into bond prices and forward rates. In such an efficient market, forward rates will predict, as accurately as is possible at the time, future spot rates. Transaction costs on UK government bonds are very low, with no stamp duties and – at least for institutional investors – no brokers' commissions, and turnover is very high. Also, because interest rates form such a major element of government policy, any expectations or comments concerning future interest rates are widely publicised. We would therefore expect forward rates to be good predictors of future spot rates.

We have already begun to explore the implications of securities market efficiency in Chapter 1. We simply need to point out here that an efficient bond market leads to the conclusion that forward rates are the best available estimates of future spot rates. Although future spot rates will doubtless turn out not to be exactly as predicted by forward rates, it will not pay most investors to spend time and money on constructing their own market forecasts. Since all that is publicly known about future interest rates is already incorporated into forward rates, it is unlikely that an investor's own views will add anything to the accuracy of the forward rates' forecasts. Despite this, much trading in bonds is based on the investors' own views of future interest rate movements which are different from those reflected in forward rates and bond prices.

The second question to be taken into account when we use forward rates as estimates of future spot rates is whether they include any systematic bias in their estimates. A systematic bias is caused by the presence of a factor that will make the estimate generally more likely either to be higher or lower than the actual value.

The various hypotheses about the accuracy of forward rates are based on different views about the presence or absence of such bias and the cause of such bias if it is present. The four most widely held hypotheses are outlined in Example 4.3. It is important to note that these hypotheses are not necessarily mutually exclusive. The simplest and perhaps the most intuitively appealing hypothesis in Example 4.3 is the expectations hypothesis, and perhaps for this reason it has tended to be the focus of much of the voluminous literature on interest rate theory. While it has been comprehensively shown that the expectations hypothesis cannot fully account for the term structure of interest rates, few would suggest that expectations do not play a part, or indeed a very significant part, in the formation of interest rates.

The *expectations hypothesis* states that forward interest rates are unbiased estimates of future interest rates. So, for example, the rate of 5.08%, calculated in the previous

Example 4.3 Interest rate hypotheses

Hypothesis	Argument	Effect
1. Expectations	Every forward rate is the best market estimate of the relevant future spot rate.	Forward rates can be used as estimates of expected spot rates.
2. Liquidity premium	Lenders prefer to lend short. Borrowers prefer to borrow long. So investors require a liquidity premium to compensate for the interest rate risk of holding longer-term securities than they wish to hold. The premium increases with maturity of the investment.	Forward rates are over-estimates of future spot rates since they include a premium for agreeing to lend long.
3. Inflation premium	Risk is mainly inflation risk, that is, uncertainty about future actual inflation since only expected inflation is incorporated into interest rates. The shorter the term of lending, the better the lender can estimate inflation. So lenders prefer to lend for short periods, and forward rates include an inflation premium to compensate lenders for uncertainty about future inflation.	Forward rates are overestimates of future spot rates since they include a premium for inflation risk.
4. Market segmentation	In order to reduce interest rate risk, both borrowers and lenders match their assets and liabilities. For example, banks will prefer short-term gilts and pension funds long-term gilts.	The premium or discount in the forward rate for a particular maturity will depend on the demand and supply for that maturity.

Box 4.2 Biased and unbiased estimators

In many situations (both in finance and in everyday life) the best available estimate of a particular variable in a population is the sample mean, and this is often also an unbiased estimate. The mean heights of repeated samples of 100 males drawn at random from the adult population would vary a little, but the mean of those sample means would be very close to the actual mean height of the population as a whole. A good example of a best available estimate that is neither the sample mean nor unbiased is if we were to estimate the number of students enrolled on a course from the numbers attending weekly lectures. The best available estimate is not the mean of the weekly attendance samples but the highest such attendance, and as it cannot exceed the true value but may well fall short of it, this estimate is more likely to be too low than too high, so it is systematically biased. 'Bias' in a statistical context is an objective statistical concept and has nothing to do with the subjectivity of, for example, a 'biased' political opinion.

---

example, was the market's best estimate on 5 December 2003 of the actual one-year spot rate for the year commencing on 5 December 2009, without any inbuilt biases.

A major implication of the expectations hypothesis is that investors need not worry about the maturity of the bonds they buy. For example, if Ms Vortex wishes to make a seven-year investment in bonds, she can buy a seven-year zero, or alternatively she can buy a six-year zero, followed by a further one-year zero. The expected seven-year holding period return from both these investment strategies is the same. If Ms Vortex buys a seven-year zero, she will get an annual return of about 4.84% for the seven years. If she buys a six-year zero, she will get a return of just 4.80% for six years, but by reinvesting the proceeds for the seventh year at the significantly higher expected rate of 5.08% she will increase her overall return for the seven years to 4.84%.

We can use the same mathematics to demonstrate that Ms Vortex could also achieve the same result by buying an eight-year zero and selling it after seven years. In the previously worked example, we used the known spot rates for six and seven years to calculate the implied future one-year spot rate at year 6. In order to solve this new problem, we first use the same method to calculate the implied future spot rate at year 7 as follows:

$$1 + r_{7,8} = \frac{\left(1 + r_{0,8}\right)^8}{\left(1 + r_{0,7}\right)^7}$$

Substituting actual values for $r_{0,7}$ and $r_{0,8}$:

$$1 + r_{7,8} = \frac{\left(1 + 0.04870705\right)^8}{\left(1 + 0.04842769\right)^7}$$

$$r_{7,8} = \frac{1.462964}{1.392417} - 1$$

$$r_{7,8} = 1.050665 - 1 = 0.050665 = \textbf{5.07\%}$$

The second step is to find out how much an investment of £1 in an eight-year zero at a yield of 4.8707% would be worth if it were sold at the end of year 7 at a price that would yield the new owner a return of 5.0665% for the remaining year of its life. For this we go right back to our basic present value equation 3.4:

$$P_o = \frac{C_n}{(1+r)^n}$$

and calculate its future value after seven years, F_7, as

$$F_7 = \frac{£1 \times (1+0.048707)^8}{(1+0.050665)} = £1.392417$$

which we recognise as the denominator in our first step above.

All that remains to do is to calculate what annual rate of return $r_{0,7}$ would have been achieved if an investment of £1.00 today were to yield a single payment of £1.392417 in seven years' time. Again, using basic present value arithmetic we can say

$$(1 + r_{0,7})^7 = 1.392417$$

$$(1 + r_{0,7}) = \sqrt[7]{1.392417} = 1.048428$$

$$r_{0,7} \qquad = 0.048428 = \textbf{4.84\%}$$

This is exactly the same as the current spot rate for seven years.

What this calculation shows is that although the eight-year zero is set to produce a return of 4.87% p.a. over its full life, its price at the end of just seven years will be slightly depressed by the fact that at that point it will reflect the significantly higher one-year return of 5.07% p.a., thus reducing the overall yield for seven years to the current seven-year spot rate of 4.84% p.a. So the expected return from all three strategies is exactly the same – if current spot rates correctly reflect future spot rates.

The problem with the expectations hypothesis is that the risk inherent in each of the maturity strategies is not the same, even if the expected return were the same. If Ms Vortex wishes to invest for a period of seven years, she will ensure a certain nominal return by buying a seven-year zero. But if instead she buys a six-year zero and then has to reinvest at the end of six years, she runs the risk that the one-year rate at year 6 will not be the 5.08% currently predicted and thus her return is not certain.

The *liquidity premium hypothesis* is based on the view that investors usually want to lend for a short time and borrowers (in the case of gilts, this is the UK government) wish to borrow long. So, for example, Ms Vortex would have to be paid a premium to invest in, say, a ten-year bond when she only wishes to invest for two years.

The *inflation premium hypothesis* is based on the idea that the risk of greatest concern to the investor is not interest rate risk but inflation risk. If inflation can only be forecast accurately a short time ahead, investors will prefer to lend short term, as under the liquidity preference argument. So again, forward rates will include a premium to persuade investors to lend long. Finally, the *market segmentation hypothesis* presumes that the demand and supply for each maturity of bond will be different, with the premium being positive or negative according to whether borrowers outnumber lenders or vice versa for that maturity.

In the United Kingdom, as we have seen in Figures 4.1 to 4.3, a typical government bond yield curve is humped. This provides some support for the market segmentation hypothesis. Short-dated bonds are in demand as liquid investments or reserves by financial institutions. Long-dated bonds are in demand for the long-term investment needs of pension funds and of life insurance companies managing pension and life policy business. But there is less demand for the 6–14 year maturity bonds and that can cause the 'hump' in this maturity band. This hump is also frequently visible in other countries' government bond yield curves, notably that of US Treasuries.

OBSERVING THE REACTIONS OF BOND PRICES TO INTEREST RATE CHANGES

Changes in current short-term interest rates, or in market expectations of short-term interest rates in the future (as reflected in forward rates), will change the spot rates used by the market to discount the future cash flows of a bond. This change in the applicable discount rates will in turn affect the bond's present value or price.

We now need to explore exactly how changes in actual and expected interest rates affect the value of bonds with different patterns of cash flow according to their coupons (if any) and remaining periods to maturity.

Plotting changes in spot and forward rates

We shall study the effect of changing interest rates by comparing the prices and yields on benchmark gilts at the close of business on Friday 5 December 2003 (these are already familiar to us from Tables 3.6, 4.2 and 4.5, and from Figure 4.3) with the closing prices and yields for a date exactly five weeks later, Friday 9 January 2004. The two sets of prices and yields for conventional benchmark issues are displayed side-by-side in the two sets of three columns in the left left-hand section of Table 4.7. Comparison of these figures shows that yields fell and prices rose during this five-week period. The next column headed 'Change in red. yield %pa' shows by how much the redemption yield of each bond had fallen in the period. For most maturities except for the very shortest and those over 20 years, the reduction in annual redemption yield lies in a narrow range between 0.20% and 0.24%. This kind of movement is known as a *parallel shift* in the yield curve.

As we have already seen, the complex and varying cash flow patterns of coupon-paying bonds give only an indirect insight into the structure of actual and expected interest rates for different periods starting today (spot rates) or in the future (forward rates). If we want to appreciate fully what has changed in the interest rate landscape between our two chosen dates, we first need to construct a matrix of spot and forward rates for the later (January 2004) date, for comparison with the matrix we have already constructed in Table 4.5 for the earlier (December 2003) date. The matrix of spot and forward rates for 9 January 2004, constructed by means of regression analysis from conventional and stripped gilt prices, is shown in Table 4.6.[1] The two key sets of rates in this matrix are:

○ the figures in the first column, showing spot rates from 'today' (in this case, 9 January 2004) for periods of whole years ranging from 1 year to 25 years: and

---

1   Close analysis of Tables 4.5, 4.6 and 4.7 will reveal two minor sources of discrepancies:

○ Tables 4.5 and 4.6 display spot and forward rates for periods of the same length (one year, two years etc.) but starting and finishing on different calendar dates, whereas the two redemption yields for each bond are for remaining lives of slightly different length but the same calendar maturity date.

○ There are small differences between the observed spot rates at which strips trade and the implied spot rates underlying the valuation of coupon-paying bonds: these are mainly because of the differing forces of supply and demand in the markets for the two types of bond.

Table 4.6 Spot and implied forward interest rates derived from gilt-edged market prices as at 9 January 2004

Year	0	1	2	3	4	5	6	7	8	9	10	11	12	13	14	15	16	17	18	19	20	21	22	23	24
1	4.04																								
2	4.22	4.40																							
3	4.36	4.52	4.64																						
4	4.46	4.60	4.70	4.76																					
5	4.53	4.65	4.74	4.79	4.81																				
6	4.58	4.69	4.76	4.80	4.82	4.83																			
7	4.62	4.71	4.77	4.81	4.82	4.83	4.83																		
8	4.64	4.73	4.78	4.81	4.82	4.82	4.82	4.82																	
9	4.66	4.74	4.78	4.81	4.82	4.82	4.82	4.81	4.80																
10	4.67	4.74	4.78	4.80	4.81	4.81	4.81	4.80	4.79	4.78															
11	4.68	4.74	4.78	4.80	4.80	4.80	4.80	4.79	4.78	4.77	4.75														
12	4.68	4.74	4.77	4.79	4.79	4.79	4.78	4.77	4.76	4.75	4.74	4.72													
13	4.68	4.74	4.77	4.78	4.78	4.78	4.77	4.76	4.75	4.73	4.72	4.70	4.68												
14	4.68	4.73	4.76	4.77	4.77	4.76	4.75	4.74	4.73	4.71	4.70	4.68	4.66	4.64											
15	4.67	4.72	4.74	4.76	4.75	4.74	4.74	4.72	4.71	4.69	4.68	4.66	4.64	4.62	4.60										
16	4.67	4.71	4.73	4.74	4.74	4.73	4.72	4.70	4.69	4.67	4.66	4.64	4.62	4.60	4.57	4.55									
17	4.66	4.69	4.71	4.73	4.73	4.71	4.70	4.68	4.67	4.65	4.63	4.62	4.59	4.57	4.55	4.53	4.50								
18	4.64	4.68	4.70	4.71	4.71	4.69	4.68	4.66	4.65	4.63	4.61	4.59	4.57	4.55	4.53	4.50	4.48	4.46							
19	4.63	4.67	4.68	4.70	4.69	4.67	4.66	4.64	4.63	4.61	4.59	4.57	4.55	4.53	4.50	4.48	4.46	4.43	4.41						
20	4.62	4.65	4.66	4.67	4.66	4.65	4.64	4.62	4.60	4.59	4.57	4.55	4.53	4.50	4.48	4.46	4.43	4.41	4.39	4.37					
21	4.61	4.63	4.65	4.65	4.64	4.63	4.62	4.60	4.58	4.57	4.55	4.53	4.50	4.48	4.46	4.44	4.41	4.39	4.37	4.35	4.33				
22	4.59	4.62	4.63	4.63	4.62	4.61	4.60	4.58	4.56	4.54	4.52	4.50	4.48	4.46	4.44	4.41	4.39	4.37	4.35	4.33	4.31	4.29			
23	4.58	4.60	4.61	4.61	4.60	4.59	4.58	4.56	4.54	4.52	4.50	4.48	4.46	4.44	4.42	4.40	4.37	4.35	4.33	4.31	4.29	4.27	4.26		
24	4.56	4.58	4.59	4.59	4.58	4.57	4.56	4.54	4.52	4.50	4.48	4.46	4.44	4.42	4.40	4.38	4.35	4.33	4.31	4.29	4.27	4.26	4.24	4.22	
25	4.55	4.57	4.58	4.57	4.56	4.55	4.54	4.52	4.50	4.48	4.46	4.44	4.42	4.40	4.38	4.36	4.34	4.32	4.30	4.28	4.26	4.24	4.22	4.21	4.19

Table 4.7 Conventional gilts and gilt strips: prices, redemption yields and holding period returns, 5 December 2003 and 9 January 2004

		Conventional coupon bonds									Strips							Future implied spot rates
		05 Dec 03			09 Jan 04			Change in red. yield %pa	Capital gain % flat	Holding period return % p.a.*	05 Dec 03		09 Jan 04		Change in red. yield % p.a.	Capital gain % flat	Holding period return % p.a.	Change in red. yield % pa
		Clean price	Yield Int.	Red.	Clean price	Yield Int.	Red.				Price	Red. yield	Price	Red. yield				
Maturity	Coupon																	
Under 5 years																		
07 June 04	5.00%	100.54	4.973	3.893	100.49	4.976	3.750	-0.143	-0.05	4.45	98.09	3.907	98.52	3.737	-0.170	0.44	4.57	
07 Dec 05	8.50%	107.72	7.891	4.419	107.79	7.886	4.190	-0.229	0.06	8.57	91.52	4.486	92.32	4.246	-0.241	0.88	9.13	-0.251
07 Dec 06	7.50%	108.05	6.941	4.594	108.40	6.919	4.380	-0.214	0.32	10.32	87.16	4.639	88.12	4.407	-0.232	1.10	11.50	-0.244
07 Dec 07	7.25%	109.17	6.641	4.707	109.74	6.607	4.500	-0.207	0.52	12.09	82.95	4.731	83.99	4.522	-0.209	1.25	13.06	-0.251
07 Mar 08	5.00%	101.05	4.948	4.722	101.83	4.910	4.510	-0.212	0.77	13.00	81.93	4.749	82.99	4.543	-0.206	1.29	13.49	-0.251
5–10 years																		
07 Mar 09	4.00%	96.36	4.151	4.791	97.45	4.105	4.560	-0.231	1.13	15.95	77.87	4.824	79.20	4.578	-0.246	1.71	17.82	-0.256
07 Dec 09	5.75%	104.86	5.484	4.808	106.03	5.423	4.570	-0.238	1.12	17.12	75.03	4.847	76.49	4.593	-0.255	1.94	20.28	-0.256
25 Nov 10	6.25%	108.19	5.777	4.850	109.55	5.705	4.610	-0.240	1.26	18.89	71.30	4.894	72.84	4.646	-0.248	2.16	22.50	-0.248
12 Jul 11	9.00%	125.92	7.147	4.874	127.37	7.066	4.640	-0.234	1.15	19.16	69.54	4.904	71.09	4.663	-0.241	2.23	23.26	-0.238
07 Mar 12	5.00%	100.74	4.963	4.889	102.31	4.887	4.660	-0.229	1.56	21.22	66.93	4.928	68.56	4.685	-0.243	2.43	25.32	-0.226
27- Sep 13	8.00%	123.97	6.453	4.891	125.78	6.360	4.670	-0.221	1.46	21.68	62.15	4.940	63.75	4.720	-0.220	2.57	26.85	-0.198
10–20 years																		
07 Sep 14	5.00%	100.64	4.968	4.922	102.53	4.877	4.700	-0.222	1.88	24.55	59.12	4.952	60.78	4.729	-0.222	2.82	29.40	-0.174
07 Dec 15	8.00%	127.62	6.269	4.924	129.82	6.162	4.700	-0.224	1.72	24.25	55.50	4.969	57.29	4.736	-0.233	3.22	33.61	-0.152
25 Aug 17	8.75%	137.65	6.357	4.937	140.17	6.242	4.720	-0.217	1.83	25.45	51.05	4.951	52.73	4.743	-0.208	3.30	34.43	-0.119
07 June 21	8.00%	136.15	5.876	4.900	138.94	5.758	4.700	-0.200	2.05	27.25	42.77	4.913	44.40	4.721	-0.192	3.80	39.62	-0.095
Over 20 years																		
07 Mar 25	5.00%	101.98	4.903	4.849	104.50	4.785	4.660	-0.189	2.47	30.67	36.23	4.836	37.79	4.654	-0.182	4.31	44.90	-0.079
07 Dec 28	6.00%	117.13	5.123	4.814	120.07	4.997	4.630	-0.184	2.51	31.30	30.80	4.768	32.24	4.598	-0.170	4.69	48.86	
07 June 32	4.25%	91.81	4.629	4.779	94.40	4.502	4.610	-0.169	2.82	34.05	26.48	4.718	27.81	4.558	-0.160	5.02	52.37	
07 Mar 36	4.25%	91.82	4.629	4.748	94.54	4.495	4.580	-0.168	2.96	35.52	22.61	4.665	23.74	4.523	-0.142	5.03	52.44	

* Note that the annualised holding period return is very slightly overstated because the effect of having to fund initial accrued interest purchased has not been allowed for.

○ the final figure in each line, showing the forward one-year rate at each of the annual horizons shown at the head of the corresponding column.

In the final column of Table 4.7 ('Change in forward one-year rate % p.a.') we have calculated, from a comparison of the forward one-year rates shown at the end of each line in Tables 4.5 and 4.6, the corresponding changes in such rates for the maturity dates of each of the benchmark bonds. The figures in this final column of Table 4.7 show a small but significant difference from the changes in the overall redemption yields of the bonds. This is because of the way in which (a) the forward rates combine with each other to generate the spot rates for different maturities, and (b) these resulting spot rates then feed into the observed redemption yields of bonds with differing coupons and maturities.

We should note two particular features of the comparison in this case:

○ Forward one-year rates at all time horizons up to about seven years (to the end of 2010) reveal an almost uniform drop of 0.25% p.a., whereas the drop in redemption yields is initially lower than this. This reflects the fact that the very short-term spot rate (under one year) has fallen by much less than 0.25%: this exercises a proportionately larger effect on the shorter than on the longer-term spot rates and hence on the redemption yield of short-term gilts.
○ Beyond the seven-year horizon, the drop in forward rates tapers off quite steeply, but as the number of years increases, the marginal impact of any change in the final year"s forward rate on the spot rate decreases: so the redemption yields (based as they are on spot rates) decline more slowly than the forward rates.

In the next section we will shall study how these changes have affected the values of strips, which are synthetically created zero-coupon bonds from coupon-bearing bonds. But first it might be useful to sum up our findings by showing in graphic form the subtly different shifts in spot and forward rates between our two dates. These are shown in Figures 4.4(a) and (b).

How changes in rates affect zeros and strips

The next step is to see how these changes in yields have affected the actual prices of strips, as shown in the column headed 'Capital gain % flat', which shows by what percentage the present value of each strip has changed in response to the change in the relevant measure of yield. Here we shall be recalling, and further developing, some of the general principles we outlined earlier in this chapter (page 104).

Principle 1: As return increases, present value decreases, and vice versa.
As the return has decreased for every maturity, the present value of all strips has increased as expected.

Principle 2: A given change in the rate of return has a smaller impact on nearer than on more remote cash flows.
The capital gain on the strips also increases as maturity lengthens. When the rate of return or yield r is reduced, the value of the denominator $(1 + r)^n$ in the basic cash flow equation also falls, thus increasing the present value of the cash flow or numerator. But

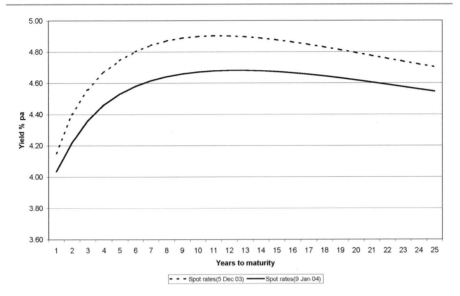

Figure 4.4(a) Spot rates for gilts as at 5 December 2003 and 9 January 2004

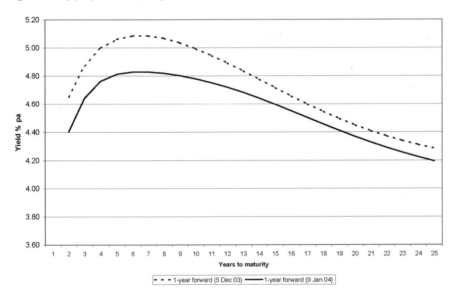

Figure 4.4(b) Forward one-year rates for gilts as at 5 December 2003 and 9 January 2004

the actual proportion by which any given reduction in r reduces the value of the denominator $(1 + r)^n$ depends also on the size of n. This was illustrated very clearly in Table 4.1. If the annual rate of return increases from 4% to 5%, the present value of a cash flow due in two years falls by 1.90% whereas that of a cash flow due in five years falls by 4.67%. This is because the discount factor for the two-year cash flow has changed from

$$\frac{1}{\left(1+0.04\right)^2} = 0.924556$$

to

$$\frac{1}{\left(1+0.05\right)^2} = 0.907029$$

or by just 1.90%, whereas the discount factor for the five-year cash flow has changed from

$$\frac{1}{\left(1+0.04\right)^5} = 0.821927$$

to

$$\frac{1}{\left(1+0.05\right)^5} = 0.783526$$

or by the much larger margin of 4.67%.

A particularly revealing example of how Principles 1 and 2 may work against each other can be seen from a comparison of the capital gain on the two longest-dated strips in Table 4.7. Despite the significant difference in their maturities – 28.5 years and 32.2 years – the increase in value of the longer-dated strip is only very marginally greater than that of the shorter-dated strip. This is because its redemption yield has fallen by only 0.142%, whereas the redemption yield of the shorter-dated issue has fallen by 0.160%.

Principle 3: As return increases, present value falls at a reducing rate.
As Table 4.7 plots just a single change in rates, it is not really possible to see this principle at work here, but we shall return to it later in this section.

Principle 4: As a bond approaches its final maturity, if the applicable rate of return remains static, the clean price of the bond approaches 100.00.
The premium that investors are prepared to pay for a bond whose coupon is greater than the required rate of return becomes smaller as the bond approaches maturity, as does the discount that investors demand for acquiring a bond whose coupon is smaller than the required rate of return.

Through careful analysis of the constituent cash flows of a fictitious bond we were able to show this principle at work in Table 4.1. But the operation of this principle is much more clearly visible in the 'Price' columns for strips in Table 4.7. Every strip is an identical zero-coupon bond, so the fact that their prices increase towards 100.00 with shortening maturity perfectly illustrates Principle 4.

How changes in rates affect coupon bonds

The next step is to analyse the effect on coupon bonds of the same changes in actual interest rates and in underlying interest rate expectations. As coupon bonds represent collections or blends of zero-coupon bonds, we would expect to observe both similarities and differences when we compare the behaviour of coupon bonds with that of zero-coupon bonds under the same circumstances of interest rate changes.

Before studying the main differences, we should dispose of one minor but nonetheless interesting anomaly, which is in fact explained by Principle 4. The present value or market price of the shortest-dated gilt in Table 4.7, the 5% due 7 June 2004, has apparently defied Principle 1 by losing value when returns fell. When we evaluate the capital gains observed between the two dates, we have to remember that under Principle 4, if yields had remained constant, all bonds priced above par would have lost a little in value (remember that the capital loss represents the difference between the interest yield and the redemption yield), so the true capital gain achieved by the fall in redemption yield is actually higher than the 'raw' gain computed simply from a comparison between the starting and finishing prices. Conversely, all bonds priced below par would have gained a little in value, so part of the 'raw' gain registered between the two dates is in fact a natural appreciation of the bond which would have occurred anyway. This is the explanation for the fact that one bond – the 5% due 7 June 2004 – in fact lost capital value despite the fall in yields. As it is very close to its redemption date, if yields remained unchanged its market value would be approaching 100.00 at an almost linear rate with the passage of time. This means that if yields had not fallen between 5 December 2003 and 9 January 2004, its value would have fallen to about 100.43, so that the actual value of 100.49 on 9 January 2004 represents a *relative* gain compared with the value registered on 5 December 2003.

We now compare the capital gain registered by each of the coupon bonds with that achieved by the strip of corresponding maturity. Two facts stand out:

○ In every case, the coupon bond registers a lower capital gain than the strip with the same maturity, but the relationship between the two is neither fixed nor linear.

○ Whereas in the case of the strips, the capital gain increases more or less smoothly with maturity (an apparent exception – the two longest-dated strips – was easily explained by reference to the different changes in return), in the case of the coupon bonds the rate of increase is very uneven. In some cases, and quite contrary to what Principle 2 would lead us to expect, an increase in maturity is actually accompanied by a decrease in capital gain. The series of eight issues starting with the 4% due 7 March 2009 underwent almost identical changes in yield, yet they can be divided neatly into four pairs of adjacent issues, in each of which the issue with the shorter maturity registered – apparently contrary to our expectation – a *bigger* capital gain than its longer-dated neighbour.

These two aspects of the effect of interest rate changes on coupon bonds are closely linked with each other. A coupon bond is equivalent to a portfolio of zero-coupon bonds with maturities matching each of its coupon dates and its final repayment date, so we should expect it to behave not like a single zero-coupon bond with the same final maturity but rather in some way that reflects the weighted average of the constituent zero-coupon bonds. In the next section we develop this idea into a single comprehensive measure which enables us to predict the sensitivity of any bond issue to a given change in interest rates, and we shall find that the same measure gives us a powerful tool for choosing between different bond issues in the context of our chosen fixed income investment strategy.

DURATION: A COMPREHENSIVE MEASURE OF SENSITIVITY TO INTEREST RATES

Defining duration

We shall use the simplified data presented originally in Table 4.1 as a basis for exploring further this idea that a coupon bond should behave similarly to a portfolio of zero-coupon bonds. The 5% bond with a remaining life of five years is equivalent to a portfolio of five zero-coupon bonds: four of them have a nominal (i.e. repayment) value of £5 each when they mature at one-year intervals starting in one year's time, while the fifth has a nominal value of £105 and matures in five years' time. At an annual redemption yield of 5%, their present values are £4.76, £4.54, £4.32, £4.11 and £82.27 – total £100.00. When the yield increases to 6%, each of them loses value in proportions that increase with their maturity; the one-year zero loses just 0.94% of its value, whereas the final five-year zero loses 4.63%. The overall loss in value of 4.21% represents a blended or weighted average – weighted, that is, according to the respective present values of the constituent zero-coupon bonds. See Table 4.1 on page 105.

We can define the *weighted average life* as the result of dividing the sum of the time-weighted present values by the sum of the present values themselves, i.e. £454.60 divided by £100.00, or 4.5460 for the five-year 5% coupon bond. We calculate this in Table 4.8.

Table 4.8 Weighted average life of cash flows of 5% bond at 5% redemption yield, with five years remaining life

Years to maturity	Nominal cash flow	PV of cash flow	Time-weighted PV
1	5.00	4.76	4.76
2	5.00	4.54	9.07
3	5.00	4.32	12.96
4	5.00	4.11	16.45
5	105.00	82.27	411.35
Totals		100.00	454.60
Weighted average life (years)			**4.5460**

By way of comparison, what would happen to the present value of a zero-coupon bond with a remaining life of 4.5460 years, if the redemption yield rose from 5% to 6%? At 5% annual redemption yield, its value P_5 per £100.00 nominal would be

$$P_5 = \frac{100.00}{(1 + 0.05)^{4.5460}} = 80.107549$$

At 6% annual redemption yield its value P_6 would be

$$P_6 = \frac{100.00}{(1 + 0.06)^{4.5460}} = 76.725817$$

The percentage change in value, which we shall denote with dP, is therefore

$$dP = \frac{76.725817 - 80.107549}{80.107549} \times 100.00$$

$$= \frac{-3.378550}{80.107549} \times 100.00$$

$dP = -4.21\%$

which is the same as the change in value for the five-year 5% coupon bond with a weighted average life of 4.5460 years.

The technical name for the weighted average life of a bond's cash flows calculated in this way is **duration**, or **Macaulay's duration** (to distinguish it from the associated concept of **modified duration** introduced later in this chapter), as one way of looking at it is the average length of time for which the original investment is outstanding. The calculation of duration D as presented in Table 4.8 can also be expressed in the form of the equation:

$$D = \frac{\left(1 \times \dfrac{C_1}{(1+r)} + 2 \times \dfrac{C_2}{(1+r)^2} + 3 \times \dfrac{C_3}{(1+r)^3} + \ldots + n \times \dfrac{C_n}{(1+r)^n} \right)}{\dfrac{C_1}{(1+r)} + \dfrac{C_2}{(1+r)^2} + \dfrac{C_3}{(1+r)^3} + \ldots + \dfrac{C_n}{(1+r)^n}}$$

where r is the redemption yield and the terms C_i are the periodic cash flows. As the denominator is identical with the present value or price P, further simplification is possible until we have the general equation

$$D = \frac{1}{P} \sum_{i=1}^{i=n} i \times \frac{C_i}{(1+r)^i} \tag{4.3}$$

No matter what the coupon or the maturity, every bond's duration can be determined using the formula given in equation 4.3. The greater the duration of a bond, the more sensitive it is to changes in interest rates.

We can now use duration to explain the apparent anomaly we noted in the price behaviour of the medium-dated gilts in Table 4.7, and to make a number of useful general statements about the price sensitivity of bonds. Closer inspection of Table 4.7 shows that there is a common feature in each of the pairs of issues where the shorter-dated bond apparently contradicted our Principle 2 by registering a larger capital gain for a given fall in yield than its longer-dated neighbour. In every case, the shorter-dated issue has a significantly lower coupon than the longer-dated issue, and therefore a longer duration. So we can say:

○ Lower coupon bonds have longer durations than higher coupon bonds with the same final maturity, because a higher proportion of the present value of the overall investment is represented by the final coupon and capital repayment, and a correspondingly lower proportion is represented by the intervening coupon payments. For any particular maturity, *the lower the coupon of the bond, the longer its duration.*

○ *The longer a bond's duration, the more volatile its price*, because we know from Principle 2 and from our study of the actual price behaviour of strips that the sensitivity of a zero-coupon bond to interest rate changes increases with its maturity.

○ As no bond can have a duration longer than its final maturity, and only a zero-coupon bond has a duration that is as long as its maturity, *a zero-coupon bond is more sensitive to interest rate changes than any other bond with the same maturity.*

Finally we should note that although we need only three values to calculate a bond's duration – its coupon, its maturity date and its redemption yield – only the first two of these are fixed features of the bond itself. The third value, the redemption yield, is a function of current market conditions; and *as it changes, so does the bond's duration.* This important fact follows directly from Principle 2:

> *Principle 2: A given change in the rate of return has a smaller impact on nearer than on more remote cash flows.*

As interest rates go up, the more remote cash flows lose present value more quickly than the nearer ones, so that they represent a diminishing proportion of the bond's overall present value. They therefore carry a correspondingly diminishing weight in the calculation of the bond's duration, so duration falls as interest rates rise. This gives us a sound theoretical basis for our empirical observation of Principle 3:

> *Principle 3: As return increases, the present value falls at a reducing rate.*

So as return increases, a bond's duration decreases. Duration corresponds to the maturity of a zero-coupon bond with the same sensitivity to interest rate change, so if a bond's duration is falling, this means that its own sensitivity to interest rate change is also falling. This is exactly the observation from Table 4.1 that led us to formulate Principle 3.

Applications of duration

Of what use is duration to the bond investor? There are two main uses. First, using duration, the investor can quantify the interest rate risk of any bond portfolio in a single number and is therefore able to work out how to hedge that amount of interest rate risk, either through bond futures (discussed in detail in Chapter 8) or by matching the durations of the assets and liabilities of the fund. Second, the investor can use duration, or a simple variant of it known as modified duration, to work out approximately how much a particular bond price will move for a given change in interest rates.

Hedging

One of the advantages of duration as a risk measure is that the duration of a portfolio of bonds is simply the weighted average of the durations of the individual bonds. For example, suppose that Ms Vortex has two bonds in her portfolio priced at £96 and £120 respectively. She has £1000 nominal of each bond, and their durations are 3 and 10 respectively. The market values of the two bonds are therefore $0.96 \times £1000 = £960$ and $1.20 \times £1000 = £1200$. The duration of the portfolio D is the weighted average of the individual durations as follows:

$$D = \frac{3 \times 960 + 10 \times 1200}{960 + 1200} = 6.9$$

So the duration of the portfolio is 6.9 years.

As we shall see in Chapter 8 on financial futures, we can use this number to decide how many futures contracts to sell in order to neutralise any exposure to interest rate risk. If the duration of the futures contracts sold is also 6.9, then if interest rates go up, any loss on the portfolio would be exactly matched by the gain on the repurchase of the futures contracts sold. The bonds in the portfolio would go down in price if interest rates fell, whereas a profit would be made on the bond futures position taken out since the futures contracts could be bought back for less than the price at which they were sold.

Alternatively, pension funds and life insurance companies can insure themselves against interest rate risk on their future liabilities by buying a portfolio of bonds with the same duration or average life as their portfolio of liabilities. For example, suppose that an insurance company works out the duration of its liabilities to be ten years. It could make sure that these liabilities could be met (if they are expressed in nominal terms) by buying a portfolio of bonds with a duration of ten years: a single zero-coupon bond with a maturity of ten years would do the trick. However, a portfolio of coupon-bearing bonds such as bonds with longer maturities than ten years but with an average duration of ten years would also fit the bill. Why would this be so?

One can think of the interest rate risk of the coupon-bearing bonds in terms of a see-saw. If interest rates were to fall over the ten-year period, the reinvestment rates achieved on the coupons would be less than 10% and would drag down the overall return. However, because the bonds would have maturities in excess of ten years, when they came to be sold at the end of the ten-year period, they would have experienced a price rise because required yields had fallen. If the average duration of the assets is fixed to be equal to the average duration of the liabilities, the reinvestment loss on the portfolio of coupon bonds will be exactly offset by the price gain made on their disposal. Similarly, if interest rates were to rise during the ten-year period, the reinvestment gain would be exactly offset by a capital loss on disposal.

Even if liability matching is not an issue, the duration of a portfolio can be used as a means of guaranteeing returns to investors. We have seen that, if a ten-year time horizon for the investor were appropriate, buying ten-year bonds would not guarantee the investor the redemption yield on the portfolio because the reinvestment risk would not be offset by any price gain or loss on disposal: ten-year maturity bonds would always be worth exactly £100 on maturity. It is the case, however, that if a portfolio of bonds with a ten-year duration were acquired, the yield to maturity on the portfolio could be locked in. The simplest possible portfolio with a duration of 10 is a ten-year zero-coupon bond; clearly, there is no reinvestment risk in this case and the redemption yield is locked in. Similarly, with coupon bonds, if the duration of the portfolio is ten years, the redemption yield can also be guaranteed. This has enabled insurance companies to offer investment products where a return is guaranteed over a number of years, protecting investors from downside risk.

Thus, the duration of a portfolio of bonds is more important than their average maturity when it comes to considering their exposure to the interest rate risk first mentioned in Chapter 2.

Estimating price changes

Duration can also be used to estimate the change in price of a particular bond, and this is useful for both hedging and taking risk.

Duration, as well as being thought of as the average life of a bond, can also be defined as its elasticity with respect to a percentage change in interest rates. Formally, it is

$$D \quad = - \frac{\% \text{ change in price}}{\% \text{ change in } (1+r)} \tag{4.4}$$

D is obtained by differentiating the price of a bond with respect to $(1 + r)$ in equation 3.1, which sets the price of a bond P equal to the sum of the present values of the cash flows discounted by $(1 + r)^n$. Note that there is a minus sign because of Principle 1: the price moves in the opposite direction from the redemption yield.

Rearranging equation 4.4 we can write

% change in price $= -D \times$ % change in $(1 + r)$

or

$$\frac{dP}{P} = -D \times \frac{d(1+r)}{(1+r)}$$

where dP and $d(1 + r)$ are the absolute changes in price P and in $(1 + r)$ respectively. Since $d(1 + r)$ is the same as dr, and taking P over to the right-hand side, we have

$$dP = -D \times P \times \frac{dr}{(1+r)} \tag{4.5}$$

We can try out this equation on the bond data in Table 4.1. We calculated that at an annual redemption yield of 5%, a 5% bond with a remaining life of five years has a duration of 4.546 years. Using equation 4.5 to calculate how much the price will change if the redemption yield were to rise to 6%, we have

$$dP = -4.546 \times 100.00 \times \frac{0.01}{(1+0.05)} = \frac{-4.546}{1.05} = -4.33$$

In this case, as the original present value of the bond was 100.00, the expected change in price is equal to the expected percentage change in price, so this also will be -4.33%.

This is not far from the change of -4.21% calculated in Table 4.1, but on the other hand we have preserved full accuracy to 12 decimal places in our calculation, rounding our results for display purposes only, so the price fall of -4.33% is a significant *overestimate* and is too large to be explained by rounding error. Before we try to explain this discrepancy, let us see what happens if we apply equation 4.4 to a 1% p.a. *fall* in redemption yield. Now we have

$$dP = -4.546 \times 100.00 \times \frac{-0.01}{(1+0.05)} = \frac{4.546}{1.05} = 4.33$$

which is exactly the same calculation as for the 1% rise in yield, except with the sign reversed. In this case the equation has led to an equally significant *underestimate* of the true change in price: we know this to be +4.45% from the detailed calculation in Table 4.1, which showed that a 1% fall in yield from 5% to 4% would increase the value from 100.00 to 104.45.

MODIFIED DURATION AND CONVEXITY

In fact, equation 4.4 provides us only with a *close approximation* of the price change. This is where Principle 3 comes into play:

Principle 3: As return increases, the present value falls at a reducing rate.

In other words, the line plotting value against return or yield is downward sloping, but the slope of the line becomes shallower as yield increases. But equation 4.4 describes a *linear* relationship between change in price and change in yield. In fact it describes the straight line representing the tangent to the price/yield curve at point *r*. This is why it produced an identical result (except for the change in sign) for a given upward or downward shift in yield.

As we can see from Figure 4.5, if we use this tangent to predict the change in value for a given change in yield, we will always *overestimate* the *fall* in value for a given increase in yield, and we will always *underestimate* the *rise* in value for any fall in yield. Another way to appreciate this is to recall our finding that duration is a function not only of maturity and coupon but also of yield. As yield increases, duration falls. But equation 5.4 estimates the fall in price for, say, a 1% increase in yield as if the duration remained constant as the yield increases. In fact, duration starts falling as soon as yield starts increasing, so that the average rate at which value reduces across a 1% increase in yield will be lower than the rate at which it is reducing at the start of the process.

Although the tangent materially under- and overestimates the actual change in price for significant changes in yield, it is useful as an approximation for small changes.

The linear nature of equation 4.4 becomes even clearer if we rearrange it in the following way:

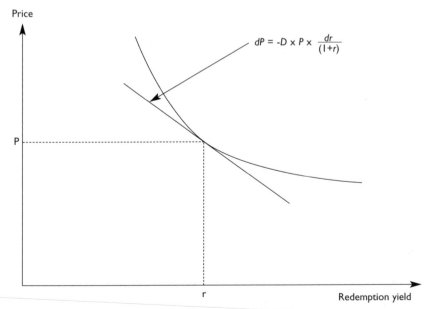

$$dP = -D \times P \times \frac{dr}{(1+r)}$$

Figure 4.5 Relationship between price, yield and duration

$$dP = -\frac{D}{(1+r)} \times P \times dr$$

$$(4.6)$$

We call the expression $\dfrac{D}{(1+r)}$ the **modified duration** or **MD**. Then we can write simply

$$dP = -MD \times P \times dr$$

$$(4.7)$$

If we assume a 1% change in interest rates, dr has the value 1 and can be ignored. So the modified duration in fact represents the linear estimate of the price change for a 1% change in yield. This is also called the **basis point value (BPV)** when applied to an interest rate change of 0.01% or 1 basis point.

The non-linear relationship between price and yield which was captured in Principle 3 and described by the curve in Figure 4.5 is known as a bond's **convexity**, because the curve is convex to the origin: that is, if you were to imagine yourself standing at the origin of the graph the curve would appear to you to be convex. The tendency of equation 4.4 to overestimate potential losses and to underestimate potential gains is captured in a market saying:

'Convexity is the investor's friend.'

This is just another way of saying that the convexity effect helps bond investors. Duration alone underestimates any gains from yields falling, whereas it overestimates losses when yields rise. Of course, if traders are short in bonds, the convexity factor will work against them. Another way of thinking about convexity, looking at Figure 4.5, is that it is the second derivative of the rate of change of P with respect to $(1 + r)$. It is the rate of change of the tangent to the curve. Sophisticated investors and traders look at both the duration and convexity of their positions.

HOW DURATION AND CONVEXITY AID INVESTMENT STRATEGY

Now that we have developed a comprehensive toolkit for comparing bonds with different maturities and coupons and for assessing the sensitivity of different bonds to changes in interest rates, we can see how an investor can use these tools to put a chosen investment strategy into practice. It might be worth repeating the two major types of strategy we identified in the Introduction.

○ **Passive strategy ('follow the market').** Investors accept the market's expectations of future interest rates implicit in bond prices. They then attempt either to minimise interest rate risk by matching the maturities of the bonds with the maturities of their liabilities or to minimise inflation risk by investing short term or buying index-linked bonds.

○ **Active strategy ('beat the market').** Investors compare their own expectations of future interest and inflation rates with those of the market and choose those bonds that will do best if their forecast proves to be more accurate than that of the market. If, for example, they believe that interest rates will decline over the next year by more than is predicted by the market and is currently reflected in bond prices, they will invest in those bonds that are the most sensitive to changes in interest rates, which will therefore experience the biggest price rises if the forecast is correct. They will invest in securities that are more sensitive than the present value of their future liabilities and will therefore increase in value more than the liabilities if the forecast turns out to have been accurate.

To these two major strategies we could add a third, more tactical approach, which is perhaps more appropriate for a trader than for a long-term investor:

○ **Exploiting market anomalies (arbitrage).** Traders take no particular view of the future movement of interest rates but seek instead to identify bonds that are either overpriced or underpriced in relation to other comparable issues. By selling the overpriced issue and buying the underpriced issue, they attempt to make trading profits when (or perhaps if) fundamentals reassert themselves and one or both of the issues falls back into line with the rest of the market.

We shall now look at these strategies in more detail.

Passive strategy ('follow the market')

In the case where investors adopt a passive interest-rate strategy, they are happy to accept the market's implied forecasts of future interest rates. They therefore have no motive to try to make additional gains by deliberately mismatching the maturities of their assets and liabilities. If, for instance, they thought interest rates were going to fall by more than the market anticipated, they would have a reason for investing in bonds with a significantly longer duration than their liabilities, so they could make additional profits if their forecast proved to be better than the market's. But if they are prepared to accept the market's forecast, their only concern is to ensure that their assets and liabilities are matched in terms of their sensitivity to interest rate changes, so that whatever happens, they do not get any unpleasant surprises.

For these passive investors, duration is the key to matching investment assets with payment liabilities. Even in the simplest case – where investors wish to hedge against a single future payment that is fixed in both amount and timing – they should choose a zero-coupon bond with exactly the same maturity and hence duration. This may be difficult if they are very selective about the quality of their investments (for instance, if they are not prepared to accept any credit risk over and above that of government bonds), and if they need to cover a liability running into tens of millions of pounds. As we saw earlier in this chapter, the relatively new market in UK government bond strips may not be able to satisfy such a need.

In the absence of a perfect match in terms of amount and timing of cash flows, investors must use duration to select alternative bond investments that, having a different cash flow profile from that of the investors' liabilities, nevertheless have the same price sensitivity to interest rate changes – in other words, the same duration. Once they have put in place an investment portfolio with exactly the same present value and duration as their liabilities, investors are said to be *immunised* against interest rate risk, but we need to be careful not to read too much into this technical use of the common idea of immunisation. Just as in real life, immunisation against a disease does not last for ever, needs periodic boosters, and in some circumstances may become partially or totally ineffective, so also in its financial sense immunisation needs to be kept under constant review.

We shall illustrate some of these complications by going back to Table 4.1 and assuming that an investor with a liability of £100 million due in 4.546 years' time covers her liability by buying at par (i.e. at a price of exactly £100.00 per £100.00 nominal) an amount of £100 million nominal of the 5% bond having a remaining life of five years and trading at an annual redemption yield of 5%. As long as interest rates do not move markedly from their starting level of 5%, then the present values of the investor's liability and of her bond hedge will move very closely in line with each other. But what will happen if, for example, interest rates go down to 3%? Table 4.1 shows that the present value of the bond hedge will rise by a total of 9.159% to £109.159 million (these figures are shown to three decimal places for greater clarity). But the present value of her liability, which has the characteristics of a zero-coupon bond as it consists of a single future cash flow, will not increase by as much. The present values P_5 and P_3 of a 4.546-year zero-coupon bond, evaluated at annual yields of 5% and 3% respectively, will be the following percentages of nominal value:

$$P_5 = \frac{100.00}{(1.05)^{4.546}} = 80.108$$

and

$$P_3 = \frac{100.00}{(1.03)^{4.546}} = 87.426$$

The increase from 80.108% to 87.426% of nominal value represents an increase of 9.136%, so the present value of the investor's liability would increase to only £109.136 million, which is some £23,000 less than the value of the asset hedge. Why has this gap opened up between the present values of the asset and the liability? The reason is that while the asset and liability had the same duration at the starting yield of 5%, the zero-coupon bond (or any equivalent single-cash flow instrument) has a constant duration equal to its maturity, whereas the duration of a coupon-paying bond or equivalent series of periodic cash flows changes as the yield changes. Specifically, the duration of a coupon-paying bond increases as yields fall (the disproportionate increase in present value of the more remote cash flows increases the weighted average life of all the cash flows). So by the time that yields have fallen from 5% to 3%, the duration of the coupon-paying bond hedge has increased and its rate of appreciation for any given fall in yield has also increased. Conversely, if yields increase, the duration of the coupon-paying bond will shorten and it will lose value at a slower rate than the zero-coupon bond or single-cash flow liability. This effect is due to convexity.

While a potential discrepancy of £23,000 in the hedging of a £100 million position is unlikely to cause a serious problem, a more intractable difficulty arises when we consider what happens when either the liability or the asset hedge experiences a cash flow, as will happen in the above case when the first coupon is received on the 5% bond held as a hedge against the single-payment liability. If interest rates have not changed at all, the investor will now hold a four-year bond worth £100 million and a cash balance of £5 million, so the value of her asset will have increased by exactly £5 million. The present value of her liability too will have increased by exactly the same amount, as its nominal value will now be discounted at a rate of $1.05^{3.546}$ instead of $1.05^{4.546}$. The durations still match too: the duration of the £100 million bond asset can now be shown to be 3.72 years, but as the duration of the £5 million cash balance is zero, the weighted average duration of her portfolio of assets is still 3.546 years, exactly matching her liability. The problem is this: what should she do with the £5 million cash balance in order to preserve her immunisation?

The only watertight solution to this problem would be to invest the proceeds of the coupon payment in a zero-coupon bond with a maturity of 3.546 years. Any other course of action would expose her to either or both of two risks: the value of the asset hedge could begin to diverge from that of the liability, or the duration of the asset hedge could diverge from that of the liability. In either case, the investor loses her immunisation.

Active strategy ('beat the market')

In this case, investors disagree with the market's interest rate expectations and are prepared to back their own judgment by mismatching their assets and liabilities. Whereas there is theoretically only one way of perfectly achieving a fully matched passive strategy, there are of course a potentially infinite number of ways of implementing a mismatched strategy. Active investors need therefore to specify as closely as possible the parameters of their disagreement with the market. We take a simple example from the spot and implied forward interest rates as at 9 January 2004, as plotted in Table 4.6. The one-year spot rate was 4.04% and the two-year spot rate was 4.22%, reflecting the fact that (according to the expectations hypothesis) the market expects the one-year rate in one year's time to be 4.40%:

$$1 + r_{1,2} = \frac{(1 + 0.422)^2}{(1 + 0404)}$$

$$r_{1,2} = \frac{1.0862}{1.04} - 1$$

$$r_{7,8} = 1.0440 - 1 = 0.0440 = \mathbf{4.40\%}$$

Suppose that Mr Grey believes that the market significantly underestimates the level of the one-year rate in one year's time. He can back this judgment in several ways. For instance, he can sell an existing holding of a two-year zero-coupon bond and switch the proceeds into a bond with just one year to maturity. He will thus incur an opportunity cost equivalent to the two years' return at 4.22% p.a. which he has forgone; but as long as he is correct and can reinvest the proceeds of his shorter-duration bond (when it matures) at a rate higher than the market's expectation of 4.40%, he will beat the market overall.

Simple strategies like this tend to overlook the dynamic and continuous nature of the market; it is quite artificial (and can be quite dangerous) to divide up the future into discrete segments and aim to maximise the return in each segment as if it were a separate theatrical performance. A more sophisticated strategy would be to seek to exploit the shape of the yield curve on a rolling basis. Suppose that Mr Grey considered that the short end of the yield curve shown in Figure 4.3 was likely to stay unchanged for the foreseeable future. He could exploit this by buying a two-year zero-coupon bond (for example, a gilt strip), selling it after just one year and then repeating the exercise for as long as rates remained in his favour, as follows:

Step 1:   Buy £100 nominal of 2-year zero at a yield of 4.22%

$$\text{Cost} \quad = \quad \frac{£100.00}{(1+0.0422)^2} = £92.07$$

Step 2:   Sell after one year at a yield of 4.04%

$$\text{Proceeds} = \frac{£100.00}{(1+0.0404)} = £96.12$$

His annual holding period return would then be

$$\frac{£96.12-£92.07}{£92.07} = 0.0440 = 4.40\%$$

As long as Mr Grey confined himself to the short-term end of the yield curve, the potential for profit or loss from his 'beating the market' strategy would remain relatively modest. At the opposite end of the maturity spectrum, the risks and rewards become very much larger. For instance, we can see from the capital gains on strips shown in Table 4.7 that if, over a comparatively short period of five weeks in 2003–04, Mr Grey had speculated (wrongly) on an increase in interest rates by very marginally mismatching an 11-year liability with a ten-year hedge, he would have lost 0.25% of his capital invested.

Exploiting market anomalies ('arbitrage')

The final case is that of the trader or arbitrageur who may not have a long-term investment strategy but seeks to make gains out of temporary mispricing of securities in the market, regardless of the general level or movement of interest rates.

Suppose Miss Vortex is given the information in Example 4.4 and is told that Bond *A* is cheap and Bond *B* is dear. If she already holds Bond *B*, a simple way to enhance returns on her portfolio would be to sell Bond *B* and to buy Bond *A*.

Let us suppose that Ms Vortex has no particular view on interest rates and wishes to maintain the interest rate risk exposure of her portfolio at current levels. She can do this by doing a *duration-weighted switch*. Suppose that she has £1000 nominal of Bond *B* in her portfolio which she sells.

How much of Bond *A* should she buy? She begins by using equation 4.7 to calculate the value of *dP* for each of the bonds, assuming the same yield shift of, say, 1%.

$$dP_A = -6.80 \times 100 \times 0.01 \tag{4.8}$$

Example 4.4 Bond switch with neutral interest rate risk

Bond	Coupon	Maturity (years)	Price (£)	Yield (%)	Modified duration
A	8%	10	100.00	8	6.80
B	12%	4	106.44	10	3.16

$$dP_B = -3.16 \times 106.44 \times 0.01 \tag{4.9}$$

Since Bond *A* has a higher duration than Bond *B* it is riskier in interest rate risk terms. In order to maintain her exposure to interest rate change at its current level, Ms Vortex will need to hold less of Bond *A* than she did of Bond *B*. To calculate by how much she must scale down her holding in order to maintain her risk exposure, we divide equation 4.8 by equation 4.9:

$$\frac{-3.16 \times 106.44}{-6.80 \times 100.00} = 0.49$$

So Ms Vortex should replace £1000 nominal of Bond *B* with £490 nominal of Bond *A*. If the bonds move back into line and become fairly priced, she should make money by carrying out the switch – regardless of what happens to interest rates.

One question that arises here is what Ms Vortex should do with the surplus cash arising from the fact that she has only partially reinvested the proceeds of selling Bond *B* in Bond *A*. Ignoring accrued income, she has realised £1064.40 from selling £1000 nominal of Bond *B* at £100.00, and has reinvested just £490 in that nominal amount of Bond *A* priced at par. What does she do with the remaining uninvested proceeds of £574.40? Clearly she cannot do anything that would upset or in any way modify her exposure to interest rate risk, so her choices are very limited. The only asset with no interest rate risk at all is an asset with a duration of zero, and the only asset that meets that very strict criterion is cash. But cash has the drawback that it earns very little return, so in practice Ms Vortex would probably compromise and invest the surplus in extremely short-term interest-bearing government debt, i.e. in Treasury bills. Nevertheless, arbitrageurs do generally work on very small margins, as market anomalies tend to be both small and short-lived, so Ms Vortex would need to calculate very carefully to ensure that the loss of carry on her temporary holding of cash or near-cash did not eat too deeply into the prospective profit from her main arbitrage strategy.

OTHER FIXED INTEREST SECURITIES

The discussion of holding period returns of gilts and the importance of the yield curve and the term structure of interest rates applies to all types of fixed interest securities. In this section, we briefly describe the types of fixed interest securities other than government bonds such as gilts, concentrating on the differences rather than the similarities.

'Other' fixed interest securities traded via the stock exchange can be divided into two main groups:

○ 'other' public fixed interest securities, which include local authority (municipal) stocks and sterling bonds, known as *bulldogs*, issued by foreign governments
○ 'private' fixed interest securities, that is, issued by corporations and not governments and which include five sub-categories: eurobonds, debentures and loans, preference shares, and securities with embedded options such as convertibles.

Convertibles entitle the holder to convert from a fixed interest security into a company's equity, and form a neat link between this chapter on fixed-interest securities and the next chapter, Chapter 5, on equities.

In today's markets, ordinary shares (equities) and eurobonds dominate the more old-fashioned forms of company finance such as debentures and preference shares. This was not always the case. In the nineteenth century, companies could only borrow short-term from the banks. Any long-term finance had to come from the stock market, in the form of debentures, unsecured loan stock, preference shares or convertible stock. In recent years, banks have been willing to lend longer-term to companies and the corporate bond market has become dominated by the eurobond market, at least for larger companies.

We shall now look at each type of private fixed-interest security in turn.

Eurobonds

Since private fixed interest securities are issued by companies and financial institutions rather than government bodies, the risk of non-payment of interest attached to these types of securities is greater than for government bonds. Because of this higher additional risk, the returns available on company fixed interest securities are higher than those on government bonds. Each company debt issue is given a credit rating by agencies that specialise in such rankings, the most famous being Standard & Poor's (S&P) and Moody's. The ratings vary slightly but essentially range from AAA (triple A) for the best rating to C or D for the worst. An example of investment grade, high-yield and emerging market bonds issued in a number of currencies, with the spread over the equivalent currency government bond, is given in Table 4.9.

The eurobond market is regulated by neither the FSA nor the Bank of England. It is an international market but issues are listed on the stock exchange in London. Issues can be by UK or non-UK companies, and the bonds are sold to an international clientele. In 2005, 111 eurobonds worth £34.4 billion were issued by UK companies, and a further 110 eurobonds worth £13.5 billion were issued by foreign companies. The advantages of the eurobond market from the issuer's point of view are access to an international investor clientele and a wide variety of types of bond. Bond issuers can also use the swap market, described in Chapter 8, to swap into another type of loan, if desired. In addition, since there is little regulation of this market, the documentation required for an issue is less than for a traditional debenture or loan issue.

Eurobonds are issued in bearer form, with interest paid annually. They were originally bought by individual investors who held them to maturity. (The archetypal eurobond investor was said to be a Belgian dentist seeking to avoid payment of tax!) As the market has grown, so institutional investors have now become the main investors in eurobonds. The smallest denomination is typically 1000 currency units compared with any amount for gilts, and coupons on eurobonds are paid annually rather than semi-annually as for gilts and US Treasury bonds.

The way in which the accrued interest is calculated for eurobonds differs from the accrued interest method for gilts. The eurobond method is known as the '30/360' method, because traders in eurobonds assume there are 30 days in each month and hence 360 days in each year. Also, accrued interest can be more important in cash terms since coupons are only paid annually, on provision of the coupon which has been detached from the bond certificate. For example, if a 10% coupon sterling eurobond pays interest on 2 April

Table 4.9 Bond yields and bond spreads, 4 December 2006

GLOBAL INVESTMENT GRADE

Dec 1	Red date	Coupon	S*	Ratings M*	F*	Bid price	Bid yield	Last chge yield	Mth's chge yield	Spread vs Govts
■ US $										
KFW Int Fin	01/07	4.75	AAA	Aaa	AAA	99.90	5.40	+0.02	+0.11	+0.17
CIT Group	04/07	7.38	A	A2	A	100.19	6.72	–	+0.52	+1.71
GE Capital	06/07	5.00	AAA	Aaa	n/a	99.88	5.23	-0.05	-0.14	+0.18
Depfa Pfandrbnk	10/07	3.38	AAA	n/a	AAA	98.54	5.19	–	-0.09	+0.09
Goldman Sachs	01/08	4.13	AA-	Aa3	AA-	98.92	5.13	-0.01	-0.06	+0.04
Citigroup	02/08	3.50	n/a	Aa1	AA+	98.32	5.01	-0.06	-0.25	-0.05
Canada	11/08	5.25	AAA	Aaa	AAA	101.22	4.59	-0.10	-0.32	+0.05
DaimlerChrysler	09/09	7.20	BBB	Baa1	BBB+	103.99	5.62	–	+0.07	+0.97
Wal Mart	08/09	6.88	AA	Aa2	AA	104.46	5.07	-0.02	-0.06	+0.55
Du Pont	10/09	6.88	A	A2	A	104.87	5.02	-0.05	-0.09	+0.51
Philipps Petr	05/10	8.75	A-	A1	A-	111.47	5.10	+0.02	-0.01	+0.59
Unilever	11/10	7.13	A+	A1	A+	107.46	5.00	-0.06	-0.34	+0.57
Bank America	01/11	7.40	A+	Aa3	A+	110.02	4.69	-0.04	-0.12	+0.24
JP Morgan	02/11	6.75	A	A1	A	105.94	5.14	-0.01	-0.15	+0.69
France Telecom	03/11	7.75	A-	A3	A-	109.95	5.11	-0.02	-0.06	+0.66
Petronas	05/12	7.00	A-	A1	A-	108.57	5.18	-0.07	-0.13	+0.73
Goldman Sachs	11/14	5.50	AA-	Aa3	AA-	100.87	5.36	-0.01	-0.13	+0.90
Italy	09/23	6.88	A+	Aa2	AA-	119.03	5.17	-0.03	-0.30	+0.74
Pacific Bell	03/26	7.13	A	A2	A	111.72	6.08	-0.03	-0.26	+1.54
Deutsche Tel	07/13	5.25	A-	A3	A-	97.91	5.63	–	–	+1.24
DaimlerChrysler	01/31	8.50	BBB	Baa1	BBB+	121.12	6.72	+0.02	-0.02	+2.15
FHLMC	03/31	6.75	AAA	Aaa	AAA	124.97	4.97	–	-0.22	+0.43
GE Capital	03/32	6.75	AAA	Aaa	AAA	117.61	5.46	-0.02	-0.15	+0.89
Gen Motors	11/31	8.00	BB+	Ba1	BB	109.28	7.19	–	-0.26	+2.63
■ Euro										
Dresdner Fin	01/07	4.00	A+	A1	A	99.99	3.95	+0.24	+0.37	+0.59
Eurohypo	02/07	4.00	AAA	Aaa	AAA	100.02	3.75	+0.06	+0.20	+0.28
BNG	05/07	2.88	AAA	Aaa	AAA	99.63	3.66	-0.07	-0.07	+0.12
ING Bank	07/07	5.63	AA	Aa2	AA	101.02	3.74	-0.01	-0.05	+0.24
TPSA Eurofin	12/08	7.75	BBB+	Baa1	BBB+	104.59	5.32	-0.04	-0.05	+0.69
BAT Int Fin	02/09	4.88	BBB+	Baa1	A-	101.92	3.95	-0.07	-0.11	+0.36
VW Int Fin	05/09	4.13	A-	A3	A-	100.66	3.83	-0.06	-0.08	+0.24
SMBC Int Fin	06/09	8.50	A-	A2	BBB+	107.99	5.09	-0.04	-0.13	+0.58
Depfa Pfandrbnk	01/09	3.75	AAA	Aaa	AAA	100.24	3.63	-0.03	-0.08	+0.01
Mannesman Fin	05/09	4.75	A-	A3	A-	101.92	3.91	-0.03	-0.10	+0.32
Deutsche Fin	07/09	4.25	AA-	Aa3	AA-	101.19	3.76	-0.03	+0.03	+0.17
Repsol Int Fin	05/10	6.00	BBB	Baa1	BBB+	105.90	4.10	-0.04	-0.12	+0.51
Elec de France	10/10	5.75	AA-	Aa1	AA	107.04	3.77	-0.03	-0.04	+0.17
HVB	09/11	5.00	AAA	Aa1	AAA	105.13	3.80	-0.03	-0.11	+0.20
■ YEN										
Tokyo Elec	11/06	2.80	MATD	MATD	MATD	100.00	2.80	–	+2.11	–
Nippon Teleg	07/07	2.50	AA-	Aa1	AA-	101.29	0.47	+0.01	+0.10	-0.01
Toyota Motor	06/08	0.75	AAA	Aaa	n/a	100.08	0.70	–	+0.04	+0.08
KFW Int Fin	03/10	1.75	AAA	Aaa	AAA	102.61	0.95	-0.04	+0.04	-0.01
Chubu Elec	07/15	3.40	NR	Aa3	AA-	113.82	1.58	-0.05	-0.11	–
■ £										
DaimlerChrysler	12/06	7.50	BBB	Baa1	BBB+	100.01	3.63	-1.67	-1.99	-1.30
HBOS	04/08	6.38	AA	Aa2	AA+	101.19	5.32	+0.01	-0.05	+0.25
Network Rail	03/09	4.88	AAA	Aaa	AAA	99.37	5.10	-0.05	-0.08	+0.17
Boots	05/09	5.50	BBB	Baa2	BBB	99.85	5.48	-0.07	-0.13	+0.56
France Telecom	03/11	7.50	A-	Baa1	A-	107.88	5.41	-0.04	-0.12	+0.63

US $ denominated bonds NY close; all other London close. *S - Standard & Poor's, M - Moody's, F - Fitch.

Source: Reuters

continued overleaf

Table 4.9 continued

HIGH YIELD & EMERGING MARKET BONDS

Dec 1	Red date	Coupon	S*	Ratings M*	F*	Bid price	Bid yield	Day's chge yield	Mth's chge yield	Spread vs US
■ HIGH YIELD US$										
TNK-BP	11/07	11.00	BB+	Baa2	BB+	104.31	6.08	-0.03	-0.16	+1.65
Gazprombk	10/08	7.25	BB+	A3	n/a	102.58	5.79	-0.08	-0.18	+1.36
Gazprom	03/13	9.63	BBB	n/a	n/a	119.50	5.85	-0.06	-0.25	+1.42
Kazkommertsbk	04/13	8.50	BB+	n/a	BB+	107.46	7.02	-0.06	-0.09	+2.59
■ HIGH YIELD EURO										
Gaz Capital	09/10	7.80	BBB	n/a	BBB-	111.00	4.58	+0.05	+0.04	+0.15
Fiat Fin	05/11	6.75	n/a	Ba3	BB-	107.40	4.86	-0.04	-0.15	+0.43
■ EMERGING US$										
Ukraine	06/13	7.65	BB-	B1	BB-	107.75	6.19	-0.04	-0.14	+1.76
Mexico	03/15	6.63	BBB	Baa1	BBB	107.63	5.46	-0.04	-0.16	+1.03
Brazil	03/15	7.88	BB	Ba2	BB	111.69	6.05	+0.04	-0.13	+1.62
Turkey	03/15	7.25	BB-	Ba3	BB-	103.00	6.77	+0.01	-0.06	+2.34
Peru	05/16	8.38	BB+	Ba3	BB+	116.94	5.99	-0.03	-0.01	+1.56
South Africa	06/17	8.50	BBB+	Baa1	BBB+	121.79	5.72	-0.02	-0.11	+1.29
Philippines	01/19	9.88	BB-	B1	BB	128.06	6.49	+0.07	-0.15	+2.06
Colombia	02/20	11.75	BB	Ba2	BB	142.56	6.81	–	+0.04	+2.38
Venezuela	09/27	9.25	BB-	B2	BB-	124.13	7.02	+0.04	-0.05	+2.59
Russia	03/30	5.00	BBB+	Baa2	BBB+	112.98	5.66	-0.01	-0.08	+1.23
Ecuador	08/30	10.00	CCC+	Caa1	n/a	88.06	11.62	+0.76	+1.68	+7.19
Argentina	12/33	8.28	B+	n/a	n/a	101.70	8.11	-0.15	-0.08	+3.68
■ EMERGING EURO										
Brazil	02/10	11.00	BB	Ba2	n/a	120.38	4.01	-0.03	-0.09	-0.42
Poland	02/11	5.50	BBB+	A2	BBB+	106.36	3.83	-0.04	-0.12	-0.60
Turkey	02/17	5.50	BB-	Ba3	n/a	97.75	5.80	–	-0.07	+1.37
Argentina	11/26	11.75	DEF	DEF	CC	30.00	39.15	-0.20	-0.01	+34.72

US $ denominated bonds NY close; all other London close. *S*- Standard & Poor's, M - Moody's, F - Fitch.

Source : Reuters

Source: *Financial Times*, 4 December 2006.

each year and the settlement date for the purchase of the bond is 16 August, the accrued interest would be calculated as follows:

Number of days accrued

April 2–30	=	28
May	=	30
June	=	30
July	=	30
August	=	16
Total	=	134

Accrued interest

$$\frac{134}{360} \times 10 \quad = £3.72$$

Care must be taken when comparing the redemption yield on a eurobond with the redemption yield on a gilt. Since gilts pay coupons semi-annually, we showed in Chapter 3 how the yield is calculated on semi-annual cash flows and then multiplied by two to give an annual figure. Thus, if both a gilt and a eurobond have 10% redemption yields, the gilt's true yield would be understated relative to that of the eurobond, because no account would have been taken of the compounding potential of the semi-annual coupon. In order to make accurate comparisons, the eurobond yield must be reduced to a semi-annual equivalent or the gilt yield compounded up. In this case, we could compound the true semi-annual yield of 5% on the gilt as follows:

$$(1 + .05)^2 - 1 = 0.1025$$
$$= 10.25\%$$

yielding an extra 25 basis points compared with the eurobond.

Debentures and loans

This consists of debentures and loan stocks. *Debentures* are secured forms of fixed interest debt. Should the borrower default, the debenture holders can appoint a receiver to sell those assets of the company that represent their security and to reimburse them with the proceeds, whether or not the company is still operating. This security is either a *fixed* charge on a particular asset such as property or a *floating* charge. A floating charge gives the debenture holders more powers, and means that investors are secured on all the assets of the company. The managers can buy and sell these assets until the company defaults, at which time the floating charge 'crystallises' and the debenture holders can sell as many assets as they need to get the money they are owed. Debenture holders are usually protected by a trust deed which specifies exactly their rights in the event of default and also places restrictions on the company, for example limits on other debt it can issue.

Unsecured loan stock is less protected against default risk in that it has no security. In the event of default, it is only ranked with all the other unsecured creditors, for example suppliers to the company.

So in addition to inflation and interest rate risk, to which gilts are subject, investors in company debentures and loan stocks are concerned with whether the income of the company will be sufficient to enable it to fund the interest and capital repayments on the securities – that is, with default risk. They are similarly interested in the company's ability to repay its debts in the event of its being wound up before the due repayment date.

Interest paid on both these types of debt capital is deducted from the company's pre-tax profits and so the cost to the company of the interest payments is net of the associated corporation tax liability. From the investor's point of view, the returns and yields on these securities are calculated exactly as for gilts, and income from these investments is taxed at the investor's personal tax rate.

Preference shares

These are not strictly speaking fixed interest securities since preference shares are equity and not debt securities and so pay dividends rather than interest. However, because of the fixed nature of most preference shares' dividends, they are valued in the same way as fixed interest securities and are for that reason included in this chapter rather than Chapter 5 on Equities.

Preference shares form part of the share capital of the company and so holders can be viewed as part-owners of the company. In return for accepting a fixed rather than a variable amount of dividend, preference shareholders rank before ordinary shareholders who are entitled to whatever is left after all creditors, debt holders and preference shareholders have been paid. Preference shareholders suffer less uncertainty of income than ordinary shareholders since they know how much income they expect to get. However, the company does not have to pay the preference dividend as it does with debt interest. It is in the interests of the ordinary shareholder for the company to pay the preference dividend since no ordinary share dividends can be paid until it has done so. With *cumulative preference shares,* all previous years' unpaid preference share dividends have to be made up before any ordinary dividends can be paid. Also, preference shares usually rank before ordinary shares, but after debt capital, on a winding up of the company.

It can be seen that preference shares occupy a middle position between debt capital and ordinary shares. Preference shareholders are not strictly subject to default risk, as are other fixed interest securities, since they are part-owners of the company and not creditors who can put the company into liquidation. However, they do run the risk of not receiving a fixed dividend payment or being fully repaid on winding up. Their risk is greater than the debt holders' default risk but less than the ordinary shareholders' uncertainty of income.

Another difference between preference shares and debt capital is their tax position. Preference and ordinary share dividends are paid out of profits after payment of corporation tax. This is in contrast to interest on debt capital which is paid out of the company's pre-tax profits and hence is allowable against the company's tax bill. This tax disadvantage has contributed to the decline of the preference share as a source of funds for companies. The main reason for the continued presence of preference shares on the stock market is the fact that the majority, although perhaps issued in the 1930s or before, are irredeemable.

Securities with embedded options

There are a variety of securities that have an embedded option: that is, the option – but not the obligation – to switch from one kind of security to another. We shall discuss how to value options such as these in Chapter 9. For the moment, we just describe how they work in more detail, in particular, convertibles, bonds with warrants, and investor put and issuer call options.

Convertibles

Convertible unsecured loan stock and convertible preference shares (convertibles for short) lie somewhere between straight debt and equity in terms of risk for the investor, and it has been this compromise in terms of risk and return that has given them their popularity. Companies with high debt–equity ratios that were consequently unable to issue more debt in the markets were able to issue convertibles. Also, investors, worried about equities after the Crash of 2000 and yet unwilling to give up the profit potential inherent in equities, were happy to invest in convertible debt, which offered the comparatively greater security of fixed interest debt if the ordinary shares did not do well combined with the possibility of switching into shares at a later date if they did do well.

So why buy convertibles? One reason is that convertible preference shares, for example, also offer the holder an income advantage over the purchase of straight equity. Holders of the convertible preference shares will receive a fixed dividend whereas holders of the ordinary shares will receive a variable (lower) dividend. However, for most healthy companies, ordinary share dividends are expected to grow, and at some point in the future the income advantage will switch to the ordinary shareholders, at which point it will be optimal for the convertible holders to convert.

This concept of convertibles as equity plus an income advantage represents the traditional way of viewing convertibles and is still used. A more modern method is to use option valuation techniques which take into account the value inherent in the *option* to convert; the traditional method assumes that investors always do convert.

The modern method views a convertible as a straight bond plus the option to convert into shares at a fixed price. For this reason the coupon on a convertible is lower than that on a straight bond to reflect the value of the embedded option. Unfortunately, the options inherent in convertibles are somewhat more complex than traded options. There are several reasons for this. First, there is usually a variety of possible conversion dates instead of just one on traded equity or equity index options. A second disadvantage when valuing the option element of a convertible is the determination of the exercise price. With a traded option, the price paid when switching or exercising the option is fixed. With a convertible, the exercise price is the value *at conversion* of the fixed income security given up. This value will change depending on the interest rates prevailing at the *estimated* optimal conversion date.

Bonds with warrants

The eurobond market has seen the invention of a very wide range of bonds, from *plain vanilla* to such *exotic* creations as 'heaven and hell' bonds, for example! Banks have been expert in designing bonds in order to tempt investors. Bonds with **warrants** are an example of this, and were devised in the 1980s to raise money for companies, often Japanese, that were not well enough known in the euromarkets to raise money via plain vanilla issues. Warrants are exactly the same in concept as options in that they offer the investor the right to buy shares at some date or dates in the future at a fixed price. The warrants issued with eurobonds were seen as sweeteners which would be of interest to investors wishing to gain a leveraged way into the seemingly ever-rising Japanese stock market. The warrants were detachable from the bonds, allowing investors to choose the level of risk they wished to bear – straight bonds, warrants, or a combination – unlike convertibles, which are an inseparable mixture of debt and options.

One major difference between the options embedded in convertibles and warrants and the traded options which will be discussed in more detail in Chapter 9 is that embedded options usually involve the issuing of new shares by the company when the embedded options are exercised. This causes what is known as dilution of the equity, by creating more shares, but has a positive effect on total earnings by either extinguishing the interest liability on the convertible or receiving exercise payments on the warrants. Thus, the effect on earnings per share when exercise of the embedded options takes place can be positive or negative, depending on the number of shares issued relative to the money taken in. The other major difference between embedded options and traded options is that the embedded options usually have much longer lives than the traded options discussed in Chapter 9.

In the 1980s, Japanese companies were quick to take advantage of this low-cost funding; some companies managed to raise money at an interest cost of less than 1%. However, there was the prospect of substantial dilution when the warrants expired in the early 1990s. This risk evaporated with the crash in Japanese share prices in early 1990, which wiped out the likelihood of investors wishing to exercise the many warrants that they held, and led to a fall in popularity among investors of bonds with such warrants. Nevertheless, bonds with warrants attached have recovered their popularity in other markets.

Investor put and issuer call options

One further example of embedded options is the call and put options written into the terms of corporate bonds. There are two main kinds, investor put and issuer call options.

An *issuer call option*, which may be included in government bonds as well as corporate issues, typically gives the issuer the right to call the bond in early at a fixed price, usually at a premium to nominal value. Whether the bond is called or not will be a function of interest rates. The undated gilts we came across in Chapter 3 have embedded government call options. They are still in existence – have not been called – because the coupon on the bond is lower than interest rates have been since the bonds became callable. If interest rates had been lower than the coupon, the issuer would call the bond and refinance at the new, lower rate. Since the issuer has the option to act in the best interests of the borrowers, lenders will require a yield premium to compensate them for the risk that the bonds will be called when alternative investments are offering a lower return. Notice also that an investor wishing to fix duration is unlikely to choose a callable bond. If the bond is called early the duration will fall to zero.

Investor put options give investors the right to return the investment they hold to the issuer at a fixed price. An example might be a convertible bond, with a call option for investors to convert into equity, also having a put option to convert into a plain vanilla bond. This type of option is of value to investors, and so will reduce the cost of the initial issue. Relatively high-risk issuers may be required to give such a put option to investors to enhance the attractiveness of the bond issue sufficiently to encourage them to reinvest.

SUMMARY

This chapter has discussed how to make investment decisions concerning fixed interest securities, a subject often neglected in investment texts. The chapter has concentrated on government bonds, by far the most important type of fixed interest security traded on the UK stock exchange, since the valuation of other types of fixed interest security is based on the method used for bonds.

The chapter then described how, given the prices of different maturity and coupon bonds, the underlying term structure of interest rates could be derived. It was seen that the spot and forward rates implicit in the term structure could be used to derive market estimates of future interest rates more accurately than was possible with redemption yields. Given this knowledge, investment decisions could then be made according to investor beliefs (relative to market estimates) of future interest rates.

The measures used in Chapter 3 to describe bonds were then examined to see how they could help investors to choose between bonds. One of the main requirements was a tool to be able to quantify the interest rate risk of each bond. This was found to depend on the coupon and on the maturity of the bond, and a single number, known as duration, was derived to measure this interest rate risk accurately. Armed with the duration of each bond, investors can calculate how many bonds or futures contracts to buy or sell in order to hedge their interest rate risk.

Finally, this chapter has looked at other types of fixed interest security, in particular unibonds, debentures and loans, preference shares and securities with embedded options such as convertibles.

REVIEW EXERCISES

For these exercises you will need to use the following information:

Today's date is 6 December 20X1, and today's dealings in the gilt-edged market are for settlement on 7 December 20X1.

Mr Short is the manager of a bond fund which is allowed to invest only in (a) UK government bonds with a remaining life of not more than five years, and (b) bank deposits with a term of not more than six months.

The following are the only outstanding conventional sterling UK government bonds with a remaining life of five years or less:

Issue	Coupon	Clean price	Final maturity
A	5%	100.7371	7 June 20X2
B	8%	103.6482	7 December 20X2
C	6.75%	102.8990	7 June 20X3
D	9.5%	108.5480	7 December 20X3
E	4%	97.1646	7 June 20X4
F	9%	110.1537	7 December 20X4
G	4%	94.5168	7 June 20X5
H	15%	135.1373	7 December 20X5
J	2%	87.5030	7 June 20X6
K	15%	143.2368	7 December 20X6

1. Calculate the zero-coupon (spot) interest rate for each of the ten periods from 7 December 20X1 to the final maturity dates of issues A-K, starting with six months (Issue A) and going up to five years (Issue K).
2. Calculate the implied future six-month spot rates for each of the nine successive six-month periods beginning on 7 June 20X2.
3. Calculate the interest and redemption yields for each of the issues A–K.
4. Plot on a graph the values you have calculated in Exercises 1 and 2, and for each of the two sets of data sketch in the 'line of best fit'. Explain the relationship between the two curves you have sketched.
5. Now add to your graph the points you have calculated for the redemption yields in Exercise 3. How are these values related to the curves you have sketched?
6. On the basis of the pure expectations hypothesis of interest rates, what conclusions can be drawn from your calculations with regard to market expectations of future interest rates?
7. How might you modify your conclusions in Exercise 6 above, in the light of other hypotheses about interest rate determination?
8. Calculate the duration and the modified duration for each of the issues A-K. When you compare the durations with the remaining lives, do you notice any particular anomalies?

9. Assume now that the market experiences a sudden shock, such that the current and all future implied 6-month spot rates increase immediately by (a) exactly 1% p.a. ('Scenario A') or (b) 5% p.a. ('Scenario B'). For each of these scenarios:
    a. Calculate precisely the percentage change in value of each of Issues A–K.
    b. Estimate the percentage change in value using the duration-related approximation.
    c. Comment on the discrepancies between your calculations in (a) and your estimations in (b).

10. Assume that Mr Short had had the skill or the good luck to predict correctly that Scenario B was about to happen. How would he have arranged his portfolio to maximise the benefit of the shift in market rates?

11. Assume that Mr Short had positioned his portfolio for Scenario B but in fact neither Scenario A nor Scenario B materialised: instead, all six-month rates (actual and expected) fell by 1% p.a. What percentage loss would the portfolio suffer as a result of the measures undertaken in Exercise 10?

12. Assume that all rates, actual and implied, remain completely unchanged for six months, i.e. until 7 June 20X2. What would be the annualised holding period return for each of Issues A–K for the six-month period from 7 December 20X1 to 7 June 20X2?

Sample answers to the review exercises can be found on the companion website.

Part III
Equities

5 Equities: analysis and valuation

Learning objectives for this chapter

After studying this chapter you should be able to

○ describe the principal features of equities and related securities
○ describe the market mechanisms for issuing new equities
○ describe and apply the principal models for valuing equities, including dividend yield, price–earnings ratios and free cash flow.

INTRODUCTION

The subject of this chapter is the analysis and valuation of *ordinary shares* (or *equities*). These are by far the most important type of security issued by UK companies. As we saw in Chapter 1, at the end of 2004 there were 1575 outstanding equity issues by UK ~~mpanies~~ on the London Official List (or Main Market) with a total market value of ~~billion~~, or about 100 times the value of the 567 issues of other domestic ~~companies (excluding international securities such as eurobonds).

~~alised economy emerged in the late nineteenth and early twen-
~~gan to raise much-needed capital by issuing securities
interest securities, including both debt and *preference*
~~on form of security issued. Then, as the need for capital
~~npany owners became unable to raise additional debt on
~~rned to issuing ordinary shares, thereby encouraging
fully in the risk and return of their companies. Ordinary
ct of unlimited returns, but come with the downside of being

last in the queue after debt holders, creditors and preference shareholders in the event of liquidation. But investors, eager for high returns, were willing to accept the greater risk of ordinary shares because their liability on fully paid-up shares was limited to the amount they invested. If a company goes into liquidation with liabilities exceeding its assets, individual shareholders, unlike sole traders or members of a partnership, do not have to provide additional funds from their assets to make good the shortfall facing the creditors. Also shares, unlike debt securities, seemed to offer the prospect of unlimited participation in the upside benefits of economic growth.

As the stock market developed, both UK and overseas companies came to UK investors for funds. A glance at a *Stock Exchange Official Year Book* of 50 years ago reveals that UK and overseas corporate securities of many more different types were in issue than are quoted today. Securities such as redeemable preference shares, convertible debentures and deferred ordinary shares abounded, with a company possibly having well over a dozen different types of security in issue, offering a wide variety of different levels of risk and return. A careful scrutiny of today's Official List will show that the variety of these securities has diminished significantly, and that their value in relation to that of ordinary shares is now almost negligible.

The decline in the significance of domestic listed securities other than ordinary shares as a source of capital can be attributed to several factors:

○ the nationalisation and subsequent reprivatisation of the utilities; for example, 590 companies were merged when the gas companies were nationalised in 1948, but only one new company was floated on the stock exchange when the industry left the state sector in 1986
○ takeovers and mergers
○ the general decline in popularity of fixed interest securities in the UK since the middle of the twentieth century (discussed in Chapter 1)
○ the lower costs associated with larger issues of a single type of security, both at original issue and in terms of ongoing compliance with investor and stock exchange requirements.

Preference shares of various types and convertible unsecured loan stocks (convertible into ordinary shares) are still issued, but pure equity is by far the most important type of finance raised through the issuance of domestic securities on the London market (though equity in turn is dwarfed by the figures for issuance of eurobonds, discussed in Chapter 4).

However, as well as providing an equity market for UK companies, the London stock exchange offers the same to international companies. Indeed, as we saw in Chapter 1, Table 1.3, 351 companies with a market value of £1971.64 billion were also listed on the London stock exchange. Since 2004, the London stock exchange has attracted a large number of overseas companies, many of them from the former Soviet Union, and by late 2006 the number of international companies listed was 430 from 55 different countries. As well as the Main Market, the London stock exchange also operates the Alternative Investment Market (AIM), a market specialising in companies without a track record. By end 2004, a further 1021 companies with a market value of £31.75 billion were listed on AIM.

This chapter concentrates on the analysis and valuation of ordinary shares. The first section details their fundamental characteristics, and is followed by a description of the

---

Box 5.1 A case of 'Any security you like – as long as it's an ordinary share'?

Three of the five largest UK companies with a primary listing on the London stock exchange, Vodafone, HSBC and GlaxoSmithKline, have no listed domestic securities in issue other than their ordinary shares. The two largest UK listed companies, BP and Shell, each have two listed domestic issues of preference shares, but their total value of less than £20 million for each of the two companies is negligible in comparison with the market value of their ordinary shares, which was £130 billion (BP) and £122 billion (Shell) on 31 October 2005.

By way of contrast, if on the same date we look just below the FTSE 100 index of the largest listed companies, we find that the leading industrial and commercial property investment company Slough Estates has a more varied range of securities in the Official List. Apart from its ordinary shares, valued at just under £2 billion at 30 September 2004, it had three other listed issues with an aggregate market value of about £150 million, comprising

○ cumulative convertible redeemable preference shares (redeemable by the company at their face value between 2006 and 2011 if not already converted into ordinary shares by their holders)
○ 11¼ per cent mortgage debenture stock (a domestic debt security secured on the company's fixed assets) due in 2019
○ 12¾ per cent unsecured loan stock due in 2009.

---

major ways in which ordinary shares are issued to investors. The chapter then goes on to consider the advantages and disadvantages of the most commonly used measures of returns on shares, as well as the more complex problem of how the expected holding period return on a share can be estimated. The chapter continues with a description of some of the major share valuation models used in practice.

DESCRIPTION OF ORDINARY SHARES

Ordinary shares are issued by limited liability companies as risk capital; each share represents a proportionate claim on the residual income (after all expenses and charges, including interest due to lenders) have been accounted for, and on the proceeds of the residual assets (after all other creditors and claims have been paid off when the company is finally wound up).

Under UK company law, shares must have a ***nominal value*** (or ***par value***) just as bonds do, but this can be very different from the market value or price of the share and – unlike the nominal value of a bond – it has nothing at all to do with any final repayment value. For example, a 25p nominal share can have a market price of, say, 437p. The actual nominal value of a share may reflect the original amount of money raised by issuing shares (since UK company law prohibits the issue of shares at a price below their nominal value) but it is more likely to be a hangover from the tradition in the UK of keeping nominal (or par) values below £1. Ordinary shares are usually described simply by the name of the company that issued them and by the nominal value.

Most ordinary share prices are given in the *Financial Times (FT)*, which lists the share prices of all those companies whose shares are traded on the Main Market of the stock exchange and that are willing to pay an annual fee to the *FT*. The shares are divided into a standard 37 subsectors listed in Appendix 5.3 to this chapter. There is a separate section in the *FT* for companies listed on AIM, classified according to the ten high-level industries of the FTSE system.

Example 5.1 (overleaf) shows details of the shares listed under the headings of Food & Drug Retailers, and Food Producers and Processors. Note that these tables include not only UK companies with their primary listings in London but also the secondary listings of foreign companies whose primary listing is on a foreign exchange.

Example 5.1(a), published on Saturday 7 January 2006, shows the format in which the editions of the *FT* published on Tuesday to Saturday include a report on the previous day's market activity. The figures represent the position at close of business on the previous trading day, in this case Friday 6 January 2006. Explanation of the columns is as follows:

Notes:	Symbols and letters in this column convey a wealth of useful information. For instance the symbols † and ‡ indicate respectively a recent increase or reduction in the level of dividend, and the symbol ♦ indicates that the company is involved either in a merger or takeover or in a capital reorganisation.
Price:	This is the closing **midprice** (i.e. the average of the bid and offer price) on the previous trading day.
Chng:	Price change (in money terms) since the close on the previous day.
2005/06 high low:	Highest/lowest closing price recorded so far in 2005/06.
Y'ld:	The **dividend yield** is calculated from the total dividends payable in respect of the company's most recent financial year, expressed as a percentage of the current share price; this is analogous to the interest-only yield on bonds, discussed in Chapter 3, and is explained later in this chapter.
P/E:	Price–earnings ratio, that is, the latest share price expressed as a multiple of the latest year's reported **earnings per share**. This too is explained later in this chapter.
Vol '000s:	Number of shares traded during the day's trading session. A close approximation to the value of the day's turnover can be calculated by multiplying the volume by the closing price.

Example 5.1(b), published on Monday 9 January 2006, a weekday, is in a slightly different format. As the immediately previous trading day is still the previous Friday, some of the information reported on Saturday is repeated here, and some additional information is provided. The new columns here are as follows:

W'k % Chng:	Price change (in percentage terms) since the close on the Friday one week earlier.
Div:	Total dividend payable for the latest year.
Div cov:	The number of times the latest year's dividend was covered by the company's after-tax earnings for that year.
Mcap £m:	The **market capitalisation**, that is, the latest share price multiplied by the number of shares in issue, in millions of pounds.
Last xd:	The date on which the share last went ex dividend.

Shares printed in bold, such as Tesco, are constituents of the FTSE 100 index of leading shares, accounting in aggregate for some 83 per cent of the total value of all UK shares traded on the main market.

Superficially, it would appear from the *FT* listings that an investor wishing to invest in a certain sector of the UK economy would best achieve that objective by investing in the ordinary shares of some or all of the companies listed under the appropriate sector of the stock market. But closer examination of the two sectors we have shown in Example 5.1 will yield some useful insights into the relationship (or perhaps the lack of it) between an international market such as the London stock exchange and underlying economic activity in its host country.

Example 5.1 FT daily share service for selected sectors as reported on (a) Saturday 7 January 2006 (left-hand table) and (b) Monday 9 January 2006 (right-hand table)

	Notes	Price	Chng	2005/06 high	low	Y'ld	P/E	Vol '000s
FOOD & DRUG RETAILERS								
AllncUniChem	♠†	806½	−8½	875	720	2.4	16.4	3,064
Dairy Fm $	s	210	−2	222½	123	2.0	19.7	46
Euro Home Retail	†	88xd	......	195	86½	3.8	62.0	10
Greggs	♠†	4622	−78	4950	3620	2.2	20.0	15
JardnMt$	†	976¾	−3	1056½	827½	2.4	6.4	216
Morrison		196	+1¼	224	161½	1.9	49.1	6,988
Sainsbry	♠	319¾xd	−1¼	323¾	264¾	2.4	−	13,914
Tesco	♣♠†	321¾	−3	335¾	294¾	2.4	16.9	53,509
Thorntns		156¾	−3¼	176	125½	4.3	17.4	21
UtdDrug		247½xd	−3½	270	213¼	1.5	Φ	101
WhitrdCh	♦	89¾	......	190	65	4.2	9.4	6
FOOD PRODUCERS								
AngloEst	♠	239	.....	249½	156½	1.9	14.7	26
ArlaFdsUK		69½	+1	74	52	2.0	Φ	1,792
AscBrFd	♠	857xd	+2	863	728	2.1	16.1	1,831
CadbSchw	♣†	559	+1	594	466½	2.3	22.5	6,712
Carr'sM	♠	557½xd		607½	456½	2.9	Φ	5
Conafex R	♥	97¼	+¼	97¼	60½	−	17.2	
Cranswck	♠†	615xd	+12	665½	511	2.5	13.8	59
Dairy Cr	♠†	532xd	+1	547	400½	3.9	14.8	223
Devro	♠†	126	+¼	139	120½	3.2	16.7	168
Fyffes €		158	−2¾	179¼	133½	3.0	−	21
Glanbia	†	170	−¼	280½	156¾	2.2	−	21
Grncore €	♠	243½xd	+6	263	203¾	3.6	−	5
HighldM$		60¾	−1	66¾	48¾	7.4	7.1	14
IAWS €		870¾	+5¾	894¾	750¾	0.9	−	7
Kerry A €	†	1289	+1	1450¾	1165	0.8	−	25
NstlRg SFr		£175 9/32	−2 5/32	£177 7/16	£135 15/32	2.0	22.8	733
Northern	♠†	152	.....	173	143¾	6.1	−	1,812
PGI	z	55	+1	66	16½	0.4	−	126
PremierFds	†	299	−¾	341¾	264	4.6	41.8	1,994
REA		268½	......	277½	215	−	11.3	5
RHM		263½xd	+1¼	320	247	2.0	−	2,542
RichmdFd		601½xd	......	683½	455½	1.7	Φ	0
RWiseman	♠†	296½	+1½	300	233½	2.8	14.5	58
Sygen	♠♦	63	......	63¼	36	1.3	33.5	0
Tate&Lyl	♠†	576xd	−5½	587	440	3.4	14.7	2,443
TigerBrd R		1436	+77	1436	800½	2.6	18.6	−
TongtHuR		758¼	+2	758¾	434¾	2.9	37.2	20
Unilever	♠†	577½	+4	602½	487½	3.4	26.9	11,335
N/Vtg €	†	£39 7/16	......	£41¼	£33 13/32	3.3	29.6	3,009
Uniq	♠	105	−¼	191½	104	6.7	−	493

	Notes	Price	W'k % Chng	Div	Div cov.	Mcap £m	Last xd	City line
FOOD & DRUG RETAILERS								
AllncUniChem	♠†	806½	0.7	19.15	2.6	2,917	3.8	4290
Dairy Fm $	s	210	−4	Q7.6c	2.5	2,829	17.3	3178
Euro Home Retail	†	88xd	......	3.35	0.4	42.4	14.12	3080
Greggs	♠†	4622	−1.7	102.0	2.3	562.5	31.8	2774
JardnMt$	†	976¾	−2.0	Q40.85c	6.6	5,932	17.8	1114
Morrison		196	1.3	3.7	1.1	5,211	26.10	3422
Sainsbry	♠	319¾xd	1.4	7.8	−	5,443	23.11	3904
Tesco	♣♠†	321¾	−2.9	7.8	2.4	25,283	28.9	4197
Thorntns		156¾	0.5	6.8	1.3	104.6	2.11	5041
UtdDrug		247½xd	−5.4	5½c	Φ	544.8	30.11	1261
WhitrdCh	♦	89¾	......	3.8	2.5	21.4	28.9	1580
FOOD PRODUCERS								
AngloEst	♠	239	−2.4	8c	3.6	95.0	8.6	1618
ArlaFdsUK		69½	9.4	1.4	Φ	124.6	22.6	1292
AscBrFd	♠	857xd	2.1	18.0	3.0	6,784	30.11	1674
CadbSchw	♣†	559	1.7	12.7	2.0	11,646	14.9	2030
Carr'sM	♠	557½xd	0.9	16.0	Φ	44.9	14.12	2075
Conafex R	♥	97¼	1.1	−	−	11.2	4.0	−
Cranswck	♠†	615xd	8.4	15.2	2.9	274.0	30.11	2270
Dairy Cr	♠†	532xd	−2.7	20.6	1.7	660.6	14.12	1632
Devro	♠†	126	−1.8	4.0	1.9	203.4	20.9	2496
Fyffes €		158	0.8	6.89c	−	552.3	14.9	1425
Glanbia	†	170	2.6	5.36c	−	498.0	7.9	1601
Grncore €	♠	243½xd	4.7	12.63c	−	475.7	30.11	2905
HighldM$		60¾	0.1	Q30c	1.9	367.3	14.9	−
IAWS €		870¾	3.5	11.89c	−	1,088	6.4	2583
Kerry A €	†	1289	0.6	14½c	−	2,411	19.10	2838
NstlRg SFr		£175 9/32	1.2	Q80%	2.2	70,730	20.4	5239
Northern	♠†	152	0.3	9.1	0.1	747.8	27.7	3536
PGI	z	55	......	0.2	−	53.7	28.9	2125
PremierFds	†	299	......	13.75	0.5	732.2	26.10	−
REA		268½	......	−	−	67.5	12.99	3749
RHM		263½xd	−.8	5.3	−	917.6	21.12	−
RichmdFd		601½xd	0.6	10.0	Φ	141.5	7.12	1200
RWiseman	♠†	296½	2.6	8.2	2.5	213.7	24.8	4146
Sygen	♠♦	63	0.4	0.8	2.3	186.0	26.10	2587
Tate&Lyl	♠†	576xd	2.3	19.6	2.0	2,805	7.12	4173
TigerBrd R		1436	11.6	Q405c	2.1	2,436	4.7	−
TongtHuR		758¼	1.6	Q240c	0.9	787.8	24.8	−
Unilever	♠†	577½	0.2	19.59	1.1	16,665	16.11	4347
N/Vtg €	†	£39 7/16	−1.3	1.82c	1.0	22,535	9.11	−
Uniq	♠	105	−.7	7.0	−	120.6	30.11	4344

The first thing to note is that the *FT* does not distinguish explicitly between UK companies with their primary listing in London and foreign companies with a secondary listing here. Some (but by no means all) of the latter can be identified by the indication that the price (or the dividend) is quoted in foreign currency, but for definitive listings of UK and foreign companies we would have to go to the stock exchange's own Official Lists. In Example 5.2 we show just the UK companies in each of the two sectors, arranged in descending order of market capitalisation as at 6 January 2006; the final column shows the cumulative percentage of the market capitalisation of each sector.

Example 5.2 Market capitalisation of UK companies, selected sectors, as at 6 January 2006

Food & drug retailers	Mkt cap £m	Cum. % of sector	Food producers & processors	Mkt cap £m	Cum. % of sector
Tesco	25,283	63.9	Unilever	16,665	39.1
Sainsbury	5,443	77.7	Cadbury Schweppes	11,648	66.5
William Morrison	5,211	90.9	Associated British Foods	6,784	82.4
Alliance Unichem	2,917	98.3	Tale & Lyle	2,805	89.0
Greggs	563	99.9	RHM	918	91.2
Thomtons	105	99.9	Northern Foods	748	92.9
Whittard of Chelsea	21	100.0	Premier Foods	732	94.7
			Dairy Crest Group	661	96.2
			Arla Foods UK	425	97.2
Total	**39,543**		Cranswick	274	97.9
			Devro	203	98.3
			Robert Wiseman Dairies	214	98.8
			Sygen International	186	99.3
			Uniq	121	99.6
			Richmond Foods	142	99.9
			Carr's Milling Industries	45	100.0
			Total	**42,571**	

Questions that might come to mind include the following:

○ To what extent, and in what sense, does each of the two lists of UK companies 'represent' that sector of the UK economy?
○ To what extent do the relative capitalisations of the companies reflect their UK market share within their sectors?

We shall look at each sector in turn, drawing on figures from the latest available published information (as of January 2006) for each of the companies mentioned and for their respective industries. If we first look at the food retailers we find that:

○ **Tesco** was in fact, as the numbers suggest, the largest food retailer in the UK, but its market share was only 30 per cent, barely half of its 63.9 per cent share of the sector's market capitalisation. Furthermore, some 50 per cent of its sales are now made outside the UK, and an undisclosed but significant percentage of its UK turnover is in non-foods.

○ The then second-largest UK food retailer does not actually appear in the table at all, because **Asda** was a subsidiary of the US group Wal-Mart. UK-based activity in some sectors (notably, volume car manufacturing) is not represented at all by domestic securities listed on the London stock exchange.

○ **Sainsbury** and **Morrison** were much closer to the model of a UK food retailer, and their market shares were not dissimilar to their proportions of the sector's capitalisation.

○ The three next-largest UK food retailers do not figure in the table at all, and each for a different reason:

    ○ **Somerfield** had recently been taken over by a group of private investors and had therefore disappeared from the stock market

    ○ the turnover of the foods division of **Marks & Spencer** was not separately disclosed, and the company itself was listed in a different sector under General Retailers

    ○ the **Waitrose** chain of supermarkets is a division of another general retailer, John Lewis, which is not a publicly traded company at all but a partnership company with a unique ownership structure.

Turning now to drug retailing:

○ While some of the above companies do have significant drug retailing operations within their supermarkets, only **Alliance Unichem** was predominantly engaged in drug distribution, but over 80 per cent of its business was not retail but wholesale (in fact, the full definition of the drugs subsector in the FTSE / DJ classification system makes it clear that – despite its title – wholesalers are included as well as retailers); and its published figures did not split out its UK business from the 'Northern Europe' segment – which anyway accounted for less than half of its business.

○ The largest drug retailer in the UK was in fact **Boots**, but as drugs accounted for less than half of its turnover it was listed in the General Retailers sector. Boots has now merged with Alliance Unichem to form Alliance Boots!

The significance of non-UK operations becomes even greater when we look at the three largest companies in our second sector, Food Producers and Processors.

○ **Unilever**'s turnover in non-foods accounted for 50 per cent of the total: in Unilever's accounts UK turnover was not shown separately, but was included in a total for Europe, which represented barely 40 per cent of worldwide turnover.

○ Only 16 per cent of **Cadbury Schweppes**' sales were in the United Kingdom; and the company is listed under food producers despite the fact that 40 per cent of the company's worldwide sales were not foods but beverages, and beverages are specifically excluded by the full FTSE /DJ definition of this sector (they represent the other sector within the Food & Beverage supersector).

Box 5.2 A special case: the dual-listed company

Two different classes of securities are listed against the name of Unilever in Example 5.1. The first is in respect of the primary listing in London of the ordinary shares of Unilever PLC, whilst the second refers to the ordinary shares of Unilever NV, a Netherlands company whose primary listing is in Amsterdam. In order to understand the significance of these two entries, we need to be familiar with the peculiar corporate structure known as the dual-listed company.

A dual-listed company or DLC is not to be confused with a company that has its primary listing in one country and maintains one or more secondary listings on foreign exchanges; most of the largest companies on the London main market also maintain secondary listings on the New York stock exchange, and many of them maintain further listings on other foreign exchanges (for instance, HSBC in Hong Kong). A DLC is perhaps best described as one of a pair of 'Siamese twins', where two companies, each with its identity, its own share register and its own market listing in its home country, effectively combine their operations and cash flows into a single enterprise (usually under a unified management team) and share the economic benefits of the combined business according to a predetermined ratio.

The oldest and possibly best known DLC structure was that of Royal Dutch (a Dutch company) and Shell (a UK company) which combined to form the Royal Dutch/Shell group in 1907, with the Dutch and UK parent companies sharing the benefits in the ratio of 60:40, until the dual structure was abandoned in favour of a more conventional unitary structure in 2005.

Similarly, in Example 5.1, Unilever PLC and Unilever NV are respectively the UK and Dutch parent companies of the Unilever Group, which arose out of the 1930 merger of the UK company Lever Brothers and the Dutch company Margarine Unie. The shareholders in the two Unilever parent companies share the benefits of ownership of the Unilever group of operating companies in such a way that each share in 'NV' is theoretically worth 6.67 shares in 'PLC'. Other DLCs in the FTSE 100 index of leading shares include Reed Elsevier (also a UK/Dutch partnership), two mining groups, BHP Billiton and Rio Tinto (both UK/Australian operations), and Carnival (a twinning of two cruise-ship operators, Carnival Corp of the United States and the UK company Carnival plc).

The central problem arising from the DLC structure is the challenge it presents to the efficient markets hypothesis. In truly efficient international markets, the market capitalisations of the two parent companies in a DLC structure would reflect more or less exactly the ratio of their interests in the shared enterprise, but in practice this is seldom the case and more often than not the discrepancy is both significant and persistent. For instance, from the price of the 'PLC' share shown in Example 5.1, we would expect the shares in 'NV' to have been worth 577½p × 6.67 or £38.52 each, whereas in fact the price was the equivalent in euros of £39.44, a premium of about 2.4 per cent to the expected value. We return to this problem in our final review of open issues in finance in Chapter 13.

○ **Associated British Foods** – despite its title – made nearly 50 per cent of its sales outside the United Kingdom; and its UK clothing subsidiary accounted for nearly 20 per cent of its worldwide sales.

Two further problems that arise in connection with stock market sectors will be discussed in later chapters:

○ The dominance of one or two companies in a sector makes it very difficult to achieve in practice the portfolio efficiency gains that can theoretically be obtained by means of diversification. This is discussed in more detail in Chapters 7 and 12.

○ The size of a company's underlying business enterprise cannot be reliably or conclusively judged from the value of its ordinary share capital, as different companies rely to differing extents on debt capital as a partial source of financing. This is discussed in greater detail in Chapter 7.

A final peculiarity worth identifying at this stage is the difference between ordinary shares that have voting rights, and ordinary shares that have no such rights or whose rights are formally restricted by the company's *articles of association*. This type of capital structure was originally used by family-controlled companies as a means of raising new equity funds without sacrificing control of the business to outside investors. A small number of ordinary shares with voting rights continued to exercise control over the company while the majority of shareholders held non-voting ordinary shares, identical in nearly all respects save for the right to vote in general meetings on matters affecting the overall direction and governance of the company.

For example, Marks & Spencer had this dual share structure until 1966 when the 'A' ordinary shares were enfranchised. The London stock exchange has long encouraged companies to have only one class of voting ordinary share. An example of a surviving exception to this trend is Daily Mail and General Trust, whose capital structure consists of just 20 million voting shares of 12.5p each, which are not listed on the stock exchange but are majority owned by Harmsworth family interests, and 381.4 million non-voting 'A' shares of 12.5p each, which are listed on the stock exchange and ranked near the bottom of the FTSE 100 at the end of October 2005 with a market capitalisation of some £2.6 billion. The reason this structure survived longer in newspaper and similar industries was as a means of preventing supposedly 'undesirable' operators from acquiring controlling interests in mass media enterprises.

Other classes of share, such as the various types of preference share, rarely have any voting rights, though they might temporarily acquire such rights if (for example) the company falls into arrears in payment of their dividends. This lack of voting rights can be a serious drawback. If the preference shareholders of a target company in a takeover bid have no say in the matter, they might find themselves left out in the cold, with no bid for their shares at all. Following the takeover, they might be left holding a very minor class of security of a subsidiary of a much larger group, and they will find very little market interest or liquidity in their investment.

Two special classes of equity-related security are *convertible preference shares* and *warrants*, each of which confers on the holder the right (but not the obligation) to subscribe for ordinary shares at a predetermined price on or between fixed future dates. As far as votes are concerned, warrants are unlikely to carry any voting rights, whereas issues of convertible preference shares might have voting rights in the event of a takeover or a reconstruction, and such voting rights would ensure that this type of shareholder is not penalised by major changes to the company.

Fixed interest securities, whether issued by companies or by governments, have fixed repayment conditions; even undated securities, which have no mandatory repayment dates, invariably have provisions for voluntary repayment by the issuer. Ordinary shares, however, like many issues of preference shares, are usually irredeemable. Ordinary shares thus have an indefinite life, unless the company is wound up, voluntarily or involuntarily, or there is some scheme to reduce the share capital, or the company is taken over. So except when the company is forced into liquidation, the voting shareholders have a say in whether their shares should be repaid or acquired. However, if 90 per cent of a company's shares have been acquired or are held by another company, the remainder can be compulsorily purchased if total control is desired.

The attraction of ordinary shares is their limited liability and possibly unlimited returns. Investors in fully paid ordinary shares can never lose more than 100 per cent of their investment but their return on the shares can be far greater than this. For this reason, the probability distribution of returns on shares is not quite normal: returns can never be less than -100 per cent but can exceed +100 per cent.

Fixed interest securities have specified income, in the form of the periodic coupon and the repayment on maturity. Although the holding period rate of return can vary according to changes in price of the fixed interest security, the returns on fixed interest securities will on average be less volatile than those on ordinary shares, where both the income and the future share price are uncertain.

Because of this extra volatility of share price and income, and hence of holding period return, shares are in general riskier than fixed interest securities. As a result, ordinary shareholders require a risk premium for taking on this additional risk: that is, a return in excess of the return on less risky investments, such as gilts. We saw in Chapter 2 that risk could be measured by the standard deviation of the probability distribution of returns. In fact, in Chapter 7, we shall find that the relevant measure of risk for an ordinary share is its risk relative to other shares and to the stock market as a whole, since shares are not usually held in isolation but as part of a diversified portfolio.

The remaining sections of this chapter will focus on the characteristics and valuation of pure equity securities: that is, ordinary shares.

ISSUANCE AND LISTING OF ORDINARY SHARES

We start by considering the various ways in which company shares become listed on the stock exchange. We consider separately the cases of

○ a company whose ordinary shares are to be listed on the stock exchange for the first time
○ a further issue by a company whose ordinary shares are already listed.

Initial listings of ordinary shares

A company may have one or more reasons for seeking a listing for the first time. A listing can:

○ give the company access to a wider pool of capital
○ make its shares more marketable and therefore more attractive to investors
○ enable founders and other existing holders to realise all or part of the gain on the capital appreciation of their shares
○ enhance the company's image in the business community and in the wider world

○ facilitate the takeover of other businesses through the ability to offer marketable shares in exchange for another company's shares.

A company listing its shares for the first time has several alternative courses of action open to it, depending on its motivation and on whether it or its existing shareholders wish to raise new funds immediately.

In an ***Introduction*** the existing shares of a previously private company are listed and admitted for trading on the stock exchange. No new money is raised for the company itself and there is no immediate transfer of shares from the existing investors to new investors, but the existing shareholders gain access to a ready market for their shares and potential shareholders gain the opportunity for the first time to buy into the company. All parties benefit from access to an efficient pricing mechanism, as privately held companies are notoriously difficult to value. Even though no new money is raised in an introduction, the requirements of the Financial Services Authority (FSA) (as the UK Listing Authority) and of the stock exchange must be still be met. The principal requirements for any listing of a company's shares on the Official List are that:

○ at least 25 per cent of the shares must already be adequately spread among investors
○ the company must have a satisfactory track record of profitable operation
○ the company must have access to sufficient working capital to maintain its operations for the next 12 months
○ the company must conform to prescribed standards of disclosure and corporate governance.

In all cases other than an introduction, the listing of the previously private company will be accompanied by the simultaneous sale of some shares to new investors. There are four basic variations on this theme, depending on the source of the shares that are sold, and on how the shares are distributed to new investors.

If the immediate purpose of the listing is just for the existing shareholders in a privately held company to take some profits (or reduce their risk) by selling part of their shareholdings on the open market, then the shares offered for sale in the listing will be part of those already in issue. The sellers will be the existing investors, and they (not the company) will receive the net proceeds of the sale. But if the purpose of the listing is also to raise new funds for the company, then the shares offered for sale will be newly issued for this purpose by the company. It is possible to combine these two variants, so that an offer can include both new and old shares.

If the shares are to be offered for sale to the investing public at large, the issue is called an ***initial public offering*** or ***IPO***. If they are placed instead with a small group of institutional investors, the issue is called a ***placing***. 'IPO' has now replaced the traditional 'flotation' in market jargon, reflecting the increasing adoption of US terminology and practices in the UK markets.

In the case of an IPO, the offer will usually be made on the company's and/or the existing investors' behalf by an investment bank in the form of an offer for sale at an agreed fixed price. The sale of new shares is normally underwritten by the investment bank. In other words, if potential investors are not interested in the offer for sale at the agreed price, the investment bank (and other financial institutions acting as sub-underwriters) contracts to buy any new shares not taken up by investors at the agreed price. In this way, the company can be sure of receiving the funds whatever happens to the stock market during the offer period. The underwriters charge a fee for underwriting and sub-underwriting which, under the UK system, is around 2–5 per cent of the amount of the issue.

A typical IPO is made by a private company which has grown to the extent that existing investors needed to realise profits or spread their risk, and the company itself needs to access a wider pool of funds to finance its further expansion. However, since the 1980s, a new source of IPOs came from the massive programme of privatising previously nationalised businesses. These companies were often utilities, such as British Telecom and British Gas, which had a long track record of offering a service at a low cost rather than of attempting to maximise shareholder wealth. Other privatisations were simply the sale of shares in companies that had previously been listed on the stock exchange but had been bought by the government when they, or companies that owned the shares, experienced financial difficulties, as was the case with Rolls-Royce.

If an offer is oversubscribed, as many primary issues and privatisations were in the 1980s, the issuing company and their financial advisers can choose what is known as an allotment policy. The normal mechanism is to divide applications into bands according to the number of shares applied for, and to allot percentages of the total available to each band. In this way, preference can be given to large or small applicants as desired. Before the privatisation programme, it was normal to favour large bidders since this reduced the administrative costs of maintaining the shareholder register. With privatisations, however, the government attempted to encourage small shareholders by favouring the smallest bidders. As Table 1.2 shows, however, the long-run trend away from direct private ownership of shares was not halted by this. Many successful applicants simply sold their shares at a profit to the investing institutions as soon as the shares were quoted on the market – a process known as *stagging* a primary issue.

A public offer that is oversubscribed is considered to be a success, although too much unsatisfied demand, reflected in the shares immediately trading at a substantial premium to the offer price, could imply that the shares were sold too cheaply. In Chapter 13 we shall review some evidence that suggests IPOs are in fact systematically overpriced rather than the reverse.

An alternative method of primary issue which aims to maximise the amount of money raised by the sale of the shares is the new issue by means of a *tender offer*. In this case, would-be investors bid the price that they are prepared to pay for the shares and those with the highest bids get the shares. This method does not require underwriting, thereby saving the issuer fees, but does expose the issuer to the risk of selling the shares at an unsatisfactory price or, if a minimum share price to be tendered is imposed, having a rump of shares unsold. The other disadvantage is that it requires investors to be confident of the price they are prepared to pay for the shares, since there will be no quick profits in the form of a premium over the offer price, as is the case in a fixed price offer. A variant of the new issue by tender method allows investors to bid either a particular price of their choice or the average price at which the shares are allotted. In this way, the government was able to use the new issue by tender method for one or two privatisations without frightening away less sophisticated investors. However, most new issues, whether privatisations or not, use the fixed price method in order to maximise interest in the new issue.

In recent years, the *book-building* method has taken over from other new issue methods. With this system, the managers of the issue ask for indications of interest from investors, in terms of both the amount they might bid for and the price at which they will bid. The managers will have given an indication through a minimum price. Book building therefore aids price and demand discovery, as the final price reflects investor demand and makes it less likely that shares will rise to a substantial premium over the offer price when listing takes place.

A further alternative is a *placing,* in which there is no offer for sale to the investing public at large. Instead, the investment bank arranges for substantial blocks of the shares to be purchased by a small syndicate of investing institutions. This has both advantages and disadvantages for the issuer or sellers of the shares. The costs of a placing are normally lower than for a public offering, and there is less uncertainty, because the investment bank negotiates a mutually acceptable price for the deal. Formal underwriting is therefore unnecessary, though the price achieved for such block transactions may include an implied discount which has a similar effect in terms of reduced net proceeds of sale. A disadvantage is that, in a placing, the company does not immediately achieve the same breadth of name-recognition in the market as it would from a full-scale public offer. Conversely, to the extent that the shares are, at least initially, still quite tightly held, it could be some time before an active secondary market develops, and this temporary restriction in the liquidity of the shares is another reason that investing institutions participating in a placing might look for a discount. In 2005, 30 per cent of funds were raised through placings and the remainder through public offerings.

For new shares to be listed on the London stock exchange Main Market, a number of minimum criteria have to be satisfied, specifically a minimum amount of £700,000 of shares issued, a three-year track record, at least 25 per cent of the shares in total held in public hands, and sufficient working capital for the next 12 months, as well as good corporate governance requirements. There are no such minimum conditions for companies listing their shares on AIM, and so less protection for potential investors. Some international companies listing on the London stock exchange comply with the domestic company **listing requirements**. However, many international companies coming to the London stock exchange list what are known as **global depositary receipts** or **GDRs.** GDRs are negotiable certificates held in the bank of one country representing a specific number of shares of a stock traded on an exchange of another country. The attraction for some issuers of using GDRs is that they have less onerous listing rules and corporate governance requirements. For example, they allow a company with a single shareholder holding 90 per cent of the shares to list on the London stock exchange. GDRs are sold to the investing institutions rather than uninformed retail investors, and cannot form part of a stock market equity index.

Subsequent issues by listed companies

Once a company is listed, further issues may occur when it seeks to raise additional risk capital via an issue of shares or when, in a takeover, new shares in the bidding company are issued to the shareholders of the company being acquired, in consideration for the sale of their shares to the bidding company. Such issues are sometimes referred to as **secondary offerings,** or in US terminology, *seasoned equity offerings (SEOs)*. We need to be careful not to confuse secondary offerings either with the secondary *market* (the day-to-day trading of shares already in issue) or with the secondary *listing* of a company's shares on an exchange other than that of its home country.

It is convenient to distinguish two types of secondary issues, depending on whether the new shares are issued for cash or in exchange for shares in another company. In the former case, the new shares are issued to raise money either to fund expansion or to strengthen the company's balance sheet, for instance by using the proceeds to repay borrowings. The commonest case of an issue for exchange into the shares of another company is when one company takes over another, not by paying shareholders in cash for their shares but by exchanging new shares of its own for those in the target company.

Additional equity funds for companies listed on the stock exchange are usually raised by means of **rights issues,** where existing shareholders are entitled to subscribe for new shares at a fixed price, usually below the existing price, in a fixed ratio to their existing shareholdings. General offers for sale by companies whose shares are already listed (as opposed to companies coming to the stock exchange for the first time, as was discussed above) are severely restricted in order to protect existing shareholders from what is known as **equity dilution.**

For example, suppose the ordinary shares of Crumbly Cakes plc are quoted at 100p. A rights issue of one-for-four is announced, with the subscription price set at 80p per share. Mrs Tooth holds 1000 shares and is therefore entitled to purchase 250 new shares at 80p each. She will then hold 1250 shares and these shares should be worth, other things being equal, their previous market value plus the new funds invested.

However, as the new shares have been issued at a discount to the existing market price, in most cases a rights issue will cause the share price to fall after the issue, in the case of Crumbly Cakes plc from 100p to 96p.

1000 existing shares at 100p	= £1000
New funds invested: 250 new shares at 80p	= £200
Expected value of investment	= £1200

As Mrs Tooth now holds 1250 shares, the value of each share after the rights issue (*ex rights*, in market terminology) will be

$$\frac{£1200}{£1250} = 96p$$

This is known as the **theoretical ex-rights price** (or **TERP**) of the share. Of course, the announcement of a rights issue may also be accompanied by good or bad news about the company. The funds may be needed either to take advantage of a profitable new project or to strengthen the company's flagging financial structure, and this might cause the share price to settle at a new level either higher or lower than the TERP.

If Mrs Tooth does nothing, the value of her existing shares would in this case fall from £1000 to £960. So, in the case of a rights issue, action must be taken, either to take up the rights to buy new shares or to sell the rights to someone else. These rights will be worth approximately the difference between the subscription price and the price of the share after the rights issue:

Ex rights price   =   96p
Subscription price   =   (80p)
Value of one right   =   16p

Mrs Tooth has rights to 250 new shares, so the sale of her rights would theoretically raise $250 \times 16p$ or £40, which would exactly compensate her for the diminution in the value of her 1000 shares.

The management of the company may arrange to sell any shareholders' rights not taken up and to distribute the proceeds of the sale to those shareholders. In such instances, the shareholders may take no action if they so wish without financial loss. However, in cases where the amount is small, the management may sell the rights not taken up and use the proceeds for the benefit of the company.

If Mrs Tooth sells her rights, she will have reduced her level of investment and percentage holding in Crumbly Cakes plc. A third alternative is for Mrs Tooth to sell just sufficient of her existing shares to be able to take up the rights on the remaining shares without having to invest 'new' money. She would then maintain the level of her investment at £1000.

Rights issues are usually underwritten by a syndicate of investment banks. In other words, if investors such as Mrs Tooth choose not to take up their rights (for example, if the share price falls below the subscription price on the new shares and the rights thus become worthless), the investment bank, and other financial institutions to which it sub-underwrites, contract to buy any new shares for which the rights have not been taken up. In this way, the company can be sure of receiving the new funds, whatever happens to its share price between the offer date and the closing date of the issue. An alternative to underwriting is a *deep-discount rights issue*, where the subscription price is set so far below the current share price that there is little or no risk that the share price will fall below the subscription price during the three weeks or so of the issue period. In this way, the costs of underwriting, usually around 2% of the funds raised, can be avoided. However, deep-discount issues are not as common as underwritten rights issues, since to raise the same amount of money as with a conventional rights issue, more new shares would have to be issued. If, as is usual, dividends per share are maintained at pre-rights issue levels, a deep-discount rights issue would involve companies in substantially increased dividend payments.

A further case of new issuance by a company whose shares are already listed is in a *merger* or *acquisition* (M&A), where Company A takes over Company B by acquiring either all or most of Company B's voting share capital. Under the terms of its offer for the shares, it might acquire those shares either by paying cash, or by issuing new securities of its own in exchange for the shares in Company B, or by offering a mixture of cash and securities. The most common type of security used in such offers is ordinary shares, since one risky security is replaced by another. The shareholders of Company B can then decide whether to sell any shares received and reinvest elsewhere, or retain the shares and hold an investment in Company A. The possible advantage of shares over cash to the shareholders of Company B is that, by holding on to the Company A shares they receive, they can delay any crystallisation of capital gains tax.

Box 5.3 Rights issue case study: Prudential plc

Prudential plc is the second-largest listed UK life insurance group. In late 2004 it ranked as about the 25th largest share issue in the FTSE 100 index. Before the market opened on the morning of 19 October 2004, with its shares having closed on the previous day at 458p and its market capitalisation at £9,265 million, the company surprised the market by announcing a one-for-six rights issue at 308p, a discount of almost 33 per cent to the market price, to raise about £1 billion of new money to finance expansion. The theoretical ex-rights price was as follows:

Six existing shares at 458p each	=	2748p
One new share at 308p	=	308p
Value of seven shares	=	3056p
Value of one new share (TERP)	=	437.5p

The theoretical value of the rights, being the difference between the theoretical ex-rights price of 437.5p and the subscription price of 308p, was just under 120p.

But the market took the news very badly, because recent statements by the directors had been taken to imply that the company had sufficient resources to cover its immediate plans. It was also felt that the rights issue had been made necessary only by the failure of the company's protracted efforts to sell its controlling interest in Egg, its internet banking operation. As a result, as can be seen from Figure 5.1, the shares fell in heavy trading in the course of the next three days, not just to the theoretical ex-rights price of 437.5p, but to a low of 386p, an effective fall of some 11.8 per cent below the expected value, against a background of a broadly unchanged level for the FTSE 100 index itself, before staging a modest recovery.

Despite the protests of institutional shareholders and their demands for the resignation of the chief executive officer, Jonathan Bloomer, it was announced on 11 November 2004 that investors representing 92 per cent of the shares had in fact taken up their rights. The remaining shares were placed in the market at 419p, so that after the company had received

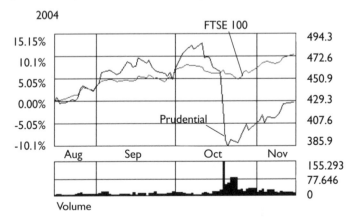

Figure 5.1 Prudential plc share price, trading volume and performance against the FTSE 100 index, August–November 2004
Source: Prudential plc.

the subscription price of 308p per share and the incidental expenses of the issue had been paid, those investors who had not taken up their rights received 110p per share for those rights – slightly, but not disastrously, less than the expected value of 120p. The market price of the shares was now 430p, or about 1.7 per cent below the theoretical ex-rights price, while the FTSE 100 index meanwhile had risen by some 3.6 per cent, so that the shares were effectively about 5 per cent down on their value relative to the rest of the market immediately before the initial announcement. The rights issue had been underwritten by three investment banks, but the successful placing in the market of the rights not exercised by shareholders relieved them of their liability.

As for the CEO Mr Bloomer, he was reported to have followed Mrs Tooth's third alternative. He held 692,000 Prudential shares before the issue, so he received rights over 115,000 new shares. In order to maintain the amount of his investment in the company in money terms, he sold his rights to 86,000 shares for about 97.5p each, and the £84,000 raised by this exercise substantially met the cost of exercising his rights over the remaining 29,000 shares, which at 308p each cost £90,000.

Two other types of share issue should be mentioned for the sake of completeness. Neither of them involves the raising of new money or any change in the value of the company itself.

In a *scrip* issue (also known as a **bonus** or *capitalisation* issue) new shares are issued to existing shareholders, in proportion to their existing holdings (as for a rights issue) but no payment is required. Whereas in the case of both takeovers and rights issues, the value of the company issuing the shares changes, in the case of scrip issues, there should be no fundamental change in the value of the company. As an example of a scrip issue, say Crumbly Cakes issued one new share free for each two existing shares held. No money would change hands. Mrs Tooth would then hold, instead of 1000 shares, 1500 shares. Since the value of the company would remain the same, other things remaining constant, each share would be worth:

$$\frac{£1000}{£1500} = 66.67p$$

and Mrs Tooth's total investment in Crumbly Cakes would still be worth £1000. An accounting change would take place in the sense that, within the shareholders' funds section of the balance sheet, the share capital would be increased and the reserves (usually, the *accumulated profit*, also known as *retained earnings*) would be reduced, by the amount of the scrip issue. The significance of this paper transaction is that whereas accumulated profit is eligible to be distributed to shareholders by way of dividend, share capital cannot normally be distributed in this way.

Why do companies make scrip issues? One reason might be to reduce the share price, since UK company share prices were traditionally below £10. It can be seen, for example, in Example 5.1 that the only UK company in the selected sectors to have an ordinary share price significantly in excess of £10 is the bakery chain Greggs, which has the highly unusual share price of £45.48. However, this convention for low share prices is disappearing, particularly for internationally traded UK shares,

---

Box 5.4 Acquisition case study: Wm Morrison/Safeway

On 9 January 2003, the UK's fifth-largest listed supermarket chain, William Morrison, announced an agreed all-share offer for the fourth-largest chain, Safeway. Before the announcement, Safeway shares were trading at 222p and Morrison at 210p. By offering 1.32 of its own shares for each Safeway share, Morrison was effectively valuing Safeway shares at 277p, a premium of 25 per cent to the current price and equivalent to a market capitalisation of £2.9 billion. The market's immediate reaction was to mark Morrison's shares down by 9 per cent to 192p, and to mark Safeway up by 20 per cent to 266p. These moves reflected three separate strands in the market's initial analysis of the proposed deal.

As in almost every takeover, the would-be acquirer was prepared to pay a substantial premium over the current market value in order to acquire a business which it felt could be run more profitably than by the incumbent management, usually (as in this case) by realising economies of scale and operational synergies from a larger business combination. But by offering such a large premium, Morrison was risking overpaying for control of Safeway. In other words it ran the risk of transferring to the shareholders in Safeway a disproportionately large share in the combined enterprise and hence in the expected gains from the takeover.

The markdown of Morrison's share price to 192p meant that the offer for Safeway was now worth only 192p x 1.32 = 253p. But the Safeway share price in fact rose further than this, to 266p. This reflected a market belief that despite the fact that the Morrison bid had been agreed by the Safeway directors (that is, they had agreed to recommend it for acceptance by their shareholders), other bidders might yet emerge who were prepared to outbid Morrison.

This subsequently became one of the most protracted takeover bids on record. All the other major supermarket chains, as well as some other interested parties, let it be known that they were also potential bidders. This raised serious competition policy issues which took the authorities a year to resolve. In the event, the Morrison bid was successful, and although it formally lapsed at one stage and had to be revived, it finally went through on substantially the same terms as first agreed, and the companies were formally merged in March 2004.

In early 2004, before the acquisition was consummated, Morrison and Safeway had ranked around 68th and 75th respectively in the FTSE 100 index. The merged company subsequently occupied a place around 50th in the index.

---

because shares in the United States, Europe and Japan traditionally have much higher quoted share prices than in the United Kingdom.

Another reason for a scrip issue is that it provides a method of paying non-cash dividends. If Crumbly Cakes announces a scrip dividend of 1/20 new share for each existing share held, what effect will this have on Mrs Tooth's investment?

Existing holding 1000 shares
Scrip dividend $\frac{1}{20} \times 1000 = 50$ shares
Ex dividend holding 1050 shares

Again, no money has changed hands so the value of the company should therefore remain the same. Mrs Tooth's ex dividend holding must still be worth £1000, and so the ex scrip share price will be £1000/1050 = 95.25p. Mrs Tooth has not received any cash dividend. She can, however, sell her scrip entitlement of 50 shares at 95.25p if she wants income from the shares. She would thus realise approximately £47.50 and might be liable to capital gains tax on the proceeds. Mrs Tooth would then be left with 1000 shares worth £952.50. She could, of course, sell part of her existing holding if she wished, without a scrip issue, and achieve the same effect.

If Crumbly Cakes had chosen to pay a cash dividend, say, of 4.75p per share, instead of making a scrip issue, Mrs Tooth would have received £47.50 dividend (on which she would be liable for income tax) and be left with shares worth, ex dividend, 100p – 4.75p or 95.25p per share, giving the same total of £952.50.

So a scrip issue may affect the tax position of the investor differently from dividends, and alter the balance sheet of the company, but it does not change the fundamental value of the company or the value of Mrs Tooth's investment. If the company announces some other news at the same time as a scrip or rights issue, such as increased profits, or if the issue is felt to be telling the market something about the company's future prospects, the ex-scrip price might be greater than the theoretical price calculated in the above examples.

Finally, a company can effect a *share split* by subdividing its existing share capital into smaller nominal units. For example, a company with 100 million 50p shares in issue could replace these shares with 200 million new 25p shares, by issuing two new 25p shares in exchange for every existing 50p share. Again this is a paper transaction which would have no effect on the value of the company, and in the case of our example we would expect the new shares to trade at exactly half the value of the old shares. The primary motive for a share split might be to make the share price more manageable for trading purposes, although, as mentioned above, the trend is towards higher share prices and nominal values.

We end this section with a cautionary story which shows that even an issue for such a blue-chip company as BP can still go spectacularly wrong.

Box 5.5 Cautionary tale: the BP issue of 1987

In 1979 and 1983, the UK government had raised £830 million from the successful placing in the market of 12 per cent out of its total holding of about 45 per cent in the shares of BP. In autumn 1987 it planned to sell the remaining 32.5 per cent in a public offer, which was to be accompanied by an issue of £7.25 billion in new shares by the company itself. This operation combined the largest ever privatisation issue and the largest ever corporate fundraising. The issue was underwritten by several hundred institutions in the UK, the United States and Europe. Terms were announced on 15 October 1987; the offer price of 330p represented a discount of about 6 per cent to the market price of 350p.

On 19 and 20 October the market fell by over 20 per cent and BP shares dropped to 286p, leaving the underwriters with the prospect of losses of up to £1 billion. The institutions put intense pressure on the UK chancellor, Nigel Lawson, to cancel or change the terms of the issue, but he stood his ground and insisted that events like those of October 1987 were precisely the reason that underwriters were allowed to charge their generous commissions in more normal times.

VALUATION MEASURES FOR ORDINARY SHARES

We saw in Chapter 2 that the two most important valuation criteria for any security were its expected return and its risk. Risk could be measured by standard deviation and expected return R by the expected holding period return,

$$R = \frac{D_1 + (P_1 - P_0)}{P_0} \qquad (2.1)$$

where

$P_0 =$ the cost of the security
$D_1 =$ the expected income to be received during the period
$P_1 =$ the expected value of the security at the end of the period.

In Chapter 4, we looked at surrogate measures for the holding period return on bonds and other fixed interest securities, the interest yield and the redemption yield. The interest yield, given by

$$\frac{D_1}{P_0}$$

is a measure of the income yield from the security. This measure takes no account of the capital gain or loss element, given by

$$\frac{(P_1 - P_0)}{P_0}$$

because P_1 cannot be determined with certainty during the life of the bond. However, P_1 is usually known with certainty at maturity, since it must then equal the redemption value. An estimate of total holding period return can therefore be made, provided the bond is assumed to be held to maturity, and this return, converted into an annual average, is termed the redemption yield.

In the case of ordinary shares, any estimate of expected holding period return is subject to much greater uncertainty. Since there is usually no fixed redemption date or redemption value for shares, P_1 is not known for any point in the future. Also, D_1 is not certain since the size of the future dividend is at the discretion of the company and depends on future profitability. Alternative summary measures have to be used for ordinary shares.

Dividend yield

The dividend yield is the equivalent for ordinary shares of the interest yield for bonds. It is merely the income element of the holding period return

$$\frac{D_1}{P_0}$$

ignoring the capital gain or loss element

$$\frac{(P_1 - P_0)}{P_0}$$

Dividends on UK company shares are usually paid twice yearly, in the form of an interim and a final dividend, but some companies (for instance, BP) follow the US practice of paying dividends quarterly. The value of these dividends is determined by the directors of the company, subject to the approval of the shareholders in their annual general meeting, and is usually announced a few weeks before payment. The amount of future dividend payments is not known until shortly before they are paid. The dividend yield given in the *Financial Times* refers to last year's known interim plus final dividends and not the unknown dividends for next year. The dividend yield calculated is thus D_0/P_0 and not D_1/P_0 and represents part of the historic rather than the expected holding period return. In the case of bonds, D_1 is always equal to D_0 and so D_1/P_0 is known with certainty. With ordinary shares, there is no guarantee that D_1 will exceed D_0 or even equal it, although the company might maintain a more or less explicitly stated policy of steady dividend growth.

As we have already seen, a tentative indicator of future dividends can be found in the symbols under Notes next to the company names in Example 5.1. These give some idea of trends in dividend payments – an indication of what D_1 might be relative to the D_0 given. For example, the symbol † shows that the most recent interim dividend (the first half of D_1) has been raised relative to last year's interim (or resumed), and the symbol ‡ shows that the interim dividend has been reduced or passed.

In Chapter 3, we saw that the interest yield on a bond was a function of its coupon – a low coupon gave a low interest yield and a high coupon a high interest yield. The interest yield gave no indication of the total return to be expected on a bond, that is, the return including a capital gain or loss on disposal. Similarly, with ordinary shares, dividend yield is no measure of the total expected return, which will consist of both income and any capital gain or loss. The UK companies listed in Example 5.1 have dividend yields on ordinary shares varying between 0.4% and 6.7%. These yields will be more a reflection of company dividend policy than of company profitability, although an unusually high dividend yield might indicate a low share price and hence a company in difficulties. So, as with interest yield, we find dividend yield an incomplete measure of expected return.

Dividend payout and cover

The accounting profit reported after deduction of tax, interest on any corporate borrowings and preference share dividends is known as the *earnings available to ordinary shareholders*. These earnings, divided by the number of shares in the company, give the *earnings per share* (or *eps*). It is up to the company's directors to decide how much of these earnings will be paid out as dividends. For example, in recent years, companies making losses or reduced profits have sometimes chosen to maintain the same level of dividend, paid out of previously undistributed past earnings, rather than reduce it in line with current earnings. Any earnings not paid out are termed *retained earnings* and can be reinvested by the company to yield future profits, although a company with a high dividend policy and low retained earnings can finance future investments with borrowings or a new equity issue instead.

Example 5.3 compares the holding period return of two companies with identical earnings, prospects and risk but with different dividend payout policies.

In this simplified example we can see that Company X pays out all the period's earnings as dividends. Since it has no retained earnings, the value of the company would in theory remain unchanged, wit $P_1 = P_0 = 100$p. Company Y pays a smaller dividend of 10p per share, retaining 40p per share within the company. Company Y should therefore be worth 40p per share more at the end of the period, so $P_1 = 140$p. Both companies yield the same holding period return, with Company X's being provided entirely in the form of divi-

Example 5.3 Impact of dividend policy on holding period return

	Company X	Company Y
Number of issued shares	100	100
Share price P_0	100p	100p
Earnings for ordinary shareholders	£50	£50
Earnings per share	50p	50p
Dividend	£50	£10
Dividend per share	50p	10p
Retained earnings	0	£40
Retained earnings per share	0	40p
Share price P_1	100p	140p
Holding period return =	$\dfrac{50 + (100 - 100)}{100}$	$\dfrac{10 + (140 - 100)}{100}$
=	50%	50%

dend and Company *Y*'s partly from dividend and partly from capital gain on the share.

In practice, Company *X* and Company *Y* could differ in their investment policies: for example, Company *Y* might invest its 40p per share retained earnings profitably and Company *X* might not borrow an equivalent amount to invest. In this case, Company *Y*'s share price would increase by more than 40p to reflect its increased future profits. However, if investment policy were the same for these two companies, dividend policy would be irrelevant. In this example, both companies have identical prospects and risk, and identical earnings of 50p per share, and so should yield the same total return to the investor. Thus earnings and not dividend yields are indicators of total returns. Unfortunately, as we shall see below, earnings figures as reported in company accounts are not always good indicators of future profitability.

As was mentioned earlier, an additional problem the dividend yield has when compared with interest yield is that dividends are expected to grow whereas interest payments generally are not. However, in cases where companies try to maintain a stable dividend policy, some attempt can be made to estimate future dividends from past dividends. For example, a company could maintain a regular 5 per cent growth in dividend or always pay out a constant proportion of earnings. In this latter case, it would be said to have a constant *dividend payout ratio*, which is given by the equation

$$\text{Dividend payout ratio} = \frac{dps_0}{eps_0}$$

where dps_0 = dividend per share in year 0 and eps_0 = earnings per share in year 0.

We can see from Example 5.3 that Company *X* has a dividend payout ratio of 50p/50p = 100%, whereas company *Y*'s ratio is 10p/50p = 20%.

The reciprocal of the dividend payout ratio is termed the *dividend cover*:

$$\text{Dividend cover} = \frac{eps_0}{dps_0}$$

What does dividend cover tell us? From our example, we see that Company X has dividend cover of one and Company Y has dividend cover of five times. A dividend cover of one in the case of Company X would seem to imply that a downturn in earnings might force Company X to cut its dividend next year. On the other hand, a dividend cover of five in the case of Company Y would appear to imply that Company Y can afford to maintain the present level of dividend payments in the future even if it suffers a severe drop in earnings.

The major problem with the use of dividend cover for such conclusions is that the level of a company's earnings might give a very misleading picture of its ability to pay dividends. Dividends are paid out of cash flow whereas the earnings figure is an accountant's calculation which includes non-cash items such as depreciation. Also, dividends may be paid out of reserves on the balance sheet but not out of share capital or the share premium account. So a company might have high reported earnings and yet have insufficient cash or distributable reserves to maintain its dividend payments. As we shall see in the next section, any measure that uses reported earnings is subject to difficulty of interpretation.

We conclude this section by looking at the five-year earnings and dividend record of two companies from Example 5.1, Sainsbury and Tesco (see Example 5.4). According to the figures in the *Financial Times,* Sainsbury's dividend yield of 2.4% is the same as Tesco's. An analysis of the underlying position shows just how misleading the comparison of these raw figures can be.

Even a cursory examination of these figures shows that Tesco has shown stronger and more consistent earnings growth, so that it has been able to pay increasing dividends to its shareholders without increasing its payout ratio, which is both lower and more stable than that of Sainsbury. The latter's shareholders, having been lulled into a false sense of security by the apparently smooth growth in dividends (though not in underlying earnings) in the years 2000–04, experienced a rude awakening when earnings collapsed and the dividend was halved in 2005. In short, Tesco shareholders are prepared to accept a lower dividend payout because they are confident that the dividend will increase steadily over the coming years. In the next section we shall see how this confidence is translated mathematically into a higher share price.

Example 5.4 Sainsbury and Tesco: earnings per share and dividends 2000–05

	2000	2001	2002	2003	2004	2005
Sainsbury						
Earnings per share (pence)	18.30	14.50	19.10	23.70	20.70	8.60
Dividend (pence)	14.32	14.32	14.84	15.58	15.69	7.80
Dividend payout ratio (%)	78.3%	98.8%	77.7%	65.7%	75.8%	90.7%
Dividend growth (%)		0.0%	3.6%	5.0%	0.7%	-50.3%
Tesco						
Earnings per share (pence)	10.36	10.87	12.33	14.10	16.45	18.53
Dividend (pence)	4.48	4.98	5.60	6.20	6.84	7.56
Dividend payout ratio (%)	43.2%	45.8%	45.4%	44.0%	41.6%	40.8%
Dividend growth (%)		11.2%	12.4%	10.7%	10.3%	10.5%

Price–earnings (p/e) ratio

One of the two summary measures provided in Example 5.1 is concerned with dividends – the dividend yield – and yet we have seen that dividend measures provide inadequate estimates for holding period return. The problem lies in the fact that, for any ordinary share, future earnings, dividends and share prices are unknown. The only information available concerns the current share price and past earnings and dividends.

The second summary valuation measure listed in Example 5.1 is the *price–earnings* or *p/e ratio,* which uses two known figures, the current share price divided by the latest earnings per share. Thus,

$$PE_0 = \frac{P_0}{eps_0}$$

Because they are ratios, the dividend yield and dividend cover can be used for comparative purposes, unlike the net dividend per share. This use for comparison also holds true for the p/e ratio, and is its major attraction. For example, the p/e ratios of the ordinary shares in the Food and Drug Retailers sector are given in the penultimate column of Example 5.1(a). The ratios for the major UK companies range from 16.9 to 49.1, and because they are ratios, it makes sense to ask questions such as 'Why is Morrison's p/e ratio almost three times that of Tesco?'

What does the p/e ratio tell us? That investors are willing to pay 16.9 times last year's reported earnings for Tesco shares compared with 49.1 times Morrison's reported earnings. In some sense, Morrison's earnings could be said to be more expensive, and this could be because they are expected to grow faster than those of Tesco in the future. So the comparison of p/e ratios is an attempt by the investor to use currently available information to find out something about the future expected growth in earnings.

Unfortunately, the expected growth rate in earnings is not the only factor affecting a company's p/e ratio. For example, the p/e ratio will also be affected by the uncertainty surrounding future earnings. Morrison and Tesco could have the same expected growth rate, but the variability (standard deviation) of the predicted earnings growth could be higher for one than for the other, because of a riskier business activity or higher financial leverage, or both. (This is explained further in Chapter 7.) In this particular case, Morrison's very high p/e ratio is primarily because the most recent year's published earnings were extraordinarily low as a result of the exceptional costs of the acquisition of Safeway. This suggests that if the price the market is prepared to pay for the shares is in fact a 'normal' multiple of a 'normal' year's profit, then that price – expressed as a multiple of an exceptionally poor result in one particular year – will be very high.

Before we go on to discuss how the p/e ratio can be used to estimate expected holding period return, several problems which arise when using the p/e ratio must be mentioned. First, the latest year-ends for companies that are to be compared may well be several months apart. For example, in November 2005 the p/e ratio for Company *X* could be determined from earnings for the year ended 30 September 2005 whereas the p/e ratio for Company *Y* could be calculated from earnings for the year ended 31 December 2004, nine months earlier. The earnings for the more recent period could be higher because of inflation, reducing *X*'s p/e ratio relative to *Y*'s. Alternatively 2004 could have been a recessionary period for the industry in question or for the economy as a whole, with many companies' earnings unduly depressed, giving Y an unnaturally high P/E ratio relative to X.

This cyclicality problem can be emphasised in another way. Suppose Crumbly Cakes plc trades on a p/e of 5, and when its latest earnings are announced, these are declared to be only half those of the previous year. However, the company confidently expects to recover from the downturn and return rapidly to its normal earnings level. Because of this, the share price (which reflects the market's unchanged view of the company's long-term prospects) does not fall, so the p/e ratio doubles to 10; and yet Crumbly Cakes has not become a high-growth company overnight. An extreme example is when a company declares zero earnings. Should it have an infinitely high p/e ratio? In short, two companies could have high p/e ratios for completely different reasons, one because it is a high-growth share and the other because of a sudden – but believed temporary – plunge in profits.

One way of getting round this problem is to 'normalise' the earnings, that is, to calculate the p/e ratio using an earnings figure that the analyst believes to be a reflection of the trend in earnings rather than the peaks or troughs. Another method of avoiding this problem is to compare industries rather than to compare individual companies. This is because companies in an industry are subject to the same economic cycles and not infrequently have the same year end. Also, because the p/e ratios are weighted averages for each industry, anomalies caused by individual companies are reduced. However, a major problem with the p/e ratio, which affects its use in any context, is the quality of the earnings per share figure. First, as already noted, the eps is an accounting approximation to an economic determination of income. It is difficult to know how well accounting earnings reflect the economic profits of a company, and how a historic earnings figure can indicate the extent to which future cash flows will be affected by economic changes. Economic profits, by definition, can only be assessed by taking a view of the future. Accounting profits are the results of calculations based on conventions in which such a view plays only a limited part, and which also depend on personal judgements.

Second, different companies use different accounting practices to arrive at their earnings figures, and so the earnings and hence p/e ratios might not be comparable. For example, suppose that two companies are identical in all respects save in their method of accounting for depreciation of fixed assets. Depreciation is simply an accounting device for charging the cost of an asset against the profits earned in more than one accounting period; it has no effect on the company's cash flows or on its aggregate profits over the life of the asset. Nor do different accounting policies for depreciation affect the companies' tax payments, as tax allowances for capital expenditure are fixed independently of a company's own accounting policy. So two companies that are identical in all respects except for their depreciation policies should have the same market value, but as their different depreciation policies result in their reporting different eps figures, their shares should trade on different p/e ratios.

Despite these fundamental problems with both the meaning of the p/e ratio and its use for comparative purposes, the p/e ratio is still commonly used as a summary measure by investors and their advisers, as evidenced by its appearance, however qualified, in the *Financial Times*.

This attitude towards the p/e ratio's usefulness lies behind the accounting profession's concern over providing clear guidelines for the calculation of eps – eps is forecast by analysts as a key means of estimating future share prices.

Box 5.6 More than meets the eye in 'like-for-like' sales figures

In Box 5.4 we saw how Wm Morrison issued new shares to acquire the competing business of Safeway in a takeover which was first announced in January 2003. As the extract below from a *Financial Times* article of 1 November 2002 shows, Safeway had been regarded as a takeover target for some time. In this article the then chief executive officer of Safeway complained about what he saw as the unfair way in which analysts used the idea of 'like-for-like' sales to calculate both the underlying profitability and the growth potential of super-markets – two key factors in assessing an appropriate p/e ratio and hence a value for the company.

Safeway chief launches attack on City analysts

Carlos Criado-Perez, Safeway chief executive, has accused city analysts of wilfully misrepresenting the supermarket group's trading performance.

In an interview with the *Financial Times*, Mr Criado-Perez said he thought the City was ignoring the truth about Britain's fourth biggest supermarket chain because it was interested in fuelling rumours of a takeover bid for the group.

Safeway shares have fallen sharply as sales growth has slowed. It has been touted as a break-up opportunity for financial buyers or a target for Wal-Mart, Mr Criado-Perez's former employer.

His criticism centres on the analysis of like-for-like sales figures – the measure that strips out the effects on trading of new store openings. His comments are likely to be seen as an attack on the whole system of valuing retail groups.

Like-for-like figures are the most market sensitive information released by retailers. However, they are not covered by any accounting standards and many retailers have routinely used the regulatory gap to present the figures in as flattering a light as possible.

Mr Criado-Perez, who joined Safeway three years ago, said a proper analysis of its performance showed it was performing in line with Tesco and J. Sainsbury.

'Analysts chose to ignore elements that are very important in what is called like-for-like,' said Mr Criado-Perez. 'It makes the measure just a nonsense.' In the supermarket sector, he said, Tesco and Sainsbury both included stores with extra selling space added.

'When all you look at is like-for-like we are totally handicapped by that measure. But most analysts chose to ignore that. I feel angry about this,' he said. Interest in Safeway was driven 'either by things that sell newspapers or things that make more excitement in the stock market'.

Mr Criado-Perez said he still had two years to go in his five-year campaign to rebuild Safeway. 'There is a lot more pain we need to carry in our back pack. But I didn't come to Safeway to sell it or do a takeover. I believe there is a successful independent future.'

Estimate of holding period return

We saw in Chapter 2 that the two most important measures describing a share were its expected holding period return and its risk, measured by the standard deviation of the expected returns. The two summary measures discussed so far, gross dividend yield and the p/e ratio, have not proved of much help in estimating either risk or return. We have to find alternative means.

The simplest way to express a one-period expected holding period return is

Expected holding period return $= \dfrac{D_1 + (P_1 - P_0)}{P_0}$

(5.1)

where D_1 is the expected income to be received during the period, P_1 the expected value of the security at the end of the period, and P_0 the cost of the security.

If the share is held for n periods or years, in each of which income is received, as we saw in Chapter 2 (Example 2.4), equation 5.1 could be rearranged and extended to give

$$P_0 = \dfrac{D_1}{(1+r)^1} + \dfrac{D_2}{(1+r)^2} + \dfrac{D_3}{(1+r)^3} + \ldots \dfrac{D_n}{(1+r)^n} + \dfrac{P_n}{(1+r)^n}$$

(5.2)

where P_n is the value of the security at the end of n years and D_i the income to be received in the ith year. But since P_n could be viewed as the present value of the future dividends from year $(n + 1)$ onwards, the equation for P_0 could be written as the present value of *all* future dividends.

$$P_0 = \dfrac{D_1}{(1+r)^1} + \dfrac{D_2}{(1+r)^2} + \dfrac{D_3}{(1+r)^3} + \ldots \dfrac{D_n}{(1+r)^n} + \ldots$$

(5.3)

In equation 5.1, r represents the one-period expected holding period return. In equations 5.2 and 5.3, r is the expected annual rate of return whatever the holding period. But we saw in Chapter 3 when considering the redemption yield for gilts that there was no reason why it should be the same in year 1 as it is in year n, since interest rates and required rates of return will vary according to time. So equation 5.2, for example, should be written:

$$P_0 = \dfrac{D_1}{(1+r_1)^1} + \dfrac{D_2}{(1+r_2)^2} + \dfrac{D_3}{(1+r_3)^3} + \ldots \dfrac{D_n + P_n}{(1+r_n)^n}$$

(5.4)

However, in the case of ordinary shares, the future P_n and all the future D_i are uncertain and must be estimated. So the approximation inherent in using r for all years instead of R_i is less important (since r must of necessity be a rough estimate) than in the case of bonds, where the D_i and P_n (at redemption) are known for certain and an accurate assessment of the implicit r_i can be made.

Dividend valuation models

Equations 5.2 and 5.3 are known as dividend valuation models for shares. How can we use them to estimate the expected annual holding period return r?

If we look at equation 5.2, we know P_0 and so we need to estimate the dividend stream $D_1, D_2 \ldots D_n$ expected during the holding period and the end-of-period share price P_n. The holding period can be as long or short as desired and will probably reflect how far into the future the investor feels able to predict the cash flows D_i. This type of dividend valuation model, given in equation 5.2, is known as a finite horizon model, since we consider the cash flows up to a finite horizon in year n.

The dividend stream must be estimated from knowledge of the company's dividend policy and from expectations concerning the company's future prospects, since dividends ultimately depend on the cash flows generated by the company. Even if the company has a declared dividend policy, for example a constant percentage growth or constant payout ratio, it will not be able to maintain this policy if insufficient cash flow is generated.

How can P_n be estimated? It represents the company's share price in n years' time, and its value will depend on market views at time n of all future cash flows attributable to the share beyond year n. Since it is impossible to estimate with any degree of accuracy such a share price P_n, one method would be to estimate the p/e ratio and earnings per share n years hence, because

$$P_n = eps_n \times \frac{P_n}{eps_n}$$

so

$$P_n = eps_n \times PE_n$$

Despite the problems inherent in the use of p/e ratios and earnings per share which were discussed earlier, investors may feel more confident about estimating the future earnings per share figure and p/e ratio than their product, the future share price P_n.

The p/e ratio of a company will vary according to expected future growth and risk, and the stage of the economic cycle prevailing. These must be considered from the point of view of year n. The eps figure in year n will also depend on many factors, including the company, the industry and the economy as a whole.

Earnings forecasts now form part of the equity analyst's key function. Earnings per share are forecast two years out, plus a long-run forecast, so that these numbers can be plugged into a dividend valuation model. Information providers such as Reuters and Bloomberg publish these analyst forecasts from which a 'consensus' forecast can be derived. However, earnings are affected by accounting conventions and policies, which makes them more difficult to estimate than cash flows.

As a result of the problems of estimating P_n, either directly or indirectly through PE_n and eps_n, the alternative method for estimating r is to use equation 5.3, obviating the need to estimate P_n. In other words, we consider an infinite horizon model. Since it would be a Herculean task to estimate with any degree of accuracy all the future dividends the company will ever pay, simplifying assumptions concerning future dividends must be made. For example, if it can be assumed that all future dividends will grow by a constant percentage g, equation 5.3 becomes

$$P_0 = \frac{D_1}{(1+r)^1} + \frac{D_1(1+g)}{(1+r)^2} + \frac{D_1(1+g)^2}{(1+r)^3} + \ldots \frac{D_1(1+g)^{n-1}}{(1+r)^n} + \ldots \tag{5.5}$$

As each term after the first in equation 5.5 is calculated by multiplying the previous term by a fixed ratio:

$$\frac{(1+g)}{(1+r)}$$

equation 5.5 is a geometric series. As long as r is greater than g, we can use the standard formula for the sum to infinity of an infinite geometric series to simplify equation 5.5 to

$$P_0 = \frac{D_1}{r-g} \tag{5.6}$$

And we can rearrange this as

$$r = \frac{D_1}{P_0} + g \tag{5.7a}$$

or

$$r = \frac{D_0(1+g)}{P_0} + g \tag{5.7b}$$

This is known as *Gordon's dividend growth model*.

To use Gordon's growth model, all that is needed to estimate r is last year's dividend D_0, the current share price P_0 and the expected dividend growth rate g. For example, if we use the data on Tesco in Example 5.1, assuming a current share price of 321¾p, and a rate of 11% for the annual growth in dividends, we find from equation 5.7b that

$$r = \frac{7.56(1+0.11)}{321.75} + 0.11$$

$r = 13.61\%$

If we look at the data on Sainsbury in Example 5.4, we see immediately one of the big problems associated with Gordon's growth model in practice: what value would we take for g, given that there is no clear historical trend in Sainsbury's dividend?

The assumption of constant growth in expected dividends is a simplification of reality. Problems can arise using this model if the company currently does not pay any dividends but is expected to do so in the future, or if it is a small, rapidly growing company with a high dividend growth rate, say 25% per annum. We can see that, in equation 5.6, if g is large, r will not be much greater than g, and so the denominator will be very small. As the value of g approaches that of r, the share price will approach infinity and will become hypersensitive to small changes or inaccuracies in either g or r. Since in practice we do not see companies with infinitely large market values traded on the stock exchange, we can assume that such very high growth rates will not last for ever. This leads us to another form of finite horizon model.

$$P_0 = \frac{D_1}{(1+r)} + \frac{D_2}{(1+r)^2} + \ldots + \frac{D_n}{(1+r)^n} + \frac{D_n(1+g^*)}{(R-g^*)(1+r)^n} \tag{5.8}$$

where dividends are expected to grow at an annual rate of g until year n, after which the annual growth rate will be a smaller rate g^*. The final term of equation 5.8 is the value, as at year n, of all dividends beyond year n, discounted back to the present day at rate r.

An alternative way of using the dividend valuation model is to transform it into an earnings model. Since the dividend payout ratio for period K_i is defined to be

$$K_i = \frac{D_i}{eps_i}$$

we can write

$$D_i = K_i eps_i$$

and equation 5.3 becomes

$$P_0 = \frac{K_1 eps_1}{(1+r)} + \frac{K_2 eps_2}{(1+r)^2} + \frac{K_3 eps_3}{(1+r)^3} + \ldots + \frac{K_n eps_n}{(1+r)^n} + \ldots \tag{5.9}$$

This type of model allows the investor to forecast future earnings instead of dividends. However, some assumption still has to be made about dividends. It could be assumed, for example, that the dividend payout ratio will remain constant, say at $K = 40\%$. So equation 5.9 would become

$$P_0 = \frac{K.eps_1}{(1+r)} + \frac{K.eps_2}{(1+r)^2} + \frac{K.eps_3}{(1+r)^3} + \ldots + \frac{K.eps_n}{(1+r)^n} + \ldots \tag{5.10}$$

where $K = 0.4$.

If the same simplification of constant growth is applied to earnings as was applied to dividends, we get

$$P_0 = \frac{K.eps_0(1+g)}{(1+r)} + \frac{K.eps_0(1+g)^2}{(1+r)^2} + \frac{K.eps_0(1+g)^3}{(1+r)^3} + \ldots + \frac{K.eps_0(1+g)^n}{(1+r)^n}$$

$$P_0 = \frac{K.eps_0(1+g)}{r-g} \tag{5.11a}$$

or

$$P_0 = \frac{K.eps_1}{r-g} \tag{5.11b}$$

This is the same as Gordon's growth model, since the assumption of constant growth g in earnings and a constant dividend payout ratio must also give constant growth g in dividends. So the constant growth version of the dividend valuation model can be used either by forecasting dividend growth explicitly or by forecasting both earnings growth and a dividend payout ratio. Unfortunately, as we saw earlier, the evidence is that there is in practice no such trend in earnings growth, which means that the simplifying assumption of constant earnings growth (as well as constant dividend payout and constant dividend growth) must be viewed as an approximation to reality.

Before we leave the earnings version of the dividend valuation model, let us take a further look at equation 5.11a. If we divide both sides by eps_0, we get

$$PE_0 = \frac{K(1+g)}{r-g} \tag{5.12}$$

The left-hand side of the equation is simply the p/e ratio, and the equation, written in this way, allows us to see exactly which factors affect the p/e ratio. The term g reflects earnings growth, K shows how much of earnings is paid out as dividends, and r, the holding period return, gives an idea of the riskiness of the share (since the higher the required r, the riskier must be the share). We can now see that the p/e ratio will be greater the higher the earnings growth, but also the higher the dividend payout ratio and the lower the risk of the share. So despite the limitations of the model, it does allow us an insight into the factors that are likely to affect the value of a share.

All the above methods of estimating holding period return, whether from finite or infinite horizon models, require estimates of future dividends, earnings or share prices. Each model is based on the same fundamental equation for the value of a share, equation 5.2, which simply states that the current value of a share, given by its share price, must be equal to all the future cash flows attributable to that share discounted by a rate of return that reflects its risk.

Figure 5.2 shows a small sample of the large number of different share valuation models that can be derived from equation 5.2. The choice of model will depend on investors' subjective estimates of which variables they can best forecast, for example dividends or earnings, growth rates or future p/e ratios.

Free cash flow valuation model

There are potentially serious flaws in all of the valuation models we have discussed so far, over and above the obvious fact that they are based on more or less subjective judgments about the course of future events. Models based on earnings forecasts are exposed to the criticism that the published earnings of a company are based not so much on objectively determined cash flow as on the application of various accounting concepts (including that of accruals) which significantly affect both the timing and the amount of profit reported. Models based on expected dividends ignore the fact that the level of dividend

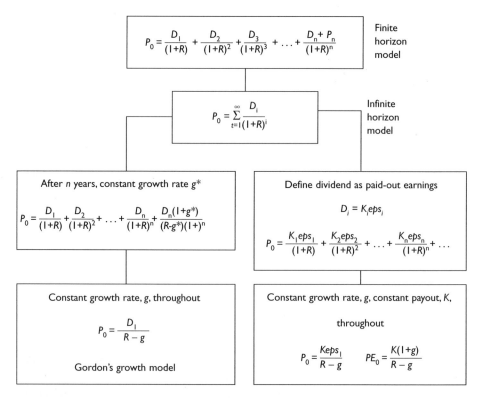

Figure 5.2 Alternative share valuation models

is subject to arbitrary manipulation by management and is therefore not a reliable measure of the underlying value of the company's cash-generating potential.

Critics of both models argue that as investment in shares (as in anything else) is essentially a matter of 'cash out, cash in', the only truly rigorous way of valuing shares is to estimate the company's future ability to generate cash that is potentially freely available for distribution to the shareholders, and to discount that future 'free' cash flow at a rate equivalent to the expected return on equity. The process of estimating free cash flow is a complex one and lies outside the scope of this book, but the basic principle is to adjust future expected after-tax operating profits (calculated in accordance with normal accounting principles) to take account of (a) non-cash items such as depreciation, (b) changes in working capital (debtors, creditors and stocks) which affect the company's cash flow but are not directly reflected in its reported profit, and (c) net cash invested in fixed assets to maintain and expand the company's productive capacity.

Although this approach is theoretically more rigorous than the models based on dividends or reported earnings, it still takes as its starting point the figures reported (or to be reported) in the accounts, so it cannot entirely escape the criticism that it is vulnerable to the subjective influences of accounting policies. However, it is generally agreed that – so long as sufficient information is available to make reliable estimates of the inputs into the model – it offers a more realistic basis for a valuation process which, it has to be remembered, is more of an art than a science.

RISK

Whichever model is employed to estimate the expected holding period return r, it is useful to think of r as being made up of a basic return required on a riskless investment, say a very short-term gilt, plus a premium for the uncertainty of the future cash flows. Thus we can write

$$r = R_F + \text{risk premium} \tag{5.13}$$

where R_F is the riskless return, which will change as interest rates and hence required rates of return change. This serves as a useful check to any estimates of r: the figure calculated should always be greater than the redemption yield on gilts because of the greater risk of holding shares.

The expected holding period return on a share cannot be calculated in isolation from its risk, which can be measured, as we saw in Chapter 2, by the standard deviation of the probability distribution of returns. How should the standard deviation be assessed? Strictly, we need to estimate not only all expected future cash flows but the probability distributions of all such flows. This would in practice be a daunting task. Luckily, the risks attached to particular shares have been found in general not to change rapidly over time, so that risk can usually be fairly adequately measured by the standard deviation of past returns.

Thus, given the expected holding period return and risk of two shares being considered as potential investments, investors can use their attitude to risk and return (utility function) to decide which share they prefer. However, if investors are considering adding a share to their existing portfolio, knowledge of the expected holding period return and standard deviation of each share is not sufficient for them to make their decision. Each share cannot be considered in isolation but must be considered in the light of its impact on the portfolio as a whole. This portfolio approach will be considered in more detail in Chapters 6 and 7, where we will see that the return on a share reflects only that part of the risk of the share which is common to the stock market as a whole. The remaining risk on any share can be avoided through diversification, by holding a portfolio of shares.

This portfolio approach will also provide an alternative method of deriving the required rate of return of a share and of measuring its risk, known as the Capital Asset Pricing Model, or CAPM. This method is based on a measurement of each share's risk and return relative to the stock market as a whole, and offers a different, but not incompatible, means of estimating r from that offered by any of the versions of the dividend valuation model. It would thus be prudent to estimate the expected holding period return using one of the valuation models described above and the CAPM in Chapter 7. If the returns obtained from the two methods are approximately the same, more reliance can be placed on the estimates.

FUNDAMENTAL ANALYSIS

In practice, many investment analysts do not use these share valuation models to determine the expected holding period return but prefer to use them instead to derive estimates of what P_0 should be, given an assumed holding period return r. This is done to determine what they believe to be the 'intrinsic' value of the share. As we shall see in Chapter 12, trying to determine an intrinsic value for a share presupposes that the current share price is in some sense an incorrect value for the share and that the analyst is better able to value the share than the market as a whole. These assumptions are clear in the following definition of intrinsic value: 'the value that the security ought to have and will have when other investors have the same insight and knowledge as the analyst'. If the intrinsic value obtained from a share valuation model exceeds the actual price, the share is considered undervalued and it is recommended for purchase. If the intrinsic value is less than the actual price, the share is considered overvalued and recommended for sale. This method of valuing shares, known as *fundamental analysis*, is the most common form of investment analysis. Estimates of future earnings and dividends are still needed, but the intrinsic present value is the unknown as opposed to r.

Estimates of r must therefore be found from other sources. In practice, either the CAPM estimate of the required rate of return, described in Chapter 7, is used, or an arbitrary risk premium, based on intuition or judgement, is added to the current yield on gilts, as in equation 5.13, or it is assumed that the average rate of return achieved over some holding period in the past is a good estimate of the future holding period return. However, the historic rate is unlikely to be a good estimate of the future rate, as earnings and dividends will of course change over time; so, more importantly, will the riskless rate of return, even if the risk premium remains constant.

The basic premise for fundamental analysis is that the market is not 100 per cent efficient – in the sense that some of the securities sold on it will later prove to have been wrongly priced, and that greater returns than expected given the shares' risk can be made from spotting such share bargains. Far more time is spent by analysts on such activities as fundamental analysis than on calculating the 'fair' rate of return on a share bought at a fair price, given the risk. As we shall see in Chapter 12, which introduces such commonly used investment techniques as technical and fundamental analysis, there is a real question whether, for the small investor, such activities are likely to be worthwhile.

SUMMARY

This chapter has looked at ordinary shares or equities. We first described ordinary shares as listed in the *Financial Times*. We then looked at how shares are listed on the stock market, either as an introduction, initial public offering or IPO, or placing. We also looked at how shares can be issued as a secondary equity offering, or SEO, and considered in particular the rights issue method, which gives rights to the new shares to existing shareholders, pro rata to their existing holdings.

This chapter also examined ways in which ordinary shares are valued. The major characteristics of ordinary shares and their methods of issue were described as well as measures used to compare equities – dividend yield, dividend cover and p/e ratios. The advantages and disadvantages of these measures were discussed, the major disadvantage being that none of them provided an estimate of total holding period return. The chapter then described how the expected holding period return could be derived from estimates of future earnings or dividends, this model being known as the dividend valuation model. All the different versions of the basic model require subjective estimates of future income from the share and these estimates depend on a multitude of factors, including company, industry and general economic influences. The major use to which these valuation models are put in practice is not, in fact, to determine expected holding period return, but, assuming a value for r, to determine an intrinsic share price to see whether the share is undervalued or overvalued and should be bought or sold.

REVIEW EXERCISES

1. Look in the *Financial Times,* and visit the website of the London stock exchange (www.londonstockexchange.com), for up-to-date information on companies in the Food and Drug Retailers and Food Producers sectors (see Example 5.1).
   a. How has the composition of the sectors changed since the dates shown in Example 5.1? Have any of the companies listed in Example 5.1 disappeared from the listing, and have any new companies appeared? Try to find out the reasons for any such changes. (Tip: visit the 'Investor Relations' section of the companies' websites)
   b. With regard to those companies that are still listed, what changes do you notice in:
      i. their market capitalisations?
      ii. their dividend yields?
      iii. their p/e ratios, both in absolute terms and relative to each other?
   Again, visit the companies' websites, and use press and any other available information sources, to find explanations for any changes you observe.
2. Blue Boxes plc has just announced a rights issue of 2 million new shares. The pre-announcement share price was 145p and the rights issue involves the issue of one new share (for every existing three shares held) at a price of 115p.
   a. What will be the theoretical ex rights price and the value of the rights?
   b. How much new money will be raised (before transaction costs)? What will those transaction costs consist of?

    c. Mr Brown already holds 3000 shares. Outline the main alternatives available to him. Can Mr Brown simply do nothing without suffering a financial loss?

3. Advanced Electronics plc expects to pay a dividend of 20p per share at the end of the present year. The dividend is then expected to grow at a 15% rate for three years, then at a 10% rate for the next three years, and at 5% for ever more.

    a. What value would you place on the share if a 9% rate of return were required?

    b. Would your valuation change if you expected to hold the shares for only three years?

4. The reverse yield gap is the gross redemption yield on gilts less the gross dividend yield on shares. If the gross redemption yield is, say, 10% and the gross dividend 4%, the reverse yield gap is 6%. What does this imply about the return on equity relative to the return on gilts?

5. Bloomington's Boutiques plc has 76,000,000 shares in issue. The current share price is 313p. It paid a dividend of 8p per share last year and is expected to pay 8.8p per share next year on forecast earnings of £11.7 million after tax.

    a. Assuming the dividend is expected to grow at a constant rate in perpetuity, what is the return on the share?

    b. Calculate the expected earnings per share, p/e ratio, dividend yield and dividend cover. Explain the significance of each of these ratios.

    c. Suppose the current redemption yield on gilts is around 4%. This is higher than Bloomington's dividend yield. Does this mean that Bloomington's can raise share capital more cheaply than the UK government can borrow in the gilt market?

    d. How would you decide whether to buy Bloomington shares? What further information would you require?

6. How would you expect inflation to affect the value of your equity investments?

7. Visit the 'Investor Relations' section of Tesco's website and update the information shown in Example 5.4. In the text we came to the conclusion that on the basis of the data for 2000–05, Gordon's dividend growth model offered a reasonable guide to the expected rate of return on Tesco's shares. How (if at all) would you modify that conclusion in the light of Tesco's subsequent earnings and dividend record?

Sample answers to these review exercises can be found on the companion website.

APPENDIX 5.1: UK TAXATION OF INVESTMENT INCOME

UK companies pay corporation tax on their profits, which are calculated after deduction of interest paid on bonds and on other debts for borrowed money. Dividends are paid out of after-tax profits. This disparity in the tax treatment of interest and dividends means that when they are received by the investor, the dividends have been paid out of income that has already been taxed, whereas interest has been paid out of pre-tax income. To tax the investor equally on both types of investment income would therefore result in dividend income being taxed twice and interest income once only, although some classes of investor (notably, approved pension funds, which are discussed in more detail in Chapter 10) are exempt from all tax on investment income. Without some further corrective provision, such a *classical tax system* would involve economic *double taxation* of the same income: once as part of the company's profits, and then again in the shareholders' hands when the company pays dividends. Different countries use different methods to mitigate this potential for double taxation. The UK's current rules, which are described below, represent a combination of what are known as the *imputation system* and the *schedular system*. The rules were altered significantly in 1999 with the abolition of *advance corporation tax* (*ACT* for short).

Until 1999, when UK companies paid dividends, they were also required to pay an amount of ACT, latterly at the rate of 25% of the net dividend paid. The ACT paid could then be credited against the company's mainstream corporation tax liability against its profits when that became due. Shareholders, meanwhile, were taxed on the gross dividend amount, i.e. the sum of the actual dividend receipt and the ACT amount, but were entitled to a tax credit equal to the ACT. So in giving shareholders a tax credit for the ACT, the system 'imputed' some of the company's tax liability to the shareholders. The tax credit could be used against the shareholder's own liability to tax on the dividend. Exempt investors, such as approved pension funds, could reclaim the tax credit from the Inland Revenue. So could an individual investor who had no liability, whether because of the lack of any other income or by virtue of investing through a tax-advantaged 'wrapper' such as a *Personal Equity Plan* (*PEP*).

In 1999, ACT was abolished. UK dividends still attract a tax credit (albeit at a lower rate than previously – see below for details), but the credit is in a sense only notional since it no longer bears any relation to the corporation tax paid by the company. In addition, the tax credit is generally no longer repayable. Pension funds (and other tax exempt investors, such as charities) lost the entitlement to repayable tax credit on 6 April 1999. The right to repayment was retained for shares held in PEPs and *ISAs (Individual Savings Accounts)*, but only until 5 April 2004. Only non-portfolio corporate investors in certain overseas jurisdictions now have any right to repayment of the tax credit, and even then only a fraction of the credit is repayable.

In effect, therefore, the tax credit just reduces the applicable tax rate for those investors paying tax on UK dividends. At present, the tax credit is equal to one-ninth of the net dividend, or one-tenth of the gross amount. The basic rate of tax on UK dividend income is 10%, which compares with 22% for other income. So for basic-rate taxpayers the credit fully satisfies their tax liability: they have no more to pay. For higher-rate taxpayers, the marginal rate of tax on UK dividends is 32.5% (instead of 40%, which is the rate for other income): after taking account of the credit, the remaining liability is 22.5% of the dividend or 25% of the net dividend received.

The tax situation becomes more complex when we consider that just as the total return on an investment includes not only dividend or interest income but also the capital gain or loss on disposal, so also the tax implications of realised capital gains or losses need to be taken into account. An individual investor pays capital gains tax (CGT) on such gains at his or her marginal rate of income tax, which for a higher rate taxpayer is 40% – substantially more than the effective 25% rate paid on dividend income. For most investors, however, the impact of CGT is mitigated by taper relief, which provides that once an asset has been held for three years, the chargeable percentage goes down annually by 5% of 40% (i.e. by 2% of the gain itself) to a minimum of 24% after 10 years. So the effective rate of CGT for a higher rate taxpayer is 24% after a holding period of ten years or more. However there is also an annual exempt amount, £8800 for 2006–07.

A specially accelerated rate of taper relief, which reduces the effective CGT rate to 20% after just one year and to 10% after two years or more, applies in the special case where the asset on which the gain is realised qualifies not as a portfolio asset but as a business asset. The criteria for recognition as a business asset are rather complex, and in the case of a security listed on the main market will usually be satisfied only if the investor is either an employee of the company in question or controls more than 5 per cent of the voting capital. But interestingly, as the AIM market is technically not classified as a recognised stock exchange for the narrow purpose of Inland Revenue rules, all shares traded on that market are classified as business assets, regardless of the investor's individual circumstances, so that CGT on AIM shares is 10% for any investor who has held the shares for at least two years.

APPENDIX 5.2: FTSE SHARE INDICES

FT industrial ordinary shares index

The first important UK share index was the Financial Times Industrial Ordinary Shares Index, started in 1935 and based on 30 major industrial shares. Similarly, in the United States, the most famous index was the Dow Jones Industrial Average, also based on 30 shares, although originally based on 11 shares when it started in 1884. The limited size of these indices is a function of their age, since both predate the era of electronic computers, and this limitation has led to their replacement by indices on larger samples of shares as technology has advanced.

The original purpose of both indices was to measure market movements over the short term and not to provide any estimates of market return (they ignore dividends) or to act as benchmark portfolios. Their object was to help predict market trends and to provide measures of market volatility. To this end, the FT 30 (as it is known) was constructed as an unweighted geometric mean. All the shares in the index were given equal weighting and the same emphasis was given to a 10 per cent increase in price to 55p of a share quoted at 50p as to a 10 per cent increase in price to 550p for a 500p share. The relative sizes of the companies and the relative share prices were ignored. What counted was the percentage change in share price: that is to say, the share's volatility.

FTSE indices

Since 1984, when the FTSE 100 index was introduced as the London market's 'flagship' index, the system of indices has evolved. This now encompasses the whole of the Main Market as follows:

○ The FTSE 100 Index includes the top 100 share issues in descending order of market capitalisation, accounting typically for about 83 per cent by value of the total market.

○ The FTSE 250 Index includes the next 250 issues in descending order of market capitalisation, accounting typically for about 13–14 per cent of the total market.
○ The FTSE 100 and FTSE 250 indices make up the FTSE 350 Index.
○ The FTSE SmallCap Index is designed to include in descending order of market capitalisation sufficient of those companies too small to qualify for the FTSE 350 Index until a point is reached where the FTSE 350 and FTSE SmallCap indices combined account for about 98 per cent by value of the total market. This is quite difficult to manage very precisely in practice; what happens is that the review panel periodically set a market capitalisation level which roughly corresponds to the 98 per cent cut-off point, and all companies that meet that level are included. About 300–350 companies comprise the FTSE SmallCap Index.

The FTSE 350 and the FTSE SmallCap indices together make up the FTSE All-Share Index. The FTSE 250 and 350 indices were originally developed as a compromise between the FTSE 100 (which does not necessarily reflect the movements of the market as a whole, but is small enough to permit continuous recalculation during trading) and the FTSE All-Share Index, which is fully representative of the market but has too many constituents to permit continuous recalculation.

Companies that are too small to be included in the FTSE SmallCap Index are included in the FTSE Fledgling Index.

All of these indices apart from the FTSE 100 are on two alternative bases – with and without investment trust companies (ITCs). ITCs, which are described in more detail in Chapter 10, are companies that invest their capital in portfolios of other companies' shares, so to include them in the index calculation creates risks of (a) double-counting (to the extent that they invest in shares in their own section of the index) and (b) distortion (to the extent that they invest elsewhere in the UK indices or overseas).

Calculating returns on indices

When calculating returns on indices rather than on individual shares, care should be taken as to whether the returns on the index include dividends or not. Many commonly quoted share indices around the world do not include dividends, because they are being quoted to show short-term price movements and not longer-term returns.

The exclusion of dividends means that indices have to be adjusted before they can be used as true benchmarks for portfolio managers, although major index providers do produce returns with and without dividends.

This Appendix ends with some additional notes on the flagship i   the FTSE 100.

FTSE 100 Index

The most popular index today is the FTSE 100 Index, which w
in response to the need for an index enabling futures and o[
linked to the performance of the UK stock market. The FT 3(
too few shares in it to be representative of the market as a wh
long history, these shares tended to over-represent the ma[

under-represent the services sector which had grown in the 1970s and 1980s. It was also a geometric index and thus did not reflect a portfolio that could realistically be held by investors. This is vital for an index to which futures contracts are linked since, as we shall see in Chapter 8, in order for the futures contract to be correctly priced, investors must be able to carry out arbitrage when there is mispricing, for instance, by buying futures and selling the underlying shares when the futures contract is cheap.

The FTSE 100 Index is a weighted arithmetic index of the top 100 share issues in terms of market capitalisation; it thus mirrors a real portfolio, includes both service and manufacturing companies, and yet has sufficiently few shares to be calculable on a continuous basis.

The FTSE 100 Index was first calculated on 3 January 1984, when it was given the base level of 1000. It has functioned on every working day since then with the exception of 16 October 1987, when a hurricane in the south of England prevented sufficient market-makers from getting to work. Coincidentally, the biggest one-day fall in the index was just four days later, when it fell by 12.22 per cent; and its biggest one-day rise was on the next day, by 7.89 per cent. The highest level the FTSE 100 has reached to date was on the last trading day of 1999 when it reached 6930.2.

Constituents of the FTSE 100 are reviewed quarterly in March, June, September and December. Changes to the constituents can be prompted by new listings on the exchange, mergers and acquisitions, or (most commonly) an increase or decrease in a company's capitalisation relative to the market. A reserve list of the five largest companies outside the index is maintained, so that if a company falls out between quarterly review dates (for instance, because of a takeover), the first reserve automatically joins the index immediately.

Most importantly, although membership of the index is based strictly on market capitalisation, that is, on a company's entire ordinary share capital valued at the current market price, the weightings of the constituent companies in the index itself are *free float weighted*. The free float in a company's shares is the proportion of the share capital which is considered to be 'investable', that is, potentially available for trading on the open market at any time, and specifically excludes known large long-term holdings, such as the family holdings of the Sainsbury and Weston families in J Sainsbury and in Associated British Foods respectively.

A neat example of the workings of the reserve list and of the free float system was provided on 8 March 2004, when Wm Morrison completed its takeover of another FTSE 100 constituent, Safeway. The latter was immediately removed from the FTSE 100 index, to be replaced by the then first reserve, the Chilean mining company Antofagasta, which was included with an *investability weighting* of just 40 per cent, as some 60 per cent of the shares were in the hands of the chairman and his family and therefore considered unlikely to be available for trading.

A comparison of the largest five companies at the launch in 1984 and 20 years later is indicative of the changes in the market and in the economy at large. Table 5.1 lists the largest five companies at the launch in January 1984 and 20 years later.

Predictably, oil continues to figure heavily, but the key differences are:

> replacement of two traditional manufacturing companies with just one
> ceutical company

○ the appearance of two banks, and of a mobile telephone company (which did not even exist in 1984), in the top five.

Table 5.1 The largest five companies in the FTSE 100 Index

a) At the launch in January 1984

Rank	Company	Market value (£m)
1	British Petroleum Co.	7,401
2	Shell Transport & Trading Co.	6,365
3	General Electric Co.	4,915
4	Imperial Chemical Industries	3,917
5	Marks & Spencer	2,829

b) 20 years later

Rank	Company	Market value (£m)
1	BP	100,518
2	Vodafone Group	97,429
3	HSBC	97,035
4	GlaxoSmithKline	76,361
5	Royal Bank of Scotland Group	48,598

APPENDIX 5.3: FTSE ACTUARIES SHARE INDICES BY INDUSTRY CLASSIFICATION

FTSE Actuaries Share Indices
Produced in conjunction with the Faculty and Institute of Actuaries

UK series
www.ft.com/equities

	£ Stlg Nov 29	Day's chge%	Euro Index	£ Stlg Nov 28	£ Stlg Nov 27	Year ago	Actual yield%	Cover	P/E ratio	Xd. adj. yld	Total Return
FTSE 100 (100)	6084.4	+1.0	7028.2	6025.9	6050.1	5423.2	3.13	2.46	12.96	191.44	3414.55
FTSE 250 (250)	10666.1	+1.6	12320.7	10497.2	10493.6	8327.9	2.12	2.45	19.24	218.37	5774.81
FTSE 250 ex Inv Co (220)	11174.4	+1.5	12907.8	11005.9	11002.6	8620.8	2.19	2.51	18.22	234.52	6122.36
FTSE 350 (350)	3189.0	+1.1	3683.7	3155.4	3166.0	2788.4	2.98	2.46	13.63	94.92	3648.94
FTSE 350 ex Inv Co (320)	3179.4	+1.0	3672.6	3146.4	3157.2	2779.9	3.00	2.47	13.49	95.31	1868.78
FTSE 350 Higher Yield (99)	3882.3	+0.7	4484.5	3853.7	3865.7	3497.7	3.88	1.99	12.94	138.91	4083.44
FTSE 350 Lower Yield (251)	2428.9	+1.4	2805.7	2394.9	2403.6	2051.6	2.00	3.46	14.47	55.97	2091.15
FTSE SmallCap (328)	3647.85	+0.3	4213.73	3635.65	3674.23	3200.60	1.83	1.43	38.33	67.04	3918.78
FTSE SmallCap ex Inv Co (232)	3532.60	-0.1	4080.60	3537.58	3574.58	3108.91	2.11	1.48	31.94	73.29	3884.57
FTSE All-Share (678)	3134.48	+1.0	3620.72	3102.17	3113.33	2741.05	2.94	2.44	13.92	92.14	3635.88
FTSE All-Share ex Inv Co (552)	3121.40	+1.0	3605.62	3089.91	3100.99	2729.73	2.98	2.45	13.67	92.90	1866.82
FTSE All-Share ex Multinationals (611)	1207.32	+0.9	1155.87	1196.29	1200.52	973.64	2.89	2.22	15.60	33.46	1511.71
FTSE Fledgling (247)	4183.51	+0.3	4832.49	4170.64	4193.56	3583.86	1.70	†	†	65.82	5839.37
FTSE Fledgling ex Inv Co (149)	5138.95	+0.5	5936.03	5114.48	5138.69	4399.94	1.81	†	†	82.37	7082.40
FTSE All-Small (575)	2430.11	+0.3	2807.08	2422.07	2446.05	2125.09	1.81	1.12	49.35	43.78	3346.34
FTSE All-Small ex Inv Co (381)	2491.07	-0.1	2877.50	2492.89	2517.40	2185.67	2.08	1.12	43.04	50.41	3478.79
FTSE AIM All-Share (1156)	1017.6	-0.2	1175.5	1019.3	1027.3	1012.0	0.52	†	†	7.30	991.11
FTSE Sector Indices											
Oil & Gas (20)	7654.12	+0.4	8841.47	7620.88	7616.21	7546.01	3.10	3.09	10.42	239.05	4503.24
Oil & Gas Producers (14)	7374.77	+0.4	8518.79	7345.63	7342.08	7483.51	3.14	3.10	10.30	232.57	4467.12
Oil Equipment & Services (6)	10294.18	+3.1	11891.08	9983.93	9890.82	-	1.02	2.30	42.68	102.05	6119.46
Basic Materials (21)	4686.60	+1.3	5413.61	4626.80	4685.10	3657.02	1.71	5.84	10.03	83.17	3654.18
Chemicals (8)	3610.30	+2.3	4170.36	3529.94	3592.23	2705.29	2.15	2.44	19.09	63.80	2488.27
Forestry & Paper (0)											
Industrial Metals (1)	2407.22	+0.4	2780.64	2397.59	2404.81	1342.02	1.50	4.15	16.06	37.31	1749.40
Mining (12)	14679.45	+1.2	16956.62	14499.37	14681.23	11189.62	1.68	6.29	9.49	262.06	5957.14
Industrials (141)	2706.24	+1.6	3126.05	2663.42	2678.21	2186.35	2.27	2.37	18.62	62.23	2111.76
Construction & Materials (15)	5330.61	+1.3	6157.53	5264.73	5261.16	4059.19	2.33	2.44	17.55	112.56	3893.97
Aerospace & Defence (11)	2972.11	+1.6	3433.16	2924.11	2950.90	2709.57	2.41	2.62	15.85	61.04	2469.74
General Industrials (6)	2354.23	+1.7	2719.44	2313.99	2310.76	-	3.73	2.05	13.08	90.53	1860.95
Electronic & Electrical Equipment (14)	2420.58	+0.7	2796.07	2404.04	2416.22	1882.89	1.67	3.26	18.31	40.85	1693.64
Industrial Engineering (18)	3439.50	+1.4	3973.05	3393.53	3419.36	2788.35	2.33	2.61	16.46	86.18	3106.32
Industrial Transportation (12)	4146.85	+0.8	4790.13	4115.00	4106.41	2925.53	3.08	1.29	25.07	115.57	2429.31
Support Services (65)	4205.52	+1.9	4857.90	4128.10	4152.75	3516.21	1.99	2.24	22.41	94.13	3362.28

Consumer Goods (48)	8109.25	+0.7	9367.21	8048.98	8023.36	7139.98	2.48	14.03	227.75	4244.39
Automobiles & Parts (2)	5060.42	+1.8	5845.42	4970.23	4973.67	5087.64	1.74	13.41	206.67	3701.52
Beverages (5)	6058.23	+0.1	6998.02	6051.08	6041.30	5327.69	2.01	16.85	180.54	3202.05
Food Producers (14)	4232.24	+0.9	4888.77	4193.11	4190.04	3918.56	3.26	10.02	119.41	2645.79
Household Goods (14)	6525.41	+1.4	7537.67	6434.63	6449.08	—	3.18	14.76	135.15	3477.43
Leisure Goods (6)	3247.25	-0.6	3750.98	3268.43	3272.43	3108.89	3.01	80.00†	93.25	2026.66
Personal Goods (4)	6812.76	+0.4	7869.60	6788.52	6853.13	5102.15	1.65	26.64	112.14	3619.37
Tobacco (3)	18908.33	-0.7	21841.52	18781.46	18528.50	16819.83	3.29	15.79	623.14	7925.83
Health Care (31)	6544.90	-2.7	7560.19	6370.71	6364.73	6444.86	2.74	16.31	191.13	3261.69
Health Care Equipment & Services (13)	3458.64	+0.7	3995.17	3434.48	3435.66	3618.33	1.00	27.31	39.51	2530.80
Pharmaceuticals & Biotechnology (18)	9119.93	+2.8	10534.68	8867.83	8858.90	8879.16	2.84	15.98	274.21	3979.32
Consumer Services (114)	3855.26	+1.0	4453.32	3817.39	3826.89	3202.11	2.27	20.07	90.41	2639.85
Food & Drug Retailers (6)	4574.56	+0.6	5284.20	4547.93	4569.54	3485.34	2.31	27.33	101.64	3905.74
General Retailers (41)	2633.00	+0.2	3041.45	2627.95	2638.53	2112.40	2.52	27.44	79.55	2125.61
Media (33)	4186.59	+1.4	4836.04	4130.18	4130.08	3822.10	2.30	21.21	100.87	1864.84
Travel & Leisure (34)	5981.94	+1.6	6909.90	5887.26	5898.17	4722.99	2.01	13.31	105.38	4268.83
Telecommunications (9)	2361.11	+1.1	2727.38	2334.63	2343.28	2048.10	4.34	20.90	97.14	1567.01
Fixed Line Telecommunications (7)	3457.56	+0.6	3993.92	3437.75	3444.65	2777.55	3.95	15.00	91.83	1977.99
Mobile Telecommunications (2)	3048.83	+1.4	3521.79	3008.19	3021.32	—	4.50	24.62	139.54	1775.00
Utilities (13)	6547.56	+0.4	7563.26	6522.07	6573.97	4802.41	3.18	17.46	197.24	4462.61
Electricity (6)	7138.57	+0.7	8245.95	7086.27	7168.40	5141.31	2.22	14.29	186.41	6033.00
Gas Water & Multutilities (7)	6050.81	+0.1	6989.45	6043.02	6074.54	4503.00	3.90	21.00	201.64	4140.11
Financials (240)	7087.00	+0.9	8186.38	7026.68	7071.34	6063.03	3.44	12.97	243.94	4416.94
Banks (9)	10767.73	+0.6	12438.08	10706.68	10793.95	9662.00	4.28	12.00	456.68	5229.59
Nonlife Insurance (18)	1475.30	+1.5	1704.15	1453.49	1451.59	1167.33	3.26	19.13	48.52	1668.59
Life Insurance/Assurance (9)	5951.29	+1.9	6874.49	5841.35	5890.33	5024.31	2.96	15.76	189.14	3675.27
Real Estate (45)	5396.05	......	6233.12	5397.04	5402.32	3824.03	1.76	8.14	85.89	4416.89
General Financial (33)	6494.13	+1.0	7501.55	6430.68	6435.59	4766.51	2.09	14.64	139.46	4909.47
Equity Investment Instruments (126)	5626.65	+1.9	6499.49	5519.37	5541.71	4917.11	1.41	47.44	81.50	2412.67
Non Financials (438)	3049.44	+1.1	3522.48	3015.69	3023.01	2689.69	2.73	14.36	83.67	3119.66
Technology (41)	439.35	+2.7	507.51	427.87	427.13	432.75	1.31	22.83	5.49	478.14
Software & Computer Services (30)	554.76	+3.1	640.82	537.84	538.64	526.29	1.55	27.13	8.29	609.71
Technology Hardware & Equipment (11)	380.85	+1.1	439.93	376.64	371.88	421.14	0.50	13.60	14.75	1.99	401.75

■ **Hourly movements**

	8.03	9.00	10.00	11.00	12.00	13.00	14.00	15.00	16.00	High/day	Low/day
FTSE 100	6058.4	6046.9	6072.7	6069.0	6062.0	6053.3	6067.7	6080.1	6089.5	6098.6	6046.7
FTSE 250	10590.4	10597.5	10631.6	10652.0	10640.5	10614.8	10626.2	10657.0	10657.0	10670.6	10575.3
FTSE SmallCap	3639.00	3645.58	3644.82	3645.91	3644.34	3642.47	3641.37	3644.17	3644.98	3648.47	3639.00
FTSE All-Share	3120.02	3115.62	3127.98	3127.31	3123.86	3119.00	3125.52	3132.19	3136.21	3140.32	3115.62

Time of FTSE 100 Day's high: 16:06:45 Day's low: 9:00:15. FTSE 100 2005/06 High: 6254.9 (16/11/2006) Low: 5506.8 (14/06/2006)
Time of FTSE All-Share Day's high: 16:07:00 Day's low: 9:00:00. FTSE All-Share 2005/06 High: 3216.53 (16/11/2006) Low: 2797.98 (14/06/2006)

Further information is available on http://www.ftse.com. © FTSE International Limited 2006. All Rights reserved. "FTSE", "FT-SE" and "Footsie" are trade marks of the London Stock Exchange and The Financial Times and are used by FTSE International under licence. † Sector P/E ratios greater than 80 are not shown. or changes to FTSE Fledgling Index constituents please refer to www.ftse.com/indexchanges. ‡ Values are negative.

Source: *Financial Times*, 30 November 2006

6 Portfolio theory

CHAPTER CONTENTS

Learning objectives for this chapter

After studying this chapter you should be able to

- ○ describe how diversification can improve the risk–return characteristics of a portfolio
- ○ calculate the risk and return of a two-asset portfolio under varying assumptions about correlation between the portfolio components
- ○ calculate an optimum combination of a two-asset portfolio
- ○ describe the role of individual indifference curves in the application of portfolio theory
- ○ appreciate the practical implications and the theoretical and practical problems surrounding portfolio theory.

INTRODUCTION

In Chapter 2 we discussed how to measure the two most important characteristics of a security – its return and its risk. We decided that, for each security, investors would compare the expected return from a range of probable outcomes with the risk of the security, as measured by the standard deviation S of the probability distribution of returns. If the probability distribution of returns on a security or portfolio is normal then S is a sufficient measure of the risk of that security or of a portfolio of securities. Investors would only need to consider the expected returns and standard deviations when they are choosing securities for their investment portfolios. The assumption that investors are assumed to be risk averse means that they would choose those securities that offered the most return for a given level of risk or the least risk for a given level of return.

However, we did not consider the effects of combining securities; we looked only at how to compare individual securities with each other as mutually exclusive potential investments. We did get an indication that combining securities into a portfolio might be a sensible way of reducing risk, in particular, by the process of pooling independent investments. The problem with securities is that their returns are not entirely independent of each other. If the FTSE 100 Share Index goes up, an investor will expect most company shares to show an upward trend, whether or not they are in the FTSE 100 Share Index. There are market-wide influences, such as changes in interest rates or tax rates, which will affect the prices of all securities to a greater or lesser extent. We shall see in this chapter that, despite this common market influence, our basic assumptions about investor behaviour mean that it still makes sense to combine securities even if their returns are to some extent correlated with each other. In fact, it is irrational to invest all one's resources in a single security, as one can almost always achieve a higher return for a given level of risk by holding a portfolio with at least two securities.

Portfolio theory offers a framework for investors to decide which of the myriad possible combinations of available securities or portfolios give them the best return for each level of risk. They can then choose the portfolio that has the optimal risk–return relationship for their own circumstances. For example, an individual investing his own money on the stock market might prefer a high-risk, high-return portfolio whereas a pension fund manager might choose a lower-return portfolio because she feels unable to accept more than a certain level of risk. Each investor will end up with what is known as an efficient portfolio (which provides the highest possible return for the level of risk incurred); but each investor will probably hold a different efficient portfolio according to his or her individual risk–return preference.

We shall see in Chapter 7 that by making some additional assumptions (such as the availability of a risk-free interest rate for investing and borrowing) we can construct a model known as the *Capital Asset Pricing Model (CAPM)*. This is simpler to use than portfolio theory, but the additional assumptions of the CAPM (pronounced 'Cap M') are in some respects less realistic than those underlying the basic portfolio theory. For this reason, portfolio theory is still widely used. We shall see in Chapter 11 that because there is no world-wide risk-free security, CAPM cannot easily be extended to an international framework. However, portfolio theory does offer us a suitable model for determining optimal international portfolios.

This chapter now goes on to explain how the results of portfolio theory were obtained and what they mean in practical terms to the investor. Some mathematics is involved, since you need it to understand implications of the theories, but we try to keep this to a minimum. The first part of the chapter considers a portfolio of only two securities and shows how investors can decide on a combination of these two securities which is optimal for them in the context of their own particular utility function. The result is then extended to portfolios containing any number of securities. Finally, the chapter discusses the general implications of portfolio theory for investment and the problems inherent in its use. Chapter 11 will explore the international dimension of portfolio theory.

RISK AND RETURN OF TWO-SECURITY PORTFOLIOS

In order to understand how combining securities into a portfolio can reduce risk, we shall start by looking at the simplest case, where two securities are combined, and then extend the results to any size of portfolio. Suppose an investor is considering securities A and B, which have the characteristics detailed in Example 6.1.

Example 6.1 Return and risk of securities A and B

Probability	% return	
	Security A	Security B
0.25	20	45
0.50	10	25
0.25	0	5
1.00		
Expected return	$E(R_A)= 10\%$	$E(R_B)= 25\%$
Variance of returns	$V_A = 50\%$	$V_B = 200\%$
Standard deviation of returns	$S_A = 7.1\%$	$S_B = 14.1\%$

The investor could choose which of these securities he (or she) prefers if he calculates the utility he would derive from the risk–return relationships of each security. But what would happen if, instead of buying only A or only B, he bought both A and B in proportions W_A and W_B such that $W_A + W_B = 1$?

If we call the resulting combination of A and B, portfolio P, what can we say about P's expected return and risk? First, the expected return of P is given by the equation:

$$E(R_P) = W_A E(R_A) + W_B E(R_B) \tag{6.1}$$

That is, the expected return $E(R_P)$ of portfolio P is the weighted average of the expected returns of $E(R_A)$ and $E(R_B)$ of A and B respectively. For example, if the investor had half his portfolio in A and the other half in B, we would have $W_A = W_B = 0.5$. So,

$$E(R_P) = 0.5E(R_A) + 0.5E(R_B)$$
$$= (0.5 \times 0.10) + (0.5 \times 0.25)$$
$$= 0.175$$
$$E(R_P) = 17.5\%$$

But what can we say about the *risk* of the portfolio? Would this also be simply the weighted average of the risks of the constituent securities? The answer is that it depends on the extent to which those returns are correlated with each other.

The variance of any security, as we saw in Chapter 2, can be written as

$$V_i = S_i^2 = \sum_{i=1}^{i=n} (R_i - E(R))^2 p(R_i) \tag{6.2}$$

which is just the sum of the probabilities of each return (R_i) multiplied by the square of the difference of each R_i, from the expected return $E(R)$. In exactly the same way, the variance of the portfolio return can be written

$$V_P = S_P^2 = \sum_{i=1}^{i=n} (R_{pi} - E(R_p))^2 p(R_{pi}) \tag{6.3}$$

If we allow for the fact that P is made up of $W_A A + W_B B$ in equation 6.3 we get

$$V_P = W_A^2 S_A^2 + W_B^2 S_B^2 + 2\, W_A W_B \sum_{i=1}^{i=n} (R_{Ai} - E(R_A))(R_{Bi} - E(R_B))p(R_i) \tag{6.4}$$

How we get this equation is explained in more detail in Appendix 6.1. This expression for the variance of P is not quite the weighted average of the variances of A and B, S_A^2 and S_B^2, as was the case for the expected return of P. In equation 6.4, the expression for the variance of P includes a complex-looking term at the end which describes the relationship between the returns of A and B. This term (excluding the proportions $2W_1 W_2$) is called the *covariance* of returns of A and B and is written COV_{AB}:

$$COV_{AB} = \sum_{i=1}^{i=n} (R_{Ai} - E(R_A))(R_{Bi} - E(R_B))p(R_i) \tag{6.5}$$

What does the covariance of returns between two securities mean? In each state of the world (expressed by different probabilities $p(R_i)$), the return is compared with its expected value for both securities. If the return on A is greater than its expected value and the return on B in the same state of the world is greater than its expected value, then that term in COV_{AB} will be positive, and similarly, if the returns on A and B are less than their expected values in the same state of the world. So, if two securities do well (better than expected) or badly (worse than expected) in the same state of the world, they will have a positive covariance. If the returns of A and B are on different sides of the expected value, for each state of the world, covariance will be negative. If they are sometimes on the same side of the expected value and sometimes on different sides, the signs will cancel out to give a covariance of around zero.

The correlation coefficient, written $CORR_{AB}$, is defined to be the covariance divided by the product of the standard deviations of A and B:

$$CORR_{AB} = \frac{COV_{AB}}{S_A S_B} \tag{6.6}$$

The reason for bothering to define the correlation coefficient is that it can only take values of between -1 and +1. It is merely another way of expressing the amount of covariance between the returns of two securities which has the property that it can never be greater than 1. If two shares' returns move together in perfect unison, they will have a correlation coefficient of +1. If they move in exactly opposite directions, $CORR_{AB}$ will be equal to -1. If they are totally independent, so that if they move together it is by chance, they will have $CORR_{AB} = 0$.

Rearranging equation 6.6 to give

$$COV_{AB} = CORR_{AB} S_A S_B$$

and substituting for COV_{AB} in equation 6.4, we get

$$V_P = W_A^2 S_A^2 + W_B^2 S_B^2 + 2 W_A W_B S_A S_B CORR_{AB} \tag{6.7a}$$

This equation is also known as the portfolio risk equation, in this case for two assets A and B. Equation 6.7a can also be written as:

$$V_P = W^2_A V_A + W^2_B V_B + 2W_A W_B S_A S_B CORR_{AB} \tag{6.7b}$$

Taking the positive square root gives us an equation for the standard deviation of a portfolio of two assets, A and B:

$$S_p = | \sqrt{W^2_A V_A + W^2_B V_B + 2W_A W_B S_A S_B CORR_{AB}} |$$

Where $| |$ signifies the modulus or positive, in this case, square root.

The detailed proofs of the equations for the variance, standard deviation and covariance and correlation coefficients of a two-security portfolio are set out in Appendix 6.1. We now investigate the effect of different values of $CORR_{AB}$ on the risk of the portfolio returns. We begin by considering three special cases: perfect positive correlation, perfect negative correlation and zero correlation. In each case we evaluate the portfolio risk equation in theoretical terms for the chosen value of the correlation coefficient. Throughout the rest of this chapter our examples are based on the two securities A and B in Example 6.1.

We shall end this section with some observations based on the actual types of correlation most commonly observed in the world of real investments.

Perfectly correlated securities

First, let us look at the securities A and B described in Example 6.1. We can calculate the covariance and hence the correlation coefficient from the information we have:

$$COV_{AB} = \sum_{i=1}^{i=n} (R_{Ai} - E(R_A))(R_{Bi} - E(R_B))p(R_i)$$

$$= (0.20 - 0.10)(0.45 - 0.25) \times 0.25 + (0.10 - 0.10)$$
$$(0.25 - 0.25) \times 0.50 + (0 - 0.10)(0.05 - 0.25) \times 0.25$$

$$= 0.10 \times 0.20 \times 0.25 + 0 + -0.10 \times -0.20 \times 0.25$$

$$COV_{AB} = 0.01$$

So
$$CORR_{AB} = \frac{COV_{AB}}{S_A S_B} = \frac{0.01}{0.071 \times 0.141}$$

$$CORR_{AB} = 1.0$$

This means that the returns of the two securities move perfectly in unison, which was intuitively obvious from looking at Example 6.1.

Substituting $CORR_{AB} + 1$ into equation 6.7 we get:

$$V_P = W_A^2 S_A^2 + W_B^2 S_B^2 + 2W_A W_B S_A S_B$$

The right-hand side of this equation is a standard expression of the form

$$x^2 + y^2 + 2xy$$

which is another way of writing the 'perfect square'

$$(x + y)^2$$

Substituting $W_A S_A$ for x and $W_B S_B$ for y, we can write

$$V_P = (W_A S_A + W_B S_B)^2$$

And as the standard deviation of the portfolio return is the square root of the variance, we can then write

$$S_P = W_A S_A + W_B S_B$$

In other words, if the returns on two securities are perfectly positively correlated, the risk of the portfolio return, as measured by its standard deviation, is just the weighted average of the risks of the constituent securities' returns.

As we have already seen, the expected return on portfolios consisting of shares A and B is also the weighted average of the returns of the two shares. This means that there is a linear relationship between the risk and return of all possible portfolios consisting solely of shares A and B in differing combinations. This is illustrated in Figure 6.1.

To sum up our conclusion on perfect positive correlation: the bad news is that where the returns on two shares are perfectly positively correlated, no advantage is to be gained

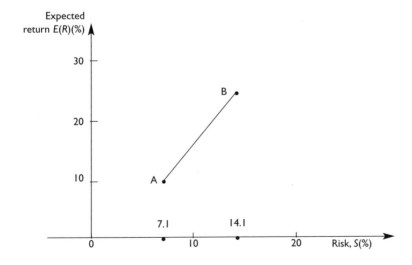

Figure 6.1 Risk and return of two perfectly positively correlated securities

from combining them, as there is no element of risk reduction by means of diversification. The good news is that $CORR_{AB}$ is less than 1, so the right-hand side of the portfolio risk equation must be *less* than the weighted average and so the risk of the portfolio must be *less* than the weighted average of the risk of its constituent securities.

This means that, provided two securities are not perfectly positively correlated, some advantage in the form of an improved risk–return relationship can be gained by combining them. We continue now by looking at the other two special cases, where $CORR_{AB} = 0$ and where $CORR_{AB} = -1$.

Unrelated securities

Suppose that $CORR_{AB} = 0$. In this case the two securities A and B are completely unrelated. They are not affected by any common factors and any similar movements will occur by chance. Equation 6.7 becomes:

$$V_P = W_A^2 S_A^2 + W_B^2 S_B^2$$

The significance of this is that for any combination of two securities, the portfolio risk will be lower if the returns on the two securities are entirely uncorrelated than if they are at all positively correlated, because even the smallest positive value for the correlation coefficient would reinstate a positive third term in the portfolio risk equation.

As we discussed in Chapter 2, events such as houses being destroyed or the deaths of individuals are generally unrelated to each other, so any two insurance policies covering such eventualities would have returns which were uncorrelated: that is, have a zero correlation coefficient. We can now quantify the benefits that can be gained from the pooling of risks. Suppose that an investor holds equal amounts of two investments which have the same expected return and the same risk S_i, and have zero correlation with each other. The variance of the portfolio return will be

$$V_P = 0.5^2 S_i^2 + 0.5^2 S_i^2 = 0.25 S_i^2 + 0.25 S_i^2 = 0.5 S_i^2 = \frac{S_i^2}{2}$$

and the risk or standard deviation of portfolio returns can be calculated by taking the square roots of both sides:

$$S_P = \frac{S_i}{\sqrt{2}}$$

This conclusion can be generalised to show that the risk of holding a portfolio of n uncorrelated investments, each with risk S_i, would be given by the equation

$$S_P = \frac{S_i}{\sqrt{n}}$$

In short, the portfolio risk would steadily decrease by a factor equal to the square root of n. The independence between events insured, reflected in zero correlation coefficients, represents the rationale behind the principle of pooling. Unfortunately, the returns of financial securities are not independent in the same way. Before we consider the actual correlations between market securities, we need to look at the third special case, that of perfectly negative correlation.

Perfectly negatively correlated securities

The returns on two securities in a portfolio are said to be perfectly negatively correlated if they move in exactly the opposite direction from each other. We showed how securities A and B in Example 6.1 were perfectly positively correlated. Suppose we now reverse B's returns to be 5% when A's are 20%, and 45% when A yields 0%. This would mean that B underperformed when A outperformed and vice versa. In this example, A's and B's returns would be perfectly negatively correlated.

The portfolio variance equation for this case is almost the same as for the case of perfectly positively correlated securities, except that the third term becomes negative as follows:

$$V_P = W_A^2 S_A^2 + W_B^2 S_B^2 - 2W_A W_B S_A S_B$$

The right-hand side of this equation is similarly a standard expression of the form

$$x^2 + y^2 - 2xy$$

which is another way of writing the 'perfect square'

$$(x - y)^2$$

Substituting $W_A S_A$ for x and $W_B S_B$ for y, we can write

$$V_P = (W_A S_A - W_B S_B)^2$$

And as the standard deviation of the portfolio return is the *positive* square root of the variance, this becomes:

$$S_P = W_A S_A - W_B S_B$$

This case offers not only the prospect of less risk (for all possible combinations) than the uncorrelated portfolio, but also a unique combination where the risk is eliminated completely, where

$$W_A S_A = W_B S_B \tag{6.8}$$

so that

$$S_P = 0$$

We can find this combination quite easily by rearranging equation 6.8 so that it reads

$$\frac{W_A}{W_B} = \frac{S_B}{S_A}$$

In other words, if two perfectly negatively correlated securities are combined in inverse proportion to the ratio of the standard deviations of their respective returns, the resulting portfolio will yield a constant return and hence be riskless.

This combination can be calculated for our sample securities A and B in Example 6.1 by substituting the actual values for their standard deviations:

$$\frac{W_A}{W_B} = \frac{14.14}{7.07}$$

So

$$\frac{W_A}{W_B} = \frac{2}{1}$$

and as

$$W_A + W_B = 1$$

it follows that $W_A = {}^2/_3$ and $W_B = {}^1/_3$.

This combination is shown as point Q in Figure 6.2. Point P is the equally weighted portfolio of A and B.

Small positive correlation between securities

What implications do the above results have for investors? If they can find two securities that are not perfectly positively correlated, that is, that have $CORR_{AB} < +1$, then they can combine them into a portfolio and expect to get the weighted average of their expected returns with less than the weighted average of their risk. In other words, they will have reduced risk without sacrificing an equivalent amount of return. Provided two securities do not have $CORR_{AB} = +1$, investors can always do better than just holding one risky security.

The less correlated the returns of two securities, the more investors can reduce risk by combining them. If they can find two securities that have $CORR_{AB} = -1$, they can reduce their risk to zero while still getting a weighted average of expected returns.

Unfortunately, the returns on risky securities are not usually negatively correlated or even entirely independent of each other, since they are subject in varying degrees to at least some common influences. The correlation coefficient between two securities will probably be small and positive, for example $CORR_{AB} = 0.3$.

If we substitute a value of 0.3 for $CORR_{AB}$ into the portfolio risk equation (6.7), we get

$$V_P = W_A^2 S_A^2 + W_B^2 S_B^2 + (2W_A W_B S_A S_B \times 0.3)$$

This is not a perfect square and so gives a curve of possible combinations rather than a straight line. This curve is shown in Figure 6.3 with A taken, as before, to have an expected return of 10% and a standard deviation of 7.07% and B an expected return of 25% and a standard deviation of 14.14%. If, for example, we assume equal proportions of A and B are held, we still get

$$E(R_P) = (0.5 \times 0.10) + (0.5 \times 0.25)$$

$$E(R_P) = 17.5\%$$

but risk is reduced to less than the weighted average:

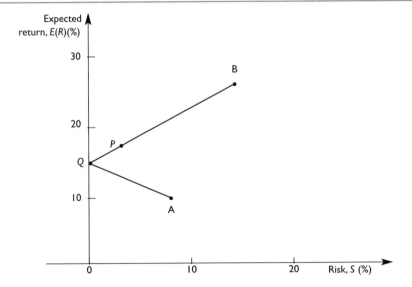

Figure 6.2 Risk and return of two perfectly negatively correlated securities

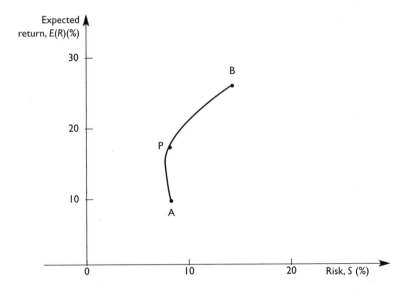

Figure 6.3 Risk and return of two securities with correlation = +0.3

$$V(R_p) = (0.25 \times 0.005) + (0.25 \times 0.02) + (2 \times 0.5 \times 0.5 \times 0.0707 \times 0.1414 \times 0.03)$$
$$V(R_p) = 0.0064$$
$$\boldsymbol{S(R_p) = 8.0\%}$$

This particular combination is shown as *P* on Figure 6.3.

We have shown how investors can reduce risk by holding different combinations of two securities instead of just one on its own. It is likely that the securities they will consider will provide a curve of possible combinations as in Figure 6.3. Investors then have to decide which point on the curve AB they prefer: that is, which portfolio maximises their utility. To show how this can be done we first discuss how indifference curves can be derived for each investor from knowledge of his or her utility function. These indifference curves will then be used to determine the investor's optimal portfolio.

INDIFFERENCE CURVES

As we saw in Chapter 2, each investor has a utility function which quantifies his or her attitude towards risk and return at different levels of wealth. If we consider a risk-averse investor, her utility of wealth function may describe a curve as in Figure 6.4.

This curve implies a certain trade-off relationship between risk and expected return. For example, we found in Chapter 2 that Mr Black could use his utility function as a tool to distinguish between two securities that offered different expected returns and different risks.

An investor's risk–return trade-off can be expressed more directly by using the utility function to determine the investor's indifference curves. For example, if the investor requires 10% t return for accepting a standard deviation of 12%, and for an additional 3% of standard deviation he requires an additional 4% of return, we can draw his 'indifference curve' – by identifying the risk–return combinations between which he is indifferent. From the above information we know that he is indifferent between a security which offers 10% expected return and has $S = 12\%$ and a security which offers 14% and has S 3% higher at 15%. If we plot these and other points on a graph we will get a curve as shown in Figure 6.5, assuming that the additional return required by the investor for taking on more risk increases more rapidly than the risk itself.

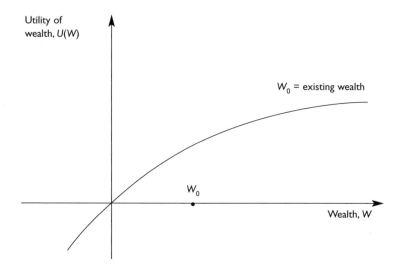

Figure 6.4 Utility curve of a risk-averse investor

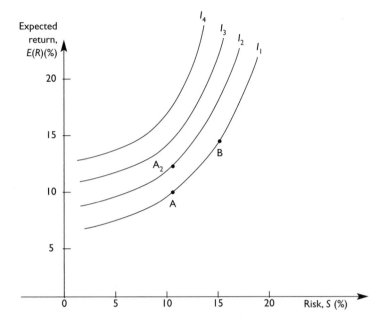

Figure 6.5 Indifference curves of a risk-averse investor

We know that I_1 will curve upwards because we are dealing with a risk-averse investor who requires an increasing amount of extra return for taking on each unit of additional risk, as measured by standard deviation. Each investor will have a different curve, although of the same basic shape, because each investor will differ in how he or she trades off risk against return.

In fact each investor will have an infinite number of parallel indifference curves I_1, I_2, I_3 and so on. They will be indifferent between any point on I_1, say between A and B, but they will not be indifferent between a point on I_1 and a point on I_2. Compare points A and A_2. Both have the same risk but A_2 has a higher expected return. Investors will obviously prefer to be on I_2 rather than I_1. In fact, they will aim to get on the highest possible indifference curve, in order to maximise their utility, but once there they will be indifferent to where they are on that curve.

Once the utility function of an investor is known, his or her indifference curves can be drawn. These curves are used in deciding which portfolio the investor should choose to maximise his or her utility. Suppose that A and B are the only securities the investor can buy and that they are as described in Figure 6.6 with $CORR_{AB} = 0.3$. Any combination of securities A and B lies on the curve AB. If the investor plots his indifference curves on this graph, as is done in Figure 6.6, we can see that he would prefer B to A because B is on a higher indifference curve than A.

We also know that the investor could do better than buying A on its own by investing in P, a portfolio containing equal quantities of A and B and with a standard deviation of 8%, as described earlier. However, the investor can maximise his utility in this case by investing in portfolio R. At this point, one of his indifference curves is a tangent to the curve AB. This is the highest indifference curve he can reach (any higher one would not touch a portfolio on AB) so R must be his optimal portfolio.

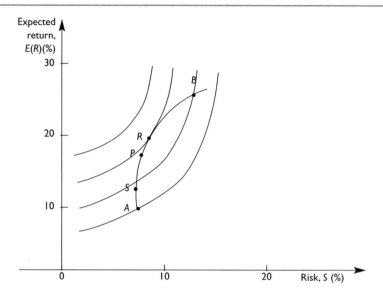

Figure 6.6 Optimal combination of two securities with correlation = +0.3

So unless securities *A* and *B* are perfectly positively correlated, an investor can always reach a higher indifference curve and hence achieve greater expected utility (a better risk–return trade-off) by investing in a combination of the two securities.

MINIMISING PORTFOLIO RISK

As long as the correlation coefficient of the returns on two securities is less than +1, any combination of them into a portfolio will have a risk that is less than the weighted average of their individual risks, while still having an expected return exactly equal to the weighted average of their individual returns. But we have also seen that if the correlation coefficient is sufficiently low, some combinations of the two securities will have a risk that is not only lower than their weighted average but is also lower than the risk of the less risky of the two assets on its own. In such a case, as the risk–return line makes its way up from *A* to *B*, it starts by curving left towards the y-axis before changing direction and heading off to *B*. The point where this curve comes closest to the y-axis represents the unique combination of *A* and *B* that has a lower portfolio risk than any other possible combination. How can we find this point? Specifically, how much of *B* do we have to add to *A* in order to achieve maximum risk reduction?

The slope of the curve at this point is vertical, which means that the rate of change in risk, in relation to a change in return, is momentarily zero. We shall use differential calculus to find this point, but first we have to give some thought to the labelling and calibration of the vertical y-axis. In all our equations so far, the y-axis has represented return, but return does not figure anywhere in the portfolio risk equation, and anyway we want to find the turning point of the risk–return curve not in terms of return but in terms of portfolio weightings. The solution to this is that as the portfolio return is a strict linear function of the portfolio weightings, all we need to do is to redefine the y-axis as the proportion of Y in the portfolio, and recalibrate it so that the point corresponding to the expected return on A is zero and the point corresponding to the expected return on B has the value $+1$.

The next step is to eliminate the complication of having two proportions W_A and W_B. As we are trying to find a specific value for W_B we shall replace W_A with $(1 - W_B)$.

The portfolio risk equation, expressed in terms of variances rather than standard deviations, now reads:

$$V_P = W_B^2 V_B + (1 - W_B)^2 V_A + 2W_B (1 - W_B) S_A S_B CORR_{AB}$$

Multiplying the brackets:

$$V_P = W_B^2 V_B + (1 - 2W_B + W_B^2) V_A + (2W_B - 2W_B^2) S_A S_B CORR_{AB}$$

To find the slope of this curve at any point the equation is differentiated with respect to W_B

$$\frac{dV_P}{dW_B} = 2W_B V_B - 2V_A + 2W_B V_A + 2S_A S_B CORR_{AB} - 4W_B S_A S_B CORR_{AB} \qquad (6.9)$$

Note that we are here differentiating x with regard to y, rather than (as more usually) y with regard to x, but the mathematical principle and procedure are the same.

At the turning point of the curve:

$$\frac{dV_P}{dW_B} = 0$$

Equating the portfolio risk equation 6.7 to zero gives:

$$2W_B V_B + 2W_B V_A - 4W_B S_A S_B CORR_{AB} = 2V_A - 2S_A S_B CORR_{AB} \qquad (6.10)$$

Solving this equation for W_B:

$$W_B = \frac{V_A - S_A S_B CORR_{AB}}{V_B + V_A - 2S_A S_B CORR_{AB}} \qquad (6.11)$$

We can now calculate the proportion of B in the minimum risk portfolio of A and B for any value of the correlation coefficient of A and B.

If we keep the correlation coefficient at 0.3 as it was in our earlier example, we have

$$W_B = \frac{50 - (7.07 \times 14.14 \times 0.3)}{200 + 50 - (2 \times 7.07 \times 14.14 \times 0.3)}$$

$$W_B = \frac{50 - 29.99}{200 + 50 - 59.98}$$

$$W_B = \frac{20.01}{190.02} = 0.105$$

So investing 89.5 per cent of available funds in share A and the remaining 10.5 per cent in share B will give a minimum level of risk:

$$V_P = W_A^2 S_A^2 + W_B^2 S_B^2 + 2W_A W_B S_A S_B CORR_{AB}$$

$$V_P = (0.895^2 \times 50) + (0.105^2 \times 200) + (2 \times 7.07 \times 14.14 \times 0.3)$$

$$V_P = 47.89$$

$$S_P = \sqrt{V_P}$$

$$\mathbf{S_P = 6.92}$$

and

$$E(R_P) = 0.895 \times 10.00 + 0.105 \times 25.00$$

$$\mathbf{E(R_P) = 11.58}$$

So the minimum risk portfolio shown in Figure 6.6 as point S has a standard deviation of 6.92% and an expected return of 11.58%.

It is worthwhile repeating this exercise for different coefficients of A and B. We suggest that you start by experimenting with reductions in the correlation coefficient below the level of +0.3, and then see what happens when the correlation coefficient is steadily increased towards +1. What do you notice?

○ As you reduce the correlation coefficient towards its minimum possible value of -1, the optimal proportion of B increases, at a gradually slowing rate, until it reaches a maximum value of exactly one-third at which point the portfolio risk is zero. This is in line with our finding for the perfectly negatively correlated securities, which can be combined into a riskless portfolio if their proportions are the inverse of their respective standard deviations. In the case of A and B, the ratio of their standard deviations is 1:2, so the riskless combination is given by the proportions of 2:1.
○ When you increase the correlation coefficient above the starting point of +0.3, both the optimal proportion of B and the amount of risk reduction achieved by that optimal proportion decrease quite steadily, until at a correlation coefficient of +0.5 no further absolute risk reduction is possible.

We can see why this happens if we look at the numerator in equation 6.11. When this numerator is equal to zero, the optimum proportion of W_B will also be zero. But if

$$V_A - S_A S_B CORR_{AB} = 0$$

then

$$V_A = S_A S_B CORR_{AB}$$

Dividing both sides by S_A gives

$$S_A = S_B CORR_{AB}$$

and

$$\frac{S_A}{S_B} = CORR_{AB}$$

This shows that the critical point is reached when the correlation coefficient is equal to the ratio of the two standard deviations. In the case of shares A and B, the ratio of the shares' standard deviations is exactly 2:1, so the point at which no further absolute reduction in risk can be gained from combining the shares is a correlation coefficient of +0.50. (In theory, further risk reduction could be achieved at higher positive values of the correlation coefficient by holding a minus position in B and investing more than 100 per cent in A, in effect by selling B short and investing the proceeds of sale in A, but this possibility is not explored further here.)

EXTENSION TO A MULTI-ASSET PORTFOLIO

So far we have considered only the simplest possible portfolio, one consisting of just two shares. Although the computations become more complex, the mathematical principles affecting risk and return of portfolios containing more than two shares are just the same.

We start by analysing the familiar portfolio risk equation for a two-security portfolio into its constituent parts. Each of the three terms in the familiar equation

$$V_P = W_A^2 S_A^2 + W_B^2 S_B^2 + 2W_A W_B S_A S_B CORR_{AB} \tag{6.7a}$$

expresses the weighted covariance between two securities in the portfolio, *including the covariance of each security with itself*, which is just another way of looking at its variance. This can be represented in the form of a matrix as in Example 6.2.

Example 6.2 Variance–covariance matrix: two-security portfolio

	Share A (weighting W_A)	Share B (weighting W_B)
Share A (weighting W_A)	$W_A^2 COVAR_{AA} = W_A^2 S_A^2$	$W_A W_B COVAR_{AB}$ $= W_A W_B S_A S_B CORR_{AB}$
Share B (weighting W_B)	$W_A W_B COVAR_{AB}$ $= W_A W_B S_B S_A CORR_{AB}$	$W_B^2 COVAR_{BB} = W_B^2 S_B^2$

The two cross-terms plotting the covariance of A with B are identical with each other so they are combined in the third term of the portfolio risk equation. The total risk of the portfolio is therefore made up of the individual variances of the securities and of their covariances with each other, weighted according to their proportions in the portfolio. Note that the weightings automatically add up to 1 as follows:

$$W_B = (1 - W_A)$$

So

$$W_A^2 + W_B^2 + 2W_A W_B \quad = W_A^2 + (1 - W_A)^2 + 2W_A(1 - W_A)$$
$$= W_A^2 + 1 + W_A^2 - 2W_A + 2W_A - 2W_A^2$$

All the W_A and W_A^2 terms cancel out, leaving a value of 1 for the expression as a whole. We can now extend this to three securities, as shown in Example 6.3.

Example 6.3 Variance–covariance matrix: three-security portfolio

	Share A (weighting W_A)	Share B (weighting W_B)	Share C (weighting W_C)
Share A (weighting W_A)	$W_A^2 COVAR_{AA} =$ $W_A^2 S_A^2$	$W_A W_B COVAR_{AB} =$ $W_A W_B S_A S_B CORR_{AB}$	$W_A W_C COVAR_{AC} =$ $W_A W_C S_A S_C CORR_{AC}$
Share B (weighting W_B)	$W_B W_A COVAR_{AB} =$ $W_B W_A S_B S_A CORR_{AB}$	$W_B^2 COVAR_{BB} =$ $W_B^2 S_B^2$	$W_B W_C COVAR_{BC} =$ $W_B W_C S_B S_C CORR_{BC}$
Share C (weighting W_C)	$W_C W_A COVAR_{CA} =$ $W_C W_A S_C S_A CORR_{CA}$	$W_C W_B COVAR_{CB} =$ $W_C W_B S_C S_{RB} CORR_{CB}$	$W_C^2 COVAR_{CC} =$ $W_C^2 S_C^2$

We can generalise this result for any number of securities if we adopt the convention of using i to denote the lines in the matrix and j the columns, as follows:

(6.12)

$$E(R_P) = \sum_{i=1}^{i=n} W_i E(R_i)$$

$$V_P = \sum_{i=1}^{i=n} W_i^2 S_i^2 + \sum_{i=1}^{i=n} \sum_{j=1}^{j=n} W_i W_j COV_{ij}$$

(6.13)

Equation 6.12 states that, just as in the case of a two-security portfolio, the expected return of the portfolio is the weighted average of the expected returns of the constituent securities. Similarly, equation 6.13 is the sum of the variance and covariance terms COV_{IJ}. Equation 6.13 looks complex because, in order to be able to calculate the variance of the portfolio we have to know not only the variance of each of the n securities, but also the covariance COV_{ij} or correlation coefficient $CORR_{ij}$ of each pair of securities. With the two-security portfolio, we had only one covariance term. With the n security case we have many more covariance terms $((n^2 - n)/2)$.

However complicated the equations for n securities look, the same basic results apply. For example, as with two securities, the risk of any combination of n securities will be less than the weighted average constituent risks unless each pair of securities is perfectly positively correlated, which is an extremely unlikely event. Having decided that a portfolio of securities should always be held rather than one security on its own, we again face the problem of deciding which combination of these n securities is optimal for the investor.

Suppose $n = 10$, that is, the investor has ten securities to choose from. She has a choice

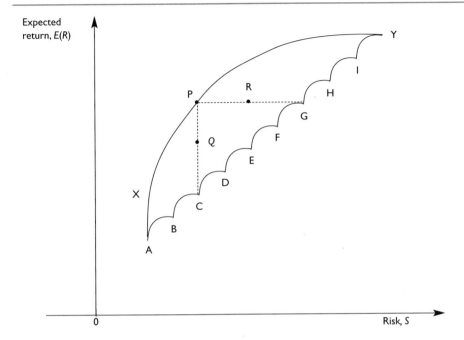

Figure 6.7 Opportunity set with ten securities

of ten different portfolios with only one security in them, 45 portfolios with two securities in them, right up to one portfolio with ten securities in it. In fact she has a choice between 1023 possible portfolio combinations of the securities. The formula for the number of possible combinations of m securities out of a choice of n securities is

$$_nC_m = \frac{n!}{(n-m)! \times m!}$$

where $n!$ ('factorial n') represents the product of all numbers from 1 to n. For example, $6! = 6 \times 5 \times 4 \times 3 \times 2 \times 1 = 720$. Note that by convention $0! = 1$.

The investor also has a virtually infinite choice of variations in the proportions in which she can hold the securities in each possible portfolio. If we draw these possible portfolios on a graph, as in Figure 6.7, we find that they all fit into a shape which resembles an umbrella. This is because each pair of the n securities is likely to have a small positive correlation coefficient and so the possible combinations of each pair of securities will lie on a curve joining the securities. This will give the serrated edge AB, BC and so on. Combinations of more than two securities will similarly lie on curves inside or on the umbrella. All possible portfolios are said to make up the *opportunity set* available to the investor.

The curve XY is called the *efficient frontier*. This means that all the portfolios lying on the curve joining X and Y are efficient in the sense that they are superior to portfolios in the opportunity set. A portfolio can always be found on XY that has a higher return for the same risk or a lower risk for the same return than any other possible portfolio not on XY. For example, in Figure 6.7 P offers a higher expected return than C or Q for the same risk and P offers a lower risk than G or R for the same expected return.

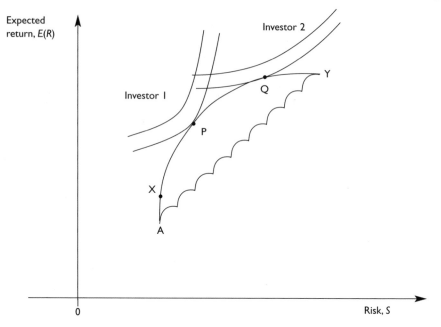

Figure 6.8 Optimal portfolios from ten securities for investors with different utility functions

How do investors choose between efficient portfolios on *XY*? They simply draw their indifference curves and, as in Figure 6.8, choose the point where their indifference curve is a tangent to *XY*. So investor 1 would choose portfolio *P* as optimal while investor 2 would opt for portfolio *Q*.

Investors 1 and 2 would probably choose different portfolios from the same efficient frontier because they no doubt have different attitudes to the relationship between risk and return (although both are risk-averse) which will be reflected in different utility functions and indifference curves. Also, investor 2 might not even have the same opportunity set and efficient frontier as investor 1, because he or she might have different views on the expected returns and risks of the ten securities in question. This would lead him or her to a different umbrella altogether.

PRACTICAL IMPLICATIONS FOR THE INVESTOR

Portfolio theory allows investors to choose the particular combination from the set of all available securities that will maximise their utility. How is this done in practice? For each security, the investor has to estimate its expected return $E(R_i)$, its variance V_i, and its covariance COV_{ij} or correlation coefficient $CORR_{ij}$ with every other security in the set. The investor then plots these figures in a matrix like the one shown in Example 6.4. The weightings corresponding to efficient portfolios can be calculated manually using graphical analysis, calculus or quadratic programming (see Elton et al. 2003 for details) but in practice it is easier and quicker to use a computer. Example 6.5 illustrates how different portfolios could be constructed from three shares *A, B* and *C*.

Note that in this example, we have allowed negative amounts of securities to form part

Example 6.4 Determination of optimal three-security portfolio

Security	Expected return (%)	Standard deviation (%)	Covariances (%)		
A	6	4	$COV_{AA} = 16$	$COV_{AB} = 12$	$COV_{AC} = 16$
B	8	6		$COV_{BB} = 36$	$COV_{BC} = 12$
C	10	8			$COV_{CC} = 64$

Example 6.5 Some efficient portfolio combinations of A, B and C

Portfolio no.	Proportions held of A, B, C			Expected return $E(R_P)$ (%)	Standard deviation S_P (%)
	W_A	W_B	W_C		
(1)	0.33	0.33	0.21	7.5	4.3
(2)	0.41	0.35	0.24	7.7	4.4
(3)	0.30	0.40	0.30	8.0	4.6
(4)	0.13	0.48	0.39	8.5	5.1
(5)	-0.19	0.63	0.56	9.5	6.1

of the portfolio – in other words, it is assumed that securities can be sold short. In practice, this might not be possible. However, the computer program used to determine the efficient frontier can be adjusted to incorporate the requirement that all $W_i \geq 0$.

How will investors choose between these efficient portfolios? If they know their utility function they have two choices. They can calculate the utility they will get from each efficient portfolio and choose the one that offers them the highest utility; or they can plot their indifference curves against the efficient frontier and choose the portfolio where the tangent indifference curve touches the efficient frontier, as in Figure 6.8.

In practice, investors will probably not know their utility function or be able to plot their indifference curves. What they can do is specify a minimum acceptable level of expected return or a maximum acceptable level of risk. For example, they could require their portfolio to have minimum risk given an expected return of at least 8.5%; pension funds, for instance, might have the objective of earning a return of 4% more than the risk-free bond rate of 4.5% (at the time). Alternatively, an investor might be unwilling to accept a level of risk higher than 20% (measured by variance) if acting as a trustee for those who cannot afford to lose more than a certain amount. If the former requirement held, portfolio (4) in Example 6.5, which yields an expected return of 8.5%, would be chosen as optimal. If the latter restriction held, portfolio (2), with a standard deviation of 4.4%, would be preferred.

SIZE OF OPTIMAL PORTFOLIO

Investors can now choose the combination out of n securities that is optimal for them. It might include only two securities or it might include all n securities, depending on their correlation coefficients. The question that investors will now no doubt ask is how many securities they should consider in the first place. What would n be? They know they should diversify to gain the benefits of risk reduction, but to what extent? Small investors will be particularly concerned to know the answer to this question since their transaction costs will increase with the number of securities they buy.

We now examine what happens to the risk of a portfolio as we increase its size. We can see from equation 6.13 that the variance of a portfolio of n securities is equal to the sum of the weighted variance terms plus the sum of the weighted covariance terms.

If we assume that the n securities are all held in equal amounts, that is, that for each security

$$W_i = \frac{1}{n}$$

it can be seen that the relative significance of the variance terms diminishes as the number of securities increases. For larger n, the risk of the portfolio will largely depend on the average covariance between the securities. Obviously, as n becomes large enough to include all securities in the stock market, so the risk of the portfolio will come to be identical with the risk of the stock market.

How quickly does the risk of a portfolio decrease and tend towards the average market risk as we increase n? Experiments have been carried out on different sizes of randomly selected portfolios of UK shares, and one example is shown in Figure 6.9. In this study, portfolios containing from 1 to 50 securities were chosen and the average risk of each size of portfolio calculated. This average risk was then expressed as a percentage of the average risk of holding only one share.

We can see from Figure 6.9 that average risk initially decreases very rapidly as we increase the number of securities held. But each time another security is added, risk is reduced by a smaller amount, and no matter how many securities are held, risk cannot be reduced on average to below 34.5% (in this particular study) of the risk of holding only one share. This reinforces the view we already held that there is a certain amount of risk common to all shares quoted on the stock market which cannot be diversified away. This is intuitively obvious since if investors held all quoted UK shares, they would certainly not be holding a riskless investment!

These results have two major implications for investors. First, small investors need only diversify by holding 10 to 15 shares to have substantially reduced risk from holding one share and to have removed most of the non-market risk from their portfolios. For example, by holding ten randomly selected shares in equal amounts, an investor can on average diversify away 90 per cent of the shares' non-market risk. Second, institutional investors do not need to hold vast numbers of securities to be diversified. The extra reduction in risk gained by holding 150 rather than 50 securities is very small and may well be more than outweighed by the additional transaction and monitoring costs involved in holding the extra 100 shares.

So far, in discussing how many securities investors should hold, we have considered *naïve diversification* (randomly chosen securities held in equal amounts) and average levels of risk for different sizes of portfolios. This misses the more dramatic reductions in risk that can be achieved by carefully selecting securities and then calculating efficient frontiers, known as *Markowitz diversification*. It may be that two negatively correlated

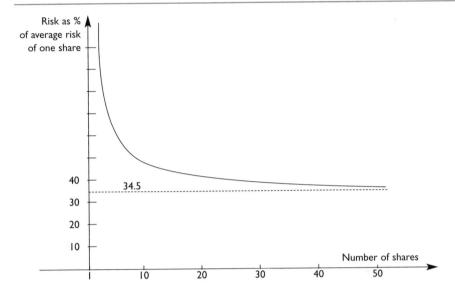

Figure 6.9 The effect on risk of the number of securities in a portfolio
Source: Solnik (1974).

shares could be found, in which case a minimum risk portfolio would include only those two shares. If another share were added it would add risk. So, on a naïve diversification policy, at least ten shares should be held to reduce risk close to the average market risk level, whereas a careful examination of covariances could lead to a smaller but equally efficient portfolio.

PROBLEMS WITH PORTFOLIO THEORY

When portfolio theory was first discussed in the 1950s, it was not widely accepted by analysts and investors. There were two main reasons for this. First, if n securities are to be considered, estimates of the value of n expected returns, n variances and $(n^2 - n)/2$ covariances have to be made. That meant that over 45,000 data items had to be calculated for a portfolio of 300 different securities, at a time when computers were both very slow and very expensive to run.

Second, the investment research departments of stockbroking firms were usually organised on an industry basis, so who was to determine the covariance of returns of a timber company with those of a shoe retailer? In any case, the only way such variances and covariances could be estimated was by looking at past data and assuming that underlying factors affecting the securities would be the same in the future, so that values based on past frequencies could be used for future probabilities. This was relatively straightforward for returns and variances, but calculations of covariances were much less robust.

One further potential problem with portfolio theory is that it is only a one-period model. The one-period model restriction means that all investment decisions must be made at the beginning of the period and no changes can be made during the period, whereas a multi-period model would allow changes at the beginning of each period and so perhaps achieve greater utility. Investors usually consider investment policy for several years (or periods) ahead, and wish to maximise their expected utility of wealth at the end of the whole period. However, it can be shown that, if certain assumptions concerning the utility function of the investor are made (for example, if the utility function is a logarithmic one, $U = f(\ln(W))$), then investors will maximise their overall expected utility by considering each period separately. Thus, they can use the portfolio theory approach in each individual period.

But despite the problems in using portfolio theory which derive from the cumbersome nature of the required input data, as computers evolved and the use of more quantitative techniques in investment analysis gained wider acceptance, portfolio theory began to be used in determining optimal portfolios.

Portfolio theory does offer a framework for each investor to determine his or her optimal portfolio from inputs which can be derived subjectively or from past data. For example, the theory can be applied to net-of-tax returns, thus allowing for the particular tax position of the investor. This would lead to different portfolios for different investors even if each started out with the same expected gross returns and risk for each security. Also, as was mentioned in the introduction to this chapter, portfolio theory can be applied to the determination of optimal portfolios in an international context. If the expected returns, risks and correlation coefficients are estimated in sterling terms (again usually relying to some extent on past data), optimal international portfolios can be found for UK investors. Similarly, if the returns and risk data are calculated in terms of euros, optimal international portfolios for eurozone investors can be determined. Finally portfolio theory can also be applied successfully to the asset allocation problem, namely what proportions of equities, bonds, cash and, say, property to have in a particular portfolio.

SUMMARY

This chapter has looked at how investors can decide on an optimal portfolio of securities. It was discovered that not only should the expected return and risk (measured by standard deviation) of each security be considered, but also its correlation or covariance with the other securities in the portfolio.

Since most shares quoted on the UK stock market are correlated positively, but less than perfectly, with each other, combining them into a portfolio will actually reduce the risk to investors to less than the weighted average of the individual risks of the securities. However, the expected return on a portfolio is equal to the weighted average of the expected returns of the constituent securities. So, it will always pay investors to diversify, provided the securities in their portfolio are not perfectly positively correlated.

Investors, knowing their utility function and indifference curves, can then find a portfolio that is optimal for them from the efficient frontier of portfolios: that is, from those portfolios that offer the best expected returns given their risk. This method of finding the optimal portfolio is termed _Markowitz diversification_, and involves careful consideration of all the securities and how they relate to each other. Investors can also reduce risk by going for 'naïve' diversification, where they simply invest equal amounts in randomly selected securities. Naïve diversification will reduce risk substantially, but will involve a portfolio with more securities and a worse risk–return ratio than the more rigorous Markowitz diversification.

REVIEW EXERCISES

1 Shares A and B have the following characteristics:

Share	Expected total return (% p.a.)	Standard deviation of expected returns (%)
A	12%	8%
B	18%	16%

Complete exercises (a) and (b) below for each of the following correlation scenarios:
Correlation coefficient of expected returns:

Scenario A: -1.00
Scenario B: 0.00
Scenario C: 0.30
Scenario D: -0.80

a. Calculate the expected return and risk of several portfolios containing different proportions of A and B, including at least the following three:
   i. $1/3$A and $2/3$B
   ii. $½$A and $½$B
   iii $2/3$A and $1/3$B
b. Plot all of your portfolios on a graph of expected return against risk.
   i.   Which proportions of A and B do you think will maximise expected return given the risk?
   ii. Which proportion of A and B do you think will give the minimum possible risk, regardless of return?

2. The expected return and variance-covariance matrix of shares X, Y and Z is as follows:

Share	Expected total return (% p.a.)	Standard deviation of expected returns (%)	Correlation coefficients X	Y	Z
X	10.50%	7.80%	1.00	0.30	0.90
Y	14.25%	11.70%	0.30	1.00	0.10
Z	17.60%	17.60%	0.90	0.10	1.00

a. Calculate the expected return and variance of equally weighted portfolios of:
   i.   X and Y
   ii. X and Z
   iii. Y and Z.
b. Comment on the difference between the risk of the XZ portfolio and the risk of the YZ portfolio.
c. Calculate the expected return and variance of a portfolio consisting of equal amounts of X, Y and Z. Compare your results with those for the two-security portfolios.

3. Suppose two shares P and Q have the following risk and return characteristics, and that their returns are perfectly negatively correlated.

Share	Expected total return (% p.a.)	Standard deviation of expected returns (%)
P	9%	11%
Q	15%	23%

a. What will be the expected return and risk of an equally weighted portfolio?

b. What portfolio weights for P and Q will lead to a perfectly hedged portfolio?

c. Plot your results on an expected return and risk graph.

d. Can you suggest any securities whose returns might, in practice, be negatively correlated?

4. Mrs Peach intends to invest in three securities, J, K and L, each with expected return of 15% and variance of 150%. The three securities all have returns which are totally uncorrelated with each other.

   a. What will be the expected return and risk of Mrs Peach's portfolio if she holds the three securities in equal amounts?

   b. What if Mrs Peach puts 40% in J, 40% in K and 20% in L?

   c. Estimate the weights for J, K and L which would lead to a minimum risk portfolio for Mrs Peach.

   d. Would Mrs Peach be right to go for a minimum risk portfolio?

5. 'Three hundred equities, if they are rightly chosen, are sufficient as a selection ground for most portfolios. I feel that increasing the number of shares under consideration to an unmanageable number is no way of diversifying.' Does this statement conflict with the results of portfolio theory?

Sample answers to the review exercises can be found on the companion website.

APPENDIX 6.1: PROOF OF THE PORTFOLIO RISK EQUATION

The variance V_i of the return on any security i can be written as

$$V_i = S_i^2 = \sum_{i=1}^{i=n} (R_i - E(R_i))^2 p(R_i)$$

(A6.1)

or, if we are calculating the variance from an unweighted raw data set of every possible outcome rather than from a probability-weighted table of outcomes,

$$V_i = S_i^2 = \frac{1}{n} \sum_{i=1}^{i=n} (R_i - E(R_i))^2$$

(A6.2)

In exactly the same way, the variance of the portfolio return can be written

$$V_P = \frac{1}{n} \sum_{i=1}^{i=n} (R_P - E(R_P))^2$$

(A6.3)

As the return on the portfolio in each period is made up of the weighted proportions of the returns on A and B, this equation can be expanded in the form

$$V_P = \frac{1}{n} \sum_{i=1}^{i=n} [(W_A R_{Ai} + W_B R_{Bi}) - E(W_A R_A + W_B R_B)]^2$$

(A6.4)

As the terms W_A and W_B are constants, we can use the equation

$$E(W_A R_A) = W_A E(R_A)$$

to rearrange equation A6.4 in the form

$$V_P = \frac{1}{n} \sum_{i=1}^{i=n} [W_A R_{Ai} + W_B R_{Bi} - W_A E(R_A) - W_B E(R_B)]^2 \qquad (A6.5)$$

This can be further rearranged to

$$V_P = \frac{1}{n} \sum_{i=1}^{i=n} [(W_A R_A - W_A E(R_A)) + (W_B R_{Bi} - W_B E(R_B))]^2 \qquad (A6.6)$$

and then to

$$V_P = \frac{1}{n} \sum_{i=1}^{i=n} [W_A (R_{Ai} - E(R_A)) + W_B (R_{Bi} - E(R_B))]^2 \qquad (A6.7)$$

If we now expand the terms in square brackets we get:

$$V_P = \frac{1}{n} \sum_{i=1}^{i=n} [W_A^2 (R_{Ai} - E(R_A))^2] + \frac{1}{n} \sum_{i=1}^{i=n} [W_B^2 (R_{Bi} - E(R_B))^2] \qquad (A6.8)$$

$$+ \frac{1}{n} \sum_{i=1}^{i=n} [2 W_A W_B (R_{Ai} - E(R_A))(R_{Bi} - E(R_B))]$$

We can make more sense of this cumbersome equation by first taking the W_A and W_B terms out of the square brackets thus:

$$V_P = \frac{W_A^2}{n} \sum_{i=1}^{i=n} [(R_{Ai} - E(R_A))^2] + \frac{W_B^2}{n} \sum_{i=1}^{i=n} [(R_{Bi} - E(R_B))^2]$$

$$+ \frac{2 W_A W_B}{n} \sum_{i=1}^{i=n} [(R_{Ai} - E(R_A))(R_{Bi} - E(R_B))] \qquad (A6.8a)$$

Then, if we recall that for any security i

$$V_i = \frac{1}{n} \sum_{i=1}^{i=n} (R_i - E(R_i))^2 \qquad (A6.2)$$

we can simplify at least the first and second of the three elements in equation A6.8a and rewrite it as

$$V_P = W_A^2 V_A + W_B^2 V_B + \frac{2 W_A W_B}{n} \sum_{i=1}^{i=n} [(R_{Ai} - E(R_A))(R_{Bi} - E(R_B))] \qquad (A6.9)$$

So the variance of the return on a two-security portfolio is made up of the variances of the returns on the individual securities, each multiplied by the square of its proportion in the portfolio, plus a third term which we now need to analyse in more detail. It is the product of

$$2W_A W_B$$

and

$$\frac{1}{n}\sum_{i=1}^{i=n}[(R_{Ai}-E(R_A))(R_{Bi}-E(R_B))] = COV_{AB} \tag{A6.10}$$

This last expression, which is called the *covariance of returns on A and B* (COV_{AB}) looks a little like the variance of the return on a single security, but with one important difference. Instead of multiplying the difference between each value of $(R_{Ai}-E(R_A))$ by itself, we multiply it by the concurrent value of $(R_{Bi}-E(R_B))$.

The covariance of A and B is closely related to two other statistical measures which are not only more familiar but also intuitively easier to understand, namely their standard deviations S_A and S_B and their correlation coefficient $CORR_{AB}$. The relationship is expressed by the equation

$$CORR_{AB} = \frac{COV_{AB}}{S_A S_b} \tag{A6.11}$$

This can be rearranged as

$$COV_{AB} = S_A S_B CORR_{AB} \tag{A6.12}$$

The effect of dividing the value of the covariance between the returns on two securities by the product of the standard deviations of those returns is to index the covariance relationship in relative terms such that it can only take values between -1 and +1.

We can now express our equation for the variance of returns on a two-security portfolio in its definitive form. First, we can rewrite equation A6.9 in the form

$$V_P = W_A^2 V_A + W_B^2 V_B + 2W_A W_B COV_{AB} \tag{A6.13}$$

Then, substituting from equation A6.12 we can write

$$V_P = W_A^2 V_A + W_B^2 V_B + 2W_A W_B S_A S_B CORR_{AB} \tag{A6.14}$$

This is a little untidy, because it contains both variance and standard deviation terms. Remembering that the variance is the square of the standard deviation, we can rewrite it using standard deviation terms throughout as follows:

$$V_P = W_A^2 S_A^2 + W_B^2 S_B^2 + 2W_A W_B S_A S_B CORR_{AB} \tag{A6.15a}$$

Equation A6.15a expresses the risk of a two-security portfolio in terms of its variance. As standard deviation is the positive square root of the variance, we can also state the risk of such a portfolio in the form of equation 6.15b:

$$S_P = |\sqrt{W_A^2 S_A^2 + W_B^2 S_B^2 + 2 W_A W_B S_A S_B \, CORR_{AB}}| \qquad \text{(A6.15b)}$$

where $|\ \ |$ represents the modulus or positive square root.

Equations A6.15a and A6.15b are fully interchangeable with each other, and we use whichever of them is easier to manipulate in a given context.

7 The Capital Asset Pricing Model

CHAPTER CONTENTS

Learning objectives for this chapter

After studying this chapter you should be able to

- ○ describe how the extension of portfolio theory into the Capital Asset Pricing Model (CAPM) offers a comprehensive theoretical framework for calculating the expected return on any security
- ○ calculate the expected return on a security from given data about the historical relationship between its return and the return on the market as a whole (beta)
- ○ describe the principal factors determining the beta of a security
- ○ describe in detail the assumptions and results of CAPM, as well as its practical implications for portfolio managers
- ○ appreciate the principal potential shortcomings of CAPM, both in theory and in practice.

INTRODUCTION

In Chapter 6 we saw that the use of portfolio theory to find an optimal portfolio requires a computer program and a potentially large variance–covariance matrix. This has hindered general acceptance of portfolio theory, despite its usefulness. We also saw, in the section on the size of the optimal portfolio (pages 213–15), that however much investors diversify and however many securities they include in their portfolio, a naïve diversification policy cannot reduce aggregate risk below a certain minimum level. If they keep increasing the number of securities in their portfolio, eventually they will hold every security in the stock market, and thus bear the risk of the market itself, which cannot be eliminated or reduced by any further diversification.

This concept of undiversifiable market risk is fundamental to the development of the more rigorous *Capital Asset Pricing Model* (*CAPM*, usually pronounced

'Cap-em'). The CAPM shows that the risk of any security can be divided into two parts: an element reflecting the undiversifiable market risk, and an element specific to the share, which can be diversified away by holding the share as part of a large portfolio. The CAPM is a much stronger model than portfolio theory, because it not only prescribes optimal portfolios for investors but also derives an equation for the relationship between the expected return and the risk of any security.

By making certain assumptions in addition to those made by portfolio theory, the CAPM shows that all investors will hold, not different portfolios derived from different opportunity sets (as in portfolio theory), but different amounts of the same portfolio. This portfolio of securities that all investors will hold is the market portfolio: that is, the portfolio consisting of all securities in the market, weighted according to their market capitalisations. All investors will adjust to their particular risk–return requirements by combining their holding of the market portfolio M with positive or negative amounts of a risk-free security such as Treasury bills. Investors wishing to take on more risk than is offered by the stock market as a whole will borrow money and invest further in M. This will increase the risk of the investment through *leveraging up*. In contrast, more cautious investors who want a lower risk than that of the market as a whole will put only a small part of their money into M and will invest the rest in risk-free securities.

The relationship between the risk and return of any security, which is found in the CAPM, is an equally strong result. This equation is known as the *securities market line*. It shows that there is a linear relationship between the risk and expected return of any security. The risk for which the investor is actually rewarded is not the total risk (represented by the standard deviation or variance of returns) but only a proportion of it, namely the element reflecting the undiversifiable market risk. Any risk arising from holding the share on its own and not as part of a diversified portfolio will not be rewarded.

The CAPM has far-reaching implications for investment decision making. Investors who assume that securities are valued according to the CAPM will not use techniques such as fundamental analysis to select investments, but will simply select securities on the basis of the risk and expected return predicted by the CAPM. Such investors will expect only a fair return for the risk they bear, as opposed to fundamental analysts who expect to earn better than average returns as a result of their share selection skills. These differing investment strategies are discussed in more detail in Chapter 12.

This chapter starts with a description of the *market model*, which forms the empirical basis of the CAPM. We then introduce the assumptions underlying the CAPM and derive its results. We devote a whole section to the practical application of the results of the CAPM, for example how we can use the notion of market risk, called *beta*. The chapter continues with a discussion of some of the theoretical and practical problems posed by the CAPM, and concludes with an introduction to more complex models than the CAPM, including *arbitrage pricing theory*.

THE MARKET MODEL

Definition of the market model

It was not surprising that a simplification of portfolio theory would be proposed, especially as securities do seem to be subject to some common influences. We have already noted the tendency towards positive correlations in their returns. Sharpe (1963) postulated that this correlation is caused by a common 'market' response. This led him to suppose that the expected return of any security could be expressed as a linear function of the expected return of the market as a whole. The expected return of the market could be approximated by using the return on a suitable stock market index. This would lead to an equation of the form

$$E(R_i) = a_i + b_i E(R_M) \qquad (7.1)$$

for each security i, where

$E(R_i)$	is the expected return on security
a_i and b_i	are constants specific to that security
$E(R_M)$	is the expected return on the market as a whole.

In practice the return R_i would not necessarily turn out to be equal to its expected value, so, if past data on returns were used, an equation of the form

$$R_i = a_i + b_i R_M + e_i \qquad (7.2)$$

would be found, where R_i and R_M were the actual returns for security i and the market as a whole, and the residual term e_i was the difference between the actual and expected result. The expected value of e_i would be zero.

Such a simple model is obviously based on some quite strong assumptions. It presupposes that the only common factor affecting all securities is the return on the market. Mathematically, this is expressed by requiring the covariances between all values of e_i to be 0: $COV(e_i, e_j) = 0$ for all i, j. Sharpe's model also requires $COV(e_i, R_M) = 0$ for all i, which means that the size of the error term e_i is unrelated to the size of the market return. Other common influences such as industry factors or economic influences affecting only some securities are ignored.

It would be convenient for investors if Sharpe's market model worked in the real world, but as yet we have no theoretical foundation for such a model. However, as we shall see in the next section, the validity of such a market model can be proved theoretically if certain additional assumptions are made about the stock market and investor behaviour.

Advantages of the market model

How does this market model help us? It radically reduces both the number of variables needed to determine efficient portfolios and the number of calculations needed to find these variables. All we need for each security is a_i, b_i and the variance of the error term $V(e_i)$. We begin by plotting actual past values of R_i and R_M against each other, as in Figure 7.1. Then we use the technique of *regression analysis* to find a linear relationship between them (the *line of best fit*) by minimising the sum of the vertical distances of the points from the line.

For example, we could plot monthly total returns (that is, dividends plus/minus capital gains/losses) over the past five years. The intercept of the line fitted to the points by

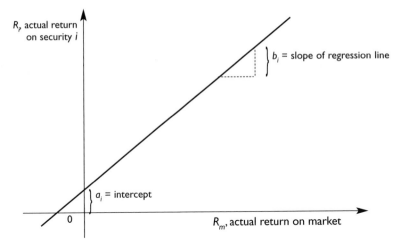

Figure 7.1 Calculation of coefficients in $R_i = a_i + b_iR_M + e_i$

regression would give a_i, the slope of the regression line b_i, and the variance of the error terms would be calculated from the regression analysis by the computer. We could then assume that these values will hold in the future for each security. Alternatively, if we expect any specific changes, we can estimate a_i, b_i and $V(e_i)$ subjectively. The variance of the market V_M and its expected return $E(R_M)$ must also be estimated. In all, a total of only $3n + 2$ data items are required for an n-security portfolio. For example, with 30 securities, the market model requires only 92 data items whereas portfolio theory requires no fewer than 495.

The expected return and variance of any portfolio P are then

$$E(R_P) = a_p + b_p E(R_M) \tag{7.3}$$

$$V_p = b_p^2 V_M + \sum_{i=1}^{i=n} W_i^2 V(e_i) \tag{7.4}$$

where a_p and b_p are the weighted averages of the constituent securities' a_i and b_i, and the W_i are their weightings.

$$a_p = \sum_{i=1}^{i=n} W_i a_i$$

$$b_p = \sum_{i=1}^{i=n} W_i b_i$$

and

$$\sum_{i=1}^{i=n} W_i = 1$$

The attractions of the simpler model are obvious.

THE CAPM THEORY

Assumptions of the CAPM

The market model's attempt at explaining security returns is attractive in its simplicity, but we have as yet no theoretical foundation for believing that we can cut corners in this way. We have seen that as long as we accept the assumptions of portfolio theory and the fact that it is a one-period rather than a multi-period model, it leads to some interesting results. However, to get any further we need to introduce some additional assumptions:

1. The securities market is perfectly competitive, frictionless and in equilibrium, which means that:
   - ○ there are no taxes, no transaction costs and no restrictions on short-selling (i.e. selling shares you do not yet own)
   - ○ all relevant information is available to all investors simultaneously and free of charge
   - ○ securities are infinitely divisible (so can be bought and sold in any quantity) and they all have a market price
   - ○ no single investor can affect the market price by buying or selling securities
   - ○ all investors are rational maximisers of expected utility.
2. All investors agree on a period under consideration for investment purposes (say, one month or one year) and have identical expectations regarding the probability distributions of security returns for that period.
3. Unlimited amounts of money can be borrowed or lent by all investors at the risk-free rate; if inflation exists, it is fully anticipated in interest rates.

Assumption 1, which requires the absence of potentially distorting factors such as taxes and transaction costs, is obviously unrealistic in the context of the real world. However, if too many real-world complexities are introduced into a model at an early stage, no analysis of the basic return relationships of securities or of how investors behave can be made. The validity of the model can be tested empirically to see if it reflects what actually happens in the market and, if necessary, complexities can be added at a later stage.

Assumption 2 is important since the CAPM requires investors to have the same opportunity set of portfolios and the same efficient frontier. Portfolio theory does not require this; all investors can derive their own set of efficient portfolios, map their own indifference curves on to them and choose their own optimal portfolios without concerning themselves with other investors' preferences or expectations.

Assumption 3 is also crucial to the derivation of the CAPM, because the existence of risk-free lending and borrowing extends the range of opportunities available to the investor. By risk-free we mean without any of the risks described in Chapters 1 and 2. If investors buy government fixed interest securities (equivalent to lending money free of default risk), they might still be subject to inflation risk and interest rate risk. We deal with inflation risk here by assuming that inflation is fully anticipated in interest rates. Interest rate risk can be avoided if a zero-coupon fixed interest security is chosen that matures exactly at the end of the period in question.

In practice, the security that most clearly satisfies the conditions is a **Treasury bill**, a zero-risk, zero-coupon government security. Treasury bills are also very short-term securities with a life of not more than six months, thereby reducing interest rate risk and inflation risk to a minimum. However, even if an almost risk-free investment can be found, the assumption that any investor can also borrow money at the risk-free rate is more difficult to envisage in the real world.

Results of the CAPM

When we add these further assumptions to those already made by portfolio theory, we now have the capital asset pricing model (or CAPM) from which we can derive interesting insights into how the risk and return of securities are related and how rational investors will behave.

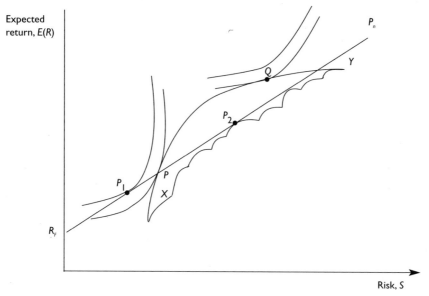

Figure 7.2 Optimal portfolios with risk-free borrowing and lending (1)

First of all, we can say that all investors face the same opportunity set of risky securities and portfolios and the same efficient frontier XY, as shown in Figure 7.2. They may, however, choose different optimal portfolios according to their different indifference curves, for example P and Q.

The risk and return characteristics of the risk-free asset are shown as R_F in Figure 7.2; because it has no risk, its x-value is zero so it is located on the y-axis. The introduction of risk-free borrowing and lending possibilities both increases and improves the alternative portfolios available to each investor. For example, the investor who initially chose P can now, as well as choosing P, also move up and down the line $R_F PP_n$. If she borrows money at the risk-free rate of interest, R_F (or 'leverages up'), she can move along $R_F PP_n$, say to P_2, having increased the risk of her investment in P by using some borrowed money. If she lends, she can move along $R_F PP_n$ say to P_1, having reduced the amount invested in the risky portfolio P and hence her overall investment risk.

For example, what would happen if an investor were to divide his available funds between portfolio P and the risk-free asset? What would be the risk and expected return characteristics of the resulting portfolios? We can fall back on basic portfolio theory for the answers, as the investor now effectively owns two assets – the risk-free asset and a composite asset in the form of portfolio P_1. With suitable modifications to the familiar notation, using the subscripts P, F and P_1 to denote the portfolio P, the risk-free asset and the portfolio P_1 respectively, we can describe the expected return on such a portfolio P_1, with W_F invested in R_F and W_P invested in P, with the equation

$$E(R_{P_1}) = W_F R_F + W_P E(R_P) \qquad (7.5)$$

As $W_F = 1 - W_P$, we can rearrange equation 7.5 as

$$E(R_{P_1}) = R_F + W_P(E(R_P) - R_F) \qquad (7.6)$$

In other words, the expected return of such a portfolio will be the risk-free rate plus the same proportion of the difference between the expected return on portfolio P and the risk-free rate as portfolio P occupies in the new portfolio P_1.

What is the risk of the new portfolio P_1? Here again we can use the portfolio variance equation 6.7b from Chapter 6:

$$V_{P1} = W_P^2 S_P^2 + W_F^2 S_F^2 + 2W_P W_F S_P S_F CORR_{PF} \qquad (7.7)$$

But in this case the portfolio risk equation can be radically simplified because one of the two assets is risk-free. The risk-free asset is so called because the variability of its return is zero. This means that S_F is also zero and the whole of the second of the three terms in the equation is zero and can be ignored. The third term is also zero, not only because it too contains S_F but also because COV_{PF} is zero.

In short, for a portfolio P_1 consisting partly of the risk-free asset and partly of portfolio P of risky assets, the second and third terms of the portfolio variance equation can be ignored, leaving only:

$$V_{P1} = W_P^2 S_P^2 \qquad (7.8)$$

or

$$S_{P1} = W_P S_P \qquad (7.9)$$

So the risk of the portfolio is directly proportional to the weighting of the risky portfolio P within it – just as the expected return is. In other words the risk–return relationship for a portfolio consisting of two assets, one of which is the risk-free asset, is not the familiar risk-reducing curve of portfolio theory but a straight line, because it says that the expected return and the risk of any portfolio consisting of the risk-free asset and the risky portfolio P will be directly proportional to the amount of P in the portfolio.

The possibility of moving up and down $R_F PP_n$ enables investors to increase their utility by moving to a higher indifference curve. For the particular investor we have considered, if she invests partly in the risk-free asset and moves to P_1, she will have reached a higher indifference curve and thereby increased her utility.

But this is not the end of the additional opportunities created by the CAPM. Our investor no longer has to restrict herself to portfolio P which was optimal without the risk-free borrowing and lending possibilities. It can be seen from Figure 7.3 that she would do better still by focusing her attention on portfolio M where the line from R_F is a tangent to the efficient frontier.

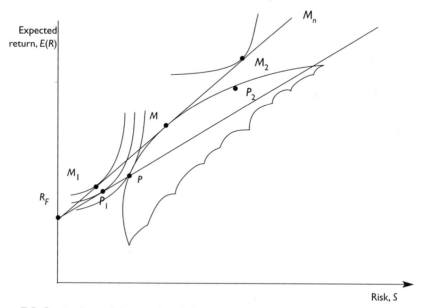

Figure 7.3 Optimal portfolios with risk-free borrowing and lending (2)

It is easy to see why not only our investor in P but all investors would maximise their utility by choosing portfolio M. They would then either borrow or invest at the risk-free rate in order to move up or down $R_F M M_n$ until they reached the point where it touched their highest possible indifference curve. This point is M_1 in the case of our original investor in P, or M_2 in the case of another, rather less cautious investor. So every investor will hold some proportion of M and either positive amounts of the risk-free asset (investing) or negative amounts (borrowing).

What securities make up portfolio M? If all investors hold M in equilibrium, M must be the total of all risky assets in the marketplace. All investors will therefore hold all risky securities in proportion to their market values, in an amount depending on the overall size of their portfolio. If they want higher risk and return than those offered by the market as a whole, they will borrow to buy more of M and move upwards and to the right along $R_F M M_n$. If they want less than the overall market risk, they will hold less M and invest some of their money at R_F, for instance by buying Treasury bills.

The model we have built up from our assumptions has told us how investors ought to behave. The surprising and counterintuitive result is that all investors should hold not different portfolios, but different amounts of the same portfolio M combined with positive or negative amounts of money invested or borrowed at the risk-free rate. Unlike portfolio theory, which leaves it open to all investors to hold their own tailor-made portfolio, the CAPM says we should hold the same security portfolio made up of all risky securities in the market in proportion to their market value, not just ten or 15 shares but several hundred securities.

The CAPM does not stop there. It also tells us something very revealing about the relationship between return and risk.

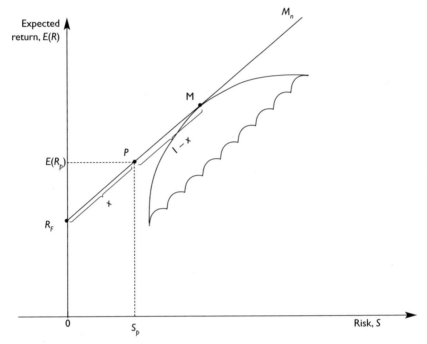

Figure 7.4 Capital market line

When we were exploring the linear relationship between risk and return in a portfolio P_1 consisting partly of the risk-free asset (or risk-free borrowing) and partly of the portfolio P, we concluded that the risk of such a portfolio was defined by the following equation:

$$S_{P1} = W_P S_P \qquad (7.9)$$

and the return by the following equation:

$$E(R_{P1}) = R_F + W_P(E(R_P) - R_F) \qquad (7.6)$$

If we now apply this result to the special case of a portfolio P combining the risk-free asset with market portfolio M, we can express the expected return in the form

$$E(R_P) = R_F + W_P(E(R_M) - R_F) \qquad (7.10)$$

and the risk in the form

$$S_P = W_P S_M \qquad (7.11)$$

It follows from equation 7.11 that

$$W_P = \frac{S_P}{S_M}$$

so that we can now rewrite the equation for the expected return on portfolio P in the form

$$E(R_P) = R_F + (E(R_M) - R_F)\frac{S_P}{S_M} \tag{7.12}$$

Equation 7.12 is known as the *capital market line*, and expresses the expected return of a portfolio which lies on $R_F M M_n$ in terms of its risk S_P. This equation is useful if we are dealing with efficient portfolios lying on the capital market line; any portfolio lying on $R_F M M_n$ must be efficient in the sense that it must be perfectly positively correlated with the market portfolio M because it is joined to M by a straight line. But we would like an expression relating the return and risk of any security, not just of portfolios lying on $R_F M M_n$. In fact, equation 7.12 can be used to derive the required expression for the expected return of any security in the market. For a detailed proof, see Appendix 7.2.

The equation for the expected return on a security i is

$$E(R_i) = R_F + (E(R_M) - R_F)\frac{COV_{iM}}{S_M^2} \tag{7.13}$$

Equation 7.13 is known as the *securities market line* since it relates the expected return of any security to its risk. This equation is similar to the capital market line but instead of expressing $E(R_i)$ in terms of its standard deviation S_i, we see that the return of a security is a function of its covariance with the market return COV_{iM}.

We have already noted, in the case of a risk-free security, that COV_{iM} is always zero, and $E(R_i)$ will be equal to R_F. If the security is risky, a premium will be required over and above the risk-free rate, which will increase with the covariance of the security with the market. The expression $(E(R_M) - R_F)/S_M^2$ is sometimes called the unit market price of risk. For each 1% increase in COV_{iM}, the expected return required of the security will increase by the market price of risk.

This has serious implications for investors when they consider adding a security to their portfolio. The only risk for which they will be rewarded will be for the covariance of the return on the security with the market return, and not its total risk measured by its variance or standard deviation. This can be seen more clearly if we simplify equation 7.13. If we let

$$\beta_i = \frac{COV_{iM}}{S_M^2} \tag{7.14}$$

then equation 7.13 can be written

$$E(R_i) = R_F + \beta_i(E(R_M) - R_F) \tag{7.15}$$

or

$$E(R_i) = a_i + b_i E(R_M) \tag{7.16}$$

where

$$a_i = R_F - \beta_i R_F$$

and

$$b_i = \beta_i$$

This looks like the market model that Sharpe suggested might hold. We have shown that, under certain conditions, it does hold and that the return of a security depends on its relationship to the market return. β_i or beta is a measure of sensitivity to the market, and it is for this sensitivity that the holder of the security is rewarded. The market portfolio M will have a beta of 1. This can be seen by substituting $\beta_i = 1$ into equation 7.16.

How do we calculate the beta of a specific security? Ideally, we would need to look at the future to determine beta. But if we can assume, as we did for standard deviations in the market model, that a past figure will be a good proxy for the future, we can plot historical returns R_i against R_M, as in Figure 7.1. β_i will then be the slope of the regression line

$$R_i = a_i + \beta_i R_M + e_i \tag{7.2}$$

where e_i is the error term of the regression.

From this approach we can also derive an equation for the risk or variance V_i, of R_i, using the following general rules:

○ The variance of the sum of two or more terms is the sum of their variances.
○ The variance of a constant is zero.
○ The variance of ax, where a is a constant and x is a random variable, is $a^2 V_x$.

In equation 7.2, we know therefore that the risk of the constant a_i is zero, and that the risk of $\beta_i R_M$ is $\beta_i^2 S_M^2$, and the risk of e_i is $S^2(e_i)$, so we can say

$$V_i = \beta_i^2 S_M^2 + S^2(e_i) \tag{7.17}$$

This equation 7.17 splits the total risk of a security, as measured by its variance, into two parts: risk relative to the market, measured by the sensitivity factor β_i, and *specific risk* or *diversifiable risk*, $S^2(e_i)$. The latter risk is called specific, because it is specific to security i, and diversifiable because it can be diversified away. We saw when looking at portfolios of n securities that total portfolio risk was quickly reduced to market risk as n increased. The risk specific to individual securities could easily be reduced through diversification. This will become clearer when we have looked at a numerical example in the next section.

The securities market line (equation 7.13) is therefore telling us that the holders of a security are rewarded only for the systematic or beta risk of their security, and not for their diversifiable risk. In other words the market assumes all investors hold diversified portfolios.

THE CAPM IN PRACTICE

How does the CAPM theory help the investor? By deriving a theoretical foundation for the market model, we have greatly simplified the calculations of the risk and return of any portfolio. The risk and return of any combination of securities can be calculated from the following inputs

- ○ the beta and diversifiable risks for each security
- ○ the risk and return characteristics of the stock market as a whole
- ○ the risk-free rate.

Estimating each of these inputs is not without practical difficulties, which depend on how far we are prepared to rely on historically observed values and simply extrapolate them into the future, and how far we wish to modify historical data to take account of our own subjective view of the future.

Understanding the historical data

Information about securities' past risks and returns is now readily available for all shares quoted on the US, UK and other major stock exchanges. The information shown in Table 7.1 for a sample of shares in the FTSE 100 index of leading shares is extracted from the London Business School's quarterly *Risk Measurement Service* for the quarter and year ended 31 December 2004. The following notes explain the significance of the columns. In Appendix 7.1 we reproduce information from the same source about individual sectors of the stock market.

The *FTSE-Actuaries Classification* is a hierarchical sector categorisation used by the FTSE.

Market capitalisation is calculated by multiplying the number of shares in issue by the closing market price for the share on the date in question. In Table 7.1 companies are ranked by 'market cap'.

Beta, as calculated in the London Business School publication, is derived from historical data (monthly returns for the past five years) using regression analysis.

Variability expresses the total risk or volatility of returns on the share, as measured by the standard deviation of percentage returns on the share. Using the properties of the normal distribution described in Chapter 2, we can say that on average the annual return on the share will fall short of its mean expected value by at least its variability in about one year in every six.

Specific risk is the risk of non-market-related fluctuations in the return. It is the $S(e_i)$ in equation 7.17.

Standard error of beta is a measure of how much reliance we can put on the beta estimate provided from our historical sampling process. It does not in itself indicate conclusively how far we can rely on our historical estimate of beta as a guide for the future value of beta, but is rather a measure of how accurately our sampling process will have identified the true *historical* value of beta. The lower the standard error term, the more confidence we can have in our estimate. See under 'R squared' below for a further discussion of this.

R squared represents the percentage of the share's overall variability that is accounted

Table 7.1 Risk and return data for the 40 largest constituents of the FTSE 100 index for Q4 2004

Company	Actuaries classification	Average capitalisation	Beta	Variability	Specific risk	Standard error of beta	R squared	Qtly abnormal return	Ann. abnormal return	Actual annual return	Net yield	P/E ratio
BP	Oil Intg	109,884	0.82	22	18	0.14	32	-9	5	16	3.0	14.8
HSBC Holdings	Banks	98,194	1.24	24	14	0.11	64	-7	-10	4	3.7	20.1
Vodafone Group	Telcomob	92,591	1.05	35	31	0.20	21	1	-9	4	2.1	na
GlaxoSmithKline	Pharmact	71,702	0.40	20	20	0.15	9	0	-8	-1	3.4	15.8
Royal Bank of Scotland	Banks	55,548	1.14	29	23	0.16	37	2	-4	10	3.0	22.2
Shell Trnspt&Trd'Regd'	Oil Intg	42,735	0.95	22	16	0.13	44	3	-1	12	3.6	13.7
Barclays Bank	Banks	37,676	1.24	27	19	0.14	51	2	8	23	3.7	13.8
HBOS	Banks	33,265	1.06	33	29	0.19	24	6	9	22	3.7	13.3
AstraZeneca	Pharmact	31,084	0.68	31	29	0.19	12	-22	-38	-28	2.3	20.4
Lloyds TSB group	Banks	26,456	1.26	30	23	0.16	42	1	-1	14	7.2	8.1
Tesco	FdrugRet	24,937	0.62	25	23	0.17	14	8	19	28	2.2	21.3
Diageo	BevDstVn	22,465	0.36	20	19	0.14	8	4	-2	5	3.7	16.2
British American Tobacco	Tobacco	19,217	0.80	30	28	0.18	17	6	11	22	4.4	33.3
Anglo American	Msc Mine	18,404	1.15	33	28	0.19	28	-15	-10	5	2.5	23.4
BT Group	Telcomfx	17,313	1.48	36	27	0.18	41	5	-4	13	4.5	12.4
Rio Tinto	Msc Mine	16,370	1.21	31	24	0.17	36	-5	-12	2	2.4	22.8
National Grid Transco	Multutil	15,318	0.64	21	19	0.14	21	3	20	30	4.1	13.8
BHP Billiton	Msc Mine	15,068	1.12	32	27	0.18	28	-3	14	28	2.2	21.6
Unilever	FoodProc	14,892	0.67	26	24	0.17	15	10	-8	2	3.6	16.0
Aviva	Life Ass	14,301	1.52	36	27	0.18	43	5	17	34	3.9	15.2
BG Group	Oil Intg	12,515	0.77	24	21	0.16	23	-10	14	25	1.0	16.2
Standard Chartered	Banks	11,412	1.33	30	22	0.16	46	-7	-7	8	3.1	22.8
Reckitt Benckiser	HshdProd	11,408	0.47	21	19	0.14	12	12	19	27	1.9	22.7
British Sky Broadcasting Gp	SubsEntN	10,784	1.03	41	37	0.22	15	11	-32	-19	1.1	34.7
Prudential	Life Ass	10,761	1.48	36	28	0.19	40	-5	-14	3	3.5	17.8
mm02	Telcomob	10,652	1.11	44	40	0.25	16	17	46	59	0	64.2
Imperial Tobacco	Tobacco	10,406	0.64	28	26	0.18	13	14	25	35	3.5	23.2
Cadbury-Schweppes	FoodProc	10,046	0.60	22	20	0.15	18	9	12	21	2.5	26.6
GUS	Ret Dept	9,466	0.88	28	24	0.17	24	-2	14	25	3.0	19.8
Centrica	Gas Dist	8,907	0.86	25	21	0.15	28	-10	4	16	2.8	18.0
SABMiller	BevBrews	8,674	0.92	28	25	0.17	25	13	41	53	2.2	30.7
Scottish Power	Electric	7,515	0.50	24	23	0.16	10	-7	6	14	5.2	15.6
Scottish & Southern Energy	Electric	7,482	0.15	18	18	0.14	2	10	31	37	4.4	16.7
Kingfisher	Ret Dept	7,255	1.15	33	28	0.19	29	-7	1	15	3.2	30.6
Legal & General Group	Life Ass	7,156	1.38	29	20	0.15	54	2	-1	15	4.5	13.3
BAE Systems	Defence	7,054	1.21	38	33	0.21	24	-4	28	43	4.0	na
WPP Group	MediaAgc	6,760	1.46	39	32	0.20	33	2	-11	6	1.2	19.2
Carnival	LeisFacl	6,741	1.26	41	36	0.22	23	9	28	43	0.9	36.8
Land Securities Group	RealEsta	6,541	0.65	18	15	0.12	31	15	36	46	2.7	22.6
BAA	Air+Tran	6,255	0.69	24	21	0.15	20	2	12	22	3.5	16.4

Source: London Business School, January–March 2005. Capitalisation in £million.

for by its market risk. Arithmetically, it is derived from the values in the *Variability* and *Specific risk* columns and is derived from the other columns as follows:

$$R^2 = \frac{(\text{Variability})^2 - (\text{Specific risk})^2}{(\text{Variability})^2}$$

The next three columns relate to a share's actual and expected (from the CAPM) return over the past quarter and year.

Annual abnormal return compares the actual holding period return for the latest year with the return that was expected on the basis of the share's estimated beta for the past five years.

Net yield is the dividend yield, a measure of income on the share, which we discussed in Chapter 5.

P/E ratio is a valuation measure for shares, again already covered in Chapter 5.

Box 7.1 Beta and investment trust companies

An important characteristic of beta can be observed by looking at the R squareds and standard error of shares in *investment trust companies* (or *ITCs*). An investment trust is a company that simply invests in the shares of other companies, so it is in effect a portfolio of shares. Research has shown that betas of portfolios of shares tend to be more stationary over time than those of individual shares, and that their returns are more closely correlated to those of the market as a whole. An important assumption implicit in our historical sampling process is that the value we are seeking to estimate is unchanged over the sampling period. Across the London market as a whole, all 35 companies with the highest value for R squared were ITCs, with values ranging from 91 down to 69 (which was still appreciably higher than the highest value shown by a FTSE 100 share, HSBC at 64). These companies also had very low standard errors, almost all of them lower than the lowest in the FTSE 100 (again, HSBC at 0.11). The low standard error for the investment trusts is therefore telling us that our beta assumption is safer for such companies than it is for a conventional industrial or commercial enterprise.

We now turn to how the numbers in Table 7.1 can be used to analyse portfolio performance.

Analysing past performance

The CAPM can be used not only for estimating expected return and risk on any portfolio, but also for assessing its past performance. For example, the performance of an actual portfolio can be compared with the performance that would have been achieved by following the recommended CAPM strategy of holding a proportion of the market portfolio M, with a beta of 1, and adjusting to the required level of risk by holding positive or negative amounts of R_F. This CAPM strategy is known as a *passive strategy*, and is discussed in more detail in Chapter 12.

As we saw in Chapter 1, the FTSE 100 index is dominated by just four sectors: banks, oils, pharmaceuticals and telecoms. Suppose that an investor, Miss Divine, had constructed a portfolio at the beginning of 2004 by investing equal amounts in the largest company in each of those four sectors: BP, HSBC, Vodafone and GlaxoSmithKline. We can use CAPM to find out whether or not she was wise to restrict herself to a small, relatively undiversified portfolio, which still contains diversifiable (or specific) risk, instead of diversifying away all specific risk to the fullest possible extent. In short, did her *active strategy* beat the passive alternative?

The only additional information required for a complete risk–return analysis of her portfolio that is not in Table 7.1 is the return on the market and the risk-free rate of interest. A way round having to estimate the expected return on the market is to calculate the *equity risk premium* or market premium, $E(R_M) - R_F$.

There is considerable argument about what the appropriate equity risk premium should be. Over the long run, it has averaged around 5–7%, depending on the time period and stock market covered, but during the stock market bubble of the late 1990s and early 2000s it was estimated to be as low as 3–4%, or less. At the height of the stock market boom, investors were viewing equities as no riskier than bonds, implying a zero equity risk premium. After the market falls of the early 2000s, the typical equity risk premium is assumed to be around 5%.

So all that remains to be estimated is the risk-free rate of interest. We saw in the CAPM assumptions that one risk-free security could be a short-term government-backed security, such as a three-month treasury bill, to reduce inflation risk and interest rate risk to a minimum. An alternative risk-free asset could be a longer-term gilt that matched Miss Divine's expected holding period.

Let us first examine the past performance of Miss Divine's relatively undiversified portfolio. We can estimate the risk characteristics of Miss Divine's portfolio P using equation 7.17,which divides the variance of total risk into two elements, market risk, $\beta_P S_M^2$, and specific risk, S_P^2.

The beta of the portfolio is simply the weighted average of the constituent shares' betas:

$$\beta_p = (0.25 \times 0.82) + (0.25 \times 1.24) + (0.25 \times 1.05) + (0.25 \times 0.40)$$

$$\beta_p = \textbf{0.8775}$$

The variance of the market risk element is the square of the portfolio beta multiplied by the market risk S_M. We can find a realistic value for the market risk S_M over the past year, for instance by using the standard deviation of the FT-Actuaries All-Share Index, which was 15% (see the end of Appendix 7.1 and Table 7.2). So the standard deviation of the market risk element is given by the equation

$$\beta_p S_M = 0.8775 \times 0.15$$

and the variance of the market risk element is given by

$$\beta_P^2 S_M^2 = (0.8775)^2 (0.15)^2$$

$$= 0.7700 \times 0.0225$$

$$\beta_P^2 S_M^2 = \textbf{0.0173}$$

The other element of risk of the portfolio, the diversifiable or specific risk, is the weighted average of the specific risks of the constituent shares.

$$\text{(Portfolio specific risk)}^2 = S^2(e_p) = \sum_{i=1}^{i=n}(W_i S(e_i))^2$$

We know that W_i^2 is 1/16 for each i, giving

$$S^2(e_p) = \frac{1}{16}(0.18)^2 + \frac{1}{16}(0.14)^2 + \frac{1}{16}(0.31)^2 + \frac{1}{16}(0.20)^2$$

$$= 0.002025 + 0.001225 + 0.006006 + 0.002500$$

$$S^2(e_p) = 0.0118$$

We should note in passing that the portfolio's overall diversifiable risk as measured by its standard deviation is lower than the diversifiable risk of any of the individual constituents of the portfolio; the square root of the variance 0.0118 is 0.1084 or **10.84%**, significantly lower than the lowest of the individual securities' specific risks, 14% for HSBC. However, diversifiable risk is still present and represents an unrewarded element of risk according to the CAPM. We shall see below whether or not Miss Divine was in fact rewarded for taking on this unnecessary risk in 2004.

To complete the picture of the portfolio's risk, we calculate the portfolio's total risk V_p, which is the sum of the market element of risk plus the specific risk. From equation 7.17 we can write

$$V_p = \beta^2 S_M^2 + S^2(e_p)$$

$$V_p = 0.0173 + 0.0118 = 0.0291$$

$$S_p = \sqrt{V_p}$$

$$S_p = 0.1706$$

We now know that the total risk or variability of Miss Divine's portfolio is 17.06% compared with an equivalent figure for M of 15%.

We can now compare Miss Divine's portfolio's performance last year with what she could have achieved under a CAPM or passive strategy. The return that could have been achieved on a gilt-edged bond bought at the beginning of January 2004 with one year to maturity was about 4%, and the return on the market in 2004 (using the surrogate of the FT-Actuaries All-Share Index from Appendix 7.1 or Table 7.2) was 13%. From these we can calculate the return on the benchmark portfolio. Note that the benchmark portfolio is designed to have the same beta risk as Miss Divine's portfolio, that is, a beta of 0.8775.

$$R_p = (1 - \beta_p)R_F + \beta_p R_M$$

$$= (0.1225 \times 0.04) + (0.8775 \times 0.13)$$

$$= 0.1190$$

$$R_p = 11.90\%$$

We can now compare this with the return Miss Divine actually achieved on her portfolio. We do this by looking at the column headed 'annual actual return' in Table 7.1 and finding the weighted average of the returns for each of the securities:

$$R_p = (0.25 \times 0.16) + (0.25 \times 0.04) + + (0.25 \times 0.04) + (0.25 \times -0.01)$$

$$= 0.0575$$

$$R_p = \mathbf{5.75\%}$$

So, whereas the stock market as a whole did quite well, Miss Divine did relatively poorly, and much worse than if she had pursued a CAPM strategy of putting 12.25 per cent of her money into the risk-free asset and the balance of 87.75 per cent into a well-diversified portfolio. The diversifiable risk she retained by not holding a diversified portfolio led to her *underperforming* the benchmark portfolio that had the same amount of beta risk, by 11.90% – 5.75% = 6.15%. This is known as the *abnormal return*, and is given in the Risk Measurement Service for each share.

At first sight, Miss Divine's strategy – spreading her money evenly across blue-chip shares in four quite different economic sectors – looks reasonable enough. But a closer analysis of the individual securities' returns in Miss Divine's portfolio reminds us of the true meaning of the term 'risk'. All of her shares performed quite markedly differently from expectation, and only BP outperformed: the other three underperformed very badly.

Would Miss Divine have fared better if, instead of investing in just one share in each of her chosen sectors, she had invested equal amounts in diversified portfolios from each

Table 7.2 Risk and return data for selected sectors of the FTSE Actuaries Indices

FTSE sector	Number of companies	Average capitalisation	Index %age	Beta	Variability	Specific risk	Standard error of beta	R squared	Qtly abnormal return	Ann. abnormal return	Actual annual return
Resources 　Oil & Gas	(20)	8,629	12.2	0.86	21	16	0.12	41	-7	5	16
Non-cyclical consumer 　goods 　Pharmaceuticals	(16)	6,986	7.9	0.54	19	17	0.12	18	-7	-18	-9
Non-cyclical services 　Telecommunications 　services	(12)	10,467	8.9	1.22	31	24	0.15	37	3	-7	7
Financials 　Banks	(10)	27,287	19.4	1.25	23	12	0.09	71	-1	-3	12
FTSE All-Share	(705)	2,042	100.0	1.00	15	1	0.00	100	0	0	13

Source: London Business School, December 2004.

of those sectors? To find the answer, we shall follow the same methodology, but substitute the following sector values (from Appendix 7.1) for the individual security values we have used previously.

The beta of this portfolio of portfolios is the weighted average of the constituent sectors' betas:

$$\beta_p = (0.25 \times 0.86) + (0.25 \times 0.54) + (0.25 \times 1.22) + (0.25 \times 1.25)$$

$$\beta_p = \mathbf{0.9675}$$

The variance of the market risk element is the square of the standard deviation of this element, which is the portfolio beta multiplied by the market risk S_M.

$$\beta_p S_M = 0.9675 \times 0.15$$

and the variance of the market risk element is given by

$$\beta_p^2 S_M^2 = (0.9675)^2 (0.15)^2$$

$$= 0.9361 \times 0.0225$$

$$\beta_p^2 S_M^2 = \mathbf{0.0211}$$

The other element of risk of the portfolio, the diversifiable or specific risk, will be the weighted average of the specific risks of the constituent sectors.

$$(\text{Portfolio specific risk})^2 = S^2(e_p) = \sum_{i=1}^{i=n} (W_i S(e_i))^2$$

We know that W_i is 1/16 for each i, giving

$$S^2(e_p) = \frac{1}{16}(0.16)^2 + \frac{1}{16}(0.17)^2 + \frac{1}{16}(0.24)^2 + \frac{1}{16}(0.12)^2$$

$$= 0.0016 + 0.0018 + 0.0036 + 0.0009$$

$$S^2(e_p) = \mathbf{0.0079}$$

Note that the portfolio's overall diversifiable risk ($\sqrt{0.0079} = 0.0889 = \mathbf{8.89\%}$) is lower than the diversifiable risk of any of the individual constituent sectors of the portfolio.

To complete the picture of the portfolio's risk, we calculate the portfolio's total risk V_p, which is the sum of the market element of risk plus the specific risk.

$$V_p = \beta_i^2 S_M^2 + S^2(e_p)$$

$$V_p = 0.0211 + 0.0079$$

$$S_p = \sqrt{V_p}$$

$$S_p = \mathbf{0.1703}$$

So the total standard deviation of Miss Divine's portfolio is 17.03% compared with an equivalent figure for M of 15%.

Next we compare Miss Divine's portfolio's performance last year with what she could have achieved under a CAPM or passive strategy. From the values we have already calculated for the risk-free rate and for the market return, we can calculate the return on a benchmark portfolio with the same beta risk as Miss Divine's portfolio: that is, a beta of 0.9675.

$$R_p = (1 - \beta_p)R_F + \beta_p R_M$$
$$= (0.0325 \times 0.04) + (0.9675 \times 0.13)$$
$$= 0.1271$$
$$R_p = 12.7\%$$

We can now compare this with the return Miss Divine actually achieved on her portfolio.

$$R_p = (0.25 \times 0.16) + (0.25 \times -0.09) + (0.25 \times 0.07) + (0.25 \times 0.12)$$
$$= 0.0650$$
$$R_p = 6.5\%$$

giving an annual abnormal return of -6.2%.

Has Miss Divine done better by investing in sectors rather than in individual securities? Table 7.3 summarises the results of the two exercises.

Table 7.3 Investing in shares and in sectors: comparison of risk and return

	Beta	Variability	Specific risk	R squared	Ann. abnormal return	Actual annual return
Portfolio of shares	0.88	17.06	10.8	59.9	-6.1	5.8
Portfolio of sector portfolios	0.97	17.03	8.9	72.7	-6.2	6.5

Source: London Business School.

The results of this attempt to spread risk by investing in sectors rather than in individual companies are both surprising and disappointing. Although the total risk remains roughly the same, by investing in sectors rather than in individual shares Miss Divine has achieved a worthwhile, though hardly dramatic, reduction in specific or diversifiable risk: market risk, as measured by the R^2 values, had increased from 59.9% to 72.7% of total risk.[1] The disappointing aspect is that the abnormal return has actually increased.

The explanation for this result lies partly in the fact that each of the individual securities in Miss Divine's original portfolio represents a very large proportion of its sector. HSBC represents 36 per cent of the total value of the banking sector in the FTSE Actuaries index, whilst the other three shares in Miss Divine's portfolio account for over 60 per cent of their respective sectors. This *lumpiness* of the market is a practical problem which affects every investment strategy in one way or another. A second reason for Miss Divine's

---

1 Remember that R squared measures the percentage contribution of market risk to total risk and is calculated as follows:

$$R \text{ squared} = \frac{(\text{Variability})^2 - (\text{Specific risk})^2}{(\text{Variability})^2}$$

unsatisfactory result lies in the relative weightings of her investments. While it might not have appeared unreasonable to invest equal amounts in her original four securities, as their individual market capitalisations lay in a relatively narrow band between £74 billion and £91 billion, the underlying sectoral weightings are quite different from each other, ranging from 7.9% for pharmaceuticals to 19.4% for banks, expressed as a percentage of the FTSE All-Share Index..

Estimating future performance

If Miss Divine wants to estimate expected return on her portfolio, all that she needs to know is the risk-free rate over her desired holding period and an expected value for the equity market premium. Suppose she again wishes to consider a one-year horizon. She can use the one-year spot interest rate implicit in gilt prices, which can be derived as we saw in Chapter 4, as her risk-free rate. Suppose that this is now 4.5%. The market premium can be estimated at 9% again on the basis of the 2004 result, or it might be more prudent to use instead a long-run average of 5%. This will give the expected return on her portfolio $E(R_p)$ as

$$E(R_p) = R_p + \beta_p(E(R_M) - R_p)$$
$$= 0.045 + 0.8775(0.05)$$

$$E(R_p) = 0.0888$$

or 8.8% p.a.

Miss Divine can expect to be rewarded only for the element of market risk, measured by her portfolio beta of 0.8775. She can expect no additional reward for bearing avoidable diversifiable risk.

Constructing a benchmark portfolio

Before we leave this example, let us consider how Miss Divine could follow the recommended CAPM strategy in practice. First of all, she should hold a proportion of the market portfolio. Obviously, it would be difficult in real life for her to hold small amounts of each risky security in issue, in proportion to its total market value, because of the enormous transaction costs involved. She would also have to buy and sell securities continually, as share prices moved, to maintain her weightings.

An alternative strategy would be to buy shares in an index fund, a fund set up specially to mirror the market portfolio as closely as possible. This type of fund restricts itself to shares (although strictly it should include all marketable assets) and it may not contain all the shares in the market, or even, say, all the approximately 700 shares in the FTSE All-Share Index (see Chapter 5 Appendix 5.3). This is because a reasonably good approximation to the share market as a whole can be obtained by holding only a few hundred shares. With that number, a beta of 1 can be achieved and there is hardly any specific risk.

Index funds were initially set up in the United States, where it is estimated that more than 30 per cent of institutional investment in equities is now in such funds. Index funds have also shown rapid growth in the United Kingdom and elsewhere, so that they are now a global phenomenon, with many countries' equity markets available to investors through funds tailored to the most representative stock market index for that country. Retail products have also been developed so that individual investors, as well as institutional investors, have access to a CAPM or passive investment strategy.

An alternative would be to invest in an investment trust or unit trust (both discussed in greater detail in Chapter 11) with a beta of 1. To achieve a beta of 0.8775, Miss Divine would then have to invest a small amount in gilts to reduce her overall exposure to market risk.

Yet another alternative strategy for Miss Divine would be to invest in a portfolio much better diversified than her present one, that has the beta that she requires of 0.8775. She would thus avoid having to invest in gilts to reach her required level of risk. In theory, she would not need to hold many more shares than she holds at the moment, since we saw in Chapter 6 that a portfolio equally divided between ten shares should on average eliminate 90 per cent of the diversifiable risk of the individual securities. But as we have seen, the lumpiness of the market – with just four shares accounting for 26 per cent of the total market – makes this more difficult to achieve in practice.

Miss Divine must therefore be holding her present portfolio either because she has not heard of portfolio theory and the CAPM or because she believes she can pick shares that will do better than predicted by the CAPM. In other words, she believes that she can pick winners. She did not succeed in 2004. It remains to be seen whether she will make up the lost ground in future years.

What determines beta?

So far we have considered beta primarily in theoretical terms. What determines the beta of a security in practice? What makes one security generally more or less responsive than another to changes in the return on the market as a whole? As beta excludes by definition all risk factors that are unique to the specific issuer of the security, we have to look further afield for a satisfactory explanation of securities' varying degrees of linkage to the market. Not surprisingly, research in this area has concentrated on the general characteristics of the industry sector in which the issuer of a specific security operates. Some industries tend to do better than others at different points in the economic cycle; and major movements in stock market prices have often been associated with outperformance or underperformance by the shares of companies in particular sectors. These trends became particularly marked in the final years of the protracted 1990s *bull market*, and continued through the three-year *bear market* from early 2000 until March 2003 and the partial recovery of 2003–06.

The primary source of market risk arises from the interaction of a company's *business operations* with the external environment, but there is a further and unrelated factor specifically affecting the expected return and standard deviation of returns on a company's shares. This is the company's *financial structure,* and specifically the ratio of debt to equity in its total financing.

How financing affects beta is illustrated by Table 7.4. In Column A we show the possible value of a company's annual operating profit across the full range of future states of the world in the next year. In this base case we assume that the company is unleveraged (that is, it is financed entirely by equity), so the entire operating profit accrues to the shareholders as their return on investment. The expected profit of £17 is the mean value

Table 7.4 How leverage affects equity risk and return

Base case £100	25% debt		50% debt		75% debt	
Equity £100	Debt £25	Equity £75	Debt £50	Equity £50	Debt £75	Equity £25
Operating profit £ (A)	Interest paid on debt £ (B)	Annual return on equity % (C)	Interest paid on debt £ (D)	Annual return on equity % (E)	Interest paid on debt £ (F)	Annual return on equity % (G)
5.90	-1.25	6.20	-2.50	6.80	-3.75	8.60
1.10	-1.25	-0.20	-2.50	-2.80	-3.75	-10.60
-1.10	-1.25	-3.13	-2.50	-7.20	-3.75	-19.40
4.80	-1.25	4.73	-2.50	4.60	-3.75	4.20
31.20	-1.25	39.93	-2.50	57.40	-3.75	109.80
17.50	-1.25	21.67	-2.50	30.00	-3.75	55.00
44.60	-1.25	57.80	-2.50	84.20	-3.75	163.40
42.40	-1.25	54.87	-2.50	79.80	-3.75	154.60
-3.20	-1.25	-5.93	-2.50	-11.40	-3.75	-27.80
26.30	-1.25	33.40	-2.50	47.60	-3.75	90.20
39.10	-1.25	50.47	-2.50	73.20	-3.75	141.40
-10.90	-1.25	-16.20	-2.50	-26.80	-3.75	-58.60
19.40	-1.25	24.20	-2.50	33.80	-3.75	62.60
4.90	-1.25	4.87	-2.50	4.80	-3.75	4.60
28.60	-1.25	36.47	-2.50	52.20	-3.75	99.40
28.90	-1.25	36.87	-2.50	52.80	-3.75	100.60
16.50	-1.25	20.33	-2.50	28.00	-3.75	51.00
8.50	-1.25	9.67	-2.50	12.00	-3.75	19.00
-3.10	-1.25	-5.80	-2.50	-11.20	-3.75	-27.40
20.90	-1.25	26.20	-2.50	36.80	-3.75	68.60
20.10	-1.25	25.13	-2.50	35.20	-3.75	65.40
36.10	-1.25	46.47	-2.50	67.20	-3.75	129.40
38.70	-1.25	49.93	-2.50	72.40	-3.75	139.80
28.70	-1.25	36.60	-2.50	52.40	-3.75	99.80
17.20	-1.25	21.27	-2.50	29.40	-3.75	53.80
29.20	-1.25	37.27	-2.50	53.40	-3.75	101.80
6.10	-1.25	6.47	-2.50	7.20	-3.75	9.40
3.90	-1.25	3.53	-2.50	2.80	-3.75	0.60
19.90	-1.25	24.87	-2.50	34.80	-3.75	64.60
-12.20	-1.25	-17.93	-2.50	-29.40	-3.75	-63.80
Expected return						
17.00		21.00		29.00		53.00
Standard deviation						
16.00		21.33		32.00		64.00

of possible profits, and the risk as measured by the standard deviation is £16. If we also assume that the shareholders require a return of 17% on their investment, the value of the shares, and hence of the company itself, is £100. It is important to note that the value of the company – that is, of its net operating assets – is in principle independent of the particular way those assets are financed. The situation is not fundamentally different from that of a private residential property, whose value is not increased or decreased by changes in the way it is financed; but what does change as the financing arrangements change is the owner's *equity interest* in the property.

In the remaining three pairs of columns we explore what would happen to the return and risk of the shares if the company were to become leveraged: that is, if debt were to be substituted for equity in different proportions in the company's overall financing structure. In each of these cases, we assume that the cost of debt is 5% p.a.; debt is cheaper than equity because the return is more secure and more stable than the return on shares.

In the first scenario (columns B and C), 25 per cent of the firm's capital requirement is provided by £25 of debt. The annual interest charge on this will be a constant £1.25, because lenders expect a fixed contractual return, regardless of the fortunes of the underlying business. This has a double effect on the expected return on equity.

First, the expected return increases. As 25 per cent of the total capital requirement has been met by lenders who require only a 5% annual return on investment, the proportionate expected return on the shareholders' residual investment has increased; in addition to the expected 17% return on 'their' 75 per cent of the company, they can expect to keep 12% of the return on the other 25 per cent. As a result, their expected return increases from 17% to (17% + (12% x 25/75)), which is 21%.

Second, the risk of the expected return also increases. At first sight, this result may not be obvious. After all, if a constant amount of interest is deducted from the operating profit, then the residual amount available to the shareholders will fluctuate by exactly the same amount as when the company was unleveraged. Although this statement is true of the absolute monetary amount of the fluctuation, it overlooks the fact that a standard deviation is always expressed in the same units as the variable to which it relates, and the variable in this case is the percentage return. Just as the percentage return increases as the value of equity on which it is earned decreases, so does the standard deviation of those returns, and in exactly the same linear fashion. So, in the case of 25% leverage, the standard deviation has increased from 16% to (16% + (16% × 25/75)), which is 21.3%. The remaining pairs of columns extrapolate these findings for successively higher levels of leveraging.

How do these observations affect security betas? The financial structure of a company has a direct and objectively measurable effect on the risk and return of its shares. If we make one further simplifying assumption, that the beta of the company's debt is zero, then we can capture this effect in a simple equation. In order to show how this works in the case of the fictitious company in Table 7.4, and in order to simplify the mathematics as far as possible, we shall assume that the company has a beta of 1.0. We also assume a risk-free rate of 5% and an expected equity risk premium of 12%. Taken together, these assumptions give us the following values:

$$R_F \qquad = 5.0\%$$
$$E(R_M) - R_F = 12.0\%$$
$$\beta_e \qquad = 1.0$$

where β_e is the beta of the company's shares, so that the expected return on the company's shares in the unleveraged state is given by the equation

$$E(R_i) \quad = R_F + \beta_e(E(R_M) - R_F)$$

$$= 5\% + 1.0(12\%)$$

$$= \mathbf{17\%}$$

When the company leverages up by taking on debt, there is no change in the company's operating profit; its overall sensitivity to market risk is unaffected by changes in the financing arrangements. What has changed is that a third party – a lender – has been added to the equation and has struck a bargain (with the company and with its shareholders) whereby it has agreed to accept less than a proportionate share of the overall operating returns *on condition that it accepts none of the associated business risk*. As the nature and magnitude of the business risk are unaffected by these arrangements, they simply become more concentrated on the shareholders' residual interest in the firm in direct proportion to the degree of leverage.

In order to express more formally what is happening here, we need to introduce a distinction between the beta of equity in the unleveraged state and the beta of equity in the leveraged state of the company. Conventionally, the former is denoted by *asset beta* with the notation β_A and the latter by *equity beta* with the notation β_E. Asset beta is admittedly not an ideal formulation as it is not always intuitively obvious to what it refers; after all, betas are associated with securities, which are not assets but liabilities of the companies issuing them. A perhaps more transparent term would be *enterprise beta*, because this draws attention to the fact that it derives from the market sensitivity of the business enterprise itself rather than from the incidental circumstances of the enterprise's financing.

If we let

V = the market value of the company or enterprise
E = the market value of the equity
D = the market value of the debt,

Such that

$$V = E + D$$

then we can readily capture the idea of the concentration of risk on to the shareholders' interest in a leveraged company with the equation

$$\beta_E = \beta_A \times \frac{V}{E} \tag{7.18}$$

In the example given in Table 7.4, we have initially assumed no leverage, and so the equity beta is equal to the asset beta, and is equal to 1. Now suppose that the company is financed instead with 50 per cent equity and 50 per cent debt, so that V/E = 2. The asset beta, reflecting the business risk, does not change. But the equity beta, reflecting both business and financial risk, will rise. From equation 7.18 we can estimate the revised equity beta:

$$\beta_E = \beta_A \times \frac{V}{E}$$

$$= 1.0 \times 2$$

$$\boldsymbol{\beta_E = 2.0}$$

Adding debt to the capital structure has increased the required rate of return on equity through a higher equity beta.

We can estimate the revised expected rate of return on equity:

$$E(R_i) = R_F + \beta_E(E(R_M) - R_F)$$
$$= 5\% + 2.0(12\%)$$

$$E(R_i) = 29\%$$

The required rate of return on the company's shares has risen from 17% to 29% to reflect the higher financial risk.

Conversely, if all we have is the value of the leveraged beta, we can use the same equation to calculate the underlying unleveraged beta of a company:

$$\beta_A = \beta_E \times \frac{E}{V}$$

As we stated earlier, this simple relationship depends on our assumption that the company borrows at the risk-free rate and that its debt has no market risk at all: that is, that its debt has a beta of zero. In practice this is seldom if ever the case, so we need to modify the above equation to take account of this added complexity. In this case, the overall market risk of the enterprise is being shared between the providers of debt and the providers of equity capital, so that if we let β_D = the beta of debt we can write

$$\beta_A = \left(\beta_D \times \frac{D}{V}\right) + \left(\beta_E \times \frac{E}{V}\right) \tag{7.19}$$

To sum up, the equity beta of a leveraged company reflects two different kinds of exposure to market risk: operating or business risk, which is inherent in the company's business enterprise and how it interacts with the external economic environment, and financial risk, which is the additional sensitivity to market risk caused by the process of leveraging up the company's financial structure.

When we compare the equity betas of two companies operating in the same sector, the first step is always to strip out the differential effects of any disparity in their financial structure, so that our analysis of their underlying business operations is conducted on a strict like-for-like basis.

PROBLEMS WITH THE CAPM

We have seen how simple it is to apply the CAPM in practice to portfolio investment. Yet we do not see all investors holding index funds (or investment trusts) with betas of 1 and positive or negative amounts of some risk-free security. In practice, each investor holds a different portfolio of shares, as predicted by portfolio theory but not by the CAPM. So what if anything is wrong with the CAPM?

No taxes or transaction costs?

First of all, we must remember the restrictive assumptions of the model: for example that there are no taxes or transaction costs. Small investors will be unwilling to buy

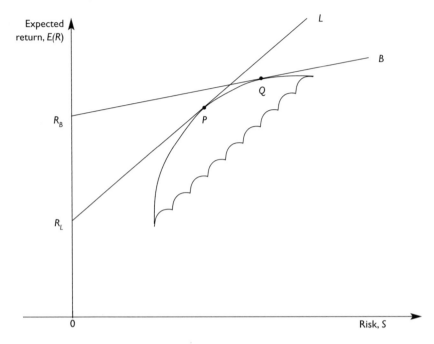

Figure 7.5 Efficient portfolios with different borrowing and lending rates

a proportion of all the securities in the stock market when they have only £10,000 to invest, although an index fund or investment trust will offer them a close surrogate for *M*. Moreover, *M* in theory should contain all marketable assets, including works of art and property and other non-financial investments. For practicalities' sake, a market index including most company shares is used to represent *M*, but this excludes a substantial number of marketable assets.

Borrowing at the risk-free rate?

Another obvious problem with the assumptions is that all investors cannot borrow and lend at the risk-free rate. If we assume that the lending rate R_L is lower than the borrowing rate R_B we get the result shown in Figure 7.5. There is no longer only one efficient portfolio *M*. The investor will choose either a point on one of the two lines $R_L P$ and *QB* or any efficient portfolio from the efficient frontier *PQ*. We can see that, with a relaxation of one of the assumptions of the CAPM, we have the result that investors will not necessarily all hold the market portfolio. However, it has been shown that other assumptions underlying the CAPM can be relaxed without affecting its major results. For example, the CAPM can still be derived without the need for a risk-free asset; a zero beta security (or combination of securities) can be used instead (Black 1972).

What is 'the market'?

Calculating the inputs for the risk-free rate and the risk and return of the market as a whole is rather more problematic. The central difficulty is the definition of 'the market'. Portfolio theory and CAPM were originally formulated in the United States at a time when cross-border equity investment into and out of the United States was much less significant than it is today, so the implicit identification of 'the market' with 'the domestic stock market' was not unreasonable. This is no longer the case. There is a high degree of cross-border investment between the stock markets of the major world economies, and the companies quoted on each country's stock market are not necessarily representative of their own country but increasingly belong to international or global peer groups. There is frequently a stronger correlation in the returns on large company shares between the US and UK stock markets than there is between large and small company shares within either of those markets. This implies that so far from there being a single discrete and homogenous pool of funds available for investment on the UK stock exchange, there are potentially many such pools of funds and 'the UK stock exchange' does not accurately or meaningfully describe an opportunity set available to any of them.

The existence and anomalous price behaviour of dual-listed companies (see Chapter 5) poses specific problems for the application of CAPM in practice. The general problems associated with the international dimension of investment will be discussed in more detail in Chapter 11.

Which market premium?

Even within the confines of a single country's stock market, there is considerable argument about what the appropriate 'market premium' or 'risk premium for equities' should be. Table 7.5 shows that in the United Kingdom, the actual average annual premium for equities when compared with government bonds in ten-year periods from 1900 onwards has been as high as 16.4%; this was in the 1950s, when the average annual inflation rate was 4.1%. In general, the equity market premium seems to have been falling during the second half of the century. The figures also show that investors in nominally risk-free assets such as government bills and bonds had a very rough ride during the period of high and volatile inflation rates in the 1970s and 1980s, whereas investors in equities posted steady gains – even after allowing for inflation – in four of the five completed decades since 1950. By contrast, the average equity market premium in the four-year period from the beginning of 2000 was *negative* 10.5%. Overall, the assumption of a long-run average of 4–5% seems to be reasonable.

Which risk-free rate?

It now remains to estimate the risk-free rate of interest. We saw in the assumptions of the CAPM that a true risk-free security would be hard to find. Two possible approximations are either a short-term, government-backed security, such as a three-month Treasury bill, to reduce inflation risk and interest rate risk to a minimum, or one of the longer-term government bonds which were discussed in Chapter 3, as was the case when we looked at Miss Divine's benchmark portfolio. It is important, though, to be consistent when choosing the risk-free rate in the equity risk premium calculation, and the risk-free rate itself. Table 7.5 also shows the historic equity risk premium relative to bills rather than bonds.

Table 7.5 UK real rates of return, inflation and premia over holding periods of various lengths between 1900 and 2004

		1900	1910	1920	1930	1940	1950	1960	1970	1980	1990	2000	2004	
Real	1900		2.0	5.3	3.8	2.0	2.1	4.3	4.9	4.6	4.9	4.6	4.0	Equity
equity	1910	1.8		8.6	4.7	2.0	2.1	4.8	5.3	5.0	5.3	4.9	4.2	premium
total	1920	0.2	-1.3		0.9	-1.1	0.0	3.9	4.7	4.4	4.8	4.4	3.7	vs bonds
returns	1930	3.1	3.8	9.3		-3.1	-0.4	4.9	5.7	5.2	5.5	5.0	4.1	
	1940	3.0	3.4	5.9	2.6		2.3	9.1	8.8	7.3	7.3	6.4	5.2	
	1950	3.0	3.3	4.9	2.9	3.1		16.4	12.2	9.1	8.6	7.2	5.8	
	1960	4.7	5.3	7.1	6.4	8.3	13.7		8.1	5.6	6.2	5.0	3.5	
	1970	5.0	5.5	7.0	6.4	7.7	10.0	6.5		3.1	5.2	4.0	2.2	
	1980	4.2	4.5	5.5	4.8	5.3	6.1	2.5	-1.4		7.3	4.5	1.8	
	1990	5.4	5.8	6.9	6.5	7.3	8.3	6.6	6.7	15.4		1.7	-2.0	
	2000	5.9	6.4	7.4	7.1	7.9	8.9	7.7	8.1	13.3	11.2		-10.5	
	2004	5.3	5.7	6.6	6.2	6.8	7.5	6.2	6.1	9.4	5.3	-8.2		
Real	1900		-0.1	1.7	1.7	1.7	2.4	4.4	4.4	4.1	4.7	4.9	4.3	Equity
equity	1910	-2.5		3.5	2.6	2.3	3.0	5.3	5.2	4.7	5.4	5.5	4.8	premium
capital	1920	-4.4	-6.3		1.7	1.7	2.8	5.8	5.5	4.9	5.6	5.7	4.9	vs bills
gains	1930	-1.8	-1.4	3.7		1.7	3.4	7.2	6.5	5.6	6.3	6.3	5.4	
	1940	-1.8	-1.5	1.0	-1.7		5.1	10.0	8.1	6.5	7.3	7.1	5.9	
	1950	-1.5	-1.3	0.4	-1.2	-0.7		15.1	9.6	7.0	7.8	7.5	6.1	
	1960	0.0	0.5	2.3	1.9	3.7	8.3		4.5	3.2	5.5	5.7	4.2	
	1970	0.3	0.7	2.2	1.8	3.0	4.9	1.7		2.0	6.0	6.1	4.1	
	1980	-0.6	-0.3	0.7	0.1	0.5	1.0	-2.5	-6.6		10.1	8.3	4.9	
	1990	0.5	0.9	2.0	1.7	2.4	3.1	1.5	1.3	9.9		6.5	1.4	
	2000	1.1	1.5	2.5	2.4	3.1	3.8	2.7	3.1	8.3	6.6		-10.2	
	2004	0.6	0.9	1.9	1.6	2.1	2.7	1.4	1.3	4.8	1.3	-10.8		
Real	1900		-2.1	-3.4	-2.0	-0.3	0.3	0.1	-0.4	-0.5	-0.2	0.3	0.3	Bond
bonds	1910	-0.2		-4.7	-2.0	0.3	0.9	0.5	-0.2	-0.3	0.1	0.6	0.6	maturity
	1920	-4.8	-9.2		0.8	2.8	2.8	1.8	0.8	0.4	0.8	1.2	1.2	premium
	1930	-0.6	-0.8	8.3		5.0	3.9	2.2	0.8	0.4	0.7	1.3	1.3	
	1940	1.0	1.4	7.1	5.9		2.8	0.8	-0.6	-0.7	-0.1	0.7	0.7	
	1950	0.9	1.2	4.9	3.3	0.7		-1.1	-2.3	-1.9	-0.8	0.3	0.3	
	1960	0.4	0.5	3.1	1.4	-0.8	-2.3		-3.4	-2.2	-0.7	0.7	0.6	
	1970	0.1	0.2	2.1	0.7	-1.0	-1.9	-1.5		-1.1	0.7	2.0	1.8	
	1980	-0.5	-0.5	1.0	-0.4	-1.9	-2.7	-3.0	-4.4		2.6	3.7	3.1	
	1990	0.4	0.5	1.9	0.9	-0.1	-0.3	0.4	1.4	7.5		4.7	3.4	
	2000	1.3	1.4	2.8	2.1	1.4	1.6	2.6	4.0	8.4	9.3		0.3	
	2004	1.3	1.5	2.8	2.1	1.5	1.7	2.6	3.8	7.4	7.4	2.6		
Real	1900		1.1	4.9	2.2	1.8	2.0	2.3	2.5	3.8	4.1	4.1	4.0	Inflation
bills	1910	1.9		8.9	2.8	2.0	2.2	2.6	2.8	4.2	4.5	4.4	4.3	
	1920	-1.4	-4.7		-2.9	-1.3	0.1	1.1	1.6	3.4	3.9	3.9	3.8	
	1930	1.4	1.2	7.5		0.4	1.6	2.4	2.7	4.7	5.1	4.9	4.7	
	1940	1.3	1.1	4.1	0.9		2.8	3.5	3.5	5.8	6.1	5.6	5.4	
	1950	0.6	0.3	2.1	-0.5	-2.0		4.1	3.9	6.9	6.9	6.2	5.9	
	1960	0.3	0.0	1.2	-0.8	-1.6	-1.2		3.7	8.3	7.8	6.7	6.3	
	1970	0.6	0.3	1.4	-0.1	-0.4	0.4	1.9		13.1	10.0	7.8	7.1	
	1980	0.1	-0.2	0.6	-0.7	-1.2	-0.9	-0.7	-3.3		6.9	5.2	4.7	
	1990	0.6	0.4	1.2	0.2	0.0	0.5	1.1	0.7	4.8		3.5	3.2	
	2000	1.0	0.9	1.6	0.8	0.7	1.3	1.9	1.9	4.6	4.4		2.3	
	2004	1.0	0.9	1.6	0.8	0.8	1.4	1.9	1.9	4.2	3.8	2.3		

Source: Dimson and Marsh (2004).

Beta – a moving target?

Finally, do betas of individual securities really remain static over time? The risk profile of a company changes gradually as the company grows and evolves, and conscious decisions to change strategy or direction can cause radical shifts in a company's overall sensitivity to market risk. The market risk characteristics of whole sectors can also change, though the evidence is that this is a more gradual process than the typical rate of change at company level. As *e* is by definition a random error term, if there is *any* detectable pattern in its value over time, then we can conclude with some confidence that the regression line that we have plotted is not telling us the whole story about the relationship between the return on the security and the return on the market. If, for instance, the error term has a tendency to become increasingly positive as time passes, this tells us that the relationship described by our regression line is tending increasingly to underestimate the return on the security. Blume (1975), among others, established a general tendency for security betas to trend towards 1.00 over time. One way to test the hypothesis that a beta is changing is to plot the value of the error term *e* for successive holding periods over time. Using exhaustive research into the behaviour of US security prices, Blume proposed a standard correction to historical beta as a basis for estimating a future beta, as follows:

$$\text{Prospective beta} = 0.33 + (0.67 \times \text{historical beta}) \tag{7.20}$$

In round numbers, this means that we should estimate future betas as having values one-third of the way between the historical value and 1.00. Although this adjustment is widely used, it must be stressed that it is ultimately based on a subjective judgment, and other interpretations of the data are possible.

ALTERNATIVES TO THE CAPM

Despite the problems associated with the assumptions underlying the CAPM, there are few simple alternatives to the CAPM that can provide estimates of the future expected return on a share. One method, already mentioned in Chapter 5, is to forecast all future dividends to be paid on the share or, more simply, to assume constant growth of such dividends (Gordon's growth model). The assumptions underlying Gordon's growth model are as restrictive as those underlying the CAPM, and the CAPM provides an intuitively logical relationship between risk and expected return as well as using market data, albeit historic, rather than subjective forecasts.

Other alternatives to the CAPM are compromises between the single-index approach of the CAPM, where expected return is a function of only one factor (namely beta or covariance with the market), and the more computationally complicated portfolio theory. These multi-index models do not have the same theoretical base as the CAPM but start off from the same point. The single-index market model was based on the observation that all share prices tend to move up or down with a market index. Multi-index models are based on the fact that variations in share prices and returns can be traced to other common factors such as industry influences or interest rate changes. The impact of such factors is discussed in more detail in Chapter 13.

Such models can be written in the form

$$E(R_i) = a_i + b_{i1}E(I_1) + b_{i2}E(I_2) + \ldots + b_{in}E(I_n) \tag{7.21}$$

where a_i is a constant, and the b_{ij} terms reflect the sensitivity of the return to the indices I_1, I_2 etc., that measure the different influences on share returns. I_1 could be a market index, I_2 an industry index and so on. Equation 7.21 can always be stated so that the index factors are independent of each other $((COVI_i, I_j) = 0$ for all i, $j)$ and this considerably simplifies the computations for calculating efficient portfolios.

Multi-index models are generally derived by putting in possible explanatory factors such as industry or interest rate indices, and seeing how well the data can be explained. Historic data are used to calculate the coefficients of the equation, and the equation can then be used to forecast expected returns, as with the CAPM. The problem with more complex models, which have more explanatory variables, is that although they explain the historic data better than simpler models (that is, they achieve a good 'fit'), they may also include random 'noise' from the data and actually explain less than a simpler model when used on other sets of data. A regression model always involves a compromise between explaining as much variation as possible and running the risk that the 'noise' included will spoil its predictive powers.

A multi-index model that statistically derives the explanatory factors affecting share returns from the actual data (rather than taking economic factors and seeing how well they fit) is that of *arbitrage pricing theory* (or *APT*). Proposed by Ross in 1976, this provides a theoretical foundation for a multi-index model with independent indices. First, it shows that with the possibility of diversification available to any investor, any non-common causes of risk ('specific' or 'unique' risk) can be diversified away as with CAPM. Second, it proves that, if shares are assumed to form an efficient market where no arbitrage profits can be made, the expected return of a share must be a linear expression of its sensitivities to the factors affecting it. Arbitrage profits are those that can be made without any risk at all – in this case, if there were some securities that were cheaply priced relative to others with the same risk. In efficient markets, where no arbitrage profits can be made, there would be no 'free lunches' of this kind. So,

$$E(R_i) = a_i + b_{i1}\beta_1 + b_{i2}\beta_2 + \ldots \tag{7.22}$$

where the β_j are the sensitivities of security i to the factors or indices affecting its returns, and the a_i, b_{ij} are constants specific to security i. These indices can be statistically derived from the data rather than by indices suggested by the researcher as in the earlier multi-index models.

Arbitrage pricing theory has gained popularity as the empirical tests have fuelled criticism of the CAPM. It has been shown reasonably successfully that a security's return is an increasing and linear function of its beta, but the foundation for such tests has been criticised by Roll (1977), who argued that the surrogates used for 'the market' are not good enough, and the tests in fact show whether or not the surrogates are efficient portfolios rather than proving or disproving CAPM. The implication of Roll's criticism is, in fact, that the CAPM is untestable. However, empirical testing of the newer APT is hindered by the failure of the model to specify exactly which factors the β_i apply to. Are they interest rate, cyclicality, industry or other factors?

Fama and French (1993) developed an empirical model based on the multi-factor approach. As well as a conventional beta risk factor, they added two others that they argue better explain equity returns, a size factor and a book value/market value of equity factor. The size factor was to allow for the fact that small capitalisation frms tended to underperform large cap firms. The book value/market value factor was to explain the relative outperformance of 'value' as opposed to 'growth' shares. This so-called Fama–French three-factor model has achieved popularity, despite the relative underperformance of value shares in the late 1990s growth-related boom.

Despite the problems associated with the CAPM and the possible shifts in research emphasis to a multi-index model of the form suggested by the APT, the CAPM is simpler in conception than the newer multi-index models, such as APT. It is therefore unlikely to hold as well as these in the real world but it is computationally simple and easy to understand and apply in practice. Although its results should be treated with caution, it offers a framework for investment decision making to the investor which 'gut feel' does not. For further discussion of the empirical evidence on CAPM and of Roll's critique, see Elton and Gruber (2003).

SUMMARY

We saw in Chapter 6 that portfolio theory provides a basis for determining efficient portfolios for all investors taking into account their individual risk–return preferences. However, the determination of these portfolios requires a substantial amount of data and calculation, and simpler models explaining the risk and return relationship of securities have been put forward which enable a much quicker analysis of portfolios to be undertaken.

The capital asset pricing model (CAPM) provides a theoretically based single index model. It shows that the reward for holding a risky security is not based on the security's total risk (its standard deviation) but only on its beta, or systematic risk – the risk that remains, assuming the security is held as part of a well-diversified portfolio. The CAPM also shows (unlike portfolio theory, which assumes all investors have individually designed portfolios) that all investors should hold the same market portfolio (all marketable assets) combined with borrowing or lending at the risk-free rate. The only difference between portfolios would be the different proportions held of M and risk-free borrowing or lending. However these results can break down if the assumptions underlying the CAPM are relaxed.

The CAPM allows the expected return and risk of a security or portfolio to be estimated so that alternative investments can be easily compared. Empirical tests of the CAPM have been carried out, but criticism of the methodology and a desire for more complete explanations of security returns have led to multi-index models. Arbitrage pricing theory is one such model.

However, the CAPM has gained acceptance, first in the United States and now worldwide, as a helpful investment decision-making tool, facilitating the choice of portfolios for the investor, whether they are investing hundreds or millions of pounds.

REVIEW EXERCISES

1. The expected return on the shares of Company A (which is financed entirely by equity) is 10% pa, the risk-free rate is 5% p.a. and the expected return on the market is 13% p.a.
   a. What is the share's beta?
   b. All other things equal, how would the share's beta change if Company A were to refinance exactly half of its equity capital with debt? Explain any assumptions you have to make in order to calculate the revised beta.

2. Assume that shares A and B are correctly priced according to the Capital Asset Pricing Model. Share A is expected to have a return of 19.8% pa and has a beta of 1.2. An annual return of 17.1 % is expected on share B, which has a beta of 0.9. Derive the securities market line.

3. Two unit trusts X and Y have betas of 0.8 and 1.3 respectively. In 2004 they achieved total annual returns of 10% and 20% respectively. Using the data reproduced in Appendix 7.1, can you say anything about their performance?

4. Sharpe postulated that a portfolio's expected return and risk could be expressed in equations 7.3 and 7.4 respectively as follows:

$$E\left(R_p\right)= a_p + b_p E\left(R_m\right) \tag{7.3}$$

$$V_p = b_p^2 V_m + \sum_{i=1}^{i=n} W_i^2 V\left(e_i\right) \tag{7.4}$$

   a. What is the main argument behind the market model?
   b. How many data itemsмre needed using the market model for a ten-security portfolio compared with portfolio theory?
   c. As the size of the portfolio is increased (n gets larger) which component in the overall ris^M V_p will become dominant and why? What will happen to the overall risk V_p?

5. Shares with betas below 1 are commonly referred to as 'defensive' whereas those with betas above 1 are known as 'aggressive'.
   a. Using the data in Appendix 7.1, identify the most defensive and aggressive industries and sectors.
   b. Why do you think the industries and sectors you have identified exhibit these characteristics?
   c. Can you think of any shares which might have a negative beta?
   d. You are trying to construct two well-diversified portfolios, one with a beta of 0.6 and one with a beta of 1.4. How would you go about constructing these portfolios?

6. Again using the data reproduced in Appendix 7.1, select one or more shares or sectors which registered an especially high abnormal return in 2004. From company websites and other sources, try to explain why the performance of these companies' and sectors' shares diverged so markedly from expectations based on their historical betas.

7. Comment on the actual and abnormal annual returns for the Non-cyclical Consumer Goods sector to 2004, using the sector data in Appendix 7.1 and the company data in Table 7.1.

8. At the beginning of 2004 Miss Cagey decided to invest in a portfolio divided into equal

holdings of the shares of five individual companies selected from five different industries, with a portfolio beta of 0.5.

a. Construct such a portfolio from the data in Example 7.1.
b. How would the portfolio have performed in its first year (i.e. in calendar 2004) compared with expectation?
c. Would she have fared any better if instead of selecting five companies from different sectors, she had put one-fifth of her money into each of five well-balanced portfolios constructed from each of those different sectors?

Sample answers to these review exercises can be found on the companion website.

APPENDIX 7.1: LBS RISK MEASUREMENT SERVICE, SECTORAL ANALYSIS FOR Q4 2004

FTSE sector	Number of companies	Average capitalisation	Index %age	Beta	Variability	Specific risk	Standard error of beta	R squared	Qtly abnormal return	Ann. abnormal return	Actual annual return	Net yield	P/E ratio
Resources	**(31)**	**7,540**	**16.3**	**0.92**	**20**	**15**	**0.11**	**48**	**-7**	**3**	**15**	**2.8**	**12.2**
Mining	(11)	5,561	4.1	1.16	29	23	0.15	37	-8	-3	11	2.3	13.0
Oil & gas	(20)	8,629	12.2	0.86	21	16	0.12	41	-7	5	16	2.9	12.0
Basic industries	**(52)**	**1,002**	**3.7**	**1.02**	**20**	**13**	**0.10**	**58**	**2**	**12**	**25**	**3.0**	**12.3**
Chemicals	(10)	1,206	0.9	1.00	22	15	0.11	50	4	5	17	3.4	15.1
Construction & building mats	(40)	929	2.6	0.94	21	15	0.11	49	2	14	26	3.0	10.4
Forestry & paper	(1)	603	0.0	1.03	31	27	0.16	26	-3	-4	8	5.3	9.8
Steel & other metals	(1)	2,241	0.2	1.33	65	61	0.21	10	-10	53	68	n.a.	n.a.
General industrials	**(45)**	**773**	**2.5**	**1.29**	**26**	**16**	**0.12**	**59**	**-1**	**11**	**26**	**3.2**	**16.9**
Aerospace & defence	(9)	2,183	1.4	1.14	27	21	0.14	41	-3	22	36	3.4	15.4
Diversified industrials	(0)	0	0.0	0.07	11	11	0.09	1	-2	-4	0	n.a.	n.a.
Electronic & electrical equip	(14)	280	0.3	1.30	47	43	0.20	18	2	-12	4	2.3	93.1
Engineering & machinery	(22)	509	0.8	1.20	26	18	0.13	51	3	4	18	3.1	15.5
Cyclical consumer goods	**(16)**	**365**	**0.4**	**1.04**	**27**	**22**	**0.14**	**35**	**5**	**2**	**15**	**3.2**	**11.6**
Automobiles	(8)	544	0.3	1.08	29	24	0.15	32	9	2	15	3.5	10.8
Household goods & textiles	(8)	187	0.1	0.66	22	20	0.14	20	-6	4	14	2.3	15.6
Non-cyclical consumer goods	**(55)**	**4,440**	**16.7**	**0.50**	**15**	**13**	**0.10**	**26**	**1**	**-4**	**4**	**3.1**	**15.7**
Alcoholic beverages	(5)	8,174	2.9	0.47	18	16	0.12	16	7	9	17	3.4	16.6
Food producers & processors	(15)	2,489	2.4	0.65	20	18	0.13	24	11	5	15	3.1	11.3
Health A	(12)	554	0.5	0.86	23	19	0.13	33	1	1	12	1.1	25.5
Personal care & house prods	(4)	3,190	0.9	0.53	20	18	0.13	16	11	18	26	2.0	19.9
Pharmaceuticals	(16)	6,986	7.9	0.54	19	17	0.12	18	-7	-18	-9	3.1	16.8
Tobacco	(3)	11,603	2.1	0.76	27	24	0.15	19	10	18	29	4.0	15.0
Cyclical services	**(206)**	**1,055**	**14.7**	**1.09**	**19**	**10**	**0.08**	**74**	**0**	**1**	**14**	**2.6**	**20.5**
General retailers	(44)	1,202	3.5	0.88	20	15	0.11	44	-4	6	18	3.2	14.6
Leisure entertain & hotels	(29)	1,246	2.5	0.93	20	14	0.10	52	6	21	33	2.2	16.7
Media & photography	(38)	1,636	4.1	1.29	29	21	0.14	47	0	-8	7	2.1	26.6
Support services	(65)	602	2.7	0.97	19	12	0.10	59	1	-10	3	2.8	19.1
Transport	(30)	900	1.9	0.99	21	15	0.11	51	5	6	19	3.0	60.9

FTSE sector	Number of companies	Average capitalisation	Index %age	Beta	Variability	Specific risk	Standard error of beta	R squared	Qtly abnormal return	Ann. abnormal return	Actual annual return	Net yield	P/E ratio
Non-cyclical services	(20)	8,123	11.4	1.15	26	19	0.13	45	3	-5	9	2.3	17.4
Food & drug retailers	(8)	4,605	2.5	0.61	21	19	0.13	20	7	6	15	2.4	25.5
Telecommunications Services	(12)	10,467	8.9	1.22	31	24	0.15	37	3	-7	7	2.3	16.0
Utilities	**(15)**	**3,803**	**4.0**	**0.53**	**14**	**12**	**0.09**	**33**	**3**	**21**	**29**	**4.2**	**15.6**
Electricity	(4)	4,562	1.3	0.50	15	13	0.10	26	1	18	26	4.4	13.6
Utilities, other	(11)	3,527	2.7	0.61	16	13	0.10	35	3	22	31	4.2	16.7
Information technology	**(43)**	**367**	**1.1**	**1.57**	**40**	**32**	**0.18**	**36**	**-1**	**-25**	**-7**	**1.1**	**64.9**
Information techn hardware	(13)	384	0.4	1.34	52	48	0.20	15	0	-33	-18	0.3	na
Software & computer services	(30)	360	0.7	1.50	41	34	0.18	31	0	-19	-2	1.5	30.0
Non-financials	**(483)**	**2,118**	**70.8**	**0.87**	**14**	**4**	**0.03**	**91**	**0**	**1**	**12**	**2.8**	**15.6**
Financials	**(222)**	**1,876**	**29.2**	**1.28**	**21**	**9**	**0.07**	**83**	**1**	**-1**	**15**	**3.6**	**15.5**
Banks	(10)	27,287	19.4	1.25	23	12	0.09	71	-1	-3	12	4.0	13.8
Insurance	(20)	460	0.5	1.27	32	25	0.16	38	-4	-15	0	3.9	9.5
Life assurance	(8)	5,279	3.0	1.46	30	20	0.14	55	2	7	23	3.9	15.0
Investment companies	(121)	301	2.5	1.25	21	8	0.07	85	2	0	15	1.9	48.5
Real estate	(34)	886	2.1	0.76	17	13	0.10	46	13	35	45	2.2	33.1
Speciality & other financial	(29)	885	1.7	1.30	26	17	0.12	59	11	-5	11	2.6	17.0
FTSE All-Share	**(705)**	**2,042**	**100.0**	**1.00**	**15**	**1**	**0.00**	**100**	**0**	**0**	**13**	**3.0**	**15.6**
FTSE 100	**(100)**	**11,757**	**82.5**	**0.99**	**15**	**2**	**0.02**	**98**	**-1**	**-1**	**11**	**3.2**	**14.7**
FTSE 250	**(250)**	**836**	**14.0**	**1.07**	**19**	**9**	**0.07**	**78**	**4**	**10**	**23**	**2.6**	**18.4**
FTSE 350	**(350)**	**3,956**	**96.4**	**1.00**	**15**	**1**	**0.01**	**100**	**0**	**0**	**13**	**3.1**	**15.1**
FTSE Small Cap	**(355)**	**155**	**3.6**	**1.07**	**21**	**13**	**0.10**	**63**	**1**	**1**	**14**	**2.1**	**138.6**

Source: London Business School Risk Measurement Service, January–March. 2005.

APPENDIX 7.2: DERIVING THE EXPECTED RETURN ON A SECURITY FROM THE CAPM

A portfolio consisting of W_i invested in share i and $(1 - W_i)$ in the market portfolio M will have the following expected return and risk (as measured by standard deviation):

$$E(R_P) = W_i E(R_i) + (1 - W_i (E(R_M)) \tag{A7.1}$$

$$S_P = [W_i^2 V_i + (1 - W_i)^2 V_M + 2W_i(1 - W_i)COV_{iM}]^{0.5} \tag{A7.2}$$

Note that we are using alternative notation here (V rather than S^2 to denote the variances, and the square root as a power of 0.5) purely in order to make the next steps easier to follow.

Using differentiation we can determine the change in the expected return and risk of the portfolio for a given change in W_i:

Change in expected return =

$$\frac{dE(R_P)}{dW_i} = E(R_i) - E(R_M) \tag{A7.3}$$

Change in risk =

$$\frac{dS_P}{dW_i} = \frac{1}{2}\left[W_i^2 V_i + (1 - W_i)^2 V_M + 2W_i(1 - W_i)COV_{iM}\right]^{-0.5}$$
$$\times \left[2W_i V_i - 2V_M + 2W_i V_M + 2COV_{iM} - 4W_i COV_{iM}\right] \tag{A7.4}$$

Portfolio M already contains share i in proportion to its market value. Portfolio M is the optimal portfolio, so we would not expect investors to want to add to their holdings of individual shares. So by substituting $W_i = 0$ into the above equations we can determine the change in expected return and risk for a given change in W_i at this equilibrium point.

The change in expected return is unchanged at

$$dE(R_P)/dW_i = E(R_i) - E(R_M) \tag{A7.5}$$

but the change in risk becomes much simpler with

$$\frac{dS_P}{dW_i} = \frac{1}{2}\left[V_M\right]^{-0.5} \times \left[-2V_M + 2COV_{iM}\right] \tag{A7.6}$$

As

$$V_M^{0.5} = \sqrt{V_M} \tag{A7.7}$$

we can rewrite this as

$$\frac{dS_P}{dW_i} = \frac{1}{2}\left[\frac{2COV_{iM} - 2V_M}{\sqrt{V_M}}\right]$$

$$\frac{dS_P}{dW_i} = \frac{COV_{iM} - V_M}{S_M} \tag{A7.8}$$

So the slope of the risk/return trade-off at point M is

$$\frac{dE(R_P)/dW_i}{dS_P/dW_i} = \frac{E(R_i) - E(R_M)}{(COV_{iM} - V_M)/S_M} \tag{A7.9}$$

But we have already determined the risk/return trade-off for portfolio M as this is the slope of the capital market line:

$$\text{Slope} = \frac{E(R_M) - R_F}{S_M} \tag{A7.10}$$

Equating these two equivalent slopes we have

$$\frac{E(R_M) - R_F}{S_M} = \frac{E(R_i) - E(R_M)}{(COV_{iM} - V_M)/S_M} \tag{A7.11}$$

Rearranging and solving for the expected return on share i we get

$$E(R_i) = R_F + (E(R_M) - R_F)\frac{COV_{iM}}{S_M^2} \tag{A7.12}$$

which we showed as equation 7.13 in this chapter.

Part IV
Risk Management
Products

8 Financial futures

Learning objectives for this chapter

After studying this chapter you should be able to

- ○ describe the principal features and benefits of derivative instruments
- ○ describe the mechanisms of the financial futures markets
- ○ describe the principal features of each of the main types of financial futures contract, and the relationship between each and its underlying cash market product
- ○ calculate a fair price for a futures contract from given data from the cash market
- ○ use financial futures as a tool for enhancing the risk–return characteristics of portfolios of cash market instruments.

INTRODUCTION

In Chapter 1 we identified two key functions of financial markets. They provide mechanisms for governments, companies and other organisations to raise funds from investors and for investors to manage the risks and returns arising from their investing activities.

Since the 1970s, stock markets and other financial markets have shown increasing volatility: that is, a greater tendency to move up or down in a random, unpredictable manner. Volatility makes it difficult for investors to predict with accuracy the likely return on an investment. Investors run the risk of making short-term losses on their portfolios even if their long-run expectations are for a reasonable return. The last quarter of 1987, which included the crash of 19 October, and the long bear market that followed the bursting of the stock market bubble of the late 1990s, taught investors that shares in particular can go down as well as up. Investors therefore need a means of protecting themselves against the adverse effects of market volatility, and the years since the early 1970s have seen the development of risk-management products designed to do just this.

Without such specially developed instruments the only way to adjust investment risks and returns is to buy and sell the investments themselves. If Mr Jitter owns 1000 Vodafone shares and decides, for whatever reason, that he would like to eliminate temporarily his risk exposure to Vodafone, the surest way to achieve this objective is by selling his shares on the secondary market to another investor. But this has two disadvantages.

○ It is relatively expensive. The sale involves transaction costs, and if he subsequently changes his mind and decides that the original level of risk was acceptable to him after all, buying his shares back will involve a second set of costs.
○ Although selling the shares definitely protects Mr Jitter from the loss he would incur if his misgivings about Vodafone prove to be justified, what will happen if those fears prove to be groundless and – contrary to his expectation – Vodafone shares actually go up in value? Mr Jitter will have missed out on the gain that he would have realised if he had retained his shares, and will therefore suffer an opportunity cost.

In response to this kind of situation, the financial markets now offer a wide and sophisticated range of *derivative* instruments enabling investors to achieve the desired adjustments to their risk and return profiles without having to trade in the *underlying* securities, and in some cases without sacrificing all the potential gains. But these risk-management products do more than just meet the cautious investor's desire for a measure of insurance. The same products can be used by more speculative market participants to replicate the risk and return characteristics of an underlying investment without having to commit in hard cash more than a fraction of its market value. This also has the effect of drastically reducing the associated transaction costs.

Possibly the easiest way to understand how such instruments began to evolve is to consider a variant on a conventional securities transaction. Normally, securities are bought and sold for more or less immediate settlement (usually called *spot settlement*, because the transactions are settled on the spot). Suppose that we were to vary this so that we could agree today all of the terms (including, of course, the price) on which we would buy and sell a security for some more distant date in the future. Such an agreement would need to be wholly independent of any changes in market prices between the contract date and the settlement date; otherwise there would be no real point in entering into the agreement. Although settlement of such a contract (called a *forward contract*, to distinguish it from a *spot contract*) would be some way in the future, it would have the desired effect of immediately changing the parties' risk profiles.

○ Buyers would be immediately exposed to the effects of changes in the price of the underlying security, because they would be committed to buy at a fixed price, even if the market price were to rise or fall between the contract and settlement dates.
○ Sellers would have no further exposure to the market price, as they would now have a committed buyer at a fixed price.

Such a transaction has certain advantages over the conventional spot transaction:

○ Buyers do not have to pay the purchase price immediately (this is useful if their objective is to fix now the price at which they will be able to invest when an expected source of funds materialises at a future date).

○ If at any time between contract date and settlement date the parties change their minds, they can cancel the transaction and avoid all or nearly all of the transaction costs of the original deal, by agreeing that the party who has lost money since the contract was made (the buyer, if the price has subsequently fallen; the seller, if it has risen) will simply pay a cash difference to the party that has made an equal but opposite gain.

It would be tempting to think that a forward transaction might have a further benefit for sellers, namely that they would not immediately lose the benefit of the running yield on the underlying security. But we shall see later in this section that this potential advantage is automatically neutralised by a very similar pricing mechanism to the one we met when we studied the term structure of interest rates in Chapter 4.

Although a forward transaction offers some additional flexibility when compared with the standard spot contract, it still falls some way short of meeting all the requirements of an ideal risk-management product. Three shortcomings in particular stand out:

○ As it is a private, bilateral *over-the-counter (OTC)* contract, a party who subsequently changes his mind can get out of the contract only if the other party has had a simultaneous and exactly opposite change of heart. Such a coincidence is very unlikely in the real world. Suppose, in our example above, that Mr Jitter had adjusted his Vodafone position by selling his 1000 shares on a forward basis, but subsequently – during the period between doing the deal and the forward settlement date – decided that he had after all been too cautious and now wished to reverse the forward sale. If his original forward purchaser were unwilling to reverse the transaction Mr Jitter would have to find a new trading counterparty who was willing to sell him 1000 Vodafone shares for the same settlement date as his original forward sale. This could be difficult, and it would certainly be cumbersome and expensive, with two extra sets of transaction costs.

○ Another disadvantage of the private bilateral nature of the forward transaction is that each party has a credit exposure to the other. Suppose again that after Mr Jitter has sold his 1000 Vodafone shares on a forward basis, the market price goes down (exactly in accordance with the expectation that prompted him to sell), but his dealing counterparty has gone bankrupt in the meantime and the administrator of his bankruptcy repudiates the contract with Mr Jitter. Being now deprived of his forward sale at the guaranteed price, Mr Jitter will suffer exactly the loss that the forward transaction was designed to eliminate. But credit risk is a double-edged weapon in a trading situation; if the market price moved against Mr Jitter and not in his favour, the failure of the counterparty might relieve him of the obligation to honour a loss-making contract.

○ The forward transaction is in a sense just like the spot transaction in that the outcome is fixed. The parties must honour it at the agreed price, regardless of how prices have moved in the meantime. One party is thereby forced to realise a loss, and his or her loss is the other party's gain. Such a contract is essentially symmetrical and does not have the key asymmetrical property of a true insurance contract, which is designed to protect the insured party from loss while allowing him or her to enjoy all or nearly all the benefit of any gain (less the cost of the insurance premium paid).

In this and the next chapter we shall see how the markets have responded to these previously unfulfilled needs by creating a wide range of financial futures and options contracts. In this chapter we look at financial futures, which solve the problems inherent in bilateral forward trading. We also explore *interest rate swaps* and *cross-currency swaps*, which are OTC products for managing long-term interest rate and foreign exchange exposure arising from financing and investing activities. In Chapter 9 we explore the more complex world of options, which uniquely satisfy the need for a true insurance product with asymmetric outcomes.

The remainder of the chapter begins with a general description of the major characteristics of financial futures contracts, their market mechanisms and pricing principles. We then describe in detail the specific features and pricing characteristics of the three main types of futures contract. Then we explore the advantages that futures enjoy over trading in the underlying cash products. We conclude the main section on financial futures by seeing how futures contracts can be used as surrogates for the underlying securities for trading and investing purposes, as well as for hedging interest rate risk and equity risk. In a final section we describe swaps, which have become the major bilateral OTC product for the management of longer-term interest-rate and currency risks.

FINANCIAL FUTURES MARKETS

A futures contract is a legally binding agreement, concerned with the buying, or selling, of a standardised product, at a fixed price, for cash settlement (or physical delivery) on a given future date.

(Euronext.liffe)

As we saw in the introduction to this section, the simplest instrument for managing financial risk is the forward contract in which two parties agree to execute a transaction at some future date, on terms which are fully specified at the outset. We used as a fictitious example a forward sale and purchase of shares, but in fact the most common forward contract traded today is the *forward foreign exchange contract*: that is, a contract for the exchange of one currency for another at a fixed rate on a fixed future date. We describe the characteristics of this contract and the reasons for its continued success in greater detail in Chapter 11 (on international investment). Opinion is divided on whether a forward contract can properly be termed a derivative contract at all, as it is not a separate type of contract derived from an underlying cash market contract but is simply a variant of the cash market contract itself, differing only in the legally quite minor matter of the settlement date.

When it comes to the management of risks arising from securities rather than from foreign currency transactions, private bilateral forward contracts have generally given way to exchange-traded financial futures contracts. The term *financial futures contract* is applied to futures contracts on equities, stock market indices, interest rate products and foreign exchange, in order to differentiate them from futures contracts on commodities.

Futures contracts are forward contracts that are standardised in terms of their quantity, quality and settlement dates and terms, and are traded exclusively through an organised market or exchange which not only provides a trading forum but also guarantees the fulfilment of all contracts traded there. The channelling of trading activity into standardised contracts on a public exchange has many benefits in terms of improved liquidity, transparency and flexibility, as well as eliminating or substantially reducing credit and settlement risks and transaction costs.

Financial futures originated in the United States in the early 1970s. Although the first contracts were not actively traded, successful currency futures were introduced on the Chicago Mercantile Exchange (CME) in 1972 and interest rate contracts on both the Chicago Board of Trade (CBOT) and the CME in 1975. It is significant that the financial contracts were set up by exchanges that already specialised in meat and grain futures contracts. The first European exchange was the London Financial Futures Exchange (LIFFE) established in 1982, and since then there has been rapid growth in both Europe and the Far East in financial futures exchanges. LIFFE is now part of the Euronext group which has been renamed Euronext.liffe and includes the derivatives exchanges of Amsterdam, Brussels, Lisbon, London and Paris. The evolution from floor-based physical markets to screen-based electronic markets is rapidly reducing the significance of the geographic location of an exchange.

Financial futures contracts are based on the following four major cash markets:

○ short-term fixed-rate interest-rate products such as interbank deposits
○ long-term fixed-rate interest-rate products such as government bonds
○ individual company shares and equity market indices
○ foreign currencies based on forward exchange rates.

Euronext.liffe currently offers futures contracts in the first three of these categories on the following specific products

○ short-term interbank deposits denominated in sterling, US dollars, euros, Swiss francs and Japanese yen
○ UK, German and Japanese government bonds, and interest-rate swaps in US dollars and euros (interest rate swaps are described on page 295)
○ UK and European equity indices, as well as on individual shares in a large number of major UK and European companies.

As we shall see in the next chapter, Euronext.liffe also offers options contracts on nearly all of these futures contracts as well as on some of the underlying cash products themselves. Euronext.liffe also offers futures and options contracts on four soft commodities (cocoa, coffee, sugar and wheat), but these are beyond the scope of this book. This product range undergoes a process of almost continuous evolution and development in response to investor demand and the ever-increasing competitive pressure from other exchanges.

As the primary focus of this book is investment in marketable securities, we concentrate on the second and third of the contract types listed above, but we shall begin with an examination of futures on short-term fixed-rate interbank deposits, for two reasons. First, the exceptional degree of precision and transparency demonstrated by the short-term money market makes it an ideal medium for exploring the mathematics and economics of financial futures, and second, short-term money market interest rates play a key role in the determination of prices for other financial futures contracts such as those on bonds and equity-related products.

We shall not describe currency futures contracts in this chapter since, in London in particular, the bilateral forward foreign exchange market is dominant. LIFFE closed down its currency futures contracts in 1990 because they had failed to achieve sufficient volumes to offer viable competition to the long-established forward currency market. We describe the forward currency market in Chapter 11, and restrict our analysis here to representative contracts of the other three types currently traded on Euronext.liffe: short-term interest rate, long-term bond and equity-linked futures contracts.

In order to define and understand a financial futures contract, we need to understand:

○ what product is being bought and sold
○ how the financial futures market works
○ how a financial futures price is determined.

In the next section we consider each of these three characteristics of financial futures contracts in general terms before, in the following sections, using the same framework for a detailed analysis of our representative sample of specific contracts.

COMMON CHARACTERISTICS OF FINANCIAL FUTURES CONTRACTS

Defining a financial futures contract

Depending on the characteristics of the underlying product, up to nine separate terms and conditions of a financial futures contract need to be defined in order to ensure a fully standardised product. In Table 8.1 each of these terms is introduced and described generically. In the following sections on sample contracts from each of the three major categories of futures, these terms are further specified and discussed in greater detail.

Table 8.1 Principal terms of financial futures contracts

Unit of trading	The quantity and quality of the underlying cash product; for instance, it might be a three-month interbank deposit of £500,000, or £100,000 nominal of a notional UK gilt.
Quotation basis	The way in which the price is expressed. Normally this follows the same convention as the underlying financial instrument. For example, the price of a bond futures contract is expressed as a percentage of nominal value, although as we shall see later, there are important exceptions.
Minimum price movement ('tick' size and value)	The 'tick' or minimum permitted price movement is fixed for each contract at a level which reconciles the competing requirements for precision, liquidity and ease of calculation. For example, prices in the UK gilts futures contracts are quoted to two decimal places (rather than the six decimal places employed in the cash market), so that the minimum price movement is 0.01% of £100,000, or £10.00.
Delivery (or contract) month	The specified month to which a particular futures contract relates. Most financial futures contracts have at least four delivery months a year – usually March, June, September and December – but the most heavily traded contracts have consecutive delivery months ('serial months').

continued overleaf

Table 8.1 continued

Last trading day	The day when trading in the financial futures contract stops. Where cash settlement takes place (see below on modes of settlement), the last trading day will typically be one or two business days before the delivery day. Where the delivery day can vary throughout the month, the last trading day is, in the case of the US Treasury long bond futures contract, the seventh business day before the last business day of the delivery month, and in the case of the UK long gilt futures, contract, two business days prior to the last business day of the delivery month.
Delivery day	The day that any futures contracts still open are to be settled. Some contracts will have a fixed delivery date, such as the third Wednesday of the delivery month. Others, notably bond futures contracts such as the UK gilt futures contract, may be settled on any day in the delivery month, at the option of the contract seller.
Exchange delivery settlement price (EDSP)	The price at which futures contracts are settled upon delivery. The EDSP is determined at the futures exchange, and is often an average of traded prices over a set period.
Mode of settlement	Financial futures contracts can be settled in one of two ways depending on the specification of the particular financial futures contract. *Physical settlement:* the seller delivers the underlying instrument to the buyer. *Cash settlement:* one party to the original contract will have made a loss, through having sold future contracts at a lower price, or bought them at a higher price, than the EDSP. The losing party pays the difference between the purchase or sale price and the EDSP. A cash-settled futures contract is therefore an example of a *contract for differences* or *CFD*.
Trading hours	The hours during which the exchange is open for trading of a specific contract.

Source: Euronext.liffe.

How the futures market works

Futures exchanges are similar to other organised financial exchanges in the important respect that only members of the exchange may transact business there. The most active members of futures exchanges are specialised departments or subsidiaries of major financial institutions. Other investors or traders wishing to deal in financial futures must do so as customers of a member firm.

A further feature that futures markets have in common with other financial markets is the technology-driven trend away from floor-based physical markets to screen-based electronic markets. The relatively small number of rigidly standardised products traded on a futures exchange (compared, say, with the multitude and variety of types of security traded on a large stock market) has made the transition easier for the futures markets, which have led the way in this respect.

Until the 1990s financial futures were mostly traded in physical marketplaces, where representatives of member firms came together to trade each type of futures contract in its own designated area of the exchange floor (known as a *pit*). In terms of the analysis we made in Chapter 1, these were primarily quote-driven markets, in which the traders would shout out the prices at which they were prepared to deal, with those prices influenced partly by the customer orders they had received and partly by their own trading instincts and objectives. This method of trading is known as the ***open outcry*** method. More recently, technological advances have made it possible to abandon the physical in favour of an electronic marketplace, in which members input their orders anonymously into a central computer; this makes use of complex algorithms to match buy and sell orders which agree in price and quantity.

The shift to electronic trading has contributed significantly to the globalisation of futures markets, as member firms can now input orders from any location in the world. Both the earlier open outcry and the more recent electronic trading models have made for a very high degree of market transparency and an efficient process of price discovery. A further consequence of trading electronically via a centralised order-book is the anonymity of the parties placing orders and making trades. Opinion is divided on the question whether the identity of the parties placing the bids and offers is information that participants could legitimately regard as necessary in order to build up a full picture of the market, but there is little doubt that anonymity enhances the liquidity of the market.

We now consider the four special features which together account for the unique character of futures markets:

○ the clearing house
○ margining
○ fungibility
○ cash-settled versus physical delivery.

The clearing house

An essential feature of a futures exchange is that while a transaction is concluded only when two members simultaneously have equal but opposite trading requirements, the transaction itself is legally concluded not between those members but between each of them and the exchange. Strictly speaking, it is concluded between each of them and the clearing house, as the exchange usually subcontracts the clearing and settlement process to an external firm specialising in the provision of these services. The clearing house is therefore a principal in every transaction and not merely a facilitating agent. Euronext.liffe currently uses the LCH.Clearnet, which is owned by a consortium of financial institutions.

Margining

An important consequence of the clearing house system is that the individual members are protected from the inability or refusal of a trading counterparty to honour a deal. Conversely, the credit risk arising from all the members' outstanding transactions is borne by the clearing house. The clearing house protects itself by taking a cash margin from both parties to each transaction.

Margin is payable in two forms. As soon as a deal is concluded, both parties must deposit an ***initial margin*** with the clearing house. This is fixed for each type of futures contract, and is intended to cover the maximum likely price movement in that contract over a 24-hour period. Then at the end of each day each member's open positions are **marked to market**. The market closing price for the day is compared with the prices at which the member's deals were done on that day. If members have made a loss (because the price of a contract they have bought has subsequently fallen, or the price of a contract they have sold has risen), they must deposit with the clearing house within 24 hours a further amount, called **variation margin**, equal to the unrealised loss. Conversely, parties that have made an equal but opposite profit from the transaction receive a credit to their margin account; but they may not withdraw the credit until either they conclude equal but opposite transactions in order to clear their open position or the contract finally expires.

Members' failure to meet a margin call results in their positions being closed out by the exchange, that is, the exchange eliminates its exposure to the defaulting member by entering into equal but opposite transactions with another member or members. To the extent that such transactions may result in the realisation of a loss by the exchange, the latter can reimburse itself by using the defaulting members' initial margin and any subsequent variation margin they have deposited.

There is a tension between the clearing house, which wants to maximise its protection, and the members, who want to minimise the amount of margin they have to put up. Futures exchanges have developed various ways of reconciling this conflict. For instance, a member might buy the September futures and sell an equal amount of the December futures in the same contract, in anticipation of a particular relative shift between interest rates for those two maturities. In this case, the net risk to the exchange is substantially less than if the member were to take a view on the overall direction or absolute level of interest rates by adopting an outright open position in either the September or December contract. Complex algorithms based on observed correlations between rates can be used to calculate an appropriately reduced amount of margin which still gives the exchange the necessary protection against adverse movements in market rates.

Fungibility

A further key feature of all exchange-traded futures contracts is their **fungibility**. Fungibility is the quality of unlimited interchangeability which exists, for instance, between all £20 notes or between all US$10 bills. If a friend lends you £20 she has no legal right to demand by way of repayment exactly the same banknote she lent you; any genuine £20 note is a valid discharge for the debt. In the case of financial futures, this quality of fungibility arises from two facts: all transactions in a particular futures contract involve the sale and purchase of an identical quantity and quality of a product for settlement by exactly the same method and on the same date; and one party to all transactions is the exchange or clearing house itself.

This means that if a member initially buys 20 futures in the September 2008 UK long gilt contract and subsequently sells the same number of futures in the same contract, it is of no significance that the two trades may have been executed for different customers of that member, or that two different members of the exchange supplied the other side of each trade. All that matters to the exchange is that the member has bought and sold an identical quantity of the September 2008 long gilt futures so that its account with the exchange in that contract now has a zero balance. The exchange no longer has any risk on that member as a result of his or her dealings in that contract, so any margin standing to his or her credit from those dealings may now be withdrawn by him or her (as long as he/she is up to date with his/her other margin calls!).

Cash-settled versus physical delivery

The final special feature of futures contracts that we need to consider is the settlement mechanism. In practice, most futures positions are closed out before the final settlement date of the contract by the simple expedient of entering into equal but opposite transactions, but a small proportion of contracts is usually still open at settlement date. A small minority of contract types require settlement by means of physical delivery. This means that the sellers under any contracts still open on settlement date are obliged to deliver the requisite quantity of the underlying financial instrument to the exchange or clearing house, and the buyers are similarly obliged to accept delivery. These transactions are settled at the final exchange delivery settlement price (EDSP) determined by the exchange at the moment when the contract expires, the parties' aggregate accumulated profits and losses having already been accounted for via the margining system.

Among financial futures contracts traded on Euronext.liffe, the prime example of a physically delivered contract is the UK long gilt futures contract, and the peculiar complexities of this process are discussed in more detail on page 275. Most futures contracts on Euronext.liffe, however, are ***cash-settled***: that is, the losers pay in cash for their losses and the gainers collect their gains. In practice, as soon as the exchange receives the final margin calls it already holds sufficient cash to effect these payments as a result of the daily marking-to-market process described above. In this way, if (for instance) purchasers of futures contracts wish to acquire the underlying asset, they can do so by purchasing it on the open market at the current market price (which will be the same as the EDSP). If they bought the futures at a lower price than the EDSP they will receive a compensating amount from the exchange; if they bought the futures at a higher price, they will have already paid the difference to the exchange. In either case, the result is the same: their net cost of acquiring the underlying asset is the price at which they originally bought the futures, regardless of the market price on settlement day.

Pricing of financial futures

The fundamental pricing principle of all financial futures contracts is essentially the same as the principle we used in Chapter 4 for determining forward/forward future interest rates. The fair value of an investment commencing (or settling) at a fixed future date is a simple mathematical function of (a) the price applicable to that investment in a spot transaction and (b) the cost of carry, i.e. the difference between the yield on the asset and the cost of financing it from the spot date to the future date. The practical application of this principle varies in complexity according to the properties of the underlying financial instrument. Just as we began our analysis of implied future yields on gilts by considering forward short-term interbank deposit rates, so we shall start our analysis of financial futures with the contract on short-term interbank deposits, as these are the simplest products to understand.

Except in the rarest of circumstances, there will be a difference between the price or interest rate for a spot transaction in the underlying asset of the futures contract and the price or interest rate applicable to the futures contract in the same underlying asset. This difference is referred to as the *basis*. As a futures contract approaches its final settlement date, the basis tends to reduce until the futures price ultimately converges with the spot or cash price, because at the moment when the futures contract expires the final price for the futures is the same as the cash price or EDSP.

SHORT-TERM INTEREST RATE FUTURES: THREE-MONTH STERLING FUTURES CONTRACT

Description

Table 8.2 sets out the specification of the *short sterling futures contract* on Euronext.liffe, and Table 8.3 is the trading report for this contract for Wednesday 19 May 2004. We shall use this in a numerical example.

Unit of trading

Most short-term interest-rate financial futures contracts are based on the rates for three-month fixed-rate interbank deposits (some contracts are also based on monthly averages for overnight deposit interest rates). The short sterling contract is based on the three-month sterling interbank rate for a £500,000 deposit and the three-month eurodollar contract is based on the three-month eurodollar interest rate for a US$1 million deposit. Such futures contracts effectively fix the cost of borrowing or lending money for a three-month period starting on the expiry or settlement date of the futures contract. Selling the futures is equivalent to fixing the interest rate on a borrowing for a three-month period

Table 8.2 Contract specification, short sterling contract

Unit of trading	£500,000
Quotation basis	100.00 minus rate of interest (see below for detailed explanation)
Minimum price movement ('tick' size and value)	0.01 (£12.50)
Delivery month	March, June, September, December, and two serial months, such that 22 delivery months are available for trading, with the nearest three delivery months being consecutive calendar months
Last trading day	11.00 on the third Wednesday of the delivery month
Delivery day	First business day after the last trading day
Exchange delivery settlement price (EDSP)	Based on the British Bankers' Association London interbank offered rate (BBA LIBOR) for three-month sterling deposits at 11.00 on the last trading day. The settlement price will be 100.00 minus the BBA LIBOR rounded to three decimal places. Where the EDSP rate is not an exact multiple of 0.005, it will be rounded to the nearest 0.005, or where the EDSP rate is an exact uneven multiple of 0.0025, to the nearest lower 0.005 (e.g. a BBA LIBOR of 5.43750 becomes 5.435).
Mode of settlement	Cash settlement based on the EDSP
Trading hours	07.30–18.00 London time

Source: Euronext.liffe.

Table 8.3 Trading information for short sterling futures contract on Euronext.liffe

Financial Futures

Business Day — Wed 19 May 2004

	Opening Trans	Settle	Change	Daily High	Daily Low	Lifetime High	Lifetime Low	Closing Price	CONNECT* Volume	Basis Volume	Block Trd Volume	Official Volume (Previous Business Day Tue 18 May 2004)	Open Interest	Change
Three Month Sterling														
May 04		95.455	-0.025			95.570	95.480	95.460	0	N/A	0	689	670	+167
Jun 04	95.410	95.340	-0.080	95.420	95.320	96.710 S	93.040	95.320	114,626	N/A	0	28,272	221,541	+798
Jul 04		95.230	-0.090					95.210	0	N/A	0	0	0	0
Sep 04	95.070	94.980	-0.100	95.080	94.950	96.590	93.350	94.960	104,463	N/A	0	31,406	207,580	-1,053
Dec 04	94.820	94.730	-0.110	94.840	94.680	96.480 S	93.250	94.710	146,288	N/A	0	48,488	232,609	+5,683
Mar 05	94.660	94.570	-0.110	94.670	94.520	96.380	93.290	94.550	65,913	N/A	0	17,615	154,327	+2,720
Jun 05	94.560	94.480	-0.100	94.570	94.430	96.300 S	93.290	94.460	35,593	N/A	0	9,600	116,427	+999
Sep 05	94.490	94.440	-0.090	94.520 S	94.390	96.230	94.060	94.420	17,243	N/A	0	4,378	107,607	-200
Dec 05	94.480	94.420	-0.080	94.480	94.360	96.150	94.060	94.400	14,106	N/A	0	3,994	78,882	+2,671
Mar 06	94.460	94.410	-0.070	94.460	94.360	96.100	94.050	94.390	5,265	N/A	0	2,403	45,453	+720
Jun 06	94.450	94.390	-0.070	94.450 S	94.350 S	95.970 S	94.040	94.380	1,789	N/A	0	1,809	32,382	-717
Sep 06	94.420	94.380	-0.070	94.420	94.340	95.750	94.320	94.370	1,634	N/A	0	1,707	31,876	-97
Dec 06	94.340	94.370	-0.060	94.380 S	94.340 S	95.830 S	94.250	94.360	656	N/A	0	342	12,851	-42
Mar 07	94.320	94.360	-0.060	94.380 S	94.320	95.820	94.320	94.350	152	N/A	0	0	4,897	0
Jun 07	94.350	94.340	-0.060	94.350 S	94.350 S	95.730	94.350 S	94.330	16	N/A	0	200	984	0
Sep 07	94.360	94.310	-0.060	94.360 S	94.360 S	95.620	94.360 S	94.300	13	N/A	0	0	811	0
Dec 07		94.300	-0.060			95.450	94.620	94.290	0	N/A	0	0	933	0
Mar 08		94.300	-0.060			95.250	94.500	94.290	0	N/A	0	0	566	0
Jun 08		94.300	-0.060			95.210	94.810	94.290	0	N/A	0	0	335	0
Sep 08		94.300	-0.060			94.810	94.810	94.290	0	N/A	0	0	50	0
Dec 08		94.300	-0.060			94.810	94.810	94.290	0	N/A	0	0	50	0
Mar 09		94.300	-0.060					94.290	0	N/A	0	0	0	0
									507,757	N/A	0	150,903	1,250,831	+11,649

Source: Euronext.liffe.

starting on the settlement date; buying the futures is equivalent to fixing the interest rate on a future deposit. For example, a September short sterling futures contract purchased in July has the same effect as fixing the interest rate to be earned on a three-month deposit or loan starting in September.

Quotation basis

The general level of three-month interest rates in May 2004 was between 4% and 5%, so it may seem strange that the prices of futures contracts based on those rates were around 95 (see Table 8.3). In fact, the price of a short-term interest-rate futures contract is obtained by subtracting from 100 the underlying interest rate implied in the futures market, so that (for instance) the closing or settlement price of the September 2004 contract was priced at 94.98 because market prices implied a forward rate of 5.02% for the three-month period starting in that month. Although this pricing convention may appear perverse, it is based on a very simple idea. If the price of anything at all (for instance, a house, a car or a painting) goes up, then the party who has bought it will gain and the party who has sold it will suffer a loss. But in the case of financial instruments, buyers gain if the interest rate goes *down*. Conversely, sellers and borrowers gain if interest rates go *up* after they have sold the asset or fixed the cost of their borrowing. The prices of financial futures therefore need to be expressed in such a way that they go up in the situation where the buyer gains, and the easiest way to achieve this is to express the price as 100 minus the implied interest rate, so that the price now moves in the required direction. This problem arises only with instruments like short-term deposits whose prices are normally expressed in terms of an interest rate. As we shall see in the next section, the same problem does not arise in the case of futures on long-term interest-rate products, because these are conventionally quoted not in terms of the interest rate or yield but in terms of the market value of the instrument itself, which varies inversely with interest rates and therefore moves in the required direction, going up when interest rates go down.

Minimum price movement: 'tick' size and value

Short-term interest rate futures are quoted to two decimal places, corresponding to minimum steps of 0.01% p.a. This minimum price step is known as a ***tick***. Like all the other standardising features of futures contracts, the tick serves the purpose of simplifying the trading process. As each contract represents a notional deposit of £500,000 for a quarter of a year, the tick represents an interest amount of £500,000 × 0.01% × ¼ = £12.50. Note that in computing tick values, precise daycounts are ignored and periods of exactly one quarter of a year are used instead – again, in the interests of simplicity. The use of tick price movements makes it easy for traders and investors to compute their profits and losses from futures.

Delivery month

The availability of contracts for each of the next 20 quarters creates the facility to deal in three-month futures for a continuous period, in this example of five years to June 2009.

Additionally, the provision of *serial month contracts* in the nearest two months not covered by the quarterly cycle (May and July 2004) gives additional depth and liquidity to the near end of the market.

Last trading day

As 19 May 2004 was the third Wednesday of the month, the May 2004 serial month contract expired at 11.00 London time on that day. We shall see the significance of this in more detail as we now go on to analyse the data in the columns of the trading report, Table 8.3. From the next day, Thursday 20 May, the May serial month contract will have disappeared from the report, to be replaced by the new serial month contract for August 2004.

Opening transaction

As the column header in Table 8.3 implies, this is the price at which the first transaction of the day was concluded. Note that there were no new transactions in the May 2004 contract between the opening at 7.30 and the final expiry of the contract at 11.00 on the same day.

Settle

In Table 8.3 this is an abbreviation for 'settlement price', and is the notional price at the end of the trading session, computed from the latest advertised bid and offer prices. It does not necessarily represent the price at which the last business was actually done (see 'closing price' below). In the case of the May 2004 contract, which finally expired at 11.00, the end-of-day settlement price is replaced by the EDSP. This is the actual three-month LIBOR as calculated by the British Bankers Association at that moment. Note that in the case of the final settlement price only, the price quotation is in half-ticks. Three-month sterling LIBOR was fixed on 19 May 2004 at 4.54563%. To the nearest 0.005, this gave an EDSP of 95.455.

Change

This is the difference between the current settlement price (or, in the case of the expiring May contract, the EDSP) and the previous day's closing price.

Daily/lifetime high/low

These columns in Table 8.3 show the highest and lowest prices at which the contract has actually traded on the day of the report and during its entire lifetime.

Closing price

In contrast to the settlement price (see above) this is the price at which the contract last actually traded on the day of the report.

CONNECT volume

This is a provisional value for the number of contracts traded on the electronic order-book on the day of the report. In this particular case, each of the nearest three quarterly contracts traded more than 100,000 contracts, or well in excess of a notional total of £50 billion each.

Previous business day

Definitive aggregate trading data for each day take 24 hours to compute, so that these three columns are reported with a time lag of one day. The open interest for each contract is the total number of financial futures contracts outstanding: that is, the total of all the long (bought) positions, which of course corresponds exactly to the total of all the short (sold) positions. The open interest figure reflects the number of futures contracts that have been bought or sold and remain open, in contrast to the volume figures which include *day trades*. *Day traders* open and close their futures positions within the trading day, preferring not to keep a highly leveraged position open overnight.

We finish this section by looking at how short-term interest rate futures are priced.

Pricing

From what we have already learned in Chapter 4, we can say that the price of a short-term futures contract should reflect the differences between the two cash market rates for the periods starting on the normal spot settlement date and running, respectively, to the first and last dates of the period covered by the futures contract. This relationship is captured in equation 4.2 which is reproduced again below.

$$
r_{i,j} = \left\langle \frac{\left[1 + \left(\frac{r_{0,j} \times d_{0,j}}{100 \times y}\right)\right]}{\left[1 + \left(\frac{r_{0,i} \times d_{0,i}}{100 \times y}\right)\right]} - 1 \right\rangle \times \left[\frac{y \times 100}{d_{i,j}}\right]
$$

(4.2)

We can test this relationship by applying the equation to evaluate the futures price data in Table 8.3. As Table 8.3 provides the data for the expiry date of a futures contract, we can conveniently use the British Bankers Association's LIBOR figures for the same date from Table 8.4 without the need to interpolate rates for fractional months.

According to the theoretical relationship established in Chapter 4, the June futures price should be calculable from the one-month and four-month cash market deposit rates.

Table 8.4 Sterling LIBOR as at 11.00 am, 19 May 2004 (selected maturities)

Period (months)	% p.a.	End date	No. of days from spot	Closest futures expiry
1	4.431250%	21 June 04	33	16 June 04
2	4.476250%	19 July 04	61	21 July 04
4	4.613750%	20 Sep 04	124	15 Sep 04
7	4.847500%	20 Dec 04	215	15 Dec 04
10	5.036250%	21 Mar 05	306	16 Mar 05

Source: British Bankers Association.

Substituting the corresponding values into equation 4.2 we get

$$r_{33,124} = \left\langle \left[\frac{1 + \left(\frac{4.61375 \times 124}{100 \times 365} \right)}{1 + \left(\frac{4.43125 \times 33}{100 \times 365} \right)} \right] - 1 \right\rangle \times \left[\frac{365 \times 100}{124 - 33} \right]$$

$$= 4.66125676$$

This forward rate of 4.66% (to two decimal places) would be expressed as a futures price of (100 – 4.66) or 95.34, the settlement price for the June 2004 contract in Table 8.3.

Thus, given spot money market interest rates, forward interest rates and hence futures rates are predetermined. Any significant difference between the fair futures price and the actual futures price rate would lead arbitrageurs to enter the market in order to profit from the mispricing. The constant threat of arbitrage will therefore keep the futures price in what is known as its *arbitrage channel* – the implied forward price plus or minus the transaction costs of doing the arbitrage.

We now turn from short-term to long-term interest rate futures contracts, or bond futures.

BOND FUTURES: UK LONG GILT FUTURES CONTRACT

We take as an example of bond futures the Euronext.liffe long gilt futures contract. Table 8.5 sets out the full specification of this contract, and Table 8.6 shows trading information for Wednesday 19 May 2004.

Long-term interest rate futures contracts such as the UK long gilt futures contract are generally contracts on government bonds in the currency concerned. The UK long gilt futures contract differs from short-term interest rate contracts in four important respects: unit of trading, basis of quotation, time of expiry and mode of settlement. The following analysis focuses primarily on these differences, and does not repeat explanations already given in the preceding section (for instance on trading volumes and high/low prices) where there is no material difference between the short-term interest rate and the long gilt futures contract. We first give a brief description of each of the four differences, and then analyse their considerable combined impact on the mechanics and economics of trading in the long gilt futures contract.

Unit of trading

Whereas the unit of trading for the short-term futures contract is a real cash-market financial asset (for example, a three-month interbank deposit of £500,000), the long gilt contract is based on a notional asset. Currently this is a sterling government bond with a coupon of 6% p.a. The main reason for employing a notional bond is to ensure consistency and continuity between futures contracts with successive expiry months, but – as we shall soon see when we come to consider the settlement

Table 8.5 Contract specification, UK long gilt futures contract

Unit of trading	£100,000 nominal value notional gilt with 6% coupon
Quotation	Per £100 nominal
Minimum price movement ('tick' size and value)	0.01 (£10)
Delivery month	March, June, September, December, such that the nearest three delivery months are available for trading
Last trading day	11.00 two business days prior to the last business day in the delivery month
First notice day	Two business days prior to the first day of the delivery month
Last notice day	First business day after the last trading day
Delivery day	Any business day in delivery month (at seller's choice)
Exchange delivery settlement price (EDSP)	The Euronext.liffe market price at 11.00 on the second business day prior to settlement day. The invoicing amount in respect of each deliverable gilt is to be calculated by the price factor system (see below). Adjustment will be made for full coupon interest accruing as at settlement day.
Mode of settlement	Delivery may be made of any gilt on the List of Deliverable Gilts in respect of a delivery month. Holders of long positions on any day within the notice period may be delivered against during the delivery month. Deliverable gilt issues will have the following characteristics (authors' note: this list has been slightly abridged):
	○ having terms as to redemption such as provide for redemption of the entire gilt issue in a single instalment on the maturity date falling not earlier than 8.75 years from, and not later than 13 years from, the first day of the relevant delivery month;
	○ having no terms permitting or requiring early redemption;
	○ bearing interest at a single fixed rate throughout the term of the issue payable in arrears semi-annually;
	○ being denominated in sterling;
	○ not being convertible;
	○ not being in bearer form;
	○ being anticipated by the Board to have on one or more days in the delivery month an aggregate principal amount outstanding of not less than £1.5 billion.
Trading hours	08:00–18:00

Source: Euronext.liffe.

and pricing process – these advantages are secured at the expense of considerable complexity when the contract expires.

Basis of quotation

The long gilt futures contract follows the general rule that its price is expressed on the same basis as the underlying cash market product, which in the case of a sterling-denominated bond is the price per £100.00 nominal. No adjustment is therefore necessary to make the price go in the 'right' direction, as was the case with the short-term

Table 8.6 Trading information for long gilt futures contract

Business Day — Wed 19 May 2004

Bond Products
Long Gilt

| | | | Daily | | Lifetime | | | | | | Previous Business Day Tue 18 May 2004 | | |
Opening Trans	Settle	Change	High	Low	High	Low	Closing Price	CONNECT* Volume	Basis Volume	Block Trd Volume	Official Volume	Open Interest	Change
Jun 04 106.03	105.69	-0.45	106.07	105.55	110.06	105.50	105.68	36,478	10,096	1,000	37,353	214,939	+4,136
Sep 04 105.64	105.32	-0.43	105.66S	105.22S	107.38	105.22S	105.31	4,054	0	0	647	5,901	+647
Dec 04	105.12	-0.45					105.11	0	0	0	0	0	0
								40,532	10,096	1,000	38,000	220,840	+4,783

Source: Euronext.liffe.

interest rate futures contracts. If the price of a bond goes up, buyers make a gain, and sellers suffer an opportunity cost or (if they have sold short what they do not own, in the hope of being able to buy it back later at a lower price) an actual cash loss.

Delivery day

Unlike the short-term interest rate futures contracts, each of which has a single expiry time and date, and therefore a single EDSP, the long gilt contract can be settled on any day in the delivery month by means of the short position (the seller of the futures) giving two business days' notice to the exchange of his or her intention to settle. Only the seller can give notice in this way. The exchange computer then allocates the contracts being settled by the seller to appropriate holders of corresponding long positions.

Mode of settlement

As the notional bond does not exist in the market, it is not possible to cash-settle the long gilt contract. It is therefore settled through physical delivery of one of a predetermined range of actual gilts issues. The main criteria for determining whether an issue is deliverable are set out in Table 8.5, and a list of the actual issues meeting those criteria is shown in Table 8.7. The main criteria can be summed up by saying that the issue must be a 'plain vanilla' single-dated conventional gilt with a remaining life of between 8¾ and 13 years from the first day of the delivery month.

There remains just one question, and it is a very big one: for any given settlement price for the notional 6% gilt represented by the futures contract, what is the equivalent price at which the seller will invoice the buyer for delivery of each actual gilt issue that meets the criteria for deliverability?

Pricing of bond futures: the principle of 'cheapest-to-deliver'

Exactly the same valuation technique applies to all futures and forward contracts: they differ from the value of the underlying cash instrument by the cost of carry. In the case of bond futures, there is one complication. Since a number of bonds can be delivered (the choice of bond being at the option of the seller), determination of the fair price of the futures contract must assume that a particular bond will be chosen. In practice, this is less difficult than it sounds since there is always one bond that is *cheapest to deliver.*

We need to establish a standard 'rate of exchange' (known as the *price factor* or *conversion factor*) between the notional bond and each of the deliverable bonds, so that (for example) a seller of futures knows exactly how much of which bond to hold as a *hedge*. By convention, the price factor between the futures settlement price and the equivalent settlement price for each deliverable gilt issue is computed on the basis of the ratio between their prices if the yield on each of them were exactly equal to the coupon on the notional bond on the first settlement date in the settlement month.

Table 8.8 shows, for the June 2004 futures contract, what would be the prices of each of the deliverable gilts, on 1 June 2004 if they were trading on a yield of exactly 6% p.a. The price of the notional gilt would of course be exactly 100.00. Note that, as we would expect, the prices of deliverable gilts with coupons below 6% would be less than 100.00 and the prices of gilts with coupons above 6% would be more than

Table 8.7 Initial list of deliverable gilts against the June 2004 long gilt futures contract

List of deliverable gilts

Long gilt contract (6% coupon) – price factors and accrued interest delivery Month: June 2004

Gilt ISIN* code	Coupon	Redemption	Price Factor	Daily Accrued	Initial Accrued	June 2004 Delivery Days
GB0008921883	8.00	27 Sep 13	1.1410760	21.739130	1,413.043478	1234-78901-45678-12345-890
GB0031829509	5.00	7 Sep 14	0.9240793	13.586957	1,154.891304	1234-78901-45678-12345-890
GB0033280339	4.75	7 Sep 15	0.8986086	12.907609	1,097.146739	1234-78901-45678-12345-890
GB0008881541	8.00	7 Dec 15	1.1646196	21.857923	-153.005464	1234-78901-45678-12345-890

Key: *International Securities Identification Number
Price Factor: price factor expressed as a fraction of par.
Daily Accrued: accrued interest per day on £100,000 face value.
Initial Accrued: accrued interest on £100,000 face value as of the last day of the month prior to the delivery month.
Delivery days: – = non business day.
Invoicing Amount: (1000 x EDSP x Price Factor) + Initial Accrued + (Daily Accrued x Delivery Day in Month).
Issue Date: 12 May 2004

Source: Euronext-liffe.

Table 8.8 June 2004 long gilt contract: calculation of prices of deliverable gilts at different yields

		Market yield on first settlement date						
	Coupon	3.00%	4.00%	5.00%	6.00%	7.00%	8.00%	9.00%
Notional gilt	6.00%				100.00			
Deliverable stock								
Maturity	Coupon							
27/09/2013	8.00%	**140.39**	**130.86**	**122.12**	**114.11**	106.75	99.98	93.76
% change from 6% yield price		23.03%	14.68%	7.02%	0.00%	-6.45%	-12.38%	-17.83%
07/09/2014	5.00%	117.55	108.35	99.99	**92.41**	85.52	79.25	73.54
% change from 6% yield price		27.21%	17.25%	8.21%	0.00%	-7.46%	-14.24%	-20.42%
07/09/2015	4.75%	116.62	106.75	97.86	**89.86**	**82.65**	**76.15**	**70.28**
% change from 6% yield price		29.78%	18.79%	8.90%	0.00%	-8.02%	-15.26%	-21.79%
07/12/2015	8.00%	148.38	136.62	126.02	**116.46**	107.82	100.00	92.92
% change from 6% yield price		27.41%	17.31%	8.21%	0.00%	-7.42%	-14.13%	-20.21%

Note: 8% Treasury 2013 is the deliverable gilt with the lowest duration, that is, with the smallest percentage price rise when yields fall. 4¾% Treasury 2015 is the deliverable gilt with the longest duration, that is, with the greatest percentage price fall when yields rise.

100.00. So, for example, the price of the 8% Treasury 2013 gilt is 114.1076, rounded to 114.11 in Table 8.8.

The price factor for each deliverable gilt issue is simply the ratio of its own price at the 6% yield to that of the notional gilt. As the latter is exactly 100.00, the price factor of each deliverable is its price divided by 100. So, for example, the price factor of the 8% Treasury 2013 is 114.10760 / 100.00 = 1.1410760, as shown in Table 8.7.

Now look at what would happen to the prices of each of the deliverable gilts if yields were to move away from 6%. Because of their different maturities, coupons and durations, they would behave differently, as shown in Table 8.8. The percentage change in price as yield changes, for example, is greater for the 4¾% Treasury 2015 than for the 8% Treasury 2013.

Figure 8.1 captures the situation in graphic terms. Note that the vertical (price) axis has been rebased so that a notional index value of 100 represents the price of each issue at a 6% yield. Below this level of yield, the deliverable issue with the shortest duration, the 8% 2013, gains value more slowly than the deliverable bond with the longest duration, making it cheaper to deliver. Above this level of yield, their positions are reversed, because it is the issue with the longest duration that loses value most quickly and thus takes over the role of cheapest to deliver.

One very important effect of all of this is that the futures contract no longer behaves as if the notional were the 6% issue specified in the contract terms, but instead it effectively becomes a futures contract on the cheapest-to-deliver issue. If this were otherwise, risk-free profits could be made by selling the futures and delivering the cheapest to deliver (if any buyers could be found – for buyers would face a loss as certain as the

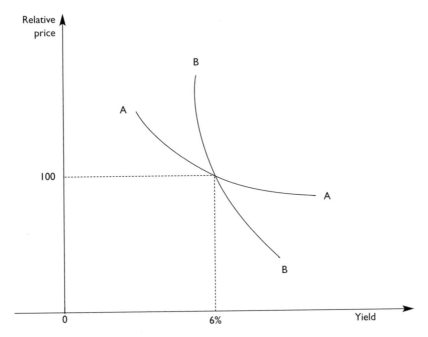

Figure 8.1 Price–yield graph for 8% Treasury 2013 (A) and 4¾% Treasury 2015 (B)
Note that in order to display relative price, the price axis has been normalised so that for each bond, 100 = market value at 6% yield.

Table 8.9 Gilts delivered against long gilt futures, March 2000 to June 2004

Coupon Month Year Expiry	5.75% 07 Dec 2009	6.25% 25 Nov 2010	9.00% 12 Jul 2011	5.00% 07 Mar 2012	8.00% 27 Sep 2013	5.00% 07 Sep 2014	8.00% 07 Dec 2015	Totals
June 04					21,033			21,033
Mar 04					11,828			11,828
Dec 03					11,277			11,277
Sep 03					9,799			9,799
June 03				8,654				8,654
Mar 03				3,047				3,047
Dec 02				6,587				6,587
Sep 02			7,679					7,679
June 02			17,327					17,327
Mar 02			10,594					10,594
Dec 01		3,091						3,091
Sep 01		12,489						12,489
June 01			5,583					5,583
Mar 01	3,872							3,872
Dec 00	899							899
Sep 00	656							656
June 00	7,359							7,359
Mar 00	5,379		1,264					6,643

Source: Euronext.liffe.

seller's risk-free profit). So in terms of Figure 8.1, the futures contract actually behaves as if it were always on the lowest line for any level of yield.

If we refer now to Table 8.9, showing actual deliveries into the long gilt contract since March 2000, we can see that in almost every case all deliveries were of a single issue, latterly the 8% 2013 which we have just calculated as cheapest to deliver for June 2004. The reason for this is that as actual yields were always significantly lower than the notional coupon, the deliverable issue with the shortest *duration* was always the cheapest to deliver.

For the sake of completeness, we should note that the settlement price of gilts against the futures contract must also include accrued interest; the conversion factor serves only to establish the ratio between the respective issues' clean prices. The columns in Table 8.7 headed 'Daily accrued' and 'Initial accrued' give the amount of accrued interest to be added to the clean price to arrive at the final settlement price, as explained in the note on 'Invoicing amount' at the foot of the table. Note that in the case of the 8% gilt due 7 December 2015, the initial accrued interest is negative, as the last day of the month prior to the delivery month lay within the ex-dividend period before the next coupon which was due on 7 June 2004.

The principle of cheapest to deliver can also be illustrated by showing the technique known as **cash and carry**, which is the market term for the practice of selling the futures and simultaneously borrowing to buy the cheapest to deliver to cover one's liability under the short futures position. In an efficient market this should yield neither profit nor loss (or a profit or loss so small that it cannot be arbitraged because of transaction costs).

Table 8.10 Cash-and-carry and cheapest-to-deliver, June 2004 long gilt futures contract

Issue details:				
Coupon	**8.00%**	**5.00%**	**4.75%**	**8.00%**
Maturity date	**27-Sep 2013**	**07 Sep 2014**	**07 Sep2015**	**07 Dec 2015**
Last coupon date	27 Mar 2004	07 Mar 2004	07 Mar 2004	07 Dec 2003
Next coupon date	27 Sep 2004	07 Sep 2004	07 Sep 2004	07 June 2004
Cash transaction details:				
Transaction date	19 May 2004			
Settlement date	20 May 2004			
Delivery date	01 June 2004			
Days in holding period	12			
Cost of financing purchase (% p.a.)	4.38%			
Redemption yield	*5.1482%*	*5.1506%*	*5.1522%*	*5.1253%*
Clean price	120.9500	98.8000	96.5800	124.8200
Accrued interest	1.1739	1.0054	0.9552	3.6066
Cost of purchase (A)	122.1239	99.8054	97.5352	128.4266
Cost of finance (B)	0.1759	0.1437	0.1405	0.1849
Coupon received 7 June	N/A	N/A	N/A	-4.0000
Total cost of cash transaction ((A) + (B))	122.2998	99.9492	97.6756	124.6115
Futures transaction details:				
Transaction price	105.6800	105.6800	105.6800	105.6800
EDSP on delivery date[1]	105.6800	105.6800	105.6800	105.6800
Conversion factor	1.1411	0.9241	0.8986	1.1646
Plus/(minus) initial accrued interest to 31 May	1.4130	1.1549	1.0971	-0.1530
Plus/(minus) daily accrued interest from 31 May	0.0217	0.1359	0.0129	0.0219
Total proceeds of futures (B)	122.0237	98.9475	96.0750	122.9459
Net profit or loss (A) – (B)	-0.2761	-1.0017	-1.6006	-1.6656

1 For ease of calculation only, it is assumed that EDSP on 31 May is same as the transaction price: any change will have been accounted for by means of variation margin and will therefore cancel out.

Figures have been rounded to four decimal places for display purposes only: actual calculations (e.g. of accrued interest, conversion factors etc) have been performed with full accuracy.

Table 8.10 shows the expected results of a cash-and-carry transaction involving (a) the simultaneous purchase of each of the deliverable gilts and sale of a June 2004 futures contract on 21 May 2004, and (b) delivery of the purchased gilts against the futures position on 1 June 2004. The total cost includes the accrued coupon interest payable on the gilts purchased, and the total proceeds include the initial accrued and daily accrued interest on the settlement price of the futures contract. For simplicity's sake, we have calculated the total proceeds on the assumption that the final settlement price of the futures contract was the same as the price at which the contract was originally sold on 21 May 2004 (i.e. 105.68); in practice, any difference between the two prices would have been exactly compensated by the variation margin credited or debited during the 11-day period when the position remained open.

The cash-and-carry transaction produces a small loss if the 8% Treasury 2013 is used, and greater losses in the other cases. This shows both that the 8% 2013 is the cheapest to deliver and that the pricing of the futures contract closely follows the cheapest to deliver.

We now turn to the third kind of futures contract, equity futures.

EQUITY INDEX FUTURES: THE FTSE 100 INDEX CONTRACT

We take as an example of equity index futures the Euronext.liffe futures contract on the FTSE 100 Index. Table 8.11 sets out the full specification of this contract, and Table 8.12 shows full trading information for Wednesday 19 May 2004.

Description

Equity index futures contracts are contracts on the basket of ordinary shares that make up the particular index. Although there are many equity index futures contracts traded world-wide, for example the US S&P 500 index futures contract traded on the Chicago Mercantile Exchange (CME), the principal such contract traded on Euronext.liffe is based on the FTSE 100 index. This index was specially designed to be the basis of a futures contract: it has only 100 shares to enable the trader or arbitrageur to replicate the futures contract with a portfolio of the underlying shares. Since it is made up of the 100 largest shares by market capitalisation, it also moves quite similarly to the broader FTSE All-Share Index which has about 700 shares in it. Fund managers holding portfolios resembling the FTSE All-Share Index can therefore use the FTSE 100 Index to hedge their portfolios, as the FTSE 100 represents over 80 per cent by value of the All-Share Index.

In practice, delivery of the 100 shares representing the FTSE 100 share index in the correct proportions would be difficult for most sellers of equity index futures contracts. As a result, the FTSE 100 index futures contract is *cash settled*. Notice in Table 8.11 how there is no nominal amount underlying the FTSE 100 futures contract, unlike, say, the £500,000 nominal value of the short sterling contract. With an equity index futures contract, a complex basket of shares, held in different

Table 8.11 Contract specification, FTSE 100 Index contract

Unit of trading	Contract valued at £10 per index point (e.g. value £45,000 at 4500.0)
Quotation	Index points (e.g. 4500.0)
Minimum price movement ('tick' size and value)	0.5 (£5.00)
Delivery month	March, June, September, December, such that the nearest four delivery months are available for trading
Last trading day	10.30 on the third Friday of the delivery month
Delivery day	First business day after the last trading day
Exchange delivery settlement price (EDSP)	The EDSP is based on the outcome of an intra-day auction on the last trading day
Mode of settlement	Cash settlement based on the EDSP
Trading hours	08:00–17:30

Source: Euronext.liffe.

Table 8.12 Trading information for FTSE 100 Index futures contract

Business Day Wed 19 May 2004

Equity Products FTSE 100 Index	Opening Trans	Settle	Change	Daily High	Low	Lifetime High	Low	Closing Price	CONNECT Volume	Previous Business Day Tue 18 May 2004 Official Volume	Open Interest	Change
Jun-04	4445.0	4470.0	+53.5	4478.0	4439.5	4608.5	4019.5	4471.0	71,938	53,034	394,508	-875
Sep-04	4464.0	4479.5	+54.0	4485.5	4458.0	4600.0	4288.5	4480.0	3,437	633	23,300	+370
Dec-04	4491.5	4511.0	+57.0	4491.5	4491.5	4607.0	4351.5	4512.0	400	0	21,123	0
Mar-05	4503.0	4522.5	+56.0	4510.5	4502.5	4510.5	4474.0	4523.5	1,652	0	506	0
									77,427	**53,667**	**439,437**	**-505**

Source: Euronext.liffe.

amounts to reflect their relative market values, underlies the futures contract. So the equity index futures contract is priced at £10 per index point. For example, if Ms Golden chose to buy one equity index futures contract for June 2004 delivery at the closing price of 4471 quoted in Table 8.12, she would be buying into the risk of a notional portfolio of shares currently worth $4471 \times £10 = £44,710$. The tick size for the FTSE 100 share index futures contract is 0.5 of an index point, equivalent to $£10/2 = £5$. So, if the futures price rose 10 index points or 20 ticks, Ms Golden's position would be in profit by $20 \times £5.00$ or £100.

Pricing

Futures contracts on equity indices can be priced by considering what happens on expiry. At that point, we have seen how futures prices are defined to converge to the underlying security prices. So, before expiry, the difference in price between a futures contract and the cash security price is equal to the difference in what is known as the *cost of carry*.

Let us consider the price of the stock index futures contract as quoted in Table 8.12. The closing price on 19 May 2004 for the September 2004 futures contract on the FTSE 100 share index was 4480, while the closing price for the index itself was 4471, implying a premium for the futures index price over the cash index price of 0.20%. And yet, on the expiry date in September 2004, the futures price must equal the cash price.

Why is the futures price trading at a 0.20% premium? Because it is cheaper to buy the futures contract on the FTSE 100 share index and hold it to expiry than to buy the 100 shares underlying the index and hold them for the same period. Buying shares implies a cash outflow which has an implied interest cost; on the other hand, buying shares provides a dividend income which can be offset against the interest cost of the shares. Since the interest rate on the money used to buy shares usually exceeds the dividend yield expected from holding shares, the cost of carrying shares is positive. In contrast (ignoring the impact of margin accounts), futures have a zero cost of carry. No money need be borrowed to buy futures contracts and no dividend income is received in return for buying futures contracts. Thus, the difference in price between the equity index futures and cash prices is the borrowing cost minus the dividend yield.

As an example, we use the September 2004 contract with the cash index and futures prices from Table 8.12. Example 8.1 calculates whether or not the futures price is fair, given the underlying cash index price and the cost of carrying the cash shares.

Both methods imply that the futures price was cheap relative to the cash price by about 0.1%. However, given that transaction costs in switching between cash and futures prices are substantially higher than 0.1%, the index futures contract was fairly priced, being higher than the cash index price by the cost of carry (allowing for transaction costs).

If the futures price were not fairly priced with respect to the underlying cash price, an arbitrage opportunity would arise. For example, suppose that, on 19 May 2004, the futures contract was trading at 4490 and the cash index at 4471. What would arbitrageurs do? They would buy the shares underlying the cash index at an index-equivalent price of 4471 and simultaneously sell the futures contract at 4490. By doing so they would lock in a profit since, assuming the same interest rate charge and expected dividends as in

Example 8.1 Determining the fair price of a stock index futures contract

Date	19 May 2004
Futures price	4480
Cash index price	4471
Interest rate	4.6% p.a. (four-month sterling LIBOR)
Expected dividend income*	53.5 or 1.1966% of 4471
Number of days to futures settlement	119

Method (1) Determine the cost of carry

Cost of carry
$$= \text{expected interest cost} - \text{expected dividend income}$$
$$= 0.046 \times 119/365 - 0.011966$$
$$= 0.014997 - 0.011966$$
$$= 0.3031\%$$

Premium of futures index price to cash index price
$$= (4480/4471) - 1$$
$$= 0.2013\%$$

Difference
$$= -0.1018\%$$

Method (2) Determine the fair futures price

Fair futures price
$$= \text{cash price} + \text{interest cost} - \text{expected dividends}$$
$$= 4471 + (4471 \times 0.046 \times (119/365)) - 53.5$$
$$= 4484.5$$

Actual futures price
$$= 4480$$

Difference
$$= -4.5/4484.5$$
$$= 0.1003\%$$

* Estimated from declared dividends not yet paid and from estimated dividends payable during the period to expiry of the futures contract.

Example 8.1, their costs per futures contract would be $4471 \times (1 + 0.0460 \times 119/365) - 53.5 = 4484.5$ and their revenue per futures contract would be 4490, leaving a gross profit per futures contract of 5.5 ticks or, at £5 per tick, £27.50. However, transaction costs would need to be deducted from the gross profit to determine the net proceeds. As a result, only arbitrageurs with access to large amounts of cash, and hence with low percentage transaction costs, could take advantage of any futures pricing anomalies. Indeed, the opposite arbitrage is more complex: if the futures price is below the fair price, say at 4475 in this example, arbitrageurs would wish to buy the futures and *sell short* the underlying securities. In the UK stock market, only certain participants can sell securities short, and thus take advantage of futures mispricing.

However, equity fund managers who wish to hold a portfolio that resembles the FTSE 100 Share Index have shares to sell from their portfolio and so are not restricted by any limitations on short selling. They could take advantage of a cheap futures contract to switch out of cash shares into the futures contract, switching back to cash shares on expiry of the futures contract or earlier if the futures price moves back to its fair level. What impact does such switching have on the portfolio's returns? It offers the fund manager the opportunity to earn more than the index return on the portfolio with no additional risk, and to capitalise on any *arbitrage* skills.

ADVANTAGES OF FINANCIAL FUTURES

The futures contract can serve two purposes:

- ○ as a substitute for the spot contract since, whether a security is bought for immediate settlement or for settlement six months later, once the later settlement date has been reached, the investor in either case holds the underlying security
- ○ as a hedge, since the spot purchase of a security can be offset by the sale of a futures contract, neutralising the risk of holding the security.

There are several factors that have contributed to the phenomenal growth of financial futures markets and to their appeal to both traders and hedgers.

Liquidity

Financial futures markets are often more liquid than the underlying securities markets. For example, there are more than 50 gilt issues for investors to choose from if they wish to invest in the UK gilt market, compared with only one futures contract. Investors wishing to buy gilts or alter the size of their exposure to the gilts market can do so more quickly and easily via the futures market than via the cash gilts. This liquidity keeps transaction costs low, and this enhances the attraction of using the futures markets as an alternative synthetic way into the underlying securities. Because of this liquidity in financial futures markets, financial futures prices often 'lead' cash prices. In other words, if traders and investors can more quickly and efficiently alter their exposure to cash securities via the futures market, the futures price will move faster than the underlying cash security prices and will be a better guide to short-term market sentiment.

Cash efficiency

A second attraction of financial futures markets is that they offer traders a cash-efficient means of taking a position in a market. Futures are traded on margin, which means that the trader has to invest only a fraction of the market value of an underlying security in order to be fully exposed to price rises or falls on that security. The margining system therefore allows traders a leveraged exposure to equity or interest rate risk. However, the leveraging effect of the margining system also means that investors can quite quickly lose 100 per cent of their investment, which is very unlikely if they invest in high-quality bonds or shares directly.

Reduced credit risk

Another advantage of the margining system is that credit risk is reduced by the intermediation of the clearing house between the two parties to every trade. So, if Mr Bull buys a futures contract from Mr Bear, each of them has the clearing house as his legal counterparty. In fact, in an order-driven electronic trading system such as Euronext.liffe, neither Mr Bull nor Mr Bear is aware of the identity of the other. All that they have to do is satisfy the exchange that they are creditworthy to do the transaction. Instead of needing to have lengthy talks with each other on their financial strength, they each place a deposit or initial margin with the exchange which is usually based on the maximum expected price movement of the futures contract in any one day. In this way, the maximum loss the futures exchange can incur is one day's adverse price movement on either Mr Bear's or Mr Bull's position, and this one-day loss is covered by the initial margin placed by each of them with the exchange. The futures exchange then requires daily settlement of any losses and records daily credits of any profits to accounts by means of variation margin. When Mr Bull, for example, wishes to realise his profits or limit his losses in the futures position, he simply sells the futures contract at the then prevailing price and closes out his account. The buying party in this case will not necessarily be Mr Bear, who might still wish to retain his futures position. If Mr Bull has made a profit, it will already be in his account; if he has made a loss, he will have already covered it by variation margin payments into his account.

Ability to go short

A further advantage of financial futures contracts is that they offer both traders and investors the ability to take what is effectively a short position in the underlying security: that is, to sell something they do not have. Traders, for example, may think the market is going down. By selling futures contracts and buying them back later after the price has fallen, they will be able to make money in a bear market. Similarly, investors can use futures contracts to limit exposure to a particular securities market or indeed to sell short a particular market.

Suppose a pension fund manager holds an equity portfolio which closely resembles the UK stock market in its composition. If she thinks that the UK equity market is going to fall and wishes to turn her portfolio into cash, she can either sell all her shares (which might take time and depress share prices anyway if her portfolio is large) or she can simply sell stock index futures against her portfolio. If she is right, the loss incurred on her equity portfolio will be counterbalanced by a profit on her financial futures position. Alternatively, she can sell more futures contracts than her share portfolio is worth. In this case, she would be like the trader and effectively have a net short position in shares.

Flexibility for small investors

Stock index futures contracts allow small investors and traders to gain short-term exposure to a stock market without having to buy a portfolio of shares, and to earn the average rate of return on a stock market instead of holding a small number of shares which might outperform or underperform the market as a whole. However, by the expiry date, small traders or investors who have bought futures contracts have to decide whether to then buy shares, stay in cash, or buy new futures contracts with a later expiry date by *rolling forward* their position.

As we have seen, financial futures markets are used by both traders and investors. A third category, *arbitrageurs*, is vital to the smooth functioning of these markets. Arbitrageurs seek to make money by exploiting anomalies between the prices of futures contracts and the underlying cash securities. It is difficult to estimate the importance of each of these three types of participant, although it is definitely the case that traders dominate in terms of volume. This may at first sight seem to imply that futures markets are only for speculators and not for investors seeking to hedge interest rate or equity risk. However, it is the traders who accept the risk that the hedgers wish to offset. Further, it is the traders who provide the liquidity and depth to the financial futures markets by always being willing to buy or sell futures contracts, and the arbitrageurs who ensure that futures are correctly priced relative to the underlying cash securities. This creates a market in which would-be hedgers can hedge in an efficient manner.

USING FINANCIAL FUTURES

Trading

The most active participants in the financial futures markets are traders who buy or sell futures contracts in order to profit from a view that the market will either go up or go down. The range of currently available financial futures contracts enables traders to take a view on many different short-term and long-term interest rate products as well as on equity markets and individual equities.

The advantages to traders of using futures contracts rather than, say, three-month Treasury bills for exposure to short-term interest rates, or equity index futures contracts

---

Example 8.2 Comparison of results from investing in the gilts cash and futures markets from 5 December 2003 to 9 January 2004: bullish scenario

Strategy A. Invest £5 million in 8% Treasury 2013

Clean price on 5 December 2003	= 123.970000
Plus 72/182 days accrued interest	= 1.582418
Dirty price	= 125.552418
Nominal amount purchased	= £5,000,000 × 100/125.552418
	= £3,982,400
Clean price on 9 January 2004	= 125.780000
Plus 107/182 days accrued interest	= 2.351648
Dirty price	= 128.131648
Value of £3,982,400 nominal @ 128.131648	= £5,102,715
Overall gain	= £ 102,715
Annualised holding period return	= £102,715 × 365/35 × 100/5,000,000
	= 21.42% p.a.

Strategy B. Invest £50,000 in 50 long gilt futures contracts

Initial margin per contract (say)	= £1,000
No. of contracts purchased	= 50
Futures price on 5 December 2003	= 107.36
Futures price on 9 January 2004	= 109.31
Tick size/value	= 0.01 / £10
Gain per contract (no. of ticks × £10)	= £1,950
Gain on 50 contracts	= £97,500
Annualised holding period return	= (£97,500 − £50,000) × 365/35 × 100/50,000
	= 991% p.a.

instead of a portfolio of shares for exposure to movements in stock market prices, are low transaction costs, speed of trading, liquidity (essential to trader who might wish to close out their position at any time to lock in a profit or limit a loss) and, most importantly, the leverage effect provided by the margining system.

For an example we shall return to the data presented in Chapter 4. There we studied the effect of the net movement in the gilts market in the five-week period from 5 December 2003 to 9 January 2004, when redemption yields fell by between 0.20% and 0.25% p.a. Suppose that Mr Fish had correctly predicted this fall in interest rates and had decided to commit £50,000 of his capital to a long position in the gilts market. Example 8.2 shows the results Mr Fish could have achieved by means of two alternative trading strategies. Under Strategy A, he would have invested £5 million in the cash market, by buying the 8% Treasury 2013 (which happened also to be the cheapest-to-deliver stock into the nearest futures contract, the March 2004); and under Strategy B he would have invested £50,000 in the futures market, by depositing this amount in initial margin on 50 futures contracts at £1000 margin each. The difference in annualised holding period returns is dramatic: a healthy 21.42% for the cash market Strategy A, but a spectacular 991% for the futures market strategy B. The reason for the discrepancy is that as the initial margin represents only 1% of the notional amount of the investment in a futures contract, Mr Fish has earned the full profit on £5 million of underlying gilts from an investment of only £50,000.

But what would have happened if Mr Fish had made the opposite prediction, and had not bought but sold 50 March 2004 gilts futures contracts on 5 December 2003 in anticipation of a fall in the market? In this case the futures market would have moved by 195 ticks against him, and he would have lost 195 x £10 on each of 50 contracts, for a total £97,500. In other words, he would have lost not only his initial investment of £50,000, but *nearly as much again*.

Note that the futures market offers the private investor like Mr Fish a ready means of exploiting a bearish view of a particular market, in this case the gilts market, simply by selling the futures contract and buying it back later. Unless he were a gilt market-maker, he would otherwise find it very difficult to take a short position in the market as he could not normally sell short, i.e. sell gilts that he did not already own.

Trading futures is fundamentally different from trading the underlying securities (whether they be shares or bonds) because the downside risk is not limited to a loss of 100 per cent of the initial investment. We saw how Mr Fish could easily have lost nearly 200 per cent of his initial investment, and there is no reason at all why a trader should not lose five or even ten times the amount of his initial margin. For this reason, outright position-taking is normally very short term and often intra-day, to reduce the risk of large swings in price. Also, traders may put a stop loss order on their positions, so that the trade is closed out once a certain futures price has been reached, limiting the loss to a manageable quantity. In our example, where Mr Fish made the wrong prediction, it is unlikely that he would have allowed the position to deteriorate to the point where he was losing nearly twice his initial investment, especially as every day when the market moved further in the wrong direction he would have had to put up further variation margin to cover his loss.

In passing, we might note that there is evidence from the cash markets that investors are in fact irrationally reluctant to realise losses on conventional investments in stocks and bonds (see further on this in Chapter 13), but this would not apply in the futures market where the variation margin mechanism forces holders of loss-making positions to realise their loss every day. However, in volatile markets or around the announcement of volatile figures, futures prices may jump right over the *stop loss* price set by the trader. It is for this reason that most small investors who wish to trade in a leveraged way in the securities markets do so via options, described in Chapter 9. Although selling options can be of similar risk to selling futures, buying options limits the potential loss to a maximum of 100 per cent of the initial investment.

Hedging

The main purpose of hedging by investors is to protect the future value of their portfolio. An investor holding a portfolio of cash, shares and bonds can take out a hedge to protect the future sale price of his or her portfolio by selling an equivalent amount of the appropriate futures contracts.

In Chapter 9, we shall look at the role of options as a possible hedge for the investor. The main difference between futures and options as hedging alternatives is that the futures contract offers certainty of outcome and therefore deprives buyers of upside potential as well as protecting them from downside loss, whereas the purchase of an option protects the downside while leaving the upside potential still open. So, if hedgers of an equity portfolio sell futures contracts against their position and then see the stock market go up rather than down as they had feared, they cannot take advantage of that upswing. They have locked in an effective selling price: if the stock market goes up, they will have to buy back their futures position at a loss, and the loss on the futures hedge will balance the gain on their portfolio.

Entering into a futures contract obliges hedgers to go through with either cash or physical settlement (depending on the type of futures contract) or to do a counterbalancing trade on the futures market – in this example to buy back the number of futures contracts they have sold. As we shall see in Chapter 9, the purchase of an option does not impose an obligation to settle (or exercise) the trade or even to do a counterbalancing trade. Hedgers can write off the initial premium they paid for the option and walk away from their hedge. For that reason, options are sometimes described as a more expensive way of hedging than futures, because futures are simply priced as the underlying cash instrument plus the cost of carry with no extra costs comparable with the option premium. What this comparison overlooks is that futures and options achieve fundamentally different outcomes, so their costs cannot be compared directly with each other. Hedging via a futures trade merely fixes the value of an asset or liability. Hedging via options offers true insurance against loss.

Determining the hedge ratio

We now turn to the problem of how many futures contracts to use as a hedge. We start by considering the hedging of a straightforward position in short-term interest rates, then we apply the same principles to the hedging of a bond investment and finally to a portfolio of shares.

Hedging a short-term interest-rate exposure

The simplest type of futures contract is the short-term interest rate futures contract. Suppose that it is 19 May 2004 and Ms Ball runs a pension fund portfolio which is due to receive a £10 million cash inflow in mid-June 2004. She would like to place the cash on three-month deposit when it is received but is concerned that before the money is received interest rates might have fallen to a level below the forward interest rate implied in the three-month short sterling futures contract. As we saw on page 271, the June short sterling futures contract settled at 95.34 on 19 May 2004, and this implies a forward interest rate of 4.66% p.a. for the period mid-June to mid-September. In order to lock in this rate, Ms Ball must buy 20 short sterling contracts since their nominal value is £500,000 each. If interest rates do fall before expiry of the futures contract, the settlement price of the futures price on expiry will have risen, creating a gain on the futures hedge to compensate for the lower interest rate that Ms Ball will earn on the £10 million deposit.

Similarly, if Ms Ball wished to hedge the interest rate on a *six*-month deposit of £10 million from mid-June, she would have to buy double the number of contracts – because twice as risky – in this example 20 June contracts and 20 September contracts to fix the effective return on her deposit of £10 million from mid-June to mid-December.

Hedging an investment in bonds

Although the same principles of hedging apply to a bond portfolio as to a short-term deposit transaction, the arithmetic can be rather more complex. If the cash position we are trying to hedge is in the cheapest-to-deliver bond issue, the futures contract offers a straightforward hedge because its value does closely track the value of the cheapest-to-deliver stock. The value of the futures contract differs from that of the cheapest to deliver only by an amount equal to the cost of carry from the present day to the futures settlement date, and this is quite small as the period involved is very short in relation to the remaining life of the stock. Where a more substantial problem arises is when we are trying to hedge a bond issue that is not the cheapest-to-deliver, or a portfolio of several different bond issues. In this case, we need to compare the relative sensitivity of the futures contract and of our bond or bond portfolio to changes in market interest rates.

Let us suppose first that Ms Ball, as part of the pension fund for which she is responsible, also held in May 2004 £2 million nominal of the Treasury 8% 2013, then the cheapest-to-deliver bond. If this is the only bond that needs to be hedged, the **hedge ratio** (the number of futures contracts that need to be sold to create a hedge) is simply the ratio of the nominal values of the gilt futures and the amount to be hedged adjusted for the conversion factor of the cheapest-to-deliver bond. There is no need to adjust for any difference in price sensitivity, since the price of the bond futures contract moves almost exactly in parallel with the price of the cheapest-to-deliver gilt. Thus, Ms Ball would need to sell:

$$\frac{\text{Nominal value of CTD gilt held} \times \text{conversion factor}}{\text{Nominal value of gilt futures contract}} \tag{8.1}$$

$$= \frac{£2,000,000 \times 1.1410760}{£100,000}$$

$$= 22.81 \text{ futures contracts}$$

if she were using the June 2004 gilt futures with which to hedge. In practice, only round numbers of futures contracts can be traded and so Ms Ball would have to slightly overhedge by selling 23 June gilt futures contracts.

But if she wished to hedge another gilt issue with the gilt futures contract, Ms Ball would have to carry out an adjustment to reflect the relative price sensitivity of the gilt she wishes to hedge and of the cheapest-to-deliver gilt which drives the price of the gilt futures contract. As we saw in Chapter 4, the price sensitivity of a bond to interest rate change can be measured by its duration. Equation 4.5 gave us a formula for estimating a price change dP given the duration D of a bond and its redemption yield r:

$$dP = -D \times P \times \frac{dr}{1 + r} \tag{8.2}$$

What Ms Ball wishes to do is to make sure that the change in value of the gilt she holds is exactly offset by a change in value of the gilt futures contract. What she therefore needs to do is to express her actual gilt holding as an equivalent risk holding in the cheapest-to-deliver gilt and then use the hedge ratio in equation 8.1 to determine the appropriate number of June gilt futures contracts to sell.

Suppose Ms Ball held, on 5 December 2003, £20 million nominal of the 8% Treasury 2021. From Table 4.7 we know that its current market price was 136.15 at a redemption yield of 4.90%, and that the cheapest-to-deliver, the 8% 2013, was priced at 123.97 to yield 4.891%. The durations of the gilts were 10.84 and 7.21 for the 8% Treasury 2021 and the cheapest-to-deliver gilt respectively.

Let us consider the impact of a uniform rise of 0.5% p.a. in redemption yield on Ms Ball's portfolio. Using equation 8.2, the market value of £20 million nominal of 8% Treasury 2021 would fall as follows:

$$dP = -10.84 \times \frac{£20,000,000 \times 136.15}{100} \times \frac{0.005}{1.0490} \tag{8.3}$$

$$dP = -£1,406,926$$

The next step is to calculate the nominal amount H of the cheapest-to-deliver that would also suffer a loss in value of £1,406,926 if the redemption yield were to rise by 0.5% p.a., as follows:

$$-£1,406,926 = -7.21 \times \frac{H \times 123.97}{100} \times \frac{0.005}{1.0489} \tag{8.4}$$

$$H = \frac{-£1,406,926}{-7.21} \times \frac{100}{123.97} \times \frac{1.0489}{0.005} \tag{8.5}$$

$$H = £33,020,463$$

Ms Ball could therefore view her portfolio as being equivalent, in interest rate risk terms, to £33,020,463 nominal of the cheapest-to-deliver gilt. She could then use the normal hedge ratio formula in equation 8.1 to calculate the number of gilt futures contracts to sell. In this case, it would be

$$\frac{£33,020,463 \times 1.140760}{£100,000}$$

= 377 futures contracts (to the nearest whole number)

However, the method used to equate Ms Ball's holding of 8% Treasury 2013 to the cheapest-to-deliver issue assumes that both issues would experience the same change in redemption yield. Although this assumption turned out to be correct in the case of the particular period we have been studying (5 December 2003 to 9 January 2004, when yields on all medium-term maturities fell by between 0.20% and 0.25%), this assumption becomes more risky as the difference in duration between the gilt to be hedged and the cheapest-to-deliver increases. The hedging calculation is also subject to the general shortcoming of the duration measure, noted already in Chapter 4 (pages 134–6), namely that it is accurate only for small changes in interest rates. Using equation 8.3, for example, we calculated that if the yield on the 8% Treasury 2021 had risen by 0.5% from 4.90% to 5.40% on 5 December 2003, the value of a £20 million nominal holding of that issue would have fallen by £1,406,926. The correct figure is actually about £1,390,000, the difference being due to the phenomenon of convexity: as the yield increases the rate at which the value falls slows down, so the application of the linear function captured in equation 8.3 would result in an overestimate of the actual loss.

Hedging a portfolio of equities

Let us again assume that it is 19 May 2004, and this time that Ms Ball has a well-diversified UK equity portfolio worth £5 million. She wishes to lock in a sale value for September 2004 equivalent to an index level of 4480, the closing price on 19 May of the September FTSE 100 share index futures contract.

The number of FTSE 100 share index futures contracts is determined by the ratio of the market value of the equity portfolio to the amount of equity exposure inherent in one equity index futures contract, which is £10 times the value of the equity index concerned. In this example, we have a hedge ratio of

$$\frac{£5,000,000}{£10 \times 4480} \tag{8.6}$$

= 111.6 futures contracts

Ms Ball would therefore sell 112 FTSE 100 share index futures contracts (leaving herself very slightly overhedged) to hedge the equity element of her portfolio. If her portfolio differed significantly in its composition from the FTSE 100 share index, she might choose to adjust the hedge ratio accordingly. One comparatively straightforward way to incorporate such an adjustment would be to take account of the portfolio's beta. The beta of the FTSE 100 is very close to 1 (as it accounts for over 80 per cent of the entire market), so a portfolio with a beta of, say, 1.2, would require 1.2 times as many futures contracts to hedge it against market movements.

SWAPS

In this final section we look briefly at another comparatively new product for the management of risks arising from potential changes in interest rates and from long-term cross-currency borrowing and investing. The *interest-rate swap* and the *cross-currency swap* are OTC products which made their first appearance in the early 1980s. This family of products developed in response to two quite separate situations.

Interest rate swaps

Two features of the capital and money markets in particular led to the evolution of the swaps market.

○ Participants in the securities and money markets frequently want to change their relative exposure to fixed and floating interest rates. For instance, the finance director of a company that has raised funds by issuing a ten-year bond at a fixed interest rate may subsequently feel that interest rates are about to fall, so she will want some way to escape from the commitment to pay what could turn out to be an uneconomically high fixed interest rate, and instead pay a short-term floating rate based on three- or six-month LIBOR until such time as long-term rates have fallen, before considering whether to lock in to a fixed rate again (hopefully, at a lower level).

○ A general feature of the debt markets is that the increased return or premium required by lenders to a riskier borrower is usually less for floating-rate than for fixed-rate products. Opinions vary about the reason for this phenomenon, which at first sight is a violation of the efficient markets hypothesis. One possible factor which might account for this apparent anomaly is that the universes of investors in the two types of debt are largely distinct from each other. Demand for floating-rate debt is driven by the banking sector, and as banks generally have (or at least consider that they have) a superior capability to assess and monitor credit risk, they can afford to accept lower credit risk premiums than other types of investor who dominate the fixed-rate debt markets. Another possible reason is that, on average, the losses incurred by investors when borrowers default may be proportionately higher on fixed-rate debt than on floating-rate debt issues.

Let us consider each of these two points in turn.

The company seeking to unwind the effect of having entered into a commitment to pay fixed-rate interest on a bond issue would appear to have two principal alternative courses of action. The first course is to ask the bond investors to accept early repayment. But the terms on which fixed-rate bonds are issued normally include a provision (**call protection**) to prevent the issuer from repaying early, precisely so that the investors will not be threatened with this type of situation. And even if the investors were to agree, they might well want to charge a premium to cover the risk that they will only be able to earn a lower rate of interest when they reinvest the proceeds of the early repayment for the balance of the original term of the bond issue. A second possible course of action is for the company to raise a new loan at a floating rate of interest based on LIBOR and to invest the proceeds at a fixed rate. The two fixed rates – on the original bond issue and on the investment of the new loan proceeds – will then cancel each other out, leaving the company with just the commitment to pay LIBOR-based floating-rate interest on the new debt. But such a course of action would be extremely cumbersome and would also be an inefficient use of the company's finite capacity to raise new capital.

An interest-rate swap enables the company to achieve its objective without either repaying or renegotiating the terms of the existing bond issue, and without any need for additional fund-raising or investing activities. The company enters into an agreement with a counterparty (normally a commercial or investment bank), whereby the company pays periodic floating-rate interest to the bank on a notional principal amount equal to the original bond issue, and the bank pays to the company periodic interest at a fixed rate on the same notional amount. In effect, the bank covers the company's obligation to pay the original fixed rate (albeit its contractual relationship is with the company and not directly with the original bondholders themselves) and the company pays a floating rate instead.

So much for the first of the two situations for which the interest-rate swap was developed. The second is more subtle but is probably more important in terms of its effect on the securities markets. We consider the hypothetical case of two issuers called Triple-A and Single-A. Triple-A has the highest credit standing and is typically a government agency of a large industrialised country. Single-A is a company with a good, but not quite the highest, credit rating. Triple-A is planning to borrow £100 million for ten years, and after considering its interest rate exposure profile has decided to issue floating-rate debt. Single-A is also planning to borrow £100 million for ten years, but wishes to borrow at a fixed rate. The terms on which each of them can borrow in the current market environment might be as follows:

	Triple-A	**Single-A**
Cost of fixed rate debt	5.00%	6.00%
Cost of floating rate debt	LIBOR – 0.125%	LIBOR + 0.125%

Single-A thus pays a premium of 1.00% for fixed rate debt, but only 0.25% for floating rate debt, over the rates paid by Triple-A.

Without the benefit of the interest-rate swap mechanism, each borrower would issue debt in the appropriate market – Triple-A in the floating rate market at LIBOR – 0.125%, and Single-A in the fixed rate market at 6.00%. But the interest-rate swap enables both parties to save interest costs, in a rare example of a genuine win-win situation, by issuing debt not in the market corresponding to their own needs but in the market where they enjoy the greatest competitive advantage (or, in the case of Single-A, the least competitive disadvantage) and then swapping their interest payment liabilities just as the company and the bank did in our first example. The resulting structure can best be illustrated graphically (see Figure 8.2 overleaf).

The net interest rate exposure of the two parties as a result of their borrowings and the interest-rate swap is as follows.

Triple-A:
○ pays a fixed rate of 5.00% to its investors
○ receives a fixed rate of 5.50% from Single-A and
○ pays a floating rate of LIBOR to Single-A.

The fixed positive margin on the two fixed-rate elements in the structure gives Triple-A a constant saving of 0.5% on its floating rate interest liability to Single-A priced at LIBOR, so that Triple-A has effectively manufactured a floating-rate interest liability at LIBOR minus 0.5%. This is 0.375% better than the floating rate of LIBOR minus 0.125% which it could have achieved by borrowing directly from the floating rate debt market.

Single-A:
○ pays a floating rate of LIBOR plus 0.125% to its lenders

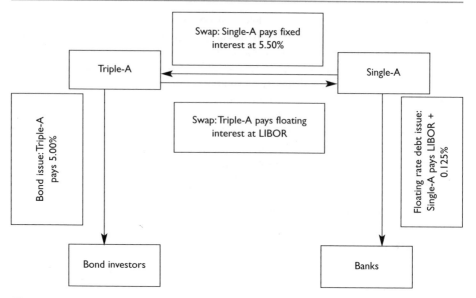

Figure 8.2 Interest-rate swap cash flows

○ receives a floating rate of LIBOR from Triple-A and
○ pays a fixed rate of 5.50% to Triple-A.

Note that it does not matter what absolute value LIBOR takes from time to time; as long as the periodic rate-fixing dates under the swap agreement are synchronised with those under Single-A's borrowing agreement with its banks, the two LIBOR elements will always cancel each other out. So Single-A is left with a constant negative margin of 0.125% from the two floating-rate elements in the structure. Adding this to the fixed rate of 5.50% that it pays to Triple-A in the remaining element, the fixed-rate leg of the swap, we find that Single-A has effectively manufactured a fixed rate interest liability at 5.625%. This is 0.375% better than the fixed rate of 6.00% which it could have achieved by issuing debt directly in the fixed-rate market.

There is a simple way of proving that our result is correct. The difference between the premiums Single-A pays in the two markets is 0.75% (1.00% in the fixed rate market less 0.25% in the floating rate market). The aggregate savings achieved by the two parties by entering into an interest rate swap must equate to the same figure as this net difference.

We should note three ways in which the practice of the swaps market differs from the theoretical model we have used for illustration purposes:

○ The rates we used are fictitious and the margins have been inflated in order to make it easier to appreciate the rationale and workings of the swap mechanism.
○ The parties do not pay gross interest to each other at the full rates set out in the swap agreement. At the end of each interest period the party with the greater liability for that period pays to the other party the difference between their liabilities to each other. So, for example, if LIBOR were set for a particular period at 8%, then at the end of that period Triple-A would pay to Single-A 8.00% − 5.50% = 2.5% on the notional prin-

cipal amount of the swap contract. Conversely, if LIBOR were set at 3.00%, Single-A would pay to Triple-A 5.50% – 3.00% = 2.50% on the principal amount. Because the parties do not lend the principal amount itself, and because the interest claims are netted out against each other, the credit risk that each incurs with respect to the other is only a very small fraction of the notional principal amount on which the swap payments are computed.

○ The end-users of swaps very rarely deal directly with each other. Instead, a firm or other organisation seeking an interest-rate swap will approach one of the major banks that make markets in swaps by quoting continuous two-way rates.

Although swaps are an OTC market and are not traded on an organised exchange, most features of the product, including the terms and conditions, documentation and settlement procedures, are largely standardised so that the market is both liquid and large. The *Financial Times* publishes a daily list of swap rates for the major currencies covering the most actively traded maturities. The rates for 20 November 2004 are shown in Table 8.13. Like any other market-maker, the bank dealing in swaps makes its profit from two sources: from the bid–offer spread and from outright position taking, that is, by taking a view on the direction of interest rates and leaving an appropriate part of its swaps book uncovered in the hope that its view will turn out to be correct.

This table tells us, for instance, that at close of business on 20 November 2006, major banks were prepared to enter into ten-year interest rate swaps in sterling with the most creditworthy counterparties on terms whereby the bank would pay 4.91% fixed if it were

Table 8.13 Interest rate swap rates

20 Nov 2006	Euro-€		£ Stlg.		SwFr		US$		Yen	
	Bid	Ask	Bid	Ask	Bid	Ask	Bid	Ask	Bid	Ask
1 year	3.88	3.91	5.40	5.42	2.19	2.25	5.29	5.32	0.69	0.72
2 year	3.87	3.90	5.30	5.34	2.31	2.39	5.07	5.10	0.89	0.92
3 year	3.85	3.88	5.26	5.30	2.36	2.44	5.01	5.04	1.05	1.08
4 year	3.85	3.88	5.21	5.26	2.40	2.48	4.99	5.02	1.20	1.23
5 year	3.85	3.88	5.15	5.20	2.43	2.51	5.00	5.03	1.33	1.36
6 year	3.86	3.89	5.10	5.15	2.46	2.54	5.01	5.04	1.44	1.47
7 year	3.87	3.90	5.05	5.10	2.49	2.57	5.03	5.06	1.55	1.58
8 year	3.88	3.91	5.00	5.05	2.52	2.60	5.05	5.08	1.65	1.68
9 year	3.90	3.93	4.95	5.00	2.54	2.62	5.07	5.10	1.75	1.78
10 year	3.92	3.95	4.91	4.96	2.57	2.65	5.08	5.11	1.83	1.86
12 year	3.96	3.99	4.81	4.88	2.59	2.69	5.12	5.15	1.98	2.01
15 year	4.00	4.03	4.70	4.79	2.62	2.72	5.16	5:19	2.16	2.19
20 year	4.03	4.06	4.52	4.65	2.64	2.74	5.20	5.23	2.36	2.39
25 year	4.04	4.07	4.39	4.52	2.65	2.75	5.21	5.24	2.48	2.51
30 year	4.02	4.05	4.29	4.42	2.64	2.74	5.20	5.23	2.55	2.58

Bid and ask rates as of close of London business. US $ is quoted annual money actual/360 basis against three-month LIBOR. £ and Yen quoted on a semi-annual actual/365 basis against six-month LIBOR, Euro/Swiss Franc quoted on annual bond 30/360 basis against six-month EURIBOR/LIBOR with the exception of the one-year rate which is quoted against three-month EURIBOR/LIBOR.

Source: *Financial Times*/ICAP plc.

paying the fixed rate, and would receive 4.96% if it were *receiving* the fixed rate; in either case, the floating side of the swap is assumed to be LIBOR, so that the price of the swap is reflected solely in the fixed rate.

Interest rate swaps, and the closely related product cross-currency swaps, play a pivotal role in the market for the new issue of bonds in two respects. A fluctuating but generally high proportion of total new issuance is determined by activity and opportunities in the swaps market, as issuers seek to use the swaps product to exploit competitive advantages they enjoy in particular markets. Second, the pricing of swaps relative to the benchmark government bond rate for each currency and maturity is regarded as a key determinant of the condition of the market. As the government bond rate is a risk-free rate, and the swap rate is the rate for a prime banking or corporate counterparty, the size of the spread between the two tells us a lot about how relatively risk-averse the market is at any partic-ular point in time. When confidence is high, the spread narrows as investors require a smaller premium for taking on private-sector risk rather than investing in risk-free bonds. When the financial system is under stress (as, for example, after the Asian and Russian financial crises of 1997 and 1998 respectively), the spread widens as investors run for the protection of risk-free assets in what is popularly known as a ***flight to quality***.

Table 8.13 shows fixed rates for sterling swaps. The yield curve for gilts at that time was exactly the same shape but at the lower level of 5.00% to 3.85%, showing that swap spreads were more or less even at 0.40% to 0.45% across the maturity spectrum. The extent to which swap spreads are driven by global investor sentiment is clear from Figure 8.3, which shows swap spreads for both sterling and US dollars for the period from 1995 to 2003.

Some statistics illustrating the growth and scale of the global market for interest rate swaps and other OTC derivatives are reproduced at the end of the next section.

Figure 8.3 Ten-year sterling and US dollar swap spreads, 1995–2003
Source: Bank of England.

Cross-currency swaps

Once the principle of the interest-rate swap became established, it rapidly became clear that it could be harnessed to exploit any comparable yield differential in the capital or money markets, as long as the benefit of exploiting the differential was not outweighed by the transaction costs of the swap itself.

One area where such differentials have historically been sufficiently high to justify the use of swaps is in the relative rates (that is, relative to the appropriate risk-free rate) charged to one and the same borrower in different national and international bond markets. A prime German industrial company might enjoy better name recognition in the eurobond market than an equivalent US company, which in turn might have a comparable competitive advantage in the US dollar market. If each of two such companies had similar but opposite requirements to raise funds in the other's 'strong' currency, they could save money by issuing securities in their own currency or market and then swapping the payment obligations with each other (in most cases, via a bank, as in the case of interest-rate swaps). In a typical cross-currency swap, unlike in a single-currency swap, the full principal amounts are exchanged at the outset and re-exchanged on final maturity, and the periodic interest payments are also made on a gross rather than a net basis. Even so, the credit risk is mitigated by the fact that each party enjoys a full right of set-off of its own obligations against the obligations of the other, in the event that the latter defaults on its own payment.

Table 8.14 Global OTC derivatives market turnover by instrument: average daily turnover in April 2004, in billions of US dollars

Instrument	1995	1998	2001	2004
A. Foreign exchange instruments[1]	**45**	**97**	**67**	**140**
Currency swaps	4	10	7	21
Options	41	87	60	117
Other	1	0	0	2
B Interest rate instruments[2]	**151**	**265**	**489**	**1,025**
FRAs	66	74	129	233
Swaps	63	155	331	621
Options	21	36	29	171
Other	2	0	0	0
C. Estimated gaps in reporting	4	13	19	55
D. Total	**200**	**375**	**575**	**1,220**
Memo:				
Turnover at April 2004 exchange rates[3]	180	410	690	1,220
Exchange-traded derivatives[4]				
Currency instruments	17	11	10	22
Interest rate instruments	1,204	1,371	2,170	4,521

1 Adjusted for local and cross-border double-counting.
2 Single currency interest rate contracts only.
3 Non-US dollar legs of foreign currency transactions were converted into original currency amounts at average exchange rates for April of each survey year and then reconverted into US dollar amounts at average April 2004 exchange rates.
4 Sources: FOW TRADE data; Futures Industry Association; various futures and options exchanges.

Source: Bank for International Settlements.

Table 8.14 shows a summary of statistics for turnover in OTC derivatives, including interest-rate and currency swaps, gathered from 52 countries and collated by the Bank for International Settlements in Basel. This is a triennial survey, and the comparative figures for the previous three surveys going back to 1995 make clear the rapid growth in the use of these instruments. One reason that the cross-currency sector is much smaller, and is growing less rapidly, than the single-currency sector is that the kind of differentials that drive cross-currency swaps may be narrowing as markets in the major countries become increasingly integrated with each other and global investor sentiment becomes more homogenous.

One area where previously discrete markets have become largely integrated and homogenised is of course the eurozone: that is, the countries in the European Union that have adopted the euro as a single currency. There is now no exchange risk for investors based in any of these countries buying euro-denominated bonds issued by the government of any other country in the zone. There is also a unified interest rate structure for the entire euro market, because if different countries tried to set their own interest levels in the common currency, the opportunity for risk-free arbitrage would swiftly bring them back into line with the rest of the eurozone.

While the advent of the euro has undoubtedly made a very positive contribution to the development of the capital markets, it does pose an awkward technical problem. Despite the fact that the general level of interest rates for all euro instruments is determined by the European Central Bank in Frankfurt, the market still makes small (but non-negligible) distinctions in its assessment of the creditworthiness of different national governments issuing euro-denominated bonds. For this reason there is now no longer a single benchmark risk-free rate to serve as a cornerstone for the entire euro capital market as there is, for instance, in the sterling or US dollar markets.

The market responded to this awkward side-effect of the single currency with typical resilience by identifying instead a rate that, unlike the slightly differing bond rates of national government bond issues, is still uniform across the entire euro market, and that is the fixed rate for single-currency interest rate swaps in euros. This reflects the fact that whereas different governments in the eurozone pay slightly different rates for their debt, the market has a single rate at which it transacts fixed rate swaps in euros for a given maturity with prime counterparties. This rate is now used as the basis for the Swapnote® futures contract on Euronext.liffe, which is a contract on a notional fixed-coupon bond priced according to the swaps curve and (unlike the gilt futures contract) cash-settled.

SUMMARY

Thirty years ago, investors could afford to ignore the then relatively new market in derivatives, and financial futures in particular. Since then, the derivatives markets have experienced phenomenal growth, in Europe and the Far East as well as in their original home market of the United States. Now, financial futures and options have become an integral part of investors' tools, with which they can adjust the risk and return profile of their portfolio in order to protect against heightened interest rate risk, currency risk and equity market risk.

Financial futures contracts have found widespread appeal among both hedgers and traders. Indeed, the liquidity in the major financial futures markets is such that the futures price leads the underlying cash instrument's price as a market indicator. Contributing to the popularity of financial futures markets are their liquidity, low transaction costs, simplified credit risk, and the way they can be used by traders to create short positions and by hedgers to neutralise interest rate, currency or equity market risk. Financial futures have also helped fund managers in a number of areas: in particular, trading and hedging stock market risks.

In this chapter we have looked in detail at three types of futures contract: short-term interest rate futures, bond futures and equity index futures. In particular, we have looked at how they are priced relative to the underlying cash equivalents. We then looked at the advantages of financial futures, and how to hedge cash positions with futures contracts: in other words, how to determine the appropriate hedge ratio. We concluded the chapter with a discussion of interest rate and cross-currency swaps. Chapter 9 looks at another derivatives product, options, in more detail.

REVIEW EXERCISES

1. What are the main differences between forward and futures contracts?
2. What are the advantages to the trader of using futures contracts?
3. What are the advantages to the hedger of using futures contracts?
4. In the text, we used equation 4.2 and the market data reproduced in Table 8.4 to establish a fair rate for forward three-month LIBOR, as of 19 May 2004, for the period commencing 21 June 2004.
   a. Calculate fair forward rates, as of 19 May 2004, for three-month LIBOR for the periods commencing 20 September and 20 December 2004.
   b. How do these implied rates compare with the prices for the September and December 2004 short sterling futures contract, also quoted on 19 May 2004, as shown in Table 8.3?
   c. How would you explain any discrepancies?
5. Table 8.6 reproduces trading data for the long gilt futures contract on Euronext.liffe for 19 May 2004.
   a. Interpret the figures shown for 'Official Volume' and 'Open Interest' for the June and September contracts for the previous trading day.
   b. Suggest a possible reason why the September contract is trading more cheaply than the June contract.
6. Using the Euronext.liffe and DMO websites, explore the long gilt futures market as of the date when you do these exercises.
   a. In which month does the next futures contract settle?
   b. According to the exchange's website, which gilt issues are deliverable into the next futures contract? Can you verify the list from the details of each issue's terms published on the DMO website?
   c. According to the exchange's website, what are the price factors for the deliverable gilts?
   d. Following the method shown in Table 8.8:
      i. Try to verify the price factors
      ii. Determine which of the deliverable issues is currently the cheapest-to-deliver.
7. Assume that the current level of the FTSE 100 index is 5765, the short-term interest rate is 4% p.a., the expected dividend yield 2.5% p.a., and the FTSE 100 futures contract due to expire in exactly three months' time is standing at 5800.

    a. Calculate the difference between the current futures price and a theoretically fair price.

    b. How might the difference be exploited by

       i. an existing investor in the constituent shares of the FTSE 100 index?

      ii. a speculator?

8. To what extent would a short position in the FTSE 100 index futures contract protect against loss an investor whose portfolio consisted of the ten biggest share issues in the FTSE 100 index itself, assuming that her holdings were weighted proportionately to the ten companies' market capitalisations?

9. In the text ('Hedging an investment in bonds' on page 293) we assumed that Miss Ball wished to use long gilt futures to hedge an investment in £20 million nominal of the 8% Treasury 2021. Assume instead that she held £20 million nominal of the 7¼% Treasury maturing on 7 December 2007.

    a. Calculate the hedge ratio for this holding (hint: you will first need to calculate its duration).

    b. Comment on the suitability of the long gilt futures contract for a hedge of this type.

10. Miss Bountiful is considering switching 50% of her £3 million equity portfolio into gilts. She would like to do an immediate futures sale in order to be able to take her time over selling the shares. If the cash value of the FTSE index is currently trading at 5873, how many FTSE 100 index futures contracts should she sell?

Sample answers to the review exercises are on the companion website.

9 Options

CHAPTER CONTENTS

Learning objectives for this chapter

After studying this chapter you should be able to

○ describe in detail the principal features of call and put options on financial products
○ calculate the profit or loss from each of four basic options transactions
○ value options according to the general binomial and the Black–Scholes methods
○ use options as a tool for enhancing the risk–return characteristics of portfolios of cash market instruments.

INTRODUCTION

Options are the second major category of risk management product and the last of the basic building blocks of finance to be discussed in this book. Chapter 8 showed that financial futures offer considerable flexibility in the management of the risks and returns arising from transactions in the underlying cash products, but futures do not overcome one shortcoming of such transactions. A futures transaction has to be settled on the agreed terms, regardless of changes in market conditions between contract date and settlement date, so that the outcome for both parties is fixed at the outset. Such a transaction lacks the essential feature of a genuine insurance contract: the ability to eliminate or to limit potential losses without having to sacrifice the potential gains.

Options overcome this shortcoming by giving just one party to the contract (the *option buyer* or *option holder*) the right to require the other party (the *option seller* or *option writer*) to complete a specified transaction in an underlying financial asset on predetermined terms on or before a fixed future date. This is an essentially asymmetric contract in which the option buyer has a right but no obligation, and the option seller has an obligation but no rights. Clearly, buyers will exercise their options only if it is in their interest to do so: for instance, if the option gives them the right to buy an asset at a price below its current market price. The range of possible profits and losses arising from an option for buyers therefore lies between zero (where there is no benefit for them in exercising their options and they simply walk away from them, leaving them to expire unexercised) and some positive value.

The mean or expected value of an option to the buyer is always positive. The range of possible outcomes for the seller or writer is the exact mirror image of this, so for sellers the mean or expected outcome is negative. As rational participants in the financial markets do not voluntarily or knowingly enter into transactions with negative expected outcomes, the seller of an option requires the buyer to pay an initial premium based on the expected cost of the outcome. The expected cost of an option depends on several different factors, and varies continuously throughout its life, so the valuation of options is considerably more complex than any other operation we have encountered so far.

There are two types of option:

○ a *call option* confers on the buyer the right, but not the obligation, to buy a fixed quantity of an underlying asset at a fixed price (the *exercise price* or *strike price*) on or before a specified date in the future (the *exercise date* or *expiry date*)
○ A *put option* confers on the buyer the right, but not the obligation, to sell a fixed quantity of an underlying asset at a fixed price on or before a specified date in the future.

Options that offer the holders the right to exercise at any time up to and including the expiry date are known as *American-style options. European-style options* entitle the holders to exercise their options only on the expiry date itself. A useful mnemonic for the two types of option is:

○ 'E' stands for Europe and for Expiry
○ 'A' stands for America and for Anytime.

Although holders of an American-style option have the right to exercise throughout the life of the option, we shall see later that they are usually more likely to realise any profit before expiry by selling their option rather than by exercising it.

The expiry date of an options contract may vary from a few weeks (for options on specific equities and equity indices), to many years (in the case of options that are embedded in the terms of security issues). An example of the latter is a double-dated conventional gilt. This is a combination of a single-dated bond issue sold by the government to investors and maturing on the later of the two dates, and a call option sold by investors to the government, giving the latter the right but not the obligation to buy the bonds back on a date of its own choosing between the first and second dates.

It is important to understand that the idea of buying or selling appears twice in the description of any option contract. The option is a right to buy or to sell an underlying asset; and the right is itself bought by one party and sold by the other. So if you buy a put option you are *buying* the right to *sell*, and if you sell a call option you are *selling* the right to *buy*. The two types of option – call and put – are fundamentally different from each other, so that, for instance, buying a call is not the opposite of selling a put. As we shall see later in this chapter, the consequences of failing to maintain this distinction can be disastrous. The easiest way to avoid the risk of confusion is to think of options primarily in graphical terms. Each of the four possible options transactions (buy or sell, call or put) has its own distinctive and simple payoff graph, and once you have mastered these you are much less likely to make potentially expensive mistakes.

The facility to buy and sell options on a wide variety of instruments has been one of the most interesting developments for investors in recent years. Options offer investors a flexible and cost-effective way of creating a wide variety of risk and return alternatives from the same underlying security. Options allow investors to take a view not only on prices in a market but also on the volatility or risk of that market.

Although options on ordinary shares have existed in the United Kingdom in one form or another since the seventeenth century, interest in options on shares listed on the UK stock exchange took off in the 1980s following the opening of the traded options market in 1978. Early growth in UK traded options was not as rapid as had been widely expected. Hopes had been high after the huge success of the Chicago Board Options Exchange. However, reasons for the initial relative lack of success in the United Kingdom seem to have been tax disadvantages for institutional investors (disadvantages which have now been removed) and a perception by institutional investors and private investors alike that options were a risky investment.

This concept of options as risky and speculative is not a recent one. Dealing in options was officially banned on the London stock exchange from 1734 to 1860 and again from 1939 to 1958. The first ban was as a result of speculation leading to the South Sea Bubble which burst in 1720. The second was imposed as part of general restrictions on share dealings during wartime, but despite pressure from would-be dealers in options it was not relaxed until more than ten years after the end of the war. The idea that options are used for speculation also appears to be confirmed by the fact that the biggest options market in the world (which includes equity index options) is based in Chicago, the home of commodity markets with their tradition of speculation, rather than in New York, the site of the New York Stock Exchange. Options are similar to futures in that only a small amount of money need be spent initially to gain exposure to a large underlying securities position. This, as we shall see later in the chapter, can lead to large percentage gains or losses, and this type of trading activity will clearly attract speculators.

Options also have the property of regularly becoming completely worthless, if the underlying asset price on expiry has moved contrary to the purchaser's expectations so that there is no profit to be made from exercising the option. Whereas a share becomes completely valueless only if the company's liabilities exceed its assets so that nothing is left over for the shareholders in the liquidation, a put or call option can become worthless, whatever the solvency of the enterprise that issued the underlying asset.

It is these characteristics of options that lead to the view that options are speculative investments. What is often not appreciated is that options enable investors to vary the risk element in shares in both directions. In other words, investors may either increase or decrease expected return and risk by trading in options. For example, institutional investors such as insurance companies which, as we shall see in Chapter 11, are generally considered to be risk averse in their attitude to investment, are frequent sellers or writers of call options. By simultaneously holding shares and writing call options on those shares, they can reduce their risk to less than that of simply holding the shares.

Another major difference between options and the securities we considered in earlier chapters is that traded options do not represent direct claims on the underlying assets of the issuer. A shareholder, for example, holds the right to some fraction of the earnings and assets of the company, whereas a call option holder merely has the right to buy at some time in the future shares that are already in issue, representing only a potential claim on the company's assets. Shareholders hold securities issued by the company, providing funds for the company in return for future income. Option holders have no initial or direct relationship with the company whose shares they have an option to buy or sell. They have simply entered into an agreement with another party, the option seller or writer, concerning the possibly future purchase or sale of shares at a predetermined price. The writing of such option contracts has no impact on the company's issued share capital, and neither the writer nor the purchaser has any direct relationship with the company. However, options attached to or embedded in other securities are not independent of the issuer. For example, warrants attached to convertible bonds entitling the bondholders to convert their bonds into shares are a complicated kind of embedded option (put option on bonds and call option on shares) which can be exercised by requiring the issuer to issue new shares to the holder. And, as we saw, when investors buy double-dated gilts, they are simultaneously buying a bond and selling a call option directly to the issuer.

This chapter begins by describing in turn the four basic options transactions, the purchase and sale of call and put options. Using options on a leading UK equity (BP) as an example, we explore the implications of each type of transaction, and compare and contrast them with purchases and sales of the underlying security in the cash market. The main differences are the much smaller outlay and the much higher leverage of an options contract compared with a cash transaction, and the asymmetric profit and loss features of the option which give it its unique value as a means of both hedging and speculating. There follow two rather more mathematical sections in which the two models for valuing options are explained: the general binomial method and the Black–Scholes formula. After this we investigate further the crucial role played by volatility in the pricing and application of options. A final section shows how options can be used to hedge portfolio risk.

It should be noted that the Black–Scholes option valuation model looks difficult to use, and it is the most complex model in this book. However, in practice, this is irrelevant since the calculations can be done by a very simple computer program. All that is needed is an understanding of the factors affecting the value of an option. The computer will do the rest.

FINANCIAL OPTIONS: GENERAL DESCRIPTION

Exchange-traded option contracts are just like exchange-traded futures in one respect: their terms are standardised as to quantity, quality, delivery and settlement terms. Whereas the easiest financial futures contract to analyse is the short-term interest rate contract, in the case of options it is usually best to start with options on individual company shares. Table 9.1 shows the standard terms for Euronext.liffe option contracts on each of the indi-

Table 9.1 Contract specification, individual equity option contracts

Unit of trading	One option contract normally represents rights over either 1000 or 100 shares
Quotation	Pence per share
Minimum price movement (tick size and value)	The tick size is fixed for each share at either 0.5 or 0.25 pence per share. Depending on whether the unit of trading is 1000 or 100 shares, the tick values of one option contract are therefore either £5.00 and £2.50 (for the 1000-share contracts) or 50p and 25p (for the 100-share contracts).
Expiry months	The three nearest quarterly expiry months from the cycle March, June, September and December. In addition, options on a 'focus group' of about 12 shares comprising the leading companies in the principal industry sectors are available for (a) two near-dated serial expiry months and (b) three longer-dated quarterly expiry months beyond the standard three-quarter cycle.
Exercise	Exercise by 17:20 on any business day, extended to 18:00 for all series on a last trading day
Last trading day/time	16:30 on the third Friday in expiry month
Settlement day	Four business days following the day of exercise or last trading day
Trading hours	08:00–16:30

Source: Euronext.liffe.

vidual UK company shares in the FTSE 100 index. Table 9.2 is an extract from the 4 May 2004 trading report in options on shares in BP plc.

As a sector leader and as one of the three largest companies traded on the London stock exchange, BP belongs to the Euronext.liffe 'focus group', so that in addition to the three regular quarterly expiry months (June, September and December 2004) options were also available for the serial months May and July 2004 and for the longer-dated quarterly months March, June and December 2005. The extract reproduced as Table 9.2 shows only the four nearest expiry months: May, June, July and September 2004. For each expiry date, the currently available exercise prices are listed in bold type down the middle of the table, and the corresponding data for call and put options at this strike price are shown respectively to the left and to the right of the strike price.

The most important sections of the report for the purpose of our analysis in this chapter are described below and discussed in greater detail in the following sections of this chapter. In many cases their meaning will be clear from what we have already learned in Chapter 8 about financial futures.

Underlying price

This is the closing price of the underlying share in BP, which was 492.5p at close of business on the day in question. Note that the suffix 'H' is used throughout the report to indicate a halfpenny.

Settle[ment] price

This is based on the latest advertised bid and offer prices before the market closed. It may not correspond to the price at which the last deals were actually done.

Equity Options — Interim

Table 9.2 Options on shares in BP: report for 4 May 2004

Calls

BP plc (BP)

May 04 — Indicative a-t-m Vol 19.66 — Underlying Price 492H — Time to expiry: 17 Days

Settle Price	Delta	Volatility	Blk Trd	OTC Facility Volume	Total Volume	Official Volume	**Open Int	Daily High	Daily Low	Change	Exercises
163	1.00	31.86	0	0	0	N/A	N/A			0	0
133	1.00	29.98	0	0	0	N/A	9			0	0
103	1.00	28.28	0	0	0	N/A	22			0	0
73	1.00	25.36	0	0	0	N/A	252			0	0
33	0.97	21.48	0	0	0	N/A	1,226			0	0
4H	0.34	19.27	0	0	5	N/A	2,807	4	4	0	0
CAB	0.00	18.30	0	0	0	N/A	N/A			0	0
CAB	0.00	17.49	0	0	0	N/A	N/A			0	0
Total			0	0	5	N/A	4,116			0	0

Jun 04 — Indicative a-t-m Vol 19.12 — Underlying Price 492H — Time to expiry: 45 Days

Settle Price	Delta	Volatility	Blk Trd	OTC Facility Volume	Total Volume	Official Volume	**Open Int	Daily High	Daily Low	Change	Exercises
213	1.00	31.64	0	0	0	N/A	N/A			0	0
183	1.00	31.10	0	0	0	N/A	1			0	0
163	1.00	29.63	0	0	0	N/A	1,800			0	0
133	1.00	28.16	0	0	0	N/A	3			0	0
103	1.00	25.16	0	0	4	N/A	89			0	0
73	1.00	22.66	0	0	40	N/A	2,640	102	102	0	0
35	0.84	21.16	0	0	40	N/A	5,021	74	74	0	0
9	0.40	18.69	0	0	101	N/A	7,644	34 S	34 S	0	0
H	0.05	19.00	0	0	0	N/A	2,269	9	8H	0	0
CAB	0.00	18.99	0	0	0	N/A	N/A			0	0
CAB	0.00	18.99	0	0	0	N/A	N/A			0	0
Total			0	0	185	N/A	19,467			0	0

Jul 04 — Indicative a-t-m Vol 19.08 — Underlying Price 492H — Time to expiry: 73 Days

Settle Price	Delta	Volatility	Blk Trd	OTC Facility Volume	Total Volume	Official Volume	**Open Int	Change	Exercises
192H	1.00	25.05	0	0	0	N/A	N/A	0	0
163	1.00	25.05	0	0	0	N/A	N/A	0	0
133	1.00	25.05	0	0	0	N/A	N/A	0	0
103	1.00	25.05	0	0	0	N/A	N/A	0	0
73H	0.95	23.45	0	0	0	N/A	44	0	0
38	0.78	20.46	0	0	50	N/A	50	0	0
13	0.44	18.79	0	0	215	N/A	215	0	0
2	0.09	18.60	0	0	0	N/A	300	0	0
CAB	0.01	18.29	0	0	0	N/A	N/A	0	0
CAB	0.00	18.23	0	0	0	N/A	N/A	0	0
Total			0	0	609	N/A	609	0	0

Sep 04 — Indicative a-t-m Vol 19.54 — Underlying Price 492H — Time to expiry: 136 Days

Settle Price	Delta	Volatility	Blk Trd	OTC Facility Volume	Total Volume	Official Volume	**Open Int	Daily High	Daily Low	Change	Exercises
192H	1.00	30.68	0	0	0	N/A	N/A			0	0
163	1.00	29.38	0	0	0	N/A	N/A			0	0
133	0.97	28.08	0	0	0	N/A	5			0	0
104H	0.94	26.43	0	0	0	N/A	156			0	0
76H	0.89	23.44	0	0	0	N/A	63			0	0
44H	0.72	21.23	0	0	4	N/A	1,246	44HS	44HS	0	0
19H	0.47	19.18	0	0	4	N/A	5,505	19HS	19HS	0	0
4H	0.17	18.11	0	0	0	N/A	532			0	0
1	0.04	18.11	0	0	0	N/A	N/A			0	0
Total			0	0	8	N/A	7,507			0	0

Puts

May 04 — Indicative a-t-m Vol 19.29 — Time to expiry: 17 Days

Exercise Price	Settle Price	Delta	Volatility	Blk Trd	OTC Facility Volume	Total Volume	Official Volume	**Open Int	Daily High	Daily Low	Change	Exercises
330	CAB	0.00	32.30	0	0	0	N/A	N/A			0	0
360	CAB	0.00	30.23	0	0	0	N/A	N/A			0	0
390	CAB	0.00	28.43	0	0	0	N/A	19			0	0
420	CAB	0.00	24.83	0	0	0	N/A	289			0	0
460	1	-0.09	21.04	0	0	0	N/A	1,114			0	0
500	14H	-0.69	18.92	0	0	40	N/A	2,297	14H	14H	0	0
550	51	-0.99	18.13	0	0	0	N/A	60			0	0
600	111	-0.99	16.22	0	0	0	N/A	30			0	0
Total				0	0	40	N/A	3,809			0	0

Jun 04 — Indicative a-t-m Vol 19.37 — Time to expiry: 45 Days

Exercise Price	Settle Price	Delta	Volatility	Blk Trd	OTC Facility Volume	Total Volume	Official Volume	**Open Int	Daily High	Daily Low	Change	Exercises
280	CAB	0.00	33.89	0	0	0	N/A	N/A			0	0
300	CAB	0.00	33.38	0	0	0	N/A	101			0	0
330	CAB	0.00	32.00	0	0	0	N/A	103			0	0
360	CAB	0.00	30.35	0	0	0	N/A	130			0	0
390	CAB	-0.01	28.34	0	0	35	N/A	4,139			0	0
420	11	-0.04	25.28	0	0	0	N/A	3,832	1	1	0	0
460	4	-0.18	21.09	0	0	40	N/A	460	4 S	4 S	0	0
500	18H	-0.60	19.00	0	0	40	N/A	594	17	17	0	0
550	61	-0.97	18.98	0	0	0	N/A	25			0	0
600	111	-0.99	18.62	0	0	0	N/A	N/A			0	0
650	151	-0.99	18.37	0	0	0	N/A	N/A			0	0
Total				0	0	115	N/A	9,384			0	0

Jul 04 — Indicative a-t-m Vol 19.01 — Time to expiry: 73 Days

Exercise Price	Settle Price	Delta	Volatility	Blk Trd	OTC Facility Volume	Total Volume	Official Volume	**Open Int	Change	Exercises
300	CAB	0.00	24.78	0	0	0	N/A	N/A	0	0
330	CAB	0.00	24.76	0	0	0	N/A	N/A	0	0
360	CAB	0.00	24.78	0	0	0	N/A	N/A	0	0
390	H	-0.02	25.08	0	0	0	N/A	N/A	0	0
420	1H	-0.06	23.48	0	0	0	N/A	65	0	0
460	6	-0.22	20.49	0	0	0	N/A	155	0	0
500	21	-0.57	18.70	0	0	0	N/A	6	0	0
550	6H	-0.95	18.58	0	0	0	N/A	N/A	0	0
600	111	-0.99	18.22	0	0	0	N/A	N/A	0	0
650	151	-0.99	18.22	0	0	0	N/A	226	0	0
Total				0	0	0	N/A	226	0	0

Sep 04 — Indicative a-t-m Vol 18.85 — Time to expiry: 136 Days

Exercise Price	Settle Price	Delta	Volatility	Blk Trd	OTC Facility Volume	Total Volume	Official Volume	**Open Int	Daily High	Daily Low	Change	Exercises
300	CAB	0.00	30.39	0	0	0	N/A	4			0	0
330	H	-0.01	29.21	0	0	0	N/A	160			0	0
360	2	-0.03	27.92	0	0	0	N/A	23			0	0
390	2	-0.06	25.99	0	0	0	N/A	514			0	0
420	4	-0.11	23.08	0	0	0	N/A	2,785			0	0
460	11H	-0.28	20.50	0	0	3	N/A	3,110			0	0
500	27	-0.54	18.50	0	0	0	N/A	201	12	12	0	0
550	63	-0.96	17.39	0	0	0	N/A	N/A			0	0
600	110H	-0.99	17.39	0	0	0	N/A	N/A			0	0
Total				0	0	3	N/A	6,797			0	0

Business Day: Tue 4 May 2004. Prev Business Day: Mon 3 May 2004. Change: Mon 3 May 2004 / Tue 4 May 2004.

Source: Euronext.liffe

Volatility

This is the volatility of the share price as *implied* by the settlement price of the option, and is discussed more fully from page 344. Volatility is a key determinant of option value.

Indicative a-t-m vol[atility]

For each type of option (put and call) and for each expiry date, this is an interpolated estimate of what would be the implied volatility of an option with a strike price exactly equal to the current market price of the share. Such an option is described as being ***at-the-money*** (abbreviated to ***a-t-m*** or ***ATM***).

CALL OPTIONS

There are just four basic transactions in options:

○ purchase of call option
○ sale of call option
○ purchase of put option
○ sale of put option.

All options-based strategies, however complex and sophisticated, are constructed from the above four basic building blocks, either on their own or in combination with a cash transaction or transactions in the underlying asset. We shall consider each of these basic transactions in turn, using the appropriate option on BP shares as an example in each case.

Purchase of call option

From Table 9.2, we suppose that on 4 May 2004 Mr Choice buys one BP call option contract with an exercise price of 460p per share and due to expire in July 2004. It is an American-style option which Mr Choice can exercise at any time up to and including the expiry date. The current price for such a contract (that is, the premium that Mr Choice has to pay to induce an option seller to grant him the option) is 38p per share, equivalent to 38p × 1000 = £380 for the contract. (See Unit of Trading in Table 9.1.) The current BP share price is 492.5p and so the option will entitle Mr Choice to buy BP shares at below the current market price. Such an option is termed ***in the money*** (or ***ITM***) since Mr Choice could buy the option, immediately exercise his right to buy the shares at 460p, and then sell them at 492.5p to make 32.5p profit per share, before any transaction costs. Conversely, a call option such as the 500p July BP contract, where the exercise price exceeds the current share price, is referred to as ***out of the money*** (or ***OTM***), because it would not be worth exercising at the current market price of the share. If the strike price of an option is exactly equal to the share price, it is described as being *at the money* (*ATM*). In practice, as the share price rarely corresponds exactly to one of the available option strike prices, market practice is to describe the option with the strike price closest to the share price as the *at-the-money contract*.

Common sense tells us that the value or cost of an in-the-money call option must be more than the profit that could be made on immediate exercise. If it were less, then the certain prospect of a guaranteed risk-free profit would attract a potentially unlimited volume of demand from would-be option buyers, and this could be satisfied only if option writers were willing to incur equally certain losses on a similar scale. The option purchased by Mr Choice is in fact priced by the market at 38p per share, compared with the 32.5p per share profit that could be made if the option were exercised and the shares sold immediately. The amount by which the current market price of the underlying asset exceeds the strike price of a call option is the *intrinsic value* of the option. Later in this chapter we explore in detail the factors that determine the amount by which the total value of a call option exceeds its intrinsic value. In this example, this additional value amounts to 38p minus 32.5p, or 5.5p per share.

Ignoring for the moment the possibility that Mr Choice might sell or exercise the option before expiry, let us assume instead that he holds the option until expiry. How will Mr Choice decide whether or not to exercise his option on expiry? This will depend on the market price of BP shares on the expiry date, which is 16 July (the third Friday in the month), 73 days from the date when he bought the option. There are just three possibilities: either the share price will be below the strike price, or it will be above the strike price, or it will be exactly the same as the strike price. These three possibilities exhaustively describe all relevant alternative states of the world on 16 July 2004. We consider each of them in turn.

Price of underlying asset below strike price on option expiry

If the BP share price on expiry is less than 460p, there will be no point in exercising the option. Even if the circumstances of the fall in price have not given Mr Choice second thoughts about the merits of buying BP shares, it would be cheaper for him to acquire the shares by buying them in the normal way in the market than by exercising his option to buy them at the strike price of 460p. His total loss on the option contract, if the option is not exercised, will be 38p × 1000 = £380. This represents a 100 per cent loss of his option premium. But if he had bought 1000 BP shares in the market at 492.5p on 4 May, not only would his initial investment have been much larger at £4925 but his potential loss would also have been much greater. If, for instance, the BP share price had fallen to 300p during the 73 days following his purchase, Mr Choice would have lost £1925. In a worst-case scenario (the complete failure of the company in circumstances where shareholders received no payout) he could lose all £4925 of his investment. But even in this worst-case scenario, Mr Choice's maximum loss from buying the call option cannot be more than the £380 premium he paid.

In short, at any market price on expiry below the strike price, Mr Choice does not exercise his option, but instead accepts a fixed loss equal to the premium he has paid.

Price of underlying asset above strike price on option expiry

If the BP shares are quoted in the market at more than 460p on the expiry date, the exercise price will be less than the market price and it will benefit Mr Choice to exercise. When he has exercised his option, he can then decide whether to keep the BP shares he has acquired or immediately sell them. Suppose the BP share price on expiry rises from its present level to 550p. If Mr Choice immediately sells the shares he has acquired by exercising the option, he will make a profit of 90p per share (550p – 460p). However, he paid

38p per share for the right to exercise at 460p and this must be deducted from the 90p per share to arrive at his net profit on the overall transaction, which is 52p per share or £520 on the option contract. In practice this profit of £520 would be reduced a little by the transaction costs incurred by Mr Choice, but we have omitted these from our analysis for the sake of simplicity.

It is important to recognise that it would still pay Mr Choice to exercise if the market price on expiry were only, say, 490p. He would still be able to make 30p per share by exercising his right to buy the shares and selling them immediately. In this way he could recover 30p of the 38p per share cost of the option, for a reduced overall net loss of 8p per share. A common mistake is to assume that it becomes worthwhile to exercise a call option only when the market price exceeds the strike price by an amount at least equal to the premium paid. But at the time of exercise the premium is a sunk cost and no longer plays any part in the decision whether to exercise or not. That decision depends purely on whether the market price is above or below the strike price.

We can sum up this section by saying that if the market price on exercise is higher than the strike price, the option buyer's overall profit or loss is equal to the market price less the strike price less the premium paid.

Price of underlying asset exactly equal to strike price on option expiry

We refer to this rather unlikely outcome only for the sake of theoretical completeness. In the event that the actual cost of shares in the market (excluding transaction costs) were exactly the same as the strike price, then Mr Choice might exercise the option if he wished to keep the shares, as he would thus acquire them without incurring commission.

Purchase of call option versus purchase of share: similarities and differences

The key similarity between the purchase of a call option on a share and the purchase of the underlying share itself is that the profit potential is unlimited. For every penny the share price exceeds the purchase price of the share (or, in the case of the call option, the strike price plus the premium), the purchaser makes a penny profit. The potential profit is unlimited, as there is no theoretical upward limit to any share price.

We can also identify three key differences between buying a call option on shares and buying the underlying shares themselves.

○ The investment outlay required for a call option is smaller. In order to acquire exposure to an underlying amount of 1000 BP shares, the option route entails an initial outlay of just £380 whereas to purchase the shares in the normal way in the markets would cost £4925.

○ The downside risk in *money* terms is smaller for a call option. The maximum amount Mr Choice can lose on his option is £380, by leaving the option unexercised. However, Mr Choice can lose much more in money terms on the shares themselves if the price falls substantially below his purchase price. In this example, Mr Choice would lose £1925 from holding shares if the share price fell to 300p.

○ The *percentage* gain or loss is greater on an option purchase than on a share purchase.

Relative to the amount invested, for any given change in the value of the shares, Mr Choice stands to make a greater percentage gain or loss on the option than on the shares themselves. This implies, from our knowledge of the relationship between expected return and risk, that the purchase of a call option is riskier than the purchase of the underlying shares.

We said earlier that each of the basic four options transactions is associated with a unique payoff diagram for the profit or loss immediately before expiry. Figure 9.1(a) is the first of our four basic payoff diagrams, and summarises our findings for the purchase of a call option. Figure 9.1(b) shows the equivalent payoff for a purchase of the shares themselves.

Figure 9.1(a) illustrates the potential gain or loss to Mr Choice on the BP option just before expiry, depending on the underlying share price S and the exercise price $X = 460p$. We can see that Mr Choice makes a loss on his option investment unless the share price S reaches 498p, equal to the exercise price of 460p plus the cost of the option C of 38p. Beyond that, his profit amounts to $(S - X)$ per share minus the cost of the option C, giving a profit of $S - (X + C)$.

Figure 9.1(b) shows the equivalent gain or loss on the underlying shares. This is simply the difference between the cost of the share, in this case, 492.5p, say S_0, and the share price on expiry S.

Who buys call options?

Call options are typically bought in a number of circumstances.

○ They are bought on their own, by investors who simply want to 'wait and see' before deciding definitely to buy a share that interests them.
○ They are bought on their own or in combination with other options as part of a more complex strategy designed to exploit temporary or relative changes in prices.
○ A speculator might buy a call option as a less risky way of gambling on a price rise than buying the share itself. For this kind of relatively risk-averse speculator, the premium is a price worth paying in order to limit the downside risk.
○ Arbitrageurs might buy a call option because they think the option itself is undervalued. As we shall see later in this chapter, this would be the case if they thought the market price of the option reflected an underestimate of the volatility of the underlying share. But if they were to buy a call in anticipation of an increase in perceived volatility feeding through into a higher option price, they would need to protect themselves against the effect of any change in the intrinsic value of the option, so they would have to hedge their position by short-selling the appropriate volume of underlying shares.

Sale of call option

The profit or loss for the option seller on expiry of a call option is the exact mirror image of that experienced by the buyer, and is charted in Figure 9.2. Just as the buyer suffers a fixed loss if the market price on expiry is lower than the exercise price, but stands to make a theoretically unlimited profit if the price rises above the exercise price, the seller earns

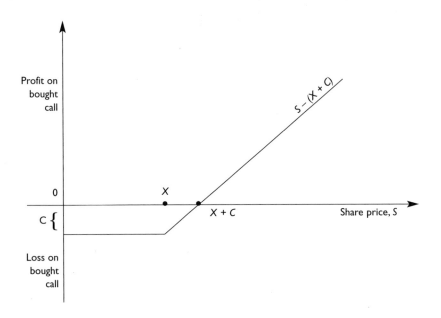

Figure 9.1(a) Profit or loss on a bought call option immediately before expiry

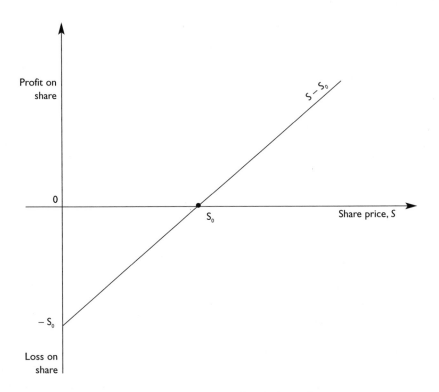

Figure 9.1(b) Profit or loss on purchase of underlying share

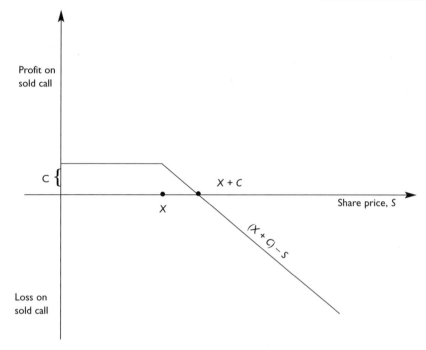

Figure 9.2 Profit or loss on a sold call option immediately before expiry

a fixed income below the exercise price but faces a potentially unlimited loss above it. The seller's breakeven point is where the market price on exercise is equal to the sum of the exercise price and the premium he or she has received. In our case of the 460p BP July 2004 call options, if the market price on expiry is 498p, option sellers will have to sell shares at 38p below their market value, exactly wiping out the 38p they have gained from the premium. Note that this calculation is the same, whether sellers already own the shares or not. If they own them, they suffer an opportunity cost by having to sell at 460p an asset they could otherwise have sold on the open market at 498p; if they do not already own them, they have to buy them on the open market at 498p and immediately deliver them to the call option buyer for just 460p.

Who sells call options?

The asymmetric payoff profile shown in Figure 9.2 appears to make selling a call option in isolation (rather than as an element in a more complex trading or investing strategy) a risky and fundamentally unattractive proposition. So why sell call options?

○ Investors might sell out-of-the-money call options on shares they own in order to collect the premium and thus enhance the overall return from them. Of course they are running the risk that if the price of the shares begins to go up they will find it progressively more unattractive to cancel their position by buying back the option, because as the share price approaches the breakeven (at-the-money) point, the call option will become more expensive.

○ For speculators, selling a call option in isolation is in principle an unattractive strategy, as their upside is strictly limited to the premium, whereas the downside is potentially unlimited. They will sell call options if they think the price is stable and will rise above the breakeven point, $X + C$.

○ Arbitrageurs might sell a call option because they felt the market was overestimating, and hence overcharging for, the volatility of the share. If they were right, and if the market began to recognise that they were right, the option price would go down, giving speculators the opportunity to buy the option itself back at a lower price than the one they paid. As such speculators would not wish to take an outright risk on the price of the underlying share, they would need to hedge their option position by buying an appropriate volume of the underlying.

PUT OPTIONS

Purchase of put option

We now turn to put options. We begin by supposing that on 4 May 2004 Mr Jitter, who owns 1000 BP shares but fears an imminent fall in the share price, buys one BP put option contract with an exercise price of 500p per share and due to expire in July 2004. From Table 9.2 on page 310, the current premium for such a contract is 21p per share, equivalent to $21p \times 1000 = £210$ for the contract. The current BP share price is 492.5p, so the option will entitle Mr Jitter to sell BP shares at higher than the current market price. Just like a call option to buy shares at a price below the market, a put option to sell shares above the market price is *in the money* since Mr Jitter could buy the option, buy shares in the market at 492.5p (if he did not already own them) and immediately exercise his right to sell the shares at 500p for a profit of 7.5p per share, before any transaction costs. Conversely, a put option such as the 460p July BP contract, where the exercise price is lower than the current share price, is *out of the money*, because it would not be worth exercising at the current market price of the share.

Let us assume again that he holds the option until expiry. How will Mr Jitter decide whether or not to exercise his option on expiry? Clearly this will depend on the market price of BP shares on the expiry date, 16 July 2004. We examine here the two principal possibilities in turn, namely that the market price on expiry is higher or lower than the strike price. The unlikely case of the market price on expiry being equal to the strike price is the same for a put option as for a call option, as discussed on page 313.

Price of underlying asset above strike price on option expiry

If the BP share price on expiry is above 500p, there will be no point in exercising the option. Even if the circumstances of the rise in price have not allayed Mr Jitter's concerns about the BP share price, it would be more profitable for him to sell the shares in the normal way in the market than by exercising his option to sell them at the strike price of 500p. His total loss on the option contract, if the option is not exercised, will be $21p \times 1000 = £210$. This represents a 100 per cent loss of his option premium, but if he had sold 1000 BP shares in the market at 492.5p on 4 May, his potential loss could have been much greater in money terms. If, for instance, the BP share price had risen to 550p during the 73 days following his sale, Mr Jitter would have missed out on a further profit of 57.5p per share or £575 in total. As there is no upward bound to the share price, there is no theoretical limit to this potential opportunity cost. But if Mr Jitter buys a put option instead of selling the shares, his maximum loss cannot be more than the £210 premium he paid.

In short, at any market price on expiry above the strike price, Mr Choice does not exercise his option, but instead accepts a fixed loss equal to the premium he has paid.

Price of underlying asset below strike price on option expiry

If the BP shares are quoted in the market at less than 500p on the expiry date, the exercise price will be more than the market price and it will benefit Mr Jitter to exercise. Suppose the BP share price on expiry falls from its present level to 430p. If Mr Jitter exercises the option to sell at 500p, he will reduce by 70p the loss he would otherwise have made on his shares, which are now worth only 430p on the open market. However, he paid 21p per share for the right to exercise at 500p and this must be deducted from the 70p saving to arrive at his net gain on the overall transaction, which is 49p per share or £490 on the option contract.

Note that this calculation is the same, whether buyers of the option already own the shares or not. If they own them, they make a gain by being able to sell at 500p an asset they could otherwise have sold on the open market at only 430p; if they do not already own the shares, they can buy them on the open market at 430p and immediately deliver them to the put option seller for 500p, thus making an immediate profit of 70p.

Once again, it is important to recognise that it would still pay Mr Jitter to exercise if the market price on expiry had fallen only to, say, 490p. He would still be able to save 10p per share by exercising his right to sell the shares at 500p. In this way he could recover 10p of the 21p per share cost of the option, for a reduced overall net loss of 11p.

We can sum up by saying that if the market price on the exercise date is lower than the strike price, the put option buyer's overall profit or loss is equal to the strike price *less* the market price *less* the premium paid.

Purchase of put option versus sale of share: similarities and differences

The key similarity between the purchase of a put option on a share and the sale of the underlying share itself is the profit potential. Whereas in the case of the purchase of a call option or of a share this is unlimited, in the case of the put option and share sale the potential saving or profit is limited by the fact that the value of the share does have a lower bound – zero. Nevertheless, the purchaser of a put option and the seller of the underlying share do share a common potential profit profile. For every penny the share price falls, each of them gains a penny per share.

There are two key differences between buying a put option on shares and selling the underlying shares themselves. The downside risk in *money* terms is smaller for the buyer of the put option. The maximum amount Mr Jitter can lose on his option is £210, by leaving the option unexercised. However, Mr Jitter can lose much more in money terms on the shares themselves if he sells them and the price then rises substantially. Also, the *percentage* gain or loss is greater on a put option purchase than on a share sale. For any given change in the value of the shares, Mr Jitter stands to make a greater percentage gain or loss on the option than on the shares themselves.

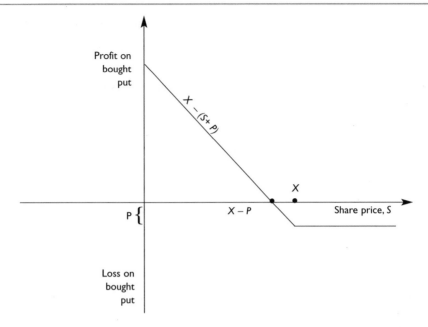

Figure 9.3(a) Profit or loss on a bought put option immediately before expiry

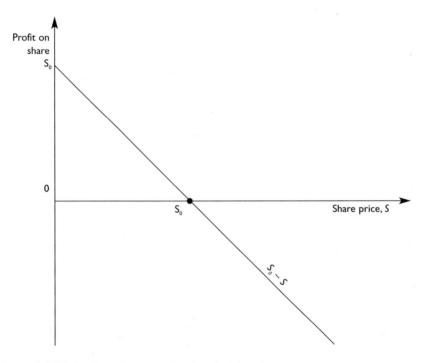

Figure 9.3(b) Profit or loss on sale of underlying share

Figure 9.3(a) is the payoff diagram for the purchase of a put option. Figure 9.3(b) shows the equivalent payoff for a sale of the underlying shares.

Figure 9.3(a) illustrates the potential gain or loss to Mr Choice on the BP option just before expiry, depending on the underlying share price S and the exercise price $X = 500p$. We can see that Mr Choice makes a loss on his option investment unless the share price S falls below 479p, equal to the exercise price X of 500p minus the cost of the option P of 21p. Below that point, his profit amounts to $(X - S)$ minus the cost of the option P, giving a net profit of $X - (S + P)$.

Figure 9.3(b) shows the equivalent gain or loss on the underlying shares. This is simply the difference between the cost of the share, in this case, 492.5p, say S_0, and the share price on expiry S.

Who buys put options?

Put options are typically bought in a variety of circumstances.

○ They may be bought on their own, by investors who either want temporary portfolio insurance or wish to wait and see before deciding definitely whether or not to sell a share in their portfolio.

○ They may be bought on their own or in combination with other options as part of a more complex strategy designed to exploit temporary or relative changes in prices.

○ A speculator might buy a put option as a less risky way of gambling on a price fall than selling the share itself. For this kind of relatively risk-averse speculator, the premium is a price worth paying in order to limit the downside risk.

○ Arbitrageurs might buy a put option because they think the option itself is undervalued. As we shall see later in this chapter, this would be the case if they thought the market price of the option underestimated the probable price volatility of the underlying share. If they were to buy a put in anticipation of an increase in volatility feeding through into a higher option price, they would need to protect themselves against the effect of any change in the intrinsic value of the option, and to this end they would have to hedge their options position by buying the appropriate volume of underlying shares.

Sale of put option

The profit or loss for the option seller on expiry of a put option is the exact mirror image of that experienced by the buyer, and is charted in Figure 9.4. Just as the put buyer suffers a fixed loss if the market price on expiry is higher than the exercise price, but stands to make a gain if the price falls below the exercise price, so the put seller earns a fixed income above the exercise price but faces an increasing loss below it. The seller's breakeven point is where the market price on exercise is equal to the net of the exercise price minus the premium he or she has received. In our case of the 500p BP July 2004 put options, if the market price on expiry is 479p, put option sellers will have to buy shares at 21p above their market value, exactly wiping out the 21p they have gained from the premium.

The worst that can happen to put option sellers is that the company issuing the shares fails and the shares become worthless. The seller of the put option still has to pay out to the buyer; options are not invalidated by liquidation of the company issuing the underlying asset, or indeed by any other event.

Who sells put options?

As with the sale of call options, the asymmetric payoff profile shown in Figure 9.4 makes selling a put option in isolation (rather than as an element in a more complex trading or investing strategy) a risky and fundamentally unattractive proposition.

○ Investors or potential investors are unlikely to have a use for selling put options, as all they offer is a premium income in return for the risk of being forced to pay more than the market price to add to the investor's holdings.

○ For speculators, selling a put option in isolation is also an unattractive strategy, as the upside is strictly limited to the premium, whereas the downside (though no longer completely unlimited, as was the case with the sold call option) is typically a large multiple of the fixed upside.

○ Arbitrageurs might sell put options because they felt that the market was over-estimating, and hence overcharging for, the volatility of the share. If they were right, and the market began to recognise that they were right, the option price would go down, giving the speculators the opportunity to buy the option itself back at a lower price than the one they paid. As such a speculator would not wish to take an outright risk on the price of the underlying share, he or she would need to hedge the option position by short-selling an appropriate volume of the underlying.

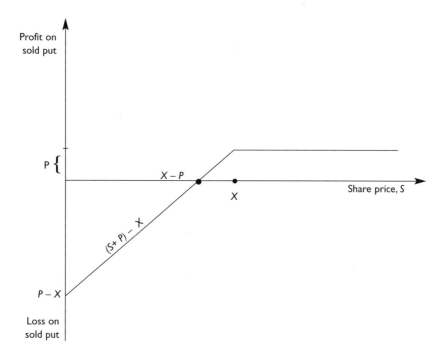

Figure 9.4 Profit or loss on a sold put option

Combinations of options

This graphical way of looking at options also allows us to examine combinations of different options, all based on the same underlying share. For example, the simultaneous purchase of a put and a call option on a share, with the same exercise price and expiry date, called a 'straddle', would lead to the profit pattern shown in Figure 9.5 on expiry.

Since the holder of a straddle will make money if the share price moves substantially up or down, an investor in a straddle will be someone who believes that the future price changes in that particular share, whatever their direction, have been underestimated by the market (as reflected in the market price of the straddle).

Other types of option combinations include a 'strip' (the purchase of two puts plus one call) and a 'strap' (two calls plus one put). The number of possible variations is vast, allowing different amounts of risk to be borne, by speculating on or hedging against a variety of possible share price movements. The website of Euronext.liffe lists a total of 56 separately identifiable options strategies, with such exotic names as 'short iron butterfly' and 'long jelly roll', but it is important to recognise that all of these strategies are ultimately constructed out of combinations of the four basic building blocks we have presented here: the purchase and sale of call and put options.

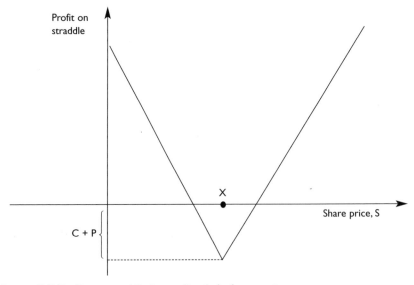

Figure 9.5 Profit on straddle immediately before expiry

BASIC OPTION VALUATION

We discuss the valuation of options in three stages. In this first part we identify in a non-quantitative way the main factors affecting the value of an option contract. In the next section we examine in detail two mathematical models for valuing options, the binomial model and the Black–Scholes formula. In the final section we take a look at the key role played by volatility in option valuation.

Intrinsic value

So far, we have made just two general observations about the value of an option. First, we met the idea of intrinsic value, which is the profit which could be made by buying and immediately exercising an in-the-money option. We have also observed that in practice the market gives any option a value higher than just its intrinsic value, so that even when an option is out-of-the-money and has no intrinsic value, it still has some value in the market.

Time value

So the first question to ask is, why should options have any value over and above their intrinsic value? The answer is that at any time other than immediately before expiry, an increase in the price of the underlying asset could increase the existing intrinsic value of a call option or create intrinsic value for a call option that currently has none; conversely, a fall in the price of the underlying asset would increase the intrinsic value of a put option. It seems reasonable to suppose that the greater the remaining time to expiry, the greater the probability that such a change will occur. In the case of the BP call options shown in Table 9.2, the strike price that is least out-of-the-money (by just 8p) is 500p, and the indicative price of call options with this strike price increases with the remaining time to expiry shown in Table 9.3.

Table 9.3 Impact of time on BP 500p call options

Month of expiry	Days to expiry	Price (p)
May	17	4.5
June	45	9.0
July	73	13.0
September	136	19.5

A 500p call option, regardless of its time to expiry, has no intrinsic value when the market price of the underlying asset is 492.5p, so the whole of the value of such an option is attributable to the time factor, referred to as the ***time value*** of the option. Intrinsic value and time value together account for the whole of the value of any option.

The next step is to make a further analysis of the factors that contribute to time value. The first such factor to be considered is not really a new one, but is just a reflection of the degree to which the option is either in-the-money or out-of-the-money. The more an option becomes in-the-money, the more probable it becomes that it will be exercised, so the value of the right not to exercise falls correspondingly. The more an option goes out-of-the-money, the less probable becomes the likelihood of exercise, so the value of the right not to exercise also falls. By definition, the value must be greatest when the option is at-the-money: that is, when there is a 50/50 chance of exercise.

We can see this clearly if we look at the September 2004 BP call options, which have 136 days to expiry. The third column in Table 9.4 shows the amount by which each strike price is in-the-money or out-of-the-money at the current market price of 492.5p for the underlying share. The fourth column shows the time value, which is the total value of the option minus (in the case of the ITM options) the strike price. The highest time value is for the call option nearest to at-the-money (X is 500p).

Table 9.4 Time values of September 2004 BP call options

Strike price (p)	Option price (p)	ITM (+) OTM (−) (p)	Time value (p)
330	163.0	+162.5	0.5
360	133.0	+132.5	0.5
390	104.5	+102.5	2.0
420	76.5	+72.5	4.0
460	44.5	+32.5	12.0
500	19.5	−7.5	19.5
550	4.5	−57.5	4.5
600	1.0	−107.5	1.0

All we have actually done so far is to suggest a reason for the relative amount of time value for different levels of intrinsic value. What we have not done is to identify the factors determining the *absolute* level of time value. It turns out that there are just two: the expected volatility of the price of the underlying asset, and the risk-free interest rate. Of these, the expected volatility almost always exercises the dominant influence on the value of the option.

Expected volatility of the underlying asset

In order to appreciate the link between volatility and value, we consider in Figure 9.6 two shares, A and B, where B is riskier because of its greater volatility, as evidenced by the higher standard deviation of possible future prices. Suppose that these shares currently have the same price S, and that call and put options can be bought on each, with the same expiry date and the same exercise price X; in this example the call option will be out-of-the-money, and the put option will be in-the-money. How – in a commonsense way – might *writers* of such options go about the task of calculating their risk? One way would be to say that the expected cost of writing any option is the product of two factors: the *probability* of exercise multiplied by the *expected loss* on exercise.

Without putting actual values on these two elements, we can appreciate them in relative terms from Figure 9.6. As the area under each of the curves encompasses all possible outcomes, we can assign the same value 1 to the area under both curves (as a probability of 1 is equivalent to certainty). We should note that the areas under each of the four non-overlapping segments A_1, B_1 etc. are identical. If we consider first the case of the out-of-the-money call options at strike price X, we are concerned with two factors:

○ the proportion of the total area under the curve that lies above X: this is the area where the option will be exercised, so its area represents the probability of exercise
○ the probability-weighted average of all the possible outcomes above X: the expected loss to the writer on exercise is the difference between this weighted average and the strike price X.

In order to appreciate the relative values of the call options on the two shares, we are concerned only with the differences in the parts of their two curves that lie within the in-the-money area. There are clearly two such differences: the in-the-money area for the call option on B is greater than the area for the call option on A by an amount equal to the area

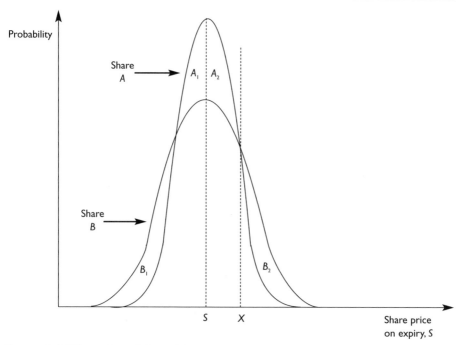

Figure 9.6 Effect of variability of share price on option value

of the segment B_2, so the probability of exercise is greater for B; and the in-the-money area for the call option on B lies on average further from X than does the in-the-money area for A, so the probability-weighted expected loss on exercise will be also greater. As both elements are greater, the cost of the call option on B must be higher than the cost of the equivalent option on A.

When we consider the expected cost of the put option, it is perhaps a little less easy to see the interplay of the two factors. In this case we are concerned with the shape of the two curves *below* X, which is the in-the-money area for a put option. Considering each of the two factors in turn, the area under curve B is actually less than that under curve A, because the combined area in segments A_1 and A_2 is greater than the area in segment B_1, so the probability of exercise of the put option on B is less than that of A, despite the fact that B is the riskier share; but on the other hand the probability-weighted cost of exercise is clearly much higher for B than for A, because the area B_1 lies much further away from X than do A_1 and A_2. In fact, it can be proved mathematically that the increase in the probability-weighted cost of exercise outweighs the decrease in the probability of exercise itself, so that the overall expected cost of the in-the-money option is always higher for the share with higher volatility.

An important footnote to this is that, as we saw in Chapters 6 and 7, when we consider investing in a share, only part of the total risk of the share is relevant – the part known as beta or market risk – since the remainder can be diversified away. However, when we consider investing in options, the *total* risk or volatility is relevant since the value of the option depends on the *total* price movements of the share.

The risk-free interest rate

The purchasers of call options acquire the right to buy something in the future. By not having to buy the shares now, they are in effect saving money that they could invest until it is (possibly) needed at expiry. So the higher the prevailing interest rate, the more valuable the option. We can see this most clearly by considering the case of increasingly deep in-the-money call options. As it becomes progressively more certain that such an option will be exercised, the significance of the volatility of the underlying asset becomes secondary and the transaction assumes more and more the character of a simple purchase on credit. In these circumstances it makes sense that the cost of the option approximates to an interest charge for credit for the period of the option.

What may be a little surprising is that the relevant interest rate affecting the value of a call option is the risk-free interest rate. In the next section we shall see that it is possible to create a perfect replica of the purchase of a call option on a particular number of shares by buying a lesser number of the shares (in a ratio known as the *hedge ratio*) and borrowing cash from the bank. Such a strategy could be used to create a completely riskless hedge against the sale of a call option to another investor: the value of the call option sold would fluctuate by exactly the same amount as the value of the combined portfolio of shares and cash loan. As all risk would be eliminated by this strategy, the appropriate interest rate for valuation purposes is the risk-free rate.

Before we move on to consider in detail the two mathematical models for valuing options, it is worth emphasising that when valuing options, we are concerned with share prices and not share returns. The future share price is relevant, since this is what determines the future return on the option. Dividends are not paid to option holders and are only of interest in so far as they affect the future share price; share prices usually fall when shares go ex-dividend. At this stage, we assume for simplicity that no dividends are paid during the life of the option, although we shall relax this assumption later.

How do we build all these factors into an actual price for a specific option? The short answer is, by constructing a probability distribution of total returns on the underlying asset.

There are two commonly used methods for valuing options, the binomial model and the Black–Scholes formula. Both methods are based on the assumption that the value of an option must be identical with the cost of replicating an identical position using a combination of the underlying asset and the basic products of the cash market – deposits and loans. Where the two methods differ from each other is in the mathematical models they employ.

THE BINOMIAL METHOD OF OPTION VALUATION

Valuing the call option

We shall begin by using the binomial model, which is mathematically the simpler model, to value a call option. We then describe how the value of a put option can be calculated from the known value of a call option. In the next section we explore the other option valuation method, the Black–Scholes formula.

The binomial method starts from the simplistic assumption that on the expiry date of the option there will be only two possible states of the price of the underlying asset: it will have either gone up or gone down by a predetermined amount. This assumption makes it possible to use basic four-function mathematics to arrive at an initial approximation of the value of an option. This initial approximation is in fact an overestimate, but the same basic method can then be used in a progressively more refined form in order to achieve an increasingly accurate estimate of the true value of the option.

We assume that the shares in Company X currently trade at 500p, and that we want to value a three-month European-style call option with an at-the-money strike price of 500p. For simplicity, we assume that the call option is an option on just one share (and not on 100 or 1000 shares). For reasons that will soon become apparent we also need to assume a value for the risk-free rate for borrowing and lending – say, 4% p.a. We also assume that the share is not expected to, and in fact does not, declare any dividends during the option period.

Step 1: Calculate upstep and downstep

For the moment we assume that on the expiry date the share will have a value of either 550p or 454.5p: that is an 'upstep' of 50p or 10%, or a 'downstep' of 45.5p or 9.09%.

Step 2: Calculate spread of outcomes from purchase of call option

The next step is to calculate the spread of possible outcomes of buying a call option. If the share value goes up to 550p, the result is a profit of 50p. If the share goes down to 454.5p, the option will not be exercised and will expire worthless; the outcome is therefore neither profit nor loss. So the result will be either a profit of 50p or a profit of zero, and the spread between the possible outcomes is 50p.

Step 3: Calculate the equivalent share portfolio

We then calculate how many shares we would have to buy in order to replicate precisely the same spread of outcomes. If we were to buy one share at 500p, the upstep would produce a profit of 50p and the downstep a loss of 45.5p, so the spread would be 94.5p. This is too wide a spread, so we need to buy only a fraction of a share. In practice, of course, it is not possible to buy fractions of shares, but we do the calculation in this way to preserve simplicity while we establish the ratio between one call option and the equivalent number of shares in the replicating portfolio. The size of the required fraction is obtained by dividing the spread of outcomes for one option by the spread of outcomes for one share.

$$\frac{\text{Spread of option outcomes}}{\text{Spread of share outcomes}} = \frac{50 - 0}{50 - -45.5} = 0.5236$$

We can prove this as follows:

Cost of 0.5236 shares at 500p per share	=	261.8p
Value of 0.5236 shares at 550p (upstep)	=	288.0p
Value of 0.5236 shares at 454.5p (downstep)	=	238.0p
Difference between upstep and downstep values	=	50.0p

This ratio is known as the **delta hedge ratio**.

Box 9.1 Normal and lognormal distributions

We explain later how the values of the 'upstep' and 'downstep' might rationally be chosen, but for the moment we comment only on the fact that the selected values for the upstep and downstep are not obviously symmetrical in money terms; the upstep is an increase of 10% whereas the downstep is a fall of only 9.09%. In fact there is an underlying symmetry in these two unequal intervals, and there are two ways of understanding it. An intuitive way is to say that either the future value will be 110 per cent of the current value, or the current value will be 110 per cent of the future value. A more technical way of expressing the relationship is to say that in terms of their natural logarithms the two possible outcomes are symmetrically distributed about the current value, as follows:

$\ln(500.0) = 6.214608$
$\ln(550.0) = 6.309918$
$\ln(454.5) = 6.119198$

The natural logarithms of the upper and lower possible future values are respectively 0.09531 more and less than the natural logarithm of the current value, because 0.09531 is the natural logarithm of 1.1, the common factor linking the upstep and the downstep.

Elsewhere in this book we have used the normal distribution to model possible returns on securities. In practice, there are two reasons why this might not be ideal for modelling future values of a share or an equity market index: first, the value cannot fall below zero, but has no theoretical upward limit; and second, share values tend on average to go up rather than down. For both of these reasons, it makes sense to model future share values with a distribution that is skewed to the right. One such distribution which is mathematically easy to understand and to manipulate is the lognormal distribution: that is, a distribution of data whose values are skewed to the right but whose natural logarithms are normally distributed. We can see this if we go back to our example: 550p is farther than 454.5p from our central value of 500p, but their natural logarithms are equidistant from it.

Step 4: Calculate bank loan

So far we have calculated that a purchaser of 0.5236 shares will experience the same spread of outcomes as the purchaser of one call option. But that is not at all the same thing as saying that their financial positions will be identical with each other. The purchaser of the share starts by having to invest 261.8p, and in three months will have either 288p or 238p. The purchaser of the call option starts by investing only the premium (which is what we are trying to calculate) and in three months will have either 50p or nothing at all. How can we modify the situation of the share purchaser so that both her investment and her outcomes are absolutely identical with those of the option purchaser?

The key to this problem is the fact that in the case of the downstep the option purchaser will have nothing in three months' time. We can replicate this situation for the share purchaser by assuming that she borrows at the outset the amount of money that, when repaid with interest in three months' time, will exactly use up all the proceeds of selling the fractional share at the lower price – leaving the purchaser in exactly the same position as the option buyer, with nothing at all. So we must assume that our share purchaser partially finances her fractional share purchase by borrowing the present value of 238p. Using the risk-free rate of interest, this gives us a value for the initial bank loan of

$$\frac{238p}{\left(1 + \frac{0.04 \times 3}{12}\right)} = 235.6p$$

The outcomes for the share purchaser are now identical with those for the option purchaser. In the event of the downstep, the share purchaser will be left with nothing after repaying the bank loan with interest. In the event of the upstep, she will have a share worth 288p, will have to pay out 238p to redeem the borrowing, and will be left with exactly 50p profit.

Step 5: Calculate option premium from initial investment

We can now calculate the option value. The share purchaser has borrowed 235.6p from the bank and has bought a fractional share for 261.8p. The shortfall of 26.2p must be provided from her own resources as an initial net investment in the over-all strategy. On the basis that the outcome of this strategy is, on the assumptions we have made, in all cases identical with the outcome of purchasing a call option, the value of a call option must be the same as the cost of the alternative strategy, otherwise arbitrage would bring the prices together. So the value of the call option must also be 26.2p.

The risk-neutral approach

What we have discussed so far is referred to as the *replicating portfolio* approach to the binomial method of option valuation. A second approach, called the *risk-neutral method*, gives the same result and has the additional advantage of introducing the idea of the relative probability of different outcomes.

We assign the probability p to the upstep and the probability $(1 - p)$ to the downstep. Since there is an absolute certainty (under our chosen assumptions) that one of these outcomes or returns will happen, then the probability-weighted sum of these returns must be equal to the risk-free rate of interest for the period in question. So, in our example, with the risk-free rate set at 4% p.a., or 1% for three months:

$[p \times 0.10] + [(1 - p) \times -0.0909] = 0.01$

$0.10p - 0.0909 + 0.0909p = 0.01$

$0.1909p = 0.1009$

$p = 0.5285$

So the probability of the upstep is 0.5285 or 52.85%. We can now use this to calculate the value of the option. There is a 0.5285 probability that it will have a value of 50p on expiry, and a $(1 - 0.5285)$ or 0.4715 probability that it will expire worthless. Its expected value is therefore the present value of 50p times 0.5285 or

$$\frac{50p \times 0.5285}{\left(1 + \dfrac{0.04 \times 3}{12}\right)} = 26.2p$$

This is exactly the same result as we obtained from the replicating portfolio approach.

Refining the binomial model

Clearly the assumption that in three months' time a share could have just two possible values is a gross oversimplification. How can we refine this approach? One way would be to divide the three months into two or more shorter periods and assume that the value of the share could go up or down in each period. The upstep and downstep need to be scaled down to take account of the shorter period. In fact, the standard formula that is used to calculate the size of the upstep in the binomial method is

$$1 + \text{upstep} = u = e^{\sigma\sqrt{t}}$$

where

    e = base for natural logarithms = 2.7183
    σ = annual standard deviation of returns
    t = time interval in years.

The downstep is then defined as

$$1 + \text{downstep} = d = \frac{1}{u}$$

We can use these equations to calculate the standard deviation of returns on Company X's share, because we know that $1 + \text{upstep} = 1 + 10\% = 1.1$, so $u = 1.1$ and

$$1.1 = e^{\sigma\sqrt{0.25}}$$

So

$$\ln(1.1) \quad = \sigma\sqrt{0.25}$$

$$0.09531 = \sigma\sqrt{0.25}$$

$$\sigma \qquad = \frac{0.09531}{\sqrt{0.25}}$$

$$\sigma \qquad = \frac{0.09531}{0.5}$$

$$\sigma \qquad = \mathbf{0.1906}$$

We can now calculate the size of the upstep and downstep for Company X's share for periods of 1.5 months:

$$1 + \text{upstep} = u = e^{0.1906\sqrt{0.125}} = 1.0697$$

So the upstep for the first period is 6.97%, giving a higher share price of 534.86p, and the lower share price is 500p / 1.0697 = 467.41p. Continuing on the same basis into the second period we get possible values of 572.15p, 500p and 436.95p, as shown in Example 9.1.

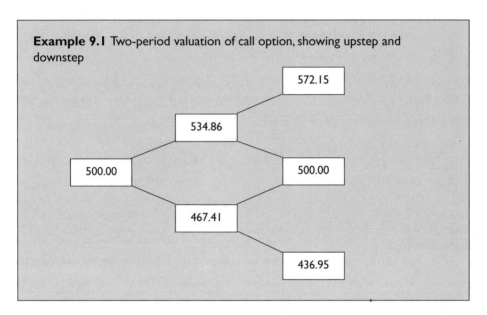

Example 9.1 Two-period valuation of call option, showing upstep and downstep

572.15

534.86

500.00

500.00

467.41

436.95

In order to calculate the value of the call option today, we first need to know its possible values in 1.5 months' time. We do this by considering in turn each of the two pairs of possible share prices at expiry.

If the share rises in the first period to 534.86p, then two possible prices at expiry will be 572.15p and 500p. The spread of outcomes for a call option with strike price 500p is 72.15p, because at a share price of 572.15p the option is worth 72.15p and at 500p it is worthless. In this case the spread of outcomes for owning one share is 72.15p, so the delta hedge is exactly 1. As in our original single-period example, we complete the replicating portfolio by borrowing an amount which, when repaid with interest at the risk-free rate, will exactly match the lower value of the share, that is 500p discounted for 1.5 months at 4% p.a. or 497.51p. So the replicating portfolio at 534.86p is made up as follows:

Buy one share at 534.86p	=	534.86p
Borrow 497.51p at risk-free rate for 1.5 months	=	-497.51p
Value of call option at 1.5 months	=	37.35p

If the share falls to 467.41p in the first period, the calculation is much easier. Whether it takes the upstep or the downstep in the second period, the call option will be worthless on expiry. The spread of option outcomes is zero, so the hedge ratio is zero; no shares need to be bought to replicate the option, and no borrowing needs to be taken out.

If we now move back one stage further, to the starting date of the transaction, we can see that the possible values of the option at the end of the first period will be 37.35p and zero, and the spread of option outcomes is 37.35p. The spread of outcomes for owning one share in the first period, however, is 534.86p – 467.41p, or 67.45p. The delta hedge ratio is 37.35 / 67.45 or 0.5537, so we complete the replicating portfolio as follows:

Cost of 0.5537 shares at 500p per share	= 276.9p
Value of 0.5537 shares at 534.86p (upstep)	= 296.2p
Value of 0.5537 shares at 467.41p (downstep)	= 258.7p
Difference between upstep and downstep values	= 37.5p

We need to borrow an amount that with interest at the risk-free rate of 4% p.a. will grow to 258.7p in 1.5 months, which is 257.4p. So the full replicating portfolio at the beginning of the three-month transaction is as follows:

Buy 0.5537 shares at 500p per share	= 276.9p
Borrow 257.4p at risk-free rate for 1.5 months	= -257.4p
Value of call option	= 19.5p

Example 9.2 shows the same data for periodic upsteps and downsteps as was shown in Example 9.1, with the corresponding value of the call option shown in brackets beneath each share value.

We notice two key differences when we compare the results of the two-period and

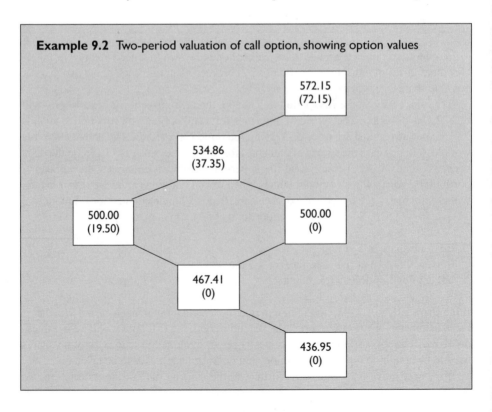

Example 9.2 Two-period valuation of call option, showing option values

Example 9.3
Ten-stage binomial tree

NodeTime:
| 0.0000 | 0.0250 | 0.0500 | 0.0750 | 0.1000 | 0.1250 | 0.1500 | 0.1750 | 0.2000 | 0.2250 | 0.2500 |

single-period calculations obtained from the same set of assumptions: first, the spread of possible share prices on expiry is wider and there are more data points within it, and second, the calculated value of the call option at the beginning of the option contract is lower. We can generalise from this result by saying that as we divide the overall life of the option into smaller and smaller periods (see Example 9.3 for an example of a ten-stage binomial tree), the distribution of possible final prices will tend towards a normal distribution. The closer a value lies to the centre of the distribution, the greater the number of paths that will lead to it and thus the higher the probability of its occurrence. By contrast, the maximum and minimum values can be reached by only one path each (all upsteps or all downsteps), and as the number of alternative paths increases, the probability of the share price taking either of these extreme paths will decrease, and the calculated value of the option will reduce, albeit at a reducing rate.

Valuing the put option

Before we describe the Black–Scholes formula for valuing options, we look at two ways of valuing put options based on what we know so far.

Using the replicating portfolio approach

Using the replicating portfolio approach to the binomial method, we would need to reverse all the constituent parts of the portfolio. Buying a call option is similar to a bet on a price rise, so the equivalent portfolio consists of a long position in the underlying share. Similarly, buying a put option is similar to a bet on a price fall, so the equivalent portfolio would be a short position in the underlying share; and instead of partially financing the purchase with a bank loan, we will be using the proceeds of a short sale of the share to put towards a bank deposit.

We shall use the same basic assumptions about upstep, downstep and risk-free interest rate as we used to evaluate the call option on Company X's share, except in this case we shall evaluate a three-month at-the-money put option with a strike price of 500p.

The range of possible outcomes for the option is a profit of 500p – 454.5p, or 45.5p if the share goes down, and zero if the share goes up, because in the latter case the put option will expire worthless. The range of possible outcomes for a purchase of one share is exactly as it was in the case of the call option: 550p – 454.5p = 95.5p. The hedge ratio is obtained by dividing the spread of option outcomes by the spread of share outcomes: 45.5p / 95.5p = 0.4764. We therefore need to sell 0.4764 shares at 500p. Note that the hedge ratio for a put is always the hedge ratio for the corresponding call, minus 1.

The associated bank transaction is a little more difficult to understand. In the case of the replicating portfolio for the call option, the purpose of the bank borrowing was to ensure that both the option transaction and the replicating portfolio had a zero outcome in the worse of the two possible cases, which for a call option was represented by the downstep. In the case of a put option, the zero-outcome case is when the share follows the upstep and makes the option worthless. In order to replicate the zero outcome with the replicating portfolio, we need to deposit with the bank an amount that, with interest earned at the risk-free rate, will be sufficient to buy back on expiry the share or fractional shares that were sold short at the outset. So the full replicating portfolio for the put option will look like this:

| Sell 0.4764 shares at 500p | = +238.22p |
| Deposit with bank the value of 0.4764 shares at 550p, discounted for three months at 4% p.a. | = -259.42p |

This leaves an initial shortfall of 21.20p which has to be provided from our own resources; this is equivalent to the value of the put option.

Using put–call parity

However, if we already know the value of a call option with the same strike price and expiry date as the put option we are trying to value, there is a much quicker way of doing the calculation. Consider the following strategy, consisting of three elements which would be put in place simultaneously at the outset:

○ Buy one share for amount S.
○ Buy one put (strike price X) for amount P.
○ Sell one call (with the same strike price and expiry as the put) for amount C.

What will happen on expiry of the two options? As always, this depends on the share price on expiry.

○ If the share price is higher than the strike price X, we shall have no reason to exercise our put option, but the call option will be exercised against us. The result is that we shall have to sell our share and we shall receive X.
○ If the share price is lower than the strike price X, the call option against us will expire worthless, but we shall exercise our put option. The result is that we shall sell our share and receive X.
○ The third possibility is that the share price on maturity is exactly X. In this case, three things could happen: the call option could be exercised against us; or if it is not, we could exercise our put option; or both options could lapse and we could sell our share in the market. In every case, we finish with X.

So the result of the strategy is that on the expiry date we receive X. What would we be prepared to pay for a guaranteed receipt of X at a future date? The answer is: the present value of X, discounted at the risk-free rate of interest. Note that the outcome is entirely independent of the risk of the underlying security, so that we use the risk-free rate of interest rather than the expected rate of return on the underlying security.

We can use this finding to express a relationship between S, P, C and the present value of X, which we shall denote by $PV(X)$. The net cost of investing in our three-legged strategy must be equal to the present value of the outcome, so

$$S + P - C = PV(X) \tag{9.1}$$

Equation 9.1 expresses the key principle of *put–call parity*, which we can use as an alternative way of calculating the value of the put option on the shares of Company X.

$$S = 500$$
$$C = 26.2$$
$$PV(X) = \frac{500}{\left(1 + \dfrac{0.04 \times 3}{12}\right)} = 495.05$$

Substituting into equation 9.1:

$$500 + P - 26.2 \quad = 495.05$$

$$P \qquad\qquad\qquad = 495.05 + 26.2 - 500$$

$$P \qquad\qquad\qquad = \textbf{21.25}$$

After allowing for rounding errors, the resulting value of 21.25p for the put option is close enough to the value of 21.2p that we calculated by means of the replicating portfolio.

BLACK–SCHOLES OPTION VALUATION

The valuation model most commonly used in practice by investors and traders is the one formulated in the early 1970s by Fischer Black, Myron Scholes and Robert Merton, using the technique of combining written call contracts with the purchase of shares in such a way as to obtain a totally risk-free, hedged investment. The model is universally referred to as the Black–Scholes model. The contribution of this team to the development of finance theory was recognised in 1997 with the award of the Nobel Prize for economics to Merton and Scholes (Black had died in 1995).

Description of Black–Scholes

According to the Black–Scholes model, the fair value of a European-style call option C on a non-dividend-paying share is given by the following:

$$C = SN(d_1) - Xe^{-rt}N(d_2) \tag{9.2}$$

The fair value of a European-style put option P on a non-dividend-paying share is given by

$$P = Xe^{-rt}N(-d_2) - SN(-d_1) \tag{9.3}$$

where

S	= underlying share price
X	= exercise price
r	= ***continuously compounded*** risk-free interest rate
t	= time to expiry, measured in years
$N(d_i)$	= the probability that a variable modelled by a standard normal distribution (that is, a normal distribution with mean 0 and standard deviation 1) will have a

value equal to or less than d_i. These probabilities can be obtained from published tables or by using the appropriate key or function on a financial calculator or computer spreadsheet program (for instance, NORMSDIST in Microsoft Excel). See Appendix 9.1 for a table of probabilities for the standard normal distribution.

The specific $N(d_i)$ values in the Black–Scholes model depend on the four variables in the main formula and on a fifth variable, the expected volatility of returns in the underlying share as measured by their standard deviation.

There are two ways of writing the formulas for the $N(d_i)$ values. For the purpose of this analysis we shall use the form that makes it easier to appreciate how a change in one variable affects the value of the $N(d_i)$ value and hence of the call option itself. This is as follows:

$$d_1 = \frac{\ln(S/Xe^{-rt})}{\sigma\sqrt{t}} + \frac{\sigma\sqrt{t}}{2} \qquad (9.4)$$

$$d_2 = \frac{\ln(S/Xe^{-rt})}{\sigma\sqrt{t}} - \frac{\sigma\sqrt{t}}{2} \qquad (9.5)$$

For a fuller explanation of the relevance of the $N(d_i)$ and the Black–Scholes model generally, see Hull (2003). The d_i terms can also be written in the form

$$d_1 = \frac{\ln(S/X) + (r + \sigma^2/2)t}{\sigma\sqrt{t}}$$

$$d_2 = \frac{\ln(S/X) + (r - \sigma^2/2)t}{\sigma\sqrt{t}}$$

and this is the form used below to show how the basic Black–Scholes formula is modified to take account of dividends.

Equation 9.5 can also be written conveniently in the form

$$d_2 = d_1 - \sigma\sqrt{t} \qquad (9.6)$$

Before getting into the detail of Black–Scholes, it is a good idea to list in full the assumptions on which it is based. These are as follows:

○ The standard deviation of returns on the share is constant.
○ The share can be sold short without any limitation.
○ There are no transaction costs or taxes.
○ The share is infinitely divisible into fractional shares.
○ Prices move smoothly over time and do not 'gap' up or down.
○ The shares can be traded continuously.
○ The risk-free rate of interest is constant and is the same for all maturities.

Equation 9.2 looks complex, but it becomes more manageable if we begin by temporarily ignoring the $N(d_i)$ terms and return to them later. This simplification gives us

$$C = S - Xe^{-rt} \tag{9.7}$$

In this simplified form, equation 9.7 states that the value of a call option is equal to the market value of the share, less the present value of the strike price discounted from expiry to the present time at the risk-free rate. In fact, the equality expressed in equation 9.7 always holds at the moment of expiry, but it also represents a lower bound for the call option value at any point in its life. We can show that this is so by considering two alternative investment portfolios, as in Example 9.4.

Example 9.4 Determining a lower bound for value of a call option C

Investment portfolio	Value at expiry date of option	
	$S_1 \geq X$	$S_1 < X$
Portfolio A:		
Buy call option for C	$S_1 - X$	0
Invest Xe^{-rt}	X	X
Total	S_1	X
Portfolio B:		
Buy share for amount S	S_1	S_1

Portfolio A consists of buying a call option with an exercise price of X at a cost of C and of investing at the risk-free rate an amount Xe^{-rt} which, with interest, will be worth X on the expiry date. If the share price on expiry S_1 is greater than or equal to the exercise price X, the call option will be worth the difference, $S_1 - X$, and the risk-free investment will be worth X, giving a total of S_1. If the share price on expiry is less than X, the call option will be worthless and the value of portfolio A will simply be X.

Portfolio B consists only of the underlying share, purchased for S, whose value on the expiry date has been defined as S_1. Thus, if S_1 is greater than or equal to X on expiry, portfolios A and B will have identical values. But if S_1 is less than X on expiry, the value of portfolio A will be greater than the value of portfolio B, since X is greater than S_1 in that case.

Since the value on expiry of portfolio B can never be more than that of A but can be less, we can write

Cost of $B \leq$ Cost of A

or

$$S \leq C + Xe^{-rt}$$

or

$$C \geq S - Xe^{-rt}$$

We can now see that is a lower bound for the value of a call option at any point in its life, as predicted by equation 9.7.

We can also find an upper bound for the value of a call option, since the value of C can never exceed the value of the underlying share S. For example, if the exercise price were zero, the value of the option would at most be the value of the free gift – the share. If the exercise price were positive, there would be a cost to acquiring the share and the value of C would be less than S.

The solid lines in Figure 9.7 represent the upper and lower bounds that we have derived for C. The dotted line shows the general shape of the curve for the value of C at any earlier point in time as given by the Black–Scholes formula in equation 9.2. This diagram shows the value of C at a particular point in time, say T, where there remains a period t to expiry. However, we can see that, as C approaches expiry, it must become less valuable since there is less time for the share price to increase. Thus, the dotted line will get closer and closer to the lower bound, $S - PV(X)$, as the option moves to expiry. Simultaneously, the value of $PV(X)$ will approach X as the expiry date nears, and so the right-hand bound, $S - PV(X)$, will move towards the value $S - X$. On expiry, provided $S > X$, the call option will be on the boundary itself, since it will then be worth exactly $S - X$. Prior to expiry the option is worth more than the lower limit (as we can see from the prices for BP call options shown in Table 9.2), given the potential for the share price to rise further.

We now need to consider the significance of the $N(d_i)$ terms which modify the values of S and Xe^{-rt} in the Black–Scholes formula. Formal proof of the Black–Scholes formula lies beyond the scope of this book, but there are two alternative and equally helpful ways to understand its workings.

Black–Scholes as a replicating portfolio

We said at the beginning of this section that both the binomial model and the Black–Scholes formula are based on the idea of perfectly replicating or hedging a call option with a portfolio consisting of a purchase or sale of shares and a bank loan

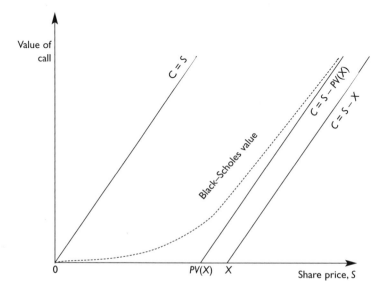

Figure 9.7 Upper and lower limits of value of call option

or deposit. The binomial realisation of this concept is based on discrete mathematics: that is, it assumes that prices move in discrete steps and that time is divided into discrete intervals. Black–Scholes uses the continuous mathematics of calculus to create a more realistic model based on the perception that time is an infinitely divisible continuum and that the range of possible stock prices, while not continuous, is divided into so many small steps that a continuous model is a closer approximation to reality.

The two terms on the right-hand side of the Black–Scholes formula represent the equivalent in continuous mathematics (calculus) of the two elements in the replicating portfolio which we met in the description of the binomial model.

○ $N(d_1)$ is the hedge ratio, so that $SN(d_1)$ is the amount to be invested in the share in the replicating portfolio model.
○ $N(d_2)$ is the probability that the option will be exercised, and Xe^{-rt} is the present value of the exercise price, so $Xe^{-rt}N(d_2)$ is the present value of the amount expected to be received on expiry. It corresponds to the amount of the initial bank loan to be borrowed at the risk-free rate r in the binomial model.

A key feature of the formula is that d_1 must always be at least as large as d_2, as the $(\sigma\sqrt{t})/2$ term (which must be greater than or equal to zero) is added to the common term $(\ln(S/Xe^{-rt}))/(\sigma\sqrt{t})$ in d_1, whereas it is subtracted from it in d_2. $N(d_1)$ must therefore also always be larger than $N(d_2)$. It follows from this that the difference between $SN(d_1)$ and $Xe^{-rt}N(d_2)$ must be greater than or equal to the difference between the share price S and the present value of the exercise price Xe^{-rt}, as the former is being scaled by a larger factor than the latter. This finding tallies with our observation that the call option is always worth at least its intrinsic value. Similarly, when S becomes very large, so do both the d_i terms, so the value of the $N(d_i)$ terms approaches 1 and C approaches $S - X$. Again, this is in line with our observation that the further in-the-money a call option is, the smaller is its time value.

Black–Scholes as the probability-weighted value of exercise

The outcome of a call option is the product of two factors:

○ The probability of exercise, which is the same as the probability that the market price on exercise will be higher than the strike price.
○ The value of exercise, which is the present value of the probability-weighted market price for all cases where it is above the strike price on expiry.

As was noted above, the cumulative normal distribution probability $N(d_2)$ is in fact the probability of exercise. So, by rearranging the Black–Scholes formula in the form

$$C = N(d_2) \times e^{-rt}\left(Se^{rt}\frac{N(d_1)}{N(d_2)} - X\right)$$

(9.8)

we can say that the second term, that is

$$e^{-rt}\left(Se^{rt}\frac{N(d_1)}{N(d_2)} - X\right)$$

is the present value of the probability-weighted market price for all cases where the option will be exercised.

Black–Scholes for dividend-paying shares: the Merton formula

One of the assumptions of the basic Black–Scholes model is that the underlying share does not pay a dividend during the option period. As a dividend is paid to the owner of the share, but not to a buyer of a call option, the basic formula needs to be adjusted to reflect this fact. There are two ways of doing this.

An easy but approximate method is simply to reduce the value of S by an amount equal to the present value of the amount of the expected dividend. The more rigorous method is to use Merton's modification of the basic Black–Scholes formula, which treats the dividend income as if it is paid and compounded continuously. The Merton value for a call option is:

$$C = Se^{-qt}N(d_1) - Xe^{-rt}N(d_2) \tag{9.9}$$

and for a put option is

$$P = Xe^{-rt}N(-d_2) - Se^{-qt}N(-d_1) \tag{9.10}$$

where q = continuously compounded dividend yield.

The d_i terms are also slightly modified. Using the alternative forms of equation 9.4 and 9.5 shown on page 337,

$$d_1 = \frac{\ln(S/X) + (r + \sigma^2/2)t}{\sigma\sqrt{t}}$$

$$d_2 = \frac{\ln(S/X) + (r - \sigma^2/2)t}{\sigma\sqrt{t}}$$

We modify these for the Merton formula as follows:

$$d_1 = \frac{\ln(S/X) + (r - q + \sigma^2/2)t}{\sigma\sqrt{t}}$$

$$d_2 = \frac{\ln(S/X) + (r - q - \sigma^2/2)t}{\sigma\sqrt{t}}$$

Valuing the call option

The use of the Black–Scholes formula to obtain an exact value of C requires either a good calculator and some probability distribution tables (such as those provided in Appendix 9.1) or, more simply, a computer program that can be used interactively. As an example, we shall use the Black–Scholes formula to calculate a fair value for the 460p September 2004 BP call option shown in Table 9.2. Assuming BP was expected to pay dividends of 15p per share annually, equivalent to a 3% yield, we use the Merton version of the formula. The variables are as follows:

S = 492.5
X = 460
r = 0.04 (the risk-free rate in May 2004)
q = 0.03 (the annual dividend as a percentage of the share price)
t = 136/365 or 0.372603
s = 0.1954 (the indicative ATM volatility of BP shares shown in Table 9.2)

We calculate first the necessary values for the d_i and $N(d_i)$ terms:

$$d_1 = \frac{\ln(492.5/460) + (0.04 - 0.03 + 0.1954^2/2)0.372603}{0.1954\sqrt{0.372603}}$$

$$= \frac{0.068268 + 0.010839}{0.119275} = 0.663232$$

$$N(d_1) = 0.746410$$

$$d_2 = \frac{\ln(492.5/460) + (0.04 - 0.03 - 0.1954^2/2)0.372603}{0.1954\sqrt{0.372603}}$$

$$= \frac{0.068268 - 0.003387}{0.119275} = 0.543961$$

$$N(d_2) = 0.7067$$

Finally, we incorporate these into the main formula:

$$C = \left(492.5 \times e^{-0.03 \times 136/365} \times 0.74641\right) - \left(460 \times e^{-0.04 \times 136/365} \times 0.7067\right)$$
$$C = 363.520665 - 320.272869 = 43.247796$$

The value of about 43.25p is close to the published settlement price of 44.5p. One reason for the small discrepancy in valuation could be that the assumptions underlying the Black–Scholes model are not wholly appropriate for realistic option valuation. For example, although we have not derived the Black–Scholes formula from first principles, we are aware of one of the major assumptions: that written calls and shares can be combined in such a way as to produce a perfect hedge against changes in share price throughout the life of the option. This is not feasible in practice because of transaction costs. Other assumptions that might not be robust are the particular model of dividend yield behaviour underlying the Merton model and the fact that traded options are American rather than European, allowing investors to opt for early exercise if they so choose. However, the difference in value between the market price of the option and its Black–Scholes value is small and is more than covered by the bid–ask spread on the options.

Valuing the put option

If we want to calculate the fair value of the 460p September 2004 BP put option, we can use Black–Scholes in one of two ways. As we already know the value of the call option with the same expiry date and strike price, we can calculate the value of the put by applying the principle of put-call parity. If we do not know the value of the corresponding call option, we can use the full Black–Scholes formula, either in the form of equation 9.3 for a non-dividend-paying share or in the form of equation 9.10 for a dividend-paying share.

According to the principle of put–call parity, the value of the share plus the value of the put option minus the value of the call option is equal to the present value of the exercise price, as shown in equation 9.1. Using the Black–Scholes technique of continuous compounding, this equation would then become

$$S + P - C = Xe^{-rt} \tag{9.11}$$

In the case of a dividend-paying share like BP, the share price S also needs to be discounted from the expiry date to the present at the continuously compounded dividend yield rate q, so that we have:

$$Se^{-qt} + P - C = Xe^{-rt} \tag{9.12}$$

$$P = Xe^{-rt} - Se^{-qt} + C$$

Substituting the values for the BP option we have

$$P = 460 \times e^{-0.04 \times 136/365} - 492.5 \times e^{-0.03 \times 136/365} + 43.24$$

$$P = 453.1949 - 487.0254 + 43.24 = 9.4095$$

This value of 9.4p is again close to the indicated closing settlement price of 11.5p shown in Table 9.2.

Alternatively, we could use the full Black–Scholes formula (Merton version) for determining the value of the put option:

$$P = Xe^{-rt}N(-d_2) - Se^{-qt}N(-d_1) \tag{9.13}$$

Note that in both the basic and the Merton versions of the formula for put options the $N(d_i)$ terms have become $N(-d_i)$ terms because we are now interested in the opposite side of the normal distribution of possible share prices. In the case of the call option, we were concerned with the cumulative probability that the share price will be above a given value of X, whereas in the case of the put option we are concerned with the cumulative probability that the share price will be below X. The value of $N(-d_i)$ is always $1 - N(d_i)$.

Using the same variables as before, equation 9.13 gives us

$$P = \left(460 \times e^{-0.04 \times 136/365} \times 0.3118\right) - \left(492.5 \times e^{-0.03 \times 136/365} \times 0.267515\right)$$

$$P = 141.3062 - 130.2866 = 11.0196$$

Again, this is acceptably close to the settlement price of 11.5p.

THE ROLE OF VOLATILITY

Most investors and traders in the markets use Black–Scholes (or variants) for their option valuation models. There thus appears to be substantial agreement on how to price call and put options on equities. However, it may still be the case that Mr Choice regards, for example, the BP July 460 call as cheap and that another investor regards it as expensive. How can this happen?

The answer is: by allowing for disagreement, not over the model itself but over the inputs. Given that there is little room for argument over the share price, the exercise price, the risk-free rate of interest, the time to expiry and the dividend yield, any difference of opinion between investors must stem from differing expectations concerning the future volatility of the share.

The fact that the only option valuation model input over which the investor can argue is that of volatility has an interesting implication. If the Black–Scholes model is the industry standard for option valuation, as it appears to be in practice, the model can be used in two ways: to calculate the value of a call option from the other input variables including volatility, or to calculate the market's implied estimate of volatility from the other input variables including the observed value of a call option. So far we have been using it in the first of these two ways. We have taken the input values provided, including the figures for volatility, to calculate fair values for the call and put options, and we came up with results that were slightly different from market prices. But we could equally well have used the market prices for the options to calculate a value for volatility, and this is done in Table 9.2 under the heading 'indicative a-t-m volatility'.

This ability to determine *implied volatilities* from option prices has led to a new method of trading and investing in securities. If Mr Choice is bullish about BP shares and also has a view on their future volatility, he can choose an option strategy to suit his view. For example, if he thinks that volatility will be higher than the value implied in the current call option price, he will buy the option. If he is right, the option will become more valuable (all other things remaining the same) as the actual volatility of the share increases. Similarly, if he is comparing several alternative options on the same share, he might choose to buy the option with the lowest implied volatility since this is effectively the best value for money. On the other hand, if he believes that the BP share will be less volatile than implied in the call option prices, he may well consider an alternative investment strategy that involves selling options. If Mr Choice has no view on prices but a view on increased or decreased volatility in the future, he could buy or sell a straddle (a strategy referred to on page 322).

The importance of volatility in option pricing means that investors always have to be aware of their view on both prices and volatility. For example, if Mr Choice thinks that prices are going to fall and he wishes to make money out of this, he has two choices, assuming that he has no underlying equity portfolio position. He can either buy a put option, which involves a money outlay and makes money if the share price falls, or he can sell a **naked call**. A sold naked call option is one where the writer has no underlying equity position. It brings the writer a limited amount of money in the form of the option premium if the price stays stable or falls, but loses potentially unlimited amounts of money if he is wrong and the price rises instead. This is because the seller or writer of options has the obligation to deliver if the buyer of the call option chooses to exercise the right to buy. In this case, Mr Choice would lose money since he would have to buy shares in the market at a higher price in order to sell them at a lower, fixed price to the call option buyer. Figure 9.8 highlights the different profit profiles of the two alternative strategies if he holds the options positions to expiry.

However, what Figure 9.8 does not make clear is the volatility strategies implied by each alternative. This will be of importance if Mr Choice decides to unwind his strategy before expiry. Buying a put option involves being long of volatility; selling a call option involves being short of volatility. So, Mr Choice will make more money by buying a put option when compared with selling a call option if the price falls sharply and the market for the share becomes more volatile – as happened during the crash of 1987. Buyers of put options before the crash benefited from both the price drop and increased implied volatility when they came to sell their put options after the crash. On the other hand, Mr Choice would make more money from a sold call option position if the price stays stable or falls a little and the market for the share stagnates, with reduced volatility. In that case, Mr Choice could buy back his option at a relatively cheaper price, reflecting the reduced implied volatility as well as the lower share price.

Finally, we should note that the implied volatility in put and call options on the same share for the same maturity and the same exercise price might be different. It is quite common for puts to be priced at higher volatilities than calls: as we shall see in the next section, institutional investors are frequent writers of call options, thus depressing their price relative to equivalent put options. For example, in Table 9.2, the implied at-the-money volatility on the June 2004 BP options is 19.37% for the put and 19.12% for the call.

One further point, particularly relevant to put options, which must be borne in mind when using the Black–Scholes model is that the formula actually gives the value for a European option: that is, one that can only be exercised on maturity. In

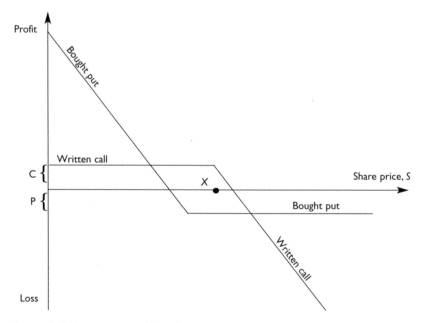

Figure 9.8 Comparison of bought put and sold call strategies

the same way as the problem of dividends is ignored in the basic Black–Scholes option valuation model, the assumption that the option is European is made in order to simplify the option sufficiently to be able to value it at all! However, this difficulty is not insuperable. We can see that the American-style options must be worth at least as much as equivalent European ones because of their additional right to exercise before expiry. However, they might be worth no more than European ones since it is usually more profitable either to sell the option or to hold the option to expiry rather than to exercise it before expiry. This is because exercise of the option realises the intrinsic value but abandons the time value, whereas a sale of the option preserves both elements in its value. So the Black–Scholes formula which gives the value of European options will usually also give the value of American options provided there are no complications such as dividends.

If a dividend is due before expiry, however, the investor might do better to exercise before the share goes ex-dividend and collect the dividend, rather than wait until expiry to exercise and thus forfeit the dividend payment. So in the case of an option on a dividend-paying share, the option must be valued twice, assuming first that it will be exercised on expiry, and second, that it will be exercised before the shares go ex dividend. It might be that the option will be more valuable if exercised before the shares go ex div and thus, in this case, an American option will be more valuable than an equivalent European option.

USING OPTIONS TO IMPROVE PORTFOLIO PERFORMANCE

As well as combining different types of option to speculate on share price movements, we can combine options with shares, either to reduce the risk to an investor of substantial price changes in their shares or to improve the risk–return balance of his portfolio. Options can be used to reduce risk as well as to increase risk through their leverage characteristic. We are now in a position to summarise the basic hedging strategies using options, and to compare them with the futures hedging strategies encountered in the last chapter.

In Chapter 8 we used the futures contract on the FTSE 100 index to illustrate the use of futures for hedging purposes. In order to facilitate a comparison of options with futures, we shall use the options contract on the same index to illustrate the hedging properties of options. Table 9.5 sets out the contract specification, and Table 9.6 shows an excerpt from the trading report for 4 May 2004. The underlying asset – in this case the FTSE 100 index of 100 leading shares – is described in detail in Appendix 5.2.

Fundamentally, options on a stock market index, such as on the FTSE 100 Index, can be treated in a similar way to individual equity options. They can be valued in the same way, and trading and hedging strategies can be adopted with either type of option. The mechanics of exchange-traded options are similar in most respects to futures, albeit with a couple of modifications. Buyers of options do not have to post initial or variation margin, but they do have to pay the premium in full at the outset of the transaction. Option sellers, who can incur potentially unlimited losses, are subject to margining requirements in exactly the same way as both parties to a futures transaction. If several trades in individual equity options and index options are done, margin credits and debits can be netted off.

Options on the FTSE 100 Index differ from options on individual shares in that the FTSE 100 Index options are cash settled on expiry whereas exercise of an individual share option involves the exchange of cash for actual physical shares.

Table 9.5 Contract specification, FTSE 100 Index option contract

Unit of trading	Contract valued at £10 per index point (e.g. value £45,000 at 4500.0)
Quotation	Index points (e.g. 4500.0)
Minimum price movement (tick size and value)	0.5 (£5.00)
Exercise price and exercise price intervals	The interval between exercise prices is determined by the time to maturity of a particular expiry month and is either 50 or 100 points, or in exceptional circumstances 25 points
Expiry month	Nearest eight of March, June, September, December, plus such that the nearest four calendar months are available for trading
Exercise	Exercise by 18.00 London time on the last trading day only. Note: this is a European-style option
Last trading day /time	10.30 on the third Friday of the expiry month
Delivery day	First business day after the last trading day
Exchange delivery settlement price (EDSP)	The EDSP is based on the outcome of an intra-day auction on the last trading day
Mode of settlement	Cash settlement based on the EDSP
Trading hours	08:00–16:30

Source: Euronext.liffe.

Options on the FTSE 100 Index do not refer to a fixed number of stock index 'units'; rather, as for the FTSE 100 Index futures contract described in Chapter 8, options are acquired on a notional sterling amount of the contract which varies with the level of the index. For example, if 100 call options were bought on the FTSE 100 Index at the strike price of 4575 shown in Table 9.5, the underlying value of the shares in which the option buyer has an interest would be $100 \times 4575 \times £10 = £4,575,000$.

Returning to our hedging strategies, we will now look at the position of an investor, Ms Maze, who is holding a diversified portfolio of shares worth in total £5 million. We assume, for simplicity that the behaviour of this portfolio will mirror that of the FTSE 100 Share Index; in other words, if the index goes up or down by 10%, Ms Maze's portfolio will also rise or fall by 10%. How Ms Maze might use the futures and options markets to improve the performance of her portfolio depends on her outlook and appetite for risk. We consider three basic scenarios:

○ she does not expect significant short-term price movements in either direction and is happy to continue holding her portfolio, but would like if possible to enhance its yield without incurring an unacceptable measure of additional risk
○ she is not concerned about the market's long-term prospects, but is nervous that a short-term setback could trigger a significant fall in prices
○ she is seriously worried about the market's future direction.

Table 9.6 Options on the FTSE 100 Index

Equity Index Options

Calls — Business Day Tue 4 May 2004 — Indicative a-t-m Vol 11.93 — Underlying Price 4549H — Official Volume 4549H
Puts — Business Day Tue 4 May 2004 — Time to expiry: 45 Days — Prev Business Day Mon 3 May 2004 — Indicative a-t-m Vol 11.93

Call Settle	Call Delta	Call Vol	Call Open Int (Prev Bus Day)	Exercise Price (Jun 04)	Put Settle	Put Delta	Put Vol	Put Open Int (Mon 3 May 2004)
2014H	1.00	45.13	660	2525	CAB	0.00	45.13	3,518
1964H	1.00	45.11	N/A	2575	CAB	0.00	45.11	N/A
1915	1.00	44.96	N/A	2625	CAB	0.00	44.96	149
1865	1.00	44.69	N/A	2675	CAB	0.00	44.69	N/A
1815H	1.00	44.30	N/A	2725	CAB	0.00	44.30	1,212
1765H	1.00	43.81	N/A	2775	CAB	0.00	43.81	N/A
1716	1.00	43.22	N/A	2825	CAB	0.00	43.22	6,735
1666H	1.00	42.55	N/A	2875	CAB	0.00	42.55	N/A
1616H	1.00	41.82	N/A	2925	CAB	0.00	41.82	1,105
1567	1.00	41.03	N/A	2975	H	0.00	41.03	N/A
1517	1.00	40.20	N/A	3025	H	0.00	40.20	10,958
1467H	1.00	39.34	N/A	3075	H	0.00	39.34	N/A
1417H	1.00	38.03	N/A	3125	H	0.00	38.03	3,713
1368	1.00	37.18	N/A	3175	H	0.00	37.18	2,285
1318H	1.00	36.39	N/A	3225	H	0.00	36.39	19,905
1269	1.00	35.65	N/A	3275	H	0.00	35.65	55
1219	1.00	34.92	25	3325	1	0.00	34.92	14,522
1169H	0.99	34.16	N/A	3375	1	-0.01	34.16	998
1120	0.99	33.35	290	3425	1H	-0.01	33.35	19,428
1070H	0.99	32.46	N/A	3475	1H	-0.01	32.46	31
1021	0.99	31.59	1,590	3525	2	-0.01	31.59	26,789
972H	0.99	30.72	N/A	3575	2	-0.01	30.72	804
922H	0.99	29.84	550	3625	2H	-0.01	29.84	22,511
873	0.98	28.91	N/A	3675	3	-0.02	28.91	870
823H	0.98	28.03	62	3725	3H	-0.02	28.03	24,643
774H	0.98	27.17	N/A	3775	4	-0.02	27.17	1,594
725H	0.97	26.31	1,290	3825	5	-0.03	26.31	33,602
677	0.97	25.43	13	3875	5H	-0.03	25.43	440
628	0.96	24.50	7,036	3925	6H	-0.04	24.50	26,753
578H	0.95	23.01	N/A	3975	7	-0.05	23.01	0
530H	0.95	22.07	14,167	4025	8H	-0.05	22.07	40,949
482H	0.93	21.28	10	4075	10H	-0.07	21.28	5,492
433H	0.92	19.70	13,898	4125	11	-0.08	19.70	2,805
386H	0.91	18.95	328	4175	14	-0.09	18.95	28,619
339	0.89	17.66	13,261	4225	16	-0.11	17.66	24,674
292H	0.86	16.67	813	4275	19H	-0.14	16.67	5,617
247H	0.83	15.66	12,753	4325	24	-0.17	15.66	22,808
203H	0.78	14.58	1,157	4375	30	-0.22	14.58	21,794
163	0.72	13.80	42,382	4425	39	-0.28	13.80	30,279
125H	0.65	13.07	782	4475	51	-0.35	13.07	1,535
90H	0.56	12.19	22,159	4525	66H	-0.44	12.19	10,036
63	0.45	11.68	2,143	4575	88H	-0.55	11.68	1,150
40H	0.35	11.15	31,637	4625	116	-0.65	11.15	4,342
24H	0.24	10.71	9,228	4675	149	-0.76	10.71	153
13H	0.16	10.45	34,537	4725	188H	-0.84	10.45	127
7	0.09	10.22	3,541	4775	231H	-0.91	10.22	18
5H	0.05	10.15	31,969	4825	277H	-0.95	10.15	358
3H	0.03	9.92	8,686	4875	325H	-0.97	9.92	20
1H	0.01	9.69	19,073	4925	374	-0.99	9.69	65

Source: Euronext-liffe.

Strategy A: Enhancing risk and return

We need to begin this section by sounding a cautionary note. In an efficient market there is no such thing as a *free lunch*; it is not possible systematically to earn excess returns, as extra return usually comes with extra risk. Nevertheless, the asymmetrical nature of options payoffs does offer a tempting opportunity for investors who slightly disagree with the market to earn a modest additional return by backing their own judgment.

In this scenario, Ms Maze's basic view is that the market is unlikely to rise or fall very far in the near future. She might also believe that the volatility implied in current options prices is excessive: that is, that they reflect an overestimate of future volatility. How can she exploit this view to enhance the return on her £5 million portfolio? The answer is that she can write (i.e. sell) out-of-the-money index call options. Her return is the premium income. It is best to divide the potential risks into two parts.

If the market rises but does not reach the exercise price before expiry, Ms Maze will keep the premium and suffer no additional loss. However, she will have an uncomfortable time. Although the option will not acquire any intrinsic value as long as the market price does not actually reach the exercise price, one element in the time value of the option will increase as the probability of exercise increases. This means that if Ms Maze begins to have doubts about the wisdom of her strategy, the cost of unwinding it (by buying back the call options she has written) might become unacceptably high. We can appreciate this indirectly from the prices for call options on BP shares shown in Table 9.2. With the current share price at 492.5p, Ms Maze could earn a one-off return of 4.5p or nearly 1% by writing four-month (September 2004) calls at 550p, which are 57.5p out of the money. We can get some idea of what it would cost her to buy the position back if (for instance) the price rose to within 10p of the exercise price just a couple of weeks before expiry, by looking at the price of the imminent (May 2004) 500p calls. At 4.5p this would exactly wipe out all her extra return (and would not compensate her at all for all those sleepless nights).

If the market does rise above the strike price, then Ms Maze begins to incur actual losses compared with the alternative 'do nothing' strategy of continuing to hold her shares. Suppose that she sells the June index call options with a 4675 strike price. As each options contract represents an underlying position of $4675 \times £10$ or £46,750, she might sell 107 contracts for a total underlying value of £5,002,250, which is very close to the value of her portfolio at the current index level of 4549. The strike price is nearly 3% above the current index value, and the premium income of 24.5 points per contract or $24.5 \times £10 \times 107 = £26,215$ represents a return of nearly 0.52% on the value of the portfolio. But what happens if the market is higher than 4675 on expiry of the options on 18 June? The index options contract is cash settled, which means that although Ms Maze does not have to part with her shares, she has to pay out in cash £1070 (£10 times 107) for every point by which the actual index value exceeds the strike price. This will wipe out the gain from premium income above the level of 4692. What she has done is effectively to cap the value of her portfolio at £5 million $\times 4675 / 4549$, or about £5,138,000, until 18 June. However, she has not actually sold her portfolio at this level. Once she has paid up for her loss and the option has been fulfilled, she is free to enjoy the benefit of any further upward movement of the market. But what would be very annoying for her would be to find that the rise in the market up to 18 June turned out to be a **spike** and the market subsequently fell back again. If that were to happen, she would be in the unhappy position of not gaining from the rise, but still losing on the subsequent fall because of the fixed maturity of the options.

Strategy B: Short-term nervousness

In this case Ms Maze is happy with the long-term prospects but is nervous that a short-term setback could get out of control. Her fundamental decision is whether she is so nervous that she wants to get out of the market altogether, or just wants temporary insurance. If the former, then she can either sell her shares or sell index futures (see Strategy C).

The problem with this strategy is that if Ms Maze's fears prove groundless and the market actually rises, she will have to buy back her portfolio or her futures position at higher prices and will have suffered an irrecoverable opportunity cost equal to the amount by which the market has risen. This risk might be too great for her if all she wants is temporary insurance, which she can purchase by buying out-of-the-money put options. This is where options really come into their own, because (unlike futures, which offer for each maturity just a single dealing price, which is the forward price implied by the spot price and the cost of carry) they offer a choice of expiry dates and of strike prices. Investors can therefore choose whichever contract best fits their own strategy and level of risk aversion. A comparatively risk-averse investor would be willing to pay 51 points for the protection afforded by a put at 4475, less than 2% below the current market level. A more relaxed investor may be content to purchase long-stop insurance 7 % below the current level by paying just 16 points for the 4225 put option. In this respect, the choice of strike price for a put option is very similar to the choice of an excess on a motor insurance policy.

It is worth pointing out that Strategies A and B are not mutually exclusive. If Ms Maze is nervous about a possible downturn, she is likely to be more relaxed about the risk inherent in writing call options against her portfolio, and in this way she can use the income from Strategy A to reduce the cost of her insurance Strategy B.

Strategy C: Serious concern

This is the case where Ms Maze's concern has risen to the level where she is seriously considering getting out of the market altogether, if only on a temporary basis until the situation becomes clearer. Her choice is either to sell the shares or sell the futures either on the index or on the individual shares.

The overall effect of all three strategies is the same: from the moment she sells her shares or sells the futures (for whatever settlement date), she ceases to have any risk on the shares or on the market. Her level of return will also revert to a money-market rate close to the risk-free rate. As we saw in Chapter 8, even if she sells the futures and continues to receive dividends on her shares until the settlement date, any difference between the dividend yield and the short-term money-market rate will be incorporated into the futures price.

Her choice between the alternative strategies for exiting the market will therefore depend on other factors, including the ease, cost and speed of executing the transactions – and of reversing them if she changes her mind. On all counts, as we saw in Chapter 8, the futures market is usually superior to the cash market as a medium for overall portfolio risk management.

However, an alternative and equivalent strategy is to sell a call and buy a put, both at-the-money, on the FTSE 100 equity index. Use Figure 9.2 and 9.3(a) to see why!

SUMMARY

This chapter has described the market in options. A call option offers the investor the right to acquire a share on or before a particular date at a fixed price. A put option offers the holder the right to sell a share at a fixed price on or before the expiry date. Options traded on Euronext.liffe, the London International Financial Futures Exchange, were described, in particular individual equity options and options linked to the FTSE 100 equity index.

Investment in options was compared with investment in the underlying shares themselves, and it was found that combinations of different options or combinations of options with ordinary shares allowed investors to increase or reduce return and risk relative to the return and risk of simply holding ordinary shares. Upper and lower limits to the value of a call option were found, and factors affecting the value of a call option discussed. This led to two explicit valuation models for call options, the binomial model and the Black–Scholes model. A discussion then followed on how to apply the Black–Scholes model to value both call and put options, and of the role of volatility in option pricing.

The remainder of the chapter looked at how to use options for hedging portfolios and for enhancing their risk–return characteristics

REVIEW EXERCISES

1. Forward contracts, futures contracts and options contracts constitute the three principal families of risk-management instruments for participants in the securities markets.
   a. What are the principal similarities and differences between these three types of instrument? Clearly distinguish between fundamental differences in the ways they react to changes in the value of the underlying, and merely 'mechanical' differences in the ways they are executed and settled.
   b. Explain the pros and cons of using each type of instrument from the point of view of:
      i. an existing long-term investor in securities
      ii. a potential investor in securities
      iii. a speculator
      iv. an *arbitrageur*.
2. Which variables affect the value of a call option on a share? Derive boundaries within which the value of a European call option must lie.
3. In late January, shares in Quiver plc were quoted at 697p. Mr Wellie wishes to buy a three-month call option on 1,000 shares. The call option is priced at 58p per share and the exercise price is 650p.
   a. Identify and quantify the two components in the price (premium) of the call option.
   b. Assuming that the risk free interest rate is 4% pa, what would be the fair price for a put option on shares in Quiver with the same exercise price and date as the call option described above?
   c. Shortly before the exercise date in April, shares in Quiver fell to 625p. Would Mr

Wellie have exercised his call option and what would have been his overall profit or loss on the transaction?

d. Ms Stiefel already owned 1,000 Quiver shares and was nervous about a possible fall in their value, so she bought put options on her shares at the price you calculated in (a) above. Would she have exercised her option, and what would have been the overall profit or loss on the transaction?

4. Suppose it is early September and an investor believes the annual results of International Manufacturing, due shortly, will cause a sharp rise in the share price. The shares can be bought at 320p or the October call options, with an exercise price of 280p, at 50p.

   a. If his prediction is correct and the shares rise to 350p while the options rise to 80p, what profit will he have made (ignoring any transaction costs) if:

     i.   he has bought 2000 shares?

     ii.   he has bought two October 280p call option contracts for 1,000 shares each?

   b. Using your results from part (a), discuss the advantages of buying options rather than shares.

5. In the text we illustrated the binomial method for valuing a call option by assuming that a share currently worth 500p could have a value of either 454.5p or 550p in three months' time.

   a. Using the same method, but assuming instead that the share is very much more volatile and that the downstep and upstep are 400p and 625p respectively, recalculate:

     i.   the fair value of the call

     ii.   the delta or hedge ratio

     iii. the size of the bank loan

     iv. the probability of exercise.

   b. Comment on the validity of your results, compared with the result obtained in the text for a downstep and upstep of 454.5p and 550p.

6. The current price of shares in Company Q is 30p. The volatility (standard deviation) of the share price is 40% and the risk-free rate is 10% pa.

   a. Using the Black–Scholes model, determine the fair value of a six-month European-style call option with an exercise price of 40p.

   b. What would the call option be worth if the current share price were

     i.   40p?

     ii.   50p?

7. The current price of shares in Company T is 20p. The volatility (standard deviation) of the share price is 36%, the risk free rate is 8% pa.

   a. Using the Black–Scholes model, determine the fair value of a six-month European-style put option with an exercise price of 30p.

   b. How good an estimate of the value of an American put option would you expect the Black–Scholes model to give if the put option were substantially:

     i.   in the money?

     ii.   out of the money?

8. Using the data on BP options reproduced in Table 9.2, test the principle of put–call parity for a variety of exercise dates and exercise prices.

   a. Allowing for possible differences between bid and offer prices, does the principle hold, or do you notice any discrepancies in your calculations?

b. What feature of the BP share, ignored in the basic formulation of the put–call parity principle, might explain any discrepancies you do observe?

9. Look at current market prices of BP call options to see if they behave as the theory would predict. For instance:

a. Follow BP options as they approach maturity. Do their prices behave in the way you would expect?

b. Compare two BP call options with the same maturity but different exercise prices. Which call option has the higher value?

c. Compare two BP call options with the same exercise price but different maturities. Which option is worth more?

d. Use the Black–Scholes model to value any BP call option with the shortest maturity.

e. Does your answer give the same as the market price? If not, why do you think you get a different answer?

f. What complications would have to be taken into account if you applied the Black–Scholes model to valuing longer maturity traded call options, for example, with an exercise date over six months away?

Sample answers to the review exercises can be found on the companion website.

APPENDIX 9.1: AREA UNDER THE STANDARD NORMAL DISTRIBUTION FUNCTION

$\int_0^z f(z)dz$

z	0.00	0.01	0.02	0.03	0.04	0.05	0.06	0.07	0.08	0.09
0.0	0.0000	0.0040	0.0080	0.0120	0.0160	0.0199	0.0239	0.0279	0.0319	0.0359
0.1	0.0398	0.0438	0.0478	0.0517	0.0557	0.05%	0.0636	0.0675	0.0714	0.0753
0.2	0.0793	0.0832	0.0871	0.0910	0.0948	0.0987	0.1026	0.1064	0.1103	0.1141
0.3	0.1179	0.1217	0.1255	0.1293	0.1331	0.1368	0.1406	0.1443	0.1480	0.1517
0.4	0.1554	0.1591	0.1628	0.1664	0.1700	0.1736	0.1772	0.1808	0.1844	0.1879
0.5	0.1915	0.1950	0.1985	0.2019	0.2054	0.2088	0.2123	0.2157	0.2190	0.2224
0.6	0.2257	0.2291	0.2324	0.2357	0.2389	0.2422	0.2454	0.2486	0.2517	0.2549
0.7	0.2580	0.2611	0.2642	0.2673	0.2704	0.2734	0.2764	0.2794	0.2823	0.2852
0.8	0.2881	0.2910	0.2939	0.2967	0.2995	0.3023	0.3051	0.3078	0.3106	0.3133
0.9	0.3159	0.3186	0.3212	0.3238	0.3264	0.3289	0.3315	0.3340	0.3365	0.3389
1.0	0.3413	0.3438	0.3461	0.3485	0.3508	0.3531	0.3554	0.3577	0.3599	0.3621
1.1	0.3643	0.3665	0.3686	0.3708	0.3729	0.3749	0.3770	0.3790	0.3810	0.3830
1.2	0.3849	0.3869	0.3888	0.3907	0.3925	0.3944	0.3962	0.3980	0.3997	0.4015
1.3	0.4032	0.4049	0.4066	0.4082	0.4099	0.4115	0.4131	0.4147	0.4162	0.4177
1.4	0.4192	0.4207	0.4222	0.4236	0.4251	0.4265	0.4279	0.4292	0.4306	0.4319
1.5	0.4332	0.4345	0.4357	0.4370	0.4382	0.4394	0.4406	0.4418	0.4429	0.4441
1.6	0.4452	0.4463	0.4474	0.4484	0.4495	0.4505	0.4515	0.4525	0.4535	0.4545
1.7	0.4554	0.4564	0.4573	0.4582	0.4591	0.4599	0.4608	0.4616	0.4625	0.4633
1.8	0.4641	0.4649	0.4656	0.4664	0.4671	0.4678	0.4686	0.4693	0.4699	0.4706
1.9	0.4713	0.4719	0.4726	0.4738	0.4738	0.4744	0.4750	0.4756	0.4761	0.4767
2.0	0.4772	0.4778	0.4783	0.4788	0.4793	0.4798	0.4803	0.4808	0.4812	0.4817
2.1	0.4821	0.4826	0.4830	0.4834	0.4838	0.4842	0.4846	0.4850	0.4854	0.4857
2.2	0.4861	0.4864	0.4868	0.4871	0.4875	0.4878	0.4881	0.4884	0.4887	0.4890
2.3	0.4893	0.48%	0.4898	0.4901	0.4904	0.4906	0.4909	0.4911	0.4913	0.4916
2.4	0.4918	0.4920	0.4922	0.4925	0.4927	0.4929	0.4931	0.4932	0.4934	0.4936
2.5	0.4938	0.4940	0.4941	0.4943	0.4945	0.4946	0.4948	0.4949	0.4951	0.4952
2.6	0.4953	0.4955	0.4956	0.4957	0.4959	0.4960	0.4961	0.4962	0.4963	0.4964
2.7	0.4965	0.4966	0.4967	0.4968	0.4969	0.4970	0.4971	0.4982	0.4973	0.4974
2.8	0.4974	0.4975	0.4976	0.4977	0.4977	0.4978	0.4979	0.4979	0.4980	0.4891
2.9	0.4981	0.4982	0.4982	0.4982	0.4984	0.4984	0.4985	0.4985	0.4986	0.4886
3.0	0.4987	0.4987	0.4987	0.4988	0.4988	0.4989	0.4989	0.4989	0.4990	0.4990

Source: Copeland and Weston (2004).

Part V
Institutional and International Investment

10 Investing institutions

Learning objectives for this chapter

After studying this chapter you should be able to

○ identify and describe the main types of institutional investor active in the securities markets
○ identify and analyse historical trends in these institutions' activities in the securities markets
○ describe how these institutions' underlying objectives, and the regulatory regimes within which they operate, determine their investment strategies and behaviour
○ appreciate how the behaviour of major investor groups and their relationship with company managements impacts the securities markets.

INTRODUCTION

This chapter stands apart from the others in this book, in the sense that it is not directly concerned with how to value particular securities, or how to value an investment portfolio. It is concerned instead with a group of principal actors on the stock exchange investment stage: that is, with those financial institutions that are the major investors in stock exchange securities. No book on investment can ignore these institutions – pension funds, insurance companies, investment trusts and unit trusts – first because they are the intermediaries through which the vast majority of people knowingly or unknowingly invest in stock market securities, and second because their presence is now so dominant that every aspect of investment, from performance measurement to the role of market makers and analysts, is affected by their existence.

The role of these institutions as major investors in stock exchange securities is clearly highlighted by their holdings of UK shares, as shown in Table 10.1, which lists the proportionate holdings of UK shares by different investor types.

Individual investors

The figures in Table 10.1 show how rapidly the holdings of the UK investing institutions have grown over the past few decades. When we allow for the fact that the overwhelming

Table 10.1 Percentage ownership of UK listed equities by type of investor 1963–2004

	1963	1969	1975	1981	1989	1990	1991	1992	1993	1994	1997	1998	1999	2000	2001	2002	2003	2004
Rest of the world	7.0	6.6	5.6	3.6	12.8	11.8	12.8	13.1	16.3	16.3	24.0	27.6	29.3	32.4	31.9	32.1	32.3	32.6
Insurance companies	10.0	12.2	15.9	20.5	18.6	20.4	20.8	19.5	20.0	21.9	23.5	21.6	21.6	21.0	20.0	19.9	17.3	17.2
Pension funds	6.4	9.0	16.8	26.7	30.6	31.7	31.3	32.4	31.7	27.8	22.1	21.7	19.6	17.7	16.1	15.6	16.1	13.7
Individuals	54.0	47.4	37.5	28.2	20.6	20.3	19.9	20.4	17.7	20.3	16.5	16.7	15.3	16.0	14.8	14.3	14.9	14.1
Unit trusts	1.3	2.9	4.1	3.6	5.9	6.1	5.7	6.2	6.6	6.8	6.7	3.0	2.7	1.7	1.8	1.6	2.0	1.9
Investment trusts					1.6	1.6	1.5	2.1	2.5	2.0	1.9	1.9	1.9	2.1	2.2	1.8	2.3	3.3
Other financial institutions	11.3[1]	10.1[1]	10.5[1]	6.8[1]	1.1	0.7	0.8	0.4	0.6	1.3	2.0	4.1	5.1	4.6	9.9	10.5	11.1	10.7
Charities	2.1	2.1	2.3	2.2	2.3	1.9	2.4	1.8	1.6	1.3	1.9	1.4	1.3	1.4	1.0	1.1	1.2	1.1
Private non-financial companies	5.1	5.4	3.0	5.1	3.8	2.8	3.3	1.8	1.5	1.1	1.2	1.4	2.2	1.5	1.0	0.8	0.7	0.6
Public sector	1.5	2.6	3.6	3.0	2.0	2.0	1.3	1.8	1.3	0.8	0.1	.01	0.1	–	–	0.1	–	0.1
Banks	1.3	1.7	0.7	0.3	0.7	0.7	0.2	0.5	0.6	0.4	0.1	0.6	1.0	1.4	1.3	2.1	2.2	2.7
Total[2]	100.0	100.0	100.0	100.0	100.0	100.0	100.0	100.0	100.0	100.0	100.0	100.0	100.0	100.0	100.0	100.0	100.0	100.0

1 Includes investment trusts
2 Components may not sum to the total because of rounding

Source: Office for National Statistics.

majority of foreign holders of UK shares are also institutions, the aggregate percentage of institutional ownership of UK shares has doubled from about 35 per cent in 1963 to about 70 per cent in 2004. We saw in Chapter 3 that the growth in their control of the UK gilt market has been even more rapid, with only 25 per cent of gilts in issue in the mid-1960s being held by investing institutions, compared with over 66 per cent by 2003. For reasons which will be described later in the chapter, this growth represents a substantial increase in the assets of these institutions, and has led to their being the most powerful class of investors in the stock market today.

Pension funds and insurance companies are now the two major types of domestic investing institution. Investment trusts have suffered a decline relative to unit trusts as an investment medium for the personal investor, because of the greater ability of unit trusts to market themselves via investment intermediaries such as insurance brokers.

The decline of the individual investor

Table 10.1 also documents the simultaneous decline in importance in the stock market of the individual investor, also called the retail investor, a decline which is most marked in the context of UK equities. This decline was not reversed or even slowed by the major privatisations of the 1980s, in which shares in companies being denationalised, such as British Telecom, British Gas, and water and electricity companies, were actively aimed at small investors with the declared aim of widening share ownership. Demutualisations of building societies and mutual insurance companies also increased individual share ownership in the 1990s. As a result, the number of shareholders went up from 3 million in 1979 to 15 million by 1997, although this figure has since fallen to around 11 million. Most individual investors tend to have relatively small holdings. The percentage of equities they hold has fallen from over 28 per cent of the total in 1979 to under half that figure today. However, individual investors have not abandoned stock exchange investment. They have merely moved from direct to indirect investment of their savings in quoted securities, either because they have had no choice, as in the case of an employee required to contribute to a pension fund, or because of the tax and other advantages of investment in, say, a long-term insurance savings policy.

This growth in the use of intermediaries for channelling private sector savings has many implications in the investment field. For example, there may be duplication of investment analysis by stockbrokers and the investment institutions. Also, there has been increased demand for the regulation of these intermediaries, which culminated in the Financial Services Act 1986 and its replacement, the Financial Services and Markets Act 2001, and for increased transparency in performance measurement. Retail investors who deal direct with stockbrokers, and listen to their advice without having to take it, are largely responsible for their own investment decisions. An investor in a life assurance policy, on the other hand, transfers the responsibility for investment decisions to a third party for a long period of time.

The rise of the investing institutions

The growth in the influence and scope of pension funds seems originally to have taken the City and the government by surprise. For example, Harold Wilson, in the parliamentary debate following the publication of the Wilson Committee's Report on

Box 10.1 Rise and fall of the small shareholder

In their annual reports, many companies publish a table showing the distribution of share-holdings by size. Because their share prices differ from each other, and because each company chooses its own cut-off points, it is not possible to make precise comparisons, but the general picture is clear. The information in Table 10.2 was collected from the 2004 annual reports of BT, mm02 (as the mobile telephone division of BT was called when it was spun off from BT as a separate public company in 2001), and Vodafone.

Table 10.2 Distribution of shareholdings by size, selected companies

Company	Date	Shareholdings valued at less than …	…were held by (number of holders)…	… representing … (% of all holders)	… representing … (% of all shares in issue)
BT	31 Mar 04	£1600	1,126,143	70.20%	4.60%
mm02	31 Mar 04	£1200	1,233,418	78.15%	5.58%
Vodafone	31 Mar 04	£1300	461,540	74.54%	0.21%

The relative importance of small shareholders on the share registers of BT and mm02 reflects their status as classic 1980s privatisation issues.

In early 2005, mm02 (which simultaneously renamed itself as 02) underwent a capital restructuring, the primary objective of which was to enable it to commence paying dividends for the first time. Faced with the prospect of what it regarded as the unwelcome adminis-trative burden of servicing nearly 1 million small shareholders' dividends, the company sought to shed this load by offering to buy back up to 300 million shares, or about 3.5 per cent of its share capital, at a premium of about 5 per cent to the current market price, and then place these shares in the market.

On successful completion of this operation the company was able to announce:

The Company's Scheme of Arrangement will enable some 833,000 [i.e. more than 50 per cent by number] of its shareholders, owning up to 1000 shares, to realise the value of their shares and secure a premium without incurring dealing charges. At the same time the Company has secured a long term reduction in the costs of servicing its shareholders whilst remaining one of the 10 most widely held public companies in the UK, with more than ninety percent of its shareholder base made up of retail shareholders.

Financial Institutions published in 1980, referred to 'the pension fund revolution having occurred with no formal notice, and without debate or decision in this House'. One of the points made by the Wilson Committee was the lack of accountability of the pension funds to their beneficiaries, despite the volume of assets under their control. In 1980, pension funds controlled assets of approximately £55 billion, and yet many did not provide annual reports and accounts to present or future pension-ers. Despite these warning signals, by 1991 pension funds controlled £357 billion of assets and were still regulated only by general trust law, which failed to stop fraud on a massive scale by Robert Maxwell, and on a less dramatic but nonetheless tragic scale in a number of other sizeable pension funds.

While legislation introduced in the 1990s to improve protection against outright fraud appears to have been largely successful, other equally pressing issues have emerged. The prolonged stock market boom of the 1980s and 1990s left many company pension funds so well placed to meet their future liabilities that they were able to take contribution holidays. But the sharp downturn in equities markets from 2000 onwards, the less rosy outlook for future corporate earnings and dividends, and a rapid and largely unforeseen increase in life expectancy for retired people, put many pension funds back into deficit. As a result, companies were faced with the choice of closing schemes to new and possibly existing members, or setting aside large amounts from current profits to make good the deficits.

The increase in importance of both pension funds and life insurance companies as investment institutions has been largely the result of active government encouragement. Life assurance companies benefited from major tax advantages attached to life assurance policies until 1984, in the form of full tax relief at the taxpayer's marginal (i.e. highest) income tax rate on life assurance premiums; since that date, there are still certain advantages for particular types of life assurance savings schemes, especially for the higher rate taxpayer. Life assurance companies have also benefited from less stringent constraints on marketing, allowing them to employ salespeople who can 'cold call' potential policyholders at home. These advantages dated from the days when pension schemes were not widespread and pension benefits, such as they were, did not provide an adequate retirement income. Individuals catered for their own retirement through savings schemes related to life insurance, and to encourage this, the government accorded tax relief and marketing advantages for such investments.

Despite the reduction in tax incentives for individuals to save via life assurance policies, life assurance companies have continued to grow, this time helped by the government offering financial incentives to encourage private sector pension schemes. Since 1975, when legislation was introduced in the Social Security Pensions Act, companies have been obliged either to contract into the State Earnings Related Pension Scheme (SERPS) for their employees, or to provide their own scheme on equivalent or better terms. These privately organised pension schemes are either run as pension funds separate from the company, or managed by a bank or an insurance company on behalf of the company. In 1986, the Social Security Act also allowed employees (as well as the self-employed) to take out personal pension plans which are tied to individuals rather than to the company for which they work. At the same time, they offered financial incentives for employees to switch out of SERPS into private sector schemes. This gave a boost to life assurance companies, which are the main providers of personal pension plans. Thus, as pension schemes have spread and as benefits and hence contributions have been increased, so the assets of the pension funds (and insurance companies) have grown. Since contributions to pension schemes are generally tax-deductible at the individual's marginal tax rate, and the returns on investments made by pension funds are not liable to tax, investment in a pension fund can offer a more tax-efficient method of saving to the individual investor than does direct investment in stock exchange securities. However, aggressive selling of personal pensions has led in recent years to a number of mis-selling scandals.

Unit trusts and investment trusts, on the other hand, were not originally conceived as tax-efficient forms of saving for retirement. They were set up to offer small investors a way of holding a stake in a diversified portfolio of fixed interest securities and ordinary shares, an opportunity which was otherwise unavailable because of high transaction costs. Perhaps because unit and investment trusts have not had the same advantages of government support as insurance companies and pension funds, and also because investment trusts (as limited liability companies) have had to comply with company disclosure requirements, a greater tradition of disclosure of investment policy and investment performance has been established for these types of intermediary. For example, both the Investment Management Association (the umbrella organisation for unit trust managers) and the Association of Investment Trust Companies publish comprehensive monthly details of the past performance and the spread of investments of each unit or investment trust, albeit these are not presented on a fully risk-adjusted basis.

The next section of the chapter considers in more detail each of the four main types of investing institution: pension funds, insurance companies, investment trust companies and unit trusts. A brief description of each type of institution is given, how it arose, what its investment objectives are, and how these determine its investment strategy. The final part of the chapter is devoted to a discussion of the main areas of investment that have been affected by the growth of these investment institutions, for example the efficiency of the stock market, the role of stockbrokers and market makers, regulation, and, last but not least, the impact on the individual investor.

PENSION FUNDS

Description

From the 1960s until the turn of the century, the growth of the pension funds was the fastest of the four groups of investing institutions, rising from £2 billion of assets invested in the late 1950s to approximately £820 billion at the end of the 1990s, equivalent to over 16% annual average growth in nominal terms or 8% annual average growth in real terms. Table 10.3 gives a picture of the recent evolution of UK pension funds' assets from 1995 onwards. Unfortunately, one of the problems in talking about the pension funds and their investments is the lack of data concerning them. One reason for this is that, as we saw above, pension funds are not accountable to their beneficiaries in the same way as investment trusts are to their shareholders, and to date the level of disclosure of pension funds does not do justice to the volume of funds under their control.

Note that the section headed 'Investments in …' represents cross-holdings by pension funds in each of the other three types of institutional investment. As we explain later in this chapter, open-end funds and closed-end funds are the generic names for investments of the types represented respectively by unit trusts and by investment trust companies.

The figures in Table 10.3 show some clear trends:

○ The bursting of the stock market bubble led to a sharp fall in pension funds' total assets in 2002, largely recovered by 2004.
○ A move away from equities into bonds had become established well before 2000, although the shift is not as striking as it might appear at first sight; the increased investment in unit trusts (open-end funds) largely represents an increase in indirect holdings of equities.

This rapid overall increase in pension assets during the last 40 years of the twentieth century, whether controlled directly by pension funds or indirectly by insurance companies and unit trusts, is due, as we have already seen, to the extension of pension fund schemes to a greater proportion of the working population as a result of legislation; to

Table 10.3 Assets of UK pension funds

	end 1995		end 1999		end 2002		end 2004	
	£bn	%	£bn	%	£bn	%	£bn	%
Short-term liquid assets	26.1	5.1	32.7	4.0	30.7	4.9	57.5	7.2
UK public sector securities:								
Short gilts	14.4	2.8	21.9	2.7	11.8	1.9	11.1	1.4
Medium gilts	9.5	1.9	16.4	2.0	10.8	1.7	9.3	1.2
Long and undated gilts	4.7	0.9	17.6	2.1	14.7	2.4	20.8	2.6
Index-linked gilts	24.0	4.7	42.9	5.2	47.2	7.6	46.3	5.8
Other	0.3	0.1	0.7	0.1	0.8	0.1	0.7	0.1
	53.0	**10.3**	**99.6**	**12.1**	**85.3**	**13.7**	**88.3**	**11.0**
Ordinary shares:								
UK	256.6	50.0	357.2	43.5	186.4	30.0	180.6	22.6
Foreign	82.2	16.0	148.3	18.1	104.4	16.8	140.3	17.5
	338.8	**66.0**	**505.6**	**61.6**	**290.8**	**46.9**	**320.8**	**40.1**
Other securities (mostly bonds):								
UK companies	7.1	1.4	9.3	1.1	30.5	4.9	43.0	5.4
Foreign governments	11.7	2.3	16.7	2.0	16.0	2.6	15.1	1.9
Foreign companies	1.2	0.2	5.1	0.6	11.4	1.8	16.0	2.0
	20.0	**3.9**	**31.0**	**3.8**	**57.9**	**9.3**	**74.1**	**9.3**
Investments in:								
Open-end funds	29.4	5.7	70.1	8.5	73.3	11.8	131.1	16.4
Closed-end funds	0.5	0.1	3.8	0.5	4.1	0.7	13.1	1.6
Insurance-managed funds	19.7	3.8	42.0	5.1	40.6	6.5	67.9	8.5
	49.6	**9.7**	**115.9**	**14.1**	**118.0**	**19.0**	**212.2**	**26.5**
Loans and mortgages	0.2	0.0	0.0	0.0	0.1	0.0	0.0	0.0
Property assets	22.9	4.5	31.6	3.9	31.8	5.1	30.7	3.8
Other assets	2.5	0.5	4.4	0.5	5.8	0.9	17.1	2.1
Total	**513.0**	**100.0**	**820.9**	**100.0**	**620.4**	**100.0**	**800.7**	**100.0**

Source: Office for National Statistics.

higher earnings and benefits requiring greater contributions; to fiscal incentives offered by the government; and to the rise in the value of assets already managed, particularly during the bull markets of the 1980s and 1990s.

There are two ways in which individuals can save for their retirement. Either they can take out a ***personal pension plan***, or they might be employed by a company or other organisation which has an ***occupational pension plan*** for its own employees. Someone who takes out a personal pension plan will sign a contract with an insurance company which takes his or her contributions and invests them in a separate portfolio of assets which belongs exclusively to the individual. Once the individual reaches the chosen retirement age, the portfolio is sold and the proceeds may be used to purchase an ***annuity***. The value of the annuity will depend on how well the portfolio has been managed and how the market has performed; but it will also depend, crucially, on the level of the market at the point when the portfolio is realised, and also on the level of interest rates, because this will determine the value of the annuity purchased.

Occupational pensions are of two types. Traditionally, most such schemes were of the ***defined benefit*** type, whereby the employer promised to pay to the employee in retirement a pension based in some way on his or her earnings; either on his or her last year's earnings, or on some average of several years' earnings. A defined benefit pension might also be indexed, either against some retail prices index or, if the pensioner were lucky, against an earnings index (earnings growth tends to outstrip the growth in retail prices). The problems that began to surface from the late 1990s onwards have led an increasing number of employers to close down their defined benefit pension schemes and to replace them instead with *defined contribution* schemes, whereby one or both of the employer and the employee pays regular predetermined contributions (defined as a percentage of current salary) into a pension fund, and the value of the employee's pension on retirement is not guaranteed but is subject to all the same market factors as the personal pension plan described above.

Whether the scheme is defined benefit or defined contribution, certain features of an occupational scheme are the same. The contributions are paid into a fund which is legally entirely separate from the company. This usually operates as a legal trust, with the present and future pensioners as beneficiaries. The trustees, made up of representatives from management, current employees, pensioners and outside consultants, invest the contributions to provide pensions as required by the terms of the trust. Defined benefit pension funds are designed so that contributions from employees and the employer plus the income flow from the assets already held can normally meet the future pension payments. In the case of a defined benefit scheme, whereas the employees' contributions are usually fixed at a percentage of salary, the employer's contributions are determined by an actuarial calculation of the amount prospectively required to meet the employer's pension promises. This will depend on the characteristics of the workforce (with respect to age, sex, leaving rates, retirement ages, and so on), and the expected returns on the investment of the contributions over time. The actuary values the pension fund assets (investments) and liabilities (future pension liabilities) every three years to see if the fund is in surplus or deficit. The pension regulator, a role created under the Pensions Act 2004, will require any deficit to be covered over a period of 10 to 15 years. In the case of a defined contribution scheme, the employer will normally recommend a number of funds in which individuals can invest the company's and their own contributions. However, there is no promised pension. If the funds underperform and do not provide the expected pension, there is no obligation on the company to make up that deficit.

An actuary advising the trustees of a defined benefit fund has to be an expert in investment as well as in such matters as mortality rates. Actuaries will vary in their estimates of future cash flows according, for example, to the return they expect to be achieved from the pension fund investments over the next 10, 20 or 50 years. The more conservative the actuary's estimates of future returns on investment, the higher will be the employer's contributions to the pension fund. Less conservative actuaries will require lower contributions in the early years of the fund, with a higher probability that the employer will have to 'top up' the fund in later years. A major source of controversy in this area is the vexed question about the appropriate discount rate to be used to calculate the present value of the expected future payment obligations to pensioners, although the rate is usually based on a long-term gilt yield and this varies as gilt yields vary. The lower the discount rate, the higher the present value of the obligations, and the higher the potential fund deficit. Actuaries also encourage defined benefit schemes to reduce the risk that the assets will not be able to meet the liabilities, by encouraging them to move into bonds, particularly for the part of the fund related to pensions of employees whose entitlement is already known (such as people who have left the company's employment). However, the more that is invested in bonds, for a fund that already has a deficit, the less the fund can benefit from an upswing in the equity market.

More recently, actuaries and investment advisers have encouraged trustees to match interest rate risk more exactly. Instead of holding gilts to match known liabilities, trustees are now encouraged to lock into swap contracts, so that cash flows more exactly match liabilities 10, 20 or more years ahead.

One of the consequences of the bull equity markets of the 1980s and 1990s was the rapid rise in the value of pension fund assets (which were predominantly in equities) and the creation of a surplus of the present value of the assets in the fund over the present value of the liabilities of the fund. Indeed, in some cases, for example that of Dunlop, the pension fund became so large that it was worth more than the company itself! This led to some takeovers of companies (for example, BTR acquired Dunlop) where the acquirer was able to use the pension fund surplus to reduce future pension contributions and thus boost earnings after the acquisition. Indeed, in some cases, the acquirer was able to close the pension fund down, transfer the employees into the acquirer's own existing scheme, and take the surplus out as a reduction to the cost of the acquisition. In fear of this, many UK companies then declared pension contribution holidays themselves, reducing the cash inflows to pension funds from their previously high levels. Since 2000 the tables have turned, and more than one high-profile takeover has failed when the would-be acquirer has gained access to the books of both the company and its pension fund, and has discovered the true extent of the potential deficit that it would be assuming.

UK pension funds are exempt from income and corporation tax on their investments, except to the (usually very marginal) extent that any withholding taxes on income from overseas investment may not be recoverable. This tax exemption also includes profits from futures and options insofar as they are used for hedging rather than for trading purposes. Thus pension funds should be indifferent, other things being equal, between high and low-coupon gilts, and between dividends and capital gains on shares. Of course, other factors will influence the decision on which securities to choose, but unlike the individual investor with a high marginal tax rate, pension funds need not, in principle, take tax into account when making investment decisions.

Before we go on to discuss the investment objectives and policies of pension funds, it is useful to note that pensions do not have to be provided for via funded pension schemes, as is the norm in the United Kingdom and the United States. For example, in many continental European countries, UK-style pension funds have historically been the exception rather than the rule. Much commoner has been the unfunded or pay-as-you-go scheme, in which the company simply paid the pensions like any other trading expense out of current profits, or the government, as in the UK state pension scheme, out of current receipts. Despite the recent problems experienced by the UK corporate pension fund sector, the trend is towards the model of a separate, funded pension scheme, and there is rapid growth world-wide in pension fund assets.

Investment objectives and constraints

Given that pensions in the UK are usually funded through a separate pension fund, how are the contributions invested to provide in the best manner possible for future pension liabilities? What factors do pension fund managers take into consideration when making investment decisions?

One of the most contentious areas of defined pension fund management is how to decide on the objectives and policy of the fund. This is because there are a number of interested parties: shareholders, managers, trustees, employees, pensioners, actuaries, investment consultants and fund managers, some of whom may be taking on more than one role. Although they may all have the underlying objective for the fund of being able to pay pensions as and when required, they may have conflicting views on what the pension fund's investment objectives ought to be to do just that. In other words, given the future liabilities of the pension fund, how should its asset structure be determined and what level of risk should be assumed? For example, managers may wish to maximise the returns on the fund so that any surpluses made can be paid back to the company to boost earnings for shareholders. Trustees may wish to meet the liabilities of the fund with the minimum of risk, particularly as they are accountable for their actions. Alternatively, fund managers may have the investment objective of outperforming a specified stock market index. In practice, although trustees have the power to determine investment policy, they may have no expertise in this area and defer to the advice of investment consultants, actuaries, or fund managers responsible for the implementation of the investment policies and the management of the funds on a day-to-day basis.

The trust deed of a pension fund usually allows for the overall investment policy to be left to the discretion of the trustees, in consultation with the company and the investment advisers. The investment policy will usually be concerned with the asset mix: that is, the proportions that can be invested in each type of security, and with the desired expected return and risk constraints. Day-to-day decisions will be taken by the fund managers, who can be employees of the company, or more usually financial institutions such as investment banks or insurance companies. The pension funds managed by insurance companies will usually be in the form not of a trust fund but of a contract between the company and the insurance company. In these cases, the insurance company will normally have discretion over the investment policy.

Liabilities

Pension funds have very long-term liabilities. For example, an employee joining a company at the age of 20 will not in general become eligible for a pension for a further 40 or 45 years. We saw in Chapter 4 that one way of reducing risk is to 'match' assets and liabilities; so if, say, a pension liability will fall due in 20 years' time, an asset can be bought that will also mature in 20 years' time, and which will exactly cover the liability. It is thus likely that pension funds, with substantial long-term liabilities, will hold long-term assets. For example, as can be seen in Table 10.3, in so far as pension funds hold gilts, these are either long-dated or undated.

However, this risk reduction strategy only works if the liabilities and the assets are subject to the same economic effects. If, for example, a liability is fixed in real terms and the matching asset is fixed in nominal terms, there is a risk that the asset will not be worth enough in real terms to match the liability. Corporate pensions in the United Kingdom are usually linked to final salaries, and final salaries are typically linked to average earnings.

In recent years, UK average earnings have grown by an average of 2¾ per cent over the rate of inflation. So by investing in gilts, pension funds run the risk of not earning a high enough real rate of return, particularly if inflation is higher than expected over the investment period. This is why pension funds have been substantial investors in index-linked gilts since they were first issued in 1981, as these offer guaranteed real rates of return of 2% or so, enough to keep pace with the liabilities of final salary-related future pensions.

Another consequence of the need to match assets with liabilities that are increasing with inflation has been a search for assets that are seen to be hedges against inflation. One such type of asset is property, and this performed well in the 1970s when gilts were earning negative real rates of return in a high-inflation environment. By 1980 pension funds held 18 per cent of their assets in property. However, property became unpopular in the 1980s when it failed to act as an inflation hedge, and it underperformed equities as an asset class, and by 1995 it represented only about 5 per cent of pension fund assets. Since then, property has performed well, and pension funds have slightly increased their weighting in property as a result.

Asset mix

As can be seen in Tables 10.1 and 10.3, the emphasis in UK pension fund portfolios was historically on equities, at least until the mid to late 1990s. The attraction of equities is that, of all the securities available for investment, only equities are likely to provide a substantial real rate of return, approximately equal to GNP growth. So whereas actuaries will phrase a pension fund's objectives in terms of the need to achieve a certain real rate of return, trustees may ask fund managers to try to match a stock market index, such as the FTSE All-Share Index. The implicit assumption is that share prices will match GNP growth, providing a growth pattern to match that of the liabilities, and hence that the fund will be able to meet pension payments in the future. This assumption was brought sharply into question by the sustained stock market downturn after 2000, and that has led many pension funds to invest part of their assets in so-called 'alternative assets', most particularly hedge funds which promise absolute returns, independent of stock market movements. At the same time, the low and stable level of inflation has enabled bonds to regain some of the attraction they had lost in the volatile bond market conditions which lasted from the 1970s to the early 1990s. However, although more stable, recent low bond yields have had the effect of increasing the present value of future pension fund liabilities, and hence reducing pension fund surpluses or increasing pension fund deficits.

While UK pension funds have been steadily reducing their exposure to UK equities, the proportion of total funds invested in foreign equities remained reasonably steady at about 16–18 per cent in the period 1995–2004. One of the arguments raised against pension funds investing overseas is that UK pension fund liabilities are expressed in sterling terms, and assets denominated in foreign currencies cannot be matched to these liabilities because of exchange risk. However, as will be discussed in Chapter 11, exchange risk is not as substantial as it first appears, and the benefits of international diversification more than outweigh the added exchange risk on only part of a large portfolio. There is an entirely separate political question whether pension funds ought to invest for the good of the domestic economy. This issue was raised in a famous court case between trustees appointed by the National Union of Mineworkers and trustees appointed by the National Coal Board in 1984. The union-appointed trustees argued against

---

Box 10.2 The Boots pension fund

Although pension funds had been quietly reducing their dependence on equity investment for several years, the announcement in November 2001 that over a 15-month period ending in July of that year, the trustees of the Boots pension fund had replaced their entire equity holdings with government bonds took the financial community by complete surprise. Headlines about 'the death of the cult of equity' became commonplace, but the significance of the move was widely misinterpreted. John Ralfe, the head of corporate finance at Boots who was the architect of the new strategy, made it clear that it was based not on a simplistic 'picking-winners' view that bonds were likely to 'do better' than equities in the coming years, but rather on a relative risk assessment. He made the point that as Boots itself was already leveraged (that is, was financed partially by debt), to invest the pension fund in the equity of other, similarly leveraged companies was to expose his own company (and its present and future pensioners) to an unacceptable risk of 'double leverage'.

Just three years later, in November 2004, Boots pension fund was in the news again, when the trustees decided to shift 15 per cent of the fund's assets back into equities. This decision was prompted by the problem of finding sufficient bonds with maturities over 30 years to match the fund's longest-term liabilities. A group of 160 pensioners protested loudly about what they saw as a reckless decision to put their pensions at risk. Their spokesman was a former employee who had left the company in 2002 to become a consultant – John Ralfe. A case of the 'boot being on the other foot'?

---

international investment; academic expert witnesses put the case for portfolio theory in an international context. The academics won.

Employee and employer contributions to a defined benefit pension scheme represent a form of contractual saving from the employee's point of view. Employees have no choice about where their contributions are invested, nor can they usually decide how much to contribute; their payments are automatically deducted from their pay. This enables pension fund managers to be more or less certain of how much new money they will have to invest each month or quarter, at least in the short to medium term. This regular inflow of new money has two effects on investment strategy.

○ It allows investment managers to alter the balance of their portfolios with the new money, without having to sell part of the existing holdings. This should lead to lower portfolio turnover and transaction costs than, say, investment trusts, which have no regular new inflow of funds.

○ Pension fund managers can follow a form of investment strategy known as ***pound averaging***. By spreading the purchases of securities over the peaks and troughs of the market, pension fund managers can ensure that the average cost of these securities will be at their average prices, rather than at their peak prices, over a period. In practice, pension funds may not do this, preferring instead to keep the new money in cash until they judge that the moment is right for investment in shares or gilts, whatever the efficient markets hypothesis may say.

The evidence on whether pension fund managers are good at picking just the right moment to get in or out of a market is mixed. For example, pension funds in general withheld from investment in equities during the fourth quarter of 1974, despite the fact that shares were at what was in retrospect a 15-year low. Similarly, before the crash of 1987, they had the highest ever proportion of equities in their portfolios at over 85 per cent, compared with an average during the five previous years of 63 per cent. By way of contrast, Table 10.3 shows that pension funds reduced their proportionate investment in equities before the market falls in 2000. Between 1995 and 1999 their holdings in equities fell from 66.0 per cent to 61.6 per cent of their total assets. This was not enough to be protected from the prolonged bear market which began in 2000 and ended in March 2003. By 2002, equities represented only 46.9 per cent of their total assets.

The traditional view on asset mix in periods of low inflation, reflected in the Trustee Investments Act 1961, was that it was advisable to place the bulk of the funds in fixed interest securities such as gilts. As the rate of inflation increased in the 1960s and 1970s, asset mixes were adjusted to allow higher proportions to be invested in equities and property, which, as mentioned earlier, were viewed as better inflation hedges. By the 1980s, property had become unpopular as an inflation hedge and the cult of the equity had taken over. It became the norm for pension funds to place the bulk of their investments into both UK and overseas shares. Even the crash of 1987 did not dent their enthusiasm; pension funds still held 68 per cent of equities in their portfolios (of which 16 per cent were overseas shares) at the end of 1988, and the percentage was back up to 74 per cent (with 20 per cent in overseas shares) by the end of 1991, despite the Japanese market crash. As Table 10.3 shows, the proportion of assets held in equities fell back below 50 per cent after the 2000 to 2003 market falls.

A common way of deciding on the asset mix, taking the impact of inflation into account, is to fund the liabilities that have crystallised, such as the future pensions of employees who have left (whose pensions will be based on their known leaving salaries) with assets that have future values fixed in nominal terms – usually gilts – and to fund the uncertain future liabilities with assets that should maintain their value in real terms – usually equities.

Who benefits?

However, before the optimal level of risk in the fund, and hence the optimal asset mix, can be determined, the question must be asked who will benefit or suffer from the risks and returns of the pension fund portfolio. If, as is most common for company defined benefit pension schemes, pension benefits are fixed in relation to final earnings, the company will benefit from good performance by being able to make reduced contributions in the future, and correspondingly suffer from poor performance by being asked to make increased contributions in the future. This has been made more transparent with the phased introduction, from 2001 onwards, of UK accounting standard FRS17, and the international accounting standard IAS19, which require companies to reflect the change in the pension fund surplus or deficit in their published annual results. So in the cases where pension rights are linked to salary and not pension fund performance, the risk that the assets of the pension fund will be less than or greater than its liabilities will be felt more by the shareholders of the company than by the legal beneficiaries of the fund.

Given that in these instances the shareholders of the company may be more concerned with the risk and return of the pension fund than are the pensioners, the question of optimal asset mix should perhaps be considered from the shareholders' point of view. For example, it is likely that when the stock market as a whole does badly, and hence the pension fund's equity portfolio suffers, the company will be required to top up its contributions at a time when it too is suffering, and is least able to do so. In this way, equities in a pension fund portfolio will increase the volatility of the company's earnings and hence the risk borne by the shareholders of the company. In contrast, fixed interest investments in the portfolio would reduce this risk without affecting the pensioners' expected benefits. So by considering who actually benefits or suffers from pension fund performance in the long term, we may reach a different view of what constitutes the optimal asset mix from that usually held. Instead of investing in risky equities and property, perhaps pension fund managers should be concentrating on investing in lower-risk fixed interest securities. However, this brings us back to the inadequacy of most fixed interest investments as matches of liabilities growing in real terms.

In the case of defined contribution schemes and personal pension plans, pension rights are entirely dependent on fund performance; pensions are increased when the fund does well and reduced when it does badly. In these cases it will be the beneficiaries of the pension fund who suffer or benefit from the risk and return of the pension fund portfolio. Such pension plans are managed by an insurance company or other fund manager, and future pensioners have to trust the fund manager to decide whether the level of risk is appropriate for them. In many cases, individuals can choose which types of investments to invest in, by selecting index-linked gilt funds, US growth stocks and so on. The danger here is that individuals do not understand the level of risk they are bearing, and do not realise the benefits of having a number of funds when they, rather than the company, are taking the risk of the final outcome not being as high as expected.

A similar dilemma arises when we consider how the risk of the pension fund portfolio should be measured. In Chapter 2, we chose to measure the riskiness of securities and portfolios by their standard deviations, whereas in Chapter 7 we saw that according to the CAPM, investors are only rewarded for the beta element of risk in their portfolios, because the remaining risk of their portfolios can largely be diversified away. Applying this approach to the pension fund problem, if the shareholders of the company effectively bear the portfolio risk, the pension fund's beta will be the appropriate measure of risk, since it can be assumed that the shareholders hold these shares as part of a diversified portfolio. However, if the pensioners bear the risk, as they may do in the case of personal pensions, where their pensions are linked to their funds' performance, it must be remembered that the assets of the pension fund probably represent the major portion of their savings, especially if they are not home owners. In this case, the standard deviation as a measure of total risk might be a more appropriate measure of risk. As we shall see in Chapter 12, a risk measure appropriate to the persons at risk must be chosen before any comparable estimates of performance can be made.

INSURANCE COMPANIES

Description

We now turn to the second in our list of types of investing institution, insurance companies. UK insurance companies had assets of £4.9 billion in 1957, twice the size of the assets of UK pension funds, which were then just about to start their rapid period of growth. By 2004, as we can see from Tables 10.3, 10.4 and 10.5, UK pension funds had total assets of £800.7 billion compared with UK insurance company assets of £1,109.3

billion, 38.5 per cent more than pension funds. The insurance company assets were for two types of business, general and long-term, with £115.3 billion and £994.0 billion respectively in each.

The benefits of reducing risk through pooling by an insurance company are clear. We saw in Chapter 2 that if the risks of different events of the same type occurring are pooled, the combined risk is less than if the risks were borne separately. The degree of risk reduction depends on how independent of each other the underlying events are: that is, on the correlation between them.

For example, it has been shown that the correlation between the risks of any two houses being burgled depends primarily on their proximity to each other. It is usually possible to quantify correlations between events of this sort fairly reliably by looking at past experience. If an insurance company were to take on several thousand house contents policies, it could be reasonably certain of the likely percentage of claims on those policies, and could charge a premium to take account of the fact that the risk borne by each individual house owner would be reduced through pooling. Of course, the insurance company would need to cover its expenses; and if it was organised as a profit-making company rather than along mutual lines, it would also require a fair return for the risks borne by its shareholders, so the reduction in premium charged would not reflect in full the statistical benefit of pooling. In this type of example, historical data would give a good indication of likely future events.

As well as carrying out a pure insurance role, many insurance companies have evolved as investment intermediaries. This is partly because of the nature of life assurance itself. The term *assurance* is used where a benefit is always going to be paid (for example, if not on death then on expiry of the policy), as opposed to *insurance*, where a benefit is only paid if an event such as a theft occurs. Assurance is therefore an ideal medium for policyholders seeking to protect their dependants from financial loss caused by their premature death, while also seeking to provide an income for their own old age. Most life policies provide benefit on expiry of the term of the policy after, say, 10 or 20 years, or on earlier death. This contrasts with non-life policies, where no benefit is paid if the event does not occur during the term of the policy. Life policies therefore vary from pure term insurance, which only pays out if death occurs during the policy's term, to long-term savings schemes with an element of insurance attached, to provide the benefits earlier in the event of premature death.

The activities of insurance companies can thus be split into two: general business and long-term business (life assurance, pensions business, insurance-related long-term savings policies and long-term sickness insurance). Tables 10.4 and 10.5 give a good idea of their relative sizes, with long-term business by far the most important in terms of assets. Many insurance companies carry out both activities, and most large UK insurance companies are what is known as *composites*, although some choose to specialise in either general or in life business. However, whether specialist or composite, insurance companies are required by law to manage and report the two activities separately, to prevent cross-funding of two basically very different types of business.

General insurance

In this field, which includes household and motor insurance, policies are usually taken out for periods of one year at a time. Claims related to these policies are mostly

Table 10.4 Assets of UK insurance companies' general funds

	end 1995		end 1999		end 2002		end 2004	
	£bn	%	£bn	%	£bn	%	£bn	%
Short-term liquid assets	19.2	29.0	30.4	36.1	41.6	44.3	51.7	44.9
UK public sector securities:								
Short gilts	8.1	12.3	10.1	12.0	11.5	12.3	14.0	12.1
Medium gilts	5.6	8.5	5.0	5.9	6.0	6.3	5.1	4.5
Long and undated gilts	0.2	0.3	0.3	0.3	0.1	0.2	0.2	0.1
Index-linked gilts	0.4	0.6	0.6	0.7	0.7	0.8	0.3	0.3
Other	0.1	0.2	0.1	0.1	0.0	0.0	0.1	0.1
	14.5	**21.9**	**16.0**	**19.0**	**18.4**	**19.6**	**19.8**	**17.1**
Ordinary shares:								
UK	12.8	19.4	13.1	15.6	6.8	7.2	8.7	7.6
Foreign	2.7	4.1	3.4	4.0	1.9	2.0	1.8	1.5
	15.5	**23.5**	**16.5**	**19.6**	**8.7**	**9.3**	**10.5**	**9.1**
Other securities (mostly bonds):								
UK companies	4.2	6.4	4.7	5.6	6.9	7.3	9.9	8.6
Foreign governments	6.5	9.8	8.0	9.5	7.2	7.6	6.7	5.8
Foreign companies	1.7	2.6	2.9	3.4	5.5	5.8	9.8	8.5
	12.5	**18.8**	**15.6**	**18.5**	**19.5**	**20.8**	**26.3**	**22.8**
Investment in:								
Unit trusts	0.4	0.5	1.3	1.6	1.7	1.8	1.9	1.7
Loans and mortgages	1.3	2.0	1.1	1.3	1.1	1.1	2.4	2.1
Property assets	2.7	4.0	1.7	2.0	1.1	1.1	1.4	1.2
Other assets	0.2	0.2	1.5	1.8	1.9	2.0	1.3	1.1
Total	**66.2**	**100.0**	**84.0**	**100.0**	**94.0**	**100.0**	**115.3**	**100.0**

Source: Office for National Statistics.

settled fairly quickly (though some claims, such as those associated with Hurricane Katrina which hit New Orleans in 2005, take much longer to settle), and this reduces the insurance companies' ability to build up long-term reserves except out of profit. Clearly, the investments held to meet these claims have to be in fairly liquid form. So in Table 10.4, we can see that 57 per cent of the total assets related to general insurance business were held in short-term liquid assets and short-dated gilts in 2004, compared with an equivalent figure of under 13 per cent for long-term business. Although longer-term investments, in the form of equities and property holdings, are held by insurance companies to back the risks of general insurance, the proportion of their funds invested in this way has fallen sharply in recent years.

Long-term funds

This is mostly life assurance and pension-related business. Since we have already looked at pension funds in the previous section, we concentrate here on life assurance savings-related business. The United Kingdom is one of the most heavily 'life-assured' markets in the world. The reasons for the success of the life assurance industry in the United Kingdom are the aggressive sales techniques adopted and the success in linking life assurance to savings policies attached to mortgages or pensions.

Life assurance policies range from straightforward *annuity* business (where regular

Table 10.5 Assets of UK insurance companies' long-term funds

	end 1995 £bn	%	end 1999 £bn	%	end 2002 £bn	%	end 2004 £bn	%
Short-term liquid assets	31.6	6.3	75.5	7.9	98.9	11.3	97.7	9.8
UK public sector securities:								
Short gilts	7.2	1.4	18.2	1.9	23.9	2.7	28.1	2.8
Medium gilts	37.4	7.5	43.4	4.6	40.3	4.6	48.3	4.9
Long and undated gilts	26.9	5.4	44.8	4.7	44.7	5.1	52.0	5.2
Index-linked gilts	8.9	1.8	19.8	2.1	22.4	2.5	28.7	2.9
Other	1.6	0.3	2.3	0.2	1.8	0.2	2.3	0.2
	81.8	**16.4**	**128.5**	**13.5**	**133.1**	**15.1**	**159.3**	**16.0**
Ordinary shares:								
UK	199.2	39.9	369.9	38.9	230.8	26.3	240.0	24.1
Foreign	57.1	11.4	112.3	11.8	80.2	9.1	89.7	9.0
	256.3	**51.3**	**482.2**	**50.6**	**311.0**	**35.4**	**329.7**	**33.2**
Other securities (mostly bonds):								
UK companies	35.2	7.0	85.4	9.0	147.5	16.8	152.1	15.3
Foreign governments	8.8	1.8	18.5	1.9	19.8	2.2	20.2	2.0
Foreign companies	2.8	0.6	8.4	0.9	30.5	3.5	40.4	4.1
	46.8	**9.4**	**112.3**	**11.8**	**197.8**	**22.5**	**212.7**	**21.4**
Investment in:								
Unit trusts	38.2	7.6	84.5	8.9	65.3	7.4	95.0	9.6
Loans and mortgages	7.3	1.5	10.9	1.1	11.0	1.3	12.9	1.3
Property assets	36.1	7.2	51.7	5.4	53.1	6.0	60.9	6.1
Other assets	1.6	0.3	6.4	0.7	8.8	1.0	26.0	2.6
Total	**499.6**	**100.0**	**952.0**	**100.0**	**879.0**	**100.0**	**994.0**	**100.0**

Source: Office for National Statistics.

savings or a lump sum entitle the policyholder to an annuity in the future) to *with-profits* policies, where life assurance is only a small element of the policy and the bulk of the premiums are invested in stock market securities on the policyholder's behalf.

Given the long-term nature of life assurance policies and of the pensions business carried out by insurance companies, funds need to be invested by the insurance companies for long periods of time. If we look at Table 10.5, we can see that this is reflected in the type of securities held for long-term business. For example, in 2004, 33.2 per cent of total assets were invested in equities and a further 6.1 per cent in property. Similarly, the gilts and other bonds held were mostly those with a maturity of at least five years.

Note the significant element of cross-investment by insurance companies in the unit trust sector. Comparison of Table 10.5 with Table 10.7 shows that one-third of all investments in UK authorised unit trusts are held by insurance companies.

Both types of insurance, general and long-term, are taxed on their profits, essentially defined to be income including investment profits less expenditure including management charges. However, taxation on long-term business is complex, varying according to whether it is pension (tax-exempt), with-profits, or annuity business. The standard rate of corporation tax, currently 30 per cent, is charged on long-term business unless the profits relate to investments destined for policyholders, in which case it is reduced to the current lower rate of income tax.

This tax treatment for life assurance business has two effects. First, because they do pay tax, insurance companies are not generally gross investors like the pension funds (except on pensions business). Second, the effect of investors choosing to invest via life assurance-linked savings schemes is that the tax advantage of so doing is less than investing via a gross pension scheme, but superior to investing via a unit or investment trust. This is because payouts on *qualifying insurance policies*, for example, are exempt from income tax in the hands of the recipient, since the insurance company is already deemed to have paid tax, and this advantage will be particularly beneficial to a higher-rate taxpayer.

Investment objectives and constraints

In the same way as for pension funds, we now examine in more detail the factors affecting the investment decisions of insurance companies.

Liabilities

Originally, insurance companies concentrated on offering fixed benefits from long-term savings plans, for example a fixed lump sum or an agreed annuity. The maturities of these policies could be matched with those of long-term, fixed-interest securities, notably gilts, enabling the insurance companies to provide benefits fixed in nominal terms (subject only to the risk of changes in interest rates at which premiums and coupons on the securities could be reinvested). As we saw in Chapter 4, one way to reduce interest rate risk to a minimum is to immunise the investment portfolio. This can be done by matching the duration of the assets to the duration of the liabilities. If it does this, the insurance company is sure of being able to meet its future liabilities whether interest rates go up, stay the same or go down.

An extreme version of duration matching is cash flow matching, where every coupon and principal repayment of every bond is chosen to exactly match a particular cash flow payment on policies. A less onerous version is simply to ensure that the average durations of the assets and liabilities match, without making the cash flows exactly match. This type of risk reduction exploits the fact that duration takes into account the coupon and life of every bond to work out its likely price movement given an interest change. It does the same for a bond portfolio. Provided the estimated change in present value on the bond portfolio for a given change in interest rates is matched by the estimated change in the present value of the liabilities for the same interest rate change, the insurance company will be able to meet its liabilities.

Fixed benefit savings plans became less popular during the 1960s and 1970s, as inflation began to erode the value of the fixed benefits when received. So in the 1980s insurance companies began to market more with-profits policies linked primarily to equities rather than fixed interest securities, since equities were perceived to be a better long-run hedge against inflation. It must be remembered that insurance companies act predominantly as intermediaries for the savings elements of these policies, passing on the majority of the investment risks to the policyholders. If they cannot immunise their liabilities through duration matching, insurance companies prefer not to commit themselves on the actual benefits to be paid, usually guaranteeing only a low fixed benefit plus a bonus related to investment performance – a with-profits policy.

There are two types of with-profits policy: *endowment* and *unit-linked*. Endowment policies are sold every year and the funds invested in a large pool. Each year a certain number of the endowment policies mature and a terminal bonus is declared. The size of this bonus is a function of how well the fund has done over the past few years and of how competitive the market for life assurance is. The more competitive the market, the higher the terminal bonus will be in order to draw in new business. However, the major effect of the insurance company having the right to decide on the terminal bonus is to smooth the bonuses over time. If a policy matures in a *bull market*, the payout will not be as high as that on a unit-linked policy, which is a direct function of the value of the units on maturity; if a policy matures in a *bear market,* the endowment policyholder should do better than the unit-linked holder whose payout will reflect depressed shares prices. In other words, unit-linked holders bear more risk than endowment policyholders, who share market risk with other endowment policyholders over time.

Asset mix

However, although primarily invested in equities, many of the with-profits policies retain some gilts for diversification and risk reduction purposes. Annuity policy premiums are entirely invested in gilts with suitable maturities. As a result, a higher proportion of the long-term business liabilities of insurance companies is invested in gilts than may be the case for pension funds, less of whose liabilities are fixed in nominal terms and which may have a more aggressive approach to equity investment to meet their longer-term liabilities.

The insurance industry is heavily controlled by law, as evidenced, for example, by the careful separation of general and long-term business. The aim of the legislation is to try to prevent insurance companies from being unable to meet claims and to minimise the risk of fraud, a potential problem with any form of investment intermediary, particularly one that has control of the policyholders' funds for ten years or more.

For example, UK insurance companies involved in general business are required to maintain certain solvency margins (expressed as a ratio of net assets to net premiums written). UK legislation does not specify exactly which type of securities insurance companies must hold, in contrast to a number of countries including the United States, where insurance companies are restricted, predominantly to investing in fixed interest securities. This restriction does not, however, prevent problems since US insurers were big investors in property and *junk bonds* during the 1980s, which caused some insurance companies to declare bankruptcy.

In the UK, during the 1970s and 1980s, insurance companies found that nominal premiums and claims were increasing by more than the rate of inflation. They therefore tried to ensure that the market value of their assets also increased, in order for solvency margins to be maintained and to allow them to expand as they wished. They switched emphasis from fixed interest securities to investments such as equities which were more likely to maintain their value in real terms. However, too great a dependence on risky assets increases the probability of reduced solvency margins, and this caused some insurance companies to switch from equities back to bonds from the early 1990s onwards.

In terms of profits, general insurance companies depend to a great extent on their returns from investment to make a profit. Underwriting losses (from claims exceeding premiums paid) can be more than offset by profits generated by good management of the premiums invested. Portfolio performance can make all the difference between a profitable and loss-making general insurance company.

INVESTMENT TRUST COMPANIES, UNIT TRUSTS AND OPEN-END INVESTMENT COMPANIES

Although they have different histories and legal structures, we shall treat all these types of investing institution in the same section since they have similar investment objectives and policies.

The superficially most striking difference between the two longest established institutions, the investment trust company (ITC or *investment trust*) and the *unit trust*, is a matter of legal form: an ITC is incorporated as a limited liability company, raising capital from investors by issuing shares on the stock exchange, whereas a unit trust is not an incorporated entity at all but a trust, raising capital by issuing investment units to investors. This legal difference has a very important economic consequence. Investors in ITCs are like shareholders in any other company: unless their ITC goes into liquidation or is taken over, the only way they can realise their investment is by selling it in the secondary market at whatever price the secondary market is willing to pay, although in order to avoid the risk of a low secondary market price, some investment trusts have set dates on which they will be wound up, the investments sold, and the proceeds distributed to creditors and shareholders. Once an ITC is launched it is closed to new funds, unless it makes a rights issue, hence the generic term *closed-end fund*.

Units in a unit trust are not quoted on the stock exchange, but can be bought from or sold to the managers of the trust, who are obliged to repay existing units to investors on demand, and to issue new units to new investors wishing to participate in the trust. Since a unit trust is open to new money being invested in it, it is called an *open-end fund*. As we shall see later in this section, this difference has a crucial significance for the pricing of shares in ITCs and of units in unit trusts, and has been the subject of one of the most persistent anomalies in the application of the efficient markets hypothesis.

In 1997 UK law was amended to allow the incorporation of open-ended investment vehicles in the form of limited companies which (unlike any other type of

---

> **Box 10.3 Equitable Life**
>
> Equitable Life is the UK's oldest mutual life insurance company, with a continuous history going back to 1762. Traditionally it has been a prominent provider of insurance and annuities to the professional classes. From the 1970s onwards it wrote policies with a so-called guaranteed annuity rate (GAR), which effectively guaranteed the policy holder an annual bonus. As long as inflation and interest rates remained high, the company had little problem honouring these promises. But when interest and inflation rates fell from the mid-1990s onwards, the company found it was unable to meet its GAR promises and maintain payments to the million or so customers who did not have GAR policies. The company applied to the court for a ruling that would enable it to escape from its GAR obligations, but although successful in the lower court it lost on appeal. As a result it was plunged into the most severe financial crisis to have afflicted a major UK insurance company in modern times. In order to contain the damage it closed its doors to new business and eventually the healthy 'rump' of its business was taken over by the Halifax.
>
> One ironic feature of the protracted and tortuous litigation which surrounded this scandal was that as Equitable Life was the insurer of choice to the legal profession, it was difficult to find judges to sit on the case who did not have a personal conflict of interest!

limited company) are permitted to issue and buy back shares on a continuous basis. These are known as ***open-end investment companies*** (or ***OEICs*** – pronounced 'oiks') and correspond closely to the continental European model of a *société d'investissement à capital variable* (investment company with variable capital) or *SICAV*. The majority of new UK unitised investment funds are now launched in the form of OEICs, and some unit trusts have converted to become OEICs. OEICs are in principle cheaper to run, as several funds can be run via one OEIC structure, whereas unit trusts require one trust per fund.

Description

Investment trusts

We start with the older of the two, investment trusts, which have been in existence for more than 150 years. Originally designed to offer the small investor a way of holding a diversified portfolio, the emphasis of investment trusts had switched from being invested in fixed interest securities before the Second World War to being predominantly invested in shares. There has always been a strong international flavour to investment trust portfolios, as can be seen in Table 10.6, where 40 per cent of total UK investment trust assets were invested in overseas securities in 2004. Assets have grown from £1.1 billion in 1957 to £47 billion in 2004, representing an annual average growth rate of 8 %. This conceals a decline in real terms in the 1970s (when many investment trusts were wound up, converted to unit trusts, or taken

Table 10.6 Assets of UK investment trust companies

	end 1995 £bn	%	end 1999 £bn	%	end 2002 £bn	%	end 2004 £bn	%
UK public sector securities:								
Short gilts	0.5	1.1	1.1	2.0	0.4	1.1	0.4	0.8
Medium gilts	0.5	1.2	0.1	0.1	0.0	0.1	0.1	0.2
Long and undated gilts	0.1	0.3	0.0	0.0	0.0	0.0	0.0	0.0
Index-linked gilts	0.1	0.2	0.0	0.0	0.0	0.0	0.0	0.0
Other	0.2	0.4	0.0	0.0	0.0	0.0	0.0	0.0
	1.4	**3.1**	**1.2**	**2.1**	**0.5**	**1.3**	**0.5**	**1.0**
Ordinary shares:								
UK	19.4	44.7	28.0	48.9	19.5	51.3	23.9	50.7
Foreign	19.5	44.9	23.3	40.7	14.5	38.1	19.0	40.2
	38.9	**89.5**	**51.3**	**89.7**	**33.9**	**89.4**	**42.9**	**90.9**
Other securities (mostly bonds):								
UK companies	0.8	1.9	1.4	2.5	0.9	2.5	1.3	2.7
Foreign governments	0.3	0.7	0.7	1.2	0.1	0.4	0.0	0.1
Foreign companies	0.7	1.7	1.0	1.7	0.5	1.8	0.7	1.4
	1.9	**4.4**	**3.1**	**5.4**	**1.5**	**4.6**	**2.0**	**4.2**
Investment in:								
Unit trusts	0.3	0.7	0.1	0.1	0.0	0.1	0.1	0.3
Property and other assets	1.0	2.3	1.5	2.7	1.8	4.7	1.7	3.6
Total	**43.4**	**100.0**	**57.3**	**100.0**	**37.7**	**100.0**	**47.2**	**100.0**

Source: Office for National Statistics.

over), followed by a minor resurgence in the late 1990s and early 2000s, with numerous issues of so-called *split capital trusts* (see below, Box 10.4).

Investors in ITCs acquire the ordinary shares of the ITCs, and their return is therefore in the form of dividends and capital gains or losses from their shares. ITCs use the funds raised from shareholders to invest in a diversified or specialised portfolio of securities. New money for investment can only come from a rights issue or from borrowing, either from a bank or by issuing debt such as debentures or loan stock. This ability to raise fixed interest capital allows the ITCs to leverage and to effectively increase their beta. When interest rates are low, as in the late 1990s and early 2000s, fixed interest rate loans are commonly raised by ITCs in order to take advantage of this leverage potential.

Example 10.1 illustrates the impact of leverage on the ordinary shareholders of Wary Investment Trust. Because of the fixed interest loan stock in issue, an increase of 20 per cent in the market value of the all-equity portfolio managed by Wary Investment Trust would lead to a 27 per cent increase in the net assets belonging to Wary shareholders. However, a decline in the value of Wary's portfolio would have a similarly magnified detrimental effect on the value of Wary's net assets.

Since investment in ITCs is via the purchase of stock exchange-listed ordinary shares, one might expect an ITC's share price to be equal to the market value per share of the underlying investment portfolio which is held on behalf of the shareholders. However, this has not been the case in practice, and ITC share prices commonly stand at a discount and occasionally at a premium to their underlying portfolio or net asset value. Recent discounts have been of the order of 15–20% on average, although they can be greater. Many reasons have been put forward to explain this phenomenon, which implies that shares held through the medium of an investment trust are in some way less valuable than if they were held directly. Suggestions have included the limited marketability of some ITC shares and the fact that investment trusts do not distribute 100 per cent of the income they receive, some being absorbed by management costs and some reinvested. (To qualify as an investment trust for tax purposes, ITCs must distribute at least 85 per cent of their investment income.)

Premiums on net asset value, which sometimes exist on ITC shares, are just as difficult to explain. In these cases, investors are paying a premium for management of the portfolio. This implies either that investment trust managers are credited with superior stock selection skills (although this is unlikely to be a permanent feature – see the discussions in

Example 10.1 Effects of leverage on Wary Investment Trust shareholders

	£ million
Market value of all-equity portfolio	100
Less: 5% Loan Stock due 2020	-25
Net assets attributable to ordinary shareholders	75
If the value of the all-equity portfolio increases by 20%:	
Market value of all-equity portfolio	120
Less: 5% Loan Stock due 2020	-25
Net assets attributable to ordinary shareholders	95
representing an increase of	26.7%

Chapters 1 and 12 on efficient markets) or that they have created a portfolio that could not easily be replicated by the shareholders on an individual basis.

Whatever the reasons for premiums or discounts on the net asset value of ITC shares, their existence adds an extra dimension of risk to investment in ITC shares when compared with buying shares directly. An investor in ITC shares takes on not only the risk of the underlying investments but also the risk that the level of premium or discount will change. This will affect the holding period return in a positive or negative way depending on whether the discount, for example, has narrowed or widened.

If large discounts persist, there are various ways in which they can be reduced or removed. One method would be for a corporate to acquire 100 per cent of the ITC and realise the assets. Alternatively, a pension fund could acquire the trust and hence a ready-made equity portfolio for a relatively low cost. Aware of their vulnerability to takeover if the discounts to net asset value are large enough, ITCs have evolved a variety of methods to combat the threat. One method is to convert the ITC into a unit trust. As we shall

---

Box 10.4 Split capital trusts

Split capital trusts gave a new lease of life to the investment trust sector in the late 1990s and early 2000s: by July 2002, out of a total of 383 UK investment trusts, 111 were split capital.

In a split capital trust, the subscribed capital is divided into different share classes, each designed to meet the financial needs of a different type of investor. The three commonest types are **zero dividend preference shares, income shares** and **capital shares**.

Zero dividend preference shares (commonly known as *zeros*) receive no dividend but are entitled to a predetermined capital sum on the winding up date of the trust – provided the investments have grown over the life of the ITC at what is known as the 'hurdle rate'. The lower the hurdle rate, the less risk that the assets will not cover the capital sum. Zeros were marketed to private investors as a deferred high-yield security, with returns in the form of capital gains which could be offset against the individual annual capital gains tax allowance. Income shares typically have the right to receive all the dividend income from the underlying securities but take low priority for return of capital on winding up. Capital shares have no right to dividends but are entitled to whatever capital is left on winding up after payment in full to zero and income shareholders.

In order to be able to pay high promised dividends on income shares, at a time of low bond yields, ITC fund managers invested their funds in higher-risk corporate bonds but also in the income shares of other split capital funds. These cross-holdings, coupled with substantial bank debt, increased the risk of the split funds and the risk of the zeros and shares. Split securities began to perform badly after September 2001, and fell more than the 25 per cent the market fell in the year to October 2002. Fifty-five out of a total of 180 securities in 28 different trusts fell by more than 85 per cent during that year, including 15 zeros, 29 income shares, four capital shares and seven shares in other split capital classes. A further 29 securities fell by more than 60 per cent.

The collapse in value of these split capital trusts led to an investigation by the Financial Services Authority, the bankruptcy of some companies in the industry, and a major compensation scheme for investors who had been misled about the risks involved. But this was not the first time this had happened. Split capital investment trusts with high gearing, illiquid cross-holdings and multiple share classes were created in the United States in the 1920s and blamed for the 1929 stock market crash. Heavily regulated thereafter, and encouraged to convert into open-ended status, the US closed-end fund industry was never the same again.

see below, this automatically wipes out the discount since unit trust units are quoted at net asset value and not below it. Another is for the ITC to enter the market and to buy its own shares to support the share price. A third method is to set a fixed date for the redemption of the shares, at which point the share price must equal the net asset value. ITCs known as split capital trusts adopted this method in the late 1990s and early 2000s, typically setting a five to seven-year maturity. On the predetermined date, the assets of the trust will be wound up and distributed to the creditors and shareholders according to their priority ranking.

Another important side-effect of ITCs being organised as limited liability companies is that they are not allowed to promote the sale of their own shares. Investors buy and sell shares in ITCs exactly as they buy and sell BT shares, on the stock exchange. Unit trusts, on the other hand, can and do spend substantial amounts on marketing their units and on commissions to agents. This can explain their relatively greater success relative to ITCs in recent years, despite their higher running costs, and also the impetus behind the development of split capital ITCs.

Unit trusts and OEICs

Unit trusts are a more recent phenomenon than ITCs, only taking off in the 1960s, and – as noted above – OEICs date back only to 1997. However, unit trusts have experienced a much faster growth rate than ITCs. In 1980, ITCs managed assets worth £8.4 billion, almost double the equivalent figure for unit trusts of £4.6 billion. By 2004 the position was more than reversed, with combined assets of unit trusts and OEICs of £287 billion compared with ITC assets of only £47 billion, reflecting an average growth rate for unit trust assets of over 18% p.a. Other EU countries, such as France, Germany and Italy, have very few ITC-type investment vehicles, preferring the SICAV or unit trust structure. Also, in the United States open-end funds dominate their closed-fund counterparts.

Unit trusts, like the modern-day investment trusts, have concentrated on equity investments, with 73.6 per cent of assets invested in UK and overseas shares in 2004 (see Table 10.7).

An investor in unit trusts invests by buying units from the unit trust managers. If investors wish to invest in the trust, new units are created to meet demand and the managers invest the new money (less a *front end fee* as management charge) in securities to increase the size of the portfolio. If investors wish to disinvest, they will sell their units back to the managers and the trust will shrink in size as money is paid out, the managers in principle being forced to realise part of the portfolio in order to buy back the units from the holders. In practice, the managers will keep part of the portfolio in cash to meet such requests. They will also often be able to *match* purchasers and sellers of units on a day-to-day basis without having to touch the cash or securities in the portfolio. The managers of the unit trust buy and sell units at prices based on the underlying value of the portfolio, with the portfolio valued on a daily basis. However, there will be a small difference between the price at which they are prepared to buy units and the price at which they are prepared to sell units, the equivalent of the market-maker's bid–ask spread, and this is typically 5–8 per cent of the net asset value per share.

Although OEICs are like unit trusts in the sense that they are open-ended, issuing and redeeming shares daily on demand, an important difference is that OEICs must buy and

Table 10.7 Assets of authorised UK unit trusts

	end 1995 £bn	%	end 1999 £bn	%	end 2002 £bn	%	end 2004 £bn	%
Short-term liquid assets	5.4	4.8	6.8	3.1	8.9	4.4	11.5	4.0
UK gilts	1.8	1.6	3.6	1.6	7.1	3.5	9.,8	3.4
Ordinary shares:								
UK	59.1	53.1	119.5	53.9	82.9	40.9	130.2	45.4
Foreign	36.1	32.4	70.3	31.7	63.2	31.1	81.0	28.2
	95.2	**85.5**	**189.8**	**85.5**	**146.0**	**72.0**	**211.3**	**73.6**
Other securities (mostly bonds):								
UK companies	3.3	3.0	13.3	6.0	21.2	10.4	22.5	7.8
Foreign governments	1.1	0.9	1.3	0.6	3.3	1.6	2.3	0.8
Foreign companies	2.1	1.9	3.0	1.4	5.9	2.9	13.1	4.6
	6.5	**5.8**	**17.6**	**8.0**	**30.3**	**15.0**	**38.0**	**13.2**
Property and other assets	2.4	2.2	4.1	1.8	10.4	5.1	16.5	5.7
Total	**111.3**	**100.0**	**221.9**	**100.0**	**202.8**	**100.0**	**287.0**	**100.0**

Source: Office for National Statistics.

sell at the same price, and therefore have to rely entirely on their charges to remunerate the managers and meet their administrative expenses.

From this description of unit trusts and OEICs, we can see the major difference between them and investment trusts as investment intermediaries. The capital of an ITC is fixed (unless it borrows or has a rights issue), with the discount or premium of the share price to the net asset value reflecting current demand for the shares. The unit trust units and OEIC shares, on the other hand, are bought and sold at prices equal (except for the bid–ask spread, in the case of the unit trust) to the underlying net asset value, so that there are no discounts or premiums. Demand for unit trusts and OEICs is reflected in the number of units or shares in issue, which defines the size of the unit trust or OEIC. The price of unit trusts is always close to the underlying asset value. Demand for investment trusts, on the other hand, is reflected in the size of the premium or discount to asset value. The number of shares issued remains fixed.

Investment objectives and constraints

Regulation

Unit trusts and (to a limited extent) OEICs, as special kinds of investment intermediary not subject to the normal company and stock exchange regulation (as are investment trusts), are subject to additional controls under the financial services legislation. In order to be able to market units and shares direct to the public in the United Kingdom, they have to be authorised, although there are a number of exempt trusts subject to less onerous regulation whose units can be held by pension funds and charities. One of the more famous regulations concerning unit trusts is that, on every marketing document, the phrase 'the value of your units can go down as well as up' has to appear.

Investment trusts are regulated by Companies Acts and by all the regulations applying to companies listed on the stock exchange. Neither ITCs nor unit trusts are regulated on their management charges, provided these are suitably disclosed. Unit trust managers typically charge a 3–5% front-end fee when units are purchased, and this is deducted from the amount invested, with 0.5–1.5% of the value of the fund charged every year thereafter as a management charge. It is difficult to compare overseas unit trust charges with this, since it is common in some countries to charge lower management fees but to charge a custody fee for dealing with security transfers. ITCs typically have no front end fee although the broker will charge a commission on the purchase of the ITC shares. The annual management charge is also lower at around 0.5% of the value of the assets under management.

Both types of trusts have restrictions imposed on their investment policies. For example, unit trusts may not have more than 5 per cent in any one security, and ITCs may not have more than 15 per cent of their assets invested in any one company. This and other requirements are imposed by the Inland Revenue on ITCs before they can gain approved status and qualify for certain tax concessions (see below).

These types of restriction ensure a reasonable amount of diversification, a sensible policy according to portfolio theory. Interestingly, ITCs, which have the longer history of the two, have reduced the average number of the securities they hold over time, with an ITC holding perhaps as many as 1000 securities 80 years ago compared with around 100 now. This suggests that they realise that they can have efficient portfolios in the risk–return sense without incurring the huge transaction and monitoring costs associated with holding large numbers of securities.

If we turn now to the question of taxation, a basic problem of any investment intermediary is to provide benefits, whether from economies of scale, pooling of risk or diversification, without these benefits being eroded by tax disadvantages. For example, given the corporation tax system as applied to insurance companies, non-taxpaying investors might be at a tax disadvantage if they invested in securities via certain types of life assurance policy. Similarly, investors would be reluctant to invest via investment or unit trusts if they were taxed twice, once in the hands of the trust and once in their own hands. This potential double taxation is avoided by, for example, the dividend income from UK shares being passed on intact, and by trusts not being liable to capital gains tax on their own disposals, any such liability being incurred only by the ultimate investor.

Of course, intermediaries will benefit from any tax advantages attached to investment through their particular medium. For example, investing via a pension fund is tax exempt. *Individual Savings Accounts* (*ISAs*), which like their predecessor the *Personal Equity Plan* (*PEP*) were created by the government to encourage regular long-term saving, can currently be used as a means of investing up to £7000 each year in equities indirectly via investment trusts, unit trusts or OEICs, with no liability on the part of the investor to higher-rate tax on dividend income or to capital gains tax on disposal.

Management

Subject to all these external constraints and regulations, in the case of an investment trust company, the board of directors will determine investment policy. In the case of a unit trust, although the board of trustees will check that the investment policy is being carried out properly, the actual policy itself will usually be chosen by the unit trust managers. Management of both types of trust is mostly delegated to a management company, sometimes an outside company such as an investment bank, sometimes owned by the trust. Some management companies run a whole 'stable' of trusts, and this is particularly useful for unit trusts since one of the trusts is bound have done reasonably well in the past year and this is the one that will be promoted in the marketing literature. Each trust is characterised by its own investment policy, which may be geographic specialisation, or a stress on income, or simply offering a diversified portfolio spread across different industrial sectors and across several markets. However, it might not be the case that a UK fund is entirely invested in UK equities. It may hold some bonds or overseas equities as well. It is important to be clear on the investment objectives and the investment strategy adopted in order to be able to determine an appropriate index performance benchmark. A UK unit trust with overseas equities as well should, for example, outperform the FTSE All-Share Index since it is able to take advantage of a better risk–return trade-off from international diversification.

Figure 10.1 shows the classification system for funds currently employed by the Investment Management Association, which is the trade association for unit trusts.

Investment trusts have a fixed amount of money raised from shareholders to invest. If investors wish to leave the ITC, they do so by selling their shares in the secondary market. If enough investors wish to sell, the share price will fall relative to the net asset value and the discount to net asset value will increase. However, this will have no impact on the investment trust portfolio and hence need not affect the timing or selection of investments by the fund manager.

On the other hand, demand and supply for units do affect the cash flow available to the unit trust manager. A popular unit trust will have a regular inflow of cash to invest from the sale of new units, although it must retain a certain proportion of its portfolio in liquid assets to be able to buy back units on demand. A very popular unit trust may find itself unable to fully invest the funds it has raised, making it difficult to outperform a fully invested performance benchmark. In contrast, a unit trust that suffers a decline in popularity may well find itself with a shrinking number of units, and need to liquidate part of a carefully constructed portfolio in order to be able to buy back the units. Since management fees are a function of the value of the funds under management, managing a decreasing number of lower-priced units in a bear market has a doubly depressing effect on unit trust managers' fees. One way round this has been for unit trusts to market their units aggressively, in the hope of increasing or at least maintaining the size of the investment pool; another has been for unit trust managers to link the sales of their units to life assurance policies with regular payments into the trust over a predetermined number of years. Finally, unit trust managers encourage investors to buy *accumulation units* rather than *income units*. The latter pay dividends out to the investor; the former reinvest the dividends in the fund, giving a boost to the trust's cash flow.

Return and risk

In efficient markets it is unlikely that an investing institution can consistently achieve superior performance in the long run. This implies that a high level of portfolio turnover will be unproductive, merely resulting in unnecessarily high transaction costs, and this is certainly reflected in the poorer performance of unit trusts relative to ITCs in both the short and long term. Studies of UK unit trusts and ITCs have not found any evidence of long-run abnormal returns, leading us to conclude that the high levels of turnover in unit trusts, and to a lesser extent investment trusts, may waste some of the benefits they offer the investor in the form of diversification.

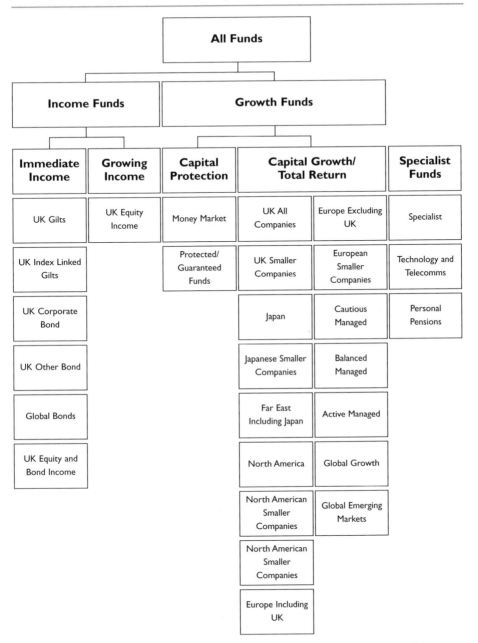

Figure 10.1 Classification of funds
Source: Investment Management Association.

As we have already seen, the objectives of both investment trusts and unit trusts are to provide the advantages of diversification. Since most trusts make clear what their investment policy is, it is relatively simple for investors to estimate the level of risk they take on by choosing a particular trust. For ITCs, the investor has the advantage of being able to look at the trust's beta. Shares in ITCs are over-represented in the lists of shares with the highest and lowest betas in the market. And regardless of their betas, what is really striking about ITCs is that they almost completely dominate the London Business School Risk Measurement Service list of the 40 shares with the lowest specific risk. This shows how ITCs do in practice provide diversification for investors.

Investment trusts with a high level of leverage (as in Example 10.1) have relatively high betas, because of the increased volatility of the ordinary shareholders' assets. Unit trusts have very limited leverage (no more than 10 per cent) and so would be expected to have a beta close to 1 for the equity market in which they are operating. In practice, though, their risk will also vary according to their investment strategy – for example, they might invest in high-beta stocks and have a high beta as a result. The Investment Management Association provides a simple risk ranking for UK unit trusts.

IMPACT OF THE INVESTING INSTITUTIONS ON THE STOCK MARKET

Having looked at each of the above types of investing institution separately, we can now consider their overall impact on stock exchange investment. As we have seen, the investing institutions are now the dominant investors in the stock market, in terms of both the proportion of securities held and turnover. As they have increased their investment portfolios and as commissions on trading securities have fallen, or in the case of gilts disappeared, so they have increased their portfolio turnover rates. This dominance of the investing institutions as the major traders in the stock market has led to larger average bargain sizes for all types of security, and to the increasing dependence of market-makers and brokers on the investing institutions for business.

Investment analysis

Following the 'Big Bang' in 1986, the average commission paid on large trades by investing institutions fell dramatically. Since then, both agency brokers and market makers have depended on large turnover to survive, and the quality of their investment analysis is one of the major factors in their getting business. Most brokers and market-makers employ large teams of equity analysts to follow companies and to make recommendations to the investing institutions. However, the quality of the analysis is not always high and may be flawed by a conflict of interest. Most of the market-making firms, and some of the agency brokers, act as brokers or investment banks to the companies on which they are advising. There have been a number of occasions on which analysts are known to have been guided away from a 'sell' recommendation on a company that brings in substantial corporate finance fees to the organisation. There may also be a conflict between the analyst and the salesperson and market-maker. The salesperson and market-maker may wish to dispose of a large *line of stock* which has been acquired on the books through normal market-making activities. They will not be happy if the analyst is recommending a 'sell' to investors.

In the United States, after the market falls from 2000, there was much debate about the quality of research into internet companies. Brokers were making more money from corporate finance and merger and acquisition activity than from investment advice. After a major investigation, some Wall Street firms that had made money from new issues of internet companies were deemed to have been over-optimistic in their broker research and in their telephone conversations to investment clients. Substantial amounts in settlement have been paid, and Wall Street brokers now have to give money to fund independent research which does not have this inherent conflict of interest. In the United Kingdom, although similar claims as to misleading advice have been made, the FSA has adopted a more hands-off approach.

Worries about the independence and quality of the investment analysis received from brokers and market makers have led to investing institutions employing their own equity analysts in-house. This is also a result of the fact that they often hold substantial percentages of particular companies' shares, which allows them privileged contact in the form of company visits and telephone calls, not available to brokers in the City. This privileged treatment could in theory lead to the investing institutions gaining access to *inside* information, information which might not be generally available to all investors.

So with privileged contacts with City analysts and with their own analysts having superior direct access to the companies in which they are investing, there does appear to be a two-tier shareholder information structure, with the smaller shareholders less well informed. However, as we can see from Chapters 1 and 12 on efficient markets, whether they have access to privileged information or not, the investing institutions do not appear to earn long-run excess returns with it. Indeed, with their greater economies of scale in investment analysis (in the sense that only one pharmaceuticals analyst is needed whether thousands or billions of pounds is being invested), there is even more reason to expect superior performance.

Finally, since the investment institutions are so dominant in trading stock exchange securities, they are clearly buying and selling from each other. Although there is little evidence of investing institutions consistently outperforming relevant benchmarks, it may well be the case that some investing institutions do consistently badly over a number of years. Given that most investing institutions make it difficult or expensive for individuals to remove their money in the short run, and that information about performance is often slow to be disseminated or is limited in content, it may take a considerable period of time for individual investors to realise the poor performance of the investing institution that they have chosen as their intermediary.

Relationships with company managements

The importance of the investing institutions as the majority shareholders in many large UK quoted companies has caused much discussion. Over recent years, this has culminated in the short-termism argument put forward by company management, angered at the ease with which their companies can be taken over. They argue that investing institutions, in particular pension funds and life assurance companies, have long-term investment horizons and should be long-term holders of the shares in their portfolios. However, they appear to hold a short-term view, since they are only too willing to accept a takeover bid, even if the incumbent management is against it. This is despite the effort company managers have put in to improve relations, by making company presentations direct to the major investing institution shareholders, and by keeping the institutions informed of projects and profits through the medium of *investor relations* managers.

Investing institutions argue that they are experts in investment and not in management, and that it is not their job to get too closely involved with company managements, else they would lose their independent stance. They point out that it is the managers of other companies who initiate the takeover bids, not the investing institutions. It is also a fact that, in the United Kingdom, takeovers are often the only way to achieve a change in management, which may well be needed if the company has been doing badly relative to its competitors. However, in the past few years, institutional investors have intervened to force board resignations, to query large payouts to serving and retiring directors, and to bring in new managers when needed. They have begun to recognise that, given the size of their percentage shareholdings, they have no choice but to help companies with ailing share prices to improve. If they attempted to dispose of their large shareholdings on the stock market, this would radically affect the share price, leading to an even greater loss on the investment.

UK investing institutions have also begun to have an influence on ethical and environmental issues, encouraging the companies in which they invest to be 'green' and to adopt a number of good **corporate governance** practices by using the votes they have as ordinary shareholders.

Impact on share prices

The investing institutions may also affect the relative pricing of different types of security. Prices of shares in the FTSE 100 share index may be affected by the investing institutions. Shares in the largest 100 companies are held by the vast majority of investing institutions, either as part of index funds or simply to gain exposure to the most important elements of the stock market. If a new issue is made of a company which will immediately form part of the FTSE 100 share index, as was the case for many privatisation issues, there is likely to be high demand from the institutions, which will drive the share price up relative to other share prices. There was also a major upheaval when Vodafone bought a German firm Mannesmann in early 2000. Shortages of stock pushed the price up to 400p at one point, with the company representing over 13 per cent of the FTSE 100 Index, falling to 250p within a few months. Such movements make it difficult for institutional investors trying to outperform indices such as these.

Since the majority of investment decisions are now made by perhaps a few hundred institutional investment managers world-wide, there may also be greater homogeneity of beliefs in respect of future returns and risks on particular securities or stock markets than when large numbers of individual investors dominate the stock market. If this is so, one of the assumptions underlying the CAPM would more nearly hold, but it could also imply greater volatility of share prices and lower liquidity in the stock market if institutional investors wish to buy and sell at the same time, creating *momentum* in share prices and major changes in sector ratings. The sudden large moivements in share prices could perhaps partly be explained by the sudden desire to sell shares of a majority of fund managers controlling billions of pounds' worth of portfolios. In Chapter 13 we look at some other explanations for the phenomenon of sudden dramatic market movements.

SUMMARY

This chapter has investigated the impact of the long-term investing institutions on stock market investment. The four main types – pension funds, insurance companies, unit trusts and investment trusts – are major holders of UK and overseas equities, gilts and international bonds, as well as being more and more involved in futures and options. Their investments, both in terms of the size of their portfolio holdings and the turnover of securities they generate, dominate the stock market. The majority of individual investors now invest the bulk of their savings devoted to securities indirectly via these investing institutions.

We looked at each of the four types of investing institution separately, concentrating on how they have evolved and discussing how their particular characteristics affect their investment objectives and policy. We showed how factors such as tax and legislation also affect the structure of their investment portfolios.

The chapter concluded with a discussion of the main ways that investing institutions have affected the stock market, in terms of the impact on investment analysis and share prices as well as on the companies in which they invest and the other investors in the stock market.

REVIEW EXERCISES

1. Among the different types of stock market investor, unit trusts and investment trusts are unique in that they both issue securities to the investing community and invest the proceeds back into the securities markets.
   a. What are the main similarities and differences between unit trusts and investment trusts?
   b. How do these differences explain the increased popularity of unit trusts over investment trusts in recent years?
   c. What are the pros and cons of investing in unit trusts and investment trusts, from the point of view of:
      i. a private investor with £100,000 to invest?
      ii. the manager of a multi-million pound life insurance or pension fund?
2. Pension funds, general and life insurance companies, unit trusts and investment trusts are the major investors in the UK stock market.
   a. In general, which types of securities do each of these investing institutions prefer, and why?
   b. Specifically, which types of gilts does each of these institutions prefer, and why?
3. What are the major arguments for and against institutional investors becoming involved in the management of the companies in which they hold shares?
4. Explain the difference between defined-benefit and defined-contribution pension schemes. Why have the latter become more popular with shareholders since the turn of the century?
5. Is there any merit in the argument that investing institutions should be limited to a maximum percentage of any one company's share capital which they can hold?
6. The Investment Trust Year Book gives ratios of management expenses/assets managed and management expenses/total gross revenue. Are high ratios good or bad for the investor?
7. Suppose a unit trust manages its portfolio as an index fund. How do you think the fund's managers should be remunerated in this case?
8. You are one of the trustees of the Widget Company's defined-benefit pension fund, which has £50 million currently invested and an annual net cash inflow of £5 million p.a. The fund is managed internally. Explain how you would:

a. Establish objectives for the fund and direct investment accordingly.
b. Evaluate the performance of the pension fund investment manager.

Sample answers to the review exercises can be found on the companion website.

11 International investment

Learning objectives for this chapter

After studying this chapter you should be able to

- ○ describe the principal features of cash and derivatives products in the foreign exchange markets
- ○ design a simple but effective hedge for the currency risk in a cross-border investment
- ○ describe and apply the principal theories about the determination and forecasting of currency exchange rates
- ○ apply the principal findings of portfolio theory and CAPM to an international context.

INTRODUCTION

So far in this book, we have mainly restricted ourselves to domestic securities (and the associated derivatives) issued on the London stock exchange by a UK company or by the UK government, and traded in sterling. But as we saw in Chapter 1, over half the market value of securities quoted on the London stock exchange is made up of overseas securities, traded in London but not necessarily in sterling. For example, a eurobond issued by IBM might be denominated and quoted in dollars, and Deutsche Bank shares might be quoted in euros. However, international investment does not have to be made via securities listed on the stock exchange in London. Foreign securities such as US Treasury bonds or Japanese equities which are quoted in markets other than the UK stock market can be bought via brokers based in London or overseas.

Indirect investment in non-UK businesses has long been available through the medium of investment trusts, set up originally in the mid-nineteenth century to enable small investors to invest in such securities as South American railway bonds. Table 10.6 showed that some 40 per cent of UK investment trusts' assets take the form of foreign securities. And as we saw in Chapters 1 and 5, even by buying the shares of UK-based companies, investors may be making another form of indirect overseas investment. Many of the largest UK companies quoted on the London stock exchange make more than half their profits (and more than half their sales) in foreign currencies. It is not at all uncommon for companies to recognise the global nature of their businesses by presenting their accounts either in US dollars (e.g. BP) or in euros (e.g. Unilever).

Prior to 1979, exchange controls were in place which effectively made it difficult for all but the most determined investor to make direct overseas investments in securities. Since 1979, the attitude to international investment has changed dramatically, with the removal of the costs and complications of exchange controls. Most foreign currency investment can now be financed with a straightforward foreign currency purchase. During the 1980s, investing institutions were quick to increase the proportions of their portfolios that were held in overseas securities. As we have seen in Chapter 10, by 2004 this proportion had risen to 15 per cent and 21 per cent in the case of long-term insurance and pension funds respectively, and was 34 per cent and 42 per cent in the case of unit trusts and investment trusts.

Despite the ease with which international investments can now be made, there are additional factors, such as exchange risk, not usually relevant when deciding on investment in UK securities, which the investor must take into account. This chapter is designed to give an understanding of the additional risks and rewards of international as opposed to domestic investment, as well as an explanation of the techniques required to evaluate international investment alternatives.

The chapter begins with a discussion of the major factor that differentiates any foreign currency investment from a sterling investment – exchange risk. This arises from the effects of exchange rate movements on the returns from overseas investments. Exchange rates can be very volatile, whether freely floating or linked in some formal way to other currencies.

Figure 11.1(a) illustrates the long-term instability of exchange rates between major currencies in the form of a graph showing average monthly exchange rates between the US dollar and the pound sterling from 1975 to 2004. Extreme fluctuations which were commonplace in the 1970s and 1990s appear to have become a thing of the past since the

Figure 11.1(a) Monthly average spot exchange rate of the US dollar to the pound sterling, January 1975 to December 2004
Source: Bank of England.

sharp fall in the value of the pound caused by sterling's enforced exit from the exchange rate mechanism (ERM) in September 1992. However, Figure 11.1(b), which covers the period from 2001 to 2004, shows clearly that significant changes in value can still occur over time and that the daily fluctuations in exchange rates cannot be ignored.

After a discussion of currency risk, the chapter goes on to explain the workings of the foreign exchange market (in particular of spot and forward exchange rates), and the ways of reducing exchange risk by hedging and matching are outlined. This leads to a discussion of the economic factors causing exchange rates to change, and hence exchange risk to exist.

The next part of the chapter shows how the underlying concepts of portfolio theory and of the capital asset pricing model (described in Chapters 6 and 7 respectively) can be extended to cover international investment decisions. It will be shown that any sterling-based investor should have not just a domestically diversified portfolio, but an internationally diversified one. This holds true whether bonds or equities are being considered. The chapter concludes with a discussion of how to apply portfolio theory techniques to international investment portfolios in practice.

FOREIGN CURRENCY RISK

What additional factors do we have to consider when investing in foreign currency securities, factors which do not have to be considered when investing in sterling securities issued by UK companies or institutions?

○ Transaction costs, as mentioned earlier, may well be higher, as may the tax burden on any proceeds from the investment. For example, dividends paid on a US share owned by a UK resident are liable to both US and UK tax. However, most countries that allow foreign investors to buy their securities (and some do not) have signed what is known as a double taxation treaty with the United Kingdom. Under these tax

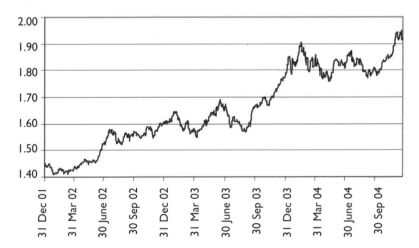

Figure 11.1(b) Daily closing exchange rate of the US dollar to the pound sterling, December 2001 to December 2004
Source: Bank of England.

treaties, each government undertakes that taxes paid abroad on such items as dividends can be offset against domestic tax liabilities. Despite these treaties the tax burden on an overseas investment may still be higher than on its UK equivalent for a UK investor.

○ For political reasons, an overseas government may withhold dividends, impose additional taxes or expropriate (for little or no compensation) assets belonging to UK investors. Although it is unlikely to happen in countries with a long history of political stability such as the United States, an uprising in a country such as occurred in the states of the former Yugoslavia in the early 1990s could lead to the expropriation of the assets of overseas investors.

Transaction costs, taxes and political risk can all be incorporated into the estimate of the holding period return for any overseas security – transaction costs and taxes directly by adjusting the cash flows and political risk indirectly by altering the probability distribution of returns. However, one other factor, which has a potentially much greater impact on holding period return than do those already mentioned, must be considered explicitly. This is the effect of changes in exchange rates, known as exchange risk, on holding period return.

An example will illustrate the potential effect of exchange risk. Suppose Mr Cook buys 100 shares in Travelog Inc, a US company, for US$50 each and holds them for one year. At the end of the year, Travelog Inc. pays a dividend of $5 per share and Mr Cook sells the shares for $60 each. Note that shares in many US and continental European companies tend to trade at higher prices per share than UK companies: coupled with the fact that brokers like to trade US shares in lots of 100, this reduces the attraction to the small investor of direct investment in US shares.

The holding period return on Mr Cook's dollar investment $R_\$$ calculated on each share is

$$R_\$ = \frac{60 + 5 - 50}{50}$$

$$R_\$ = 30\%$$

Mr Cook has had to buy dollars to make his investment in Travelog. Also, since he wishes to spend the proceeds of his investment in the United Kingdom, he will convert the dollars he receives back into pounds. If the exchange rate at the time of purchase was £1 = US$2, the investment in Travelog would have cost Mr Cook $50/2 = £25 per share, a total of £2500. Let us now imagine two scenarios for the exchange rate on disposal of the dollar proceeds. In the first, the exchange rate at the end of the year is £1 = $2.50; in the second, the exchange rate is £1 = $1.80. The holding period return in sterling terms $R_£$ will thus be:

Scenario (1):

Cost of investment per share	= £25
Proceeds per share	= $60 + $5
	$= \dfrac{65}{2.50}$
	= £26

$$R_\pounds = \frac{26-25}{25}$$

$$R_\pounds = 4\%$$

Scenario (2):

Cost of investment per share	$= \pounds25$
Proceeds per share	$= \$60 + \$5$
	$= \dfrac{65}{1.80}$
	$= \pounds36.11$

$$R_\pounds = \frac{36.11-25}{25}$$

$$R_\pounds = 44\%$$

The change in the exchange rate has had a dramatic impact on the return on investment on the Travelog shares. Whereas, for an American investor, the return would have been 30%, for Mr Cook, who invested sterling and required sterling in return, the return was either 4 or 44%. On any such dollar investment, the probability distribution of returns for Mr Cook will also be affected by exchange risk, involving greater risk than for a US investor.

This is true no matter what the original risk of the investment. If Mr Cook chose to invest in a UK gilt to maturity, his return would be certain in nominal terms. If, however, he invested in a US government bond, his sterling return in nominal terms would vary according to the exchange rate prevailing on the day he realised his investment and converted back to sterling. For example, suppose he bought a US government bond for $960, with a nominal value of $1000 and a coupon of 6% maturing in exactly one year, when the interest will also be paid. His dollar return would be

$$R_\$ = \frac{1000 + 60 - 960}{960}$$

$$R_\$ = 10.4\%$$

If the exchange rate on purchase was £1 = $2, but on sale was £1 = $2.50, that is, the dollar had depreciated in value against sterling (it took more dollars to buy £1), the sterling return $R_\pounds$ would be

Cost of investment	$= \dfrac{\$960}{} = \pounds480$
Proceeds	$= \dfrac{1060}{2.50} = \pounds424$

$$R_\pounds = \frac{424 - 480}{480} = \frac{-56}{480}$$

$$R_\pounds = -11.7\%$$

The positive return in dollars would actually be a loss in sterling terms.

The problem of exchange risk is not as daunting as appears from the above examples, but, before we can discuss how exchange risk may be reduced, we need to know more about how the foreign exchange markets work, and in particular the spot and forward markets.

FOREIGN EXCHANGE PRODUCTS

The dollar/sterling exchange rates we used in the examples were *spot exchange rates,* that is, the price paid today to receive a currency now (on the spot). Spot foreign exchange transactions are just one of the three basic types of transaction concluded in the foreign exchange market. Here are descriptions of them and of the other cash and derivative products that are associated with them:

Cash market products

A *spot foreign exchange contract* is a single transaction involving the exchange of two currencies at a rate agreed on the date of the contract for value or delivery (cash settlement) within two business days. The two-day standard settlement period for spot transactions goes back to the days when it could take up to two days to transmit the necessary instructions to banks around the world. Despite the advances in communications technology which make this no longer strictly necessary, this convention has been preserved.

An *outright forward foreign exchange contract* is a single transaction involving the exchange of two currencies at a rate agreed on the date of the contract for value or delivery (cash settlement) at some time in the future (more than two business days later). The most frequently traded maturities for forward foreign exchange contracts are one, three and six months. The relationship between spot and forward exchange rates in two currencies is based on the same basic principle of forward pricing for interest rates as was described in detail in Chapters 4 and 8, and is discussed further in this chapter.

A *foreign exchange swap* is a transaction that involves the actual exchange of two currencies (principal amount only) on a specific date at a rate agreed at the time of the conclusion of the contract (the *short leg*), and a reverse exchange of the same two currencies at a date further in the future at a rate (generally different from the rate applied to the short leg) agreed at the time of the conclusion of the contract (the *long leg*). Although a foreign exchange swap takes the legal form of two foreign exchange transactions (either a spot and a forward, or two forwards for different settlement dates), its economic impact and its commercial objective is the simultaneous loan and borrowing of two equivalent amounts in different currencies but for the same period. As in the case of forward foreign exchange rates, the relationship between the two exchange rates in a foreign exchange swap is a product of the interest rate differential between the two currencies concerned. For this reason, the foreign exchange markets are closely linked to the *eurocurrency interbank deposit* market, where banks in financial centres around the world place and accept among themselves fixed-rate, fixed-term deposits in the major currencies.

Whereas spot and outright forward exchange rates are quoted as absolute prices, the pricing of foreign exchange swaps is usually expressed not as two absolute prices (for the short leg and the long leg respectively) but as the differences between the prices. This convention follows logically from the fact that the key determinant in a foreign exchange swap is an interest rate differential. As we shall see later in this chapter, this convention also has significant practical advantages.

The foreign exchange market is a single global market. In it the major banks, financial institutions, central banks, finance ministries and the treasury departments of large multinationals are linked together by a variety of electronic means, including both order-driven and quote-driven screen-based dealing systems as well as more conventional means such as telephone. It is an over-the-counter (OTC) market, in the sense that trading does not take place on an organised physical or virtual exchange. However, the market is strictly and effectively regulated in a variety of other ways, through trade associations which publish and enforce common standards, and through formal and informal supervision by financial services regulators and central banks. A key strength of the foreign exchange market is that its dealing and settlement conventions are sufficiently uniform to promote substantial liquidity, while the essential OTC nature of the market still makes it possible for participants to strike deals with each other that meet their own precise requirements.

Closely associated with the three basic products of the foreign exchange market are a range of foreign exchange and interest rate derivative products. We have met several of these in other chapters, but they are listed again here for the sake of completeness. These products can conveniently be divided into single-currency interest rate derivatives and cross-currency derivatives.

Single-currency interest rate derivatives

A *forward rate agreement* (*FRA*) is an OTC interest rate forward contract in which the rate to be paid or received on a specific principal for a set period of time, beginning at some time in the future, is determined at contract initiation. We have already come across the FRA as the basic building-block of forward and future pricing in Chapters 4 and 8.

An *exchange-traded short-term interest rate futures contract* is the standardised exchange-traded equivalent of the FRA, and was discussed in Chapter 8.

An *interest rate swap* is an agreement to exchange periodic payments related to interest rates on a single currency, and was discussed in Chapter 8. It can be fixed-for-floating, or floating-for-floating, and based on different indices.

An *interest rate option* is an option contract that gives the right to pay or receive a specific interest rate on a predetermined principal for a set period. Included in this category are interest rate caps, floors, collars, corridors, swaptions and warrants.

Cross-currency derivatives

A *foreign exchange futures contract* is the exchange-traded equivalent of the outright forward foreign exchange contract in the cash market. The generally superior qualities of the latter contract have limited the growth of foreign exchange futures. An attempt by LIFFE to introduce currency futures contracts with small nominal values to attract retail traders and hedgers was unable to compete with the successful forward currency market already well established in London. However, both forward and futures currency prices are based on the same principle of interest rate differentials.

A *currency swap* is a transaction involving the actual exchange of two currencies on a specific date at a rate agreed at the time of the conclusion of the contract, and an agreement to exchange streams of interest payments in the currencies for an agreed period, followed by a reverse exchange at a pre-agreed exchange rate at maturity. The currency swap combines features of the short-term foreign exchange swap and the single-currency interest rate swap.

A *currency option* is an option contract that gives the right to buy or sell a currency with another currency at a specified exchange rate during or at the end of a specified period. This category also includes a number of more exotic variants such as currency swaptions, currency warrants, foreign exchange average rate options and barrier options.

Foreign exchange in practice

Example 11.1 shows an extract from the *Financial Times* giving spot, one month, three-month and one year forward exchange rates for selected currencies against the US dollar, the euro and the pound sterling, and for each of these three currencies against the others.

With two important exceptions, the rates shown in Example 11.1 are quoted in terms of how many units of the currency listed in the left-hand column are equivalent to one unit of the currency named at the head of the column. For example, the spot rates for the Swiss franc (CHF) against each of the three major currencies are:

CHF1.2000   = US$1.00
CHF1.5324   = €1.00
CHF2.2042   = £1.00

The important exceptions are that the rates shown for the pound sterling and the euro in the US dollar column are in terms of US dollar per £1.00. The general practice in the foreign exchange market is to quote foreign currencies (including the US dollar) against the pound sterling in terms of currency units per £1.00 and foreign currencies (excluding the euro and the pound sterling) against the US dollar in terms of currency units per $1.00.

Both the spot and forward markets in foreign exchange are efficient in the sense that any discrepancies in pricing which would allow arbitrage profits to be made are quickly adjusted. Any apparent anomalies are caused by restrictions in trading, for example restrictions on the purchase or sale of a particular currency or the lack of an active market in the currency. Exchange rates are therefore consistent with each other. In other words, it costs the same to buy euros directly with sterling as it does to buy euros indirectly through the dollar. We can see this using the data in Example 11.1 for both spot and forward rates.

Buying spot euros directly, £1.00 will buy €1.4384. Buying euros indirectly, £1.00 will buy US$1.8369; as US$1.2770 is required to buy €1.00, US$1.8369 will be worth €1.8369 / 1.2770 = €1.4384. Buying three-month forward euros directly, £1.00 will buy €1.4286. Buying indirectly, £1.00 will buy US$1.8242, which in turn will buy €1.8242 / 1.2769 = €1.4286. Any minor differences that might emerge are because the rates in Example 11.1 are notional mid-rates between the banks' actual buying and selling rates, and such differences would be more than eaten up by the extra transaction costs of buying currency indirectly rather than directly.

Example 11.1 Selected spot and forward exchange rates as at close of business on 27 October 2004

	Currency	DOLLAR Closing mid	DOLLAR Day's change	EURO Closing mid	EURO Day's change	POUND Closing mid	POUND Day's change
South Korea	(Won)	1124.50	-7.00	1436.04	-9.39	2065.59	-13.48
One Month		1126.35	-6.98	1438.22	-9.33	2063.92	-13.35
Three Month		1129.30	-6.95	1442.01	-9.29	2060.13	-13.56
One Year		1132.50	-7.10	1448.81	-9.29	2031.08	-13.42
Sweden	(SKr)	7.0598	-0.0086	9.0158	-0.0137	12.9682	-0.0196
One Month		7.0604	-0.0085	9.0153	-0.0136	12.9375	-0.0191
Three Month		7.0599	-0.0089	9.0149	-0.0139	12.8791	-0.0217
One Year		7.0576	-0.0127	9.0288	-0.0175	12.6575	-0.0270
Switzerland	(SFr)	1.2000	-0.0004	1.5324	-0.0010	2.2042	-0.0013
One Month		1.1986	-0.0003	1.5304	-0.0009	2.1963	-0.0011
Three Month		1.1956	-0.0004	1.5266	-0.0010	2.181	-0.0017
One Year		1.1815	-0.0005	1.5114	-0.0009	2.1189	-0.0016
Taiwan	(T$)	33.5650	-0.1300	42.8642	-0.1795	61.6555	-0.2574
One Month		33.495	-0.1430	42.7692	-0.1954	61.3762	-0.2791
One Year		32.99	-0.1600	42.2041	-0.2109	59.1659	-0.3069
Thailand	(Bt)	41.0950	+0.0850	52.4804	+0.0921	75.4874	+0.1336
One Month		41.0862	+0.0862	52.4623	+0.0945	75.2864	+0.1373
One Year		41.0925	+0.0925	52.5696	+0.1106	73.6974	+0.1414
Tunisia	(Dinar)	1.2346	-0.0002	1.5766	-0.0008	2.2677	-0.0012
Turkey	(Lira)	1477500	-5000	1886842	-6978	2714020	-10000
U A E	(Dirham)	3.6730	-	4.6906	-0.0016	6.7469	-0.0022
One Month		3.6732	-	4.6902	-0.0015	6.7307	-0.0021
One Year		3.6756	+0.0001	4.7022	-0.0006	6.5919	-0.0022
UK (0.5444)*	(£)	1.8369	-0.0005	0.6953	-	-	-
One Month		1.8324	-0.0004	0.6968	-	-	-
Three Month		1.8242	-0.0008	0.7000	+0.0001	-	-
One Year		1.7934	-0.0005	0.7133	+0.0001	-	-
Uruguay	(Peso)	27.2850	+0.0100	34.8443	+0.0018	50.1198	+0.0033
USA	($)	-	-	1.2771	-0.0004	1.8369	-0.0005
One Month		-	-	1.2769	-0.0004	1.8324	-0.0004
Three Month		-	-	1.2769	-0.0004	1.8242	-0.0008
One Year		-	-	1.2793	-0.0002	1.7934	-0.0005
Venezuela †	(Bolivar)	2490.66	-104.92	3180.70	-135.02	4575.09	-194.16
Vietnam	(Dong)	15760.00	+3.00	20126.30	-2.50	28949.50	-3.20
Euro (0.7831)*	(Euro)	1.2770	-0.0004	-	-	1.4384	-
One Month		1.2768	-0.0004	-	-	1.435	-
Three Month		1.2768	-0.0004	-	-	1.4286	-0.0002
One Year		1.2792	-0.0003	-	-	1.4019	-0.0003
SDR	-	0.66700	-	0.85175	-0.0004	1.225200	

Source: *Financial Times*.

HEDGING CURRENCY RISK

The existence of forward markets in foreign currencies allows exchange risk to be hedged, exactly as the risk of changes in commodity prices or interest rates can be hedged. A UK importer due to pay for goods in US dollars in, say, one month's time, can fix now the amount she will have to pay in sterling terms by buying the dollars forward. Suppose she owes $150,000. She could buy dollars forward, assuming the rates are as in

---

Box 11.1 The foreign exchange market in numbers

Every three years the Basel-based Bank for International Settlements coordinates a survey of the global foreign exchange market through the central banks in the main financial centres of the world. The survey conducted in April 2004 found that:

○ Average daily turnover in global foreign exchange markets was $1880 billion. The UK was the largest centre of activity with 31.3 per cent of the total.
○ Average daily turnover in OTC derivatives was $1220 billion. The UK was the largest centre with 42.6 per cent of the total.
○ The US dollar was on one side of 89 per cent by value of all foreign exchange transactions. The next most frequently traded currencies were the euro (37 per cent), the yen (20 per cent) and the pound sterling (17 per cent).
○ In single-currency derivatives, the most traded currency was the euro with 45 per cent, followed by the dollar with 34 per cent.

UK-based banks participating in the survey reported that no less than 57 per cent of their total foreign exchange activity was accounted for by foreign exchange swaps. This is evidence of the strong link between foreign exchange trading and short-term money-market activity. The remaining 43 per cent of foreign exchange business was split into spot transactions (29 per cent) and outright forwards (14 per cent). The foreign exchange market is dominated by a handful of large institutions: about 61 per cent of all trading involves just the 10 largest participants, and some 80 per cent the 20 largest.

Example 11.1, at a one month forward rate of £1 = US$1.8324. In other words, she has contracted now to pay £(150,000/1.8324) = £81,860 in one month's time for US dollars to be received at that time which she will immediately use to pay a dollar invoice. Similarly, a UK exporter due to receive payment in dollars might sell dollars forward to fix the proceeds in sterling terms.

Hedging exchange risk on equity investments

As we saw earlier, not only traders but also international investors are subject to exchange risk. How can they use the forward markets to hedge exchange risk? Could Mr Cook have eliminated exchange risk and fixed his return on Travelog Inc. shares in sterling terms?

Our starting point is the fact that investment in equities is risky because of the uncertainty of income to be received from the investment. Every such investment has a probability distribution of returns, with one return being the mean or expected return from the investment. The best that Mr Cook could do, without the advantage of perfect foresight, would be to hedge the expected return on his Travelog shares. Suppose he had expected the dividend to be $5 per share and the share price on sale $55 per share. He could have financed the cost of $50 per share by buying dollars spot and fixed the expected proceeds in sterling terms by selling $60 per share 12 months forward. If the current spot rate for buying dollars was £1 = $2 and the 12-month forward rate for selling dollars was £1 = $2.10, Mr Cook could have fixed his expected return in sterling terms.

Cost of investment per share $= £25$

Expected proceeds per share $= \$55 + \$5$

$$= \frac{60}{2.10}$$

$$= £28.57$$

Expected sterling return $E(R_£)$ $= \dfrac{28.57 - 25}{25}$

$$= 14.3\%$$

However, suppose the actual dollars received at the end of the year were $5 per share dividend and $60 per share (ex div), a total of $65. Mr Cook only sold $60 forward and so would have to sell the remaining $5 per share or $500 in total at the prevailing sterling/dollar exchange rate. Only if his actual return in dollar terms had equalled his expected return would he have completely eliminated exchange risk.

In practice, it is even more difficult to use the forward market to hedge exchange risk on risky foreign currency investments. Investments are often held for a period of months or years, and the longest liquid forward rates in many currencies are for three months (and some countries do not have a developed or efficient forward market at all). This therefore involves the forward contracts being 'rolled over' every three months. In addition, there are problems in hedging the smaller dividend cash flows as well as the attendant transaction costs of the forward transactions. However, currency hedging of equity positions is becoming ever more popular, as we shall see later in the chapter, since some institutional investors, in particular, are keen to reduce the volatility of their portfolios by hedging exchange risk.

An alternative method of hedging exchange risk is to borrow the currency in which the desired security is denominated. In Mr Cook's case, he would borrow dollars to buy Travelog shares. This method of hedging risk is known as *matching*, since Mr Cook is matching the currency and holding period of his asset (the shares) to the currency and maturity of the liability (the debt). Suppose Mr Cook borrowed dollars. To minimise exchange risk, he would borrow sufficient that, after interest, his debt would equal the expected proceeds from the Travelog shares. Mr Cook expects to get $5 dividend per share and $55 per share on sale, totalling $6000 for 100 shares. If the interest payable on the loan is 10% p.a., Mr Cook can borrow x, where

$$x(1 + 0.10) = \$6000$$

$$x \qquad\qquad = \$5454.12$$

At the end of the year, Mr Cook would use the proceeds of the Travelog investment to repay the loan (plus interest). Having borrowed $5454, Mr Cook would owe $6000 (including interest). The proceeds from the Travelog shares actually turn out to be $6500, so that the $500 not expected would have to be sold at the prevailing sterling/dollar exchange rate. As with hedging a risky investment in the forward market, Mr Cook bears exchange risk to the extent that the actual proceeds of the investment in Travelog shares are not equal to the expected amount of $6000. A further question to be resolved is what to do with the excess dollars he has borrowed at the outset of the transaction, as he borrowed $5454 but needed only $5000 for his share purchase. Theoretically he could convert it immediately into sterling, as it represents the present value of the expected profit from the transaction, but the uncertainties surrounding the transaction as a whole would make this a questionable course of action.

One final method of reducing exchange risk on equity investment should be mentioned before we consider hedging exchange risk on interest rate investments. We saw in Chapter 8 how futures contracts can be bought and sold both on equity market indices and on some individual shares. These exist for most of the major stock markets around the world and can be used as a means of investing in overseas stock markets with a minimum of exchange risk. Buying exposure to equity markets or to individual equities through futures contracts involves the payment of an initial margin and then a daily marking to market of the position.

Suppose, for example, that Ms Wan, a US dollar-based investor, decided to buy exposure to the UK stock market by buying stock index futures. If she buys exposure to £120,000 of equities, she might have to put up an initial margin to her broker of £3000 which she would have to buy at the current dollar/sterling exchange rate. If her position moved into profit immediately and stayed in profit for two weeks, she would not have to make any additional purchases of pounds. If she then sold the futures contracts, say with a £5000 profit, the £5000 plus the initial margin would have to be sold at the then dollar/sterling exchange rate. Her total exchange risk would have been limited to risk on £8000, which is less than 7 per cent of her market exposure.

Clearly, the amount of exchange risk borne by an investor in equities using futures contracts will vary according to the size of the initial margin required and of the profit or loss on the position. Investing through futures will, however, significantly reduce the exchange risk of the investment to much the same levels as achieved by using forward contracts or by matching.

Hedging exchange risk on interest rate investments

Although investment in most types of risky foreign currency securities cannot be fully hedged against exchange risk, investment in some fixed interest securities held until maturity, or money placed on fixed interest deposit, can be fully hedged. The necessary conditions are that the term of the security or deposit is equivalent to a period available on the forward or futures market (say one, three or six months) or the maturity available on a matching loan, and that the proceeds of the investment at maturity are certain in nominal terms.

We start by considering the example of money placed on deposit in eurodollars for three months. All eurocurrency and other money-market interest rates are given in annual equivalents, for comparative purposes. However, they are the simple multiples of, say, the relevant three-month rate. So, to calculate the actual interest payable on a three-month deposit, the annual interest rate given should be divided by four. Example 11.2 gives an extract from the *Financial Times* of the same day as the exchange rates in Example 11.1, showing eurocurrency rates for deposits and loans with terms up to one year in the major eurocurrencies.

We use the example of a three-month eurodollar deposit to show how an interest rate investment can be completely hedged against exchange risk. To do this, a UK investor will purchase dollars on the spot market, place them in a three-month eurodollar deposit with a fixed interest rate and simultaneously sell forward the known dollar proceeds on the three-month forward market. We use the data in Example 11.1 and 11.2 and suppose that £100,000 is invested. Example 11.3 shows how the investor can fix the rate of return

Example 11.2 Interbank deposit rates, 27 October 2004

MARKET RATES

Oct 27	Over night	Day	Change Week	Month	One month	Three months	Six months	One year
US$ Libor*	1.80250	-0.001	+0.011	-	1.96000	2.13000	2.25500	2.46375
Euro Libor*	2.06813	+0.002	-0.002	+0.011	2.09025	2.14575	2.18594	2.28125
£ Libor*	4.69625	+0.007	-	-0.248	4.83000	4.89313	4.94875	4.99375
Swiss Fr Libor*	0.64833	+0.028	+0.068	+0.063	0.62333	0.71000	0.78167	0.90833
Yen Libor*	0.03250	-0.001	-	-0.001	0.04000	0.05250	0.06500	0.09250
US$ CDs	-	-	-	-	1.89	2.04	2.17	2.35
Euro CDs	2.045	-0.010	-0.015	+0.015	2.080	2.130	2.175	2.235
US o'night repo	1.70	-0.040	-	-				
Fed. Funds eff	1.72	-0.040	-	-				
US 3m Bills	1.88	+0.010	+0.110	+0.190				
SDR int rate	2.06	-	+0.030	+0.050				
EONIA	2.06	+0.010	-	+0.020				
EURONIA	2.0525	+0.002	+0.003	+0.014				
SONIA	4.6829	+0.051	+0.037	-0.234				

* Libor rates come from BBA (see www.bba.org.uk) and are fixed at 11am UK time. Other data sources: US $ & Euro CDs: dealers; SDR int rate: IMF; EONIA: ECB; EURONIA & SONIA: WMBA.

Source: *Financial Times*, 24 October 2004.

in sterling terms in advance despite having made a foreign currency investment. For calculation purposes, we need to bear in mind that for foreign exchange and money-market dealings on Wednesday 27 October 2004, the relevant three-month period started on the spot date of Friday 29 October and ran to Monday 31 January 2005, as 29 and 30 January were non-business days. Interest therefore needs to be calculated for a period of 94 days, and on the basis of a 360-day year for the US dollar side of the transaction and a 365-day year for the sterling side.

Example 11.3 Hedging of exchange risk on a fixed interest investment

Investment = £100,000

1 Use £100,000 to purchase US dollars in spot market
£1 at $1.8369 gives $183,690

2 Place US dollars on three-month deposit

Three-month eurodollar deposit rate	= 2.13% per annum
Interest for three months	= $183,690 × 0.0213 × 94/360
	= $1021
Proceeds at end of three months	= $183,690 + $1021
	= $184,711

3 Sell US dollar proceeds forward

Three-month forward rate	= US$1.8242
Sterling proceeds of investment	= US$184,711 / 1.8242
	= £101,256

Calculate holding period return $\dfrac{101{,}256 - 100{,}000}{100{,}000} \times \dfrac{365}{94} = 4.88\%$ per annum.

Note that the effective rate of return in sterling terms (4.88%) is almost identical with the rate that could have been achieved by putting the original £100,000 on deposit in sterling at the three-month fixed deposit rate for that currency (4.89%). This is no coincidence. It is easy to see that if there were any discrepancy between the two results, arbitrage would enable the earning of guaranteed risk-free profits. This is discussed in more detail later in this chapter.

Example 11.3 shows how short-term fixed interest rate investments, such as eurodollar deposits, can be fully hedged in sterling terms. But can forward rates be used to hedge fixed interest investments with maturities of longer than one year, such as investments in foreign currency government bonds? Such securities suffer from the same problem as the foreign equity investments considered earlier: if sold before maturity, their sale price in the foreign currency is unknown and hence only the current value or the expected value can be hedged.

Suppose, for example, that Ms Grun, a sterling-based investor, buys a ten-year US Treasury bond with a view to holding the bond for six months, over which period she expects ten-year bond yields in dollar terms to fall. If she simultaneously hedges the investment by selling six months forward an amount of US dollars equal to the exected price in six months' time assuming the redemption yield is unchanged, she is effectively eliminating the currency element in her total risk and leaving only the yield curve risk open. Any change in the dollar value of the bond in six months' time (the unhedged element of the investment) will be determined exclusively by changes in the ten-year bond yield.

If, however, Ms Grun buys a ten-year US Treasury bond with a view to holding the bond to maturity, there is no uncertainty attached to the sale price (which is par) but there is no forward contract long enough with which to hedge the principal repayment on maturity. There is also the problem of finding long enough forward contracts to hedge each one of the coupon payments to be received over the life of the bond. However, it is now possible for institutional investors to enter into a currency swap with a bank. As explained on page 300, this is an agreement between the investor and the bank in which the investor promises to hand over the equivalent of the periodic US dollar coupons and final principal repayment in exchange for equivalent sterling flows in US dollars at predetermined exchange rates. This effectively creates a synthetic sterling bond for the investor which may be of a type or maturity not available in the sterling bond markets, or be cheaper than the sterling equivalent.

Interest rate parity

In Example 11.3, we showed that investors, using the eurocurrency and forward currency markets could ensure a completely certain sterling holding period return, in this case 4.88% p.a. equivalent, from a short-term, fixed interest dollar investment. As a result, they should be indifferent between investing in this way in eurodollars and investing in sterling, which will also give them a certain sterling holding period return. We can check this from Example 11.2. If the investor had instead placed the money on sterling deposit for three months, Example 11.2 tells us that it would have yielded interest of 4.89% p.a.

Thus, the three-month return would have been almost identical between the two alternatives. The discrepancy is because, for example, the foreign exchange rates are closing prices whereas the interest rates are as at 11.00, and investing in sterling via the eurodollar market and forward currency market involves two bid–ask spreads rather than just the one bid–ask spread on sterling interest rates. So the difference in returns between the two alternative sterling strategies is less than the associated transaction costs.

This phenomenon of equal returns from hedged investments with equal risks in different currencies is known as **interest rate parity.** In a perfect world, interest rate parity would always hold since, if investors could obtain different returns from investing fully hedged in different currencies, they would arbitrage the differences away. This type of arbitrage, using the forward currency markets and the money markets, is called *covered interest arbitrage*. Interest rate parity does hold in the eurocurrency markets, and in fact forward exchange rates are determined by comparing interest rate differentials. We can derive the interest rate parity formula as follows.

Let us assume that an investor has P units of currency A at his disposal and that he wants to fix his return on it for a period of d days. Using the money and foreign exchange markets, he has two alternative courses of action. The simpler course is to put the money on deposit at an annual rate of interest R_A for d days. Assuming that interest on currency A is calculated on a 360-day basis, he will receive proceeds from his maturing investment equal to

$$P\left(1 + \frac{R_A \times d}{360}\right)$$

His second course of action is to convert his money into $P(X_S)$ units of currency B at spot exchange rate X_S (where X_S is the equivalent in currency B of one unit in currency A), deposit this for d days at annual rate of interest R_B, and simultaneously sell the total proceeds of that investment for currency A at forward exchange rate X_F. The proceeds of this investment, in terms of currency A, will therefore be

$$\frac{P(X_S)\left(1 + \frac{R_B \times d}{360}\right)}{X_F}$$

Interest rate parity says that the returns from these strategies must be equal, so that

$$P\left(1 + \frac{R_A \times d}{360}\right) = \frac{P(X_S)\left(1 + \frac{R_B \times d}{360}\right)}{X_F}$$

P cancels out and the remaining terms can be rearranged in the generalised form

$$X_F = X_S\left(\frac{1 + \frac{R_B \times d}{y}}{1 + \frac{R_A \times d}{y}}\right) \tag{11.1}$$

where y is the relevant daycount basis for interest calculations in the currencies concerned, for example, 360 for US dollars and 365 for sterling.

We can illustrate equation 11.1 by using the data for three-month sterling and dollar interest rates in Example 11.2 as a check on the three-month forward rate published in Example 11.1. We shall denote sterling as currency A and the US dollar as currency B.

This gives:

$$X_F = 1.8369 \left(\frac{1 + \dfrac{0.02130 \times 94}{360}}{1 + \dfrac{0.0489313 \times 94}{365}} \right)$$

$$X_F = 1.8369 \times \frac{1.005562}{1.012601} = 1.8241$$

This is almost identical to the three-month forward rate of 1.8242 given in Example 11.1.

The forward exchange rate is therefore a strict mathematical function of the spot rate and the relevant interest rates for the two currencies concerned. It is not, as is popularly believed, what the spot rate will be on the forward settlement date. If it were the future spot rate, market participants could generate guaranteed risk-free profits by using the money markets. But we shall see later that the forward rate is an unbiased market consensus of what the future spot rate will be.

Because the forward rate is strictly linked to the interest rate differential, we can tell whether the forward rate is higher or lower than the spot rate just by comparing the interest rates and without doing any mathematics at all. If R_B is higher than R_A, then X_F will be higher than X_S. As this means that it will take more units of currency B to buy one unit of currency A in the forward than in the spot market, we say that currency B is at a forward discount to currency A, and that currency A is at a forward premium to currency B. Figure 11.1(b) showed the development of the spot dollar/sterling rate for a period of three years when sterling appreciated steadily against the dollar. Despite this upward trend in the spot value of sterling, the pound stood at a continuous forward discount to the dollar throughout this period, because sterling interest rates were always higher than dollar rates.

Although the forward exchange rate is a function of the three variables noted above, in practice the difference between the spot and forward rate (referred to as the forward premium or forward discount, depending on the currency perspective we are adopting) is relatively insensitive to typical short-term movements in the spot rate of exchange. In the above example, the difference between the spot and the three-month forward rates was that sterling was at a forward discount of $1.8369 – $1.8241 = $0.0128 or 1.28 US cents. If we now assume that the pound weakens on the spot market by half of one cent (a typical intraday movement) from $1.8369 to $1.8319 and recalculate the forward rate, we have

$$X_F = 1.8319 \left(\frac{1 + \dfrac{0.02130 \times 94}{360}}{1 + \dfrac{0.0489313 \times 94}{365}} \right)$$

$$X_F = 1.8319 \times \frac{1.005562}{1.012601} = 1.8192$$

The forward discount has apparently narrowed very slightly from $0.0128 to $0.0127 ($1.8319 – $1.8192), but if we look beyond the fourth place of decimals we can see that nearly all of this already very tiny change is caused by rounding. In other words, for small changes in the spot rate, the forward discount or premium does not change to any material extent. For this reason, forward exchange dealers save themselves (and their customers) a great deal of unnecessary work by quoting forward exchange rates not (as shown in the *FT*) in terms of absolute prices, but rather in terms of the underlying discount or premium.

There is a further reason why this labour-saving practice makes good sense. The most actively traded foreign exchange product is the foreign exchange swap: that is, the simultaneous sale and purchase of two currencies for one date (normally the spot settlement date) and their purchase and sale for a more distant date. Although a swap is structured as two linked foreign exchange transactions, it is effectively the simultaneous lending and borrowing of two currencies in equivalent amounts for the same period. Customers seeking to buy or sell one currency outright against another, whether on a spot or a forward basis, are concerned to receive as much as possible and to pay as little as possible and therefore have an interest in the absolute exchange rate. But customers seeking to do a swap are concerned only secondarily with the absolute exchange rate between the currencies; what they want is to earn as high an effective interest rate on the currency they are 'lending' (i.e. selling spot and buying back forward) and to pay as low a rate as possible on the currency they are 'borrowing' (i.e. buying spot and selling forward). In other words, they want the most advantageous interest rate differential. The interest rate differential is effectively captured in the forward discount or premium, so it makes sense for the bank to quote prices in those terms.

Interest rate parity will always hold when currency forward markets and money markets are efficient. Because eurocurrency markets are free, unregulated markets, interest rate parity does hold for the major currencies in the eurocurrency markets as we saw in Example 11.3. However, interest rate parity does not necessarily hold with other types of fixed interest investment which have returns certain in nominal terms (such as UK and US Treasury bills) or with less internationally traded currencies, since (a) treasury bill rates are for investment only (banks and companies cannot borrow at those rates) and (b) exchange controls, taxes and other government intervention may prevent investors from arbitraging away any differences in return. The general rule is that as long as the interbank markets for spot and forward foreign exchange between two currencies, and for borrowing and lending in each of those currencies, are free from sources of possible distortion, then interest rate parity between those markets will hold.

THE FUNDAMENTALS OF EXCHANGE RISK

We have seen that the major additional problem in making foreign currency as opposed to sterling investments appears to be that of exchange risk. Although for certain types of short-term, fixed interest investments, exchange risk can be fully hedged, most types of investment in risky foreign currency investments can only be partly hedged against exchange risk, if at all.

Forecasting future exchange rates

Exchange risk is the risk that exchange rates will change and adversely affect the expected base currency return on investment. Of course, if future exchange rates could be perfectly forecast by investors, exchange risk would no longer be such a problem. They would be able to calculate their expected sterling returns, allowing for forecast changes in exchange rates, and choose those investments that offered them their preferred risk and return characteristics.

There are two potential sources of forecasts of future exchange rates. First, and more simply, there are market consensus forecasts. Second, forecasts can be obtained from studying either charts of past exchange rates or the fundamental causes of changes in exchange rates, namely differential inflation and growth rates and balance of payments figures reflecting currency flows.

In Chapter 4, when analysing fixed interest securities, we found that the forward interest rates implicit in the spot interest rate term structure could be used to forecast future spot interest rates. In the simplest case, the expectations hypothesis stated that forward interest rates were the market's best estimates of future spot rates. This leads to the question whether, in the foreign exchange markets, forward exchange rates are the best market estimates of future spot exchange rates. Can Mr Cook or any investor in foreign currency securities use forward exchange rates to forecast expected future exchange rates?

The empirical evidence appears to show that, on average and in the very long term, forward exchange rates are unbiased estimates of future exchange rates. In other words, the expectations hypothesis holds for exchange rates: there is no systematic bias in forward rates. Unlike forward interest rates, which appear to include a liquidity or inflation premium in their estimates of future spot interest rates, there seems to be no premium to pay for the use of forward markets to hedge exchange risk. On average, forward exchange rates represent the market's best estimates of future spot rates, without any adjustment needed to include a charge for allowing investors and traders to hedge. The only additional cost to Mr Cook of hedging is the slightly wider bid–ask spreads he has to pay in the forward market.

Now we have established that there is no bias in the forward exchange rate estimates of future spot exchange rates, the next question to ask is how good these estimates are. If they are perfect estimates, forward rates will provide investors with the future exchange rates needed to estimate holding period returns and to make investment decisions. Unfortunately, for the investor contemplating just a single transaction or a small number of transactions, forward rates – despite their representing the market consensus – are in practice fairly poor predictors of future exchange rates, and economic forecasting models appear no better. So, if Mr Cook does not hedge exchange risk or cannot fully hedge his risky investments using the forward market, he will experience volatility in his investment returns as a result of unexpected changes in exchange rates. Forecasting techniques such as the use of forward rates or chartist methods are unlikely to help him much.

However, exchange risk is not quite as great as it might seem. Although there is no exact understanding of how exchange rates change, there are certain relationships between exchange rates, interest rates and inflation rates which ought to hold in a world where there are no barriers to trade or investment, and which do hold to a lesser extent in the real world. Using these relationships, we can predict in broad terms what will happen in the long run to exchange rates, although shorter-run movements are more difficult to forecast.

Purchasing power parity theory

The first of these relationships is known as the ***purchasing power parity*** theory, derived from the ***law of one price***. If a product is freely internationally traded, with negligible transportation costs, the law of one price says that the product should be traded for the same price everywhere. For example, if a McDonald's hamburger or a Mars bar sells for US$1 in the United States and 50p in the United Kingdom, then $1 must be worth 50p and $2 worth £1. The purchasing power parity theory (PPPT) extends the law of one price to overall price levels in each country, measured for example by a retail prices index. The PPPT is usually expressed in terms of changes in exchange rates, and says that, given the assumption of free international trade, the change in an exchange rate over a period will be equal to the relative change in inflation rates of the two countries concerned.

This can be written as

$$\frac{X_1}{X_0} = \frac{P_{ft}/P_{f0}}{P_{dt}/P_{d0}} = \frac{1 + infl_f}{1 + infl_d} \tag{11.2}$$

where

X_0 and X_1 are the spot exchange rates at the beginning and end of the period 0, t
P_f and P_d are the price levels in the foreign country and domestic country
$infl_f$ and $infl_d$ are their equivalent inflation rates during the period 0, t.

For the purpose of this exercise, the 'foreign' country is defined as the country in terms of whose currency the exchange rate is quoted. So, for example, if the two countries are the United States and the United Kingdom, the foreign country is the United States as the exchange rate is quoted in terms of dollars and cents rather than pounds and pence.

Suppose that inflation over a period is 8% in the United Kingdom and 4% in the United States, with the exchange rate at the beginning of the period $1.60 = £1. We know that

$$P_{ft}/P_{f0} = 1 + infl_f = 1.04$$

$$P_{dt}/P_{d0} = 1 + infl_d = 1.08$$

PPPT says that the exchange rate will adjust over the period to give

$$\frac{X_1}{1.6} = \frac{1.04}{1.08}$$

$$X_1 = \mathbf{1.54}$$

In other words, the pound would be expected to depreciate against the dollar to £1 = $1.54, reflecting its relatively reduced purchasing power.

PPPT cannot hold exactly as in equation 11.2 since not all goods included in a general measure of inflation are internationally traded. Also, such factors as transportation costs, time lags in price adjustments, government controls and taxes on international trade mean that, although exchange rate changes may in the long run be expected to reflect relative changes in purchasing power parity, the PPPT relationship cannot be used for accurate short-run forecasts of future exchange rates. Indeed, the failure of economic indices such as PPPT to explain short-term movements in exchange rates is a major reason that technical analysis and chartism are popular forecasting techniques for day-to-day exchange rate movements.

International Fisher effect

The PPPT is concerned with the connection between inflation and exchange rates. However, we saw in Chapter 2 that inflation also affects interest rates, with Fisher postulating that interest rates fully take account of expected (as opposed to actual) inflation. Fisher suggested an expression relating the nominal interest rate R and the real interest rate r as follows:

$$(1 + R) = (1 + r)(1 + E(infl)) \tag{11.3}$$

where $E(infl)$ is the inflation rate expected over the period.

The second fundamental relationship concerning exchange rate changes is the extension of equation 11.3 to an international context, sometimes referred to as the *International Fisher effect*. If the expression holds in each national financial market, there will be a real interest rate in each currency. If investors can freely choose in which currency to invest their money, this real interest rate must be the same everywhere, otherwise investors would arbitrage the differences away. If we consider the US dollar and sterling, for example, we can write equation 11.3 for each of them in the form:

$$(1 + R_£) = (1 + r_£)(1 + E(infl_£)) \tag{11.3a}$$

$$(1 + R_\$) = (1 + r_\$)(1 + E(infl_\$)) \tag{11.3b}$$

If the real interest rate in dollar terms is equal to the real interest rate available in sterling, we must have

$$1 + r_£ = 1 + r_\$$$

So

$$\frac{1 + R_£}{(1 + E(infl_£))} = \frac{1 + R_\$}{(1 + E(infl_\$))} \tag{11.4}$$

Rearranging equation 11.4 and subtracting 1 from each side, we get

$$\frac{R_\$ - R_£}{1 + R_£} = \frac{E(infl_\$ - infl_£)}{(1 + E(infl_£))} \tag{11.5}$$

Both equations 11.4 and 11.5 are different ways of expressing the International Fisher effect. Let us, as before, suppose that the annual rate of inflation is expected to be 8% in the United Kingdom and 4% in the United States. If nominal interest rates in the United

Kingdom are 10%, we can use equation 11.4 or 11.5 to derive the level of nominal interest rates in the United States. Using equation 11.5:

$$\frac{R_\$ - 0.10}{1 + 0.10} = \frac{0.04 - 0.08}{1 + 0.08}$$

Rearranging

$$R_\$ = 0.10 + \frac{(1 + 0.10)(-0.04)}{1 + 0.08}$$

$$R_\$ = 5.9\%$$

Interest rates will be lower in the United States, because of the lower expected rate of inflation. In both countries, however, the real interest rate will be the same:

$$(1 + r_\$)(1 + 0.04) = (1 + 0.059)$$

$$r_\$ = 1.9\%$$

$$(1 + r_£)(1 + 0.08) = (1 + 0.10)$$

$$r_£ = 1.9\%$$

The assumptions underlying the existence of a single real interest rate world-wide include, as for PPPT, that of completely free international trade, this time in interest-bearing securities. However, interest rates are often manipulated by governments as part of their economic policies and, as mentioned earlier, foreign investors might not be allowed to hold fixed interest government securities, or might be taxed more highly than domestic investors. The Fisher relationship between expected inflation and interest rates is therefore most likely to hold in the eurocurrency market.

Since it is difficult to estimate the expected inflation rates implied in nominal interest rates, studies of whether the Fisher relationship holds have looked at returns in different currencies net of actual inflation. Such studies appear to suggest that netting out actual inflation does not give the same real interest rate for each currency (see, for example, Wong and Wu 2003). As with PPPT, there are currently too many barriers and costs to international investment for different currency capital markets to offer the same real interest rate on equivalent risk investments.

Exchange risk with PPPT and International Fisher

If these two fundamental relationships, PPPT and International Fisher, did hold, international investors would not need to concern themselves with exchange risk; there would be no additional risk in international rather than domestic investment. Note that we are here ignoring political risk and any differentiation between foreign and domestic investors. Of course the fundamental riskiness of the investment (which may vary between countries) will still exist.

Example 11.4 (overleaf) shows how, if the PPPT and International Fisher relationships did hold, Mr Cook would achieve the same sterling return, without hedging, whether he invested in a sterling eurobond with one year to redemption or an equivalent dollar eurobond with the same maturity.

Example 11.4 International investment without exchange risk

Suppose that PPPT and International Fisher hold.

Assumptions:
Current spot exchange rate $/£ X_0: $1.60
Real annual interest rate on $ and £ eurobonds: 2%
Expected inflation rates: 8% (UK)
                                                       4% (US)

PPPT gives:

$$\frac{X_1}{1.60} = \frac{1.04}{1.08}$$

where X_1 = year-end exchange rate

$$X_1 = \$1.54$$

International Fisher gives the nominal interest rates that will prevail on sterling and dollar eurobonds, $R_£$ and $R_\$$.
In the United States:
$(1.02)(1.04)=(1+R_\$)$
$R_\$=6.1\%$

In the United Kingdom:
$(1.02)(1.08)=(1+R_£)$
$R_£=10.2\%$

Sterling eurobond:
Return on the sterling eurobond: 10.2%
£100 invested at 10.2%:   **£110.20**

Dollar eurobond:
Return on dollar eurobond: 6.1%
Current spot exchange rate: $1.60=£1
Year-end spot exchange rate: $1.54=£1
£100 converted initially at $1.60: $160.00
$160 invested at 6.1%: $169.80
$169.80 converted back to £ at $1.54:   **£110.20**

Unfortunately, neither of these fundamental relationships holds in the real world exactly as in Example 11.4, although exchange rates do, to some extent and in the long run, adjust for differences in inflation and nominal interest rates. So exchange risk remains a factor to be considered when investing in foreign currency securities. As we have seen, hedging on the forward market or borrowing in the currency of the investment or cross-currency swaps can provide a solution to the problem of exchange risk when investing in securities with predetermined foreign currency cash flows, but these techniques only provide a partial solution to the problem of exchange risk in overseas securities with uncertain future cash flows.

Advantages of exchange risk

However, exchange risk may not be as much of a disadvantage to international investment as it appears. It may act in such a way as to dampen the market risk of buying overseas equities or bonds. For example, the risk to Mr Cook of buying a diversified portfolio of US shares is made up of the risk of the shares (measured in terms of volatility or standard deviation of returns in the local currency) plus the exchange risk of an adverse move in the dollar relative to sterling. As we saw in Chapter 6 on portfolio theory, combining risks is not strictly additive but depends on the correlation between the return patterns. Thus, the total risk, as measured by the variance S^2, of investing in US shares for Mr Cook would be:

$$S^2 = S_M^2 + S_{Fx}^2 + 2S_M S_{Fx} CORR_{M,Fx} \tag{11.6}$$

where

S_M = standard deviation of returns on US shares expressed in US dollars
S_{Fx} = standard deviation of changes in the \$/£ exchange rate; and
$CORR_{M,Fx}$ = correlation coefficient between US equity returns and \$/£ currency movements.

The corresponding risk of investing in a portfolio of US shares for a dollar-based investor, Ms Wan, would be

$$S^2 = S_M^2 \tag{11.7}$$

In practice, the correlation coefficient between equity returns and currency movements in most markets around the world is usually around zero or slightly negative. So, if we assume 17% market volatility for US equities, 10% volatility for the \$/£ exchange rate, and a correlation coefficient of –0.1, we can see from inputting these numbers into equation 11.6 that the risk for Mr Cook of investing unhedged in US shares would be

$$S^2 = (0.17)^2 + (0.1)^2 + (2 \times 0.17 \times 0.1 \times -0.1)$$
$$S^2 = 0.0355$$
$$S = 18.8\%$$

The risk for Ms Wan, with no exchange risk, from equation 11.7 would be

$$S^2 = (0.17)^2$$
$$S = 17\%$$

In this example, exchange risk has only increased Mr Cook's risk of investing in US equities by 1.8% when compared with the risk of investing in US shares without exchange risk, as is the case for Ms Wan, although the exchange risk on its own is assumed to be 10%.

Note that the actual impact of currency risk will depend on the market and period under consideration. Standard deviation and correlation coefficient measures will vary according to the time period analysed, whether weekly, monthly or quarterly numbers are used, and according to the base currency used. However, on a global basis, exchange risk accounts for only about 15 per cent of total equity market risk. This figure is closer to 50 per cent for the global bond markets, since the typical correlation coefficient between bond returns in a particular country and its currency movements is more likely to be positive than is the case for equities. An economic explanation for the positive correlation between bond returns and exchange rate movements is that governments or central banks tend to raise interest rates (and hence depress bond prices) when their currency is depreciating. This type of intervention is known as 'leaning into the wind'.

Thus, in conclusion to this section on exchange risk, investors such as Mr Cook are free to reduce exchange risk to a minimum by hedging the expected values of their equity and bond portfolios (if a forward or swap market exists for them to do so). Alternatively, they can accept the relatively small amount of exchange risk which in practice attaches to investment in overseas stock and bond markets, particularly if only a percentage of Mr Cook's portfolio is invested in non-sterling investments.

INTERNATIONAL DIVERSIFICATION

Despite the increased volatility created by exchange risk, there may be other advantages to international investment which outweigh the potential risks. Should UK investors add foreign currency securities to their portfolios, and if so, which securities and markets should they consider?

Portfolio theory

We saw in Chapter 6 that when investors combine securities into a portfolio, they are concerned not only with the expected return and standard deviation of each security but also with the correlation coefficients between returns on pairs of securities, since these interrelationships affect the overall risk of the portfolio. This approach, which we confined to a domestic equity portfolio in Chapter 6, can equally well be applied to a global equity portfolio, where the constituent elements of the portfolio are not individual shares but individual stock markets.

Solnik (1974) showed that a naïve diversification policy on UK equities could reduce the risk of a portfolio to around 34 per cent of the average risk of holding one share (see Figure 6.9). This figure is somewhat lower at around 30 per cent for US investors because of the greater diversification potential offered by a larger stock market. He also showed how just by holding 40 securities from both US and European stock markets, the risk for a US investor would be around half that of a US portfolio of stocks with the same number of shares. This result, which emphasises the size of the risk reduction benefits that international diversification can bring, is shown in Figure 11.2. The risk reduction benefits of international diversification would therefore have

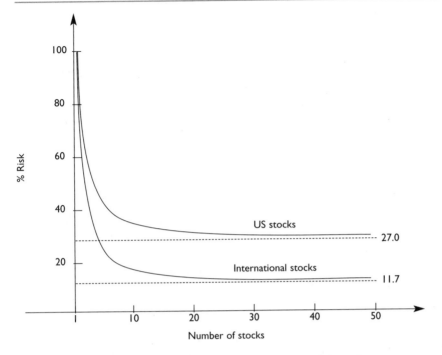

Figure 11.2 Effect of international diversification on portfolio risk
Source: Solnik (1974).

been even greater to investors from smaller markets than the US with less domestic diversification potential.

Solnik's findings were corroborated by several other contemporaneous studies. For instance, Lessard (1976) found that for 16 major countries in the period 1959–73, only 22 per cent of the overall variance in national share indices was explained by a notional world portfolio index, the rest of the variance being caused by local or regional factors.

In the 30 years or so since the seminal work of Solnik and others in this area, the issue of correlations between national stock markets has produced a flood of research which shows no sign of abating. In the whole literature of finance, possibly only the efficient markets hypothesis and the CAPM have proved to be more persistently contentious. Almost the only proposition that has gained general acceptance is that in the last quarter of the twentieth century there was a significant degree of convergence in the performance of the principal stock markets, but beyond that there is little agreement. In particular, there is disagreement on the key issue whether investors who diversify internationally achieve superior risk–return relationships by systematically hedging the pure currency component in their overall risk or by leaving it open.

Because this is such a 'live' issue we have deferred detailed consideration of it until the final chapter of the book, where we review it with the other main open issues in the theory of finance and securities. For the moment it is sufficient to assume only that the stock markets of the world are not perfectly positively correlated with each other and that the spread of correlations between all the possible pairings of markets is quite wide. The

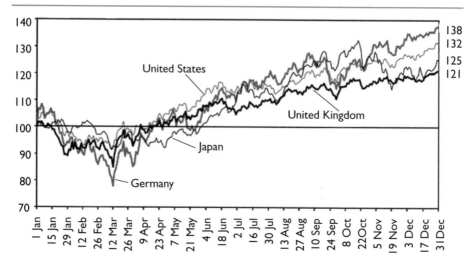

Figure 11.3 Total return index levels for 2003 (end-December 2002 = 100)
Source: Dimson and Marsh (2004).

strongest positive correlations tend to be shown by the largest and most developed markets (possibly because they tend to be dominated by multinational companies whose fortunes are least affected by narrow domestic conditions) and by pairs of neighbouring countries whose economies are closely aligned to each other. Figure 11.3 serves to illustrate in a general way the correlation between major markets by showing the index levels, on a total return basis, of four of the five largest stock markets in the world for 2003, a year which encompassed both high levels of short-term volatility and substantial longer-term price trends in both directions.

The results from portfolio theory can be used to reduce risk by concentrating on poorly correlated stock markets. To the extent that the correlation coefficients between stock markets may be lower than the correlation coefficients between shares in the same market, international diversification can generate additional reductions in risk. By using a quadratic programming computer software package and inputting return, risk, and correlation coefficient data for all these markets, a lower risk portfolio can be derived through Markowitz diversification than that achieved by naïve diversification.

Of course, there is little point in trying to reduce risk to a minimum if returns are substantially reduced as well. If returns on all foreign investments were substantially less than those available to investors on their domestic market, it might be that the benefit of reduced risk obtained from international diversification was more than offset by reduced returns.

A particular problem with international diversification is that – again by general agreement – correlations between national stock markets are not stable over time, so that the use of historic data as a basis for constructing expected values is even more fraught with difficulty than it is in other areas of finance. For instance, UK investors studying the returns and correlations of other markets in the ten years to 1990 as a basis for international diversification in the 1990s would have diverted a significant amount of their resources to the Japanese market, which in the 1980s exhibited both a very healthy level of returns and a relatively low correlation with the UK market. Unfortunately the long-term underperformance of the Japanese market, which collapsed in December 1990 and continued to fall for years afterwards, would have left them regretting their decision.

In practice, therefore, investors using a portfolio theory model to determine their optimal international equity portfolio use their own forecasts for expected returns (bearing in mind their view of future exchange rate movements) but will generally use historical estimates of market volatilities and correlation coefficients, since it is more difficult to have an intuitive feel for these. They are then offered by their computer model a range of portfolios on the efficient frontier, each with its own risk and return levels, as for the domestic equivalent. Investors can choose whichever portfolio most suits their risk preference. However, one problem with this model must be noted: a small change in expected return could radically affect the composition of the optimal portfolio, so changing views on market returns could lead to expensive rebalancing costs on portfolios.

Note that investors from different countries looking at market returns, risks and correlation coefficients for the same historical period will be shown different numbers, reflecting the use of a different base currency. This will naturally lead to different opportunity sets, efficient frontiers and optimal portfolios for different nationality investors. Also, investors within the same country may have different return expectations for markets or different tax positions, again leading to variations in optimal portfolios between investors.

Capital Asset Pricing Model

Now we have seen that portfolio theory can successfully be applied to the problem of international investment, we naturally go on to look at the role of the CAPM in an international context. As we saw in Chapter 7, the CAPM was derived in a purely national framework by US researchers with the largest stock exchange in the world and the least to gain from international investment. Can it be extended to an international framework?

There are two main ways in which the CAPM could be viewed in an international framework. One is to assume that all capital markets are *integrated*, meaning that all securities are priced relative to a world capital market. In this case, the CAPM would be a world CAPM, with world betas, of the form

$$E(R_j) = \alpha_j + \beta_j E(R_W) \tag{11.8}$$

For this to happen, investors would have to be able to invest freely in any capital market and so would naturally compare the risk and return of any security in a world-wide context.

Alternatively, each security's return could be determined, as postulated by the original CAPM, purely in its domestic market. Each country i would have its own CAPM of the form

$$E(R_{ji}) = \alpha_{ji} + \beta_{ji} E(R_{mi}) \tag{11.9}$$

where each country's risk–return relationship could be different. For there to be this multiplicity of different equations 11.9, a different one for each country, we must envisage some impediment or disadvantage to international investment to explain why investors do not value securities on an international basis and why markets are thus segmented. Factors leading to such *segmented* markets could include tax, legal or information barriers to overseas investment as well as differences in consumption preferences between investors in different countries.

There is at present no real agreement on the form that an international CAPM would take; for example, there are problems in defining a risk-free interest rate in an international CAPM context. But this view of the capital markets as integrated or segmented does give an understanding of how international diversification reduces risk. If markets were fully integrated, and investors had identical expectations and investment preferences (that is, were passive investors as opposed to the more active investors inputting expected returns into the portfolio theory model), a world CAPM would lead, as does the domestic CAPM, to the result that all investors should hold the same market portfolio: in other words, hold a proportion of all the stock markets in the world in amounts reflecting the market's relative importance. In this case, if investors chose to restrict themselves to a purely domestic portfolio, they would be bearing diversifiable risk for which they would not be rewarded.

On the other hand, if markets were segmented, international investment would also offer a reduction in risk, since risk that was systematic in a national context would become diversifiable in an international context. However, markets are segmented if there are impediments preventing investors from including non-domestic securities in their portfolios, so only those investors lucky enough to be able to circumvent the restrictions would be able to benefit from international diversification if markets were segmented.

There is some evidence that markets are partially segmented, although the tax, legal and informational barriers are gradually being removed. More and more investors are able, if they wish, to invest in international portfolios or index funds, designed to represent an international market portfolio. Thus, if they are passive investors as assumed by the CAPM, they can in practice apportion their assets between, say, Treasury bills in their domestic currency and a world index fund.

Table 11.1 shows the relative sizes of the major equities markets expressed as percentages of the total world stock market valued at the end of 2004. In this the United States represents the largest single stock market, followed by the United Kingdom, Japan, France and Germany. These five markets account for 76.2 per cent of the total global stock market capitalisation. Integrated CAPM says that all investors, regardless of which country and currency they are based in, should put the majority of their money into these five stock markets. The optimal portfolio under CAPM will include countries according to the size of their stock markets. This is in contrast to an optimal portfolio under a portfolio theory model approach, which will choose countries according to their expected returns, risks, and the correlation coefficients between countries. The CAPM model

Table 11.1 Relative size of major equities markets (end 2004)

	% of total		% of total
United States	50.7	Switzerland	2.7
United Kingdom	9.8	Canada	2.6
Japan	8.6	Australia	2.2
France	4.1	Netherlands	2.0
Germany	3.0	All others (<2.00% each)	14.3

Source: FTSE All-World Review.

assumes that investors are passive, accept the market consensus on stock market values and returns, and wish to achieve an average return on a fully diversified portfolio. The portfolio theory model assumes that investors are more active, with views different from the consensus. They will therefore expect to achieve a better risk–return ratio than investors in a global index fund by being 'overweight' in those stock markets they think will outperform and 'underweight' in those they consider overvalued.

Although there is less theoretical support for an international CAPM than for its domestic counterpart, international index funds that offer investors the opportunity to invest in countries in proportion to their stock market and bond market values have had some success (the international extensions of portfolio theory and CAPM apply equally to bonds as to equities). This has been helped by the practical difficulties investors face when attempting to select likely outperforming stocks in foreign stock markets, where they have to deal through unknown intermediaries and may not be as at ease with the local accounting methods and types of equity analysis employed. Such index funds are available to individual investors through the medium of unit trusts, but they are not as popular as the more conventional unit trusts and investment trusts which adopt a more active approach, attempting to outperform their index fund counterparts. Also, it must not be forgotten that investing in the UK stock market also exposes investors such as Mr Cook to exchange risk and to some element of international diversification, because of the large element of revenues and costs incurred overseas by UK-based companies.

Finally, most UK investors consider sterling to be their base currency. Whatever the time horizon of their investment strategy, their future liabilities are likely to be expressed in sterling terms. Both the portfolio theory and CAPM approaches to international investment should lead UK-based investors to hold a majority of non-sterling-denominated bonds or equities in portfolios that are optimal in terms of expected returns per unit of risk. This type of asset structure would expose the investors to exchange risk although, as we saw earlier in the chapter, investors who do not wish to bear the exchange risk inherent in overseas investment can, to a large extent, hedge this away. However, it is still the case that UK and other investors tend to keep a majority of their investments in securities denominated in their base currency, applying integrated CAPM only to the funds that are not dedicated to domestic investments, or adjusting the portfolio theory model to include a predetermined percentage of domestic security markets.

SUMMARY

This chapter has looked at the advantages and disadvantages to UK investors of international investment, which has become an increasingly important part of stock market investment.

The major additional factor to be considered when investing in foreign currency securities is exchange risk: the risk that the return on investment, when converted back into sterling, will be different from what was expected because of changes in exchange rates. Exchange risk can partially be hedged by using the spot and forward foreign exchange markets, both of which are efficient, or by borrowing the expected proceeds in the foreign currency. Forward rates are also the best available, albeit poor, estimates of future spot exchange rates.

Although the factors determining changes in exchange rates are as yet inadequately understood, two basic relationships ought to hold in a world with no barriers or costs to international trade. These are purchasing power parity and the International Fisher effect. If these hold, even if only in the long term and approximately, exchange risk is not as great as it originally appears. Also, because exchange rate movements and stock market returns are not significantly correlated, exchange risk is not a significant risk factor for international equity investment. The correlation between currency movements and bond market returns is more positive, making currency risk a more important element in international bond portfolios.

Exchange rate movements alter returns on overseas stock markets when expressed in sterling terms, and this reduces the correlation of these returns with those of the UK stock market. As a result, investment in these overseas stock markets can substantially reduce the portfolio risk of a UK-based portfolio. This international extension of portfolio theory shows that, unless expected returns are much lower on overseas securities (because of transaction costs, taxes or political risk), investors should not restrict themselves to domestic investment and should always take advantage of the increased returns and reduced risk available from internationally diversified portfolios determined from the investor's best estimates of expected returns, risks, and correlation coefficients allowing for exchange rate movements. An identical approach can be adopted for bond portfolios.

The CAPM, on the other hand, when applied to an international context, suggests a global index fund approach, with all investors (whatever their base currency and stock market) investing in each stock market in the world in proportion to its size. This passive approach to international investment is based on accepting the market consensus for the returns expected on each stock market.

It has now become common, particularly for UK investors who have a long tradition of overseas investment in bonds and equities, for investors to hold a significant proportion of their investment portfolios in international investments. Many countries are still limited in the proportion of non-domestic investments they can hold, but as deregulation gathers pace, the trend towards increased international investment will accelerate. However, given that the currency of consumption for UK investors is the pound sterling, most such investors will still choose to keep the majority of their investments in sterling-denominated securities.

REVIEW EXERCISES

1. Using the figures provided in Examples 11.1 and 11.2, test the hypothesis that the forward exchange rate between two actively traded, convertible currencies is determined by the interest rate differential between them, by assuming that:
   a. You are a Swiss-based investor making a fully covered investment in US dollars for one year.
   b. You are a euro-based investor making a fully covered investment in sterling for three months.

2. Mr Brooks is trying to calculate the expected return in sterling from two investments, one in Etiquette plc, a UK company, and the other in Protocol Inc, a similar US company. The current share prices are 114p for Etiquette and $26 for Protocol and the prevailing spot exchange rate is £1.00 = $1.85. Mr Brooks has asked his stockbroker for advice on the likely dividends and future share prices for the two companies in exactly one year's time. He has been given the following estimates:

Company	Estimated share price in one year's time	Estimated dividend to be received in one year's time
Etiquette plc	120p	9p
Protocol Inc	$28	$3

The broker is unwilling to commit himself on the future exchange rate; he is only prepared to give the following, admittedly very rough, probability distribution:

	Estimated spot exchange rate in one year's time	Probability of estimate
£1.00 =	1.60	0.05
	1.75	0.15
	1.85	0.25
	1.95	0.25
	2.10	0.30

a. Comment on the broker's estimate and probability distribution. How plausible do you consider it?

b. Calculate the expected one-year sterling return for Mr Brooks on each of Etiquette plc and Protocol Inc.

c. If the most pessimistic exchange rate forecast turns out to be true, how much does Mr Brooks stand to lose in sterling terms if he invests £1,000 now in Protocol?

d. If the expected earnings per share for Etiquette and Protocol are 12p and $5.14 respectively, calculate the p/e ratio, dividend yield and dividend cover for each company. Explain the meaning and relevance of each of these terms for investment decision-making and comment on the figures you have calculated for Protocol and Etiquette.

3. Miss King wishes to buy 100,000 shares in a US company, BBB Inc, which are currently quoted at $46 per share. She expects BBB to pay a dividend of $3 per share in three months' time and she expects to sell the shares three months later at a price of $55. Miss King wishes to hedge exchange risk as much as possible and her bank has provided her with the following quotations. The current spot exchange rate is £1.00 = US$1.8784 and relevant interest rates are as follows:

	Interbank deposit rates (%)	
	3 months	6 months
US dollars	5.39	5.44
Sterling	4.04	4.16

a. Should Miss King buy or sell dollars on the forward market in order to hedge her currency risk?

b. Use the interest rate parity theory to determine the equilibrium three- and six-month forward rates.

c. What rate of return can Miss King expect to earn in sterling terms and to what extent can she hedge exchange risk?

4. Assume that it is the beginning of January 2006 and that you are given the following information and estimates for the UK and for the fictitious country Molvania, whose currency is the Kuh (MK).

	United Kingdom	Molvania
Estimated inflation rate for 2006	3% p.a.	15% p.a.
Estimated required real interest rate	4% p.a.	4% p.a.
Current spot exchange rate	£1.00 = MK5.00	

a. Use the Fisher relation to estimate the nominal interest rates which will prevail in each country.
b. Use the purchasing power parity theory to estimate the expected spot exchange rate in one year's time.
c. Use the interest rate parity theory to estimate the one-year forward exchange rate.
d. Compare your estimate of the current forward rate with the expected spot rate in one year's time. What does this imply about the need to hedge using the forward markets?

5. Describe the different ways in which an investor can invest internationally, and the advantages of each.
6. What are the implications of the interest rate parity theory for transactions in the forward foreign exchange and money markets?
7. Suppose you are a UK investor considering purchasing one of the following securities on 27 October 2006. Each security has just paid its penultimate annual coupon and is redeemable at par, together with its final coupon, on 27 October 2007.

Currency	Coupon	Clean price	Current spot exchange rate £1.00 =	1-year forward exchange rate £1.00 =
Sterling	7%	101.90	N/A	N/A
US dollar	6%	103.41	US$1.8369	US$1.7934
Euro	8%	105.37	€1.4384	€1.4019

a. If you wished to make a riskless investment, which security would you choose?
b. Do your results comply with the interest rate parity theory?
c. If, however, the securities do not mature on 27 October 2007 but have a ten-year life to 27 October 2016, what, if any, exchange risk would you incur by purchasing the US dollar or euro security?

Sample answers to the review exercises can be found on the companion website.

Part VI
Strategies and Issues

12 Investment objectives, strategies and performance

CHAPTER CONTENTS

Learning objectives for this chapter

After studying this chapter you should be able to

- ○ critically assess the application of the efficient markets hypothesis to real-life situations
- ○ describe the principal differences between active and passive investment strategies
- ○ use a variety of measures to evaluate the risk-adjusted performance of different portfolio management strategies
- ○ critically assess the relevance of each measurement technique to different situations.

INTRODUCTION

In the first eleven chapters of this book we looked at different types of securities, how to value them and how to compare them through the medium of expected holding period return and risk. We also considered the advantages of portfolio investment, both domestic and international, and the different requirements of the institutional (as opposed to the individual) investor. In this penultimate chapter, we examine investors' overall strategies, from the factors they should take into consideration when quantifying their objectives to the measurement of their actual investment performance.

Before investors can make any investment decisions at all, they must decide on their objectives. Although all investors will have an implicit or unconscious investment policy, this is all too often not stated explicitly. Again, the growth of investment intermediaries has emphasised the need for clearly stated objectives. The objectives of these intermediaries have to be known before their performance can be meaningfully measured and compared. There is no point in comparing the performance of an investment trust with the FTSE All-Share Index (the most broadly based measure of UK stock market performance) if the trust's specific objective was to be 50 per cent invested in the United States and 50 per cent in Japan.

Investment managers cannot set objectives unless they know the relevant characteristics of their clients or beneficiaries. These characteristics include their appetite for risk, their desired level of return, and details of their existing wealth, their tax positions, liquidity requirements and future liabilities. Until the 1990s, the approach of investment advisers was to concentrate on the characteristics of the securities or market in which they were investing rather than on the characteristics of their clients. As understanding of the efficient markets hypothesis and the capital asset pricing model has spread, more emphasis has been placed on the construction of portfolios that are optimal in the sense of being most appropriate to the investor's risk and return requirements, rather than in the sense of optimal securities (those offering the highest expected excess returns) to put into the portfolio.

Once investment managers have established the objectives of the investor or fund, they can set about designing the most appropriate investment policy. This hinges very much on the beliefs of the individual investor or manager. The major decision is whether to follow a *passive* or an *active* investment strategy. A passive investment policy corresponds to the 'fair return for risk' approach, and will be adopted by investors who believe that markets are efficient with respect to information; in other words, that they cannot systematically earn excess returns by studying market trends or by trying to pick winners. Such investors believe that their selection skills are not sufficient to justify the search and transaction costs entailed by an active search for excess returns. All that they expect is, on average, a fair return for the risk they choose to bear. Active investors, on the other hand, follow a *picking winners* approach and try to beat the market either by searching for mispriced securities or by attempting to time investments correctly.

Investment policy does not just involve a once and for all portfolio decision. Both active and passive strategies require that the portfolio, however constructed, be amended from time to time. The frequency and extent of the portfolio revisions are also investment policy decisions, taking into account the objectives of the portfolio and the transaction costs involved.

Finally, investors will be interested in measuring the performance of their investment portfolios, for many different reasons. For example, they will wish to check (particularly if they have used an intermediary) that the investment objectives laid down have been followed. Also, they may wish to compare the performance of alternative investment funds. Performance measurement will in addition identify particular investment skills, such as the ability to pick winners, and allows comparison between active and passive investment strategies.

Despite a clear need for performance measurement, reliable techniques could not be developed before portfolio theory and the CAPM were formulated. These were the first models to establish an explicit and systematic framework for quantifying risk and return and for trading them off against each other. Once risk could be measured, comparisons could be made between portfolios of different risk. Similarly, once a passive investment strategy based on the CAPM had been identified, comparisons could be made between active and passive investment policies. Performance measurement is now commonplace, in preference to the traditional comparison with a peer group of similar funds or fund managers.

This chapter begins by continuing the discussion of the efficient markets hypothesis which was introduced in Chapter 1. It then considers possible investment objectives and the factors that must be taken into account when deciding on objectives, for example inflation and tax. The third section compares in detail the major alternative investment policies: that is, active and passive approaches to investment management. The final section describes the alternative available risk-adjusted performance measures, and discusses their relevance to the different situations in which they can be applied.

THE EFFICIENT MARKETS HYPOTHESIS REVISITED

The question whether and to what extent the markets are in fact efficient is so fundamental to considerations of investment policy that we should begin by examining in greater detail the main implications of the efficient markets hypothesis (EMH) which was introduced in Chapter 1. Fama (1970) defined three levels of efficiency, each level designed to correspond with the different types of 'picking winners' investment strategies that were used in practice to try to achieve excess returns.

- ○ In the *weak form* of efficiency, each share price is assumed to reflect fully the information content of all past share prices.
- ○ In the *semi-strong form*, the information impounded is assumed to include not only that given by all past share prices, which are of course public knowledge, but all publicly available information relevant to the share value. This includes, for example, company announcements, brokers' reports, industry forecasts and company accounts.
- ○ The *strong form* of the EMH requires all known information to be impounded in the current share price, whether publicly and generally available or not. The strong form will thus include what is known as insider information, for example details of an impending takeover bid known only to senior management of both parties to the bid.

Weak form

In Chapter 1 we saw that the major stock markets of the world appear to support at least the random walk or weak form of the EMH. Despite this evidence that excess profits cannot be made in the long run by using past share price information, investment strategies using past share price information are still popular. The two main types of such *technical analysis* are *chartism* and *mechanical trading rules*.

Chartists specialise in analysing charts and graphs of share price information, spotting past trends and patterns and using these to forecast future price movements. For example, the shape in the centre of Figure 12.1 is known as a *head and shoulders* formation. Other commonly occurring patterns include the *neckline, congestion areas* and *triangles*.

Chartists are completely uninterested in the fundamental characteristics of a share, such as, for example, the prospects for the company's high technology project in the United States. They are concerned only with price movements and also volume of trading in the share. These are then translated into patterns reflecting the elusive 'mood of the market'.

There are two problems with this type of analysis:

- ○ The choice of patterns to superimpose on the charts is a subjective decision, and is much more difficult in anticipation than in hindsight.

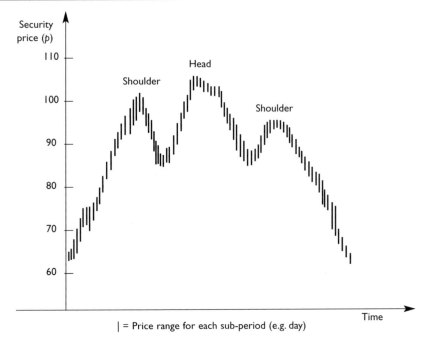

| = Price range for each sub-period (e.g. day)

Figure 12.1 Head-and-shoulders formation

○ Competition amongst chartists will compete the patterns and trends away. To make excess profits, a chartist must therefore be able to spot the pattern before all the other chartists recognise the trend. This will lead to any emerging trends being traded away and the weak form of the EMH being a valid representation of the market.

The other major form of technical analysis attempts to convert subjective impressions of trends or patterns in charts into objective mechanical rules for trading. However objective the rules may sound, they are still based on a theory of share price movement in a weak-form inefficient market.

For example, *filter rules* are designed to catch the breakout from a line, as shown in Figure 12.2 (overleaf). Within the line, the share is assumed to be trading at around its equilibrium value. As a piece of new information is absorbed, the price will break out towards its new equilibrium value. The filter rule is designed to catch the share at the *breakout point* as it moves from the old to the new equilibrium value. In an efficient market, this would not be possible, since the price would move too quickly and there would be no trend.

The object of a filter rule is to buy before the share reaches its new, higher value and sell before its new, lower value. The dilemma is which size filter to choose. Figure 12.3 shows a filter of 5%. The wider the filter, the more likely investors are to trade only on 'true' breakouts, but the later they will be in catching the trend. The smaller the filter, the likelier investors are to catch the trend early enough. However, they might be misled by false breakouts and their transaction costs will doubtless outweigh any gains they make from trading in and out of the share as opposed to simply buying the share and holding it.

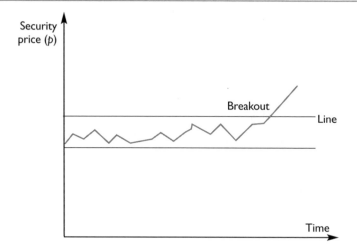

Figure 12.2 Example of line and breakout patterns

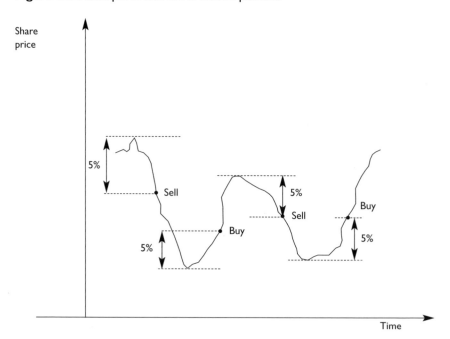

Figure 12.3 Example of filter rule

Two characteristics of these trading rules should be mentioned.

○ Where individual shares are concerned, they ignore relative risk, the shares being chosen purely on the basis of past price movements, with their fundamental and economic characteristics being ignored. Chartists believe they can afford to do this because they are looking for short-term gains, moving in and out of shares relatively frequently, rather than choosing long-term investments. However, because shares with the biggest price changes will usually be chosen under these trading rules, there may well be an emphasis on shares with higher volatility and therefore higher risk, leading investors to hold portfolios which are riskier than they perhaps realise.

○ Use of these rules will involve high transaction costs, and perhaps for this reason, they are popular with those whose commission depends on share turnover. This is no doubt one of the reasons that, when these trading rules have been tested and compared with a simple *buy and hold* strategy over a period of months or years, the buy and hold strategy has been found to yield higher returns, net of transaction costs.

No form of the EMH, including the weak form, can conclusively be shown to hold for any stock market, since it is impossible to test every possible trading rule on every possible set of share prices for excess returns. However, the weight of evidence in favour of the weak form of the EMH is generally accepted by academic opinion to be overwhelming, both in the United Kingdom and more particularly in the United States.

There are probably two main reasons for the continued popularity of technical analysis:

○ Technical analysis is popular in areas where fundamental information is lacking, in particular with market-makers and traders who need help in forecasting minute-by-minute price movements when no relevant news has been forthcoming.

○ With the advent of computerised real time data services, it now takes a few seconds to plot relative strength for a share or to plot bar charts on a gilt index, tempting otherwise rational fund managers to turn to technical analysis as a forecasting tool, even if it is secondary to fundamental analysis in their decision-making process.

Semi-strong form

The semi-strong form of the efficient markets hypothesis calls into question not only the activities of chartists but also the strategy of fundamental analysis favoured by the majority of investment professionals. Most investment analysts spend their time forecasting future earnings, dividends or returns for the companies within their chosen sector. They do this by studying economic forecasts and industry reports, by visiting the company and by analysing company accounts and statements. All of this is translated into their estimate of the share's fair value. Comparison of this fair value with the current share price generates a 'buy', 'sell' or 'hold' recommendation to clients.

Each major company is studied by many analysts, who have available to them the same public information, can make the same company visits, and pore over the same company accounts. With this in mind, the semi-strong form of the EMH, which postulates that share prices at any time fully reflect all relevant publicly available information, becomes readily believable. Any new piece of information made public will be so quickly analysed and absorbed into a new market estimate of the company's value that an investor trading on each announcement, say of unexpectedly good earnings, will act too late to be able to make consistent excess returns. Even if the market does not initially fully absorb the new information, the new share price is as likely to be an overestimate as an underestimate of the equilibrium share price reached once the information has been correctly interpreted and impounded.

The implications of the semi-strong form of the EMH for fundamental analysis, if it closely reflects reality, are far-reaching. Not only does it follow that trading on announcement of new information will not, on average and taken over time, produce excess returns, but it also implies that the best available indicator of a share's so-called intrinsic value is its current market price. So a fundamental analyst's search for undervalued shares within his or her sector using publicly available information is a waste of time. For example, a study of the intangible assets of companies could lead an analyst to believe that certain companies were undervalued and others overvalued. However, if the method of valuing intangible assets is publicly available in the notes to the accounts, other analysts will already have impounded whatever additional knowledge was contained in the notes into the share price.

Not all analysts and investors need to have fully digested and analysed the details of the accounts. All that is required is for a sufficient number of analysts and their clients to have traded in the share with that knowledge. Thus, if the semi-strong form of the EMH does hold, no investor or analyst will be able consistently to make abnormal returns from the analysis of such publicly available information. But the market value of a share will only be as good an estimate of the share's intrinsic value as the quality of the publicly available information concerning the company permits. If the information available is meagre, the market price of the share will be a correspondingly poor approximation to the share's worth. If, on the other hand, most relevant information is disclosed, the market value will be a good estimate of the share's worth. The implication for those concerned with corporate disclosure and accounting standards is therefore that careful consideration should be applied to what information is disclosed rather than how it is disclosed, since each new item of information not previously available may improve the market's estimate of the share's worth.

Such a conclusion is particularly significant for small investors whose proportionate transaction costs are high. The implication is that individual investors should not worry about investment analysis. They should simply choose a diversified portfolio of shares and concentrate on their optimum risk–reward ratio and other considerations, such as tax, liquidity and inflation proofing.

The implications of the semi-strong form of the EMH are less reassuring for investment analysts than for investors. Their main *raison d'être* is put into question. And yet, if the evidence supports the semi-strong form, why do so many people still manage to make a living out of fundamental analysis? By analysing information and trading (or recommending to clients) on that information, they ensure that share prices fully reflect the information. But if everyone believed the semi-strong form and ignored fundamental analysis, the market would become inefficient.

This paradox, which is not really resolved by the EMH, leads us to consider more recent work on markets for information. These theoretical models attempt, as the EMH does not, to take account of the role of *information intermediaries*, such as fundamental analysts, by assuming *asymmetry of information*. In these models, information is not freely available to everyone since, if this were so, security prices would obviously fully reflect all that information. Instead, they assume that information can be purchased at a cost by any investor, and that this information improves estimates of securities' expected returns. Informed investors will thus have valuable information not known to uninformed investors. Asymmetry of information will prevail.

Within this framework, let us consider the role of fundamental analysts. They acquire information, say by studying publicly available information, but at a cost. For example, there is the opportunity cost of their time, and the possible need for qualifications (such as an accounting qualification to be able to understand cash flow statements). Fundamental analysts then make use of that information by selling it (as brokers) or trading in the shares themselves. Either way, share prices will then reflect that information. This appears to lead us straight back to the paradox inherent in the EMH. If the information acquired at a cost by the analyst is fully reflected in share prices, why should investors buy information or the analyst incur costs when the price will reflect the information anyway?

In order to avoid this problem, the models have to assume that prices do not clearly reflect the information for some reason. For example, they assume that there is a certain amount of 'noise' in share prices, which no amount of information can dispel. When studying share price movements, investors will not be able to tell what proportion of the price changes are caused by information and what proportion by noise. This assumption allows for an equilibrium situation in which certain investors (and analysts) are informed and others choose to remain uninformed. No investors can improve their expected utility by changing from uninformed to informed. Certain investors will prefer to remain uninformed and to protect themselves by holding a well-diversified portfolio or index fund. Others will prefer to buy information and to use it to pick winners. On average, the cost of acquiring the information will equal the benefit from using it. So, for example, informed investors will not in the long run make excess returns after transaction costs which include the cost of acquiring information. Similarly, following the recommendations of an investment strategy based on fundamental analysis will not on average yield excess returns after transaction costs. However, informed investors might do better, on average, than uninformed investors before transaction costs, and some might on occasion do better than the average.

Trying to explain the role of fundamental analysis has led us to consider models that have a stronger theoretical framework than does the EMH. Early tests of market efficiency supported semi-strong market efficiency, although recently some tests have appeared to find stock market anomalies. However Fama (1998) argued that many apparent anomalies are due to methodological issues. We shall look further at breaches of EMH in Chapter 13, but before we leave the EMH we consider the final level of efficiency, strong form efficiency.

Strong form

The strong form of the efficient markets hypothesis states that share prices fully reflect all knowable information, whether publicly available or not. This would imply that, if only a few people knew something about a company (for example, if only a handful of senior managers and civil servants were aware that the company had just been awarded a lucrative government contract), even they would not be able to make excess profits by trading on this knowledge.

There are far fewer tests of the strong form of the EMH than of the weak or semi-strong form, because of the difficulty in obtaining share trading information on the kind of people likely to have access to non-public information. Such people are known as *insiders*. However, certain groups of potential insiders can be identified, such as directors and associates of companies and stockbrokers, on whom there is a certain amount of information available. For example, in the United States and in the United Kingdom, insiders have long been obliged to register all their share dealings in the companies to which they are insiders, and studies of these share dealings have shown that excess returns are possible. Another type of insider dealer is the specialist broker on the New York Stock Exchange who has access to a different kind of non-publicly available information: the orders to buy and sell at particular prices of his or her clients. Specialists can buy and sell on their own account with no time lag, and tests have shown that they too can, at least occasionally, make excess returns. In the United Kingdom, tests on stockbrokers' own trades and newspapers' share recommendations have also shown excess returns.

An alternative way of testing whether the strong form holds is to examine the behaviour of investing intermediaries or institutions. The economies of scale they can achieve in investment analysis and transaction costs should mean that they, of all investors, stand the most chance of being able to earn consistent long-run returns from publicly available information. Also, the relatively close relationships with the companies in which they invest (due to, for example, company visits) could lead to their obtaining information on these companies that is not generally available. So examining the performance of such institutions would provide some evidence for and against both the semi-strong and the strong forms of the EMH.

Since information on the performance of UK financial institutions is most readily available for unit and investment trusts, these are the institutions that have been studied for evidence of the possibility of long-run excess returns – the ability to pick winners. No such evidence has been found, which provides further support for the semi-strong form. As far as the strong form is concerned, the evidence is less clear-cut, however. If these institutions do not have access to non-publicly available information, a study of their performance is not a test of the strong form. In so far as they do, the validity of the strong form is supported by the lack of apparent long-run excess returns achieved by investing institutions. However, recent evidence points to excess returns achieved by some investing institutions but counterbalanced by transaction costs and fees charged to clients.

Finally, although the evidence appears to be against the strong form, implying that insider dealing can be a profitable activity, the amount of insider dealing must be perceived by the market as a whole to be relatively insignificant or else rational, risk-averse, *outsider* investors would not be prepared to invest in such a market. Indeed, regulation aimed at preventing insider dealing and providing for the rapid disclosure of information is common to all the major stock markets where turnover and investor interest is high. Insiders are more likely to make substantial excess returns in the less developed and less regulated emerging stock markets.

INVESTMENT OBJECTIVES

Investment objectives will of course vary widely according to the type of investor. For instance, an individual investor might wish to maximise her return over a ten-year period, taking on a reasonably high level of risk since she already has a substantial earned income. A pensioner would be more likely to require a constant level of income in real terms, to be achieved with minimum risk. A pension fund manager might have the objective of meeting a specified set of future liabilities at minimum overall cost.

Rather than specifying in detail particular sets of objectives, we shall concentrate instead on those factors that must be considered before any investment objectives can be set. We group these factors under five headings: consumption preferences, required risk and return, tax, inflation and asset allocation.

Consumption preferences

All investors will be aware of their own consumption preferences. These will include preferred currency of consumption, so that an investor who spends half the year in New York might require a portfolio denominated in both sterling and dollars. Also, part of the portfolio might need to be in liquid assets, to meet unforeseen liabilities and to allow the investor to pursue an active investment policy with the remainder. The preference for income or capital gain will be determined partly by the tax position of the investor but also by the need for a regular income as opposed to long-term capital growth. However, in principle capital can be turned into income by regular small sales.

The time horizon of concern to investors will vary from a few hours or days for the speculator who believes he has inside information to several decades for the pension fund manager. The time horizon will thus be a function of the future consumption needs of the investor and of the type of investment policy he or she prefers. The time horizon will also affect the investor's attitude to transaction costs. For example, if an investor wishes to invest in property in the near future, she will wish to minimise the risk and transaction costs associated with her short-term investments. On the other hand, a salaried investor with ten years to go before retirement might be willing to invest in a ***unit-linked life assurance scheme,*** where the long-term capital growth and tax advantages outweigh the relatively high transaction costs.

Attitude to risk and return

As we have seen throughout the book, investors' attitude to risk and return is the most important factor in formulating their investment objectives. Whether they wish to pursue a *picking winners* or a *fair return for risk* investment policy, investors need to state how much risk they are willing to bear and how much return they require on average in order to choose between alternative efficient portfolios. An investor whose objective is merely to supplement his earned income might aim to achieve the maximum possible return subject to a maximum level of acceptable risk. A pensioner living off her investments might aim to minimise risk subject to a minimum level of acceptable return. Risk can be expressed in terms of the standard deviation or variance of returns, if investors are considering their entire wealth and the possibility of its loss, or in terms of beta if the investment considered represents only part of their total wealth.

Since it may be difficult for an investor to be able to state the maximum standard deviation of returns that he or she will accept or the minimum return he or she requires, a simpler solution might be to face the investor with a set of alternative portfolios which lie on his or her efficient frontier, each of which will have different risk–return characteristics, and to ask the investor to choose the one he or she prefers. As we saw in Chapter 6, the efficient frontier represents those portfolios that offer the best returns given their risk. The investor will choose amongst these according to his or her risk/return preference.

Tax

Tax is also an extremely important factor in real life, although for the sake of simplicity we excluded tax from our discussion of portfolio theory and the CAPM. Tax can render certain investments unattractive to investors, as is the case with high-coupon bonds for high tax-rate investors. Similarly, tax can make certain types of investment more attractive than they would otherwise be, such as investing in equities via a pension scheme rather than directly in the stock market. Also, Individual Savings Accounts (ISAs) allow private investors to avoid capital gains tax on any gains if they hold equities for a five-year period.

Tax can therefore distort preferences for income or capital gains, high or low-coupon stocks, or direct versus indirect investment. The tax position of investors must therefore be taken into account when determining the investment objectives of their portfolios, and portfolio returns should be compared at the net-of-tax level.

Inflation

Another factor to be considered is the impact of inflation on the value of investments. Investments and liabilities can no longer be viewed purely in nominal terms. For example, the parents of a new-born child may wish to put funds aside to cover the cost of private schooling in future years. Even if they were to buy gilts with fixed nominal coupon and repayment values at exactly the right future dates, they could not be sure that school fees would remain fixed in nominal terms over the next 18 years. In fact, even if they were to invest in index-linked gilts they would probably still find themselves underprovided, because the cost of private education has historically risen by significantly more than the retail price index. Similarly, the liabilities of *final salary* (or *defined benefit*) pension schemes are related to salaries which are certainly not constant in nominal terms, and – like school fees – have historically risen faster than the retail price index. Because of this inflation risk, investment objectives must take account of inflation in assessing the investor's requirements, that is, whether the need is to keep up with inflation or merely to cover a nominal liability, such as the repayment of a fixed loan.

Most investors, whether individuals or institutions, need to maintain the value of their investments in real terms. This leads us to consider the different types of investment available in the light of how good a hedge they are against inflation.

We have already noted in Chapter 10 that investment intermediaries, in particular insurance companies, pension funds and investment trusts, all experienced losses from their fixed interest investments in the 1960s and 1970s as interest rates and inflation rates rose. From the 1980s onwards, there was a general trend (interrupted briefly by the 1987 crash, and more radically by the prolonged bear market of 2000–03) away from fixed interest investments towards equities, which were believed to represent a better hedge against inflation. According to classical economic theory, ordinary shares were supposed to maintain their value in real terms. As interest rates and the required rate of return on equities went up, so would the income of the companies as revenues and costs went up correspondingly. The overall impact on share prices would represent no change in real terms.

Let us first consider a world with no inflation. According to the dividend valuation model discussed in Chapter 5 the value of a share P_0 can be written as

$$P_0 = \sum_{n=1}^{\infty} \frac{D_n}{(1+R)^n} \tag{12.1}$$

where D_n is the dividend to be paid in year n and R is the required rate of return on the share. How will inflation affect equation 12.1? If the revenues as well as the outgoings of the firm increase in line with inflation, thus allowing dividends also to keep up with inflation, the numerator of equation 12.1 will become $D_n (1 + i)^n$ where i is the annual inflation rate expected to prevail for the foreseeable future. Similarly, the required rate of return will also adjust for expected inflation, so that the denominator $(1 + R)$ will become instead $(1 + R)(1 + i)$.

Substituting into equation 12.1 gives

$$P_0 = \sum_{n=1}^{\infty} \frac{D_n(1+i)^n}{(1+R)^n(1+i)^n} \tag{12.2}$$

The term $(1 + i)^n$ cancels out and equation 12.2 reduces to

$$P_0 = \sum_{n=1}^{\infty} \frac{D_n}{(1+R)^n} \tag{12.3}$$

which is exactly the same as equation 12.1.

From equation 12.3, we can see how the classical theory works. If, in an inflationary environment, the dividends of the company are maintained in real terms (as a result of revenues and costs going up exactly in line with inflation) and if the required rate of return also adjusts exactly for expected inflation, the current value of the share P_0 will remain unchanged, thus representing a complete hedge against inflation.

In real life, there are many reasons that the classical theory might not hold. The company's cash flows might not maintain their value in real terms for several possible reasons:

○ Prices might not keep up with costs.
○ The tax system might penalise nominal, as opposed to real, increases in profits.
○ There might be time lags between changes in costs and changes in revenues.

Furthermore, the required rate of return, R, only takes expected inflation into account. No allowance is made in equation 12.2 for unexpected inflation.

We saw in Chapter 3 that the introduction of index-linked gilts in 1981 appeared to offer a true hedge against inflation. But even index-linked gilts do not completely solve the problem of inflation, for three reasons.

○ The current supply of index-linked gilts, of around £80 billion, is by no means sufficient to hedge all the pension funds' inflation risk, let alone that of other investors.
○ Index-linked gilts are indexed to the Retail Prices Index, which is meant to reflect the cost of living of the average consumer. It might be that the investor wishes to hedge against a particular price change, such as our couple wishing to provide for school fees, and this can be greater than or less than the change in the Retail Prices Index.

○ The required real rate of return on gilts might vary, and this will affect the price of index-linked gilts. Investors cannot therefore be sure of a certain real rate of return unless they hold the index-linked gilts to maturity.

An alternative way of coping with inflation risk, as we saw in Chapter 2, is by pooling or diversification. One method, discussed in Chapter 11, is to diversify internationally. This will reduce the dependence of the investor's portfolio on domestic inflation. Another is to diversify across types of security that have different reactions to inflation.

Strategic asset allocation

Portfolio theory suggests that combining equities which have low correlation coefficients will improve the risk–return characteristics of an investor's portfolio, compared with holding just a few shares or a naïvely diversified portfolio. As we saw in Chapter 11, this argument can be extended to the international arena since the correlation coefficients between certain stock markets will be lower than between shares in the same stock market.

We can now go one step further and consider portfolios made up of combinations of different types of asset. Returns on cash and long gilts are poorly correlated in the United Kingdom, as are returns on gilts and equities. The time period chosen affects the correlation coefficients significantly, but this does not detract from the fact that spreading resources among different types of asset as well as internationally will improve the risk–return characteristics of an investor's portfolio, and this approach has been adopted (as we saw from the portfolio details given in Chapter 10) by UK pension funds and insurance companies. At one time, the British Rail Pension Fund took diversification of the asset mix one stage further by investing in Impressionist paintings as a separate asset class.

When considering the asset mix and the objectives of their investment portfolios, investors should also bear in mind the characteristics of their existing wealth. For example, if an investor works in the chemical industry, it might be sensible to include an objective to hold a smaller proportion of his portfolio than might otherwise be the case in the chemical sector. This is because the level of the investor's future earnings will be to some extent linked to the fortunes of the chemical industry. The investor would therefore reduce his risk by having an investment portfolio whose returns were poorly correlated with the chemical industry and hence his other main source of income. The choice of long-term asset mix is also called *strategic asset allocation.*

INVESTMENT POLICY

As we mentioned in the introduction to this chapter, there are essentially two types of investment policy that can be pursued by fund managers or individual investors. The first is an active investment strategy which attempts to capitalise on a particular investment skill, such as stock selection or market timing, and the other is passive, attempting merely to achieve an average return on a well-diversified portfolio.

Active investment policy

There are two main ways of attempting to actively outperform a benchmark portfolio. One is to pick stocks that do better in return terms than the stocks in the benchmark portfolio – we shall call this *stock selection*. The other is to buy and sell stocks at the right time so that they are bought at a lower than average price and sold at a higher than average price – we call this *market timing*.

Stock selectors believe that markets are in some way inefficient and/or that some securities are under- or overvalued. They believe that they can use fundamental analysis to identify undervalued stocks, and that portfolios including substantial or *overweight* holdings will therefore outperform a more diversified index benchmark. The most common kinds of techniques used to try to identify potential outperformers include more accurate earnings forecasts than the consensus, detailed analysis of the impact of accounting techniques on the declared profits, identifying stocks with high or low price/earnings ratios (according to the stage in the economic cycle), and quantitative techniques, where computers are used to identify stocks with a particular range of characteristics that the analyst believes will do well over the investment time horizon – for example, attempting to identify possible takeover candidates, or *value* or *growth* shares.

The second type of active investment policy is to attempt correct timing of purchases and sales, often through the use of technical analysis (or possibly insider information!). This can be done either at the individual security level or at the market level. One method, provided by the CAPM, would be to acquire high beta shares before a bull market and to switch into low beta shares before a bear market. This would allow fund managers or investors to alter the risk of the equity element of their portfolio without altering the amount invested in equities. Another method involves switching from equities into bonds or cash if a stock market fall is forecast, and moving into equities before a stock market rise. This technique is also referred to as *tactical asset allocation*, and can be undertaken by making a study of the typical historical relationship of, say, the yield gap between the return on treasury bills and the dividend yield on equities, and switching between treasury bills and equities according to whether the current yield gap is high or low relative to its historical average.

Tactical asset allocation involves short-term switches between asset classes, and differs from strategic asset allocation, which involves the fundamental choice of how much to put into each asset type such as bonds, domestic equities and foreign equities in the longer term. This was discussed earlier in the chapter.

Whether excess returns are created by picking winners or market timing, this implies that the investor has earned more than the expected return, $E(R_p)$, where $E(R_p)$ is given by the CAPM equation:

$$E(R_p) = R_F + \beta_p(E(R_M) - R_F).$$

The realised return, R_p, is not usually equal to the expected return, leading to an error term, e_p, from taking on specific risk:

$$R_p = R_F + \beta_p(R_M - R_F) + e_p$$

Fund managers, though, do not like to attribute any outperformance to a positive, random (according to the CAPM) value of the error term, e_p. They prefer to call it *positive alpha* by rewriting the realised CAPM equation

$$R_p = \alpha_p + R_F + \beta_p(R_M - R_F) + e_p$$

where α_p is a *persistent* element of outperformance due to investment skill (unlike the random element, e_p) – despite what the CAPM says!

Passive investment policy

The alternative investment policy is a passive approach, based on the results of the CAPM. All that is expected by the investor is a fair return for the risk involved. Thus, once the risk level has been set and an optimal portfolio (allowing for consumption prefer-ences, time horizon, tax and inflation) has been determined, all that the investor needs to do is to maintain the portfolio at its required diversification and risk levels. The turnover and transaction costs of the portfolio will be lower than that of an actively managed port-folio, as will be management fees, since there will be less need for the advice of either technical or fundamental analysts.

The passive approach to fund management has become increasingly popular over the past few years, as evidence has accumulated that the majority of fund managers do not consistently outperform a benchmark index. An *index fund* is a portfolio of equities (or bonds) that attempts to track as closely as possible a market index such as the FTSE All-Share Index for UK equities and the S&P 500 for US equities. The aim of the active investor is to outperform the relevant benchmark index; the aim of the passive investor is to achieve average performance through returns that are equal to the returns on the market as a whole, most probably through an index fund. In active fund management, success is judged by the size of the return in excess of that on the index; in index fund management, success is judged by how small is the difference between the fund's return and the index's return, known as the *tracking error*.

Hybrid investment policies

Whether an active or passive investment policy is pursued, it must be consistent. An active policy will involve high turnover, high transaction costs and relatively poor diversification (since specific risk must be borne for excess returns to be possible). A passive policy will involve low turnover, low transaction costs and high diversification. Both, however, will require some element of portfolio revision. Active investors will need to re-examine opportunities and estimates of future share price and market move-ments fairly frequently in their search for winners. Passive investors will need to revise their portfolios only when there is a change in any of:

○ the factors affecting their objectives
○ their estimates of market risk and return
○ the composition of the index or sector they are tracking.

Various compromises between the two types of investment policy are now being adopted by investors, particularly the large institutional portfolio managers. One compromise is, instead of having the entire portfolio actively managed, to split the fund into a passively managed index fund element and an actively managed element. This actively managed element might be split into three or four different funds each with specialist expertise: for example, Far Eastern, global bonds, quantitative, or futures and options. This allows the overall fund manager to keep down portfolio turnover and hence transaction costs while attempting to outperform the market with part of the portfolio. A second method is what is known as a *tilted fund*, an index fund tilted away from the index to exploit some particular investment expertise, for example the ability to identify good-value stocks or sectors likely to perform better than the market average. Tilted funds have the advantage of allowing the fund managers running them to charge higher fees than for the *plain vanilla* index funds. A third method is to create a so-called *long–short* hedge fund which is *market neutral* by having a net zero exposure to the stock market. It will have sufficient short positions in shares to counterbalance any long positions, thereby creating a zero beta portfolio. Such a fund, though, is active since it will have specific risk which will lead either to *positive alpha* or to underperformance.

PERFORMANCE MEASUREMENT

The final section in this chapter is devoted to performance measurement, which has a variety of possible uses. For instance, once the investment objectives of their portfolios have been set, investors will wish to know whether these objectives have been achieved. They may also wish to compare their portfolios' performance with the performance of portfolios that had similar objectives. For example, if an investor has placed his savings in a unit trust promising high income, he may wish to compare its performance with other high-income unit trusts. When investment is made or managed via intermediaries, performance measures also serve other functions. They help to check that the fund managers are neither fraudulent nor incompetent, and that they are keeping to their stated objectives.

Performance measures can also be used to evaluate investment policy. We saw above that there are two main investment strategies, an active investment strategy which we have called *picking winners* and a passive strategy referred to as *fair return for risk* based on the CAPM. Any actively managed investment portfolio can be evaluated not only relative to portfolios with similar objectives but also relative to an equivalent passive portfolio or index.

If we consider the quantity of performance measurement carried out in industry, such as measuring achievement against profit targets or examining variances between actual and budgeted performance, it is surprising to note how little has been done in the field of investment. Two factors probably influenced this lack of performance measurement. First, until portfolio theory and the CAPM quantified risk, there was no way that two portfolios of different risk could be compared except with a peer group with similar investment objectives. Secondly, the relative paucity of disclosure concerning the investment portfolios and policies of the investment intermediaries, especially when compared with the level of disclosure required of companies, has not allowed detailed assessments of performance.

However, as investment has become more and more institutionalised, so performance measurement has become more prevalent. Performance measures are now routinely used by trustees of pension funds as a form of monitoring and as a means of identifying the particular investment skills (or lack of them) of the managers of pension funds. Detailed performance measurement is not yet part of the services offered to private client investors, who still tend to get statements of the value of their portfolios with no information on how their assets performed relative to a benchmark or adjusted for the risk of their portfolios, but over the next few years, competitive pressures in the fund management industry, coupled with increased computerisation, will see more sophisticated measures of performance for all types of fund management.

There are four main steps in measuring the performance of a portfolio:

○ Calculate the return.
○ Adjust for risk.
○ Analyse performance in greater depth by breaking down the measure into its constituent parts.
○ Use the results to review the relevance of the measure.

Calculating return

Let us consider the calculation of the return of a portfolio run by an investing institution. Investing intermediaries have varying patterns of cash flows, and the fund managers have varying levels of control over them. For example, pension funds will have cash inflows and outflows at regular intervals, representing employer and employee pension contributions and pension payments, whereas unit trusts will experience irregular cash inflows and outflows reflecting demand for the units. So when comparing the performance of two funds, the timing of their cash flows must be taken into account. If one unit trust experiences a large inflow of funds to be invested just before a bull market whereas another experiences a cash outflow at that time, the first unit trust might well appear superficially to have done better although it might actually have achieved lower returns overall.

Suppose unit trusts *A* and *B* have identical equity portfolios and investment policies but they experience different timing of cash flows over years 1, 2 and 3, as outlined in Example 12.1. Unit trust *B* appears to have done better, with a higher terminal value of £226, because although both trusts received cash inflows of £100 during the period, unit trust *B* received its cash flow before a general market rise in year 2 and unit trust *A* only before a market fall in year 3.

Note that when we average percentage changes over time we use the *geometric mean GM* instead of the *arithmetic mean*, where

Example 12.1 Impact of timing of cash flows on performance

	Now	End of Year 1	End of Year 2	End of Year 3
Unit trust A				
Value of fund (£)	100	110	131	209
Cash inflow (at the end of year 2)			+100	
Annual rate of return (%)		+10	+19	–9.5
Average rate of return (%)	**6**			
Unit trust B				
Value of fund (£)	100	210	250	226
Cash inflow (at the end of year 1)		+100		
Annual rate of return (%)		+10	+19	–9.5
Average rate of return (%)	**6**			

$$GM = \sqrt[n]{(1 + r_1)(1 + r_2)...(1 + r_n)} - 1$$

In order to allow for the different timing of cash flows, the *time-weighted rate of return* (*TWROR*) can be used to compare the performance of unit trusts *A* and *B*, instead of simply comparing the terminal values of their portfolios. To do this, we calculate the average of the rates of return achieved in each period between cash flows. From Example 12.1, we can see that, despite the difference in timing of cash flows, unit trusts *A* and *B* are in all other respects identical, including their annual rates of return, which leads to identical TWROR of 6%

To determine the TWROR, the date on which each cash flow occurs and the value of the portfolio on each such date must be known. This may be practicable for unit trusts, which have to calculate the market value of their portfolios on a daily basis, because the bid and offer prices for units are based on the market value of the portfolio. But it may be costly for small funds that experience frequent cash inflows and outflows. In these cases it may be necessary to estimate the value of the portfolio at the time the cash flow occurred.

For example, suppose that Pequeño Trust plc achieves a return on its portfolio of 10% over a period of six months, as shown in Figure 12.4, with the portfolio increasing in value from £1000 at the beginning of the period to £1100 at the end of the six months. Suppose also that Pequeño experienced a cash outflow of £50 half-way through the six-month period. Because of this, Pequeño's TWROR must in fact be greater than 10% but it cannot be determined since the value of the fund at the date of the cash outflow is unknown.

However, the TWROR can be estimated if it is assumed that the rate of return achieved in the first three months, say *R*, was the same as that achieved in the second three months. If *x* is the unknown value of the portfolio at the half-way point, then

$$R = \frac{x - 1000}{1000} = \frac{1100 - (x - 50)}{x - 50} \tag{12.4}$$

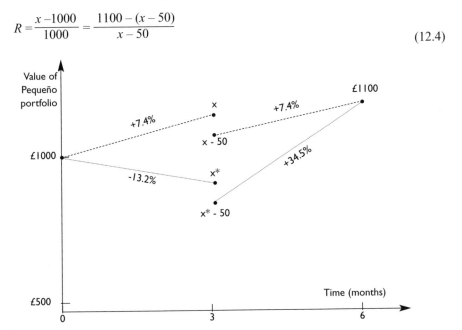

Figure 12.4 Calculating TWROR when the value of the portfolio is unknown

Cross-multiplying to solve for x in equation 12.4 gives

$$(x - 1000)(x - 50) = 1000(1100 - (x - 50))$$
$$x(x - 50) - 1000(x - 50) = 1,100,000 - 1000(x - 50)$$
$$x(x - 50) = 1,100,000$$
$$x^2 - 50x - 1,100,000 = 0$$

This is a quadratic equation of the form

$$ax^2 + bx + c = 0$$

which can be solved using a general formula

$$x = \frac{-b \pm \sqrt{b^2 - 4ac}}{2a}$$

In this particular case we take the positive square root of the $\sqrt{b^2 - 4ac}$ term, as the negative square root would give us a negative value for x, which would be nonsensical in this context.

Using the general formula to solve quadratic equations we get

$$x = £1074$$

Therefore, the return in each three-month period was 7.4%, compounding up to a six-month TWROR of 15.3%.

This method is known as the internal rate of return (or IRR) method. While it allows TWROR to be estimated, it makes no allowance for market movements during the period under consideration. It assumes that the overall return for the six months was mirrored in the two three-month sub-periods. It could have been the case that there was a downswing in the first three months followed by an upswing in the next three months.

An alternative to the IRR method uses the CAPM to take into account any such market movements when estimating x. Suppose that a suitable market index dropped from 196 at the beginning of the period to 172.5 three months later, a fall of 12 per cent. If we assume that Pequeño Trust's portfolio is well diversified and has a beta of 1.1 against the market index, we would expect the value of the portfolio to have fallen 1.1 x 12% = 13.2%. Thus an estimate of x, allowing for market movements, would be £868, 13.2% below the original £1000. This CAPM method leads to two different sub-period returns:

$$\frac{868 - 1000}{1000} = -13.2\%$$

in the first three months and

$$\frac{1100 - 818}{818} = 34.5\%$$

in the second three months. We should note that when we compound this up to a six-month TWROR we get a different result from the case where we assumed that the rate of return remained constant:

$$(1 - 0.132)(1 + 0.345) = 1.167$$

so that the overall six-month TWROR is now 16.7%.

Adjusting for risk

Having measured the return, we must now adjust for risk. Investors can use either the standard deviation or the beta of the portfolio as a measure of risk, according to whether the portfolio under consideration includes all their assets or represents only part of their well-diversified portfolio.

There are two main types of performance measure that can be derived (for either measure of risk) according to whether the risk of the particular portfolio whose performance is being measured is prespecified or not. For example, unit trusts and investment trusts choose their own levels of risk, and investors in these trusts can adjust the level of risk of their investment if they so wish, by borrowing or lending. In these cases, individual investors may wish to know which trusts offer the highest return allowing for their risk. Only by doing this will they be able to compare trusts that have different levels of risk, however that risk is measured. On the other hand, a pension fund manager might be operating under a set level of risk which has been imposed on him by the trustees of the fund. The question to be asked in this case is, given the level of risk imposed, did the pension fund manager do well or badly?

Risk measures have been developed to cater for either of these circumstances and to deal with either measure of risk. This gives rise to a matrix of performance measures, reproduced in Figure 12.5.

The two measures in the *reward per unit of risk* column give a reward–risk ratio which can be used to rank funds or portfolios. Both the *Sharpe measure*, which uses the standard deviation as a measure of risk, and the *Treynor measure*, which uses beta as a

		Reward per unit of risk	Differential return
Risk	Standard deviation	$$\dfrac{R_P - R_F}{S_P}$$ Sharpe measure	$R_P - R_{benchmark}$ where $R_{benchmark} = R_B$ and $R_B = R_F + \dfrac{(R_M - R_F)}{S_M} S_P$ Fama net gain from selectivity
	Beta	$$\dfrac{R_P - R_F}{\beta_P}$$ Treynor measure	$R_P - R_{benchmark}$ where $R_{benchmark} = R_B$ and $R_B = R_F + (R_M - R_F)\beta_P$ Jensen measure

Figure 12.5 Risk-adjusted performance measures

measure of risk, are based on the CAPM. As has already been said, no risk-adjusted measures can be derived unless a model that quantifies risk is used. Investors can then use whichever of the Sharpe and Treynor measures is more appropriate to their personal circumstances to choose the highest-ranking of the available portfolios. They can adjust to their required risk levels by borrowing or lending. For example, suppose that three unit trusts have performed as shown in Example 12.2 over the last year.

Example 12.2 Performance ranking by reward per unit of risk

Unit trust	Return (%)	Risk measure Standard deviation (%)	Beta	Sharpe measure	Treynor measure
A	12%	25%	1.3	0.16	0.031
B	10%	10%	1.1	0.20	0.018
C	13%	30%	1.4	0.17	0.036
Risk-free rate	8%				

Reward per unit of risk

Mr Adonis wishes to place the majority of his funds in one of the above unit trusts, so he is concerned with the total risk of the trust and will therefore use the standard deviation of portfolio returns as his criterion. He might choose B, which has the highest Sharpe measure. Mr Zeus wishes to place only a small part of his total portfolio in one of these unit trusts, so he is concerned only with the undiversifiable risk and will therefore use beta as his criterion. He might prefer C, which has the highest Treynor measure of performance.

Both Mr Adonis and Mr Zeus can then adjust for risk separately. If Mr Adonis wishes to bear a total risk of 20% (measured by standard deviation), he should invest all his funds in unit trust B and borrow a further 100 per cent and invest that in unit trust B as well. In practice, Mr Adonis might not be able to borrow 100 per cent of his investment at the risk-free rate. In this case, he might settle for a unit trust with a slightly lower Sharpe measure, such as trust C. He could then achieve his total required risk level by investing two-thirds of his funds in C and one-third in the risk-free asset. These proportions are calculated as follows. His total risk would be

$$S^2 = x^2 S_C^2 + (1-x)^2 S_{R_F}^2 + 2x(1-x) S_C S_{R_F} CORR_{CR_F}$$

where x is the proportion invested in fund C and $(1-x)$ is the proportion invested in the risk-free asset R_F. Since S_{R_F} is zero (as it is risk-free) we get

$$S = x S_C$$

Since the required value of S is 20% and S_C is 30%, it follows that $x = 2/3$.

Both Mr Adonis and Mr Zeus must remember that basing investment decisions on rankings derived from past returns and risk will not necessarily provide optimal returns in the future.

Differential return

The two measures denoting *differential return* (against benchmark) in Figure 12.5 can be used in cases where the risk is prespecified, which usually occurs in cases where the portfolio is managed by a fund manager. What is required in these instances is a benchmark portfolio with the same risk as the fund in question. This benchmark portfolio should represent a realistic investment alternative which was open to the fund manager. Again, the CAPM provides a suitable benchmark portfolio. For example, if we are considering beta as a suitable measure of risk, the CAPM tells us that the optimal investment policy is to hold the market portfolio (or as near as is feasible, say an index fund) and to adjust for risk by borrowing or lending at the risk-free rate. A comparison of the actual fund's performance with such a benchmark portfolio, which has the same beta, is effectively a test for *abnormal returns* or *alphas,* and a comparison of an active investment policy with a passive one. If the Jensen measure yields a positive differential (or abnormal) return, the fund manager might be beating the market because he or she is good at picking winners. Of course, a positive Jensen measure might also be due to luck, and the fund's performance over a number of periods would have to be examined to gauge whether the positive measure is more likely to be due to luck or to skill.

For instance, suppose that a company has allocated 10 per cent of its pension fund to be managed by QED investment managers. Since QED only has 10 per cent of the total company pension fund and is therefore well diversified, we can say that beta (which measures undiversifiable risk) is the appropriate measure of risk in this case. Now, suppose that the beta required by the trustees of the pension fund is 0.9. If the yield on gilts was 5% last year and the return on the FTSE All-Share Index was 17%, the return R_B on the benchmark portfolio would have been

$$R_B = R_F + \beta_P(R_M - R_F)$$
$$R = 0.05 + 0.9(0.17 - 0.05)$$
$$R = 0.158$$
$$\mathbf{R = 15.8\%}$$

If the fund managed by QED actually achieved a return of 18% with a beta of 0.9, the differential return was $18 - 15.8\% = 2.2\%$. It would remain to be seen whether this level of performance could be maintained in the future, but from the conclusions of the efficient markets hypothesis this would appear to be unlikely.

The other differential return measure of performance, which uses standard deviation as a measure of risk instead of beta, will be used in those cases where the portfolio under consideration represents the total wealth of the investor. Interestingly, if the portfolio is fully diversified, this measure will give the same differential return as the Jensen measure, since for a fully diversified portfolio there is no specific risk and the total risk of the portfolio is simply its beta risk. We can see this in equation 12.5, previously given in Chapter 7 as equation 7.17.

For each security we can write

$$V_i = \beta_i^2 S_M^2 + S^2(e_i) \tag{12.5}$$

For a portfolio the equivalent equation is

$$V_P = \beta_p^2 S_M^2 + \sum_{i=1}^{i=n} S^2(e_i)$$

(Total risk = beta risk + specific risk)

Since the specific risk of a fully diversified portfolio is zero, the second term will also be zero and the standard deviation of the portfolio will simply be equal to its beta times the standard deviation of the market:

$$S_P = \beta_p S_M$$

or

$$\beta_p = \frac{S_p}{S_M} \tag{12.6}$$

If we look at the two differential return measures in the matrix of Figure 12.5, we can see that, if the equality in equation 12.6 holds, the two differential return measures are identical.

The Jensen measure compares the performance of a portfolio P with that of a benchmark B with the same beta but no specific risk. In practice, however, the benchmark is replaced with a real-world stock market index, which will have a beta of 1 and no specific risk. In such cases, a suitable equity benchmark is chosen, say the FTSE All-Share Index for UK equities, or the S&P500 index for US equities. Such measures are routinely used for measuring the performance of institutional fund managers, particularly those managing pension fund equity assets.

If an active fund manager is benchmarked against an index, she will take on **active risk** or *relative risk* in order to achieve added value or positive relative return. If she is fully invested in equities, the active risk she takes on will be specific risk, through stock selection different from that of the benchmark index. Active risk differs from the portfolio risk we measured in Chapter 6. It is the standard deviation – not of the portfolio returns but of the *relative* returns of the portfolio and the benchmark.

So we can write

Relative return $R_{PI} = R_P - R_I$ \hfill (12.7)

Active risk $AR_{PI} = S_{PI}$ \hfill (12.8)

where R_P is the return on the portfolio, R_I is the return on the index benchmark, and S_{PI} is the standard deviation of the relative returns, $R_P - R_I$.

Suppose Ms Smith is managing the UK share portfolio for a pension fund. She has been given a performance benchmark of 1% per annum added value with an annualised active risk of no more than 4%. Given that this is a standard deviation, the pension fund trustees can convert the active risk into a probability of earning a return of less than 3% below the index – one standard deviation from the expected return of +1% relative to the index. If returns were normally distributed, this would mean a one year in six chance of a return of less than -3%.

However, there is a factor which will determine how much active risk Ms Smith is happy with, and that will depend on what is called the ***information ratio.*** The information ratio IR is the ratio of the relative return divided by the active risk, or

$$\text{Information ratio IR} = \frac{R_{PI}}{S_{PI}} \tag{12.9}$$

The information ratio can be backward-looking, that is, telling fund managers how good they have been at turning active risk into relative value. It can also be used as a number by which active risk can be multiplied to give an *expected* added value. For example, an IR of 1.0 would turn an active risk of 1% into an expected relative return of +1% relative to the benchmark; an IR of 0.5 would turn 2% active risk into the same expected outperformance. The higher Ms Smith's information ratio, therefore, the lower the active risk she would have to take on to achieve her required outperformance.

The information ratio thus measures how good a fund manager will be at turning active risk into added value. Paradoxically, the worse the fund manager, the more active risk he or she will have to take on to achieve a desired level of added value. What kinds of information ratios do real-world portfolio managers have? Grinold and Kahn (2000) suggest that only the top decile of US institutional fund managers can aspire to an IR of 1.0 over the long term, with the top quartile having IRs of over 0.5. They also suggest that only 50 per cent can aspire to a positive information ratio, leaving the bottom half performing worse than a passive investor.

These measures of relative return, active risk and the information ratio allow us to measure actual outperformance and likely outperformance in a CAPM risk–return framework.

Analysing performance in depth

We have derived various measures of performance, but they do not yet tell us how that performance was achieved. The differential return measures discussed in the last section give some indication since, by comparing the performance of the portfolio with that of a passively managed portfolio, we know that the differential abnormal return achieved must be due to some form of active portfolio management.

How can we find out which type of active investment policy was pursued? Unfortunately, the state of the art of performance measurement is still not far advanced, and as we shall see in the next section on the relevance of performance measures, there are problems in placing too much emphasis on the results obtained. However, some attempt can be made to identify the success of selectivity or timing policies, the two basic ways of picking winners.

Selectivity

We start by looking at the Jensen measure of performance. This differential return figure shows whether active portfolio management has achieved positive or negative abnormal returns. But it does not answer the question how far those abnormal returns were due to diversifiable or specific risk which would *not* have been present if a fully diversified, CAPM portfolio strategy had been adopted.

Fama (1972) graphically analysed the Jensen measure of performance as in Figure 12.6.

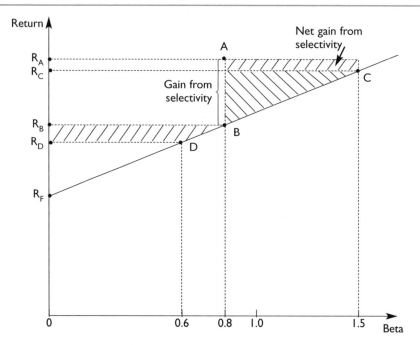

Figure 12.6 Analysis of Jensen performance measure
Source: Fama (1972). By permission of the *Journal of Finance*.

In Figure 12.6, the Jensen measure will be the difference between the actual return on the portfolio under consideration A and the return on that combination of the market portfolio and risk-free borrowing or lending which has the same beta as A. In Figure 12.5, this CAPM portfolio is represented by portfolio B. The Jensen measure is therefore given by $R_A - R_B$. Since portfolio B is fully diversified, it has only beta risk whereas A has both beta risk and diversifiable risk. The total risk of portfolio A, measured by the standard deviation of its returns, is therefore greater than the total risk of portfolio B. Because of this, it would be fairer to compare the performance of portfolio A with that of a CAPM portfolio which had the same total risk, portfolio C in Figure 12.6. C can be found by equating the standard deviation of portfolio A with the market risk of a CAPM portfolio, as in equation 12.10:

$$S_A = \beta_C S_M \tag{12.10}$$

So

$$\beta_C = \frac{S_A}{S_M}$$

If we know the total risk of portfolio A we can use equation 12.10 to find the beta of a CAPM portfolio with the same total risk. For example, suppose that the risk of portfolio A is made up as follows:

$$\beta_A = 0.8$$

Specific risk$_A$ = 25%

and that the market standard deviation of returns S_M is 20%. Substituting these values into equation 12.5 gives total risk S_A as

$$S_A = (0.8)^2(0.20)^2 + (0.25)^2$$

$$\mathbf{S_A = 0.30}$$

To find portfolio C, we substitute the necessary figures into equation 12.10 to get

$$0.3 = 0.2\beta_C$$

So

$$\beta_C = 1.5$$

Note that portfolio C has to have a higher beta than portfolio A in order to achieve a higher level of risk from market risk alone, without any specific risk at all.

We can now see that when the total risk of A is taken into account, the true abnormal return earned by A is not $R_A{-}R_B$ but the smaller $R_A{-}R_C$. Fama denoted the first measure the *gain from selectivity* and the second measure the *net gain from selectivity*.

Figure 12.6 can also be used to monitor how closely portfolio managers have kept to their objectives, provided that these were expressed either in terms of return or of beta. For instance, if the manager had been told to keep to a target beta of 0.6, compared with the actual beta of 0.8, he or she obviously added to the investors' risk, presumably in the belief that a bull market was on the way. The difference between portfolio D (which has a beta of 0.6) and portfolio B is therefore the return earned by the portfolio manager for correct timing using betas. Note, however, that this analysis will only use the beta at the beginning or end of the period or the average beta, and thus will not allow for any changes in the beta of the portfolio that might have occurred during the period under consideration.

The Fama breakdown of the Jensen performance measure gives us a way of identifying more closely the true gains or losses from a picking winners strategy based on selectivity. It shows us that we must take into account the extra risk the manager takes on in order to try to beat the market. As we saw in Chapter 7, a simple measure of how much diversifiable risk has been incurred is provided by the R^2 term in the London Business School Risk Measurement Service. This measures the extent to which the portfolio's returns are explained by market returns. In other words, it shows how much of the portfolio's total risk is explained by its beta. The higher the R^2, the more the portfolio's returns are explained by market risk and the lower the amount of diversifiable risk.

Timing

We saw above that the Fama analysis did not really help us to examine the extent to which fund managers or investors try to earn abnormal returns through correct timing of purchases and sales of particular shares or of a more general market portfolio. This is because, as mentioned earlier, this investment strategy will involve changing the risk of the portfolio over time either through changing the shares held in the equity portfolio to alter the equity portfolio's beta or through the use of equity options and futures, which can impact dramatically on the portfolio's overall beta. So performance measures which assume constant risk over a period will be of no use in this instance.

One way of examining the impact on a portfolio of changing its beta is to compare graphically the changes in beta with the changes in the market. If the manager got it right, a change to a higher beta should be mirrored by a rise in the market and vice versa. If the manager got it wrong, there should be no clear relationship between the two, as in Figure 12.7, or even a negative relationship.

This rough-and-ready appraisal of performance achieved through correct timing is obviously unsatisfactory. Our only consolation is that the evidence supporting the ability of investors to time the market correctly is weak. We have only to look at how pension funds increased (whether actively or passively) the proportion of equities in their portfolios from around 70 per cent in January 1987 to over 85 per cent just before the crash in October 1987, whereas they were net sellers of equities in early 1975, during a major bear market. It is very difficult to forecast market movements even today, as evidenced by a comment in Dimson and Marsh's overview of 2005 in the 2006 edition of their annual *Global Investment Returns*:

> When reviewing a year, it is interesting to revisit the views and forecasts that appeared in the serious financial press and from leading houses a year earlier. Looking back at these, 2005 provided many surprises. Relatively few commentators had been expecting most of the key developments that helped shape 2005 – an appreciably stronger dollar; oil above $70 a barrel; equity returns of 20% plus except in the US; a 45% return on Japanese stocks amid signs of recovery after 15 years of economic malaise; small- and mid-caps continuing to outperform; growth stocks failing to take the ascendancy; long bond yields falling rather than rising; commercial property returning close to 20% in many key markets; a continuing commodity boom; and gold above $500 an ounce.

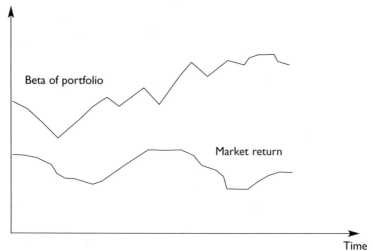

Figure 12.7 Graphical analysis of correct timing of the market

Reviewing relevance of the measure

Despite the advantages of performance measures for comparative and monitoring purposes, great care must be taken in their use. For example, we have just seen that the performance measures given in Figure 12.5 are of little use when trying to determine that element of performance that is caused by attempts to time investments correctly.

A further factor that must be taken into account when using the differential return measures is the possibility that the benchmark portfolio made up of the market portfolio and risk-free borrowing and lending is not a realistic alternative. One reason could be that a high-risk fund could not adopt the benchmark alternative and borrow at the risk-free rate (as was a problem for Mr Adonis). Rankings using the Jensen measure would thus be biased against high-risk funds. Similarly, a particular fund might be precluded from holding certain securities that form part of the market portfolio; it should not, therefore, be compared with a benchmark portfolio which in practice it could not hold.

Thought must also be given to the way betas are measured for, say, the Treynor measure. Betas may be measured in different ways against different indices, all of which might be suitable surrogates for the market portfolio. So, rankings using one index could be different from those using some other index. Further, we know that although the CAPM implies that securities' returns are determined by their betas (and the market and risk-free rates of return), in practice other variables affect security returns, such as industry factors and so on. We saw that this was the case when we considered multi-index models at the end of Chapter 7. This will provide another form of bias in the measures.

In addition, transaction costs affect performance. However much they would prefer not to, fund managers have to pay transaction costs on securities transactions. If the passive fund ignores transaction costs, the comparison is unfair.

The time horizon is also relevant. Whichever measure of performance is used, it can only be really valuable if a number of periods are examined, to separate out the effects of chance from the effects of skill. The need to consider more than a short-term horizon is acknowledged by investment trusts and unit trusts which publish five-year cumulative returns for investors to judge their performance.

SUMMARY

The emphasis of this chapter is somewhat different from that of the rest of the book since it deals with the more subjective aspects of investment, namely objectives, policy and assessment of performance. After exploring the implications of the efficient markets hypothesis in greater depth, the chapter discussed the setting up of explicit investment objectives, which must be done before a suitable investment policy can be decided on or a portfolio built up. The factors that have to be considered for investment objectives include consumption preferences, attitude to risk and return, tax, inflation and asset allocation.

The two basic types of investment policy that can be adopted can be categorised as active or passive. An active policy is based on the desire to beat the market and to make excess returns, and involves either selectivity (the search for mispriced securities) or correct timing. A passive investment policy is based on the results of the CAPM, which finds that all investors will hold the market portfolio and borrow or lend at the risk-free rate. The investor with a passive policy will therefore hold a well-diversified portfolio or an index fund and not indulge in a high-turnover, high transaction cost management strategy.

Using the results of the CAPM, performance measures can be derived which allow investors to assess how well they have done, given the risk of their portfolio, both relative to other comparable portfolios (which may have different risk) and relative to the alternative portfolio they could have constructed based on the CAPM with the same risk as their actual portfolio. However, care must be taken when using the performance measures to ensure that relevant comparisons are being made, bearing in mind the original objectives of the portfolio.

REVIEW EXERCISES

1. The risk of inflation is a serious and persistent concern to any investor in financial assets.
    a. What problems are associated with the measurement of inflation for investment purposes?
    b. What major challenges does the risk of inflation pose in the context of:
        i.   short-term investment (say, up to five years)?
        ii. long-term investment (say, over twenty years)?
    c. What investment products are available to the investor wishing to protect his or her wealth from the risk of inflation, and how effective are they?
2. Mr Dither is undecided between two investment alternatives. His stockbroker has recommended that he invest £10,000 in a portfolio of nine shares and one gilt with an overall beta of 0.9. Mr Dither is also impressed with the report and accounts of an investment trust which has the same beta of 0.9. Discuss the advantages and disadvantages of each of these investment alternatives.
3. The relationship between the efficient markets hypothesis and different investment strategies or styles is not always a comfortable one.
    a. Summarise the main characteristics of an efficient market in each of the three forms:
        i.   weak
        ii. semi-strong
        iii. strong.
    b. What are the implications of each of these three forms of market efficiency for each of the following investment strategies or styles:
        i.   technical analysis
        ii. fundamental analysis
        iii. passive investment
        iv. active investment.
4. Despite its dubious theoretical foundation, technical analysis has an enduring attraction for market operators.
    a. What are the apparent strengths of technical analysis?
    b. Why is their existence so difficult to prove or disprove?
5. You have been asked to address a group of pension fund advisers and investment analysts on the subject of efficient markets. Outline the main points you would make.
6. An efficient market implies that the net present value of any security's future cash flow is zero, whatever its risk, and yet finance managers of companies are expected to find positive NPV projects to invest in. Is there a contradiction here?

7. Data on the annual performance of six investments trusts for the last year are shown below:

Trust	Actual annual return (% pa)	Standard deviation of returns (%)	Beta
A	19	6	1.5
B	17	4	0.5
C	21	8	1.0
D	15	6	0.5
E	25	10	2.0

a. Calculate the reward to variability measure, or Sharpe index

$$\frac{(R_p - R_f)}{S_p}$$

for each trust and rank them accordingly. Assume $R_f = 9.00\%$.

b. Rank the trusts using the Treynor index

$$\frac{(R_p - R_f)}{\beta_p}$$

c. What is the essential difference between the Sharpe and Treynor indices of portfolio performance?

d. Which do you think is preferable, and why?

e. Calculate the excess return of these trusts (i.e. compared with a portfolio having the same beta) assuming last year's R_M was 13% pa. This method of judging portfolio performance is known as Jensen's measure. In what way does it differ from the Sharpe and Treynor indices?

f. Consider investment trust B. How would you break down an overall measure of performance, such as the Jensen measure, into different aspects of performance to get a better picture of how well managed the trust was, i.e. which aspects would you like to measure, and how would you attempt to measure them?

g. Suppose you are considering buying shares in one of the investment trusts listed above. What additional facts would you like to know concerning the trusts and how would you decide between them?

Sample answers to these review exercises can be found on the companion website.

13 Current issues in investment theory and practice

Learning objectives for this chapter

After studying this chapter you should be able to

- ○ describe the current work-in-progress in the field of financial theory
- ○ evaluate current developments in the securities markets in the light of the ongoing debate
- ○ be aware of critiques of portfolio theory, the Capital Asset Pricing Model and the efficient markets hypothesis.

INTRODUCTION

In this final chapter, we look more critically at the theories and models that have allowed us to develop a coherent and logical approach to investment. In particular we look at how portfolio theory, the Capital Asset Pricing Model (CAPM) and the efficient markets hypothesis (EMH) work in practice.

An underlying assumption of portfolio theory is that either investment returns are normally distributed, or investors behave as if they are. If this is not the case – for example, extreme losses occur more frequently than predicted – it will not be optimal for investors to build portfolios using only expected returns and their standard deviations. Also, portfolio theory is a single period model. Typically, investors use historic data to provide single point estimates of the risk and correlation coefficients between securities or asset classes, and derive efficient frontiers based on these estimates and their expected return forecasts. But what if the correlations and volatilities are changing over time? Which historical period and which frequency of returns (daily, weekly, monthly, annual) should be used to give the best estimates of future performance? Should more recent data be given more weight, or should a similar period in the economic cycle be used as a surrogate for what might happen next year? Finally, what about the impact of currency? Should investors look at hedged returns and risks, or take the currency risk in addition to the equity risk in their portfolios?

Turning to the CAPM, there are a number of inputs required in ⟨
return on a particular security or portfolio. These are the equity ris⟨
and the risk free rate. In practice these are problematic to estimate
data is typically used for future estimates. We shall look at some o
as well as consider the problems in using the CAPM in an internat

Finally we turn to the problems inherent in the EMH. This assumes that .....
rational and that prices react sufficiently quickly to new information to prevent arbitrage
taking place. We have already seen how this does not always apply in practice, with the
dual-listed companies mentioned in Chapter 5. There are other examples, such as the late
1990s stock market boom, in which valuations seemed to lose touch with fundamentals,
and also the prevalence of momentum trading, which even the weak form of the EMH
says is a waste of time.

We finish this chapter with a brief discussion of whether or not investors are rational
– another key assumption underlying the major investment theories. We look in particular at pension funds, which have made investment decisions that do not appear to have
maximised shareholder – or in their case pension fund member – wealth.

The issues covered in this chapter are not exhaustive. They are meant to stimulate
discussion of topics you have already covered, and to give you ideas of further problems
which inevitably occur when trying to apply investment theories in practice.

PORTFOLIO THEORY

The normal distribution

Throughout the earlier chapters of this book, we have so far been happy to accept, at least
as working hypotheses, the following basic assumptions of modern finance theory:

○ Investors are rational wealth-maximisers.
○ Investors evaluate actual and possible investments purely according to their expected
  returns and risk.
○ The normal distribution is a generally reliable model of the distributions of such
  returns, so that the standard deviation of those returns is a meaningful and useful
  measure of risk.

Later in this chapter we turn the spotlight on the behaviour of real-world investors, and test
the first and second of the above assumptions. But first we reopen the question whether
the normal distribution does in fact adequately model the realities of the financial markets.
Its use is certainly very widespread. It is central to the portfolio theory equation for the risk
of a diversified portfolio (equation 6.17), as well as to two key equations associated with
the CAPM, the capital market line (equation 7.12) and the securities market line (equation
7.13). The constant standard deviation of normally (or lognormally) distributed prices is a
key assumption of the Black–Scholes formula for option pricing (equations 9.2, 9.4 and
9.5). There is good empirical evidence too that over long periods some prices and returns
do approximate to it. For instance, Figure 13.1 (from Dimson and Marsh 2006) shows
total returns on the London stock market, expressed as a premium over the Treasury bill
rate (that is, risk-free rate) for each of the 106 discrete calendar years from 1900 to 2005.
This certainly looks very like a normal distribution, especially when we bear in mind that

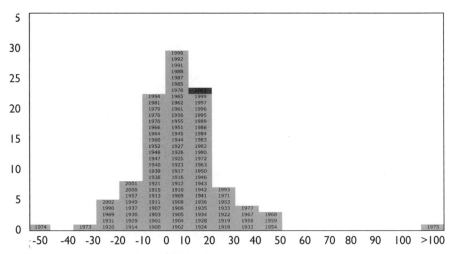

Figure 13.1 UK equity risk premium relative to Treasury bills
Source: Dimson and Marsh (2006).

the normal distribution belongs to the statistical family of continuous rather than discrete distributions: if we were to plot the data underlying Figure 13.1 not in the form of 106 successive calendar years but rather in terms of the approximately 25,000 different overlapping holding periods of 365 or 366 days encompassed in the same time series, we might well obtain something very like the familiar smooth bell-shaped curve. But on the other hand, many of the other national stock markets covered by the 2006 annual survey by Dimson and Marsh exhibit patterns of annual returns that bear at best only a tenuous resemblance to the normal distribution. This is especially true of some of the less developed markets, which may have not enjoyed the same degree or consistency of liquidity and depth as the London market.

So what is the evidence against the normal distribution? The principal charge – and it is a serious one with potentially far-reaching consequences for investor behaviour – is that it simply underestimates the frequency of occurrence of extreme events. This is commonly referred to as the *fat tail* problem. A further possible shortcoming arises from the fact that the normal distribution – like many other well-known probability distributions – is based on the idea of a very large number of identical but independent tests or readings. For instance, if we were to plot the average heights recorded in each of a very large number of independent random samples of 100 adult males drawn from the general population, we would find that the averages of the samples followed a normal distribution. The occasional incidence of a very exceptionally short or tall individual would have little or no discernible impact on the overall result. But how appropriate is this model for analysing the behaviour of a securities market? For one thing, our stock of tests is not very large, nor are they identical or necessarily independent of each other. The market is a continuum, not a succession of discrete performances, and even if it were made up of discrete performances, there is no definitively correct answer to questions such as whether – in trying to model the future – we should perhaps give more weighting to recent readings than to those drawn from the more remote past. On the other hand, there is strong evidence that the *autocorrelation* of periodic stock market returns (that is, the positive correlation between the return of each period and that of the next period) is very low, suggesting that there is little if any tendency for one year's return to influence that of the next.

Critics of the normal distribution point out that it implicitly gives undue weight to the mildly random movements that account for the bulge in the centre of the bell curve, while dismissing as mere outliers the occasional wildly random jumps (Mandelbrot and Taleb 2006). But these wildly random jumps are disproportionately important in financial markets. Whereas one very tall person in a random sample of 1000 people has exactly the same – and very small – significance as each of the other 999, the equivalent phenomenon in a financial market might have a disproportionate and lasting impact on the rest of the 'population' if it results in a price jumping from one established level to an entirely new level.

As we shall see later in this chapter when we come to consider investor behaviour, the rationality or otherwise of investor response to extreme events (or the prospect of extreme events) is a crucial issue in the study of market efficiency, so it is important to be sure that our market model accurately captures such events.

What alternative models are there to the normal distribution? One potential candidate is the so-called *power law* or *fractal law*, relating the size of an occurrence to its frequency by means of a *tail exponent* or *alpha*.[1] For instance, with an alpha of two, the frequency of occurrence would decrease by a factor of four for a doubling of the size of the occurrence. Such power laws are widely observed both in the natural world (for instance, the severity of earthquakes) and in society (such as the incidence of increased individual wealth or income). A common feature of power law distributions is that they have fatter tails than the normal distribution.

Perhaps the best known instance of a real-life challenge to the power of the normal distribution is the case of Long-Term Capital Management (LTCM), the US hedge fund that came close to collapse in August 1998. LTCM brought to bear a unique concentration of intellectual and electronic power on the task of modelling not only the possible outcomes of each of its hundreds of different positions in the financial markets, but also the correlations between them and hence the portfolio as a whole. Despite all of this, its capital of some US$4.5 billion was effectively wiped out because it was hit by a combination of price movements which – according to the model – were expected to occur only once in every 15 lives of the Earth (approximately only once in 70 billion years). It was hit by this combination not once, but twice in a very short space of time. This issue of correlation is now explored in more depth.

Correlation and volatility

One of the major outcomes from portfolio theory is that the lower the correlation between assets, the greater the benefits of diversification. We have seen how the pooling of insurance risks generally benefits from the zero or low correlation between individual risks. In an investment context, we know that holding portfolios of more than several shares allows us to benefit from low, albeit positive, correlation between their returns; and that international diversification can bring further risk reduction benefits, since individual countries' stock markets are relatively poorly correlated. Asset allocation is another

---

1.   This is not to be confused with the alpha of the market model underlying the CAPM (equation 7.1).

example of the benefits of low correlation. It might pay, for example, to hold bonds as well as cash and equities in a portfolio, even if bonds are dominated by cash and equities in the risk–return sense. This is because they allow an improvement in the overall risk–return trade-off when combined efficiently with cash and equities.

British investors have traditionally invested overseas. Before the First World War, British investors had 45 per cent of their assets in foreign securities. It was not uncommon for individual investors to have the majority of their portfolio in overseas bonds and equities, with perhaps one or two UK government bonds and railway shares. For example, in 1909 a Mr Boardman, investing through N.M. Rothschild, had investments in British government 2½% Consolidated Stock, 3% South African Transvaal Stock, 5% Rio Tinto £5 Preference Shares, 5% Argentine Buenos Ayres Water Supply Stock, 4½% Japan Sterling Bond second series, 5% Chilean bonds and 5% Brazil bonds. Currency risk was not an issue, with most countries in which he invested either on the gold standard – that is, on a fixed exchange rate with sterling – or issuing directly in sterling to attract British investors.

After the First World War, it became more difficult to invest overseas, with either direct restrictions or limits on access to foreign currency or foreign markets. In the 1950s, 1960s and 1970s, when most of the foundations of modern finance theory were laid, national stock markets had become much more self-contained than they were before the First World War. Constraints included exchange controls, withholding taxes on overseas investors' dividends, higher transaction costs, settlement and custody difficulties, limited information flows and lack of consistent international accounting standards, as well as different stock exchange regulations and legal systems. And yet it was at this time that Solnik (1974), for example, showed the benefits of international diversification through low correlation between stock markets. As emerging markets were added to the list of possible investments, they too showed historically low correlation with the major stock markets. British pension funds did begin to invest overseas as soon as they were allowed to in the 1980s. But US pension funds, as late as 1990, had no more than 3 per cent of their assets in non-US investments. By 2003, though, UK pension funds had 30 per cent of their portfolios in non-UK investments, and US pension funds had reached 15 per cent. This rise in institutional international investment in the 1980s and 1990s is mirrored in the statistics for non-resident investors in shares listed on the London stock exchange. In 1981, under 4 per cent of shares were held by non-residents, rising to 13 per cent in 1989 and continuing to rise to over 32 per cent by 2003 (Table 10.1).

In many countries, investors were unable to take advantage of low correlations until the barriers to investment fell; for example, exchange controls were abolished for UK investors in 1979. As they became able to invest overseas, so investors diversified their portfolios. As emerging markets opened to foreign investors, this broadened the opportunity set. What is interesting, though, is that as investors diversified internationally, the low correlations between markets – the reason for the diversification in the first place – increased. For example, Speidell (2004) found that the average correlation of EAFE (Europe, Australia and Far East) markets with the US S&P500 index rose from 0.55 in the mid-1980s to 0.89 in 2004. It has also been noted that correlation increases in bear markets – just when investors want the benefits of diversification! For example, Tuluca et al. (2003) studied the change in correlations between national markets in the Americas, Europe and Asia for the periods before and after the Asian crisis in 1998, and found that the average correlation between the US market and each of the other 11 markets rose from 0.45 before to

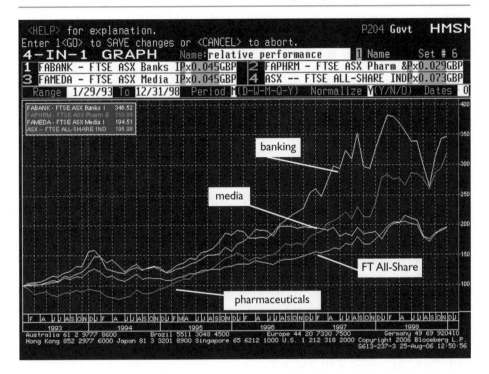

Figure 13.2 Performance of banking, media and pharmaceutical sectors relative to the FTSE All-Share Index, 1993–98
Source: Bloomberg.

0.65 afterwards. There is thus a link between correlation and volatility: when markets become volatile, correlations rise. So the benefits of international diversification are not as great as historical data would seem to imply.

The problem of changing correlations is also relevant to domestic investors, particularly institutional investors trying to outperform a stock market index. In doing so, most institutional investors will select sectors and then select stocks within a sector – the so-called *top-down approach*. However, another recent development is the decreasing correlation between sectors, making sector 'bets' more risky than they appear. For example, in the United Kingdom, 1995 saw the start of a falling out of favour of the transport and construction sectors, and an increase in popularity of the banking, media and pharmaceutical sectors, which represented, by 1998, almost 30 per cent of the value of the index. This relative popularity was very different from that of the period 1993 to 1995, as shown in Figure 13.2. Fund managers Merrill Lynch, investing around £1 billion on behalf of the Unilever pension fund, chose to continue to invest from 1995 in the so-called 'value' sectors and to underweight significantly the banking sector. This led to what became called a 'two standard deviation event'. The fund underperformed the FTSE All-Share Index by over 10 per cent in one year alone, and this led to a long and bitter court case. The rising volatility of sectors and their changing correlations had not been factored in to the fund managers' estimates of future risks and returns. Current research into this, for example, by Brooks and Del Negro

(2004), is looking at disaggregating correlations into their country, regional and sector effects. Although it is still the case that investors tend to choose country, then sector, then company, there is growing recognition that the sector effect may dominate, especially in globalised industries such as car manufacture and pharmaceuticals.

Currency

Another practical consideration with portfolio theory is the base currency to be used. The benefits of international diversification are not symmetrical. As previously mentioned, all the risk, return and correlation coefficients will change as the base currency is changed. However, in practice, as Dimson and Marsh (2006) show, over the long run most exchange rate changes are reactions to changes in relative inflation rates. So, for example, a US investor buying UK equities could expect the change in the dollar/sterling exchange rate to be offset by the difference in inflation rates between the two countries over time. Dimson and Marsh conclude that currency risk does not add greatly to the long-run risks of international equity investment. And for those investors with a relatively small or homogeneous stock market, such as Canadian, South African or Dutch investors, the benefits of diversification are greater than for, say, US investors. However, shorter-term currency volatility, which might not be in line with differences in inflation rates, may be worth hedging for those investors who are judged on short-term, say quarterly, performance.

THE CAPITAL ASSET PRICING MODEL

In Chapter 7, we touched on some of the theoretical problems with the CAPM, such as whether one could, in practice, borrow as well as lend at the risk-free rate of interest, and whether the existence of transaction costs and taxes would change the results. In this section we look at some of the real-world issues which investors have to address when using the CAPM in investment strategy.

The CAPM can be used in two ways by the investor: first, at the security or portfolio level to determine the expected return for a share or rate of return on an equity portfolio; second, to arrive at an efficient portfolio or benchmark portfolio in the risk–return sense. We shall look at each of these in turn.

Estimating the expected rate of return

By the 2000s, it had become commonplace for equity analysts to value equities using the *discounted cash flow (DCF)* valuation model. There were a number of reasons for this. First, the globalisation of stock markets meant that valuation methods already common in the United States such as DCF became more widespread. Second, a merger wave in the late 1990s had forced analysts to think of equities not just as going concerns but as targets for takeover. Since corporate finance uses DCF to value equities, analysts were forced to follow suit. And the fall in interest rates during the 1990s to lower levels than had been seen for decades made DCF, which takes interest rates explicitly into account in the discount rate, more attractive as a valuation tool than simplistic ratios. In fact, the usual method was to value companies as operating entities using the weighted average cost of capital (WACC), and one input into that was the cost of equity, which was typically estimated using the CAPM.

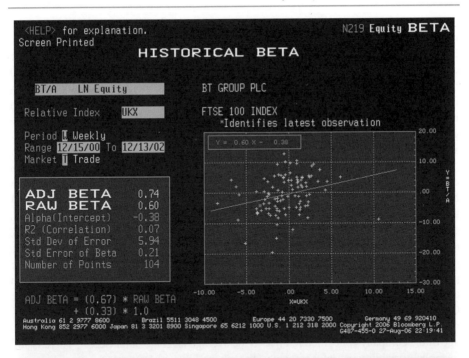

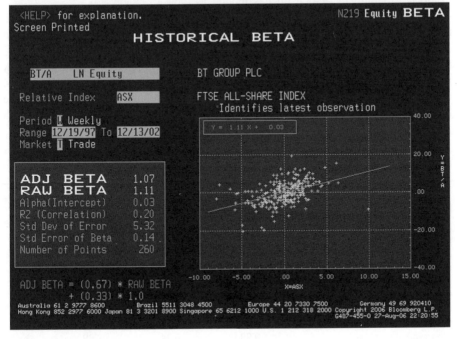

Figure 13.3 Beta estimates for BT group: weekly data 2000–02 against the FTSE 100 Index (above); and against the FTSE All-Share Index (below)
Source: Bloomberg.

There are three key inputs to the CAPM equation for the expected rate of return: the risk-free rate of interest, the beta of the share or portfolio, and the equity risk premium. In principle, the risk-free rate chosen can be the long-term government bond yield of the country concerned. Alternatively if, as in the United Kingdom, an index-linked bond market exists, it can be taken as the real index-linked bond yield plus an inflation forecast. However, emerging markets may have neither a long-term government bond nor an index-linked bond market. For consistency, it may be better to estimate a global real government bond yield and add, for the relevant country, a country risk factor (obtainable from the bond markets) and an expected inflation rate.

More problematic is the estimation of betas for individual companies. Analysts often use database providers such as Bloomberg, Reuters or Datastream to estimate betas from historical data, but these can be calculated according to different indices, over different time periods, and for different periodicities (frequencies). For example, Figure 13.3 gives estimates for a beta for BT, the UK telecoms company, which range from 0.74 to 1.07 according to the benchmark index and period chosen. This would make a major difference to any cost of equity estimate, and hence valuation of BT. Such variations in beta were particularly common during the stock market boom of the late 1990s, as companies such as BT were changing activity, often through takeovers, and also changing their leverage. Given the errors likely to be built into individual beta estimates, an alternative is to estimate sector betas. These can then be adjusted to take account of the expected future leverage of the company concerned relative to the average leverage in the sector. There is still historical variability in sector estimates, though, as Table 13.1 shows.

The historic equity risk premium over long-term government bond yields has ranged between 5% and 9% p.a. for the United States and the United Kingdom, depending on whether the arithmetic or geometric average is used and whether 20, 50 or 100 years' worth of data have been used. Which number should we take for the expected equity risk premium? An alternative to using estimates from the past is to take market forecasts, either explicitly through a questionnaire, or implicitly through market prices. For the latter, a market can be modelled using the dividend valuation model, with

Table 13.1 Developed Markets Industry Group beta ranked by change over the past five years

Industry group	5 year average beta	2003 beta estimate	Standard deviation
Utilities	0.77	0.19	1.13
Resources	0.77	0.25	0.26
Basic industries	0.84	0.48	0.21
Non-cyclical consumer goods	0.78	0.43	0.17
Cyclical consumer goods	0.88	0.60	0.30
Financials	0.90	0.73	0.20
General industrials	0.86	0.72	0.18
Cyclical services	0.84	0.71	0.35
Non-cyclical services	0.88	0.94	1.89
Information technology	1.02	1.75	5.32

Source: Merrill Lynch, Datastream. Two-year weekly regression against MSCI world index in US$. The Developed Markets data set contains the constituents of the MSCI World Developed Index. Cited in Allworthy, Debenham and Rutterford (2003).

earnings forecasts, dividend payout ratios, and long-run growth. The discount rate that equates the present value of the forecasts with the current market level is the implied rate of return on equities. Deducting the relevant benchmark bond yield gives an implied equity risk premium. Using this methodology gives lower estimates for the implied equity risk premium for most developed countries of between 3 and 4%. It is worth noting that most UK actuaries, when estimating how much more equities will return than government bonds, are currently using estimates in this range. They are doing this to be cautious about likely equity returns. However, using a lower equity risk premium in the WACC estimate for a company will increase its present value and hence its attraction as an investment.

Deriving an efficient portfolio using the CAPM

The CAPM equation linking expected return to risk shows that any investment's expected return is linked to risk relative to 'the market', and in this context, 'the market' is typically taken to be the relevant stock market. In the United Kingdom, we might argue that, looking at Figure 13.3, the FTSE All Share index is closer to representing 'the market' as a whole than the FTSE 100 Index, and so we should use the former to estimate BT's beta. However, as we have seen, most investors today invest internationally, and their benchmark 'market' might be, for example, the MSCI World Developed Market Index, or some other global equity index. In this case, although the CAPM is not an international model, investors may choose to estimate country, sector or company betas relative to a global equity index, with returns calculated in their base currency, say sterling or US dollars. This is how the sector betas shown in Table 13.1 were calculated, in this case in US dollars. Although not based on an international CAPM, this approach does help investors to see where their risk lies.

Although the CAPM assumes that investors accept the consensus expectations for returns and risks, and should thus choose passive portfolios mirroring their benchmarks, active managers also use the CAPM to manage their portfolios. In fact, active managers take *active risk* to outperform their index benchmark. By active risk, we mean the risk (measured in terms of standard deviation) of the relative return of a portfolio compared with its benchmark. Given that many conventional funds attempt to outperform a benchmark index, and given the risk that deviation from that benchmark might lead to unacceptable differences in performance, as happened with the Unilever pension fund, fund managers now often include a maximum active risk in their investment contracts with clients. For example, the fund will deviate by no more than 5 per cent in terms of active risk from the benchmark portfolio.

Tracking error is the realised active risk. However, active risk, as for beta, is estimated according to historical patterns, and as we saw in Figure 13.2 for the banking, media and pharmaceutical sectors, sector movements relative to the index can have a major impact on actual tracking error. Even if a multi-factor model, discussed at the end of Chapter 7, is used, changes in valuation between large and small capitalisation shares, between value and growth shares, between shares affected by the US dollar and those not, and so on, can quickly alter active risk and hence likely tracking error.

We now turn to the third model underpinning investment analysis, the efficient markets hypothesis.

CHALLENGES TO THE EFFICIENT MARKETS HYPOTHESIS

As we have seen already in Chapters 1 and 12, the EMH postulates three different levels or strengths of the informational efficiency of a market. By *informational efficiency* we mean that prices tend on average to adjust accurately and quickly to relevant new information of the type associated with that particular level of efficiency. As a result, excess returns cannot be earned systematically by exploiting that type of information.

The EMH itself is not particularly prescriptive about the precise chain of causation driving the process of price discovery at each level of information. So an interesting question arises: to what extent does the EMH presuppose that investors are rational: that is, that they process new information rationally in assessing its impact on the fair value of a particular share or of the market as a whole? It is possible to adopt a position accepting a degree of irrationality on the part of investors while still maintaining that the market's overall price discovery mechanism is efficient. What interests us is the question whether investor irrationality can lead not only to occasional marginal mispricing of individual shares, but also to radical and persistent under or overpricing of entire sectors, or even of the market as a whole.

A wealth of research has accumulated from the early 1990s onwards which has not so much sought simply to refute the central assumption of investor rationality by conventional finance theory, as to 'park' this assumption on one side while taking a closer empirical look at how investors actually make decisions – in short, how they behave. Unsurprisingly, this branch of academic study has acquired the general label of **behavioral finance** (the US spelling is normally employed, as US writers have tended to dominate this field of study). It is important to recognise, however, that behavioral finance does not represent a single homogeneous school of thought or world view, so much as a shared belief in the value of employing the toolkit of cognitive psychology to shed light onquestions of how economic agents interact with each other.

Behavioral finance

A common starting point for the study of behavioral finance is the observation that as human beings are famously less than perfectly rational in every other major area of decision making (whether it be in the acquisition of a house, a horse, a vintage car – or a life's companion), it actually seems almost perverse to assume that in one field alone – that of investment – they should uniquely act with perfect rationality.

This observation is reinforced by a further rather obvious fact, that even if investors were both intellectually equipped and temperamentally disposed to act in a perfectly rational manner, they could not in practice give full expression to that rationality, as there simply is not sufficient time to process all the information that might be relevant to the valuation of any particular security. Again, investment decisions share this feature with many other areas of decision making. Confronted with the impossibility of making a perfectly rational decision, people learn by experience to 'get by in order to get on', by employing **heuristics** – a set of rules-of-thumb which experience has shown to produce an acceptable preponderance of good decisions, and a bearable or containable minority of bad decisions.

It is at the next level of detail that the study of behavioral finance begins to yield really interesting results, because it now turns to question such as:

○ How do investors judge which are good decisions and which are bad?
○ How do investors determine what constitutes a bearable proportion of bad decisions?
○ How do investors develop their initial sets of heuristics?
○ How do investors adapt their heuristics to changing circumstances?

Major findings of behavioral finance

Research into these and related questions has produced a wealth of findings which modify or challenge the conventional picture of the investor as a perfectly rational wealth maximiser. We present here only a summary of some of the major findings.

○ Investors assess the historical outcomes of their earlier decisions asymmetrically, routinely attributing to their own skill those they consider to be successes, while they write off their failures to events outside their control, such as bad luck (or even conspiracy of one sort or another).

○ A similar asymmetry is apparent in the way investors view the future prospects arising from past decisions. Given identical inputs about the expected future return and risk of a security that they already hold, investors tend to reach different decisions depending upon the answer to a further, strictly entirely irrelevant, question: was the existing holding acquired at a price above, or below, the current market price? In other words, does the investor currently have an unrealised profit or an unrealised loss on the position? Generally, investors show a greater predisposition to close out an existing position if it is showing a profit rather than a loss, whereas in a perfectly rational world the only criterion for such a decision is whether the expected future return represents more or less than a fair return for the perceived risk – which has nothing to do with the relationship between the current price and the past price that the particular investor happened to have paid. What makes this tendency particularly perverse is that it actually has a tendency to maximise or to accelerate the payment of taxes.

○ Investors who *churn* their portfolios, that is, who buy and sell relatively frequently, are generally less successful than those who make relatively infrequent buy and sell decisions and then tend to live with them for an extended period. And as men are generally more active investors than women, men tend to be less successful too.

○ In their quest for positive feedback about their own earlier decisions, investors tend to show conservatism bias: that is, they focus disproportionately on new information that corroborates their decisions (and reinforces their existing heuristics), while ignoring or under-reacting to those pieces of information that suggest that the earlier decision may not have been that smart after all. Then the investors realise the error of their former ways and they over-react to the cumulative impact of all the ignored news of the past. This is a particularly interesting finding, because critics of the EMH have disagreed amongst themselves about whether real markets have a tendency to undershoot or to overshoot the new fair price following receipt of new information. Its supporters have understandably been tempted to take the view that if roughly equal numbers of critics espouse the undershooting and the overshooting views, then perhaps on average the market is getting it about right. The research finding alluded to here, however, gives some support to both the undershooting and the overshooting schools of thought, by linking them together as the two sides of the same coin.

Box 13.1 The preferences of individual investors

Individual investors have a marked preference for smaller companies' shares, as can be seen from Figure 13.4, showing the extent to which different groups invest in the shares of FTSE 100 companies and in the rest of the UK stock market. It is noticeable that unit trusts and investment trusts, which are collective investment vehicles primarily designed to reflect the preferences of private investors, show a similar pattern. At the other extreme, non-UK investors (which are predominantly institutions) show the strongest tendency to over-invest in FTSE 100 shares, doubtless because of the global reach of many of the companies in that index. Note that the FTSE 100 accounted for about 83 per cent by value of all shares listed on the London stock exchange.

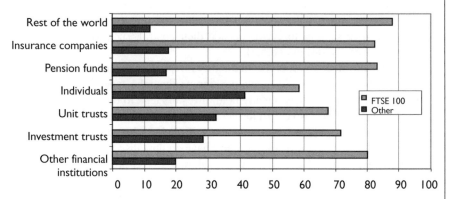

Figure13.4 Proportionate investment in FTSE 100 and other companies at 31 December 2003
Source: Office for National Statistics.

A further peculiarity of individual investors is their marked preference for shares in financial companies, and their relative lack of interest in the shares of manufacturing companies, as is shown in Figure 13.5.

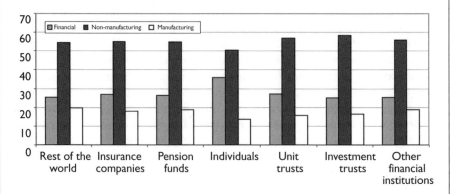

Figure 13.5 Proportionate investment in financial, manufacturing and other companies as at 31 December 2003
Source: Office for National Statistics.

○ Investors show two opposite but equally irrational tendencies in how they allow other investors' behaviour and decisions to influence their own. They *both* follow the herd (for fear of being left out) *and* demonstrate optimism bias by over-estimating their ability to pick unusual winners. As a result they tend to be overweight not only in the very largest and most high-profile shares but also among the mass of small stocks where they think the major investors might be missing 'a good story' because they cannot be bothered to do apparently uneconomic fundamental analysis. Although Example 5.8 showed that the shares outside the FTSE 100 account typically for only 16–18 per cent of the market capitalisation of the London stock exchange, individual investors hold on average over 40 per cent of their money in these stocks.

○ Individual investors tend to ignore the findings of portfolio theory by under-diversifying. This may be for a variety of less than perfectly rational reasons, including both conservatism bias (sticking with what is familiar) and optimism bias (believing in one's ability to pick winners).

○ Investors routinely oversubscribe for IPOs despite the evidence that after relative over-performance on the day of issue, shares in IPOs tend systematically to under-perform the market, inviting the conclusion that IPOs are on average overpriced and therefore offer substandard returns. This is difficult to explain, though it is tempting to conclude that some type of optimism bias is also at work here. Just as individuals have been shown chronically to under and over-estimate the statistical probabilities of the occurrence of (respectively) bad and good events in their own lives, perhaps they believe that while IPOs generally may be overpriced, 'this one is different'.

○ In partial contrast to some of the findings of conservatism bias, investors also tend to give more weight to recent events in forming their judgments about the future. They tend to extrapolate from recent events without pausing to reflect whether a recent pattern they have detected may be merely a temporary aberration, rather than the start of the new and lasting trend they think they have detected.

○ The process of developing workable heuristics is in some respects not dissimilar to the design of economic models. Just as the economist tries to make the world easier to interpret and to manipulate by eliminating extraneous and disruptive background influences from a simplified model of reality, heuristics represent the individual's attempt to focus on a few factors that really matter, rather on the whole host of factors that might be relevant in theory, but – when considered either individually or together – are unlikely to improve the quality of the final decision by enough to warrant the extra effort of considering them. This is sometimes referred to as *framing*, because the investor figuratively encloses the decision in a mental frame, determining the context within which the decision will be made, and thus consciously or unconsciously including and excluding what is considered to be respectively relevant and irrelevant to the decision. A small change in the design or location of the frame can have a significant impact on the way the problem is seen, and hence on the decision taken in an attempt to resolve it.

○ Framing is in some ways akin to the general concept of *bounded rationality*: that is, the idea that investors are not necessarily irrational but are forced by the complex practical constraints of time, money and available information, to deploy their undoubted rationality in a limited and therefore ultimately imperfect way.

○ The process of separating the factors that matter from those that do not is also related to the phenomenon of mental accounting. This refers to the observation that investors and others attach different values to the same amount of money (either a gain or a loss), depending on the identity and properties of the 'mental account' in which they choose to process it. Examples from everyday life abound. Europeans planning trips to the United States invest considerable resources of time in the process of securing the best value for money on the transatlantic air fare (perhaps because of a kind of social kudos attaching to the achievement of a better deal than one's friends). But once they are in New York or San Francisco, the much more casual degree of scrutiny they devote to a restaurant bill might mean that they lose more than the spread between the cheapest and most expensive air fares. Similarly, taxpayers routinely engage in lengthy disputes with the tax authorities about the admissibility of a claimed expense deduction which they would not notice on a restaurant bill. In short, depending on the mental account in which the item is processed, a dollar may be worth a lot less or a lot more than a dollar. And this is extremely difficult to reconcile with the fundamental assumptions of investor rationality underlying conventional finance theory.

○ Finally, and perhaps most tellingly for a body of theory that is so firmly rooted in the weighing of relative probabilities, individuals do not price uncertainty consistently with the strict mathematical models of expected outcomes. The inconsistencies are most pronounced between the theoretically equal pricings of a low-probability, high-value outcome and of a high-probability, low-value outcome. This is further bad news for the normal distribution and its already somewhat sensitive tails. Specifically, investors and others show a tendency to assess alternative courses of action not (or not only) on the basis of the weighted average and relative dispersions of their possible outcomes, but also in terms of the 'least worst outcome'. That is, they have a tendency to favour the alternative with the least bad worst-case scenario, almost regardless of its other properties. This trait is especially marked in people making judgments about the expenditure of public money, but is also observable throughout the commercial and household sectors.

The EMH and behavioral finance

How does the EMH cope with all this? Broadly speaking it has two lines of defence. It can argue that as all these investor impulses are to a greater or lesser degree irrational, their essentially random property will tend to have a broadly neutral impact on the market as a whole. However, this defence overlooks the fact that many supposedly irrational tendencies of investors take the form of herd behaviour of one type or another, in which the impact on the market as a whole is anything but neutral. EMH responds to this second argument by deploying its secret weapon – arbitrage. The arbitrageur, in the world of the EMH, is a particular kind of near-perfectly rational operator who devotes his or her energies exclusively to the identification of market mispricing, buying securities that are under-priced while selling those that are over-priced, and reversing these positions when the market comes to its senses and reprices each of them in accordance with 'the fundamentals'.

Unfortunately, as Shleifer (2000) and others have sought to demonstrate, this somewhat idealised picture of the arbitrageur does not accord with the realities of the financial markets. In theory arbitrageurs identify a security that is relatively over-priced in relation to its sector and short-sell that security, while going long of the sector as a whole (in order to protect themselves from unwelcome absolute movements in prices during the anticipated adjustment period). In practice, however, it is extremely difficult both to identify a fundamental mispricing in advance of its correction, with the degree of certainty conventionally attributed to the arbitrageur, and – this could be even more to the point – to identify the moment of maximum mispricing. Failure on the second score can easily lead to a situation where arbitrageurs, having sold short the overpriced security, sit back only to see an ever-increasing unrealised loss building up in their books whilst the market pursues its mispricing to ever higher levels. Large and growing unrealised losses are not supposed to be a feature of the landscape where arbitrageurs operate most comfortably, seeking as they do to make regular, steady, small-scale profits from exploiting pricing anomalies.

This leads us naturally to a consideration of the general problem that mispricings of individual shares, of whole sectors, and of entire markets, can persist over extended periods of time, can continue to grow, and can generally behave in ways that are still poorly understood. Two examples of the latter are the behaviour of dual-listed companies (DLCs – see Box 5.2), and the so-called closed-end investment puzzle.

Figure 13.6 shows in percentage terms the relative difference in valuation of two very large Anglo-Dutch DLCs, Shell and Unilever, over a period of 32 years from 1973 to 2005. It is clear that while their deviations from parity fluctuate quite widely, especially in the earlier years of that period, there is a clear positive correlation internally between the Shell and the Unilever mispricings. It may also be significant that both the average size of the mispricing and the amplitude of the fluctuations have tended to fall since the late 1980s. It can hardly be an accident that this coincides with a period of ever-increasing integration between the major national securities markets of the world.

The second of our market mispricing anomalies, the closed-end investment fund puzzle, is another case where the market value of a particular class of share persistently defies a 'rational' level, which can be determined, apparently objectively, from the market

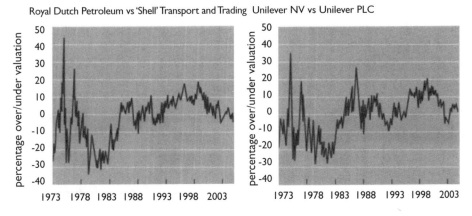

Figure 13.6 Relative difference in valuations between dual-listed companies, from 1 January 1973 to 24 January 2005
Source: McKinsey 2005.

value of other shares. As we learned in Chapter 10, a closed-end investment fund (such as an investment trust company in the United Kingdom) raises money by issuing shares to the investing public on the stock exchange, then invests the proceeds of that issue (plus the proceeds of any borrowings) in a portfolio of marketable securities. Whatever the objectives of the fund (it may, for instance, be a specialist fund concentrating on a specific industry or region), and however active or passive the investment strategy it chooses to pursue, the process of regular, transparent and comprehensive disclosure of details of its investment portfolio enables actual and potential investors to determine with some degree of accuracy the 'fair' value of the fund's net assets and hence of each share in the fund.

Yet the market values of shares in closed-end funds exhibit exactly the same form of anomalous pricing as we have observed in the case of DLCs. Most frequently, shares in closed-end funds trade at a significant but fluctuating discount to their net asset values: premiums are much rarer. And, again like DLCs, although the market prices of shares in closed-end funds defy the logic of the EMH, they do exhibit a degree of internal logic among themselves by following fairly closely a common trend in mispricing. A variety of arguments have been put forward over the years in an attempt to reconcile this phenomenon with what we would expect in an informationally efficient market. Tax undoubtedly plays some role here, as does agency theory: that is, the risk that the behaviour of the fund's own management might itself disrupt the theoretical process of shareholder wealth maximisation. But these and other such factors are at best no more than partial explanations of the overall mispricing phenomenon.

Shleifer (2000) finds an intriguing similarity between the demonstrable mispricings of closed-end investment funds and the apparent extent of over or under-valuation of small companies in comparison with the market as a whole. Individuals (as distinct from institutions) account for a disproportionate share of investment in both the small company sector and the closed-end fund sector, suggesting that there may be an identifiable individual investor psychology which at least to some extent follows different rules from that of large, professionally managed institutional investors.

Box 13.2 offers three contrasting quotations relevant to behavioral finance. The first is a ringing endorsement of EMH from one of its earliest supporters. The second is a sensationalised statement of the value of fundamental analysis, by possibly the most successful long-term investor of recent years, in brazen defiance of the semi-strong form of the EMH. And the little rhyme in the third neatly captures one of the most venerable of all technical trading rules, and implies that the conclusions of the weak form of the

---

Box 13.2 Views on the efficient markets hypothesis

'There is no other proposition in economics which has more solid empirical evidence supporting it than the efficient markets hypothesis.'

Jensen (1978)

'I'd be a bum on the streets with a tin cup if the markets were efficient.'

Warren Buffett (attrib.)

'Sell in May – and go away.'

Old London stock exchange adage

EMH count for relatively little in comparison with the imperatives of the London social calendar.

Box 13.3 offers a case study of pension funds as possible irrational investors. Did they as investors behave rationally or irrationally in changing external conditions?

Box 13.3 Irrational investors?

In the 1980s, the 'cult of equity' meant that UK pension funds were relatively heavily invested in equities, compared with funds in other countries and their historical average. By 1987, the average pension fund was 85 per cent invested in equities. One reason for this was the way in which equities were valued as assets to offset pension fund liabilities. They were valued using the dividend valuation model. When the stock market fell in 1987, pension funds did not write down their equity assets. Provided dividends were maintained, equities were worth as much as they had been before the market crash – in actuarial terms.

By the 1990s equities had recovered in value, and pension funds were in surplus when assets were compared with liabilities. Equities were still valued according to dividends, and dividends were worth more to pension funds than to individual investors, because since they were not liable to tax, they could claim back the advance corporation tax (ACT) paid by companies on their behalf. However, the surplus was in effect a tax shelter, since contributions were tax deductible and returns on the fund not taxable. In order to prevent surpluses from buidling up, the Inland Revenue imposed tax on funds where the assets exceeded liabilities by more than 5 per cent. In response, companies declared pension fund contribution holidays – that is, stopped making contributions to their funds – which had the effect of boosting earnings and as a result, directors' earnings-related bonuses. *M&A* activity also exploited pension fund surpluses. Companies were acquired not for themselves alone, but also for their pension funds, until Hanson was challenged in the courts after its acquisition of Imperial Tobacco, for attempting to close the pension fund and appropriate the surplus.

In 1997 the new Labour government abolished ACT relief for pension funds. This had the effect of reducing the actuarial value of equities in pension funds, and created deficits in some funds. Companies such as BT were required to pay millions of pounds into their pension funds to reduce deficits, even though market values of equities continued to rise. This led to a change in the way actuaries valued equities, moving to a market value method. This was encouraged by the accounting standards FRS17 and later IAS19, which required greater disclosure of pension fund surpluses and deficits in company accounts. By the end of the 1990s, pension funds were in substantial surplus and many companies had had five years or more of pension contribution holidays.

The market falls of 2000 to 2002 had an immediate impact on pension funds, given the market valuation of their equity portfolios. They suffered all the more as interest rates were at historic lows, increasing the present value of their liabilities. With greater disclosure of their deficits, and the resumption of contributions to the fund denting earnings, many companies have now decided to close defined benefit pension schemes to new, and sometimes existing, members. The method of valuation of equities has had a direct impact on economic decisions taken by pension fund trustees.

There has also been a change in the way in which pension fund investment performance is measured. In the 1990s, pension funds were judged against their peer group, so that if all pension funds decided to invest substantially in Japan or in Europe, and these markets underperformed, it did not really matter provided everyone else did badly as well. This led to highly unbalanced portfolios, particularly in a CAPM context. For example, in June 1999 UK pension funds held on average 46 per cent of their assets in UK equities, including 3 per cent in Vodafone and 3 per cent in BT, and only 2 per cent of their assets in US equities as a whole. This compared with 10 per cent in European equities, a much smaller market than the United States.

By 2000, many pension funds were also judged on performance relative to a benchmark, with the benchmark being the appropriate equity index for their share portfolios and the appropriate bond index for their bond portfolios. So, for example, UK equities were judged relative to the FTSE All-Share Index, which led to active risk being a key risk factor. However, the subsequent market falls made trustees aware that even if funds track their benchmark indices relatively closely, if the benchmark index falls 40 per cent, so does the fund. This has led to a shift in benchmark emphasis to a liability-driven benchmark, and consideration that the most relevant risk is not active risk relative to an index, but active risk relative to pension fund liabilities.

Pension fund trustees now try to structure their asset portfolios to cash flow match (immunise) their liability cash flows, which can extend 50 or more years into the future. They have also tried to diversify away from equities and invest in **hedge funds**, property funds and commodity funds to spread their asset mix across classes with relatively low correlation. However, this more rigorous approach is a bit late. The majority of UK defined benefit funds are now closed to new members. It is rather like closing the stable door after the horse has bolted.

SUMMARY AND CONCLUSIONS

In this chapter, we have taken a step back and looked more critically at some of the theories underlying investment decision making. In particular, we have looked at how some assumptions break down in practice, and at the effects this may have on investment behaviour.

We first looked at the assumptions underlying portfolio theory, the theory that quantifies the risk and return characteristics of investment portfolios made up of a number of securities. We explored the implication of investment returns not being normally distributed, in particular there being so-called 'fat tails', in other words that market crashes might occur in practice more often than predicted.

Portfolio theory shows that the lower the correlation between investments in a portfolio, the better the risk–return trade-off. Given low correlation between stock markets, international diversification is therefore likely to benefit investors. However, we found that, as markets have become more integrated and it has become easier to invest overseas, so the correlation between markets has risen, reducing the risk-reduction potential of international diversification. We also found somewhat confusing results for portfolio theory when currency is taken into account. When different currency investments are included in a portfolio, currency worsens the risk-return trade-off if short-term, say quarterly, returns are measured, making an argument for hedging the currency risk of such portfolios. However, when longer-term returns are measured, currency risk has little impact.

We next looked at the assumptions underlying the capital asset pricing model (CAPM) and considered two aspects: the use of the model to estimate the expected rate of return for an individual equity, and the use of the model to derive efficient portfolios. We found that estimating an individual equity's rate of return required the input of a risk-free rate of return, the equity's beta, and the equity risk premium. In practice, it may be difficult to estimate a risk-free rate of return, particularly in emerging markets. Beta estimates, even in developed markets, may be biased by the choice of market index used, of the periodicity of the regression (such as weekly or monthly), and of a historical period (say five years) which includes a change in capital structure of the underlying company. The equity risk premium can be estimated from historical returns, from investor expectations, or implied from current market prices using the dividend discount model. These alternative methods have at times given very different estimates leading to very different implied 'fair' equity values.

The CAPM has led investors to track the 'market' by tracking a surrogate market index, which represents an alternative passive investment strategy. In the United Kingdom, this index is typically the FTSE All-Share Index or the FTSE 100. Investors can then estimate active risk: that is, the risk that the performance of their fund will be different from that of the index. Active risk allows them to earn positive alpha, but imposing a limit on active risk reassures the client that, should the fund under-perform the index, the under-performance will not be too great. Active risk is usually measured using historical return data. In practice, though, active risk may not adequately measure the risk. Sectors may behave differently from their historical averages, so that over-weighting or under-weighting a sector such as banking could lead to much greater tracking error than forecast by the active risk measure.

The third model we explored in this chapter was the efficient markets hypothesis. This assumes that markets behave rationally through the price discovery mechanism. It does not assume that investors are perfectly rational, and this is where behavioral finance comes in. Behavioral finance considers such questions as, how do investors judge what are good or bad investment decisions? How do investors develop an initial set of heuristics (rules of thumb), and how do they change these as circumstances change? We looked at a range of results of empirical tests which provided examples of non-rational investor behaviour, such as reluctance to sell losing positions, over-subscription to IPOs, and flaws in the use of the normal distribution. We then considered whether markets might be inefficient, as a result of such irrational investor behaviour. We found two examples, one of two companies whose shares were traded on two stock markets at different prices for the same underlying assets, and the other the anomaly of closed-end fund discounts to asset value.

We concluded the chapter with a discussion of pension funds as an example of investors who might take decisions which are not rational in an investment theory sense. We explored why this might be so, and found that pension funds, in the United Kingdom, have been subject to a changing variety of regulations and requirements, which have affected their investment strategies in such a way as to make their portfolios less optimal for the ultimate beneficiaries. For example, the way in which their performance has been measured has made pension funds consider short-term returns and volatility of returns important, despite the long-term nature of their liabilities. In addition, their sponsors have taken advantage of surpluses by reducing contributions but been reluctant to fund deficits. This small case study gave you an insight into the real world of investment. Now you have learned the theories, it is time to put them into practice.

REVIEW EXERCISES

1. What are the strengths and weaknesses of the normal distribution as a model of future possible outcomes in the financial markets, and why does it have such enduring appeal?

2. What are the main problems associated with the application of portfolio theory and the CAPM in an international context?

3. What are the main problems confronting any attempt to capture the phenomena of correlation and volatility in the context of modelling possible financial outcomes?

4. Do some background reading on the case of Long-Term Capital Management (LTCM) and its near-collapse in 1998 (see suggestions for further reading on page 477). To what extent do you think that the case of LTCM calls into question the principal hypotheses and findings of conventional finance theory (as set out, for instance, in Chapters 1–12 of this book)?

5. Study the columns on personal investment in the *Financial Times* or in another broadsheet newspaper.
    a. To what extent does the investment advice given in such columns embrace the rigorous findings of conventional finance theory?
    b. To what extent does such advice play to one or other of the supposedly irrational characteristics identified in this chapter?

6. In the context of formulating a coherent and comprehensive long-term investment strategy, discuss the relative merits of skills in:
    a. Fundamental analysis.
    b. Correctly predicting crowd behaviour.

Sample answers to the review exercises can be found on the companion website.

Useful financial equations

No.	Equation	Short description
2.1	$R = \dfrac{D_1 + P_1 - P_0}{P_0}$	Holding period return
	$P_o = \dfrac{C_n}{(1+r)^n}$	Present value of any future cash flow
	$P_0 = \dfrac{C_1}{(1+r)^1} + \dfrac{C_2}{(1+r)^2} + \dfrac{C_3}{(1+r)^3} + \dfrac{C_4}{(1+r)^4} \ldots + \dfrac{C_n}{(1+r)^n}$	Present value of any series of future cash flows
2.5	$P = \dfrac{C}{r}$	Present value of a perpetuity
	$P = \dfrac{1}{r}\left(C - \dfrac{C}{(1+r)^n}\right)$	Present value of an annuity
	$F = Pe^{rt}$	Future value of a sum under conditions of continuous compounding
2.6	$(1 + \text{nominal rate}) = (1 + \text{real rate})(1 + \text{inflation rate})$	Fisher equation
2.8	$V = \displaystyle\sum_{i=1}^{i=n}\left((E(R) - R_i)^2 p_i(R_i)\right)$	Variance of returns on a security
	$S = \sqrt{\displaystyle\sum_{i=1}^{i=n}\left((R_i - E(R))^2 p_i(R_i)\right)}$	Standard deviation of returns on a security
3.2	$P = v^{\frac{s-t}{s}}\left\{d_1 + d_2 v + \dfrac{cv^2}{f(1-v)}(1 - v^{n-1}) + 100\, v^n\right\}$	Clean price of a conventional UK government bond (gilt)
4.2	$r_{i,j} = \left\langle \dfrac{\left[1 + \left(\dfrac{r_{0,j} \times d_{0,j}}{100 \times y}\right)\right]}{\left[1 + \left(\dfrac{r_{0,i} \times d_{0,i}}{100 \times y}\right)\right]} - 1\right\rangle \times \left[\dfrac{y \times 100}{d_{i,j}}\right]$	General equation for calculating an implied forward interest rate

No.	Equation	Short description
4.3	$D = \dfrac{1}{P}\sum_{i=1}^{i=n} i \times \dfrac{C_i}{(1+r)^r}$	Short-form equation for calculating duration of an asset or liability
4.5	$dP = -D \times P \times \dfrac{dr}{(1+r)}$	Duration-based estimate of change in price for a given change in interest rate
4.7	$dP = -MD \times P \times dr$	As 4.4, but based on modified duration
5.6	$P_0 = \dfrac{D_1}{r-g}$	
5.7a	$r = \dfrac{D_1}{P_0} + g$	Alternative formulations of Gordon's dividend growth model
5.7b	$r = \dfrac{D_0(1+g)}{P_0} + g$	
6.1	$E\left(R_P\right) = W_A E\left(R_A\right) + W_B E\left(R_B\right)$	Expected return on a two-asset portfolio
6.7a	$V_P = W_A^2 S_A^2 + W_B^2 S_B^2 + 2W_A W_B S_A S_B CORR_{AB}$ $S_P = \sqrt{W_A^2 S_A^2 + W_B^2 S_B^2 + 2W_A W_B S_A S_B CORR_{AB}}$	Variance and standard deviation of returns on a two-asset portfolio – general form
	$V_P = \left(W_A S_A + W_B S_B\right)^2$ $S_P = W_A S_A + W_B S_B$	Variance and standard deviation of returns on a two-asset portfolio – special case with perfectly positive correlation

No.	Equation	Short description
	$$S_P = W_A S_A - W_B S_B$$ $$\frac{W_A}{W_B} = \frac{S_B}{S_A}$$	Two-asset portfolio with perfectly negative correlation: equations for determining standard deviation and risk-free weightings
6.13	$$V_P = \sum_{i=1}^{i=n} W_i^2 S_i^2 + \sum_{i=1}^{i=n} \sum_{\substack{j=1 \\ j \neq i}}^{j=n} W_i W_j COV_{ij}$$	Variance of a multi-asset portfolio
7.12	$$E(R_P) = R_F + \left(E(R_M) - R_F\right)\frac{S_P}{S_M}$$	The capital market line
7.13	$$E(R_i) = R_F + \left(E(R_M) - R_F\right)\frac{COV_{iM}}{S_M^2}$$	The security market line
7.15	$$E(R_i) = R_F + \beta_i \left(E(R_M) - R_F\right)$$	The capital asset pricing model (CAPM)
7.19	$$\beta_A = \left(\beta_D \times \frac{D}{V}\right) + \left(\beta_E \times \frac{E}{V}\right)$$	Decomposition of beta (enterprise) into beta (debt) and beta (equity)
9.1	$$S + P - C = PV(X)$$	Options: put-call parity
9.2	$$C = SN(d_1) - Xe^{-rt}N(d_2)$$	Black–Scholes formula for valuing a call option (9.2) and a put option (9.3)
9.3	$$P = Xe^{-rt}N(-d_2) - SN(-d_1)$$	
9.4	$$d_1 = \frac{\ln\left(S/Xe^{-rt}\right)}{\sigma\sqrt{t}} + \frac{\sigma\sqrt{t}}{2}$$	Detailed definition of d_1 and d_2 terms in Black–Scholes formula
9.5	$$d_2 = \frac{\ln\left(S/Xe^{-rt}\right)}{\sigma\sqrt{t}} - \frac{\sigma\sqrt{t}}{2}$$	
11.1	$$X_F = X_S \left(\frac{1 + \dfrac{R_B \times d}{y}}{1 + \dfrac{R_A \times d}{y}}\right)$$	Calculation of equilibrium forward exchange rate from spot exchange rate and applicable interest rates

References and suggested further reading

REFERENCES

Alexander, G. (ed.) (1986) *Portfolio Analysis*, 3rd edn, Prentice Hall.

Allworthy, B., Debenham, K. and Rutterford, J. (2003) *The Cost of Capital Guide*, Merrill Lynch, London.

Bachelier, L. (1900) *Théorie de la Spéculation*, Gauthier-Villars.

Ball, R. and Brown, P. (1968) 'An empirical evaluation of accounting income numbers', *Journal of Accounting Research*, Autumn, Vol. 6 no. 2, pp. 159–78.

Black, F. (1972) 'Capital market equilibrium with restricted borrowing', *Journal of Business* (July), pp. 445–55.

Blume, M. (1975) 'Betas and their regression tendencies', *Journal of Finance*, Vol. 10, no. 3, pp. 785–95.

Brooks, R. and Del Negro, M. (2004) 'The rise in comovement across national stock markets: market integration or IT bubble?' *Journal of Empirical Finance*, Vol. 11, pp. 659–80.

Copeland, T. E., Weston, F. and Shastri, K. (1994) *Financial Theory and Corporate Policy*, Addison-Wesley, London.

Cowles, A. III (1933) 'Can stock market forecasters forecast?' *Econometrica*, Vol. 1, pp. 309–24.

Cowles, A. III (1944) 'Stock market forecasting', *Econometrica*, Vol. 12, pp. 206–14.

Dimson, E., Marsh, P. and Staunton, M. (2000) *The Millennium Book: A century of investment returns*, ABN-AMRO.

Dimson, E., Marsh, P. and Staunton, M. (2002) *Triumph of the Optimists: 101 Years of global investment returns*, Princeton, NJ: Princeton University Press.

Dimson, E., Marsh, P. and Staunton, M. (2004) *Global Investment Returns Yearbook 2004*, ABN-AMRO.

Dimson, E., Marsh, P. and Staunton, M. (2005) *Global Investment Returns Yearbook 2005*, ABN-AMRO.

Dimson, E., Marsh, P. and Staunton, M. (2006) *Global Investment Returns Yearbook 2006*, ABN-AMRO.

Elton, E., Gruber, M., Brown, S. and Goetzmann, W. (2003) *Modern Portfolio Theory and Investment Analysis*, 6th edn, Wiley.

Fama, E., Fisher, L., Jensen, M. and Roll, R. (1969) 'The adjustment of stock prices to new information', *International Economic Review*, Vol. 10, pp. 1–21.

Fama, E. (1970) 'Efficient capital markets: a review of theory and empirical work', *Journal of Finance*, Vol. 25, pp. 383–417.

Fama, E. (1972) 'Components of investment performance', *Journal of Finance*, Vol. 27, no. 3, pp 551–67.

Fama, E. (1998) 'Market efficiency, long-term returns, and behavioral finance', *Journal of Financial Economics*, Vol. 49, pp 283–306.

Fama, E. and French, K. R. (1993) 'Common risk factors in the returns on stocks and bonds', *Journal of Financial Economics,* Vol. 33, pp. 3–56.

Fisher, I. (1930) *The Theory of Interest: As determined by impatience to spend income and opportunity to invest it*, Macmillan.

Grinold, R. C. and Kahn, R. N. (2000) *Active Portfolio Management,* 2nd edn, New York: McGraw-Hill.

Hull, J. (2003) *Options, Futures, and Other Derivatives,* 5th edn, Prentice Hall.

Jensen, M. (1978) 'Some anomalous evidence regarding market efficiency', *Journal of Financial Economics,* Vol. 6, no. 2/3, pp. 95–101.

Lessard, D. (1976) 'World, country, and industry relationships in equity returns: implications for risk reduction through international diversification', *Financial Analysts Journal,* Vol. 32, no. 1, pp 32–8.

Mandelbrot, B. and Taleb, N. (2006) 'Mastering uncertainty: part 2', *Financial Times,* 24 March, p. 2.

Moore, A. (1962) *A Statistical Analysis of Common Stock Prices,* unpublished PhD dissertation, University of Chicago.

Morgan, E. and Thomas, W. (1962) *The Stock Exchange: Its history and functions,* Elek Books.

Roberts, H. (1959) 'Stock market "patterns" and financial analysis: methodological suggestions', *Journal of Finance,* Vol. 44, pp. 1–10.

Roll, R. (1977) 'A critique of the asset pricing theory's tests, part 1: on past and potential testability of the theory', *Journal of Financial Economics,* Vol. 4, No. 2, pp. 129–76.

Ross, S. (1976) 'The arbitrage theory of capital asset pricing', *Journal of Economic Theory,* Vol. 13, pp. 341–60.

Samuelson, P. (1965) 'Proof that properly anticipated prices fluctuate randomly', *Industrial Management Review,* Vol. 6, pp. 41–9.

Sharpe, W. (1963) 'A simplified model for portfolio analysis', *Management Science* (January), pp. 277–93.

Shiller, R. (2005) *Irrational Exuberance,* 2nd edn, Princeton NJ: Princeton University Press.

Shleifer, A. (2000) *Inefficient Markets: An introduction to behavioral finance,* Oxford: Oxford University Press.

Solnik, B. (1974) 'Why not diversify internationally rather than domestically?' *Financial Analysts' Journal,* Vol. 30, no. 4, pp 48–54.

Speidell, L. (2004) 'Why non-U.S. investing is essential, not optional', *Journal of Investing,* Winter, pp. 8–11.

Tuluca, S., Zwick, B. and Seiler, M. (2003) 'International versus U.S. sector diversification in the wake of the Asian crisis', *American Business Review,* Vol. 21, no. 1, pp. 67–74.

Wong, K. and Wu, H. (2003) 'Testing Fisher hypothesis in long horizons for G7 and eight Asian countries', *Applied Economics Letters,* Vol. 10, pp. 917–23.

SUGGESTED FURTHER READING

Ashton, J., Gerrard, B. and Hudson, R. (2003) 'Economic impact of national sporting success: evidence from the London stock exchange', *Applied Economics Letters,* Vol. 10, pp. 783–5.

Barber, B. and Odean, T. (2001) 'Boys will be boys: gender, overconfidence and common stock investment', *Quarterly Journal of Economics,* February, pp. 261–92.

Bedi, J. and Tennant, P. (2002) 'Dual-listed companies', *Reserve Bank of Australia Bulletin,* October.

Bernstein, P. (1996) *Against the Gods: The remarkable story of risk,* Wiley.

Black, F. (1986) 'Noise', *Journal of Finance,* Vol. 51, no. 3, pp. 529–43.

Brealey, R. and Myers, S. (2005) *Principles of Corporate Finance,* 8th edn, McGraw-Hill.

Buckle, M. and Thompson, J. (2004) The *UK Financial System: Theory and practice,* 4th edn, Manchester: Manchester University Press.

Carswell, J. (1993) *The South Sea Bubble,* Sutton.

Choudhry, M., Joannas, D., Pereira, R. and Pienaar, R. (2005) *Capital Market Instruments: Analysis and valuation,* Basingstoke: Macmillan.

Day, A. (2005) *Mastering Financial Mathematics in Microsoft Excel*, FT Prentice Hall.

Dimson, E. and Mussavian, M. (1998) 'A brief history of market efficiency', *European Financial Management*, Vol. 4, no. 1, pp. 91–103.

Golding, T., (2003) *The City: Inside the great expectation machine*, 2nd edn, FT Prentice Hall.

Hart, K. (2004) 'From bell curve to power law: distributional models between national and world society', *Social Analysis*, Vol. 48, no. 3, pp. 220–4.

Howells, P. and Bain, K. (2004) *Financial Markets and Institutions*, 4th edn, FT Prentice Hall.

Howell, P. and Bain, K. (2005) *The Economics of Money, Banking and Finance: A European text*, 3rd edn, FT Prentice Hall.

Lowenstein, R. (2002) *When Genius Failed: The rise and fall of Long-Term Capital Management*, Fourth Estate.

Malkiel, B. (2005) 'Reflections on the efficient market hypothesis: 30 years later', *Financial Review*, Vol. 40, pp. 1–9.

Martin, J. (2001) *Applied Math for Derivatives*, Wiley (Asia).

Myners, P. (2005) *Pre-Emption Rights: Final Report: A study into the impact of shareholders' pre-emption rights on a public company's ability to raise new capital*, Department for Trade and Industry.

Partnoy, F. (2003) *Infectious Greed: How deceit and risk corrupted the financial markets*, Profile.

Pike, R. and Neale, B. (2005) *Corporate Finance and Investment: Decisions and strategies*, 5th edn, FT Prentice Hall.

Roberts, R. (2004) *The City: A guide to London's global financial centre*, Profile (in association with *The Economist*).

Roberts, R., (2003) *Wall Street: The markets, mechanisms and players*, Profile (in association with *The Economist*).

Thaler, R. (1992) *The Winner's Curse: Paradoxes and anomalies of economic life*, Princeton NJ: Princeton University Press.

Vaitilingam, R. (2005) *The Financial Times Guide to Using the Financial Pages*, 5th edn, FT Prentice Hall,

Wilson, J. (1995) *British Business History, 1720–1994*, Manchester: Manchester University Press.

Glossary

Active risk The standard deviation of the relative return of a portfolio when compared with the return on a predetermined benchmark index.

American-style An option is described as American-style if it can be exercised at any time up to and including the time of expiry. See also **European-style.**

Annuity An investment entitling the holder to receive a fixed or determinable regular payment for a fixed or determinable period of time. The payment may be fixed in money terms, or it may be indexed, for instance to an index of prices, and the term may be limited to the holder's lifetime.

Arbitrage/arbitrageur Arbitrage is the exploitation, for potential profit, of market pricing anomalies which contravene (or appear to contravene) the law of one price, for instance by buying an instrument in one market and simultaneously selling it in another at a higher price. In efficient, liquid and transparent markets, opportunities for genuine arbitrage are comparatively rare. More frequently, the identification of an arbitrage opportunity depends on the validity of some more or less subjective extrapolation into the future of historically observed patterns or correlations.

At-the-money (ATM) An option is at-the-money if its exercise or strike price coincides with the current market price of the underlying.

Basis point value (BPV) This is how much a bond will change in value for 1 basis point (or 0.01%) change in the yield to maturity. This can be calculated by multiplying 0.01% by the modified duration and the dirty price of the bond.

Bear/bear market A bear is a stock market participant who believes that the market, or a specific sector or company share, is currently overvalued and therefore likely to fall in value (in the case of a sector or specific share, to fall in relation to other sectors or shares). If overall sentiment is negative about the prospects for shares, the market is said to be a bear market. See also **bull/bull market.**

Behavioral finance An approach to the subject which stresses the way that investors and others actually make financial decisions in the real world. It therefore plays down the assumptions of mainstream economics (for instance, that investors are perfectly rational, risk-averse wealth-maximisers) in favour of a more nuanced approach to the observed complexities of investor psychology, motivation and behaviour.

Benchmark issue An issue of securities (usually **bonds**) whose size and liquidity is such that its price and yield act as a reference point for the market as a whole or for an identifiable segment of the market.

Bonds Debt securities conferring on the holder the legally enforceable contractual right to receive a stream of fixed or determinable future payments.

Bonus issue See **capitalisation issue.**

BPV See **basis point value**.

Bull/bull market A bull is a stock market operator who believes that the market, or a specific sector or company share, is currently undervalued and therefore likely to rise in value (in the case of a sector or specific share, to rise in relation to other sectors or shares). If overall sentiment is positive about the prospects for shares, the market is said to be a bull market. See also **bear/bear market**.

Callable A bond is callable if the issuer has the right to prepay it voluntarily before its stated maturity date.

Call option See **option**.

Call protection Refers to any features of a bond issue's terms and conditions that explicitly or implicitly limit the issuer's ability to prepay it.

Capital shares In the context of an investment trust company (or other collective investment vehicle) with more than one category of share capital, capital shares are those which enjoy no right to periodic dividends but rely for their return on their eventual appreciation in capital value. See also **income shares** and **zero-dividend preference shares**.

Capitalisation issue A new issue of shares to existing shareholders for no new money. Also called a **bonus issue**.

Cash and carry A strategy in the futures market, whereby the investor simultaneously buys the cash instrument and sells the corresponding futures contract, in the expectation of making a net profit from (a) any income earned on the asset, less (b) the interest cost of financing the cash position (the cost of carry), plus/minus (c) the capital loss or profit arising from buying at the spot (cash) price and selling at the futures price.

Cash settlement/cash settled A futures contract is cash settled if, instead of delivering and receiving the underlying, the parties settle their long and short positions by exchanging cash amounts equal to the difference between the price at which they originally dealt and the spot price on the expiry date of the futures contract.

Certificate of deposit (CD) A document issued by a bank certifying that a sum of money has been deposited for a fixed period, either at a fixed rate or at a rate indexed (for example) to the London Interbank Offered Rate. A CD may be made out either to a named depositor or to the bearer.

Cheap A security is described as cheap if at its current price the expected return is greater than a fair return for the risk perceived to be incurred by an investor by holding it. See also **expensive**.

Cheapest-to-deliver (CTD) Financial futures contracts on bonds are usually capable of, if they do not actually require, physical settlement rather than cash settlement. Such contracts can often be settled by means of delivery of any of a number of qualifying bond issues. The relationships between the different terms of these issues and their fixed conversion factors for the purpose of futures delivery are complex, so they are not all equally economical to deliver. The issue that it is most economical to deliver is the cheapest to deliver or CTD issue. See also **price factor**.

Clean price The price of a debt security excluding the accrued positive or negative coupon interest. See also **dirty price**.

Clearing house A company or organisation which settles transactions between the participants on an organised exchange.

Closed-end (investment companies/funds) An investment company is closed-end if the shares it issues to investors cannot normally be redeemed directly by offering them back to the company itself but can only be realised by sale to other investors in the secondary market.

Collective investments Investment vehicles, such as mutual funds, which enable savers to pool their funds in ways that achieve economies and efficiencies of scale, risk diversification and management costs.

Common stock See **ordinary shares**.

Continuous compounding A theoretical mathematical model which calculates interest on the basis of compounding at infinitesimally short intervals.

Conversion factor An alternative term for **price factor.**

Convertible A bond or preference share conferring on the holder the right to exchange it on fixed or determinable terms for another security of the same or of another issuer.

Convexity As the yield of a bond increases, its value falls at a reducing rate. The curve of the graph plotting value on the y-axis against yield on the x-axis is described as being 'convex to the origin'. This quality of convexity is a complex function of the coupon and remaining life of a bond. A high-convexity bond combines superior scope for gain if interest rates fall with better protection against loss if they rise.

Corporate governance The various sets of written and unwritten rules and principles that govern the agency relationship between the shareholders of a company and the directors they appoint to manage it on their behalf and in their interests.

Cost of carry The difference between the income (excluding capital loss or profit on disposal) on an investment, and the interest cost of financing the investment.

Coupons Periodic interest payment made on a bond. So called because bonds issued in physical form (rather than electronically) have a separate coupon attached for each interest payment.

Covered call To write a covered call is to sell a call option on an underlying asset one already holds. Such an option is said to be covered because the writer is protected from the further losses that would otherwise accrue in the event that the underlying were to appreciate in value.

Cross-currency swap/currency swap An agreement to exchange two future cash flow streams in two different currencies, based on (a) a notional principal amount, and (b) any combination of fixed and floating interest rates in the two currencies.

Cum dividend/cum div A security is sold/bought cum dividend (or cum div) if the buyer is entitled to receive (a) in the case of a bond, the whole of the next interest coupon, or (b) in the case of an equity, the whole of a dividend which has been declared but not yet paid. See also **ex dividend/ex div.**

Cum rights Shares are sold/bought cum rights if the buyer is entitled to the benefit of a recently announced rights issue of the company's shares. See also **ex rights.**

Currency option A currency option gives the buyer the right to exchange a fixed amount of Currency A for a fixed amount of Currency B on a fixed date in the future. A call option on one currency in such a contract is automatically a put option on the other currency.

Current yield The periodic return on an investment represented by the income (interest or dividend) expressed as a percentage of the cost or market price.

Dear See **expensive.**

Debentures A form of debt issue similar in most economic respects to bonds.

Defined benefit pension plan A pension plan under which the *benefits* to be paid to pensioners are fixed and guaranteed, usually according to a formula based on the beneficiaries' salaries (for instance, their final salary).

Defined contribution pension plan A pension plan under which the *contributions* to be paid by the employer and/or the employee are fixed, but without any explicit or implicit guarantee as to the value of the pension which the resulting investment fund will be able to support on the employee's retirement.

Delta hedge ratio In a cash market position hedging or hedged by a derivative position, the delta hedge ratio (sometimes referred to as the hedge ratio or the delta) is the ratio of the nominal amount of the cash market position to the nominal amount of the derivative position, such that any gain in one will be exactly offset by a loss in the other.

Derivative product or instrument/derivative A derivative product or instrument (usually referred to simply as a derivative) is one whose value is primarily, but not exclusively, dependent on the value of another underlying product or instrument (usually referred to simply as 'the underlying'). A derivative has the further qualities that (a) the initial investment is very small (it can be zero) in relation to the amount that would need to be invested directly in the underlying in order to obtain the same exposure to changes in value of the underlying, and (b) it is settled at a date later than normal spot settlement for trades in the underlying.

Dilution See **equity dilution**.

Dirty price The price of a debt security including the accrued positive or negative coupon interest. See also **clean price**.

Discount a) In bonds, the difference between the par value of a security and the price (if lower than its par value) at which it is issued. b) In foreign exchange, Currency A is said to be at a forward discount to Currency B if more units of Currency A are required to buy one unit of Currency B in the forward market than in the spot market. In any pair of convertible currencies which are freely tradable in an efficient market, the currency with the higher interest rate is always at a forward discount to the currency with the lower interest rate. See also **premium**.

Discount rate a) The periodic interest rate at which future cash flows are discounted to calculate their present values. b) The rate at which a central bank acts as lender of last resort to the banking sector.

Dividend yield The **current yield** of a share.

Double-dated A double-dated bond is one that can be called by the issuer no earlier than the first of the two dates indicated (the second date being the final maturity date).

Duration The duration of a financial asset or liability expresses the sensitivity of its price to changes in interest rates. Mathematically it is equal to the remaining life (in years) of a zero-coupon bond with the same sensitivity to interest rate changes. See also **Macaulay's duration** and **modified duration**.

Earnings per share The periodic earnings of a company attributable to ordinary shareholders (after all expense and other claims, including tax and preference dividends have been provided for), divided by the average number of shares in issue during the period.

Equities See **ordinary shares**.

Equity dilution Dilution refers to the loss in value suffered by existing shareholders in a company if new shares are issued to other investors at a discount to the market value of the existing shares.

Equity risk premium The additional return earned by equities over the risk-free rate of return to compensate for the additional risk of equities.

Eurobonds Bonds issued and traded outside the country of the currency in which they are denominated. The prefix 'euro' in this sense is entirely unconnected with the single European currency, the euro.

Euromarkets/eurocurrency The euromarkets are the financial markets for instruments and products outside the country of the currency in which they are denominated. A dollar deposit held with a bank in London is a eurodollar deposit; a sterling deposit held with a bank in Paris is a eurosterling deposit. The prefix 'euro' in this sense is entirely unconnected with the single European currency, the euro.

European style An option is described as European-style if it can be exercised only at the time of expiry. See also **American style**.

Excess profit/excess return These terms can be used in two different senses. a) The amount by which a rate of investment return exceeds a fair return for the risk incurred. b) The amount by which the rate of return on a risky investment exceeds the risk-free rate.

Exchange-traded Products are exchange-traded if dealings in them take place exclusively on an organised, institutional exchange with its own comprehensive rules and regulations as regards membership, dealing procedures, disclosure standards, settlement provisions etc. See also **over the counter (OTC)**.

Ex dividend/ex div A security is sold/bought ex dividend (or ex div) if the buyer is not entitled to receive (a) in the case of a bond, the whole of the next interest coupon or (b) in the case of an equity, the whole of a dividend which has been declared but not yet paid. See also **cum dividend/cum div**.

Exercise (expiry) date The date when an option expires worthless if it has not been exercised.

Exercise (strike) price The fixed price at which the buyer of a **call (put) option** is entitled, but not obliged, to buy (sell) the underlying.

Expensive A security is described as expensive (or dear) if at its current price the expected return is less than a fair return for the risk perceived to be incurred by an investor holding it. See also **cheap**.

Ex rights Shares are sold/bought ex rights if the buyer is not entitled to the benefit of a recently announced rights issue of the company's shares. See also **cum rights**.

Factor markets The markets for the factors of production – capital and labour. See also **product markets**.

Final salary See **defined benefit pension plan**.

Financial asset An asset consisting exclusively of a claim to a fixed or determinable amount of cash. See also **real assets/real economy**.

Financial futures contract An exchange traded contract, for settlement at a date beyond the normal spot settlement date, for the purchase and sale of a standardised quantity of a standardised financial instrument. The buyer of a futures contract locks in the future rate of return on a notional investment: the seller locks in the cost of borrowing.

Fisher effect Describes the relationship between real and nominal interest rates in terms of the expected inflation rate:

$$(1 + \text{nominal rate of return}) = (1 + \text{real rate of return}) \times (1 + \text{expected rate of inflation})$$

Fixed income securities Securities offering a contractually fixed periodic income; fixed-rate bonds.

Flight to quality The tendency of investors, at times of stress and uncertainty in the markets, to avoid higher-risk investments in favour of low-risk assets such as government bonds and bank deposits. This pushes up the prices and depresses the yields on such investments, in relation to the prices and yields of riskier investments.

Floating rate notes/floaters Bonds whose coupons are not fixed in amount but are reset periodically (e.g. every three months) by reference to some benchmark such as the London Interbank Offered Rate.

Foreign exchange futures contract An exchange-traded contract for the sale or purchase of a standardised amount of a foreign currency on a fixed future date, to be settled through an exchange or clearing house.

Foreign exchange swap See **swap**.

Forward foreign exchange contract A private, bilateral over-the-counter contract for the exchange of any agreed amount of two currencies, for direct settlement between the parties to the contract on a date beyond the normal spot settlement date.

Forward (interest) rate The interest rate for the period between two future dates A and B, as implied mathematically by the two spot interest rates to the maturity dates A and B, such that no risk-free profit can be earned through dealing in any combination of the spot and forward rates.

Forward rate agreement/FRA A private, bilateral over-the-counter contract whereby two parties agree to compensate each other for the amount by which the actual market interest rate on an agreed sum of money for a fixed period commencing on a date beyond spot differs from the current implied rate for that same forward period. The buyer of a FRA receives compensation if the actual rate is higher than the contract (current implied) rate; the seller receives compensation if it is lower.

Free float The percentage of a securities issue that is considered to be available for trading; i.e. that is not in the hands of long-term investors.

Free lunch The law of one price is colloquially captured in the saying: 'There's no such thing as a free lunch.'

Fungible/fungibility Assets or instruments having common properties so that they are fully interchangeable are said to be fungible with each other. All £10 notes are fungible with each other, in the sense that any one such note can be offered in payment of a £10 debt: a lender of £10 cannot insist on being repaid with the same £10 note as he or she originally lent. Similarly, all bonds of a particular issue are fully interchangeable with each other.

Gilt-edged/gilts Securities issued in sterling by the UK government are known as gilt-edged (gilts for short) because they are not actually as good as gold but are traditionally considered to be the next best thing.

Global depositary receipt (GDR) A negotiable certificate held in the bank of one country representing a specific number of shares of a stock traded on an exchange of another country.

Hedge fund An investment fund which attempts to earn 'positive alpha', that is, more than the rate of return predicted by the CAPM given the risk, through judicious stock selection, market timing, or arbitrage.

Hedge ratio See **delta hedge ratio**.

Heuristics Decision-making rules which, although not exhaustive, have been found by experience to yield, on average, decisions that are of a reasonable quality in relation to the effort they entail, are known as heuristics. Investors who cannot practically take into consideration every single piece of information that may possibly impact on an investment decision shorten the process by employing rules they have found (or think they have found) over time to produce acceptable decisions.

Holding period return The total return earned on an investment over a given holding period, typically including both income and capital gain.

Income shares In the context of an investment trust company (or other collective investment vehicle) with more than one category of share capital, income shares are those that enjoy periodic dividends but no right to capital repayment. See also **capital shares**.

Index-linked bond Bond whose periodic interest payments and/or final repayment amount is not fixed in money terms but fluctuates in response to changes in some index, for instance of retail prices.

Information ratio The ratio of the return on a portfolio relative to a predetermined benchmark divided by the **active risk**.

Initial margin The fixed sum required to be deposited as security by each party to an exchange-traded futures contract or by the seller of an exchange-traded options contract. See also **mark-to-market** and **variation margin.**

Initial public offering (IPO) The first-time offer of a company's shares for sale through a stock exchange to the general investing public. See also **placing**.

Interbank deposit A deposit of a large (i.e. non-retail) amount of money by one bank with another, for a fixed term or repayable on call, at a predetermined fixed rate of interest.

Interest rate option An option on an interest rate (e.g. LIBOR) or on an interest-bearing financial instrument (e.g. a US Treasury bond).

Interest rate parity The thesis that investors will get equal returns from hedged investments with equal risks in different currencies.

Interest rate swap An agreement whereby two parties agree to exchange with each other, for a fixed period of years, amounts equal to the periodic interest on a fixed notional principal amount computed on two different bases, e.g. a fixed rate versus periodic floating three-month LIBOR.

Interest yield The current yield of an interest-bearing asset.

Internal rate of return (IRR) The discount rate at which the present value of the future cash flows of an investment precisely equals the current value or price, i.e. the discount rate at which the net present value of the investment is zero.

International Fisher effect This supposes that there is a single risk-free rate across currencies if securities are freely tradable world-wide.

In the money (ITM) An option is in the money if exercise would be automatically advantageous to the holder in relation to the current market price of the underlying, i.e. if the exercise price of a call (put) is lower (higher) than the current market price.

Intrinsic value The intrinsic value of an option is the amount (if any) by which it is in the money. It is one of the two elements of an option's value, and cannot be negative. The other element is **time value**.

Introduction The process whereby the existing shares of a company are listed and admitted for trading on the stock exchange for the first time, without new shares being issued or the existing shares being sold to new investors.

Investment grade In the United States, investments that meet certain minimum criteria as regards their credit quality are referred to as investment-grade securities. Many fund managers and financial intermediaries and institutions are restricted in their investments, either by law or by private contract, to investment-grade securities. See also **junk bond**.

Investment trust company/investment trust A type of closed-end investment company.

IRR See **internal rate of return**.

Jobber See **market-maker**.

Junk bond A higher-risk bond that does not meet the quality criteria required of an investment-grade security.

Law of one price In an efficient, liquid and transparent market, the same asset or instrument should theoretically trade at a single uniform price. If there were two genuinely different prices (i.e. if two different ways of achieving the same result had genuinely different costs) then there would be excess demand at the lower price and excess supply at the higher price, and the prices would converge. See also **arbitrage** and **free lunch**.

Limited liability Shareholders in a limited liability company are not personally liable for the company's debts beyond the amount of capital they have subscribed or that they have undertaken to subscribe but that has not yet been called.

Liquidity The liquidity of a market or of a financial instrument is measured in terms of the size of transaction that can be concluded without moving the market price.

Listing requirements The detailed set of rules with which an issuer of securities on a stock exchange must comply, both at the time of the initial listing and subsequently for as long as the securities remain outstanding and listed on the exchange.

London Interbank Offered Rate (LIBOR) The fixed rate at which banks in London offer interbank deposits to each other for a given currency and period.

M&A This expression is short for mergers and acquisitions, a US term to cover takeovers of companies.

Macaulay's duration Another term for **duration**. See also **modified duration**.

Market capitalisation (or **market cap**) The theoretical market value of a company, calculated by multiplying the market price of one share by the number of shares outstanding.

Marketable securities Securities issued in a form permitting or facilitating their purchase and sale in a secondary market.

Market-maker A member-firm of an exchange that is contractually bound, within certain limits, to make two-way (bid and offer) prices in specific securities to other members while the market is officially open, as a means of providing liquidity to the market.

Mark-to-market The process of periodically calculating the cumulative unrealised losses and gains of parties who have open positions in a particular cash or derivative instrument. See also **variation margin**.

Midprice The midpoint between the market bid price and the market offer price.

Modified duration Modified duration is calculated as (Macaulay's) duration divided by $(1 + r)$ where r is the present redemption yield on a financial instrument, and represents the approximate amount (subject to error caused by convexity) by which the value of the instrument will change in response to a 1% change in redemption yield.

Money purchase Another term for a **defined contribution pension plan**.

Mortgage Collateral security for a debt, consisting of a charge on property entitling the creditor (the mortgagee) to take possession and sell the property in the event of a payment default by the borrower (the mortgagor).

Mutual/mutual company A mutual company (or 'mutual' for short) has as its overriding defined objective not the maximisation of shareholder wealth but the mutual benefit of all its members.

Mutual fund Another term (common in the United States) for an **open-ended investment company**.

Naked call A call option written on an underlying that the writer does not own, leaving the writer 100% exposed (i.e. naked) to the risk that the price of the underlying will increase and cause losses.

Nominal (rate of) return A rate of investment return computed in money (cash) terms rather than in real terms.

Nominal value The stated monetary value of a financial instrument. See also **par value**.

Occupational pension plan A pension plan linked to, and forming part of, a specific employment contract. See also **personal pension plan**.

Open-end investment company (OEICs)/fund An investment company or fund is open-ended if the company is willing (or is required) continuously to repurchase outstanding shares (or units) from existing investors and issue new shares (or units) to new investors at prices closely reflecting the value of the company's own underlying net assets.

Open outcry A system of exchange trading where members call out to each other in face-to-face dealing the prices and amounts that they are prepared to deal.

Opportunity cost The opportunity cost of an income is the return that an investor could earn on the highest-yielding alternative investment that is identical in every respect, including in particular its riskiness.

Option A contract giving the **option buyer** (or **holder**), in return for the payment of a premium, the right, but not the obligation, to buy (**call option**) or sell (**put option**) a fixed quantity or amount of an **underlying** instrument at a fixed price (**exercise** or **strike price**), either on (**European-style**) or at any time on or before (**American-style**) a fixed future date (**exercise** or **expiry date**). The **option seller** (or **writer**) enters into a corresponding obligation to sell (call option) or buy (put option).

Ordinary shares Also known as **equities** or **common stock** (in the United States), ordinary shares are investments representing proportionate interests in the residual assets and income of a limited liability company after all contractual debts and other obligations have been met in full.

Out of the money (OTM) An option is out of the money if exercise would be disadvantageous to the holder in relation to the current market price of the underlying. i.e. if the exercise price of a call (put) is higher (lower) than the current market price.

Outright forward foreign exchange contract An alternative term for a **forward foreign exchange contract**.

Over the counter (OTC) A contract negotiated privately between two parties: the opposite of exchange-traded.

Par value Another term for **nominal value**.

Par yield curve (or **par coupon yield curve**) A notional yield curve showing the yields of notional bonds whose coupons would be exactly equal to their redemption yields in the current market interest rate environment.

Perpetual A bond with no contractually enforceable provision for the holder to demand repayment from the issuer (except in special circumstances, for instance a default by the issuer in the payment of periodic interest). Such a bond usually has a provision for voluntary repayment at the issuer's discretion.

Perpetuity An investment entitling the holder to receive a fixed or determinable periodic payment in perpetuity. See also **annuity**.

Personal pension plan A pension plan that is specific to the individual holder and not tied, for example, to the individual's employment contract. See also **occupational pension plan**.

Pit The trading area or trading floor of an open-outcry market.

Placing A distribution of securities to selected investors rather than by means of a public offer. See also **initial public offering (IPO)**.

Plain vanilla bond A bond with provision for (a) periodic interest payments at a single uniform fixed rate and (b) mandatory repayment on a single future date, with no provisions for early repayment save in an event of default by the issuer.

Pound averaging An ongoing strategy whereby an investor periodically invests a constant money amount in a specific security or market (rather than periodically buying a constant number or quantity of the securities), with a view to benefiting disproportionately from temporary dips in the price.

Preference shares These rank ahead of **ordinary shares** in a liquidation and are entitled to a fixed dividend in priority to any dividend payable on ordinary shares. Unlike ordinary shares, which enjoy a pro rata share in the residual assets of the company, preference shares have a fixed repayment value. In economic terms, they are therefore closer to debt than to equity.

Premium a) In **options**: the initial sum of money paid by the buyer to the seller or writer as an inducement to enter into a contract whose expected outcome is negative. b) In bonds: the difference between the par value of a security and the price (if higher than its par value) at which it is issued. c) In **foreign exchange**: Currency A is said to be at a forward premium to Currency B if fewer units of Currency A are required to buy one unit of Currency B in the forward market than in the spot market. In any pair of convertible currencies that are freely tradable in an efficient market, the currency with the lower interest rate is always at a forward premium to the currency with the higher interest rate. See also **discount**.

Present value The equivalent value in today's money of future expected cash flows, discounted at a rate that reflects the time value of money.

Price discovery The process whereby the forces of supply and demand determine market prices.

Price–earnings (or p/e) ratio The ratio of the market price of a share to the company's earnings per share (eps). It can be measured on various bases, including principally a historic basis, by reference to the latest published earnings of the company, or on a prospective basis, by reference to the expected earnings for the current accounting period.

Price factor The system of fixed factors used by the bond futures market to calculate, from the price of the contract itself, the price at which an actual qualifying bond would be delivered in settlement of an open futures position. See also **cheapest to deliver (CTD)**.

Primary market A market in which new securities are sold for the first time to investors.

Private equity fund A fund that buys companies (takes them private) with a view to adding value through leverage or improved management and then floating them on the stock market at a profit.

Product markets Markets in which good and services are bought and sold. See also **factor markets**.

Purchasing power parity The thesis that, given the assumption of free international trade, the change in exchange rate over a period will be equal to the relative change in inflation rates of the two countries concerned.

Put option See **option**.

Real assets, real economy 'Real' is here used in the opposite sense from 'financial'. A real asset is one that does not consist solely of a claim to the future receipt of cash. The real economy is the collective name for the production and distribution of goods and services.

Real rate of return, real return The rate of return (a) actually received by an investor after the effect of historical inflation has been taken into account or (b) expected by an investor after the effect of expected inflation has been taken into account.

Redemption yield The overall rate of return from a debt security, taking into account the capital gain or loss accruing to an investor when the security is redeemed (normally at par), as well as the periodic interest income.

Repurchase agreement (repo) An agreement to sell for spot settlement and simultaneously to repurchase for forward settlement at a predetermined price a stated amount of a security. A repo is in effect a secured loan.

Rights issue The issue of new shares in a company to its existing shareholders, usually on advantageous terms compared with the current market price. Such pre-emption rights may arise from the specific provision of a company's own constitution or from the general provisions of company law, and are intended to protect shareholders from dilution.

Risk In finance, risk is almost synonymous with uncertainty, and refers to the possibility that what is expected to happen will not happen.

Scrip/bonus/capitalisation issue The issuance of free new shares to existing shareholders in a fixed proportion relative to their existing holdings. In accounting terms, such an issue is reflected in the conversion of part of the retained earnings of the company into share capital.

Seasoned equity offering (SEO) See **secondary offering**.

Secondary market A market in which existing (or 'seasoned') securities are bought and sold among investors. See also **primary market**.

Secondary offering A subsequent offering of shares by a company that has already issued shares to investors at least once through an IPO or a placing. Also known as a **seasoned equity offering (SEO)**.

Securities Financial assets (representing equity or debt claims on companies, banks, governments and similar organisations) that have been issued in a form permitting or facilitating their continuing sale and purchase in a secondary market.

Sell short An investor who sells securities or another financial instrument he or she does not yet own, in anticipation of being able to buy them back later at a lower price, is said to sell short. Selling short is not permitted in some jurisdictions, and even where it is permitted it can be difficult or expensive, as it entails the temporary borrowing of the securities in order to settle the initial sale transaction.

Share capital The total number of shares either (a) actually issued by a company ('issued share capital') or (b) authorised for issue ('authorised share capital') under a company's rules as approved by its shareholders under the terms of its memorandum and articles of association.

Share split The process of subdividing the existing share capital of a company by replacing the existing shares with a proportionately greater number of shares with a correspondingly lower nominal value, for instance, the replacement of 1 million £1 shares with 10 million 10p shares. A share split is a 'paper' transaction and does not entail any exchange of cash between the company and its investors.

Short sale See **sell short**.

Single-dated bond A bond with a single mandatory repayment date.

Spike A temporary and short-lived surge in a market price.

Spot A transaction dealt for immediate settlement. The exact meaning of 'immediate' depends on the historical convention of the particular market. For example, a spot foreign exchange contract is settled two business days after the dealing date, whereas UK gilts are settled on the next business day.

Spot exchange rate The exchange rate applicable to a spot foreign exchange contract.

Spot interest rate The interest rate applicable to a loan or investment that is made on the spot date and is repaid with a single future cash flow at final maturity, without any intermediate payments of interest.

Stagging The process of oversubscribing for a new issue of securities, in the expectation of being able to dispose of them at an immediate profit when unfulfilled demand results in the market price rising above the issue price when secondary market dealings in the new securities commence.

Stock exchange An organised market for the issuance and subsequent sale and purchase of securities and (in some cases) derivative instruments based on such securities or on recognised indices of such securities.

Straddle Simultaneous purchase and sale of a call and a put option at the same exercise price and with the same exercise/expiry date.

Straight bond A bond with a fixed rate of interest.

Strips/stripping The process of separating the coupons from the principal repayment of a bond (and, in some cases, from each other) to permit their being traded separately.

Supply uncertainty premium Where investors rely on a regular supply of a certain type of securities to meet their needs and objectives (e.g. the requirement of pension fund managers for a continuous supply of low-risk long-term bonds to cover their long-term liabilities), they may be prepared to pay a premium for such securities (and hence accept lower returns than would otherwise be the case) if the supply is perceived to be irregular or uncertain.

Swap a) In the foreign exchange market, a foreign exchange swap is the simultaneous purchase and sale, for two different dates (either spot and forward, or two different forward dates) of a fixed amount of Currency A against Currency B. The amount of Currency B will vary according to the interest rate differential between the two currencies for the period between the two dates. b) In the interest-rate and capital markets, an agreement to exchange cash flows based on different interest rates on a common notional principal amount or on equivalent notional principal amounts in two different currencies. See also **cross-currency swap** and **interest rate swap**.

T-bill See **Treasury bill.**

Tender offer A method of distributing securities by inviting tenders from potential investors in a kind of auction process.

Term structure of interest rates The underlying series of spot interest rates used by the market at a particular point in time to determine the values of securities of a particular type, e.g. UK government bonds.

Theoretical ex-rights/TERPS The theoretical value to which a company's shares will move (all other things being equal) in response to a rights issue of new shares at a discount to their current market value.

Tick The minimum permitted unit of price movement for an exchange-traded derivatives contract.

Time preference for consumption The perceived preference of consumers to 'have their cake now' rather than at some time in the future. The time preference rate is the annual percentage rate that brings present and future preferences into equilibrium. A consumer who is indifferent between 100 pieces of cake today and 103 pieces of cake in one year's time is said to have a time preference of consumption of 3% per annum.

Time value The component of overall option value attributable to the probability that future changes in the value of the underlying before the option exercise or expiry date will change the intrinsic value of the option itself. It is one of two elements of an option's value, and cannot be negative. The other is **intrinsic value**.

Time value of money Measures the extent to which investors and other prefer to have money today rather than in the future: it is in effect the 'rate of exchange' between today's money and tomorrow's money.

Total return The comprehensive measure of return on an investment, which includes the realised or unrealised capital gain or loss as well as the periodic income.

Treasury bill (or **T-bill**) A short-term promissory note issued by a government, usually on a non-interest-bearing discount basis.

Undated A debt security with no mandatory repayment date is said to be undated.

Underlying, underlying asset/product The asset or product on which a **derivative** contract is primarily based.

Unit-linked life assurance/savings A method of regular periodic savings in unit trusts or mutual funds.

Unit trusts The commonest UK investment product in the category of **open-ended investment funds.**

Variation margin Additional margin charged to the loss-making party to an open futures contract, and credited to the profit-making party, as a result of the daily **mark-to-market** of open positions.

Warrant A **call option** on securities, itself issued in the form of a tradable security, either on its own or in conjunction with a conventional issue of debt or equity securities. For instance, a company may issue bonds with detachable warrants for the future purchase of its shares on specific terms.

Yield curve The line described by plotting the yields (which may be the **redemption yields** or the underlying **spot interest rates**) applicable to all securities with different periods to maturity but otherwise sharing common characteristics (e.g. all bonds issued by a government in its own currency).

Yield to maturity The total return of a bond or other interest-bearing financial asset. an alternative term for **redemption yield**.

Zero-coupon bond/zero A bond that pays no interest coupons, but yields its total return by being issued or purchased at a discount to the nominal amount that is paid out on maturity.

Zero dividend preference share A type of capital share in a split-capital investment trust company, which has priority over ordinary capital shares in a liquidation.

Index